Office 2000:
The Complete Reference

Stephen L. Nelson

Osborne/McGraw-Hill
Berkeley New York St. Louis San Francisco
Auckland Bogotá Hamburg London Madrid
Mexico City Milan Montreal New Delhi Panama City
Paris São Paulo Singapore Sydney
Tokyo Toronto

Osborne McGraw-Hill
2600 Tenth Street
Berkeley, California 94710
U.S.A.

For information on translations or book distributors outside the U.S.A., or to arrange bulk purchase discounts for sales promotions, premiums, or fundraisers, please contact Osborne McGraw-Hill at the above address.

Office 2000: The Complete Reference

1234567890 DOC DOC 90198765432109

ISBN 0-07-211859-8

Publisher
Brandon A. Nordin

Associate Publisher and Editor-in-Chief
Scott Rogers

Acquisitions Editor
Joanne Cuthbertson

Project Editor
Jody McKenzie

Editorial Assistant
Stephane Thomas

Technical Editor
Eric J. Ray

Copy Editor
Claire Splan

Proofreader
Laurie Stewart

Indexer
Jack Lewis

Computer Designers
Roberta Steele
Jani Beckwith

Illustrators
Beth Young
Brian Wells
Robert Hansen

Series Design
Peter Hancik

For Wiley Post,
The first man to circumnavigate the globe by air.
What a guy!

About the Author

Stephen L. Nelson, a best-selling author and consultant, has written more than 50 books and more than 100 articles on using computers for personal and business financial management. His books have sold more than one million copies in English and have been translated into 11 different languages.

Contents at a Glance

Contents

Part I
Introducing Office

Part II

Microsoft Word

Part III

Microsoft Excel

Part IV

Microsoft PowerPoint

Part V

Microsoft Outlook

Part VII
Microsoft Access

Part VIII

Microsoft Publisher

Acknowledgments

This book is a collective effort, and it owes a lot to many hard-working, talented people. First, I would like to thank three writers who contributed to *Office 2000: The Complete Reference*:

Pat Coleman wrote the chapters on Microsoft Word, Microsoft Excel, and Microsoft PowerPoint. She is the coauthor of several computer books and writes and edits for several publications, including *The World Almanac*.

Kaarin Dolliver wrote the chapters on Microsoft Publisher. She has coauthored with me on several other titles including books in the popular Smart Guide series published by Barnes and Noble, Inc.

Jason Gerend revised the chapter on Outlook and wrote the Web Components chapter and the Appendixes. He is a freelance writer who has worked on numerous other computer books with me as well as other authors.

I would also like to thank acquisitions editor Joanne Cuthbertson, who cracked the whip of encouragement and whose many suggestions helped make this a better book.

Thank you to Stephane Thomas, who kept contracts and chapters flying up and down the West Coast.

I also owe my thanks to copy editor Claire Splan, who lent her editorial expertise to the book, and technical editor Eric Ray, who followed doggedly in my footsteps to make sure that all the instructions in this book are accurate.

Thanks also go to project editor Jody McKenzie, who cheerfully kept everything on track, and to Jack Lewis for his excellent index.

These Berkeleyites in the editorial offices of Osborne/McGraw-Hill gave their best to the book, and for that I am very grateful: production manager Jean Butterfield; production scheduler Ann Sellers; designer Peter Hancik; illustrators Brian Wells, Beth Young, and Robert Hansen; and typesetters Jani Beckwith and Roberta Steele.

Thanks also go to Todd Young, who served as in-house editor, reviewed the manuscript, proofed pages, shot figures, collected all of the pieces and parts that make up the companion CD, acquired all the shareware programs, and generally helped organize the project.

Hercules was a single man, but if he had been married and had had children, he would have completed his labors sooner. I would like to thank my family for encouraging me and, at times, for putting up with me during the long months it took to complete this book.

Introduction

This book is a comprehensive guide to using all the programs and all the different parts of Microsoft Office 2000, the newest edition of the Office suite of programs. Put this book in a prominent place on your desk, and reach for it when you come to an impasse or you simply want to know a better way to complete a task.

The plain-language instructions in this book lay out exactly what you need to know to do a task well and then tell you, in step-by-step fashion, how to complete the task. This book does not pussyfoot around. I want you to do tasks well and do them quickly. And you should know enough to create Word documents, Excel worksheets, Access databases, PowerPoint presentations, Outlook messages, and web pages that either stand out from the crowd or are so efficient they give you the opportunity to get your work done faster and better.

In this book are instructions, tips, tricks, advice, and shortcuts for getting the most out of Word, Excel, Access, PowerPoint, Outlook, Internet Explorer, and Publisher as well as the other parts of Office 2000. What's more, this book comes with a CD on which you will find sample files for test-driving the features we explain on the pages of this book, templates for creating jazzy or useful files, and even ten shareware programs. In this book, you will also find instructions for using the new web publication features included with the Office 2000 programs.

Who Is This Book For?

This book is for everybody who either uses one of the programs in the Office 2000 suite or uses different programs in the suite to pass around and trade data. Office 2000 makes it very easy to pass data back and forth between programs. Besides telling you how to use the features in each program, the book shows you how the different programs work together. One of Microsoft's goals in designing the Office 2000 suite was to keep users from having to enter information more than once. A table created in Access, for example, can also be used in a Word document. And an outline made in Word can be turned into the text for a PowerPoint presentation. In this book, you will learn how to save lots of time by passing data among the different Office 2000 programs.

The Office 2000 suite contains the following programs:

- **Word**   A word processing program
- **Excel**   A spreadsheet program
- **Access**   A database program
- **PowerPoint**   A presentation program
- **Outlook**   A combination e-mail and personal information manager program
- **Internet Explorer**   A web browser
- **Publisher**   A page layout program
- **Shared Tools**   The clip art images, fonts, and many other features that you can take advantage of in all the programs in the Office 2000 suite

No matter which version of Microsoft Office 2000 you use, this book can help you. For the record, Microsoft offers five versions of Office 2000:

- **Standard Version**   Includes Word, Excel, PowerPoint, and Outlook
- **Small Business Version**   Includes Word, Excel, Outlook and Publisher, and has some small business tools as well
- **Professional Version**   Includes all the programs in the Small Business version as well as Access and PowerPoint
- **Premium Version**   Designed for web professionals, this version includes all the programs in the Professional version, plus PhotoDraw 2000 and FrontPage 2000
- **Developer Version**   Has all the programs that the Premium version has, plus tools for programming

The "Best Possible Way" Philosophy

In Office 2000 programs, there are almost always two ways to complete a task. Sometimes, in fact, a program offers three or four ways. Rather than waste your time explaining the two, three, or four ways, this book plunges in and explains what I believe is the best way. I chose the "best possible way" philosophy because I want to explain how to do tasks quickly and because, well, we have a lot of ground to cover. I have tried to cover all aspects of the Office 2000 programs. To do that, I had to explain the "best possible way" and not waste pages explaining all of the ways to complete a task.

As part of the "best possible way" philosophy, I also explain which program to use to complete a task and ignore a part of a program if the task can be done better in another program. For example, Word includes a rather crude spreadsheet feature for making data calculations. Rather than use a Word table, this book steers you to an Excel worksheet, since calculations are much easier to make there than they are in Word. Meanwhile, Excel includes a simple lists feature for creating a name-and-address database. But, again, why use an Excel list when an Access table is easier to use and far more powerful?

What's In This Book, Anyway?

This book is organized to help you look up the information you need quickly. To get instructions, your best bet is to turn to the index or table of contents. To get the lay of the land, the following sections explain what you will find between the covers of this book.

Part I: Introducing Office

Part I starts by providing background information so you can be a proficient user of the Office 2000 programs. It explains what the programs are and what they do, as well as how to manage Word documents, Excel workbooks, PowerPoint presentations, and so forth. You also learn how to customize the Office 2000 programs to make them do your bidding and how to use tools such as the spell checker and clip art gallery, which are common to all the programs. Last but not least, you also learn how to share data amongst the different programs.

Part II: Microsoft Word

Part II describes everything you need to know to use Microsoft Word. You learn how to work faster, how to create and use styles for consistent formatting, and how to desktop publish with Word. You also learn tried-and-true techniques for working on long reports and scholarly papers.

Part III: Microsoft Excel

Part III describes and discusses the Excel spreadsheet program. You learn what workbooks are and how to enter labels and values into worksheet cells, as well as how formulas and functions work. Part III also describes how to use the ChartWizard to create charts, how to create sophisticated PivotTables, and how to use the advanced modeling tools.

Part IV: Microsoft PowerPoint

Part IV explains how to put together a PowerPoint presentation. You learn how to create the presentation, how to embellish it with artwork and animation, and how to create speaker's notes and other amenities to ensure that your presentation is a hit. Of course, you also learn how to give a presentation.

Part V: Microsoft Outlook

Part V is divided into three chapters, one that covers how to send and receive e-mail and files, and another that explains how to use the personal information manager side of Outlook to keep track of appointments, contacts, and your to-do list. The third chapter tells you how to use newsgroups to communicate with people around the world who share your interests.

Part VI: Microsoft Internet Explorer 5.0

Part VI shows you how to get connected and start surfing the World Wide Web and local intranets using Internet Explorer 5.0. It discusses using web components to add to your web pages. And it talks about using Microsoft Outlook Express, Microsoft NetMeeting, Microsoft Chat, and Microsoft FrontPage Express.

Part VII: Microsoft Access

Part VII covers the Access database program. In this part, you learn how to create an Access database, how to create and link database tables, and how to create forms, queries, and reports. Turn to Part VII to get plain-language explanations of hideous database terms and to learn how to create useful databases that store information accurately and efficiently.

Part VIII: Microsoft Publisher

Part VIII shows you how to use Publisher to create eye-catching publications. You'll learn how to lay out a flyer, invitation, or other publication. You'll learn how to add text and graphics and finally, how to put your creation into printed form.

Part IX: Appendixes

Part IX rounds out the book with five appendixes. Appendix A describes how to install and reinstall Office. Appendix B tells how to work with Office Small Business Programs. Appendix C shows how to use Office Server Extensions. Appendix D explains how to use Office as a development tool for developing software programs. Appendix E describes what is on the companion CD included with this book, as explained next.

What's on the Companion CD?

Appendix E gives a thorough explanation of what is on the CD included with this book. The appendix also explains how to make use of the templates, sample files, and programs on the CD.

The CD contains the following:

- **Personal Testing Center TEST YOURSELF Software**   Provides a variety of options for you to assess your Microsoft Office 2000 skills. You can see where you need improvement to gain proficiency in your Offce 2000 skills. Also, if you plan to take a Microsoft Office User Specialist (MOUS) Certification test, you can use the exams included on the CD to determine if there are some areas you need to brush up on.

- **Templates**   More than 50 "Headstart" templates that you can use to create Word documents, Excel worksheets, and PowerPoint presentations. Where Headstart templates are explained on the pages of this book, you see a Headstart icon (as shown in the following section).

- **Sample Files**   Close to 200 "Learn By Example" files. Use these sample files to test and get experience using the different features that are described on the pages of this book. Where you see a Learn By Example icon (as shown in the following section) read on to learn the name of a sample file that you can use to experiment with the feature that is being explained.

- **Shareware**   Ten shareware programs that are especially worthwhile. In fact, they are the ten best shareware programs that I could find.

Conventions Used in This Book

To make this book more useful and a pleasure to read, I joined heads with the publisher to create several conventions. Following are descriptions of the conventions in this book.

Icons

Occasionally—to alert you to an important bit of advice, a shortcut, or a pitfall—you see a Note, Tip, or Caution icon and a few important words in the text.

 This is a note. Notes define words, refer you to other parts of the book, or offer background information so you can make better use of an Office 2000 program.

 This is a tip. Tips give you shortcuts and handy pieces of advice to make you a better user of Office 2000. Take a tip from me and read these tips attentively.

 This is a caution. When you see a caution, perk up your ears. Cautions appear when you have to make crucial choices or when you are about to undertake something that you might regret later.

Besides Notes, Tips, and Cautions, you also see Headstart and Learn By Example icons.

HEADSTART

As mentioned earlier in the introduction, the companion CD included with this book has more than 50 Headstart templates. To alert you to the fact that you can use a Headstart template, the Headstart icon appears along with the name of the template you can use.

LEARN BY EXAMPLE

The Learn By Example icon tells you when a practice file is available that you can use to test an Office 2000 feature. The text that accompanies these icons provides a description of the sample file and its name.

Sidebars

From time to time, information that is tangential to the main discussion is presented. When that happens, the information is put in a sidebar like this one.

Command Names

Rather than tell you to, for example, "choose Print from the File menu," this book presents commands in the order in which they are given: "Choose File | Print." After all, to choose the Print command, you have to click the File menu first, and then click Print. This convention was adopted to help you make better sense of commands and how to give them.

Bon Voyage!

I have thrown every tip, trick, and piece of useful advice that I know into this book. If you know a shortcut of your own that you would like to share with other readers, please send it to **help@stephenlnelson.com** so I can include it in the next edition of this book. For that matter, if you have a comment about the book or need advice for using a program, please send an e-mail message. Meanwhile, best of luck using Office 2000!

The Complete Reference

Office 2000

Part I

Introducing Office

Chapter 1

What Is Office?

Let's start by taking a look at Microsoft Office itself, how the parts of the Office suite of programs fit together, how this book is organized, and why you, the reader, are likely to benefit from this book. Even if you want to get on with your reading and learning, getting all this information up front will help you make better sense of Office and better use of this book.

An Overview of Office

What is Microsoft Office? This question is actually more difficult to answer than it should be. On the face of it, Office is simply five (or more) software programs sold in a bundle and installed together. If you purchase the Standard version of Microsoft Office, you get Microsoft Word, Microsoft Excel, Microsoft PowerPoint, Microsoft Outlook, and Microsoft Internet Explorer. If you purchase the Small Business edition, you get Small Business Tools instead of PowerPoint. If you purchase the Professional version of Office, you get everything that comes in the Standard version, as well as Microsoft Access, Microsoft Publisher, the Office Web Components, and the Small Business Tools. If you purchase the Enterprise/Premier version of Office, you get everything that comes in the Professional version as well as Microsoft FrontPage and Microsoft PhotoDraw. This book covers the Standard, Small Business, and Professional versions of Office 2000.

What Is Word?

You use Word to create textual documents: letters, reports, books, and so on. Figure 1-1 shows a Word document. (The files that Word creates are called *documents*.) To create a document, you simply start Word and then type in words and numbers. Chapters 7 through 11 cover working with and creating Word documents.

EXAMPLES

LEARN BY EXAMPLE
You can open the example Word document shown in Figure 1-1 from the companion CD. The sample document name, Figure 1-1 (simple Word document), shows you what a Word document looks like. If you want to experiment with the sample document, just get to work—click someplace within the document to position the insertion point and begin typing.

Note
The easiest way to open a sample document is to use Windows Explorer to view the contents of the companion CD's Learn By Example folder. When you see the sample document you want to open, double-click it.

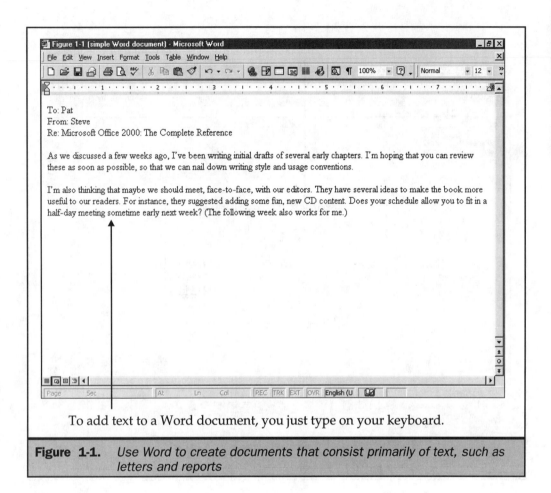

To add text to a Word document, you just type on your keyboard.

Figure 1-1.   *Use Word to create documents that consist primarily of text, such as letters and reports*

What Is Excel?

Excel lets you perform numerical analysis. By numerical analysis, I mean listing data, performing calculations on data, comparing data points, and presenting the data in a way that highlights the relationships between data points. Figure 1-2 shows a simple Excel workbook. (The files Excel creates are called *workbooks*.) In a nutshell, workbooks provide a grid of columns and rows that you use to describe and make calculations. Chapters 12 through 16 explain more about Excel workbooks, but for now note that what Figure 1-2 shows is just a simple budget. To create it, you would enter the budgeting

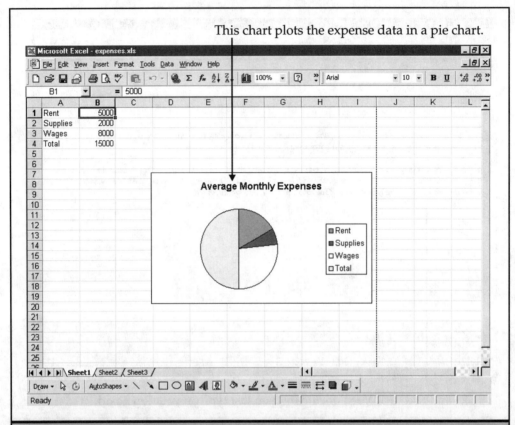

This chart plots the expense data in a pie chart.

Figure 1-2.   *Use Excel to perform numerical analysis—such as creating a budget or making a financial calculation—and to create charts*

categories Rent, Supplies, and Wages and then the budgeted amounts for these categories. You'd also create a formula to total your individual budgeted amounts.

LEARN BY EXAMPLE

*You can open the example Excel workbook shown in Figure 1-2 from the companion CD. The sample document name, Figure 1-2 (simple Excel workbook), shows you what an Excel workbook looks like. If you want to experiment with the sample workbook, just click the cell containing the number 5000—the budgeted amount for rent, type the number **2000**, and press ENTER. Notice that both the total shown and the pie chart change to reflect your alteration.*

What Is PowerPoint?

PowerPoint works much like Word does, except that rather than create pages of text, you create colorful slides that you can use to produce overhead transparencies, 35mm slides, paper handouts, or, more likely, to display directly on a movie screen. You can display PowerPoint slides in a presentation using a computer (often a laptop) connected to a special kind of projector. Figure 1-3 shows an example PowerPoint slide. Typically, PowerPoint is used to create presentations for sales calls, meetings, or speeches.

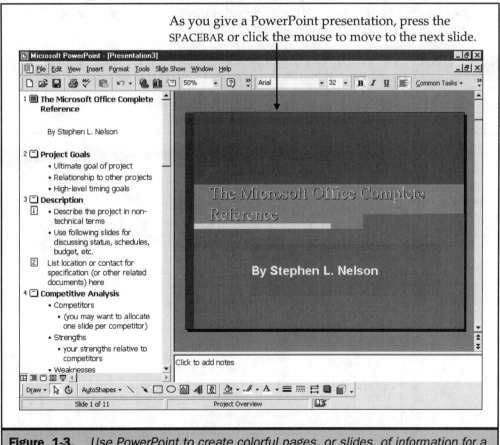

Figure 1-3.   *Use PowerPoint to create colorful pages, or slides, of information for a presentation*

LEARN BY EXAMPLE
You can open the example PowerPoint presentation shown in Figure 1-3 from the companion CD. The sample document name, Figure 1-3 (simple PowerPoint presentation), shows you what a PowerPoint presentation looks like. If you want to experiment viewing the sample document in different ways, choose the Slide Show menu's View Show command.

What Is Outlook?

Outlook is an e-mail client and personal information manager. It lets you send and receive e-mail, keep a "To Do" list, maintain an appointment calendar, and keep a list of names, addresses, and telephone numbers. Figure 1-4 shows what the message window looks like (you would use this to e-mail someone a message). Figure 1-5 shows what the Outlook appointment calendar looks like.

To use Outlook as a personal information manager, you need to first go through Outlook's setup process. Appendix A guides you through the steps of this process.

To create an e-mail message, simply fill in the To and Subject boxes, and then type your message text.

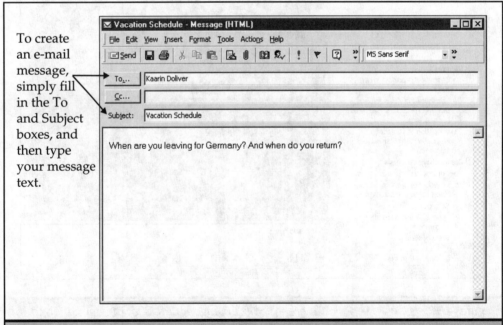

Figure 1-4.   *Outlook includes a handy e-mail program that you can use if your computer connects to a network or the Internet*

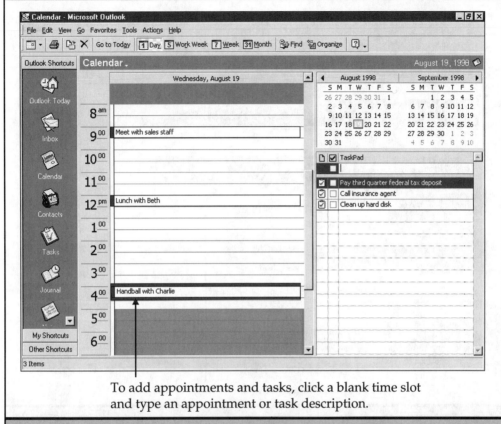

To add appointments and tasks, click a blank time slot
and type an appointment or task description.

Figure 1-5. *Outlook, as a personal information manager, includes an appointment calendar and task list manager that you can use to better manage your workday*

What Is Internet Explorer?

Internet Explorer is a suite of Internet programs. The main program in this suite is Internet Explorer itself, a web browser that you can use to view web pages on the World Wide Web and download files from web sites or FTP sites. Figure 1-6 shows what the Internet Explorer web browser looks like. The Internet Explorer suite of programs comes with a few other useful Internet tools: Outlook Express, Microsoft NetMeeting, FrontPage Express, and Microsoft Chat, to name a few. You use Outlook Express, a mail and news reader, to send and receive e-mail and read and post newsgroup messages. You can use Microsoft NetMeeting to hold an audio and video

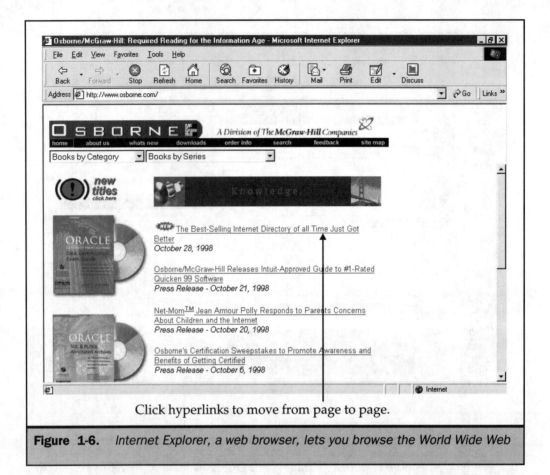

Click hyperlinks to move from page to page.

Figure 1-6.   *Internet Explorer, a web browser, lets you browse the World Wide Web*

conference online. You can use FrontPage Express to create your own web pages. And you can use Microsoft Chat to type back and forth with people in real time.

Note   *As their names imply, Outlook and Outlook Express share much of the same functionality. But they are different programs and do have several different features. Outlook is in part a personal information manager. Outlook Express is not. Outlook Express lets you work with newsgroups. Outlook borrows Outlook Express for newsgroup reading. Chapters 20 and 21 describe how to use Outlook. Chapter 22 describes how to use the newsreader features in Outlook Express. Chapter 25 describes how to use the e-mail features in Outlook Express.*

What Is Access?

Access is a database program. If you haven't used a database before, Access may sound like something that only computer experts and programmers can use. But that's not the case. Access simply helps you build and maintain lists of information, as shown in Figure 1-7. For example, if you work in a business, you maintain several lists of customer information. You keep a list of customer names, addresses, and telephone numbers, for example, as well as a list of the amounts that customers owe you. Access, as a database program, helps you keep, maintain, and better use exactly these sorts of lists. (Access calls its lists *tables*, by the way, and a collection of related tables a *database*.)

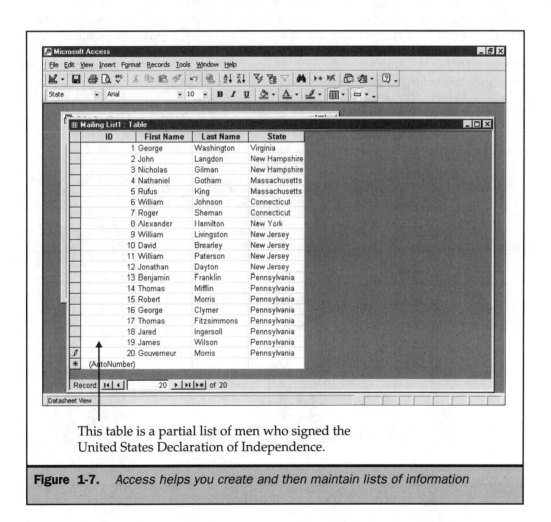

This table is a partial list of men who signed the
United States Declaration of Independence.

Figure 1-7. *Access helps you create and then maintain lists of information*

What Is Publisher?

Publisher is a page layout program used for desktop publishing. You use Publisher to create documents that require a more sophisticated layout design than what you can easily accomplish with a word processor. For example, you might use Publisher to lay out brochures, newsletters, or books. Publisher provides easy-to-use tools and numerous editing options that allow you to artfully place text and graphics on a page, as shown in Figure 1-8.

What Is FrontPage?

You use FrontPage to create web sites. FrontPage helps you organize a web site and then allows you to add all sorts of content to the individual web pages comprising the web site. With FrontPage, you don't need to know any programming language in order

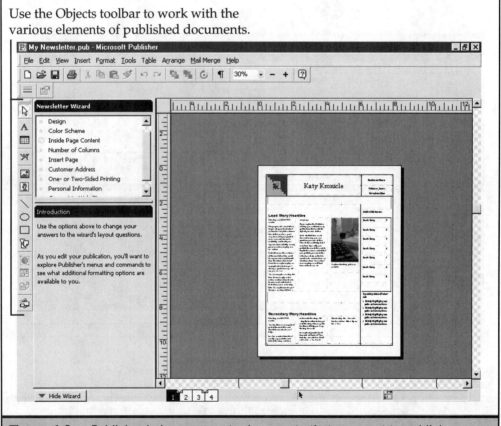

Figure 1-8.   *Publisher helps you create documents that you want to publish*

to add advanced features to your web site—you can do just about anything with the click of a few buttons. Figure 1-9 shows a web page that is part of a FrontPage web site.

What Is PhotoDraw?

You use PhotoDraw to create and manipulate graphics. PhotoDraw includes several special effects that you can apply to graphics to give them a whole new look, as shown in Figure 1-10. PhotoDraw also lets you save graphics in a variety of formats. You can use the graphics you create in PhotoDraw in a Word document, a PowerPoint presentation, or a FrontPage web site, to name a few.

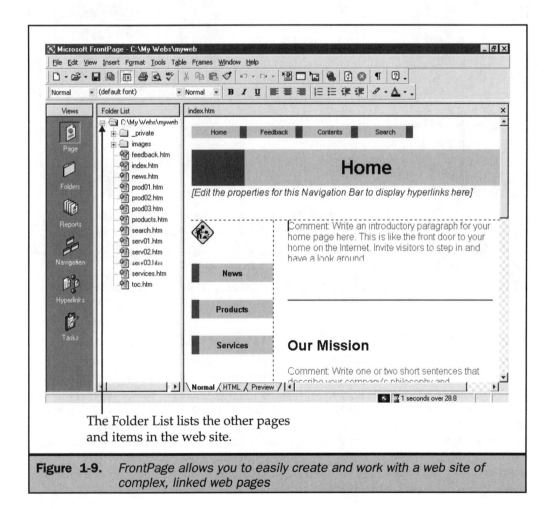

The Folder List lists the other pages and items in the web site.

Figure 1-9. *FrontPage allows you to easily create and work with a web site of complex, linked web pages*

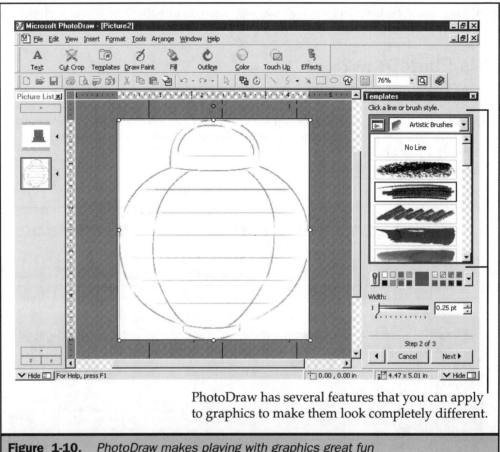

PhotoDraw has several features that you can apply to graphics to make them look completely different.

Figure 1-10.   *PhotoDraw makes playing with graphics great fun*

How the Parts of Office Fit Together

Some people mistakenly think that Office is a single program. The confusion is understandable because Microsoft markets Office in this manner. Although the Office 2000 programs are designed to work almost seamlessly together, Office 2000 still consists of several individual programs. And there is a smart strategy to learning and using the Office suite of programs. Each Office program works best for a different task: you can best compose text with Word, you can best crunch numbers with Excel, you can best manage tables of information with Access, and so on. Given this, what you want to do is learn to use the Office programs that best handle the sort of data that you work with. This makes sense, right?

In fact, this book assumes that you take this very approach: learning to use the best tool for working with a particular type of data. In this manner, you can save substantial reading and learning time by skipping coverage of features you don't need to use. And, more important, you'll get the biggest payback for your reading and learning investment since you'll be emphasizing the best tools. For example, Word includes a rather crude spreadsheet feature (called tables) that you can use to make calculations—such as for a budget. Excel's worksheets, however, are both easier to use and more powerful in what they can do. Similarly, you can use Excel to create lists of information, but for working with lots of data pieces, Access's tables feature is both easier to use and more powerful than Excel.

Regardless of which Office features you use most often, you perform many tasks in exactly the same way in all Office programs. The rest of the chapters in Part I describe and explain the various techniques and tools available to get the most out of the Office suite.

The
Complete
Reference

Office 2000

Chapter 2

Managing

Document Files

Although the different Office programs work with different types of data, their files are saved, opened, and printed in basically the same way. Because of these similarities, this chapter discusses document file management for all the Office programs. It covers saving, opening, and printing document files, as well as creating new document files, working with file properties, and searching for lost document files. If you review this chapter—and then remember even a fraction of what you read—you'll be well equipped to work with Office document files.

Saving Document Files

Any time you create a document file you want to work with again, you'll want to save the document to your hard disk, a floppy disk, or some other storage device (for example, a Zip or tape drive). Fortunately, saving document files is easy. Extremely easy.

Saving a Document File for the First Time

To save a document for the first time, click the Save button, which appears on the Standard toolbar. (You can also choose the File menu's Save As or Save command.) When the Office program displays the Save As dialog box, shown in Figure 2-1, follow these steps to save the document file:

1. Use the Save In drop-down list box to select the folder in which you want to save the document.

   If you want to save a document file in your History, My Documents, Favorites, or Web Folders folder, click the corresponding icon on the left. If you want to save a document file to your desktop, click the Desktop icon. If you want to store the document file in a new folder, click the Create New Folder button and then, when prompted by Windows, provide a name for the new folder.

2. Enter the filename you want to use for the new document file into the File Name box.

3. Click Save.

The Create New Folder button

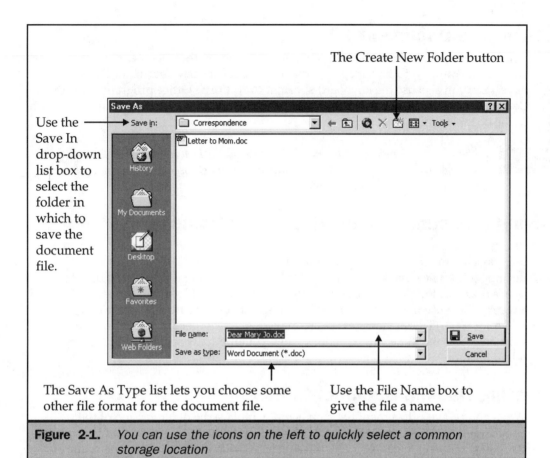

Use the Save In drop-down list box to select the folder in which to save the document file.

The Save As Type list lets you choose some other file format for the document file.

Use the File Name box to give the file a name.

Figure 2-1. *You can use the icons on the left to quickly select a common storage location*

Naming Your Document File

You can name your document files just about anything you want. For all practical purposes, there isn't a limit on the length of your document file. (You can use as many as 255 characters, for example.) Don't, however, specify a three-character file extension yourself. Let the Office program add that bit of information for you. Office programs use the file extension (as well as other information stored in the file) to identify the format of the file.

Resaving a Document File

Once you save a Document file, its new name appears on the document window's title bar. When you want to save it again, you simply click the Save button or choose File | Save. (You can also use the keyboard shortcut CTRL-S.) The Office program saves the document file in the same location and with the same name, replacing your old version of the document file.

If you've made changes to a document file since you last saved it, the Office program asks if you want to save your document file when you choose the File menu's Close or Exit commands to prevent you from accidentally losing your changes.

Saving a Document File with a New Name

You can save multiple copies of a document simply by giving the copies new names or by placing the copies in a different folder. (Typically, you'll want to give the document file a new name so that you don't get the document files mixed up.) To save a document file with a different name or in a different location, choose File | Save As. Then use the Save As dialog box to specify either a new filename or a new folder location. (This business of specifying either a new filename or a new folder location works the same way as it does when you originally specify a filename or folder location.)

Creating Backup Document Files

When you resave a document file, you actually replace the older version of the document file (the one you originally retrieved) with the new version that incorporates your most recent changes. Usually, this is exactly what you want—to replace the old version of some document file. But sometimes—particularly when someone else may later fiddle with a document file—you may want to have the Office program automatically create backup copies of your old document file whenever you save a new copy of the document file.

To automatically create a backup copy of the old versions of Word 2000 documents and Excel 2000 workbooks each time you resave a file, take the following steps:

1. Choose File | Save As.

2. When Word or Excel displays the Save As dialog box, choose Tools | General Options.

3. When the Office program displays the Save options dialog box, shown next, check the Always Create Backup Copy box (if you're working with Word) or the Always Create Backup box (if you're working with Excel).

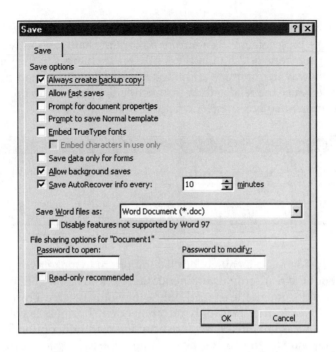

 Note *The preceding illustration shows Word's Save options dialog box. The Excel Save Options dialog box looks slightly different.*

Protecting Your Document Files and Using Passwords

If other people can grab your files—either because they can start and use your computer or because your computer connects to a network—you may want to consider using passwords for your most sensitive, confidential, or important document files. When you use passwords, people can't view document files you don't want them to see and, perhaps just as important, they can't change document files they shouldn't modify. Fortunately, this sort of control is easy to institute with both Word and Excel documents (although not with PowerPoint or Outlook) because both Word and Excel provide three levels of security in the Save options dialog box.

Note *You can control access to an Access database using passwords, too, but for Access the process works a little bit differently than it does for Word or Excel. In Access, you use the Tools menu's Security command to set passwords. Chapters 26 through 29 describe how Access works.*

Using the Read-Only Recommended Option

You can tell Word or Excel that it must require that people open a document file as "read-only." (Read-only means that someone opening the file can read the file, but not resave the file and thereby change it.) For example, if you collaborate with several other members of a project team to co-author a monthly status report, you might want to make sure that someone doesn't inadvertently make changes to the report. In this situation, one easy way to minimize (although not eliminate) the chance of such a mistake would be to use the read-only recommended option. To do this, check the Read-Only Recommended box in the Save options dialog box.

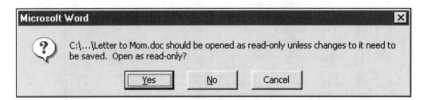

You've perhaps deduced as much, but it's important to make two quick observations about the read-only recommendation option. First of all, people aren't required to open a document file as read-only—they only receive a recommendation to do so. (In other words, the "read-only recommended" business is voluntary.) Another, somewhat less obvious characteristic of the read-only option is that someone can still save a new, modified copy of the document file as long as they use a new document filename.

Using the Password-to-Modify Option

If you want to control who can make changes to a document file but not who can read a document file, you can use the password-to-modify option. With this option, anybody can open a file. But they must open the file as read-only unless they can supply the password-to-modify password. Actually, there are numerous uses for the password-to-modify option. Any time you have a document that can't be edited but can be freely circulated, you should probably use the password-to-modify option. By using the password-to-modify option, somebody must open your file as a read-only file unless he or she can supply the password.

To enable the password-to-modify option, enter a password in the Password To Modify text box in the Save options dialog box. Your password can be up to 15 characters long, and it is case-sensitive. (For instance, if you first enter the password as all lowercase letters, you must always use all lowercase letters when reentering the password.)

 When you click OK to close the Save options dialog box, the Office program asks you to confirm the password you entered—just to make sure that you really know your password—and it reminds you to remember your password.

After you assign a password-to-modify password, the Office program prompts anyone opening the file for the password, shown next.

```
┌─────────────────────────────────────────────┐
│ Password                          [?][X]     │
├─────────────────────────────────────────────┤
│ 'Letter to Mom.doc' is reserved by Patricia A. Coleman │
│                                              │
│ Enter password to modify, or open read only. │
│ Password:  [                              ]  │
│                                              │
│   [  OK  ]   [ Cancel ]   [ Read Only ]      │
└─────────────────────────────────────────────┘
```

If you (or anyone else) can supply the correct password, you (or they) can open the document file, make changes, and then resave the document file. If someone doesn't know the password, he or she can open the file but won't be able to resave the document file. (Note, however, that someone can save a new copy of the file as long as the file gets a new name.)

Using the Password-to-Open Option

If you want to control access to the information in a document file, you can use the password-to-open option. After you assign a password-to-open password, people who know (or can guess) the password can open the document. But nobody else can. To use the password-to-open option, just enter the password into the Password To Open text box, which also appears in the Save options dialog box.

Opening Document Files

You can open recently used document files in Windows using the Documents menu on the Start menu. You can also open Office documents as you open other files using Windows Explorer or My Computer. You can open document files from within an Office program as well by clicking the Open button or by choosing File | Open.

The Basics of Opening Documents from Within an Office Program

To open an existing document, click the Open button, which appears on the Standard toolbar, or choose File | Open. When the Office program displays the Open dialog box, shown in Figure 2-2, follow these steps to open the document file:

1. Use the Look In drop-down list box or the Places bar to select the document file's storage location. If the file you're looking for isn't in the default folder, activate the Look In drop-down list box to display a list of your drives. Click the drive that contains the document file you want, and then double-click folders and subfolders until you locate your file. Alternatively, you can start looking through the folder hierarchy by clicking the Up One Level button next to the Look In drop-down list box.

Click on one of these icons to display the location's contents.

Use the Look In drop-down list box to select the folder that stores the document file.

If you see the document file listed in this box, you can double-click it to open it.

The Places bar —

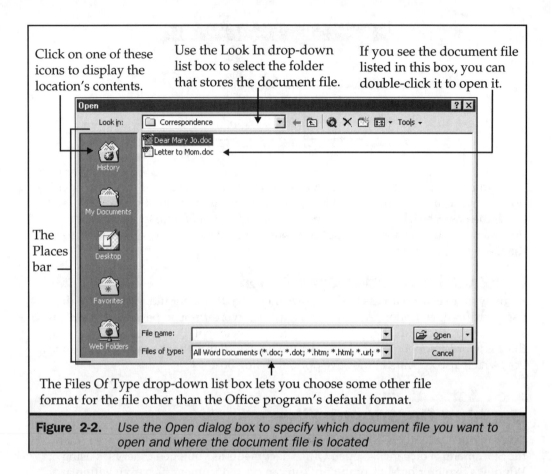

The Files Of Type drop-down list box lets you choose some other file format for the file other than the Office program's default format.

Figure 2-2.   *Use the Open dialog box to specify which document file you want to open and where the document file is located*

2. When you find the document file, double-click it or select it and click Open.

   To modify your search further, you can enter the filename into the File Name drop-down list box. Refer to "Searching for Lost Document Files" later in this chapter for more information on this feature.

   You can also typically use the File menu to reopen any of the four document files you used most recently. They are listed at the bottom of the File menu. Just click a file to open it. Chapter 4 describes how you can add more documents to the File menu.

Searching the Web

   If you click the Search the Web button in the Open dialog box, the Office program displays a Microsoft Network web page that you can use to conduct a search of the

Internet using any of the popular Internet search services. For more information about how search services work, refer to Chapter 6.

Using the Folder Icons

You can also open a document from any of the folder icons on the left in the Open dialog box. Simply click a folder to display its contents, and then double-click on the document name to open it. These same folder icons appear in the Save As dialog box. To save a document in one of these folders, simply click a folder to select it and then click Save.

Changing the Open Dialog Box's File Listing Information

One of the major advantages of using the Open dialog box to open a document file (rather than, in comparison, the Documents menu or the Windows Explorer) is that you can easily specify how you want document files listed and described. More specifically, you can use the items on the Views menu to change the way document files get listed in the Open dialog box. (Click on the down arrow next to the Views button to display the menu.) The following table identifies and describes these items:

Icon	Menu Item	Description
	List	Displays a simple list of document filenames and icons. If the current folder contains a large number of document files, the List option makes more of them visible at once than any other display option.
	Details	Displays fewer document files, but more details about each, such as file size and type. You can sort the listings differently by clicking on the Arrange Icons option and then selecting By Name, By Type, By Size, or By Date.
	Properties	Displays a simple document file listing combined with a summary of the selected file's properties from the Properties dialog box.
	Preview	Displays a simple document file listing and a preview of the selected document file.

Using the Tools Menu

Select a file in the Open dialog box, and click the Tools button to display a menu with an interesting assortment of commands.

Because the functions of a few of these commands aren't all that apparent, you may benefit from a quick review of how to use each one effectively.

Find

Choose the Find option to search for a file. See the "Searching for Lost Document Files" section later in this chapter for all the details.

Delete

You can delete a file in two ways: (1) Select the file and click the Delete button (the one with the × on it), or (2) select the file and then choose Tools | Delete.

Rename

To rename a file, select the filename and choose Rename. The Office program places a box around the filename. You can now simply type the new name for the file and press ENTER.

Print

The Print command prints one copy of the selected document using the default Windows printer. In effect, this Print command is equivalent to the Print toolbar button, which appears on the Standard toolbars of all the Office program windows.

 Later in this chapter, the section "Printing Document Files" describes in more detail how you print document files.

Add to Favorites

Use this command to add a file to your Favorites folder. Simply select the filename and choose Add to Favorites.

Map Network Drive

The Map Network Drive command displays the Map Network Drive dialog box, shown in Figure 2-3, which allows you to map, or connect to, another computer's disk

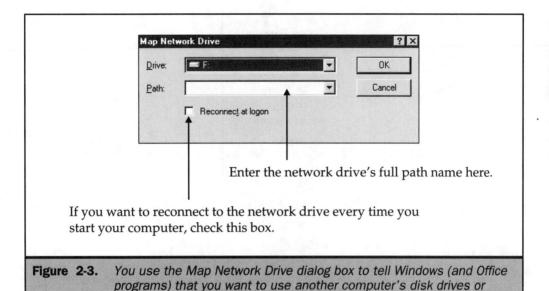

Figure 2-3.   *You use the Map Network Drive dialog box to tell Windows (and Office programs) that you want to use another computer's disk drives or storage devices*

or storage device. (To connect to some other computer's disk or storage device, by the way, your computer needs to be on a network.) After you choose the Map Network Drive, use the Path drop-down list box to provide the network drive path name in the form *computer name**disk name*. For example, if you wanted to use the hard disk drive named c$ on the computer named bobcat, you would enter **bobcat****c$** into the Path drop-down list box or select that entry from the drop-down list.

Properties

The Properties command displays the Properties dialog box for the selected document file. Document properties are covered in more detail in the section "Working with Document File Properties," later in this chapter.

Using the Shortcut Menu

If you right-click a document file listed in either the Open or Save As dialog box, Windows displays a shortcut menu of Windows file-management commands. On this menu you'll find some of the same commands that are on the Tools menu, including Print, Delete, Rename, and Properties.

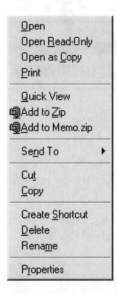

Again, because what some of these commands do isn't all that apparent, you'll benefit from a quick review of those that don't also appear on the Tools menu.

Open

This command simply opens the selected file.

Open Read-Only

Use the Open Read-Only command when you want to open a document file, even perhaps make changes to the document file, but don't want to replace the original version of the document with some, new modified document file.

 Earlier in the chapter, in the section entitled "Protecting Your Document Files and Using Passwords," this book describes how you can tell an Office program to recommend that users open a particular document file as read-only.

Open as Copy

The Open as Copy command creates a copy of the selected document file and then opens this copy rather than the original document file. When you use this command, by the way, the Office program names the new, copied document file by adding the words "Copy of" to the original document filename. For example, if you use this command to create a copy of a Word document named "Memo to Alfred," Word creates a new document named "Copy of Memo to Alfred." If you use this command to create a copy of an Excel workbook named "Next year's budget," Excel creates a new document named "Copy of Next year's budget."

Quick View

Choosing Quick View opens the selected document in a Quick View window, as shown in Figure 2-4. You can't edit the document in this window, but you can change the font size by clicking on the Increase Font Size and Decrease Font Size buttons.

The remaining items on the shortcut menu are primarily Windows commands that you'll find in most Windows programs and in Windows Explorer. If you have questions about any of these, see the user documentation that came with your copy of Windows or search for the command by name in Help.

Note *The Add to Zip program comes from the program WinZip, which you can install from the companion CD. You might also have other commands on your shortcut menu, such as a command for virus-scanning the file, depending on the programs you have installed on your computer.*

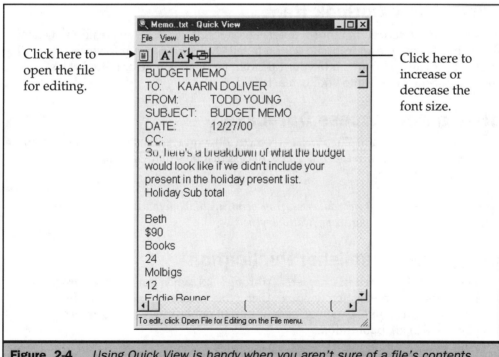

Click here to open the file for editing.

Click here to increase or decrease the font size.

Figure 2-4. *Using Quick View is handy when you aren't sure of a file's contents. For example, you might want to use Quick View before deleting a file*

Creating New Document Files

You create new document files in a variety of ways. Some programs, such as Word and Excel, for example, create new document files immediately when you start the program. And other programs, such as PowerPoint, Access, and Publisher prompt you to use wizards to create document files. In all programs, you can create new document files using the File menu's New command. Finally, in Outlook, you create new document files (or what Outlook calls "items") behind the scenes. In the paragraphs that follow, this book briefly discusses how and when you create document files with each of the Office programs.

Creating a New PowerPoint Presentation

In PowerPoint (as described in Chapters 17 through 19), you can create a new presentation when you start the program by selecting one of the new presentation options in the dialog box PowerPoint displays at startup. You can indicate that you want to run the AutoContent Wizard, or you can create a blank presentation or a presentation based on a design template.

Creating a New Outlook Item

In Outlook (as described in more detail in Chapters 20 and 21), you create a new item simply by clicking the appropriate button to tell Outlook you want to write an e-mail message, add an appointment to your calendar, jot down a note or to-do list task, or record someone's name into your contacts folder.

Creating a New Access Database

In Access (as described in Chapters 26 through 29), you typically create a new database at startup by indicating in the dialog box Access displays that you want to run the Database Wizard.

 You can also create new databases from scratch, although this book doesn't describe the mechanics of this more complicated approach.

Creating a New Publisher Publication

In Publisher (as described in Chapters 30 through 32), when you start the program, Publisher displays the Catalog window. Using this window, you can specify whether you want to create a publication using a wizard, a publication based on a design template, or a blank publication.

Creating New Word Documents and Excel Workbooks

 In Word and Excel, you actually create blank document files simply by starting the program. What's more, in both programs, you can also create blank document files by clicking the New Blank Document button, which appears on the Standard toolbar.

Using the File | New Command

Although using the New Blank Document toolbar button is the fastest way to create new documents in all Office programs, you can also choose File | New. And you'll want to do this whenever you want to create a new document based on a template. (A template is just a document file that is partially complete—either because it already stores information or because it already contains formatting.)

To create a new document file using the File menu's New command, choose the command and follow these steps:

1. Click the New dialog box tab that most closely describes the type of document you want to create.

2. When you see the document template you want to use as the basis for creating your new document file (such as the Word template shown in Figure 2-5), double-click it.

3. If a document template starts a wizard (some do), follow the wizard's instructions for completing the document.

 You can view the list of document templates in three ways. Click the buttons above the Preview box to view the templates as large icons, in a list, or in a list with file details.

Creating Your Own Document File Templates

If you use the same document file format frequently, you'll want to turn the document file into a template of your own, so you don't have to add the common content or formatting over and over to all of the documents you create. Document templates are particularly handy if you want to reuse a toolbar you've customized (as described in Chapter 4) or a macro you've created (as described in Chapter 3). To save a document file as a template, choose File | Save As and save the document file in almost the usual way. The only thing you need to do differently is select the Document Template option in the Save As Type drop-down list box, shown here:

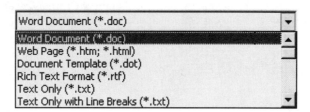

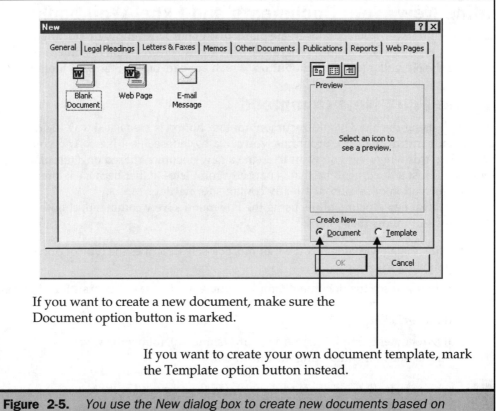

If you want to create a new document, make sure the Document option button is marked.

If you want to create your own document template, mark the Template option button instead.

Figure 2-5. *You use the New dialog box to create new documents based on existing Word or Excel templates*

Note *By default, the Office program saves document templates you create in its Templates folder so they appear on the General tab of the New dialog box. If you instead want a document template to appear on some other tab, select the Templates folder subfolder that corresponds to the tab. (In other words, if you want a document template to appear on the Memos tab, you need to store it in the Memos subfolder of the Templates folder.)*

Tip *You can create new tabs for the New dialog box by creating new subfolders in the Templates folder. You can do this using the Windows Explorer or, as described in the earlier section, "Saving Document Files," by using the Create New Folder button on the Save As dialog box.*

Working with Document File Properties

Although many of your document files will no doubt be similar in many respects, they will all have individual characteristics—properties, in other words—that distinguish them from one another. For example, they use different names, are of differing sizes, were probably created at different times, and so forth. These properties can be useful to you in a couple of important ways: they provide a valuable record associated with each document file, allowing you to describe document files, and they can make it easier for you to locate missing document files.

Describing Document File Properties

Document file properties can be divided into five general types, corresponding to the five tabs on the Properties dialog box, shown in Figure 2-6. To open the Properties dialog box, choose File | Properties.

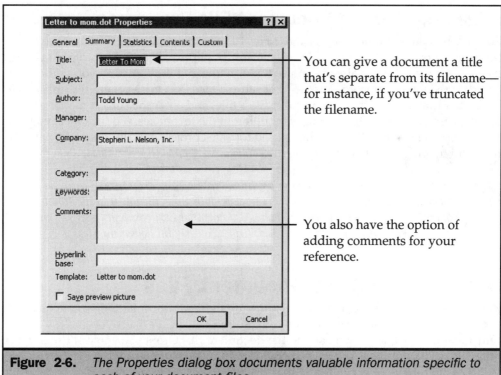

Figure 2-6.   *The Properties dialog box documents valuable information specific to each of your document files*

The General tab, as you might expect, lists general information about a document file, including its name, type, location, and size. In addition, the General tab contains statistical information also found on the Statistics tab and a record of certain file attributes.

The Summary tab (shown in Figure 2-6) lets you enter information about the document file, including its subject matter and notes or comments. In addition, you can include keywords to make file searches easier.

The Statistics tab shows when the document file was created and when it was last modified, accessed, and printed. Also included are the name of the person who last saved it (important for network users), the number of times it has been revised, the total time it has been open, and other bits of information.

The Contents tab describes the contents of a document file: the worksheets in an Excel workbook file, the headings in a Word document (if the Save Preview Picture check box on the Summary tab has been enabled), the slides in a PowerPoint presentation, and so on.

You can use the Custom tab to create properties for the active document.

Entering and Viewing Document File Properties

To describe your document files, choose File | Properties, and click the Summary tab. (In Access, you actually choose File | Database Properties.) The Office program you're using will have probably already entered your name and the company you work for, based on the information you provided at setup. Once the Office program displays the Properties dialog box, you can give your file a title, and enter the subject matter and any comments you may have, simply by filling in the text boxes. (For instance, you might make a note about assumptions used for sales projections, or you might name the client for whom you prepared the file.)

Note *To make your file easier to find later on, be as specific as you can here. If there's a keyword that you know you'll always associate with a file, include it in the summary properties. It could come in handy later. Also note that Outlook items possess a more limited set of properties than Word, Excel, and PowerPoint document files.*

Searching for Lost Document Files

You've probably had the experience of knowing there's a document file somewhere on your hard disk that you need but that you also can't locate. Perhaps you can't remember in which folder you stored the document file. Or maybe you can't remember what the document file is called. You could try just browsing through your disk in Windows Explorer. And sometimes that will work. But there are much more powerful tools available to you.

Using the Find Feature

Your first line of attack is by clicking the Tools button in the Open dialog box and choosing the pop-up menu's Find command. Selecting Find opens the Find dialog box, as shown in Figure 2-7.

By default, the Office program assumes that you want to find a "native" document file. This means that if you open the Find dialog box from Word's Open dialog box, Word thinks you want to look for a Word document. If this is not the case, select the file type criteria from the list box and click Delete. Then select File Type from the Property drop-down list box, select the correct file type from the Condition drop-down list box, and click Add to List.

If you know the directory (folder) where your file is located, select it from the Look In drop-down list box. You can search your entire disk drive by selecting it in the Look In box. Or, point to a floppy drive, if your file is on a floppy disk.

If you know part of the name of a file, and can't remember where it is, click the And option button and select File Name from the Property drop-down list box. Then select

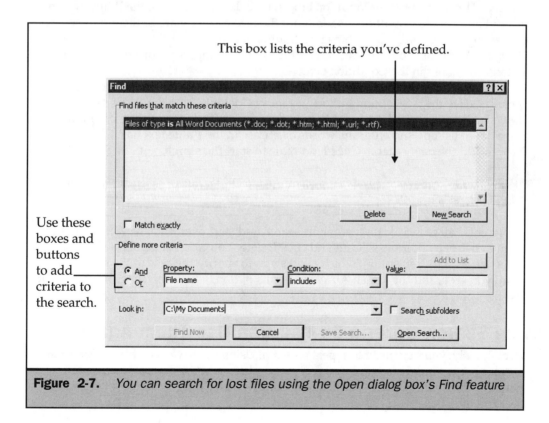

Figure 2-7. *You can search for lost files using the Open dialog box's Find feature*

Includes, Begins With, or Ends With from the Condition drop-down list box, and enter the part of the name in the Value text box. Click Add to List and then click Find Now to begin the search. The Office program displays a list of all files that match your specification in the Open dialog box.

Searching for Specific Text or Properties

If you can't remember the name of the file, you may be able to remember some specific aspect about it. You can add criteria to your search based on the aspects you know.

Use the And and Or buttons to tell the Office program whether each new criterion that you add is in addition to or instead of the previous criteria.

The Property drop-down list box lets you define which property about the Office file you remember and want to use for the search. For example, you can choose to search not only by file type or name but also by size, date, text, or any one of a number of different properties.

The Condition drop-down list box allows you to zero in on the property you entered. The listings in the Condition box change depending upon the Property you select. For example, conditions that modify the Size property are limited to those expressing numerical relationships like "more than" or "equals."

In the Value list box, you can enter either text or numbers to further define the criteria you chose in the Condition box.

For example, if you remember some piece of text that the file you're looking for includes, click the And option button and select Contents from the Property drop-down list box. Then click Includes Words or Includes Phrase from the Condition drop-down list box and enter the words or phrase in the Value text box. Click Add New to add the new criteria. Click Find Now to start the search.

> **Note**   *The Office program sometimes changes And to Or if it finds a contradiction in the criteria you select.*

To erase all criteria from a previous search and start over, click New Search. If you want to delete a criterion, select it and click Delete. You can further define your search using the Match Case option, which allows you to specify the case of the letters in the word you seek, and the Match All Word Forms option, which searches for words that use the same root as what you specify.

Saving Search Criteria So You Can Use Them Again

Occasionally, you may need to repeat a search. Using the Save Search and Open Search buttons in the Find dialog box, you can save and revisit previous searches, saving yourself much time. When you click Save Search, Office programs display the Save Search dialog box.

Save Search	? ✕
Name for this search	OK
	Cancel

To use the Save Search dialog box, simply enter a name for the search, and click OK.

To later open a saved search, click the Open Search button to display the Open Search dialog box. Select the search you want and click Open. You can delete and rename saved searches in this dialog box as well.

Printing Document Files

The Office programs all make it very easy to print their document files. As a general rule, for example, you can click the Print toolbar button to print just about any Office document file—and usually in a way you'll find acceptable. Nevertheless, it's still extremely beneficial to go beyond this simple (although highly effective) technique because in doing so you'll learn how to print Office document files that look exactly the way you want.

Printing Basics

As mentioned in the preceding paragraph, you can print the open document file—Word document, Excel workbook, PowerPoint presentation, Access database file object, or Outlook item—by clicking the Print toolbar button. When you click the Print toolbar button, you in effect tell the Office program to print the open document file in the usual way. (The "usual" way just means with all the default, or suggested, print settings.)

If you don't want to use the default, or suggested, print settings—or if you want to verify the print settings—you can choose File | Print. When you do, the Office program displays a dialog box like that shown in Figure 2-8.

Changing the Printer

Use the Name drop-down list box to specify which printer (when you use more than one printer) you want to use to print the Office document file. To specify a different printer, simply select one from the Name list box.

If you want to change the way the printer works, you can click the Properties button, which appears just to the right of the Name drop-down list box, to display the printer's Properties dialog box. Different printers provide different properties, so it's impossible to describe here which printer options you can change with the printer's Properties dialog box. Typically, however, you use the printer's Properties dialog box

Figure 2-8.   *You can use the Print dialog box to specify how an Office program such as Word should print a document file*

to specify settings such as the page orientation (landscape versus portrait, for example), the paper size, and (when your printer includes multiple paper trays) the paper source.

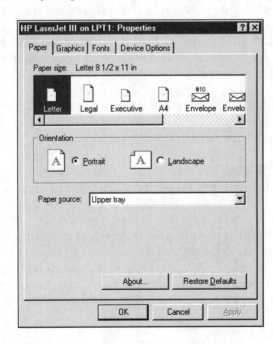

Setting the Number of Copies and Collating Them

You can tell an Office program how many copies of a document file you want to print, by entering a number in the Number Of Copies box in the Print dialog box. If you want them collated, check the Collate box. (Checking the Collate box tells the printer to print each copy complete, from the first page to the last, instead of printing all the first pages, followed by all the second pages, and so on.)

Printing to a File

Office programs let you print your document files to a file instead of to a printer. (Printing to a file means saving a copy of the document file in a form that can be read by a printer.) Printing to a file is not something you'll do with any frequency, but it can be useful when you want to print a document file later, on a different computer and printer. Printer files use the file extension .PRN.

To print to a file, check the Print To File box in the Print dialog box, and click OK. This displays the Print To File dialog box, which bears a striking resemblance to the Save As dialog box. Give the file a name and select a destination folder in the Print To File dialog box, and then click OK again.

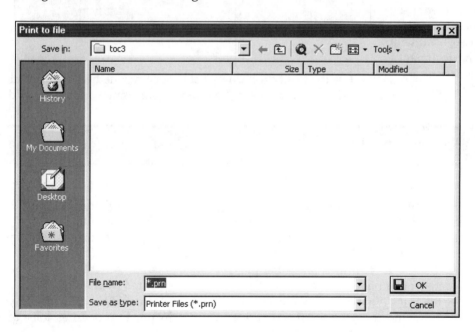

Setting Word-Specific Print Options

Word provides several print options specific to its document files, as shown in Figure 2-9: Page Range option buttons, the Print What drop-down list box, the Print drop-down list box, and the Options command button.

Use the Page Range option buttons to indicate which pages of a document you want to print.

Use the Print What drop-down list to specify whether Word should print the document itself or information associated with the document, such as Comments.

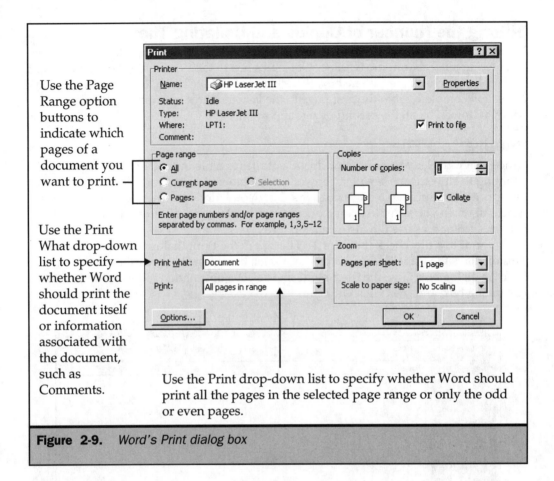

Use the Print drop-down list to specify whether Word should print all the pages in the selected page range or only the odd or even pages.

Figure 2-9.   *Word's Print dialog box*

As you might guess, you use the Page Range option buttons to indicate which pages of a document file you want to print. If you want to print the entire Word document, select the All option button. If you want to print just the current page (the page that shows in the Word document window), select the Current Page option button. If you want to print a particular page or range of pages, select the Pages option button; then enter page numbers and/or page ranges separated by commas.

Use the Print What drop-down list to specify which document file information you want to print: the document itself, a description of the document properties, a list of the comments you've used to annotate the document, and so forth.

The Print drop-down list box lets you specify which pages in the selected page range you want to print: all pages, just the even-numbered pages, or just the odd-numbered pages.

Finally, if you click the Options button, Word displays the Print options dialog box. It essentially provides a large set of check boxes you use to further refine and more precisely control how Word prints the open document. If you have questions about one of the options in the Print options dialog box, click the What's This? button and then click the check box you have a question about. The What's This? button is explained in detail in Chapter 3.

Setting Excel Workbook Print Options

Excel provides two print options specific to its document files, as shown in Figure 2-10: the Print Range option buttons and boxes and the Print What option buttons.

Use the Print Range option buttons to indicate which pages of a workbook you want to print. If you want to print the entire Excel workbook, select the All option button. If you want to print just specified pages, click the Pages option button and then use the From and To text boxes to enter page numbers or page ranges.

You can also use the Print What option buttons to specify the portion of a workbook you want to print: Selection, which means the selected range on a worksheet; Active Sheet(s), which means any selected worksheet; or Entire Workbook.

Use the Print Range option buttons to indicate which pages of a workbook you want to print.

Use the Print What option buttons to specify which sheets of a workbook you want to print.

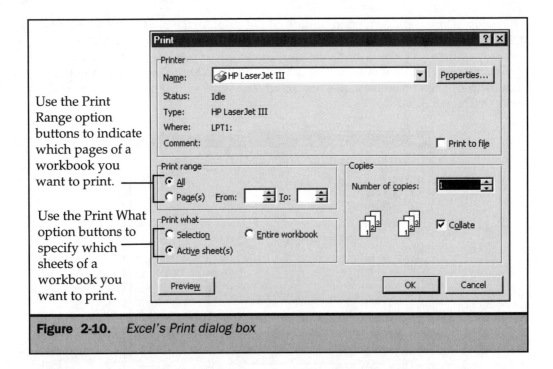

Figure 2-10.   *Excel's Print dialog box*

Setting PowerPoint-Specific Print Options

PowerPoint provides three categories of print options specific to its presentations: the Print Range option buttons and boxes, the Print What option buttons, and the check boxes that appear beneath the Print What option buttons. (See Figure 2-11.)

Use the Print Range option buttons to indicate which slides of a presentation you want to print. If you want to print the entire PowerPoint presentation, select the All option button. If you want to print only the currently selected slide, select the Current Slide option button. If you want to print just specified pages, click the Slides option button and then use the Slides text box to enter a slide number range. (The Custom Show button lets you print a subset of the presentation's slides that you've previously set up as a custom PowerPoint slide show.)

Use the Print What drop-down list box to specify what portion of a presentation you want to print: Slides (the actual slides or overhead transparencies), Handouts (pieces of paper with pictures of the slides but also plenty of extra room for taking notes), Notes Pages (speakers' note pages), and Outline View (an outline of the presentation).

    If you have a question about speaker's notes or presentation outlines, refer to Chapter 17.

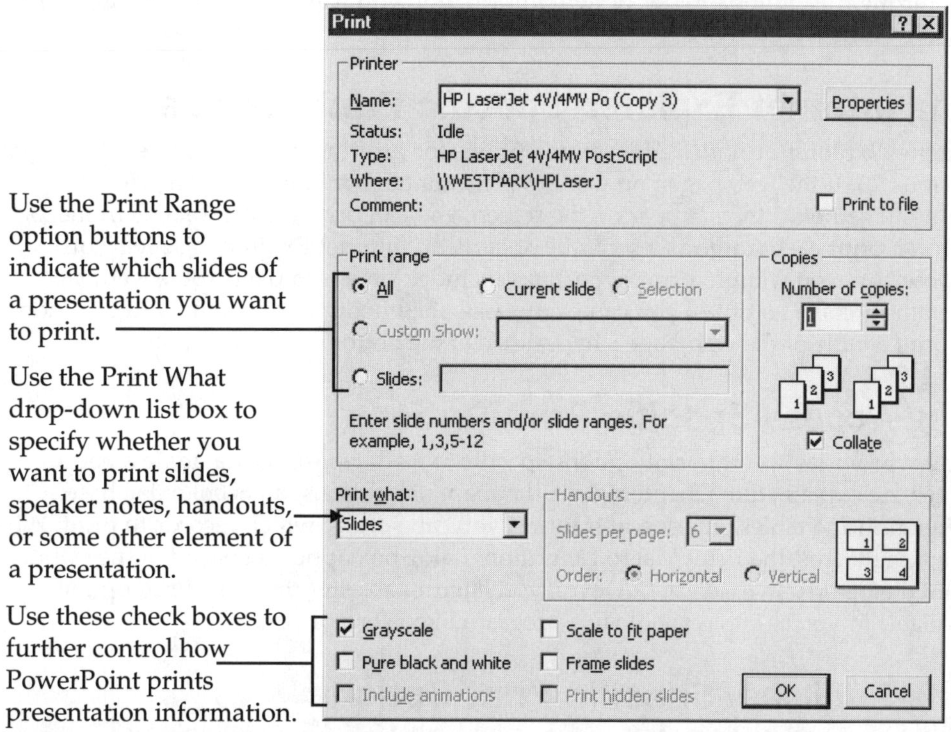

Use the Print Range option buttons to indicate which slides of a presentation you want to print.

Use the Print What drop-down list box to specify whether you want to print slides, speaker notes, handouts, or some other element of a presentation.

Use these check boxes to further control how PowerPoint prints presentation information.

Figure 2-11. *PowerPoint's Print dialog box*

Finally, the check boxes that appear beneath the Print What drop-down list box let you exert even more control over the way that PowerPoint prints slides. You can check the Grayscale box if you want PowerPoint to adjust the colors used in your presentation so that the printed copy of your presentation looks reasonable in black and white (and shades of gray). Or, you can check the Pure Black & White box if you don't want PowerPoint to use shades of gray in its black-and-white printing. You can mark the Scale To Fit Paper box if you want PowerPoint to adjust the size of the printed slides so they fit nicely on whatever paper you use to print them. You can mark the Frame Slides box if you want PowerPoint to draw a thin line around printed slides, handouts, and notes to frame the information.

Setting Outlook-Specific Print Options

Outlook provides numerous print options specific to its folders and items. But basically all these program-specific print options simply boil down to different ways of organizing the Outlook folder or item information you want to print—creating what Outlook calls a *print style*.

Setting Internet Explorer–Specific Print Options

Internet Explorer provides a few extra options for printing web pages as explained in Chapter 23. If the web page you want to print contains frames, you can print the frames together as they appear on the screen, you can print only the active frame, or you can print each frame as a separate document. Internet Explorer also lets you choose how you want to print hyperlinks included on a web page. If the web page contains links to text files, you can print these documents as well. And you can choose to print a table of the web page's hyperlinks at the bottom of the printout.

Setting Access-Specific Print Options

Access provides several print options specific to its databases or database objects, which are explained in Chapter 26. (A database object is just a part of a database.) When printing tables, queries, and forms, you can specify which records to print. When printing macros, the Print Macro Definition dialog box appears instead of the standard Print dialog box. In essence, however, you have a subset of the same print options available to you as are available in a program like Word or Excel.

Setting Publisher-Specific Print Options

Publisher, as a desktop publishing program, provides several printing options not available in any of the other Office programs. It also includes several options for preparing a publication for printing at a commercial printer. Chapter 32 is devoted entirely to these topics.

Controlling Page Setup in Office Programs

In all the Office programs, you can also use the File menu's Page Setup command to control how the Office programs print. It's by using the Page Setup command, for example, that you change the print orientation from portrait to landscape or vice versa, that you easily adjust page margins, and that you specify paper sizes.

Page Setup Basics

In Word, Excel, Outlook, and Access, you make changes to the page setup by choosing File | Page Setup. (Some Office programs also include a Setup command button on their Print dialog boxes or on their Print Preview windows, but File | Page Setup is still usually the easiest way to make page setup changes—if only because the command is always available in Word, Excel, Outlook, and Access.) When you choose the Page

Setup command, the Office program displays a dialog box—in some cases, with multiple tabs—that lets you make your changes.

Making Word-Specific Page Setup Changes

When you choose File | Page Setup in Word, you see a Page Setup dialog box like the one shown next. The Margins tab (shown here) lets you specify top, bottom, left, and right margins; gutters; and where headers and footers should appear. To specify a margin, for example, use the Top, Bottom, Left, or Right spin boxes. If you've added headers and footers to the Word document, use the Header and Footer spin boxes to indicate how far from the page's top or bottom edge the margin should be placed. Use the Apply To drop-down list box to indicate whether your margin settings apply to the entire document or from the current page forward.

Check the Mirror Margins box if you want facing pages to use the same inside and outside margins.

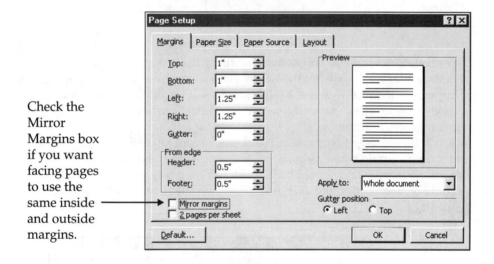

Note *A gutter is an extra amount of margin space added (usually) to the left margin for a document's binding.*

The Paper Size tab, shown next, lets you specify which size paper you're using and lets you choose a page orientation. As with the Margins tab, you can use the Apply To drop-down list box to indicate whether your paper size settings apply to the entire document or from the current page forward.

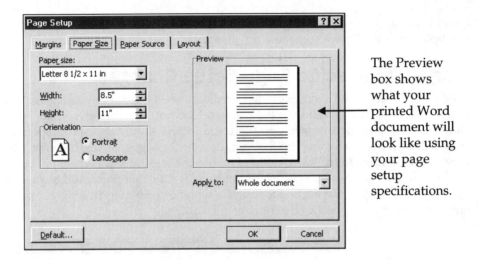

The Preview box shows what your printed Word document will look like using your page setup specifications.

The Paper Source tab lets you choose which printer tray you want to use for printing. For example, you may want the first page of a lengthy document to appear on letterhead paper, but the second and subsequent pages of the document to appear on plain, so-called "second-sheet" paper. Note that the Paper Source tab options that you see will depend on your printer.

The fourth and final Page Setup tab in Word, the Layout tab, lets you specify if a new section should start on a new page, a new column, or the next odd- or even-numbered page; how text should be vertically aligned on a page; whether line numbers should be used to number each line of the document; and whether to apply borders to the page.

If you've added endnotes to your Word document, you can check this box if you don't want them to print.

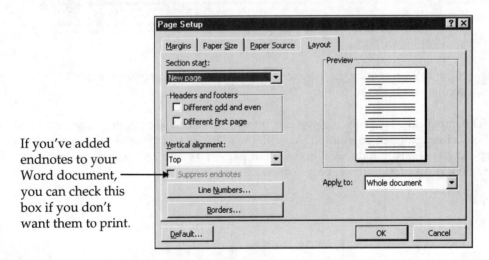

Chapter 7 describes how you can create and use Word sections.

Making Excel-Specific Page Setup Changes

When you choose File | Page Setup in Excel, you see a Page Setup dialog box like the one shown here. The Page tab lets you choose a page orientation, control the scaling of the printed worksheet, and specify which size paper you're using and the print quality you want. It also lets you specify the starting page number. How these options work will probably be obvious to you if you're familiar with Excel, but if you have questions, click the What's This? button and then the box or button you have a question about.

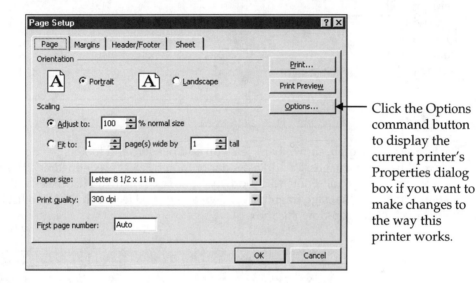

Click the Options command button to display the current printer's Properties dialog box if you want to make changes to the way this printer works.

Note   *When you scale the size of a printout up or down, Excel adjusts both dimensions proportionally. For instance, choosing 200% normal size doubles both the width and the height of a printout.*

The Margins tab, shown next, lets you specify top, bottom, left, and right margins; gutters; and where headers and footers should appear. To specify a margin, for example, use the Top, Bottom, Left, or Right spin boxes. If you've added headers and footers to the Excel workbook, use the Header and Footer spin boxes to indicate how far from the page's top or bottom edge the header or footer margin should be placed. You can also use the Center On Page check boxes—Horizontally and Vertically—to indicate how you want a worksheet range aligned on a page.

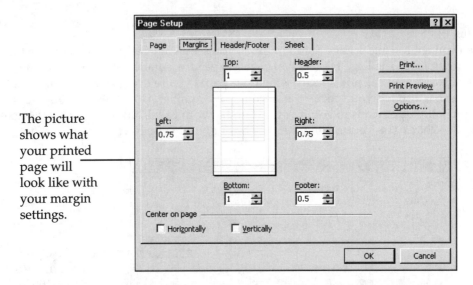

The picture shows what your printed page will look like with your margin settings.

The Header/Footer tab, shown here, lets you add headers and footers to your printed Excel workbook pages. To add a header or footer, select predefined headers or footers from the Header and Footer drop-down list boxes. When you do, Excel adds the header or footer to the page fragments shown above the Header drop-down list box and below the Footer drop-down list box.

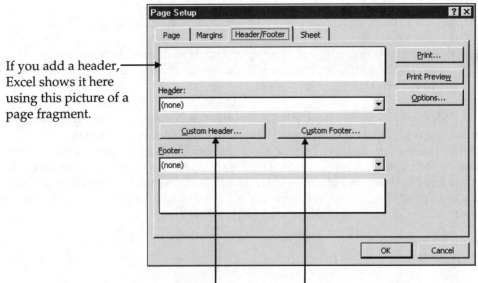

If you add a header, Excel shows it here using this picture of a page fragment.

You can click the Custom Header or Custom Footer command button to display a dialog box you can use to create your own customized headers and footers.

The fourth and final tab on Excel's Page Setup dialog box, the Sheet tab, lets you make a rich variety of page setup specifications. If you want to print only a certain range of cells on a worksheet, you can enter that worksheet range (or multiple worksheet ranges) into the Print Area text box. If you want to repeat a row or several rows at the top of each page, you can enter the worksheet range for the repeating row or rows into the Rows To Repeat At Top text box. (You use a repeating row to label your columns.) If you want to repeat a column or several columns on the left side of each page, you can enter the worksheet range for the repeating column or columns into the Columns To Repeat At Left text box.

You can click the two Page Order option buttons to see a graphic display of the effect they produce.

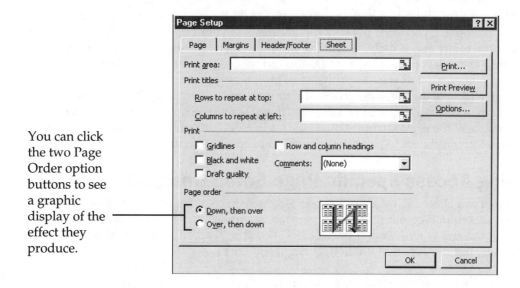

Tip   *You can click the Collapse Dialog buttons, which appear at the right end of the Print area, Rows To Repeat At Top, and Columns To Repeat At Left text boxes to temporarily shrink the Page Setup dialog box so it's possible and easy to select a worksheet range with the mouse. When you're ready to expand the dialog box, click the button again.*

If you want the worksheet gridlines to appear in the printed worksheet, check the Gridlines box. You can check the Black And White box if you want your printer to ignore background color formatting (a good option to check if you have a black-and-white printer). If you want to speed up printing of the workbook, you can check the Draft Quality box. (In this case, Excel doesn't print gridlines and most graphic images.) You can check the Row And Column Headings box to tell your printer to print the standard row and column headings (such as A, B, 1, 2, and so on) that you see on the screen, but which normally don't show up on printouts. (This option might be of interest to you if, for instance, you wanted to refer to particular worksheet cells or formulas in your printouts.) If you want to print the cell annotations that you can create using the Insert menu's Comments command, select one of the entries from the Comments drop-down list box. Finally, you can also use the Page Order option buttons to specify how Excel should break a large worksheet range into page-sized chunks.

> **Note**   *Gridlines are the light solid lines displayed on your screen that separate rows and columns. They won't show up on printouts unless you ask for them.*

Making Outlook-Specific Page Setup Changes

Outlook provides different page setup options for the type of item you select to print. For example, if you want to print appointments in your calendar folder, you have the options of printing a daily, weekly, or monthly calendar. And then you can select the range of dates you want to print. Or you can choose to print just the details of a single appointment. If you want to print e-mail messages, you can select whether you want to print a table of the messages in a folder or each one individually. You can also choose to print message attachments. Likewise, if you want to print contacts, you can choose the style of the printout: individual cards, a booklet, or a phone directory, for example. And you can choose to print the selected contacts or all contacts.

Making Access-Specific Page Setup Changes

When you choose File | Page Setup in Access, you see a Page Setup dialog box like the one shown in Figure 2-12. The Margins tab lets you specify top, bottom, left, and right margins, and where headers and footers should appear. To specify a margin, you simply use the Top, Bottom, Left, or Right text boxes.

> **Note**   *Check the Print Headings box if you want a datasheet's column headings to print.*

The Page tab, shown in Figure 2-13, lets you choose a page orientation, indicate which size paper you're using, and select a paper source. You can also specify that you want to use a particular printer by clicking the Use Specific Printer option button, clicking the Printer command button, and then selecting a printer from the dialog box that Access displays.

Using Print Preview

One of the most useful features in Word, Excel, Outlook, and Access is called Print Preview. (The Print Preview feature isn't available in PowerPoint.) It does just what its name suggests—it gives you the ability to preview what your printed page or pages will look like, before you print. Using Print Preview, you can check, among other things, the way page breaks divide up your document file, how the margins are set, and how the header and footer appear.

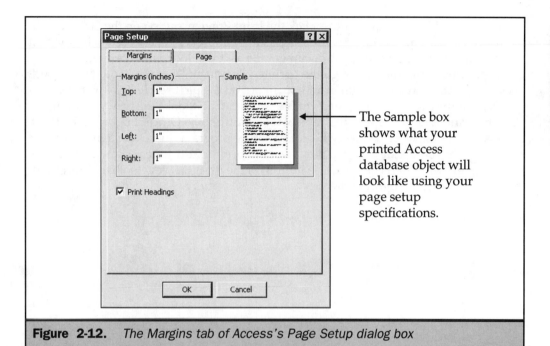

The Sample box shows what your printed Access database object will look like using your page setup specifications.

Figure 2-12.   *The Margins tab of Access's Page Setup dialog box*

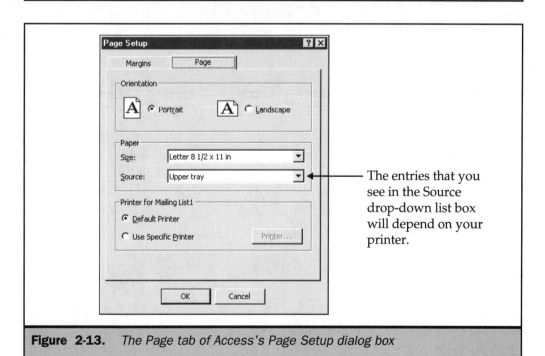

The entries that you see in the Source drop-down list box will depend on your printer.

Figure 2-13.   *The Page tab of Access's Page Setup dialog box*

INTRODUCING OFFICE

To use the Print Preview feature, click the Print Preview button on the Standard toolbar or choose File | Print Preview. Using either approach, you'll see a window that will display an entire page of your document file as it will look when printed.

To page back and forth through the "printed document," use the PAGE UP and PAGE DOWN keys. To alternately zoom in and zoom out on the picture, click the picture.

To print the document file when you've verified that it looks the way you want, click the Print button on the Print Preview toolbar. (In some Office programs, the Print command uses the label "Print," while other Office programs just show a picture of a printer.) Or, if you decide that you don't want to print the document showing in the Print Preview window, click the Close button on the Print Preview toolbar. This closes the print preview, not the document.

Chapter 3

Using the Common
Office Tools

The individual Microsoft Office 2000 programs share many of the same features, tools, and capabilities. They all use a charming little interface element called the Office Assistant to make your work easier and more fun. They check spelling in roughly the same way. They also provide common tools such as the Drawing tool.

This commonality produces a big benefit for you, the user, because it means that by learning to use a common feature, tool, or capability in one program—say Word—you've also indirectly learned how to use the equivalent feature, tool, or capability in another program such as Excel or PowerPoint. To make sure that you understand and can use all these features, tools, and capabilities, this chapter describes these common elements.

Getting Help from the Office Assistant

You are probably already familiar with the Office Assistant. The Office Assistant is the usually helpful albeit sometimes annoying interface element that, in effect, acts as a knowledge cushion between you and the program you're working with.

The Office Assistant watches your work; makes occasional suggestions for working more efficiently; passes messages back and forth between you and the program; and, when asked, attempts to answer any questions you might have.

Turning on the Office Assistant

If you can see the Office Assistant's program window on your desktop (typically on top of an Office program window, as shown in Figure 3-1), you don't have to turn it on. It's already running. If you can't see the Office Assistant and you want to use it, choose Help | Show the Office Assistant command. To close the Office Assistant, choose Help | Hide the Office Assistant command.

Using the Office Assistant

To use the Office Assistant, enter a question in the Office Assistant balloon's text box and then click the Search button. (If the balloon doesn't appear, simply click the Office Assistant.) Figure 3-1 shows the example question, "How do I print a document?"

When the Office Assistant displays a list of Help topics (essentially just essays about how to accomplish certain tasks), click the button that corresponds to the Help topic you want to read, as shown next.

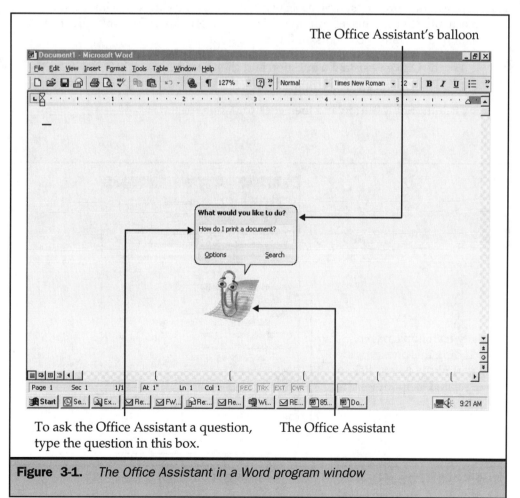

Figure 3-1. *The Office Assistant in a Word program window*

For example, if you click the Print A Document Help topic, as shown in the preceding illustration, the Office Assistant starts the Help program and displays the Help topic shown in Figure 3-2.

If the Office Assistant doesn't return any Help topics applicable to your question, you can click None Of The Above, Look For More Help On The Web button. When the Office Assistant displays the Finding Help Topics pane, you can edit your question if necessary, enter it in the text box and then click the Send And Go To The Web button to send your question to Microsoft if you have an Internet connection.

Using the Help Program

The Help program provides three basic ways in which you can access information in a Help file: a table of contents, an Answer Wizard, and an index. To display the Help information file's table of contents, follow these steps:

1. Ask the Office Assistant a question and click Search.

2. Select one of the answer buttons.

3. Click the Show button and then click the Contents tab.

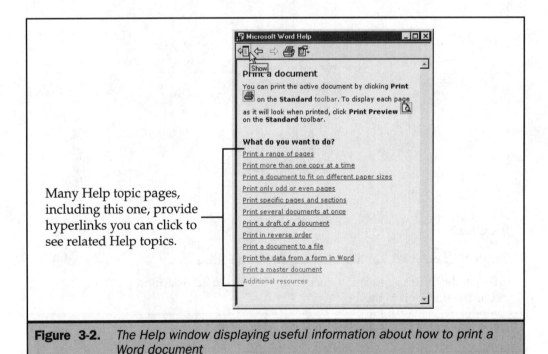

Figure 3-2. *The Help window displaying useful information about how to print a Word document*

To open the Help information file to a particular chapter, double-click one of the book icons to the left of the chapters listed in the table of contents. To open a particular chapter section, double-click it. The Help text appears in the window on the right. In Figure 3-3 you can see what all these little icons and the Help text look like.

In addition to browsing through Help using the Contents tab, you can also use the Answer Wizard or Index tab.

The Answer Wizard tab, as shown in Figure 3-4, works much the same as the Office Assistant. Type your question, click Search, and then click a topic. Its information is displayed in the window on the right. Click an underlined subtopic to display its text.

When you click the Index tab, Windows displays a two-level index of Help topics. To find a Help topic, you can scroll through this list using the PAGE UP and PAGE DOWN keys or the scroll bar. You can also type a brief description of the Help topic you want to find into the text box, as I have done in Figure 3-5. When you see the Help topic you want to read listed, just double-click it.

Customizing the Office Assistant

If you click the Options button on the Office Assistant's balloon (see Figure 3-1), Office Assistant displays the dialog box shown here. Its Options tab provides a series of check boxes that let you specify what the Office Assistant should and shouldn't do.

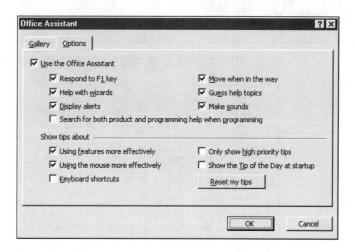

You can use the What's This? button in a window to get a more detailed description of what a check box does. To do this, click the What's This? button and then the box or button you have a question about. To learn what a box or button in a dialog box does, click the dialog box's question mark button and then click the box or button you have a question about.

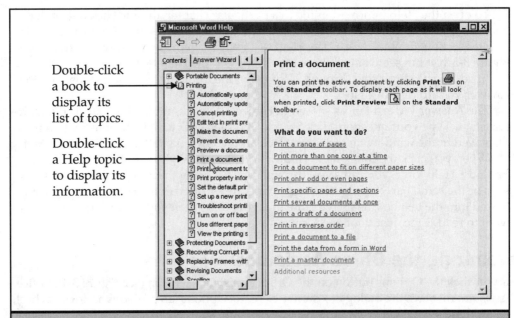

Double-click a book to display its list of topics.

Double-click a Help topic to display its information.

Figure 3-3. *When you select a topic, it is displayed in the window on the right*

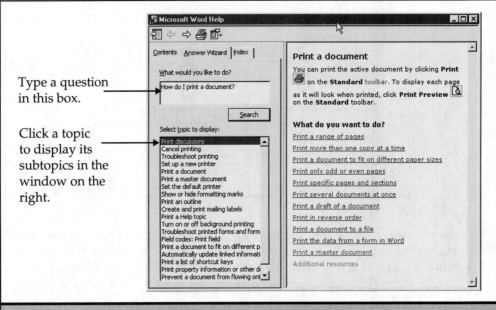

Type a question in this box.

Click a topic to display its subtopics in the window on the right.

Figure 3-4. *The Answer Wizard tab in Microsoft Word Help*

Enter the first part of the Help topic name in this box to have Word search its index.

Click the Help topic you want to read.

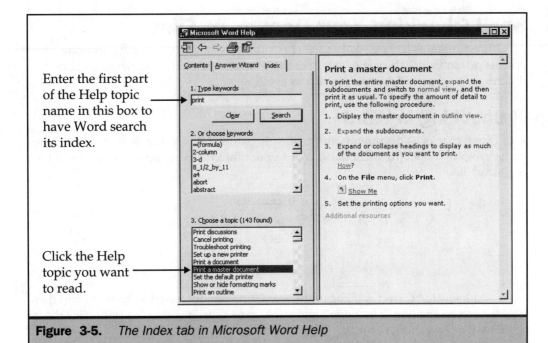

Figure 3-5.   *The Index tab in Microsoft Word Help*

The Gallery tab of the Office Assistant dialog box lets you choose a character for the Office Assistant. The default character, shown in the preceding figures and illustrations, is Clippit. You have several other choices, however, including a bouncing red dot, an Einstein-like professor (shown next), and a robot. To select a different character, use the Next and Back buttons until you see the character you want. Then click OK. You may have to insert your Office 2000 CD in your CD-ROM to install the new character.

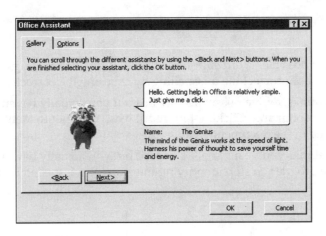

Spell Checking Your Document Files

All Office programs let you easily spell check document files. Curiously, however, the process doesn't work the same way in each Office program. The following sections describe how each Office program checks spelling

Spell Checking in Word

Word spell checks its documents automatically by default. If you type a word that's not in the program's spelling dictionary, Word underlines the possible misspelling with a red, wavy line:

If you know the correct spelling of the word, you can double-click the word and then type the correct spelling. If you don't know the correct spelling, you can right-click the word to display a shortcut menu:

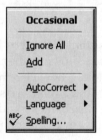

The shortcut menu provides several useful commands for dealing with the misspelled word:

- Whenever possible, Word supplies a list of alternative spellings on the shortcut menu. You can correct the misspelling by choosing the correctly spelled word.

- If Word thinks you've misspelled a word but you actually haven't, click the Ignore All command. Clicking Ignore All tells Word not to identify this word as misspelled in the document.

- If Word thinks you've misspelled a word but you actually haven't and you want the program to stop identifying the word as misspelled in this and all future documents, click the Add command. Clicking Add tells Word to place the selected word into your custom dictionary. Once you've placed a word in the custom dictionary, Word won't identify it as misspelled in any document.

- If you want Word to automatically fix this misspelling now and in the future, select AutoCorrect and then choose the correct spelling from the AutoCorrect submenu. ("Using AutoCorrect," later in this chapter, describes what AutoCorrect is and how it works.)

- If Word thinks you've misspelled a non-English word, select Language, and click Set Language to display the Language dialog box. Then select a language from the list to mark the selected text as that language.

- If you want to correct the misspelling in some way other than that already described here, click Spelling to display the Spelling dialog box. Then use the Spelling dialog box to describe how you want the misspelling corrected. For example, you can choose to ignore or change the selected occurrence of a misspelling or all occurrences of it.

Note   *If Word doesn't automatically spell check your documents, click Tools | Options, click the Spelling & Grammar tab, and then check the Check Spelling As You Type box. Note, too, that the Spelling & Grammar tab provides more than a dozen other buttons and boxes that you can use to control the way Word checks spelling and grammar in your Word document.*

Grammar Checking Your Word Documents

When Word identifies a grammar error, it places a green wavy line under the offending word, phrase, or sentence. You can fix the grammar error manually by editing the text. Or you can right-click the error to display a shortcut menu of commands similar to those you use to correct misspellings. If Word knows the correct word, phrase, or sentence, it displays it on the shortcut menu so that you can select it. Word also provides an Ignore command (which you can use to tell Word that it should ignore what it thinks is a grammar error) and a Grammar command (which you can use to display the Grammar dialog box and its additional grammar-checking buttons and boxes). To turn Word's grammar checker on or off, choose Tools | Options, click the Spelling & Grammar tab, and then check the Check Grammar As You Type box.

Spell Checking in Excel

Excel's spell checking isn't automatic, but it's still very easy. To spell check a workbook or the selected range, choose Tools | Spelling. If Excel identifies a misspelled word, it displays the Spelling dialog box (see Figure 3-6). Near the top of the dialog box, Excel displays the misspelled word and provides a list of suggested alternative spellings. If Excel is not able to supply alternative spellings, you can use the Change To text box to supply a new replacement word for the misspelled word. If the word isn't misspelled, you can click the Ignore button to ignore only this occurrence of the word or click the Ignore All button to ignore this and every other occurrence of the word.

If you want to change the misspelling to what shows in the Change To text box, click the Change button to change only this occurrence of the word, or click the Change All button to change this and every other occurrence of the word.

If the word Excel thinks is misspelled isn't actually misspelled and you want Excel to stop identifying it as such in this and all future workbooks, click the Add button. Clicking Add tells Excel to add the selected word to the custom spelling dictionary identified in the Add Words To drop-down list box. Once a word has been added to the custom dictionary, it won't be identified as misspelled any more. You typically need to do this with words and terms you've created yourself (product names, trademarks, and so on), as well as with esoteric words and terms (shoptalk, industry-specific buzzwords, and so forth).

If you want Excel to automatically correct a misspelling every time you enter it, select the correct spelling and click the AutoCorrect button. Clicking AutoCorrect tells Excel to add the selected word to its list of AutoCorrect entries.

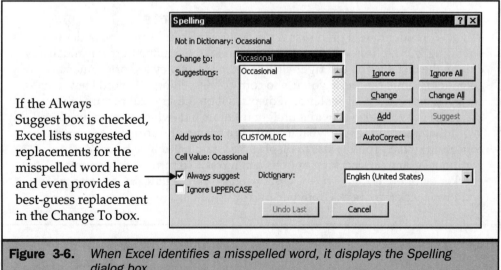

If the Always Suggest box is checked, Excel lists suggested replacements for the misspelled word here and even provides a best-guess replacement in the Change To box.

Figure 3-6.   *When Excel identifies a misspelled word, it displays the Spelling dialog box*

Spell Checking in PowerPoint

PowerPoint's spell checking works almost identically to Word's spell checking. Like Word, PowerPoint automatically checks the spelling of words as you enter them. If PowerPoint identifies a misspelled word, it underlines the word with a red wavy line. To fix the misspelling manually, double-click the word and then type a replacement. Alternatively, right-click the word and then choose one of the alternative spellings or commands from the shortcut menu that PowerPoint displays. (If you have a question about what any of the commands on the shortcut menu does, refer to the earlier discussion of Word's spell checking.)

To control how PowerPoint's spell checking works, choose Tools | Options, click the Spelling & Style tab, and then use the boxes and buttons that PowerPoint displays to describe how and when you want spell checking to occur.

Spell Checking in Access

Access's spell checking works almost identically to Excel's spell checking. To spell check the information shown in the open database object (an object is just a database building block, such as a table), choose Tools | Spelling. If Access finds a word that isn't in its dictionary, it displays the Spelling dialog box shown in Figure 3-7. Near the

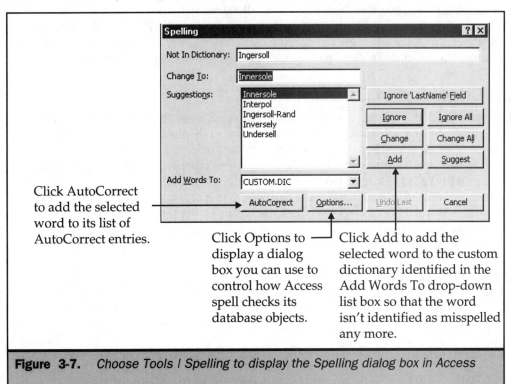

Figure 3-7. *Choose Tools | Spelling to display the Spelling dialog box in Access*

top of the dialog box, Access displays the misspelled word and provides a list of suggested alternative spellings. If Access is not able to supply alternative spellings, you can use the Change To text box to supply a new replacement word for the misspelled word. If the word isn't misspelled, click the Ignore Field, Ignore, or Ignore All button. If you want to change the misspelling to what shows in the Change To text box, click the Change button or the Change All button.

You can click the Ignore Field button to prevent Access from spell checking a field that contains textual phrases that Access won't find in its spelling dictionary: alphanumeric strings (such as product codes) and proper names (such as the names of companies and people).

Spell Checking in Publisher

Publisher's spell checking works similarly to PowerPoint's spell checking. Like PowerPoint, Publisher automatically checks the spelling of words as you enter them. If Publisher identifies a misspelled word, it underlines the word with a wavy red line. To fix the misspelling you can right-click the word and click one of the suggested spellings from the shortcut menu. Or, you can click Tools | Spelling and click Check Spelling to open Publisher's Check Spelling window. If your publication contains more than one text file or table frame, you can check the Check All Stories box to correct the spelling in all of them. To turn Publisher's automatic spell checker on or off, click Tools | Spelling and click Spelling Options to view the Spelling Options window. To hide the wavy red lines in a publication, click Tools | Spelling and click the Hide Spelling Errors button.

Spell Checking in Outlook

To spell check the information shown in an Outlook item, choose Tools | Spelling. If Outlook finds a word that isn't in its dictionary, it displays the Spelling dialog box, which is for all practical purposes identical to the Spelling dialog box that Excel shows (see Figure 3-6). Near the top of the dialog box, Outlook displays the misspelled word and provides a list of suggested alternative spellings. If Outlook is not able to supply alternative spellings, you can use the Change To text box to supply a replacement word. If the word isn't misspelled, click the Ignore or the Ignore All button. If you want to change the misspelling to what shows in the Change To text box, click the Change button or the Change All button.

To tell Outlook that it should automatically check the spelling of any items you create before you send them, choose Tools | Options, click the Spelling tab, and then check the Always Check Spelling Before Sending box. Note, too, that the Spelling tab also provides other boxes and buttons that you can use to customize the way Outlook spell checks items.

Using AutoCorrect

AutoCorrect, as mentioned briefly a handful of times already in this chapter, automatically fixes specified errors. For example, if you type the misspelling "recieve," an Office program such as Word automatically replaces your misspelling with the correct spelling, "receive."

Perhaps the most useful aspect of AutoCorrect is that it occurs automatically—without intervention from you, the user. By default, if you make a mistake that AutoCorrect knows it should fix, it fixes the mistake.

To see which mistakes AutoCorrect fixes and to add new entries to its list, choose Tools | AutoCorrect. The Office program will display a dialog box like Word's AutoCorrect dialog box shown in Figure 3-8.

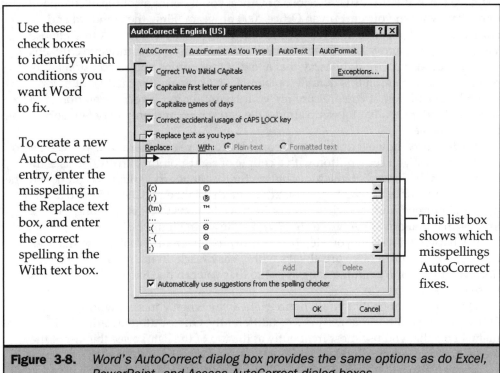

Figure 3-8. *Word's AutoCorrect dialog box provides the same options as do Excel, PowerPoint, and Access AutoCorrect dialog boxes*

Note   *Figure 3-8 shows Word's AutoCorrect dialog box, but the AutoCorrect dialog boxes for Excel, PowerPoint, and Access look and work in almost the same way. The only difference, in fact, is that the Word AutoCorrect dialog box includes three additional tabs not present on the AutoCorrect dialog boxes of other programs: the AutoFormat As You Type tab, the AutoText tab, and the AutoFormat tab. The AutoFormat As You Type and AutoFormat tabs provide boxes and buttons that you can use to control how Word's automatic formatting works. The AutoText tab lets you modify and add to the list of AutoText entries that Word will make. (An AutoText entry is a phrase or group of paragraphs assigned to a unique name. As soon as you type enough of the AutoText entry's name for Word to recognize it, Word displays the AutoText entry in a ScreenTip. If you want Word to replace the name you typed with the AutoText entry, simply press ENTER.)*

Working with Toolbars and Menus

If you've worked with earlier versions of Office, you'll notice a couple of changes immediately when you start up an Office 2000 program. First, the Standard and Formatting toolbars are displayed on one line instead of two. To check this, choose View | Toolbars, and you will see that both Standard and Formatting are checked.

You may also notice right away that a few of the buttons you're accustomed to seeing do not appear on this default toolbar—Cut, Copy, and Format Painter, for example. In addition, if you are running your computer in a screen resolution of 640 × 480, the Standard toolbar takes up almost the entire row, and only very few Formatting tools are visible.

Not to worry, however. All your favorite buttons are still there, and you can get to them easily. Do you see a button with a couple of right-pointing arrows? This is the More button. In Figure 3-9, the More button for the Standard toolbar is right next to the font window. For the Formatting toolbar, it's on the right end. Click More to display a palette of buttons, and then click Add or Remove Buttons to display a long list of buttons that you can either add or remove, as shown in Figure 3-10.

In Chapter 4, I'll show you step by step how to personalize toolbars so that the features you use most often are always within easy reach. In the following sections, however, I'll use the default arrangement so that you can become familiar with what these toolbar buttons do.

The second change that you'll notice right away when you start working with an Office 2000 program is that menus work differently. Office automatically displays menu items that you use most frequently at the top of the list. To see the rest of the menu, you click on the double down-pointing arrows at the bottom of the menu.

You can also tell an Office program that you always want to see all the items on all the menus. To do so, follow these steps:

INTRODUCING OFFICE

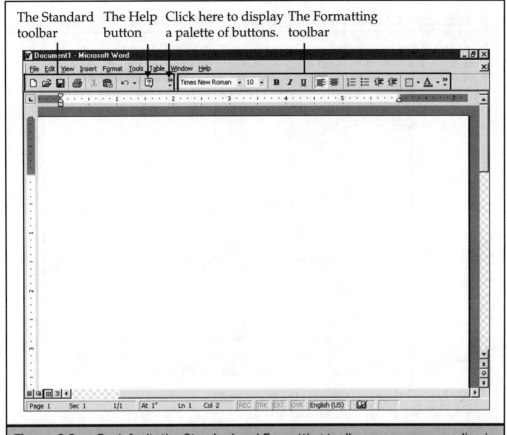

The Standard   The Help   Click here to display   The Formatting
toolbar   button   a palette of buttons.   toolbar

Figure 3-9.   *By default, the Standard and Formatting toolbars appear on one line in an Office 2000 program*

1. Choose Tools | Customize to open the Customize dialog box.

2. Select the Options tab.

3. Uncheck Menus Show Recently Used Commands First.

You can personalize your menus in many other ways, and we'll look at them all in Chapter 4.

Note   *In this book, I will always use long menus in figures and illustrations. The items on long menus always appear in the same order, so you'll be able to easily find what I'm discussing. Remember, though, that unless you are also using long menus, the items you see on your menus and those in this book will not be identical.*

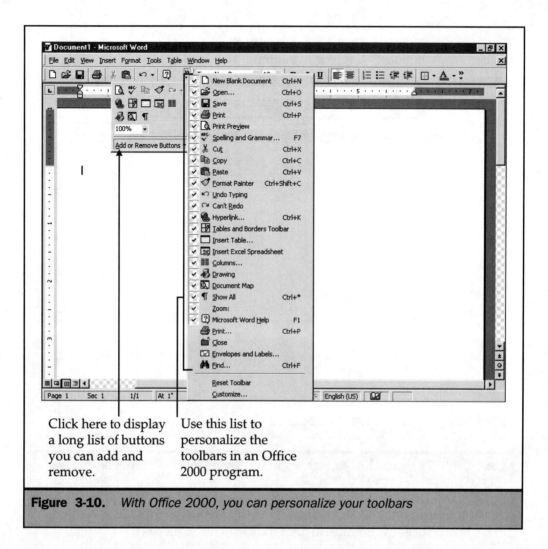

Click here to display a long list of buttons you can add and remove.

Use this list to personalize the toolbars in an Office 2000 program.

Figure 3-10. *With Office 2000, you can personalize your toolbars*

Working with the Common Editing Tools

In general, you'll use the same tools for editing much of the data you enter into and store in your Office 2000 document files. Each of the Office programs provides Cut, Copy, Paste, and Format Painter buttons—and you'll use these often. In addition, most of the Office programs also provide Undo and Redo buttons, which are equally handy. And then, of course, there are two or three Edit menu commands, which appear in most of the Office programs: Repeat, Find, and Replace. Because you'll want to use all these tools in your work with Office and because they work in the same basic manner in each of the Office programs, this chapter also describes these tools.

Tip *Table 3-1, later in this chapter, shows you what each button on the Formatting toolbar looks like, tells you the Office program in which it is available, and describes what it lets you do. And, remember, if a button I talk about in the following sections does not appear on your default toolbar, click the More button to display the button palette, and select it from that.*

Using the Cut, Copy, and Paste Toolbar Buttons

You use the Cut, Copy, and Paste tools to move and copy data within or between document files. You can, for example, move or copy text you've selected in a Word document, a worksheet range you've selected in an Excel workbook, a piece of clip art you've placed in a PowerPoint presentation, an Access database object, and even entire Outlook items. In short, you can move or copy just about anything you can select.

Note *To select text or objects in a document file, you typically click and drag the mouse across the text or click the object.*

Moving Data

To move data, for example, you use the Cut and Paste buttons in tandem, by following these steps:

1. Select the data you want to move.

2. Click the Cut button to move the selected data from the Office document file to the Windows Clipboard, a temporary storage area. (For details about the Clipboard, see the following section, "Using the Clipboard.")

3. Position the insertion point at the exact location to which you want to move the data. (You can do this by clicking where the insertion point should be placed in the document.)

4. Click the Paste button to move the data you previously stored on the Windows Clipboard—you did this in step 2—to the insertion point location.

Tip *You can use the Cut, Copy, and Paste buttons and the Windows Clipboard not only to move and copy data within a document file but also between document files. Note, too, that almost all Windows programs provide Cut, Copy, and Paste buttons, which you can use in the manner described here.*

Copying Data

To copy data, you use the Copy and Paste buttons in tandem, by following these steps:

1. Select the data you want to copy.

2. Click the Copy button to store a copy of the selected data on the Windows Clipboard.

3. Position the insertion point at the exact location to which you want to copy the data. (You can do this by clicking where the insertion point should be placed in the document.)

4. Click the Paste button to copy the data you previously stored on the Windows Clipboard—you did this in step 2—to the insertion point location.

All Office programs also let you move and copy data by dragging the selection to a new location using the mouse. You can move the selected data simply by dragging it. (This is called drag-and-drop.) And you can copy the selected data by holding down the CTRL key and then dragging the selection. As with the Cut, Copy, and Paste buttons, you can use the mouse to drag-and-drop data both within a document file and between document files. Note, however, that not every Windows program supports drag-and-drop editing. You can also drag-and-drop using the right mouse button instead of the left. When you go to drop the selection, the Office program displays a shortcut menu asking you what you want to do with the data: move it, copy it, create a link to it in that location, or create a hyperlink.

Using the Clipboard

When you copy or cut a selection from an Office program, the selection is copied to the Windows Clipboard, which, as I mentioned earlier, is a temporary storage area. When you later paste the selection, the Office program copies the selection from the Clipboard. If you copy or cut more than one selection to the Clipboard, Windows displays the Clipboard toolbar. Unlike in previous versions of Office, the Office 2000 Clipboard can hold more than one selection. The Clipboard toolbar allows you to work with the multiple selections.

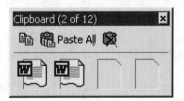

This illustration shows the Clipboard in Word, displaying the stored items. (If you don't see the Clipboard toolbar, choose View | Toolbars and choose Clipboard.)

You can use the Clipboard toolbar to paste the most recent addition or any other item that the toolbar displays. Simply click the picture that represents the item you want to paste. If you don't know which Clipboard picture represents which selection, point to the picture. Windows displays a pop-up box describing the contents of the selection.

To paste everything you've copied on the Clipboard to the active document, click the Paste All button. To erase the contents of the Clipboard, click the Clear Clipboard button (it's the one with the X on it).

Using the Paste Special Command

When you want to control the way an Office program pastes a selection, you use the Edit menu's Paste Special command instead of the Paste toolbar button. Using the Paste Special command allows you to specify the way Office formats the data you're pasting.

Normally, Office programs paste using default settings. For example, if you copy a range of cells in Excel and simply paste them in a Word document, Word retains the cells' formatting information and formats the selection as a table. But if you don't want to paste the cells as a table, you choose the Paste Special command, to display the following dialog box:

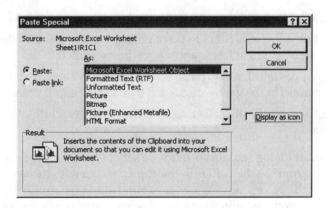

The Paste Special dialog box contains several options for pasting the selection. For example, you can paste the cells as a linked object or as a file. Say, for example, you wanted to paste the cells simply as text in a list. You would click the Paste option button, select Unformatted Text from the list, and click OK.

Excel offers more Paste Special commands for copying and moving cells within the program. Normally, when you paste a cell or range of cells within Excel, you paste the cell formatting and comments as well as the cell contents. Although normally it's okay that Excel copies all this information, if you need to, you can exercise more control over how Excel completes the copy operation. To do this, you once again need to choose Edit | Paste Special. When you choose the Paste Special command, Excel displays another Paste Special dialog box shown here, which asks what you want pasted into the destination range and how you want it pasted.

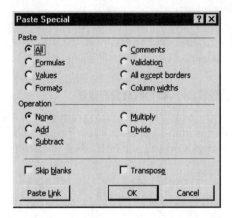

Use the Paste option button set to indicate which parts of the copied selection you want pasted into the new range:

- Selecting All tells Excel to paste everything.

- Selecting Formulas tells Excel to paste only the cell's contents. (Selecting Formulas also results in labels and values being pasted.)

- Selecting Values tells Excel to paste only labels and values. (Excel converts any copied formulas to the values calculated by the formulas if you select this option.)

- Selecting Column Widths tells Excel to copy only the width of the columns you selected.

The Paste Special dialog box also provides a set of Operation option buttons that let you arithmetically combine the values in the copied range with those in the range into which you'll paste the values: adding them, subtracting them, multiplying them, and so forth. Note that if you have questions about what one of the Paste Special option buttons does, you can click the What's This? button and then the option button you have a question about.

Using the Format Painter Button

The Format Painter button lets you copy formatting from one set of data to another set. For example, if you told Word to boldface and italicize a chunk of text, you could copy the formatting of that chunk—the boldfacing and the italicization—to some other chunk of text. Similarly, if you told Excel to format a set of numbers by adding dollar signs and decimal points, you could copy this number formatting to some other set of numbers.

The section "Using the Formatting Toolbar," later in this chapter, talks more about formatting data.

It's easy to use the Format Painter tool. You simply need to follow these steps:

1. Select the data containing the formatting you want to copy. (Typically, you do this by clicking and dragging the mouse.)

2. Click the Format Painter button.

3. Drag the mouse across the data to which you want to copy the formatting.

Using the Undo and Redo Toolbar Buttons

What the Undo and Redo toolbar buttons do may be obvious. You click the Undo button to reverse the effect of your last editing operation. And you click the Redo button to, in effect, undo the effect of your last Undo command. For example, if you've just copied data using the Copy and Paste buttons, you can click the Undo button to erase the effect of your copy-and-paste operation. If after clicking the Undo button, you realize that you've made a mistake because you did want the data copied, you can click the Redo button.

You can't undo the effect of all editing operations. In general, for example, you can undo the effect of Edit menu commands and their equivalent toolbar buttons but not the effect of File menu commands and their equivalent toolbar buttons. Occasionally, you may not be able to reverse an action because of memory limitations. For example, if you select an entire worksheet in Excel and then apply a formatting command, Excel may warn you that there is insufficient memory available to reverse the action.

It's useful to note that the Undo toolbar buttons available in Word, Excel, and PowerPoint will undo more than one editing operation. Similarly, the Redo toolbar buttons available in Word, Excel, and PowerPoint will redo more than one undo operation. To undo multiple editing operations, click the arrowhead next to the Undo toolbar button. Then, when the Office program displays a list of previous editing operations, click the oldest editing operation you want to undo. (The Office program undoes the selected editing operation, as well as every more recent editing operation.)

The Outlook Standard toolbar doesn't provide an Undo or Redo toolbar button. Outlook's Edit menu does, however, provide Undo and Redo commands.

To redo multiple undo operations, click the arrowhead next to the Redo toolbar button. Then, when the Office program displays a list of undo operations, click the oldest undo operation you want to reverse. (The Office program reverses the selected undo operation as well as every more recent undo operation.)

Note   *Access doesn't provide a Redo toolbar button—only an Undo toolbar button.*

Using the Clear Command

Most of the Office programs supply a Clear command on their Edit menus. You can use this command or its keyboard equivalent, the DELETE key, to remove the selected data. For example, if you want to remove a word, you can select the word (such as by clicking it) and then choose Edit | Clear. If you want to remove the labels and values you've entered into an Excel worksheet range, you can also choose Edit | Clear or press the DELETE key. And, predictably, you can remove items on PowerPoint slides and Outlook items in the same way: Select the thing you want to remove and then choose Edit | Clear.

Note   *Excel's Clear command works a bit differently. When you choose Edit | Clear in Excel, Excel displays a submenu listing items you can delete from the selected worksheet range. This submenu lists four commands: All, Formats, Contents, and Comments. Choose All if you want to remove everything in the selected range. Choose Formats if you want to remove the formatting of the cells in the selected range. Choose Contents if you want to remove the labels, values, and formulas entered into the cells in the selected range. Finally, choose Comments if you want to remove the comments you've used to annotate cells in the selected range.*

Using the Repeat Command

The Edit menus of Word, Excel, and PowerPoint supply a Repeat command that often lets you repeat the most recent editing command you've issued. For example, if you've just pasted the contents of the Clipboard into a document file, you can choose Edit | Repeat Paste to paste the contents of the Clipboard into a document file for a second time.

The Repeat command is a handy tool when you're making repetitive editing changes to a document file: formatting certain words to look the same way, repeatedly pasting the same Clipboard contents into a document file, inserting a series of clip art images into a document file, and so forth.

Using the Find and Replace Commands

If you've been working with a computer for very long, you've undoubtedly already come across the Find and Replace commands. As you may know, the Find command lets you search a document file for some bit of information, thereby eliminating the needle-in-a-haystack dilemma. The Replace command lets you easily make substitutions in a document—for example, swapping every occurrence of the word "Prince" with the phrase "The Artist Formerly Known as Prince." All the Office programs supply their own variations of the Find and Replace commands. But they basically work in the same manner, so the Word program's Find and Replace commands are described here. (The Excel, PowerPoint, and Access programs supply both a Find command and a Replace command, but these commands' functionality amounts to a subset of the Word program command's functionality. Outlook supplies only a Find command but it, too, amounts to a "lite" version of Word's Find command.)

Using the Edit Menu's Find Command

The Edit menu's Find command lets you search through either an entire document file or the selected portion of the document file. (If you don't select some portion of the document file before choosing the command, the Office program assumes you want to search the entire Word document, active Excel worksheet, active PowerPoint slide, or active Access database object.) To use the command, simply choose Edit | Find. When the Office program displays the Find or Find and Replace dialog box, follow these steps to describe what you're looking for and how you want the Office program to perform its search:

1. Use the Find What box to enter the word or phrase you're looking for or to activate the drop-down list to select a word or phrase from a previous search. In Figure 3-11, you can see how I have entered the word "Thorgmorton."

   The Less button shown in Figure 3-11 is a toggle switch. When you first display the Find dialog box, it's labeled More; you click it to display the complete set of Find options. Then Word renames the button Less; you click it to display only an abbreviated set of Find options.

2. Use the Search drop-down list box to indicate whether you want to search the entire document, from the insertion point forward, or from the insertion point backward.

3. Check the Match Case box if case matters in your search. If you enter "Revenues" but don't want to find "revenues," for example, case matters, and you should mark the check box.

4. Check the Find Whole Words Only box if, in order to be considered a match, what you enter in the Find What text box can't be a fragment of a larger word.

5. Check the Use Wildcards box if you want to use wildcard symbols in your search: an asterisk to represent any set of characters or a question mark to represent any single character. Note that if you don't check the Use Wildcards box, but you do use the asterisk or the question mark, Word assumes that these are actual characters you're looking for—not wildcard characters representing other characters or character strings.

If you want to look for special characters, such as those that don't actually appear on your keyboard, check the Use Wildcards box, click the Special button, and then choose the special character you want to find from the list that Word displays.

6. Check the Sounds Like box if you want to find words that are pronounced the same as what you enter in the Find What text box but that are spelled differently: *there* and *their*, *to* and *too*, and so forth.

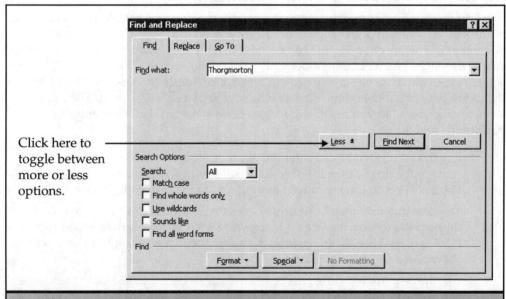

Click here to toggle between more or less options.

Figure 3-11. *The Find tab of Word's Find and Replace dialog box provides a superset of the options available in Excel, PowerPoint, Access, and Outlook*

7. Check the Find All Word Forms box if you want to find words that use the same root but may be formed differently. For example, if you're looking for the word "want," it may also make sense for you to find "wants" and "wanted."

8. If you want to find words or phrases that are formatted a certain way, click the Format button, choose one of the formatting categories from the menu that Word displays, and then use the dialog box that Word displays to describe the formatting you're looking for.

Note *If you later decide that you don't want to search for words or phrases that use formatting you've described in step 8, click the No Formatting button.*

9. After you describe the search you want to make, click the Find Next button. The Office program selects the first occurrence it can find that matches the search string you've entered into the Find What text box, and then selects the word or phrase. To continue searching, click the Find Next button again. (The Office program leaves the Find dialog box open so you can do this.) If the Office program can't find a word or phrase like the one you're looking for, it displays a message box that alerts you to this fact.

Using the Edit Menu's Replace Command

The Replace command does everything that the Find command does—and goes one step further. It lets you replace the occurrences you find of a particular word or phrase with some new word or phrase. To use the Edit menu's Replace command, first open the document you want to search and, if necessary, select the portion of the document file that you want to search so as to limit your find-and-replace operation. Then, choose Edit | Replace so that Word displays the Replace tab of the Find and Replace dialog box, as shown in Figure 3-12. Follow these steps to describe what you're looking for and want to replace:

1. Use the Find What text box to specify the word or phrase you're looking for, the so-called search string.

2. Use the Replace With text box to specify the word or phrase you want to substitute for occurrences of the search string.

3. After you describe the substitution you want to make, click the Find Next button. The Office program selects the next occurrence of the word or phrase that matches your search instructions. If you want to replace that occurrence, click Replace. Otherwise, you can click Find Next again to identify the next occurrence of the search string. To continue the substitutions, click the Replace button again. (The Office program leaves the Replace dialog box open so you can do this.) To make all the substitutions at once, click the Replace All button. When Word is finished replacing all the words matching your search string, it reports how many substitutions were made. If Word can't find a word or

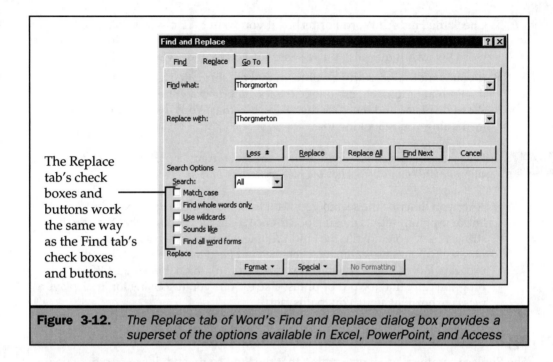

The Replace tab's check boxes and buttons work the same way as the Find tab's check boxes and buttons.

Figure 3-12. The Replace tab of Word's Find and Replace dialog box provides a superset of the options available in Excel, PowerPoint, and Access

phrase like the one you're looking for, it displays a message box that alerts you to this fact.

Working with the Formatting Toolbar

Word, Excel, PowerPoint, and even Outlook all provide a Formatting toolbar that you can use to add formatting to the information you enter into a document file: Word documents, Excel workbooks, and PowerPoint presentations.

Note *Access also provides a Formatting toolbar, but it isn't typically displayed and therefore isn't described here. Outlook provides a Formatting toolbar, but you can use it only for message items so it isn't described here either. Note, however, that the Access and Outlook Formatting toolbars work in the same basic way as the Formatting toolbars available in the other Office programs.*

Because the Formatting toolbars work in basically the same way and supply almost the same set of tools for Word, Excel, and PowerPoint, this chapter describes all three Formatting toolbars together.

Using the Formatting Toolbar

Using the Formatting toolbar's buttons is easy. You select the information you want to format. Then you click the button that represents the type of formatting you want. For example, if you want to boldface some chunk of text or a worksheet range, you select the text or range (such as by dragging the mouse across the text or cells), and then you click the Bold button. If you want to change the font, or typeface, used for a chunk of text or a worksheet range, you select the text or range and then you select a new font from the Font list box.

Remember, if you point to any toolbar box or button, the Office program displays the tool name in a pop-up box called a ScreenTip. Also, if you don't see a particular button displayed on your toolbar, click the More button.

LEARN BY EXAMPLE
You can open the sample Word document Figure 3-A (example document for formatting) if you want a simple document you can use for experimenting with the Word Formatting toolbar. You can open the sample Excel workbook Figure 3-B (example workbook for formatting) if you want a simple workbook that you can use for experimenting with the Excel Formatting toolbar. You can open the sample PowerPoint presentation Figure 3-C (example presentation for formatting) if you want a simple presentation that you can use for experimenting with the PowerPoint Formatting toolbar.

Reviewing the Formatting Toolbar's Buttons

The Formatting toolbar provides drop-down list boxes and clickable buttons you can use to change the appearance of the information you've selected in a Word document, Excel workbook, or PowerPoint presentation. Table 3-1 describes each of these boxes and buttons, but your best route for learning what these tools do is simply to experiment with them.

Perhaps not surprisingly, all the Office programs provide many more tools you can use to customize the appearance of your document file contents. Both Word and Excel's Format menus, for example, provide an AutoFormat command, which you can use to richly format a Word document or Excel worksheet range. The Word and PowerPoint Format menus also all provide a Font command, which you can use to change the font typeface, style, point size, and color and to add special effects such as underlining, shadows, and so forth.

Button	Name	Available In	What It Lets You Do
☰	Align Left	All	Left-aligns the text in the selection.
☰	Align Right	All	Right-aligns the text in the selection.
☰	Center	All	Centers the text in the selection.
Times New Roman ▼	Font	All	Selects a font (typeface) from a drop-down list box for the selection.
10 ▼	Font Size	All	Specifies a point size for the selection. You can select a point size from the drop-down list or you can enter a point size into the box.
B	Bold	All	Boldfaces the selection.
I	Italic	All	Italicizes the selection.
<u>U</u>	Underline	All	Underlines the selection.
,	Comma Style	Excel	Formats the selected worksheet range to include a comma as the thousands separator and two decimal places.
$	Currency Style	Excel	Formats the selected worksheet range to include a currency symbol, a comma as the thousands separator, and two decimal places.
.00 → .0	Decrease Decimal	Excel	Decreases the number of decimal places shown for the selected worksheet range.

Table 3-1. *Formatting Toolbar Buttons*

Button	Name	Available In	What It Lets You Do
	Increase Decimal	Excel	Increases the number of decimal places shown for the selected worksheet range.
	Fill Color	Excel	Fills the selected worksheet range using the color shown on the face of the toolbar button. (If you click the arrow next to the button Excel displays a drop-down list of colors from which you can choose your fill color.)
	Merge and Center	Excel	Concatenates the cell contents in each selected cell and then centers the new concatenated contents across the selected columns.
	Percent Style	Excel	Formats the selected worksheet range to show values as percentages and adds the percent symbol (for example, the value 1 shows as 100%).
	Animation Effects	PowerPoint	Displays the Animation Effects toolbar.
	Decrease Font Size	PowerPoint	Decreases the point size of the selection to the next smaller size shown in the Font Size list box.
	Increase Font Size	PowerPoint	Increases the point size of the selection to the next larger size shown in the Font Size list box.
	Demote	PowerPoint	Demotes the selected paragraph to the next lower level in the presentation's outline.
	Promote	PowerPoint	Promotes the selected paragraph to the next higher level in the presentation's outline.

Table 3-1. *Formatting Toolbar Buttons (continued)*

Button	Name	Available In	What It Lets You Do
	Shadow	PowerPoint	Adds a shadow to the selection.
	Highlight	Word	Highlights the selected text using the color shown on the face of the toolbar button. (If you click the arrow next to the button Word displays a drop-down list of colors from which you can choose your highlighting color.)
	Justify	Word	Justifies the text in the selection so the text is flush against both the left and right margin edges.
Normal	Style	Word	Selects a style from a drop-down list box for the selection.
	Borders	Word and Excel	Displays a list box you can use to add borders to the selection.
	Decrease Indent	Word and Excel	Reduces the indention of the selection.
	Increase Indent	Word and Excel	Increases the indention of the selection.
	Font Color	Word and Excel	Colors the text in your selection using the color shown on the face of the toolbar button. (If you click the arrow next to the button Word and Excel display a drop-down list of colors from which you can choose your font color.)
	Bullets	Word and PowerPoint	Turns the selected paragraphs into a bulleted list.
	Numbering	Word and PowerPoint	Turns the selected paragraphs into a numbered list.

Table 3-1. *Formatting Toolbar Buttons (continued)*

Using the Drawing Tools

Word, Excel, and PowerPoint share a collection of tools that allow you to draw objects such as lines, arrows, boxes, and circles to your documents files. With the common drawing tools in these programs, you can also format and edit the shapes and objects you draw.

Displaying the Drawing Toolbar

Before you can begin drawing, you need to add the Drawing toolbar to the Office program's window. In Word and Excel, you can do this by clicking the Drawing button. In PowerPoint, you choose View | Toolbars | Drawing. Once you do this, the Office program adds the Drawing toolbar to the bottom of the program window, as shown in Figure 3-13.

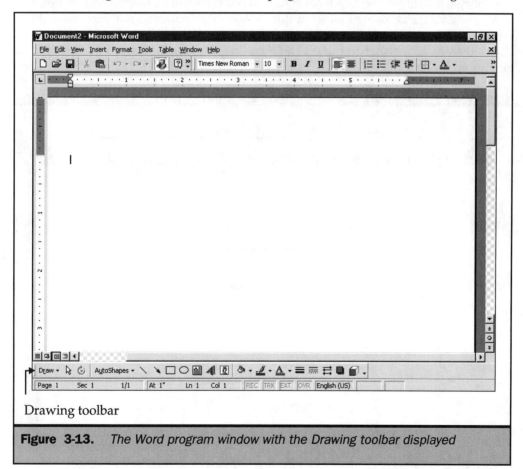

Drawing toolbar

Figure 3-13.   *The Word program window with the Drawing toolbar displayed*

To subsequently remove the Drawing toolbar in Word or Excel, you click the Drawing toolbar button again. To subsequently remove the Drawing toolbar in PowerPoint, you choose View | Toolbars | Drawing again.

Reviewing the Drawing Toolbar's Tools

The Drawing toolbar provides the same set of tools no matter which program you use it with. Table 3-2 shows the toolbar buttons and provides brief descriptions of each tool.

Drawing Objects

As Table 3-2 implies, you use the same basic procedure for drawing any object—AutoShape, line, arrow, rectangle, oval, or text box—with the Drawing add-in tool. First, you click the Drawing toolbar button or select the command that represents the object you want to draw. Second, you drag the mouse. For example, for a line or arrow, click either the Line or Arrow button and then drag the mouse between the line or arrow's endpoints:

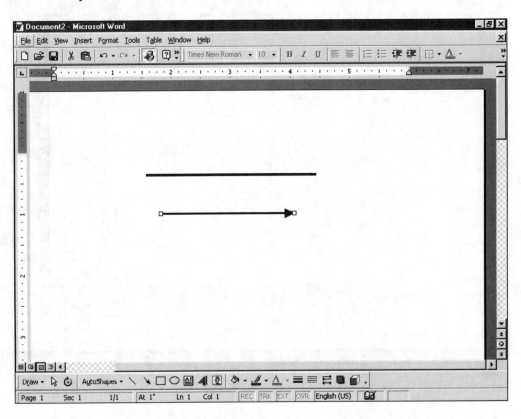

Button	Name	Description
3-D	3-D	Adds a third dimension to the selected object.
Arrow	Arrow	Draws an arrow from the point you press the left mouse button to the point where you release the mouse button. (The Office program places the arrow head at the ending point.)
Arrow Style	Arrow Style	Displays a drop-down list box of arrows so you can choose an arrow style for the selected line or arrow.
AutoShapes ▾	AutoShapes	Displays the AutoShapes menu of commands.
Dash Style	Dash Style	Displays a drop-down list box of dashed lines so you can choose a dashed-line style for the border of the selected object.
Draw ▾	Draw	Displays the Draw menu of commands.
Fill Color	Fill Color	Colors the interior of the selected object with the color shown on the face of the button. (If you click the arrow next to the button, the Office program displays a drop-down list of colors you can use for your fill color.)
Font Color	Font Color	Colors the selected text with the color shown on the face of the button. (If you click the arrow next to the button, the Office program displays a drop-down list of colors you can use for your text.)
Free Rotate	Free Rotate	Allows you to spin the selected object by dragging its rotation handles.
Insert ClipArt	Insert ClipArt	Opens the Insert ClipArt dialog box from which you can select pictures, sounds, and motion clips to insert in a document.

Table 3-2. *Drawing Toolbar Buttons*

Button	Name	Description
	Insert WordArt	Starts the WordArt add-in, which lets you turn text into colorful graphic images.
	Line	Draws a line from the point that you press the left mouse button to the point you release the mouse button.
	Line Color	Colors the border of the selected object with the color shown on the face of the button. (If you click the arrow next to the button, the Office program displays a drop-down list of colors you can use for your border color.)
	Line Style	Displays a drop-down list box of line styles so you can choose a line style (really a line thickness) for the border of the selected object.
	Oval	Draws an oval. (You identify where you want the oval by dragging the mouse between the two opposite points on the oval.)
	Rectangle	Draws a rectangle. (You identify where you want the rectangle by dragging the mouse between the rectangle's opposite corners.)
	Select Objects	Tells the Office program that it should select the next object you click or the next group of objects that you drag across.
	Shadow	Adds a shadow to the selected object.
	Text Box	Draws a text box so you can later fill it with text. (You identify where you want the text box by dragging the mouse between the box's opposite corners.)

Table 3-2.   *Drawing Toolbar Buttons (continued)*

For a rectangle or text box, you click either the Rectangle or Text Box button and then drag the mouse between the shape's opposite corners. For an oval, you click the Oval button and then drag the mouse as if you were creating an invisible box into which you want the oval to fit snugly. So you drag the mouse from one corner of this invisible box to the opposite corner. (If this doesn't make sense, just try the Oval tool, and you'll immediately see how it works.)

 To draw a square, use the Rectangle tool but hold down the SHIFT *key as you drag the mouse. To draw a circle, use the Oval tool but hold down the* SHIFT *key as you drag the mouse.*

As mentioned in the preceding table, the AutoShapes tool displays a menu of commands, and each command corresponds to a particular category of shapes. When you choose an AutoShape menu command, the Drawing add-in tool displays a toolbar-like box with clickable buttons representing different shapes:

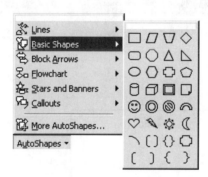

Click the button that shows the shape you want to draw and then drag the mouse in the same way you do to draw lines, rectangles, and ovals.

 When you select an AutoShape, the Drawing add-in tool also adds a yellow adjustment handle to change the shape's most prominent feature. Use the other handles to change the size of the object.

Editing, Moving, and Resizing Drawing Objects

You can most easily edit, move, and resize drawing objects by using the mouse. For example, to copy an object, click the object to select it, click the Copy button, and then click the Paste button. To move an object, simply select it and drag it. To resize an object, click the object to select it; then drag the object's selection handles. To remove an object, click it and then press the DELETE key.

You can rotate, or spin, the selected object by clicking the Rotate button and then dragging the rotation handles on the object.

 You can select more than one object by clicking the Select Objects button and then dragging the mouse from the top-left corner to the bottom-right corner of a rectangle that includes the objects you want to select. This is the same technique, by the way, that you can use to select shortcut icons on the Windows desktop.

Working with Text Boxes

You create text boxes in the same way that you create rectangle objects, except that after you've drawn the box, the Office program lets you enter text into the box.

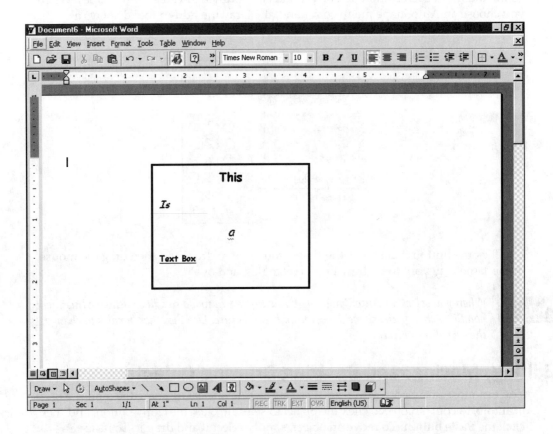

One handy feature of text boxes is that you can format the text that appears in the box, as the preceding illustration shows. You'll usually want to do this with the Formatting toolbar's buttons.

To place existing text into a text box, first select the text and then click the Text Box button.

Formatting Drawing Objects

To format a drawing object, just select the item you want to format and click the Drawing toolbar button that supplies the formatting you want to apply. Some buttons—such as the Fill Color, Line Color, Line Style, Dash Style, and Arrow Style buttons—display list boxes of formatting options. To choose an option you see listed, simply click it.

Working with the Draw Button

Clicking the Draw button displays an expansive collection of commands that you can use to further edit your drawing objects.

Grouping and Ungrouping Objects

You can group objects so that they are treated as a single object: edited together, moved or resized together, formatted together, and so on. To group a set of objects, follow these steps:

1. Click the Drawing toolbar's Select Objects button.
2. Drag the mouse from the top-left corner to the bottom-right corner of a rectangle that includes the objects you want to group. At this point, you've selected the objects.
3. Click the Draw button so that the Draw menu appears.
4. Choose Draw | Group. Notice that the selection handles now surround the group instead of the individual objects in the group.

To ungroup a set of objects you've previously grouped, follow these steps:

1. Click the grouped objects set you want to ungroup.
2. Click the Draw button so that the Draw menu appears.
3. Choose Draw | Ungroup.

Tip *You can undo the effect of your last Ungroup command by choosing Draw | Regroup.*

Restacking Objects

If you choose the Order command from the Draw menu, the Drawing add-in tool displays a submenu of commands you can use for reordering, or restacking, the drawing objects you've created. The Order submenu includes commands for moving the selected object to the foreground or background (that is, forward or backward in relation to overlapping objects or text).

Working with a Grid

If you create complex drawings or illustrations that use a rich set of individual drawing objects—lines, rectangles, and ovals, for example—you can use the Draw menu's Grid command in Word to add an invisible grid to the document file. You can then use this grid to more precisely locate your drawing objects. To add a grid, follow these steps:

1. Click the Draw button.

2. Choose the Grid command.

3. Check the Snap Objects To Grid box if you want the Drawing add-in tool to automatically move drawn objects so they are aligned against the vertical or horizontal lines in an invisible grid.

4. Use the Vertical Spacing box to specify how far apart the vertical gridlines should be placed.

5. Use the Horizontal Spacing box to specify how far apart the horizontal gridlines should be placed.

6. Use the Horizontal Origin box to specify where, starting at the left edge of the page, the gridlines should begin.

7. Use the Vertical Origin box to specify where, starting at the top of the page, the gridlines should begin.

Nudging Objects

The Draw menu's Nudge command displays a set of commands that nudge, or slightly move, the selected object. If you want to move an object left, for example, select it, click the Draw button, choose Draw | Nudge | Left. You can nudge objects in other directions by choosing one of the Nudge submenu's other commands: Right, Up, or Down.

You can nudge the selected object in even smaller, one-pixel increments by selecting the object, holding down the CTRL key, and then pressing the arrow key that points in the direction that you want to nudge the selected object.

Aligning and Distributing Objects

You can align or distribute the selected objects by using the Draw menu's Align or Distribute command. When you choose this command—you need to click the Draw button and then choose Draw | Align or Distribute—the Drawing add-in tool displays the menu shown next.

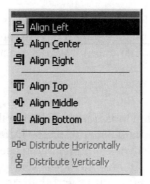

You choose the command that corresponds to the way that you want to align the selected objects. For example, if you've selected a set of ovals and you want to align them so they're all centered, choose Align or Distribute | Align Center. The other alignment commands work in the same basic way. If you want to align objects so their left edges all fall along the same line, choose Align or Distribute | Align Left. The Align or Distribute menu's distribution commands—Distribute Horizontally and Distribute Vertically—don't align the objects. Rather, these two commands rearrange the selected objects within a vertical or horizontal row.

Note *By default, the Drawing add-in tool aligns or distributes the selected objects relative to each other. If you wish, you can align or distribute the selected objects relative to the page on which the drawn objects appear by selecting Align and Distribute | Relative to Page.*

Rotating and Flipping Objects

You can use the Draw menu's Rotate or Flip command to rotate the selected object. To use this command, first select the object you want to rotate. Then click the Draw button, choose Draw | Rotate or Flip, and choose the appropriate Rotate or Flip submenu command, shown next:

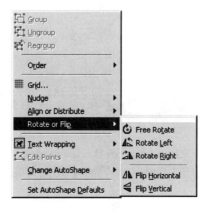

What most of the Rotate or Flip submenu commands do is obvious either from the command name or the tiny picture shown next to the command name. The only exception is the Free Rotate command, but it works exactly like the Free Rotate button, described earlier in Table 3-2.

Editing AutoShapes

The only three Draw menu commands not described in the preceding discussion—Edit Points, Change AutoShape, and Set AutoShape Defaults—let you edit AutoShapes you've added to a document file. For example, if you use the Lines AutoShape that's really a freeform shape, you can change the object's shape by selecting it, clicking the Draw button, choosing Draw | Edit Points, and then dragging the selection handles. You can also create new editing point handles by clicking anywhere on the existing shape, as shown next.

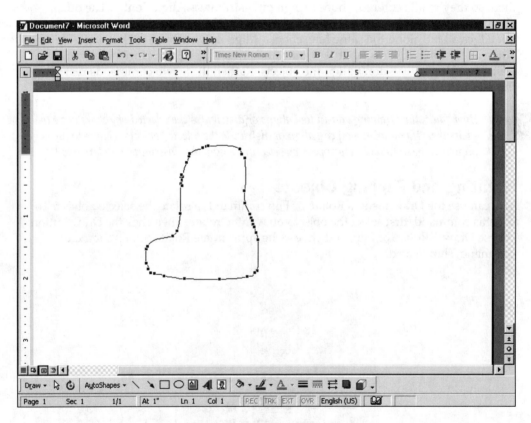

You can substitute a new AutoShape for the selected AutoShape by clicking the Draw button, choosing Draw | Change AutoShape, choosing one of the Change

AutoShape submenu commands (so the Drawing add-in tool displays a pop-up box of AutoShapes), and then choosing an AutoShape. This is easier than it sounds, so just experiment with the command if you have a question.

Finally, if you make changes to an object—perhaps you add a fill color and specify a line style—you can select the object and then use the attributes you've assigned to the object as the default for other AutoShapes. To do this, select the object (as just mentioned), click the Draw button, and then choose Draw | Set AutoShape Defaults.   .

Note   *The default AutoShape attributes you specify apply only to the active document file.*

Working with the Clip Gallery

You can rather easily add clip art images, photographic pictures, sound, and even video to your Word documents, Excel workbooks, PowerPoint presentations, and Access database objects. In fact, Microsoft Office 2000 comes with a rich set of clip art elements on its distribution CD. And you can use other clip art elements, too. (This book uses the term "clip art element" to refer not only to line art and bitmap images but also photographic images, sounds, and video clips.)

Note   *You may need to first install the Microsoft Office 2000 clip art if it wasn't installed at the same time that you installed the rest of the Office suite of programs. To do this, insert the Office CD into your CD drive, open the Clip Art folder, and then start the Clip Art Setup program. (Once you start the Setup program, follow its onscreen instructions for installing the program.)*

Inserting Clip Art into a Document File

It isn't difficult to insert clip art elements into a Word document, an Excel workbook, or a PowerPoint presentation. To add clip art images, photographic pictures, sounds, and video clips to a document file, follow these steps:

1. Choose Insert | Picture | Clip Art. The Office program opens the Insert ClipArt dialog box, as shown in Figure 3-14.

2. Click the tab that describes the type of clip art element you want to insert: Pictures, Sounds, or Motion Clips.

3. Locate the clip art element you want to insert. You can do this by clicking on a category icon and selecting a picture, sound, or motion clip.

4. Click the Insert Clip button that appears on a pop-up shortcut menu. The clip art element is inserted in the document file at the insertion point location.

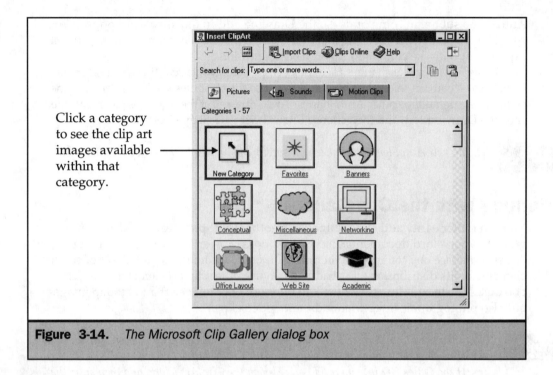

Click a category to see the clip art images available within that category.

Figure 3-14. *The Microsoft Clip Gallery dialog box*

You can find new clip art on the web if you have an Internet connection by clicking the Clips Online button. This connects you to Microsoft's web clip art gallery.

Editing Clip Art Elements

When you insert a clip art element into a document file, you can use the Picture toolbar's buttons to edit the image. To display the Picture toolbar, choose View | Toolbars | Picture. Table 3-3 identifies and describes the Picture toolbar's buttons.

If you perform a complete installation of Microsoft Office 2000, the Setup program installs the Microsoft Photo Editor program. You can also use it for editing photographic images.

Adding Clip Art Elements to the Gallery

While Office 2000 provides a rich set of clip art elements, you aren't limited to using only these items. To add other clip art images, photographic images, sounds, and motion clips, follow these steps:

1. Choose Insert | Picture | Clip Art to open the Insert ClipArt dialog box.
2. Click the Import Clips button to open the Add Clip To Clip Gallery dialog box:

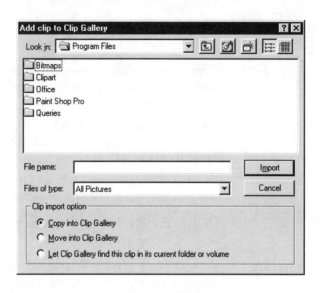

Button	Name	What It Does
⊹	Crop	Lets you crop the selected image by dragging its selection handles.
🖌	Format Picture	Displays the Format Picture dialog box.
▨	Image Control	Displays the Image Control menu, which provides settings for converting the selected clip art image to a grayscale image, a black-and-white image, or a transparent watermark image. (Note that the default image control setting, Automatic, tells the Clip Gallery to display the image using its original coloring.)
🖼	Insert Picture	Displays the Insert Picture dialog box, which works similarly to the Open dialog box. You can use this dialog box to insert another clip art element into the active document file.

Table 3-3. *Picture Toolbar Buttons*

	Less Brightness	Decreases the brightness of the selected image by removing white from the image's colors.
	More Brightness	Increases the brightness of the selected image by adding white to the image's colors.
	Less Contrast	Changes the colors of the selected image so that they show less contrast between the lightest and darkest colors used in the image.
	More Contrast	Changes the colors of the selected image so that they show more contrast between the lightest and darkest colors.
	Line Style	Displays a drop-down list box of line thicknesses you can use as a border for the selected image.
	Reset Picture	Undoes the effect of any formatting you've just applied to the selected image.
	Set Transparent	Erases whatever color you next click in the selected image, thereby allowing the document file background to show through the image and give the appearance of transparency.
	Text Wrapping	Displays a drop-down list box of options for wrapping text around the selected image. (Note that the pictures shown next to the commands show what each text wrapping option does.)

Table 3-3.   *Picture Toolbar Buttons (continued)*

3. Use the Look In drop-down list box to identify the folder holding the clip art element you want to add to the Clip Gallery.

4. When the list box beneath the Look In drop-down list box shows the clip art element file that you want, double-click it.

Click the Clips Online button to start Internet Explorer, connect to the Internet, and display the Clip Gallery Live web page. This web page contains a wealth of clip art resources, including line and cartoons drawings, photographs, and sound and motion files. You can search for a clip art resource by keyword or browse clip art by category.

Working with Macros

You can create macros in Office programs to save time performing repetitive tasks. In essence, macros let you record and then later replay a sequence of keystrokes and mouse clicks. For example, if you frequently have to change the formatting of text in an Office document file, you can create a macro that applies several formatting features simultaneously. You can then assign a keyboard shortcut or create a toolbar button for the macro. Using a macro is especially time-saving if the features included in the macro would otherwise require you to select options in dialog boxes instead of just clicking toolbar buttons. The following steps describe how you could create a macro in Word to double-space and capitalize paragraphs. Creating macros in the other Office programs works in much the same way.

1. Start Word.
2. Open a document to which you want to apply the formatting. If you want to be able to use the macro in only those documents you create using an existing custom template, open or create a new document based on that template.
3. Select the text to which you want to apply the macro.
4. Choose Tools | Macro | Record New Macro. Word displays the Record Macro dialog box shown in Figure 3-15.
5. Enter a name for the macro in the Macro Name box.
6. Click the Toolbars button to create a toolbar button for the macro. Click the Keyboard button to create a keyboard shortcut for the macro.

To create both a toolbar button and keyboard shortcut for the macro, click the Toolbars button.

■ If you click the Toolbars button, Word displays the Customize dialog box. Click the Commands tab, shown in Figure 3-16. Then drag the macro item from the Commands list to the toolbar on which you want to place the button. To rename the button, click Modify Selection and enter a new name in the Name text box. To change the button image, choose Change Button Image and select a new image. Click Close to close the Customize dialog box.

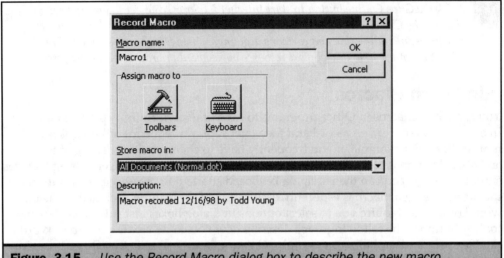

Figure 3-15. Use the Record Macro dialog box to describe the new macro

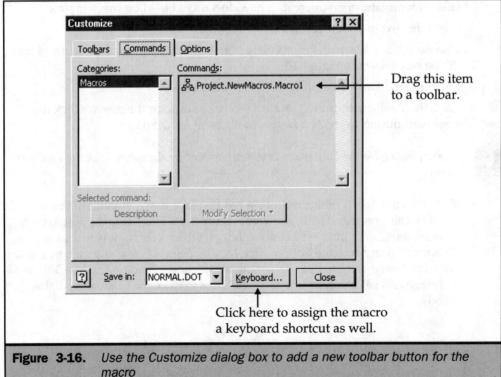

Drag this item to a toolbar.

Click here to assign the macro a keyboard shortcut as well.

Figure 3-16. Use the Customize dialog box to add a new toolbar button for the macro

■ If you click the Keyboard button, Word displays the Customize Keyboard dialog box shown in Figure 3-17. Press the key combination you want to use for the macro. If Word has an existing command applied to that shortcut, it lists it below the Press New Shortcut Key text box. When you find an unassigned keyboard shortcut, click Assign and click Close.

Tip   *CTRL-7, CTRL-8, and CTRL-9 are easy unassigned shortcuts.*

7. Word starts recording the actions you take and displays the Stop Recording toolbar, shown here:

Note   *Don't feel rushed as you record keystrokes or mouse clicks—the speed at which you issue commands doesn't affect the macro's speed.*

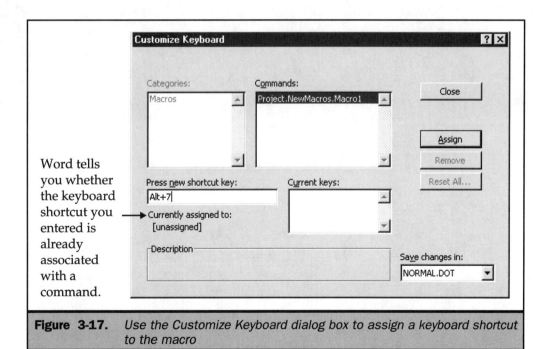

Word tells you whether the keyboard shortcut you entered is already associated with a command.

Figure 3-17.   *Use the Customize Keyboard dialog box to assign a keyboard shortcut to the macro*

8. Click Pause to pause the recording if you need to try something out before including it in the macro.

9. Click Stop when you've finished performing the steps you want included in the macro.

10. To run the macro, click the macro's toolbar button or press the shortcut key you assigned to the macro.

EXAMPLES

LEARN BY EXAMPLE

You can open the sample document Figure 3-D (a Word document with a macro) from the companion CD if you want to see how a macro works. When you open this document, Word will alert you that it contains a macro. Click Enable Macros. To run the macro, select a paragraph and click the Macro toolbar button or press CTRL-7. If the document does not open, you may have your macro security settings too high. To change your security settings, click Tools | Macro Security, and choose Medium from the Security Level tab.

The
Complete
Reference

Office
2000

Chapter 4

Customizing the
Office 2000 Programs

I mentioned in Chapter 3 that one of the new features of Office 2000 is that menus and toolbars are automatically customized as you work. Unless you manually tell an Office program not to do so by unchecking the Menus Show Recently Used Commands First option in the Customize dialog box, your menus will reflect the commands you use most frequently. In addition, you can display all the commands that are available on any menu by clicking on the More button at the bottom of a menu.

As I also mentioned in Chapter 3, most of the Office 2000 programs allow you to display the Standard and Formatting toolbars on a single line. In addition, most of the Office toolbars include a new button, called More Buttons, which you can use to access any buttons that won't fit on the toolbar. You can use the More Buttons button to quickly add and remove buttons on a toolbar. You can, however, customize Office menus and toolbar in many other ways, and I'll show you how in this chapter. For example, you can create a toolbar of your own, create your own menus, remove commands from menus, add commands to menus, and create easy-to-remember keyboard shortcuts.

Note *You'll notice that the steps in this chapter for customizing menus are very similar to those for customizing toolbars. This makes sense if you think about it, because menus and toolbars serve basically the same purpose and consist essentially of the same elements. They just have a different appearance.*

Customizing a Toolbar

Most people don't use all the buttons on the Office 2000 toolbars. If you never click a certain button, why keep it on the Standard or Formatting toolbar when you can replace it with a button you do use? For that matter, why not create a toolbar of your own with your favorite buttons or favorite commands on it? Some Office toolbars are awfully crowded. You can do yourself a favor by making them less crowded or assembling the buttons you use frequently in a single toolbar.

This section explains how to remove buttons from and add buttons to toolbars; create buttons for commands, macros, and styles; and create your own toolbar. It also explains how to copy toolbars from template to template and how to remove a toolbar when you no longer need it. And, to start with, it explains how to put toolbars on the screen, remove them, and change their size and shape.

Caution *If others share the computer you work on, you might talk to them before you change the buttons on a toolbar. A co-worker or family member who wants to click a button but discovers it isn't there any longer will receive an unpleasant surprise.*

Manipulating the Toolbars

Removing toolbars from the screen, placing toolbars onscreen, and changing the size and shape of toolbars is pretty simple. Figure 4-1 explains where to click and what to drag to manipulate toolbars. The following table gives all the details:

Displaying	Right-click on a toolbar or on the menu bar. When the shortcut menu appears, click the name of the toolbar you want to display.
Hiding	Right-click a toolbar or the menu bar. On the shortcut menu, click the name of the toolbar you don't want to display. If a toolbar is floating somewhere in the middle of the window, you can also click the toolbar's Close button (the ×) to remove it.
Repositioning	To drag a toolbar from the top or bottom of the screen to a side or the middle of the screen, click the move handle (a vertical bar at the left end of the toolbar) and drag. After you drag a toolbar onscreen, its title bar appears. To send a toolbar in the middle of the screen to the top or bottom of the screen, double-click its title bar.
Reshaping	To change the shape of a toolbar floating in the middle of the screen, gently place the cursor on a side of the toolbar. When the cursor changes to a double-headed arrow, drag the side in or out.

Larger Toolbar Buttons, Anyone?

Besides deciding for yourself which buttons should appear on toolbars, you can take advantage of three amenities that make toolbar and keyboard shortcuts easier to use and remember. Right-click on a toolbar, choose Customize to open the Customize dialog box, and click the Options tab. It offers these check boxes:

■ **Large Icons**   Makes button larger onscreen (not all buttons can fit onscreen when the buttons are enlarged).

■ **Show ScreenTips On Toolbars**   Displays a caption below a button when you move the pointer over a button. The caption tells you the button's name.

■ **Show Shortcut Keys In ScreenTips**   Displays a caption and the button's shortcut key equivalent, if there is one, below the button when you move the pointer over it.

Click and drag the border to reposition the toolbar.

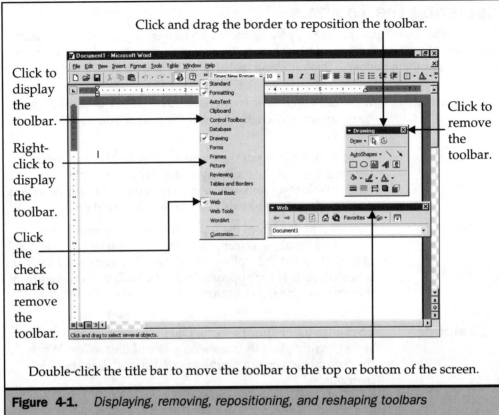

Click to
display
the
toolbar.

Right-
click to
display
the
toolbar.

Click
the
check
mark to
remove
the
toolbar.

Click to
remove
the
toolbar.

Double-click the title bar to move the toolbar to the top or bottom of the screen.

Figure 4-1. *Displaying, removing, repositioning, and reshaping toolbars*

Removing Buttons from and Adding Buttons to Toolbars

Office 2000 lets you decide for yourself which buttons appear on toolbars. Adding and removing buttons is easy, and if you change your mind later and want the original toolbar back, you can get it with a few clicks of the mouse.

Removing Buttons from a Toolbar

To remove an original button from a toolbar, click the toolbar's More Buttons button and choose Add or Remove Buttons. Then click the button you want to remove from the toolbar. To remove custom buttons from a toolbar, do the following:

1. Make sure that the toolbar whose buttons you want to remove is onscreen.

2. Right-click a toolbar or the menu bar and choose Customize from the shortcut menu. The Customize dialog box appears.

3. Move the pointer away from the dialog box and drag the button or buttons off of the toolbar. As you drag, a black × appears below the pointer. You can drop the button anywhere except on a toolbar. Click Close to close the Customize dialog box.

Note

In Word 2000, changes to toolbars apply only to a specific template. To choose a template on which to make toolbar changes, click the Commands tab in the Customize dialog box. From the Save In drop-down list, choose the template to which the toolbar changes will apply. To make changes to Word's default template, choose Normal.dot.

Adding Buttons to a Toolbar

Any command you issue in Office 2000, regardless of whether the program has assigned it a button, a place on the menu, or merely a choice in a dialog box, can be added to a toolbar. When you add a command such as What's This?, for which Office 2000 has a button image, the button is added to the toolbar. However, when you add a command for which no button image exists, such as Next Window, the command name itself is placed on the toolbar. Figure 4-2 shows toolbars with both buttons and command names.

Tip

To add the most common buttons to a toolbar, click the toolbar's More Buttons button and click Add Or Remove Buttons. Then choose the button you want to add from the pop-up menu.

To put buttons on a toolbar, follow these steps:

1. Place the toolbar to which you want to add buttons on the screen.

2. Right-click a toolbar or the menu bar and choose Customize from the shortcut menu. You see the Customize dialog box.

3. Click the Commands tab, which is shown in Figure 4-2. By clicking category names on the left side of the Commands tab, you see different sets of commands in the Commands box. Some commands offer button images, others offer only names.

4. In the Categories box, click category names to search for the command you want to add to the toolbar. The commands are listed in the Commands box on the right side of the dialog box. (The All Commands category lists all commands in alphabetical order.) Some commands offer predefined button images that you can put on toolbars; some don't. When you've found the button image or command name and it appears in the Commands box, click it.

Tip

If you have trouble telling what a command does, click the Description button in the Customize dialog box. You'll see a brief explanation of the command.

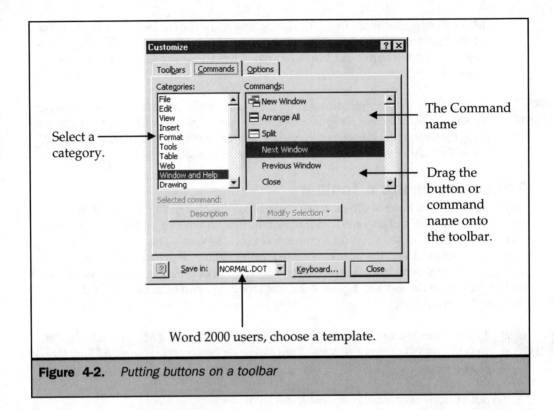

Select a → category.

The Command name

Drag the button or command name onto the toolbar.

Word 2000 users, choose a template.

Figure 4-2. *Putting buttons on a toolbar*

5. Drag the button or command name out of the Customize dialog box and place it on the toolbar. As you drag, a plus sign appears below the pointer to show that you are adding a button or command name.

Note *While you are adding buttons to the Standard or Formatting toolbar, these toolbars are displayed on two lines. Once you close the Customize dialog box, these toolbars are again displayed on one line.*

6. If necessary, arrange the buttons on the toolbar by dragging them from place to place.

7. Click the Close button in the Customize dialog box when you have finished adding buttons to the toolbar.

HEADSTART
On the companion CD is a Word 2000 template called Grandpa.dot. In this template, cumbersome toolbar buttons and esoteric commands have been removed. Meanwhile, buttons useful for writing simple documents have been added to the Standard and Formatting toolbars. Use Grandpa.dot to write letters, notes, and other simple documents.

Creating Toolbar Buttons for Macros, Styles, AutoText Entries, and More

In the previous section of this chapter, I described how to drag a button from the Customize dialog box to a toolbar. However, commands aren't the only things that can be put on toolbars. You can also place macro names, style names, AutoText entries, tables, queries, and other detritus. Because macros, styles, tables, and the like often have long names, Office 2000 gives you the chance to shorten their names when you add them to a toolbar. To create toolbar buttons for the things in Office 2000 that you name yourself, follow these steps:

1. Place the toolbar onscreen.

2. Right-click a toolbar or the menu bar and choose Customize to open the Customize dialog box.

3. Click the Commands tab (see Figure 4-2).

4. Scroll to the bottom of the Categories list. At the bottom of the list are entries called Styles, AutoText, Queries, and the like.

5. Click the type of item for which you want to create a toolbar button. When you click the item, a list of the styles, AutoText entries, queries, and whatnot that are available appears in the Commands box.

6. In the Commands box, click the item for which you want to create a button and drag it onto the toolbar.

7. Without closing the Customize dialog box, right-click on the new button you just created. You see the following shortcut menu:

8. You can accept the name that Word supplies, or you can type a button name in the Name box. If you are the decorative kind, you can also click Change Button Image and choose an image to go beside the button name.

To see an image on a button, not a name, choose the Text Only (in Menus) option.

9. Click the Close button in the Customize dialog box.

Creating Your Own Toolbar

To create a toolbar of your very own, you name the toolbar, spread it across the screen, and then call on the skills described in the previous pages to add the buttons. Creating a toolbar doesn't take long and is well worth the effort. Instead of fishing in obscure program menus or aiming the pointer at hard-to-find buttons, all you have to do is line up your favorite commands and buttons on a toolbar and take it from there.

Follow these steps to create a toolbar you can call your own:

1. Right-click on a toolbar or on the menu bar and choose Customize at the bottom of the shortcut menu.

2. Click the Toolbars tab, if necessary.

3. Click the New button. You see the New Toolbar dialog box:

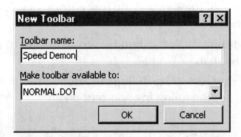

4. Type a name for the new toolbar in the Toolbar Name box. The name you enter will appear on the shortcut menu beside the other toolbar names when you right-click on a toolbar. If you are creating a toolbar for Word 2000, choose a template from the Make Toolbar Available To drop-down list.

5. Click OK. A very small toolbar with the name you typed appears somewhere in the middle of the window.

6. Double-click the title bar of the new toolbar to make it appear along the top of the screen.

7. Click the Commands tab in the Customize dialog box and add the commands. See "Adding Buttons to a Toolbar" earlier in this chapter if you need help. See also "Creating Toolbar Buttons for Macros, Styles, AutoText Entries, and More" to find out how to add other things besides buttons and commands to a toolbar.

8. To rearrange buttons on a toolbar, drag the buttons to new places.

9. To make lines appear between the buttons, drag the buttons farther apart.

10. Click Close to close the Customize dialog box.

Here is a fast way to assemble buttons from different toolbars on a single toolbar: Display the toolbars from which you want to take buttons, open the Customize dialog box, and drag the buttons to your new toolbar. Then restore the original toolbars with the Reset command in the Customize dialog box.

Restoring, Deleting, and Renaming Toolbars

It is fairly easy to go overboard when you add buttons to and remove buttons from toolbars. Therefore, this part of the chapter explains how to get an original toolbar back after you load it down with new buttons or strip it bare of its original set of buttons. It also tells how to delete a toolbar you created yourself (the subject of the next part of this chapter) and how to rename a toolbar you created.

You can't delete the toolbars that Office 2000 provides. Only toolbars you create yourself can be deleted. Likewise, you can't rename the toolbars that come with Office 2000.

Restoring a Toolbar

Suppose you make a mess out of an important toolbar, such as the Standard or Formatting toolbar, and you want the original toolbar back. To get it back, do the following:

1. Click the toolbar's More Buttons button.

2. Click Add Or Remove Buttons.

3. Choose Reset Toolbar from the pop-up menu.

4. When you are asked if you really and truly want to reset your changes to the toolbar, click OK.

Deleting a Toolbar

Think twice about deleting toolbars. After you delete a toolbar and save the document or template that the toolbar was contained in, all the work that went into creating the toolbar is lost forever. You can't get a deleted toolbar back. But if you're sure you want to delete a toolbar, do the following:

1. Right-click on a toolbar and choose Customize from the shortcut menu.

2. If necessary, click the Toolbars tab in the Customize dialog box.

3. Click the name of the toolbar you want to delete.

4. Click the Delete button.

5. Click OK when the program asks if you are sure you want to delete the toolbar.

6. Close the Customize dialog box.

Renaming a Toolbar

To rename a toolbar you created yourself, do the following:

1. Right-click on a toolbar and choose Customize.

2. Click the Toolbars tab in the Customize dialog box, if necessary.

3. Click the name of the toolbar you want to rename.

4. Click the Rename button.

5. In the Rename Toolbar dialog box, type a new name for the toolbar and click OK.

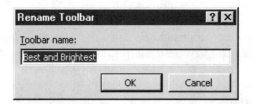

6. Close the Customize dialog box.

Changing What's on the Menus

In all the Office 2000 programs except Outlook, you can create menus of your own, remove unwanted commands from menus, move commands from menu to menu, and even get rid of menus. You customize menus in much the same way you customize toolbars. This part of the chapter explains how. By the way, if you make mincemeat out of the menus, you can always get the originals back. The following pages explain how to do that, too.

  If you share a computer with others, be sure to confer with them before you change the menus around. In Word 2000, you can confine menu changes to a single template, but menu changes to the other Office 2000 programs are for everyone to use or be confused by.

Creating Your Own Menu

As I've pointed out a couple of times, by default Office programs automatically place the commands you use most frequently at the top of the list that displays when you click on a menu. But you may favor a handful of commands from various menus and find yourself using them most of the time. In that case, you might as well put them on a single menu. That way, you will know exactly where to find them. Besides putting command names on menus, you can put font names, AutoText entries, queries, and much else.

Follow these steps to create a menu of your own:

1. Right-click on a toolbar or on the menu bar and choose Customize from the shortcut menu. You see the Customize dialog box.

2. If necessary, click the Commands tab. It is shown in Figure 4-2.

3. Scroll to the bottom of the Categories list and choose New Menu. A single option, New Menu, appears in the Commands box.

Word 2000 users can choose a template from the Save In drop-down list. By choosing a template, you tell Office 2000 to make menu changes only to documents created with the template you chose.

4. Click the New Menu option in the Commands box and drag it out of the Customize dialog box and onto the menu bar. If you do this correctly, a white box with a cross appears below the pointer as you drag.

Tip   *You can also add menus to toolbars.*

5. Right-click on the menu you just created, and, in the Name box on the shortcut menu, type a name for the menu and press ENTER. To designate a hot key for the menu, enter an ampersand (&) before the letter that is to be the hot key. For example, entering **Spee&d** makes D the hot key, and the menu name looks like this on the menu bar: Spee<u>d</u>. Be sure to choose a hot key that doesn't appear in one of the other menu's names on the menu bar. If you choose a hot key that is already in use, when you press the hot key, the Office program opens the first menu on the menu bar.

6. In the Categories box, click category names to search for the command you want to add to the new menu. (The All Commands category lists all commands in alphabetical order.) You likely have to scroll in the Commands list to find the command. Fonts, macros, queries, and other such things can be placed on menus. You will find them at the bottom of the Categories box.

7. In the Commands box, click the command, query, macro, or whatnot you want to add to the menu.

8. Drag the command out of the dialog box and onto the new menu. As you near the menu, a small gray box appears below the menu. Drop the new menu command inside that gray rectangle.

9. Repeats steps 7 and 8 to put more commands on the new menu. As shown in Figure 4-3, the new menu opens when you drag new commands onto it, and a horizontal bar shows where the command will appear on the menu.

10. Click the Close button in the Customize dialog box when you have finished creating the new menu.

Tip   *Sometimes horizontal lines appear on menus to separate commands. In Office 2000 terminology, the horizontal lines separate "menu groups." To place a horizontal line on a menu, display the Customize dialog box, click the menu, and then right-click the command that you want the line to appear directly above. Then, from the shortcut menu, choose Begin a Group and close the Customize dialog box.*

A Quick Way to Open the Files You Recently Opened

As you know if you've used an Office program for any length of time, the names of the files that were opened most recently appear at the bottom of the File menu. One of the fastest ways to open a file is to click its name at the bottom of the File menu. By default, four filenames appear, but you can add more files to the File menu by following these steps:

1. Choose Tools | Options to open the Options dialog box.

2. Click the General tab.

3. In the Entries box beside the Recently Used File List check box, enter the number of files that you would like to see on the bottom of the File menu.

4. Click OK.

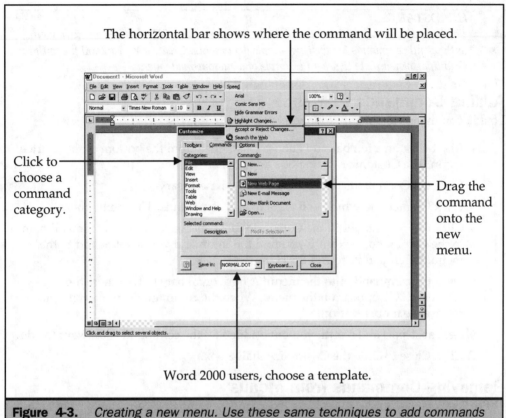

The horizontal bar shows where the command will be placed.

Click to choose a command category.

Drag the command onto the new menu.

Word 2000 users, choose a template.

Figure 4-3. *Creating a new menu. Use these same techniques to add commands to existing menus*

Adding, Removing, and Repositioning Commands

While the Customize dialog box is open, you can load an Office 2000 menu with as many commands as you desire. For that matter, you can also prune menus to remove the commands that you think are extraneous and unnecessary. And you can reposition commands in menus and reposition menus themselves on the menu bar. Read on to learn the dirty details.

HEADSTART
The Grandpa.dot Word 2000 template on the companion CD includes an extra menu with useful commands for writing simple documents. Create a Word 2000 file with the Grandpa.dot template to see an example of a custom-made menu.

Adding Commands to Menus

To add commands to a menu, follow these steps:

1. Right-click on a toolbar and choose Customize from the bottom of the shortcut menu. The Customize dialog box appears.

2. Click the Commands tab (see Figure 4-3), if necessary.

3. Click the menu to which you want to add commands. The menu opens.

4. Click category names in the Categories box, and scroll to read command names in the Commands box until you find the command you want to add to the menu. When you've found the command, click it.

5. Drag the command onto the menu. A horizontal bar shows where the command will appear on the menu. When the command is in the right place, release the mouse button.

6. Repeat steps 4 and 5 until you have added all the commands you want to add.

7. Click Close to close the Customize dialog box.

Removing Commands from Menus

Office 2000 offers a quick but reckless technique for removing commands from menus, as well as a thoughtful, conscientious technique. Both are described here.

The reckless technique is to press CTRL-ALT-- (the hyphen key). The pointer changes into a black bar. With the black bar pointer, choose a menu command that you want to remove. That's right—click the command as though you really wanted to select it. One by one, you can remove commands from menus this way.

The drawback of the CTRL-ALT-- technique is that it can't remove menu commands that offer submenus, nor can it remove commands that are grayed out. To remove those commands, you have to return to the Customize dialog box.

Follow these steps to remove commands from menus with the Customize dialog box:

1. Right-click on a toolbar or the main menu and choose Customize.

2. Click on the menu whose commands you want to remove. The menu opens.

3. One by one, click the names of the commands you want to remove and drag them off the menu.

Be sure to drag the commands away from the toolbars, menus, and Customize dialog box before you release the mouse button. If you fail to do so, you might move a command onto a toolbar or onto a different menu.

4. Click Close in the Customize dialog box when you are done pruning menus.

Removing a Menu from the Menu Bar

To remove a menu, simply right-click on a toolbar to open the Customize dialog box, and then click on the menu you want to remove and drag it off the menu bar. Be sure not to drop it on a toolbar, however, because if you do, the menu will become a button with drop-down choices on the toolbar. Close the Customize dialog box when you are finished.

Menus you created yourself are gone forever after you remove them. You can, however, restore one of Office 2000's built-in menus after you remove it. (See "Restoring and Renaming Menus," later in this chapter.)

Repositioning Menus and Menu Commands

As long as the Customize dialog box is open, you can rearrange commands on menus until the cows come home. And you can also reposition menus on the menu bar. To change the position of menus and menu commands, follow these steps:

1. Right-click on a toolbar and choose Customize from the shortcut menu. The Customize dialog box appears (see Figure 4-3).

2. To change the position of a menu on the menu bar, click the menu name, (a black box appears around it) and then drag the menu name sideways to a new position.

3. To change the location of a command on a menu, click the menu to open it, and then drag the command to a new place. A black horizontal bar shows you precisely where the command will land when you release the mouse button:

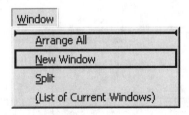

4. Click Close in the Customize dialog box when you have finished rearranging menus and menu commands.

Restoring and Renaming Menus

If you make a mess of an Office 2000 menu and want the original menu version back, all is not lost, because you can get it back very quickly. This part of the chapter explains how. It also explains how to recover a built-in Office 2000 menu that you removed and how to rename a menu.

Restoring the Commands on a Built-In Menu

Follow these steps to restore a menu to its pristine state:

1. Right-click on a toolbar and choose Customize from the shortcut menu.
2. In the Categories list, right-click on the name of the menu whose commands you wish to restore.
3. Click Reset on the shortcut menu.
4. Click Close to close the Customize dialog box.

Restoring a Built-In Menu That You Removed

If you removed a built-in menu that came with an Office 2000 program and you want to get the menu back, you have a bit of work to do:

1. Right-click on a toolbar or the menu bar and choose Customize.
2. Click the Commands tab in the Customize dialog box, if necessary.
3. Scroll to the next-to-last category in the Categories box, Built-in Menus, and click it. A list of standard, built-in menus appears in the Commands box:

4. In the Commands box, click the name of the menu you want to restore (you might have to scroll to find the menu) and drag it back onto the menu bar.
5. Click Close to close the Customize dialog box.

Renaming a Menu

To rename a menu, right-click on a toolbar to open the Customize dialog box, and then right-click the menu to be renamed. A shortcut menu appears. On the shortcut menu, delete the name in the Name box and enter a new name. To establish a hot key for the menu, enter an ampersand (&) before the letter that is to be the hot key. Be sure to choose a hot key that doesn't appear in one of the other menus names on the menu bar.

Changing Keyboard Shortcuts

This section explains how to fiddle with keyboard shortcuts. Are you particularly fond of a keyboard shortcut, perhaps a shortcut that figured prominently in WordStar or MultiMate or some other antique application that you knew and loved? If you are, you can make your favorite keyboard shortcut apply to a command in an Office 2000 program.

Following are instructions for assigning keyboard shortcuts to commands and removing keyboard shortcuts. You will also find instructions here for restoring the original keyboard shortcuts.

> **Caution**   *If you share your computer with others, be sure to speak to them first before changing keyboard shortcuts.*

Assigning a New Keyboard Shortcut

Follow these steps to assign a keyboard shortcut to a command, font, AutoText entry, query, or other directive:

1. Right-click on a toolbar or on the menu bar and choose Customize from the shortcut menu.

2. Click the Keyboard button in the lower-right corner of the Customize dialog box. You see the Customize Keyboard dialog box shown in Figure 4-4.

> **Note**   *Word 2000 users can make keyboard shortcuts apply only to documents created with a specific template. To do so, choose the template from the Save Changes In drop-down list.*

3. In the Categories list, click on the menu whose command you want to assign a keyboard shortcut to. At the bottom of the list are styles, AutoText entries, and other such items. You can assign shortcuts to those as well.

4. In the Commands list, find and click on the command, style, or whatnot to which you want to assign a keyboard shortcut. Command names are hard to understand in this dialog box because they're a combination of the menu, submenu, and command name. If you don't understand a command based on its name, check out the Description box at the bottom of the Customize Keyboard dialog box. It tells you precisely what each command does.

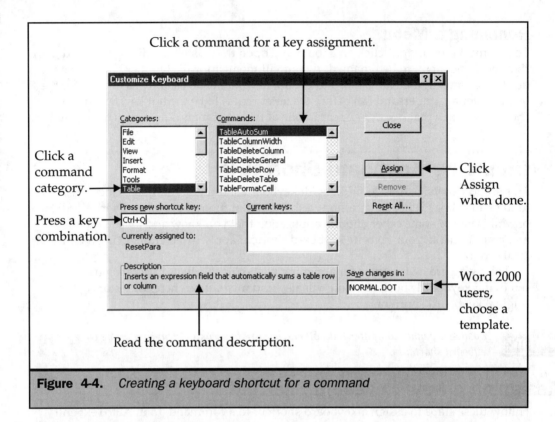

Figure 4-4. *Creating a keyboard shortcut for a command*

5. Enter the shortcut key combination in the Press New Shortcut Key box. In other words, if the shortcut key combination is CTRL-!, press the CTRL key and the exclamation point key simultaneously. Office 2000 enters the names of the keys you pressed in the box and places a plus sign between the key names.

Shortcut key combinations can begin with the CTRL key, the ALT key, or any combination of the so-called modifier keys (CTRL, ALT, and SHIFT), as well as any letter, number, or symbol. For example, the following would all be valid shortcut keys: CTRL-!, ALT-P, ALT-9, CTRL-SHIFT-N, and ALT-SHIFT-5. It's very likely, however, that the key combination you want to assign is already claimed by another command. When that is the case, the words "Currently Assigned To" and a command name appear below the Press New Shortcut Key box. Enter a new key combination, or else let yours stand if you want to override the preassigned key combination.

6. Click the Assign button.

7. Repeat steps 3 through 6 to assign other key combinations to commands, if you want.

8. Click the Close button.

9. Click the Close button in the Customize dialog box.

Removing and Restoring Keyboard Shortcuts

Following are instructions for removing a keyboard shortcut from a command and getting a program's original keyboard shortcuts back. Many an Office 2000 user has assigned keyboard shortcuts, then swiftly forgotten them and longed to have the originals back.

Removing a Keyboard Shortcut

To remove a keyboard shortcut from a command:

1. Right-click on a toolbar and choose Customize from the shortcut menu.

2. Click the Keyboard button to open the Customize Keyboard dialog box (see Figure 4-4).

3. Find the command to which the keyboard shortcut has been assigned. To do that, click a category in the Categories box, and then click the command in the Commands box. If you have trouble finding the command, read descriptions in the Description box at the bottom of the Customize Keyboard dialog box.

   When you find the command, its keyboard shortcut appears in the Current Keys box.

4. In the Current Keys box, click the keyboard shortcut you want to remove.

5. Click the Remove button.

6. Click Close to close the Customize Keyboard dialog box.

7. Click Close to close the Customize dialog box.

Restoring a Program's Original Keyboard Shortcuts

If you make a mess of assigning keyboard shortcuts to commands, you can always get the program's original keyboard shortcuts back by following these steps:

1. Right-click on a toolbar and choose Customize from the shortcut menu.

2. In the Customize dialog box, click the Keyboard button. The Customize Keyboard dialog box appears (see Figure 4-4).

3. Click the Reset All button. The program asks if you really want to unravel all your hard work.

4. Click the Yes button.

5. Click Close twice to close all the dialog boxes.

Caution *Think twice before you reset the shortcut key assignments. After you click the Reset All button, all assignments you made are lost and you have to start all over.*

Using the Tools Menu's Options Commands

At the bottom of the Tools menu on all Office 2000 programs is the Options command. When you click the Options command, you see the Options dialog box, an elaborate dialog box for customizing various parts of the program. Figure 4-5 shows the Options dialog box in the Outlook program.

Commands in the Options dialog boxes are mentioned throughout this book. For the time being, all you need to know is that the Options dialog boxes present many ways to tell the programs how you want them to operate. Moreover, if you choose a command and find that it doesn't work the way you expected, it could be that someone fooled with an option in the Options dialog box.

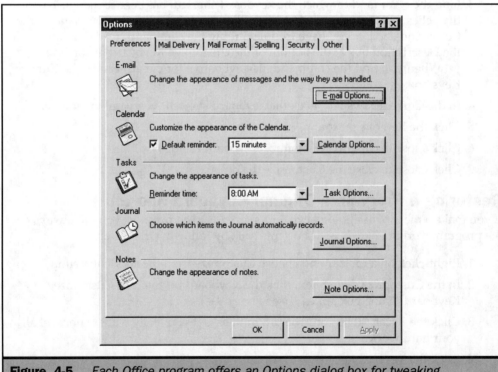

Figure 4-5. *Each Office program offers an Options dialog box for tweaking, customizing, and altering different features*

The
Complete
Reference

Office 2000

Chapter 5

Sharing Information

One of the most useful aspects of the Microsoft Office 2000 suite of programs—and, in fact, the reason it's even fair to call it a suite of programs—is that Office 2000 makes it extremely easy to share information among its individual programs and among the people using Office. You can, for example, easily move an Excel worksheet range or chart to a Word document or a PowerPoint presentation. And you can move the text, clip art, and even drawing objects you create in one program—such as Word—to one of the other programs such as PowerPoint or Excel.

Moving and Sharing Information

You can easily use information that you create with one Office program in another Office program. The process that allows you to do this is called *object linking and embedding* (formerly referred to by the acronym OLE).

Note   *You can also use object linking and embedding in many other popular Windows programs.*

You share information in two distinct ways. You can simply make a copy of the information you want to share and then paste this copied information into the other document file. This is called *embedding*. Or, you can make a copy of the information you want to share, paste this information into the other document, and tell Windows that it should update the copy any time the original information changes. This is called *linking*.

Understanding Linking and Embedding

In both linking and embedding, two files are required: a source document file and a destination document file. The program in which you create the source document file is called the *server*, while the program in which you create the destination document file is called the *client*. If, for example, you embed a picture from a PowerPoint presentation into an Excel workbook, the PowerPoint presentation is the source document file, the PowerPoint program is the server, the Excel workbook is the destination document file, and the Excel program is the client.

The data that is embedded or linked is called an *object*. Although an object is usually just a chunk of some document, an object can actually be just about anything: a file, text from a word processing program, a range of cells from a spreadsheet, a computer-drawn graphic image, a scanned photograph, a multimedia video clip—and the list goes on. The only real requirement is that the server program, as well as the client program, supports object linking and embedding, which all Microsoft Office 2000 programs do. When you embed, data created in the server program becomes a permanent part of the document file in the client program. As mentioned in the opening paragraphs of this section, even if the original data in the server document file should change, the data in the client document file would remain exactly the way it was when it was embedded.

When you link two files, however, the data itself never gets transferred to the destination document file—it remains in the source file in the server program. Instead of embedded data, the destination document file contains two other things: a marker indicating that the link to the source document file exists, and an address that tells the server where to find the linked data. As long as the link is maintained, any data changes in the server document file are reflected in the client document file.

Embedding and Linking Objects

The Office 2000 programs provide two basic ways to embed and link objects: using the Copy and Paste Special commands and using the Insert menu's Object command. This section describes both methods, because they're useful in different situations.

Embedding Using the Copy and Paste Special Commands

To embed an object using the Copy and Paste Special commands, follow these steps:

1. Select data in the source file.

2. Copy the data to the Clipboard, using whatever commands the source file application provides for that purpose. (You can probably choose Edit | Copy or click the Copy tool on the Standard toolbar.)

3. Switch to the client program. Remember that this is the program that works with the destination document file. (You can do this by clicking on the program's Taskbar button, if the program is already running. Otherwise, use the Start menu to load the program.)

4. Choose Edit | Paste Special. The client program displays the Paste Special dialog box, as shown in Figure 5-1.

5. Make sure the Paste option button is enabled.

6. If necessary, select the first item in the As list.

7. Click OK.

Embedding Using the Insert Menu's Object Command

You can also use the Insert menu's Object command to embed an object. How you use this command, however, depends on whether the object you want to embed already exists. If the object doesn't already exist, take the following steps:

1. With the client program active and the destination document file open, choose Insert | Object. Figure 5-2 shows Excel's Object dialog box.

2. If necessary, click the Create New tab to indicate that you want to create a new object.

3. Double-click the type of object you want to embed, and the appropriate program for creating the object opens.

To paste an object, select the first entry in this list box. The entry should describe what you're pasting as an object.

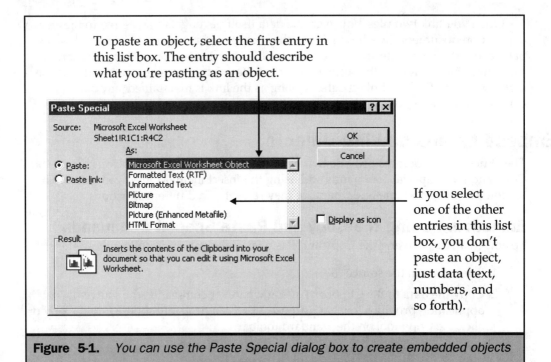

If you select one of the other entries in this list box, you don't paste an object, just data (text, numbers, and so forth).

Figure 5-1. *You can use the Paste Special dialog box to create embedded objects*

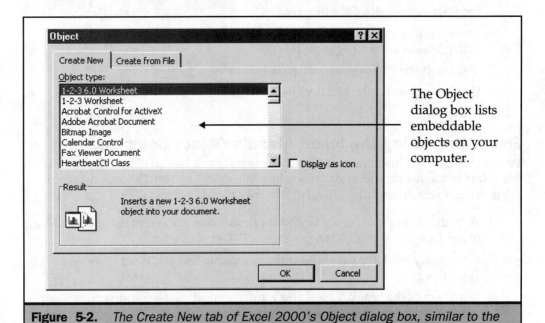

The Object dialog box lists embeddable objects on your computer.

Figure 5-2. *The Create New tab of Excel 2000's Object dialog box, similar to the Object dialog boxes of other Office programs*

4. Use the server program to create the new object.

5. After you create the new object using the server program, click away from the embedded document in the destination document to return to the client program.

Figure 5-3 shows a Word document with an Excel worksheet range embedded. Note that the Word document really uses the Excel worksheet range as a table.

LEARN BY EXAMPLE

If you want to follow along with the discussion here, open the example Word document in the Figure 5-3 (a memo with next year's budget) file on the companion CD. The example Excel workbook from which the worksheet range is copied is also on the companion CD in the file named Figure 5-A (source file for budget memo). The memo Word document without the embedded object is named Figure 5-B (client file for budget memo).

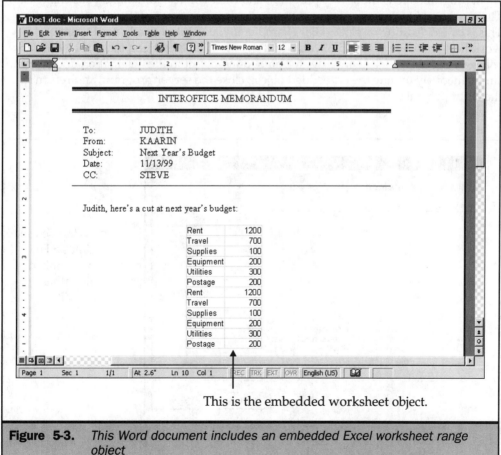

Figure 5-3. *This Word document includes an embedded Excel worksheet range object*

If the object does exist, however, take the following steps to embed it:

1. With the client program active and the destination document file open, choose Insert | Object.

2. Click the Create From File tab, shown in Figure 5-4.

3. Enter the complete path name for the file you want to link to in the File Name text box. Or, if you don't know the complete path name, click the Browse command button and then use the Browse dialog box to locate and identify the file. The Browse dialog box works like the Open dialog box, which Office 2000 programs display when you choose File | Open.

4. Click OK.

Editing Embedded Objects

If you ever need to edit an embedded object, just double-click it. When you do, the client program opens the server program, and then you use it to make your changes. The menus and toolbars for the server program replace those of the client program. This is called "editing in place." For example, if you wanted to edit the budget worksheet shown in Figure 5-3, you could double-click the object, make the necessary changes, and then click away from the embedded object in the destination document to simultaneously update the embedded object, close the server program, and return to the client program.

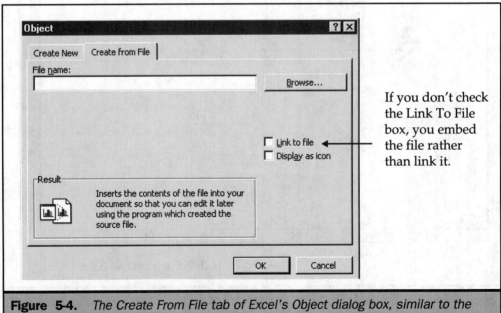

Figure 5-4. The Create From File tab of Excel's Object dialog box, similar to the Object dialog boxes of other Office programs

In order to be able to edit the embedded object, of course, you must have the server program on your computer.

Linking Using the Copy and Paste Special Commands

To link an object using the Copy and Paste Special commands, follow these steps:

1. Select data in the source file.

2. Copy the data to the Clipboard, using whatever commands the source file application provides for that purpose. (You can probably choose Edit | Copy or click the Copy tool on the Standard toolbar.)

3. Switch to the client program. (You can probably do this by clicking on the program's Taskbar button.)

4. Choose Edit | Paste Special.

5. Enable the Paste Link option button.

6. Select the list box entry that describes what you're pasting as an object. Figure 5-5 shows how I have selected to paste the link as a Microsoft Excel Worksheet Object, but the choices you will have in this box depend on what you have selected to paste.

7. Click OK.

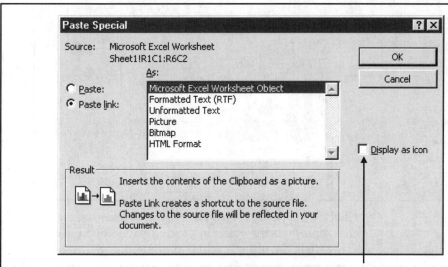

Check the Display As Icon box if you want to see an icon that represents the object in the destination document file rather than the object's actual information.

Figure 5-5. *You can also use the Paste Special dialog box to create linked objects*

Linking Using the Insert Menu's Object Command

You can also use the Insert menu's Object command to link an object. To use this approach, take the following steps:

1. With the client program active and the destination document file active, choose Insert | Object. Figure 5-6 shows PowerPoint's Insert Object dialog box.

2. Click the Create From File option button.

3. Enter the complete path name for the file you want to link to in the File Name text box. Or, if you don't know the complete path name, click the Browse command button and then use the Browse dialog box to locate and identify the file. The Browse dialog box works like the Open dialog box, which Office programs display when you choose File | Open.

4. Click OK.

Figure 5-7 shows a PowerPoint presentation with a linked Excel chart.

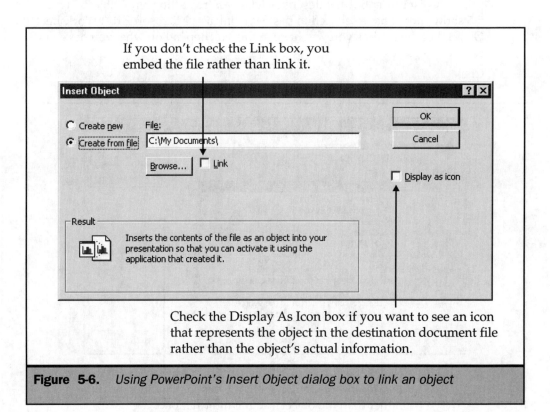

Figure 5-6.   *Using PowerPoint's Insert Object dialog box to link an object*

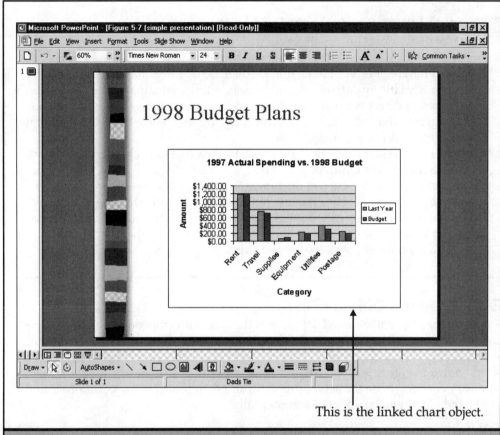

This is the linked chart object.

Figure 5-7. *This PowerPoint presentation includes a linked Excel chart object*

Note   To create a linked object, the file must already exist somewhere on your computer or, if you're connected to a network, on the network.

EXAMPLES

LEARN BY EXAMPLE
To follow along with the discussion here, open the example PowerPoint presentation in the Figure 5-7 (simple presentation) file on the companion CD. The example Excel workbook from which the chart is copied is on the companion CD and is named Figure 5-C (source file for budget chart). The PowerPoint presentation without the embedded object is named Figure 5-D (client file for budget presentation).

Manual Links vs. Automatic Links

The links that connect linked objects to their source files can be either automatic or manual. An automatic link is updated automatically whenever the server document file changes. A manual link needs to be updated manually. Although all links are automatic by default, you can change a link to manual status if you have a good reason to do so. For example, if the linked object is time-sensitive, and you don't want it to change until a certain time, you might change the link so you can update it manually at the correct time.

To change the status of a link or to update a manual link, choose Edit | Links. When you do this, the Office program displays the Links dialog box, which lists all the active links in the current document file and shows the status of each. To change a link to manual, click the link in the Links box and select the Manual option. To update a manual link, click Update Now. By clicking the Open Source command button, you can open the source document file in the client program. When you are finished, click the Close button.

Editing Linked Objects

If you ever need to edit a linked object, as is the case with embedded objects, you just double-click the object. When you do, the client program opens the server program, and then you use it to make your changes. For example, if you wanted to edit the chart object shown in Figure 5-7, you could double-click the object, make and save the necessary changes, close the server program, and then return to the client program. The linked object will be updated automatically.

In order to be able to edit the linked object, of course, you must have the server program installed on your computer.

Importing and Exporting Document Files

In most cases, you'll have no problem importing and exporting document files among Word, Excel, PowerPoint, Access, and equivalent programs such as WordPerfect and Lotus 1-2-3. You simply use the File menu's Open command to import document files and the File menu's Save As command to export document files.

Importing Using the Open Command

To import a document file created by another equivalent program, follow these steps:

1. Choose File | Open to display the Open dialog box, as shown in Figure 5-8.

For information about how to use these buttons,
see "Opening Document Files" in Chapter 2.

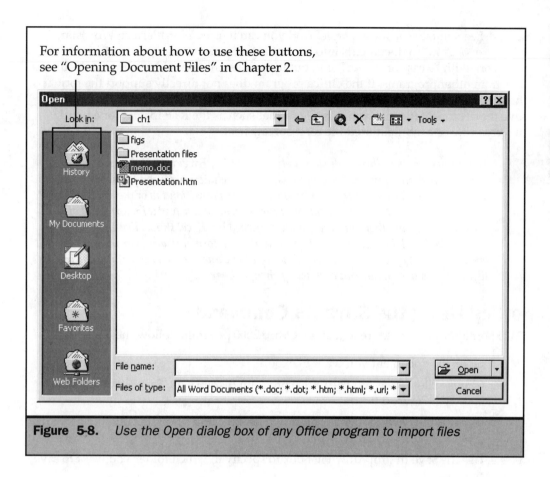

Figure 5-8.   *Use the Open dialog box of any Office program to import files*

2. Select the appropriate file type or extension from the Files Of Type drop-down
   list box.

3. Use the Look In drop-down list box to identify the folder in which you've
   stored the document file.

4. When you see the document file that you want to import, double-click it.

Note   *If you attempt to import a document file into Excel and Excel doesn't recognize or can't
easily translate the file's information, Excel may start an Import Wizard, which will ask
you questions about the file you want to import.*

As a general rule, Excel has no trouble importing document files from common
spreadsheet programs and Word has no trouble importing document files from
common word processor programs. You can import Lotus 1-2-3 and Quattro Pro

spreadsheets into Excel, for example. And you can import WordPerfect, Wordstar, WordPro, or AmiPro documents into Word. Import operations become trickier when you work with Access or PowerPoint, but it's still usually possible to import document files from other programs. If the Office program does not directly support the format of the file that you want to import, you may need to use the other (source) program to save the document file in a common file format such as the RTF format for a word processor file or a tab-delimited file for a spreadsheet.

> **Note**   *To improve compatibility with older Lotus 1-2-3 files, Excel includes special features called Transition Options. These options, which include Transition formula evaluation and Transition formula entry, can be found on the Transition tab of the Tools menu's Options dialog box. Excel automatically turns them on when you import any Lotus 1-2-3 file. Be aware that with these options turned on, Excel thinks like 1-2-3. As a result, Excel will do a few things differently than it normally does. For instance, when averaging a list of numbers, Excel will assign the value zero to any text it finds in the list. Needless to say, this can drastically change the result.*

Exporting Using the Save As Command

To export a document file created by an Office 2000 program, follow these steps:

1. Open the document you want to export.

2. Choose File | Save As. The Office program displays the Save As dialog box shown in Figure 5-9.

3. Activate the Save As Type drop-down list box, and scroll through the list of file types to find the one you want.

4. Use the Save In drop-down list box to specify in which folder you want to save the file.

5. In the File Name text box, enter the name under which you want to save the file.

6. Click Save.

Sharing Document Files with the Apple Macintosh

The programs that make up Office 2000 are highly compatible with their cousin programs that make up the Office for the Macintosh suite of programs. As a result, you can easily transfer Office document files from PCs to Macintosh computers by e-mailing them or exchanging them over a network. You can also save a document file onto a floppy disk and then read this floppy disk with the Macintosh. You just need to

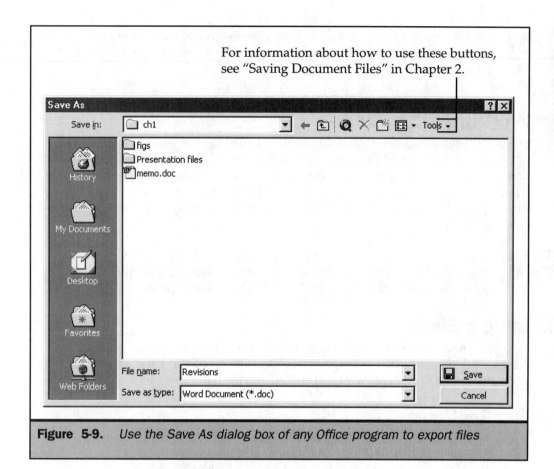

Figure 5-9.   *Use the Save As dialog box of any Office program to export files*

be sure to specify the file format as one that is acceptable to the Mac version of the Office program you're using. (You specify the file format using the Save As Type drop-down list box, which appears on the Save As dialog box.)

Newer Mac floppy disk drives generally read PC-formatted floppy drives, and the Macintosh operating system includes utilities for automatically converting PC-format files to Macintosh-format files.

You should be able to move document files from a Macintosh to a PC by following the same steps in reverse order. In other words, you use the Mac to save a file to a floppy disk and then read this floppy disk using a PC. Be sure, however, to use a floppy disk that's been formatted by a PC, because the PC isn't smart enough to read disks that have been formatted by a Mac.

The Mac version of Office doesn't have all of the features that the newest PC version of Office does. For this reason, you may lose certain non-Mac features of a document file if you move it from the PC to the Macintosh.

Working with Binder

Microsoft Office comes with a special program, called Binder, that lets you organize related Office document files so they appear to be one document. Once you've created a binder, you can open and print all the documents as a group, and you can add page numbering and headers and footers that will apply to all the documents in the binder. Although Binder may sound complicated, it's really not—especially if you understand how OLE works.

 Binder is not automatically installed when you install Office 2000. You will need to run the installation program again and select Binder to install it. Or see Appendix A for information on installing it using Office 2000 Maintenance Mode.

Creating a Binder

To create a new binder, start the Microsoft Binder program. You start Binder in the same way that you start other programs. Binder, like Word and Excel, creates a blank, or empty, binder document when you start it, as shown in Figure 5-10.

Adding Sections

You build a binder by adding sections. A section is just an Office document. (To be precise, Binder should actually call these documents objects, as described earlier in the chapter in the section, "Understanding Linking and Embedding.")

To add a section by creating a new, blank Word document, Excel workbook, or PowerPoint presentation, follow these steps:

1. Choose Section | Add. Binder displays the Add Section dialog box, shown in Figure 5-11.

2. Click the dialog box tab that represents the category of Office template that you want to use as the basis for creating a new document file. If you don't know which category you want to use, click the General tab.

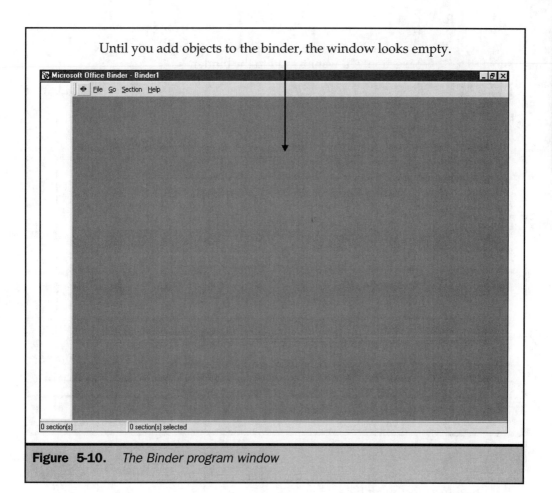

Until you add objects to the binder, the window looks empty.

Figure 5-10. *The Binder program window*

3. Double-click the template that you want to use as the model for creating a new document file. When you do, Binder adds a new section to the binder, as shown in Figure 5-12.

To add a section using a document file that already exists, follow these steps:

1. Choose Section | Add From File to display the Add From File dialog box shown in Figure 5-13.

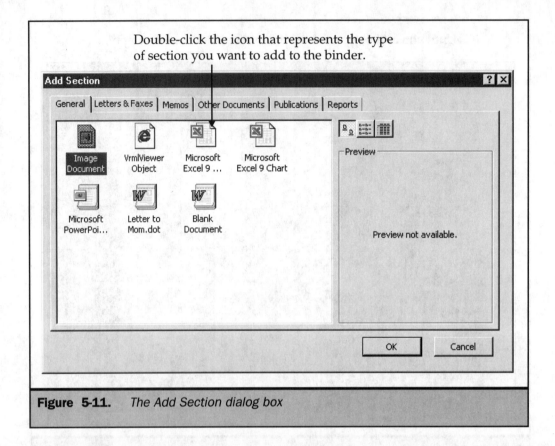

Double-click the icon that represents the type of section you want to add to the binder.

Figure 5-11. *The Add Section dialog box*

2. Use the Look In drop-down list box to select the folder in which you've stored the Office document file.

3. Double-click the document file you want to add to the binder.

Figure 5-14 shows an example binder document that includes four sections: a Word document section, an Excel worksheet section, an Excel chart section, and a PowerPoint presentation.

The right pane of the Binder
window shows the active section.

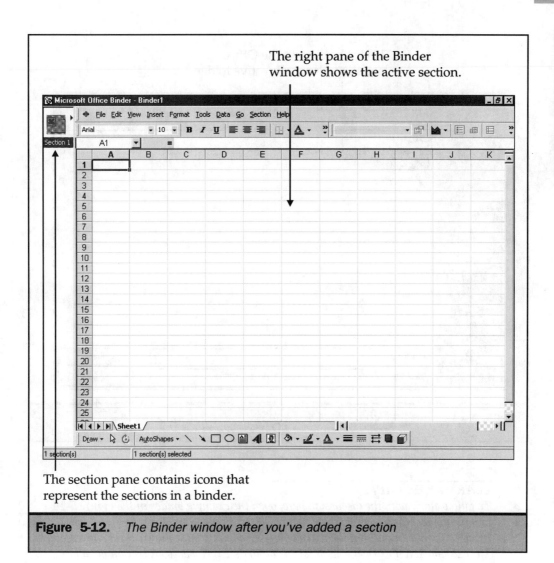

The section pane contains icons that
represent the sections in a binder.

Figure 5-12.   *The Binder window after you've added a section*

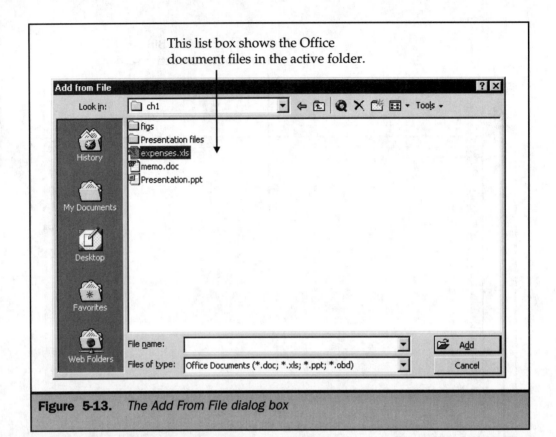

This list box shows the Office document files in the active folder.

Figure 5-13. The Add From File dialog box

LEARN BY EXAMPLE

To follow along with the discussion here, open the example binder in the Figure 5-14 (simple binder) file on the companion CD. The example Word document used for the binder's Word section is on the companion CD and is named Figure 5-E (Word section). The example Excel workbook used for the binder's Excel workbook section is named Figure 5-F (Excel workbook section). The example Excel chart used for the binder's Excel chart section is named Figure 5-G (Excel chart section). Finally, the PowerPoint presentation used for the binder's PowerPoint presentation section is named Figure 5-H (PowerPoint section).

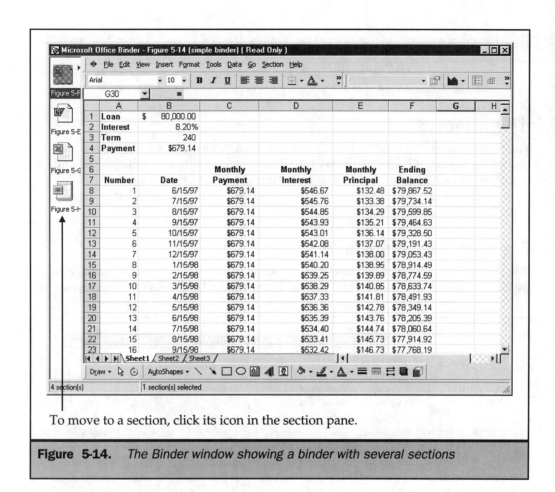

To move to a section, click its icon in the section pane.

Figure 5-14. *The Binder window showing a binder with several sections*

Working with Sections

To work with a section, you simply click its icon in the section pane. When you do this, Binder adds the server program's menus and toolbars to the Binder window. You can then work with the section the exact same way you work with a regular document file. For example, if you indicate you want to work with a Word section, you work with that section the same way you work with a regular Word document file. If you indicate you want to work with an Excel workbook section, you work with that section the same way you do with a regular Excel workbook.

Binder names your sections using labels such as "Section 1" and "Section 2" if you add them to the binder as blank documents. If you add a section using an existing file, the file-name will be used as the section label. You can rename a section, however, by clicking its name in the section pane and then typing the new name you want to use.

Printing Binders

You print binders by choosing the File menu's Print Binder command. When you choose this command, Binder displays the Print Binder dialog box, which looks and works very much like the Print dialog boxes used by other Office programs (see Figure 5-15). Unless you choose to print only the sections you've selected in the section pane, Binder prints every section.

Saving and Opening Binders

You save and open binder documents in the same basic way that you save and open regular Office documents files. Use the File menu's Save Binder As command to save a

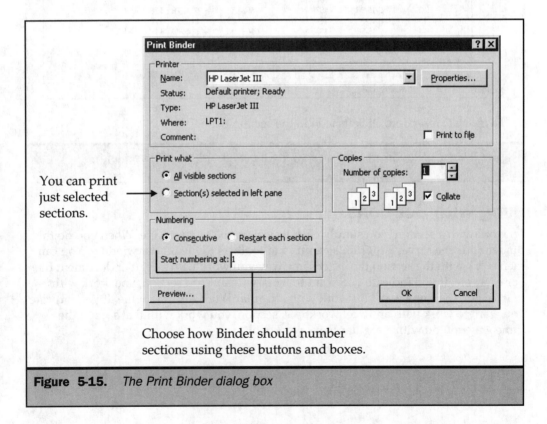

Figure 5-15. *The Print Binder dialog box*

binder document. Use the File menu's Open Binder command to open a binder document you've previously saved.

Sharing Document Files

These days it's quite likely that you will be using Word or Excel in a shared environment—on a network. Recognizing this feature of today's work environment, both Word and Excel provide special features that make it easy for you to share Word and Excel document files in workgroups. What's more, Word, Excel, and PowerPoint all provide special commands you can use to easily e-mail documents to other network users (if the network includes an Exchange server) or to somebody with an Internet mail address if your computer connects to an Internet mail server.

Note *An Exchange server is a network server that runs the Exchange server software programs. The Exchange server software, among other things, does the work of passing around e-mail messages to a network's users. In other words, when you send an e-mail message on a network that includes an Exchange server, the e-mail client (which is probably Outlook) passes the message to the Exchange server. The Exchange server then goes to the work of delivering the message to the recipient's mailbox. An Internet mail server works the same basic way. Whenever someone sends a message, the message actually gets sent to the mail server. The mail server then goes to work—typically with the help of other Internet mail servers—delivering the message to the recipient's mailbox.*

Sharing Document Files in a Workgroup

Both Word 2000 and Excel 2000 include features that make it possible to share a document file with other users. For example, Word (with the help of Windows) keeps track of the fact that more than one person has opened a Word document. And Word also provides tools for reviewing and merging the changes that multiple authors or editors make to the same document. Excel (also with the help of Windows) includes similar functionality.

 You need to be very careful when sharing documents. It's surprisingly easy to corrupt a document when multiple people share it and make changes. If you want to try Word's and Excel's document sharing capability, consider first experimenting sample documents.

Sharing Word Documents

You save and open a shared Word document in the same manner that you save and open any Word document, with one difference: You must save it to a shared drive, which is simply a drive accessible to other members of your workgroup. (Probably this means the drive is a network drive on a network file server, but the drive also could be a shared local drive on a workgroup member's desktop computer.)

The term "workgroup" simply refers to a group of people who work together. It isn't, in this context, a technical term.

When you share a Word document, the first user to open the document opens the original document. Subsequent users open copies of the document and not the original document. To alert people that they're working with a copy of a document file, Word displays a message box before it creates and opens the copy:

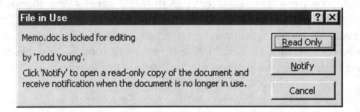

To later successfully incorporate everyone's changes into the original document, you need to do three things. First, before making any changes to the document, everyone working with a copy of the document must turn on Word's Track Changes feature. People can do this by choosing Tools | Track Changes | Highlight Changes. When Word displays the Highlight Changes dialog box, check the Track Changes While Editing box, and then click OK.

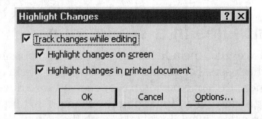

The second thing that people working with the original document and copies of the document must do is save multiple copies of the same document. Specifically, this means the person working with the original document can save the document using its original name, but everyone working with a copy of the document must save the document using a new document name. This is critical. If a user with a document copy saves the copy using the original document name, he or she may replace the original document with the copy of the document, which means that it's possible the most recent set of changes to the original document will be lost.

The final thing that somebody needs to do when multiple users share a Word document is merge the document changes. To do this, you (or someone else) needs to open the original document, choose Tools | Merge Documents, and then use the Select File To Merge Into Current Document dialog box to select the document copy with the changes you want to fold into the open document:

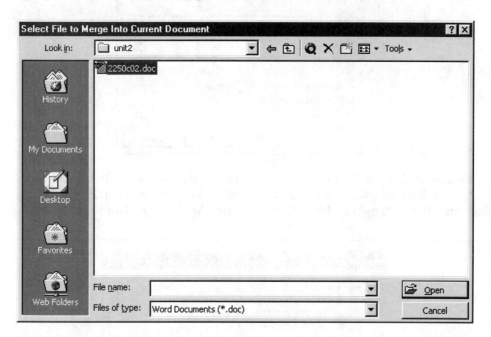

As Word adds changes from the document copy to the original document, it uses revision marks to show you where material is added or edited. You (or someone else) will later need to review these changes, resolve any conflicts, and then of course save the original document again.

 For more information about working with Word's revision marks feature and about merging documents, refer to Chapter 7.

Saving and Opening Shared Workbooks with Excel

You can also save and open an Excel workbook that you want to share just like any other workbook. As is the case with Word documents, predictably, you must store the workbook on a shared drive so other workgroup members have access to the workbook.

CREATING A SHARED WORKBOOK   As with a shared Word document, you can tell Excel that you want to share a workbook by choosing Tools | Track Changes | Highlight Changes, and then by checking the Track Changes While Editing box.

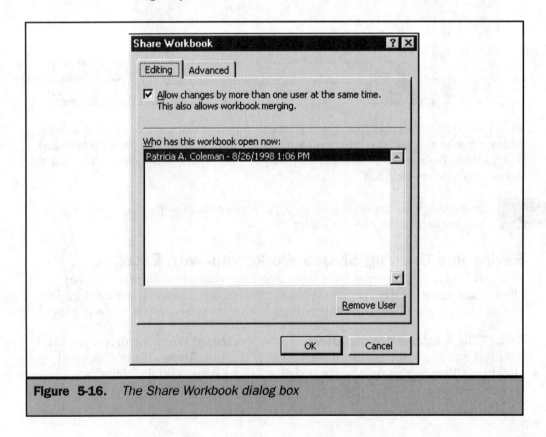

To make a file available for sharing you can also choose Tool | Share Workbook. Then, when Excel displays the Share Workbook dialog box (shown in Figure 5-16), check the Allow Changes By More Than One User At The Same Time box.

Figure 5-16.   *The Share Workbook dialog box*

You can also use the Tools menu's Share Workbook command to find out who else is working with a shared workbook besides you. When you choose the command, Excel displays a list of all current users, giving the date and time that each opened the file.

When you indicate that you want to track changes or share a workbook, Excel asks your permission to save the file again to set it up as a shared workbook. After Excel does this, it indicates that your file is now shared by inserting the word "Shared" in brackets in the Title bar after the filename.

WORKING WITH A SHARED WORKBOOK In many respects, working with a shared workbook is the same as working with an ordinary workbook. You can enter and edit numbers and text, and you can move data around within the workbook using the usual methods. You can also insert new rows and columns.

 You can't perform all editing operations in a shared workbook, however. For a lengthy list of what you can't do in shared workbooks, choose Help | Microsoft Excel Help, click the Index tab, enter the word **share**, *and click the Limitations Of Shared Workbooks topic.*

To see the changes that other people are making to a shared workbook, save the workbook. When you do this, Excel describes the changes people have made and prompts you to choose which changes you want to make and to resolve conflicts.

You can also use the Tools menu's Merge Workbooks command to fold the changes of other users into the original copy of the Excel workbook. This command works in the same basic way as the Merge Documents command described earlier in "Sharing Word Documents."

Using the File Menu's Send To Commands

The File menu's Send To submenu provides commands you can use for sharing document files over a network, using e-mail to move document files, faxing Word documents, and sending files to PowerPoint. When you choose this command, the Office program displays a submenu of commands you can use for distributing a document file:

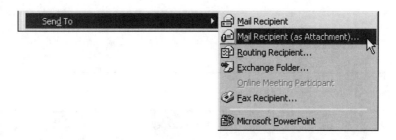

E-mailing a Document

If you choose File | Send To | Mail Recipient, for example, the Office program starts your e-mail client (probably Outlook if you're using Office), creates a new e-mail message item, and attaches the document to the message, as shown in Figure 5-17. To complete the e-mail message item, you identify the recipient, add any message text, and then click the Send button.

 For more information about creating e-mail messages with Outlook, refer to Chapter 20.

Using the File | Send To | Routing Recipient Command

If your computer connects to a network that includes an Exchange server or any mail system compatible with MAPI (Message Application Programming Interface) or VIM (Vendor Independent Messaging) mail system, you can use the Routing Recipient command on the Send To submenu. (Ask your administrator if you do not know what

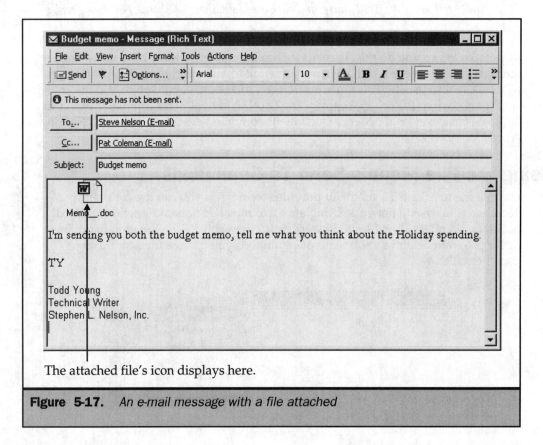

The attached file's icon displays here.

Figure 5-17. *An e-mail message with a file attached*

type of mail system you are connected to.) The File | Send To | Routing Recipient command gives you more control over how your e-mail message is sent. It's especially useful for sending a message and document file to several members of a workgroup when you want to stay posted on who has received your message and who has replied. When you choose File | Send To | Routing Recipient, the Office program displays the Routing Slip dialog box shown in Figure 5-18.

To use the Routing Slip dialog box, use the Address button to add the names of recipients to the To list box. Next, use the Subject and Message Text boxes to provide the message subject and text you want to use for the routing slip. Once you click OK, the Office program sends the message—which includes both the document file and a routing slip—to the Exchange server. The Exchange server then sends the message to each of the recipients you identified.

Note   *If you select the One After Another option, the Office program waits for a reply from the first person on your address list (in the To box) before sending your message to the next recipient.*

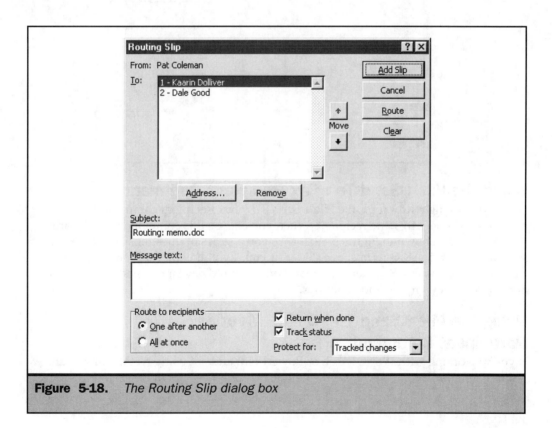

Figure 5-18.   *The Routing Slip dialog box*

To receive a notification each time the document file gets sent to a new recipient, select the Track Status option. Select the Return When Done option to route the document file back to you after all the recipients have replied.

Using the File | Send To | Exchange Folder Command

If you have Microsoft Exchange installed on your computer, you can use the File | Send To | Exchange Folder command. This command lets you post, or store, the open document in an Exchange folder. When you choose the command, the Office program displays the Send To Exchange Folder dialog box, which lets you choose the Exchange folder you want to store the document in:

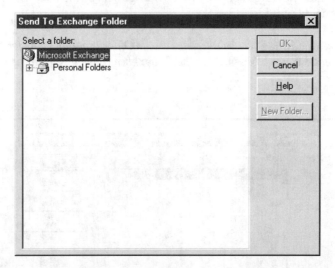

Using the File | Send To | Fax Recipient Command

If you're working with Word, the File | Send To | Fax Recipient command lets you fax the open document to some recipient. When you choose this command, Word starts the Fax Wizard, shown in Figure 5-19. It asks you a series of questions about the fax you want to send, creates a fax cover letter (if you say you want this), and then sends the fax. To use the Fax Recipient command, you need to have a fax modem installed and working in your desktop computer.

Using the File | Send To | Online Meeting Participant Command

If you're working with Word, Excel, or PowerPoint and are using NetMeeting in an online conference, you can choose the Online Meeting Participant command to send

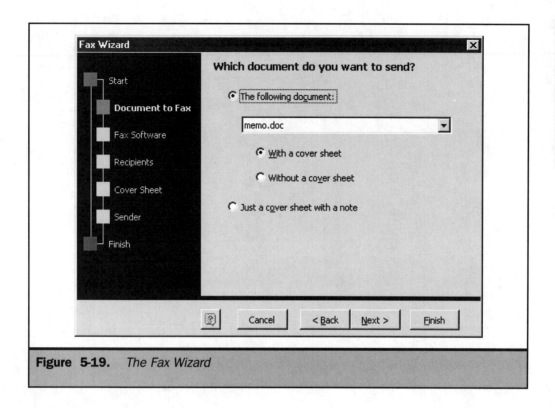

Figure 5-19. *The Fax Wizard*

the open document to those in your conference. For more about NetMeeting and how to use it, see Chapter 25.

Note *Some of the Office programs add other commands to the Send To submenu. For example, Word also adds a Microsoft PowerPoint command to the Send To submenu so you can export the open Word document to PowerPoint. Not to be outdone, PowerPoint adds a Microsoft Word command to the Send To submenu so you can export the open PowerPoint presentation to Word. PowerPoint also adds a Genigraphics command to the Send To submenu, which you can use to send a PowerPoint presentation to the Genigraphics service bureau so they'll create 35mm slides based on your presentation.*

Chapter 6

Web Publishing
with Office

151

Perhaps the most dramatic new feature of Office 2000 is the ease with which you can create and publish documents for a variety of media—for print or electronic, or to the Internet or an intranet. This chapter focuses on composing and publishing web pages, the documents that you publish to the Internet or to an intranet. In a word, creating a web page is as simple as creating a document in any Office program—Word, Excel, PowerPoint, Access, and even Outlook—and simply saving it as a web page.

Note   *Chapter 25 briefly introduces the web publishing component of Internet Explorer, FrontPage Express.*

As you may know, a web page needs to be in HTML (Hypertext Markup Language) format in order to be viewed in a web browser such as Internet Explorer. In the early days of the Internet and web browsing, you needed a working knowledge of HTML to create web pages. Later in this chapter, we'll take a look at such a page. As you'll see, it involves some rather complicated-looking coding. With Office 2000, however, just about all you need to know about HTML is that it exists and that Office programs rather easily convert any documents you create into the HTML format. Documents you create in Word, for example, retain nearly their exact same format when you save them as HTML files and later reopen them in Word.

In the first part of this chapter, we'll look at those web publishing features common to most Office components, and then we'll look at the features that are specific to each component.

Saving Office Documents as Web Pages

When you save an Office document as a web page, you use the Save As dialog box, just as you do when you save a document to your hard drive. Using this dialog box, you can save a web page directly to a web server (if you have access to one and have set up a Web folder).

   At any stage while you're creating an Office document, you can see what it will look like when displayed in your web browser. Simply choose File | Web Page Preview.

What Are Web Folders?

You use the Web Folders shortcut on the Places bar in the Save As dialog box to save, open, and manage web pages. When you click on Web Folders, you see a list of the web folders you've saved. If your list is empty and you want to publish web pages, you might need to have access to a web server that you can publish pages to. Then you need to set up a web folder by following these steps:

1. Display the contents of the Web Folders folder using Windows Explorer.

2. Double-click the Add Web Folder icon to start the Add Web Folder Wizard shown in Figure 6-1.

3. Enter the URL of your web site on the Internet or of your web server on an Intranet.

4. Click Next. The Add Web Folder Wizard validates the URL you entered and prompts you for a user name and password to be able to edit the contents of the web site or web server folder.

5. Enter your user name and password and click OK.

6. Enter a friendly name for the web folder and click Finish.

When you open or save a file to a web server, Office 2000 automatically creates a Web Folders shortcut. To manage the files you've placed on a web server, open Windows Explorer, double-click the Web Folders icon, and then double-click the web server's icon. You can browse and work with your web folders in Internet Explorer the same way you browse and work with files and folders on your computer.

After you create and format your document, follow these steps:

1. From the File menu, choose Save As Web Page to open the Save As dialog box, as shown in Figure 6-2.

2. In the File Name box, type a filename for your web page.

Figure 6-1. *Use the Add Web Folder Wizard to set up a web folder*

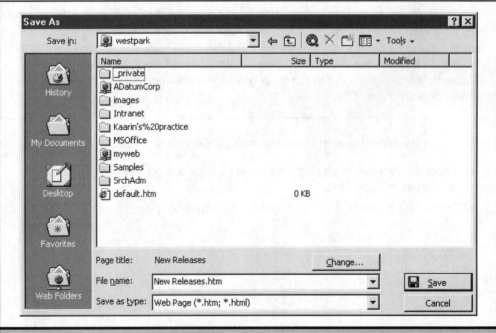

Figure 6-2. *In this Save As dialog box, click the Web Folders icon to display any web folders you have created*

3. If you want to change the proposed page title (the title that will be displayed when the page is opened in a browser), click the Change button to open the Set Page Title dialog box. Enter a new title in the Page Title box and click OK:

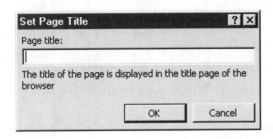

4. Choose a location on your hard drive in which to save the file, or click the Web Folders icon and select a web server to publish the document.

5. If you choose to publish your file to the web server, enter your user name and password, and then click the Save button.

 In the later sections of this chapter, we'll look at how you use the various Office components to create web pages. You'll find more information in Chapter 24.

Special Options for Saving PowerPoint Web Pages

The steps for saving PowerPoint presentations as web pages are initially similar to saving web pages in any Office component, but you have more options. In addition, you need to tell PowerPoint, for example, whether you want to save an entire presentation as a web page or only selected slides.

You can use HTML as your default PowerPoint file format if you want. This allows anyone with Internet Explorer 5 or newer to view your presentation without installing PowerPoint. You can create web pages to start with using the AutoContent Wizard. We'll look at how this works in the later section, "Web Publishing with PowerPoint."

Server Extensions

Before you can save a web page created with an Office component to a web server from within Office, the server must have either FrontPage or Office Server Extensions installed. Appendix C contains all the details. The typical Office user need not be concerned about server extensions other than realizing that they are a necessary feature for one-step web publishing.

Normally, these extensions are installed, monitored, and maintained by the network or web server administrator.

For now, I'll assume that you have created a PowerPoint presentation and want to publish all of it or selected slides as web pages. Here are the steps:

1. From the File menu, choose Save As Web Page to open the Save As dialog box, shown in Figure 6-3.

2. In the Places bar, click the Web Folders shortcut to specify the web server to which you'll save your web page.

3. In the File Name box, type a filename for your web page.

4. Verify that the Save As Type box shows the web page extension (.HTM or .HTML).

5. To change the title of your web page, click the Change button, and enter a new title in the Set Page Title dialog box.

6. Click the Publish button to open the Publish As Web Page dialog box, shown in Figure 6-4.

7. In the Publish What section, indicate whether you want to save your entire presentation as a web page, a slide, or a selection of slides.

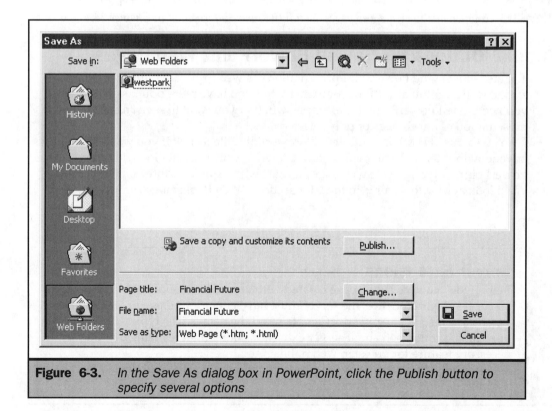

Figure 6-3. *In the Save As dialog box in PowerPoint, click the Publish button to specify several options*

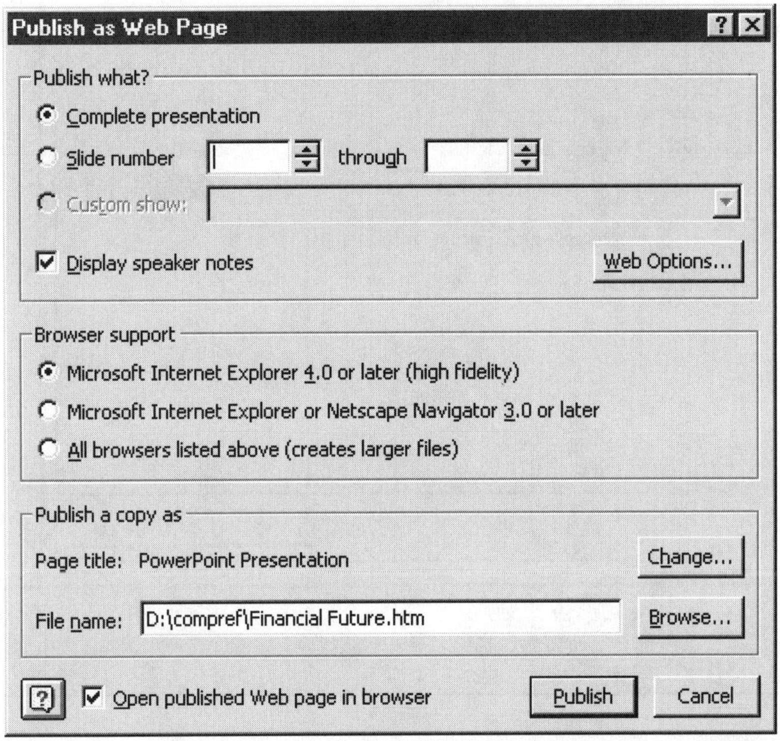

Figure 6-4. *After specifying your options in this dialog box, click the Publish button to save your presentation or slide as a web page and open it in a browser*

8. Check the Display Speaker Notes box if you want your speaker notes to display as part of your web page.

9. Now, to further define how your web page is to display in a browser, click the Web Options button to open the Web Options dialog box, shown in Figure 6-5.

10. Leave the Add Slide Navigation Controls box checked if you want to add these very handy controls to your web page. Figure 6-6 shows what these look like when they are displayed at the bottom of your web page.

11. Select the Files tab to specify filenames and locations and to choose Office as the default editor for web pages created in Office.

12. Select the Pictures tab to specify the format of picture files and to specify the size of your target monitor (if you know it, that is).

13. Select the Encoding tab if you want to save your web pages in a non-Western European alphabet.

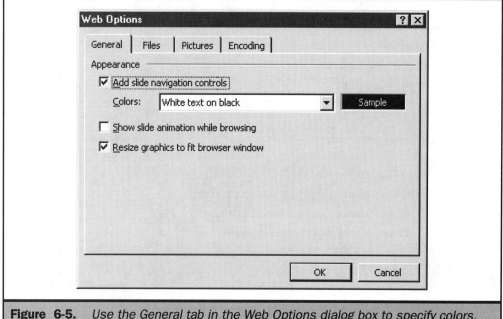

Figure 6-5. *Use the General tab in the Web Options dialog box to specify colors, animation, and graphics resizing and to add animation controls to your web page*

14. When you have specified all your options, click OK.

15. In the Browser support section of the Publish As Web Page dialog box, you can specify that PowerPoint save your presentation for Internet Explorer 4.0 and 5.0, for Internet Explorer or Netscape Navigator 3.0, or for all three browsers. When you select these options, PowerPoint writes scripts into the page's HTML coding that check the version of the browser and automatically open the appropriate version of the content.

16. In the Publish A Copy As section, change the page title or filename if you want.

17. If you check the Open Published Web Page In Browser box, PowerPoint both saves your web page and opens it in a browser when you click Publish, if you use Internet Explorer 5.0 or newer.

Special Options for Saving Excel Web Pages

Using Excel 2000, not only can you save workbooks and worksheets as web pages, but you can save them with interactivity. In other words, you can save tables and charts as web pages, and viewers who are also running Office 2000 can manipulate them.

The Navigation controls

Figure 6-6. *Use the navigation controls to show or hide the outline, expand or collapse the outline, move forward or backward in a slide show, and display your slide show in full-screen view*

Note *Because an interactive web page uses an ActiveX control, viewers must be running Internet Explorer 4.0 or 5.0 to view it properly and manipulate it.*

To save an Excel workbook or worksheet as a web page, follow these steps:

1. After creating your data, choose File | Save As Web Page to open the Save As dialog box, shown in Figure 6-7.

2. In the Places bar, click the Web Folders shortcut to specify the server where you will save your web page.

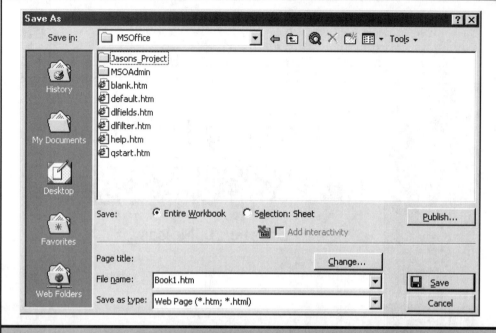

Figure 6-7. Use Excel's Save As dialog box to select a web folder, to specify whether to save an entire workbook or a worksheet, and to add interactivity to your web page

3. As you do when saving any file, make sure that the file type is correct in the Save As Type box and accept the filename that Excel suggests or type another one in the File Name box.

4. If you want to change the title that Excel suggests for your web page, click the Change button and type a new title in the Set Page Title dialog box. (This is the title that will appear at the top of your web page when it's viewed in a browser.)

5. Select whether to save an entire workbook or only a selected sheet by clicking the appropriate option button.

6. If you want your viewers to be able to use your worksheet, check the Add Interactivity box.

Note *If you select to publish an entire workbook, you'll need to click the Publish button and use the Publish As Web Page dialog box to specify that you want to include interactivity.*

7. Click the Publish button to open the Publish As Web Page dialog box, shown in Figure 6-8.

8. Click the Choose drop-down list to specify whether you want to publish previously published items (that is, update data that you've already published), a range of cells, or a worksheet.

9. Click the Add Interactivity With check box and then choose the type of functionality you want to include. Your choices are Spreadsheet and PivotTable.

Note For all the details about PivotTables, see Chapter 15.

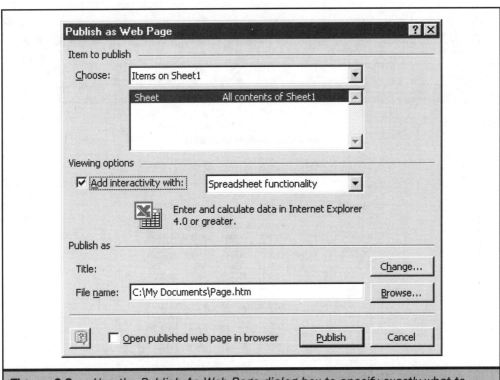

Figure 6-8. *Use the Publish As Web Page dialog box to specify exactly what to publish and the kind of interactivity it will include*

10. If you check the Open Published Web Page In Browser box and then click
    Publish, Excel saves your worksheet or workbook as a web page and opens
    it in your browser. Figure 6-9 shows a sample Excel worksheet open in
    Internet Explorer.

Using the Web Toolbar

When you're working in an Office application, you can use the Web toolbar, shown in
Figure 6-10, to link to the web or to other sources. To display the Web toolbar, choose
View | Toolbars, and click Web. The Web toolbar contains a subset of the buttons you
see on the Standard toolbar in Internet Explorer, the Address toolbar, and a button you
can click to show only the Web toolbar or all the toolbars you've selected to display.

Click the Show Only Web Toolbar button when you are displaying other toolbars to
display only the Web toolbar; then click this button again to redisplay your other

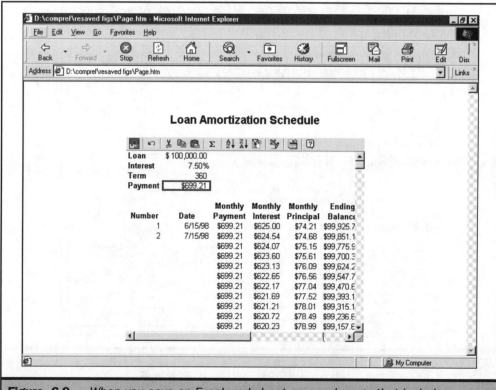

Figure 6-9. *When you save an Excel worksheet as a web page that includes
interactivity and open it in Internet Explorer 4.0 or 5.0, your viewer can
manipulate the data when you click the buttons on the toolbar*

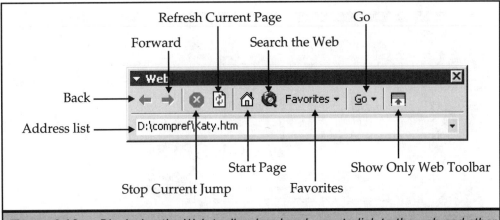

Figure 6-10.   *Displaying the Web toolbar is a handy way to link to the web and other sources while you're working in an Office application*

toolbars. The other buttons on the Web toolbar work just as they do in Internet Explorer. If you need more information, take a look at Chapter 23. Or, you could be brave and just experiment some.

Before you get going too far, you should know that while Word makes it really easy to create forms by placing controls from the Web Tools toolbar on your page, configuring your forms to work with your web server is considerably more difficult. If you use a web server that uses FrontPage or Office Server Extensions, you can open the form in FrontPage and configure it there before publishing your FrontPage web page to your web server. Otherwise, talk with your network administrator about how to configure your form to work on your web server.

Including Hyperlinks on Your Web Pages

A hyperlink is colored and usually underlined text or a graphic on a web page that, when clicked, takes you to another resource. This resource could be almost anything—a file on your hard drive, an Internet newsgroup, another web page, a sound or movie clip, a chat group, and so on. Hyperlinks are the foundation of the web and the very essence of browsing the Internet. You'll notice that the Office 2000 Help program is itself a web of hyperlinks. Clicking a link in the pane on the left opens a topic on the right, and topics themselves contain hyperlinks to still other resources.

Figure 6-11 shows the home page of the U.S. Library of Congress, a rich and elegant example of the extensive use of hyperlinks.

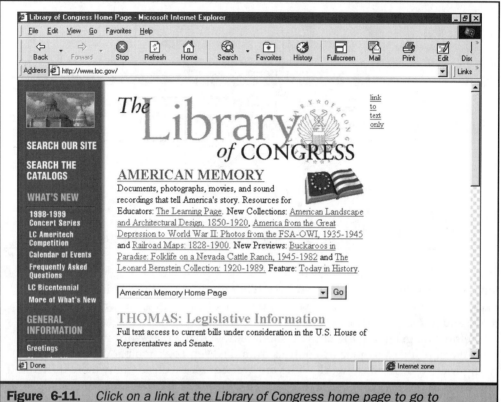

Figure 6-11. Click on a link at the Library of Congress home page to go to documents, photographs, movies, and sound recordings

---

> **Tip**   In Word, the quickest way to insert a hyperlink is to type its URL directly into the document. Word instantly formats it as a hyperlink.

Inserting Hyperlinks to a File or a Web Page

You can insert hyperlinks as you create a web page, or you can do so after your content and formatting is complete. To insert a hyperlink to an existing file or web page, follow these steps:

1. Place the insertion point where you want the hyperlink in your document, or select the text that you want to display for the hyperlink.

2. From the Insert menu, choose the Hyperlink command or click on the Insert Hyperlink button to open the Insert Hyperlink dialog box shown next.

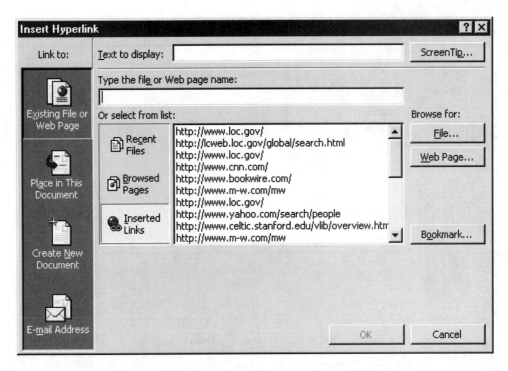

3. If necessary, click on the Existing File Or Web Page shortcut in the Link To bar.

4. The Text To Display box shows the text you selected. If you did not select text to display, type the text that you want to appear in color and underlined on your web page.

5. In the Type The File Or Web Page Name box, enter the URL or the filename of the resource to which you want to link. Or, select a resource from the list. If you don't know the URL or filename and don't see it in the list, click the Browse For File button or the Browse For Web Page button to locate it. Click OK to link to this object, or if you would like the link to connect to a location in the document, continue to step 6.

Note

Clicking the Browse For File button opens the Link To File dialog box. Select a file and click OK. You'll see the filename displayed in the Type The File Or Web Page Name list. Clicking the Browse For Web Page button opens Internet Explorer. Open the page to which you want to link, close Internet Explorer, and click the Browsed Pages button to display the list of browsed pages. Select the page from the list to display it in the Type The File Or Web Page Name box.

6. Click the Place In This Document shortcut to open the Insert Hyperlink dialog box that you can use to tell Office where in the document to link.

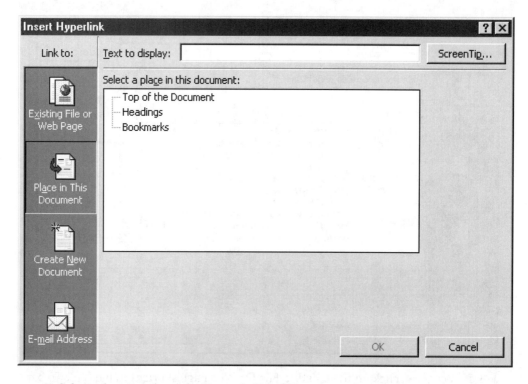

7. Select a location from the list and click OK.

You've now inserted a hyperlink in your web page. To see if it works, simply click it as you would click a hyperlink on any web page.

Adding a ScreenTip

A ScreenTip is text that appears in a little box when you place the cursor over a hyperlink. You can specify the text for a ScreenTip when you are creating a hyperlink or you can add a ScreenTip at a later time. In either case, follow these basic steps:

1. From the Insert menu, choose the Hyperlink command to open the Insert Hyperlink dialog box.

2. Click the ScreenTip button to open the Set Hyperlink ScreenTip dialog box:

3. Type your text in the ScreenTip Text box and click OK. Figure 6-12 shows a ScreenTip displayed over a hyperlink.

Formatting a Hyperlink

By default, hyperlinks are displayed in the default paragraph font, are underlined, and are in blue until they are clicked. This is a common format for hyperlinks and, therefore, has become almost universally recognizable. You can, however, display hyperlinks in a different font, in another color, and with other custom formatting in Word documents. To change the style of hyperlinks, choose Format | Style and then make your selections in the Style dialog box. For more information about modifying styles, see Chapter 9.

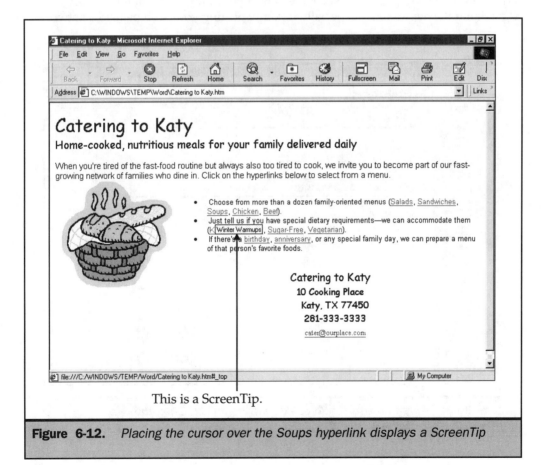

Figure 6-12.   *Placing the cursor over the Soups hyperlink displays a ScreenTip*

Inserting a Hyperlink to an E-Mail Address

The quickest way to insert a hyperlink to an e-mail address is to type it in a cell of an Excel worksheet or simply enter it directly into a Word or PowerPoint document or a field in Access. As with other hyperlinks, however, you can specify text instead of the actual e-mail address, and you can add a ScreenTip. Follow the same basic steps that you use to create any hyperlink, and in the Insert Hyperlink dialog box, click the E-Mail Address shortcut, as shown in Figure 6-13.

Enter the text to display, create a ScreenTip, enter the actual e-mail address, and add a subject line if you want. Clicking an e-mail hyperlink opens a message window in the user's e-mail program; the To box is already filled in with the address of the hyperlink, and if you included a subject line, that is also displayed.

Editing a Hyperlink

When you create and publish a web page, one of your most important tasks is maintaining the hyperlinks—especially if you're posting your web page to a network

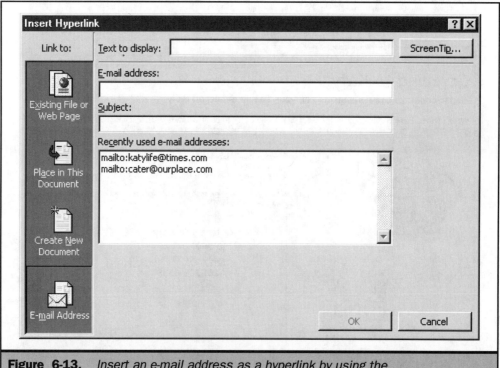

Figure 6-13. *Insert an e-mail address as a hyperlink by using the E-Mail Address shortcut*

server or to the Internet. You know how annoyed you get when you click on a hyperlink only to see a message to the effect that the site has moved or no longer exists. You may also want to edit a hyperlink for many reasons other than that its URL has changed or that the site no longer exists:

- In your web travels, you may find a resource that has much better content than the one you originally linked to.

- In the process of restructuring your web site, you may find it more efficient to restructure your folders and thus their names may need to be changed.

- You might decide that instead of text you'd like to use a picture as a hyperlink.

To do any of these things, you use the Edit Hyperlink dialog box. Follow these steps:

1. Right-click the hyperlink, select Hyperlink, and from the submenu choose Edit Hyperlink to open the Edit Hyperlink dialog box:

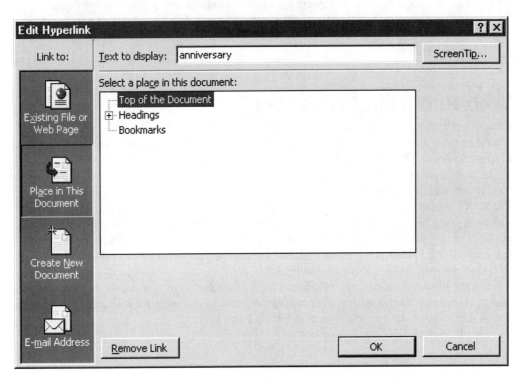

2. Now simply follow the steps for inserting a hyperlink to change a filename or a URL, to rewrite a ScreenTip, to insert an e-mail address, and so on.

To move or copy a hyperlink to another place in your web page or to another web page or document, use the Paste As Hyperlink command. First, right-click the hyperlink, choose Hyperlink from the shortcut menu, and from the submenu choose Select Hyperlink. Then choose Edit | Cut or Edit | Copy. Place the insertion point where you want to insert the hyperlink, and choose Edit | Paste As Hyperlink.

Deleting a Hyperlink

You'll find out soon enough if you haven't already tried it that the usual practice of selecting text or an object and pressing DELETE doesn't work with hyperlinks. Clicking a hyperlink opens the resource to which it points. Instead, right-click a hyperlink to display the shortcut menu, select Hyperlink, and then from the submenu, click Remove Hyperlink.

Tip *There is much more to know about hyperlinks than can be covered here. For example, you can choose to animate hyperlinks, insert hyperlinks using drag-and-drop, and insert a hyperlink to a specific location in a document. For a great deal of very good information about working with hyperlinks, open any Office Help program and search on "hyperlink."*

Web Publishing with Word

Creating a web page with Word is just the same as creating any document that you intend to print or to view electronically. You simply use all the tools you normally employ to create a document, and you save the document as a web page, as I discussed in the first section of this chapter.

Figure 6-12, earlier in this chapter, shows a web page that I created very easily as a Word document and saved as a web page. I mentioned earlier that saving a document as a web page means saving it in HTML format and that Hypertext Format Language consists of codes that tell a web browser how to display a web page. Figure 6-14 shows the underlying HTML for Figure 6-12, but I promise you that I didn't enter a single line of code. I simply created a Word document.

Let me hasten to add, however, that Word provides some special tools that you can use to make web page creation even easier and to add many more features to your web pages. Let's first take a quick look at the Web Page Wizard.

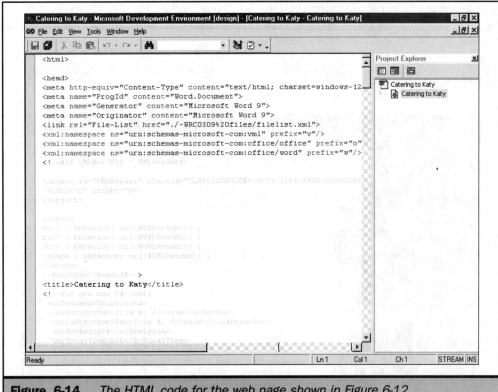

Figure 6-14. *The HTML code for the web page shown in Figure 6-12*

Using the Web Page Wizard to Create a Web Page

After you create a web page or two, you probably won't ever bother using the Web Page Wizard. But if you aren't on speaking terms with any of the tasks involved in creating a web page, stepping through this wizard will be a useful exercise. You can use this wizard to create a web site that has several pages and looks as if it were designed by a professional graphic artist. (By the way, you need browse the Internet for only a short time until you encounter pages that were definitely not created by a professional, although in the past year or so more and more people have come to realize the value of a truly well-designed, inviting web page.)

To start the Web Page Wizard, choose File | New, and in the New dialog box, select the Web Pages tab, choose Web Page Wizard, and click OK. Word displays the opening screen. Click Next, and then follow these steps:

1. In the Title and Location dialog box, enter a title for your web page, specify where you want to save it, and click Next to open the Navigation dialog box:

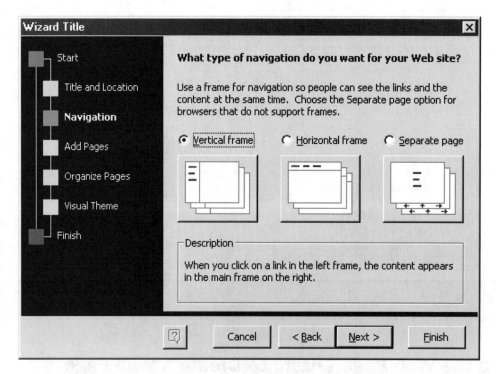

2. Select whether you want to use vertical frames, horizontal frames, or no frames. If you know you are creating a web page for a browser that doesn't support frames, choose Separate Page, or, in effect, no frames. When you've made your choice, click Next to open the Add Pages dialog box.

3. In the Add Pages dialog box, click the Add New Blank Page button to add a page; click the Add Template Page button to open the Web Page Templates dialog box and select a template; and click the Add Existing File button to open the Open dialog box and select a file to add as a page. If you want to delete a page that the wizard proposes, select it and click Remove Page. When you're done, click Next to open the Organize Pages dialog box.

4. When you use the Web Page Wizard, your pages are linked. Use the Organize Pages dialog box to change the order or rename the pages you've included. Choose Next to open the Visual Theme dialog box:

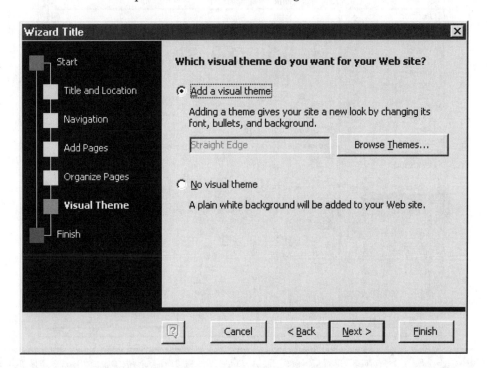

5. Click the Add A Visual Theme button and then click Browse to check out the graphic possibilities for your web page. In the Theme dialog box, select a theme on the left to see a preview of it on the right. Figure 6-15 shows the Straight Edge theme.

Note

Not all themes are installed when you install Office. If you click a theme on the left and see a message that it isn't installed, insert your Office CD and run the Remove/Install program to copy it to your hard drive. If you don't want to use a theme, click the No Visual Theme button to add a plain white background to your web pages.

6. After you select a theme and customize it to your liking, click OK, click Next, and click Finish. Figure 6-16 shows the web page structure you just created.

Tip

Remember, to check out how your web page appears in your browser, simply choose File | Web Page Preview.

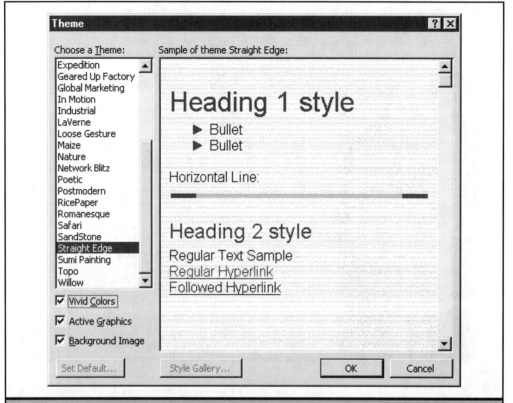

Figure 6-15. Use the Vivid Colors, Active Graphics, and Background Image check boxes to customize a theme. Experiment to see the effects in the Sample box

Understanding Frames

Frames are a handy device indeed when you are creating web pages. Simply put, a frame allows you to display more than one "page" in a web page. For example, if you select the Vertical Frame option, you could place a table of contents in the frame on the left. Clicking on a topic in the left frame displays the text for that topic in the frame on the right.

If you don't use frames, your table of contents would be on a separate page (vis-à-vis the Separate Page option). Clicking a topic on the contents page would open another page altogether that would contain the content.

By the way, unless you know you are creating a web page that will be viewed by those using an older browser, don't think twice about using frames. All the popular current browsers can display frames.

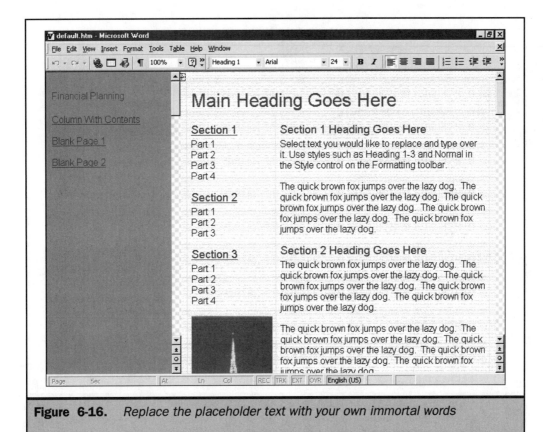

Figure 6-16.   *Replace the placeholder text with your own immortal words*

Using Word's Web Page Templates

When you create a web page layout with the wizard, you can choose a template from the Web Page Templates dialog box. But you don't need to use the wizard to select a template for your web pages. In the New dialog box, simply select the Web Pages tab, choose a template, and click OK. For example, choosing the Personal Web Page template provides this structure for your web page (see Figure 6-17).

Using the Web Tools Toolbar

Now that we've looked at some very easy ways to create web pages, let's look at the tools you can use to enhance them. The Web Tools toolbar is your one-stop shop for the tools needed to add special effects and controls to a web page. Controls, by the way, are such things as check boxes, option buttons, submit buttons, and drop-down list boxes. You see and use controls all the time when you're browsing the Internet. For example, often when you're filling out a form, you'll use a drop-down list box to select the abbreviation for your state.

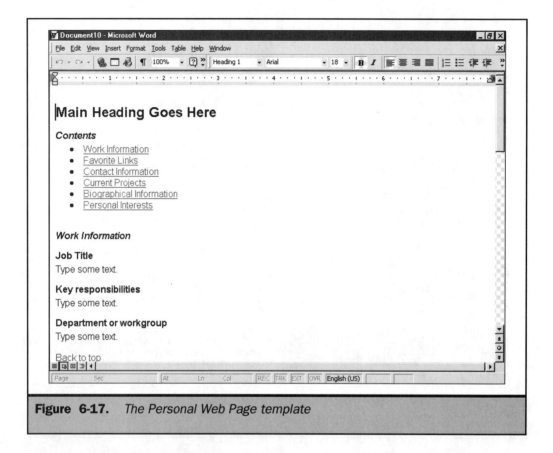

Figure 6-17.   *The Personal Web Page template*

Placing a control on your web page is easy. Simply place the insertion point where you want the control and then click on the control in the Web Tools toolbar, shown in Figure 6-18. To display the Web Tools toolbar, choose View | Toolbars and then click Web Tools.

In this section, I'm going to walk through the basics of using this toolbar. I won't describe how to use each one in detail, but many of these tools work in a similar fashion. You can follow these basic instructions for using the tools I don't describe in detail. In addition, see Appendix D for information about using Microsoft Script Editor.

Working in Design Mode

When you're adding controls and special effects to your web pages, you work in Design Mode. The Design Mode button is a toggle; whenever you click a button to add a control, it automatically becomes the Exit Design Mode button. When it's in this state, click it to display the control as it will appear when you view your page in a browser. For example, if you add a check box to your web page, the check box is empty in

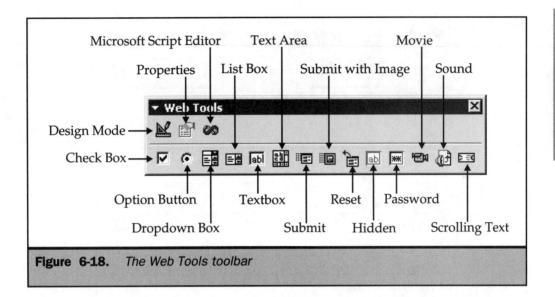

Figure 6-18. *The Web Tools toolbar*

Design Mode. When you exit Design Mode, you can check and uncheck your check box just as you would check or uncheck a check box in any Office dialog box. Try it—you'll see what I mean.

Inserting Scrolling Text

When you're browsing the Internet, you run into scrolling text everywhere. Sometimes it's effective, and sometimes it's annoying, so you want to exercise care when using this feature. But it's very easy to add scrolling text to a web page. Place the insertion point in your web page where you want to add scrolling text, and then click the Scrolling Text button to open the Scrolling Text dialog box, shown in Figure 6-19.

Follow these steps to specify how you want scrolling text to appear in your web page for viewers using Internet Explorer:

1. In the Behavior drop-down box, select whether you want text to scroll, slide, or alternate. Experiment with these settings to see how each works in the Preview box.

2. If you want a background color for your scrolling text, click the Background Color drop-down box and select the color. Again, you'll see the effect in the Preview box.

Tip   *If you want text to display in white on a dark background, select the background color, make your other choices in the Scrolling Text dialog box, and click OK. The scrolling text box is selected. Choose Format | Font, and select White as the font color. For information on formatting, see Chapter 3.*

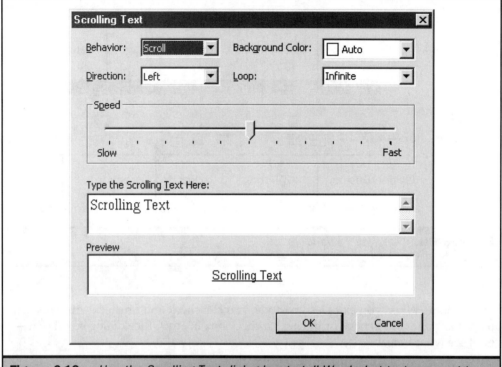

Figure 6-19.   Use the Scrolling Text dialog box to tell Word what text you want to scroll, how fast to scroll it, for how long, in what direction, and which color to place behind it

3. In the Direction drop-down box, select a direction for the text to scroll—left or right.

4. In the Loop drop-down box, select the number of times you want text to scroll—1, 2, 3, 4, 5 times or infinite (forever or until the viewer closes the web page, whichever comes first).

5. Adjust the slider bar to set the speed of the scroll.

6. Type the text you want to scroll in the Type The Scrolling Text Here box.

If you've selected text before you open the Scrolling Text dialog box, the text you type will appear in the same style as the text you selected. You can also change the font and size of the text after you close the Scrolling Text dialog box by using the Format menu's Font command.

7. When the scrolling text appears as you want, click OK to close the Scrolling Text box. The scrolling text appears in a text box in your page, and you can use the usual formatting tools to edit it.

Inserting a Drop-Down Box

Now, let's look at how easy it is to insert that drop-down list box of state abbreviations I mentioned earlier. Place the insertion point in your web page where you want the drop-down box, be sure you are in Design Mode, and click the Dropdown Box button. Word inserts a drop-down box, and it is selected.

 To move a drop-down box or any control, simply drag its handles.

Now follow these steps to insert the text for your drop-down box:

1. Click the Properties button to open the Properties dialog box:

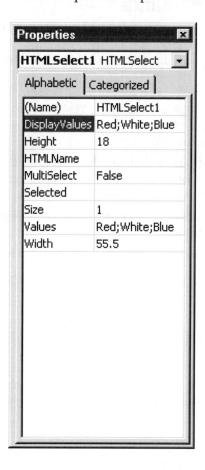

2. Click in the box beside Display Values, and enter the text you want to display. Separate each item with a semicolon, and don't space between items. For example, if you want to display Red, White, and Blue, type **Red;White;Blue**.

3. When your list is complete, click the Close button.

4. Click the Exit Design Mode button, and then click the down-arrow in the drop-down list box. Voilá! Your list box is populated with the selections you typed.

Enter text for a list box in exactly the same way.

To insert a check box or an option button, simply click the corresponding button. You can enter a label either before or after you insert the button. To move a button, drag its selection handles

Inserting Movies and Sounds

To insert a movie in your web page, click the Movie button to open the Movie Clip dialog box, shown in Figure 6-20.

Follow these steps to specify how your movie will perform:

1. In the Movie drop-down list box, select the movie file you want to include.

2. Use the Alternate Image and Alternate Text boxes to specify a picture or text that will display in the event that your viewer's browser can't display movies or in the event that the browser is in text-only mode.

3. In the Playback Options section, use the Start drop-down list to specify whether the movie starts as soon as the viewer opens the page, when the viewer's mouse button is over the movie icon, or on both occasions.

4. Use the Loop drop-down list to specify whether the movie plays 1, 2, 3, 4, or 5 times or plays indefinitely.

5. Click OK to close the dialog box. You'll see the movie icon displayed in your web page.

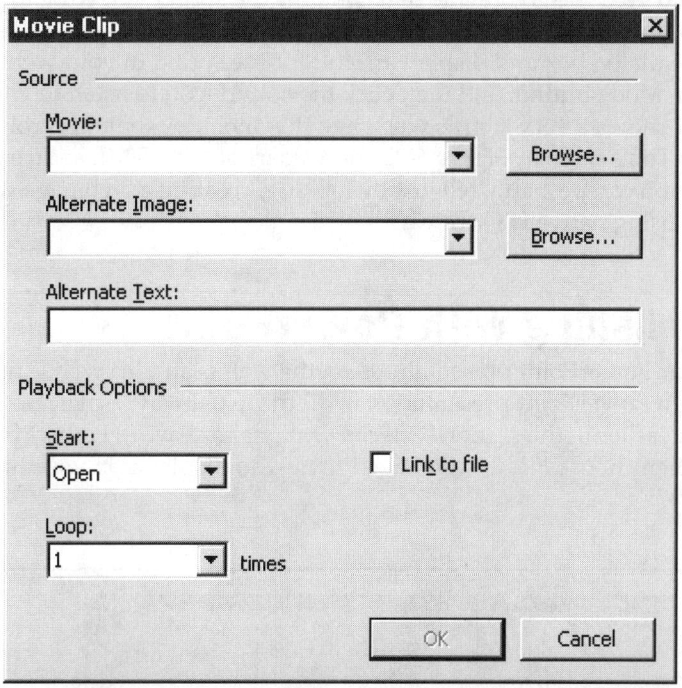

Figure 6-20. *Use the Movie Clip dialog box to insert a movie in your web page, but be careful. Movie files can load slowly and display in unpredictable ways, depending on the hardware and software of the viewer's computer*

To insert a background sound in your web page, click the Sound button to open the Background Sound dialog box:

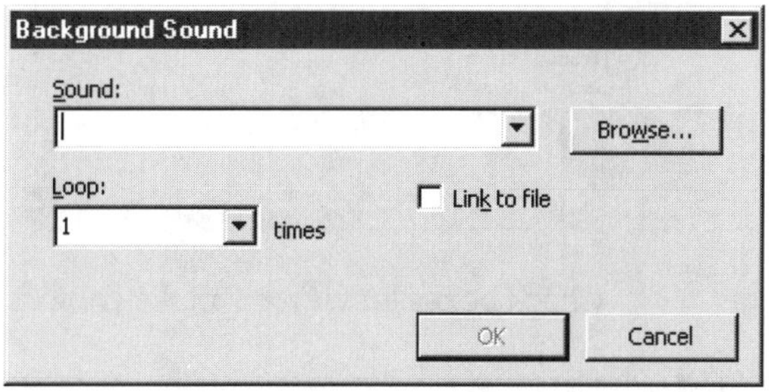

In the Sound box, specify the file that contains the sound you want to play, and in the Loop drop-down list box, specify the number of times the sound will play. Click OK to close the dialog box and display an icon for the sound in your web page. Click the Exit Design Mode button, and then click the sound icon to listen to your selection.

Figure 6-21 shows a very simple web page that includes some controls inserted by using the Web Tools toolbar. Figure 6-22 shows part of the HTML source code for this web page. As you can probably tell just by looking, creating a web page with Word is a lot easier than using native HTML.

Web Publishing with PowerPoint

Publishing your PowerPoint presentations on the web is an idea whose time has come. You can create a PowerPoint presentation in all the usual ways, save it as a web page (as I discussed earlier in the section "Special Options for Saving PowerPoint Web Pages"), and then choose File | Web Page Preview to display it in your browser.

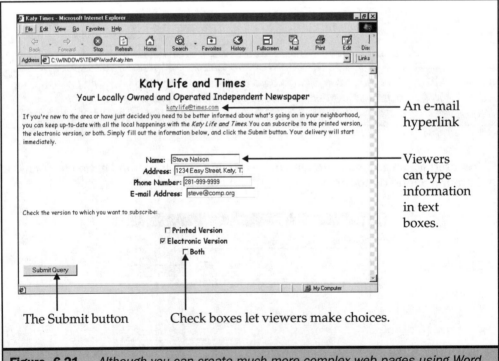

Figure 6-21.   *Although you can create much more complex web pages using Word, this example shows the use of simple text boxes, check boxes, a Submit button, and an e-mail hyperlink*

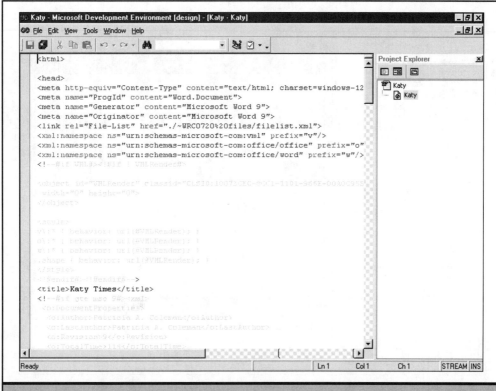

Figure 6-22. *The HTML source code for the web page shown in Figure 6-21. To view the HTML any time while you are creating a web page, choose View | HTML Source*

Figure 6-23 shows a PowerPoint presentation in Normal view, and Figure 6-24 shows the same page in Web Page Preview. As you can see, the outline level 1 headings appear in the frame on the left, and the slide appears in the main frame on the right. You simply click a heading to display that slide.

Using the AutoContent Wizard to Create a Web Page

You can also use the AutoContent Wizard to create a web site. Choose File | New to open the New Presentation dialog box, select AutoContent Wizard, and click OK to display the first screen of the wizard. Click Next, and then follow these steps:

1. In the Presentation Type dialog box, click a category button and click a presentation type in the list on the right.

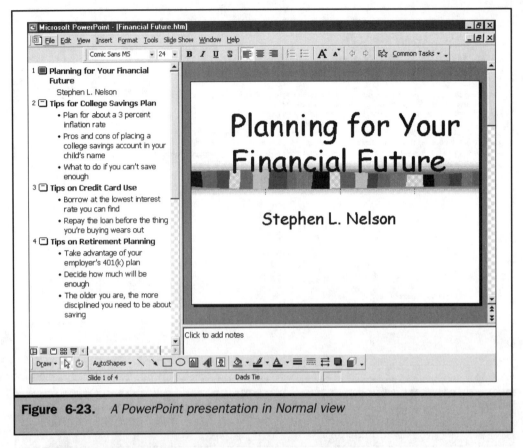

Figure 6-23. *A PowerPoint presentation in Normal view*

2. Click Next to open the Presentation Style dialog box:

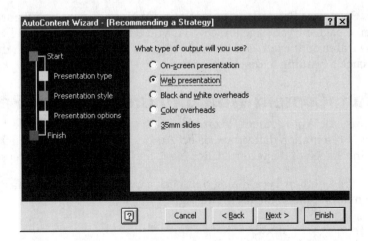

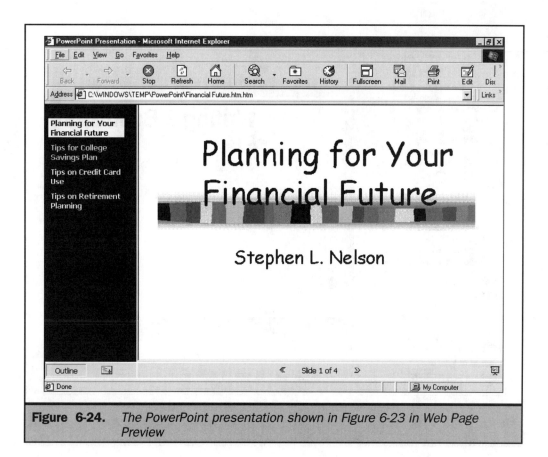

Figure 6-24.   *The PowerPoint presentation shown in Figure 6-23 in Web Page Preview*

3. Click the Web Presentation option button and then click Next.

4. Enter a title for your presentation and, optionally, a footer. Click to remove the check marks if you don't want the date the presentation was last updated and the slide number to appear in your web page.

5. Click Next and then click Finish to view your document.

Figure 6-25 shows the document in Normal view. In this case, I chose the General category and the Generic presentation style.

You can now replace the placeholder text with content of your own. For information about creating PowerPoint presentations, see Part IV of this book.

Figure 6-25. *The results of using the AutoContent Wizard to set up a structure for a presentation you plan to use on the web*

Online Collaboration or Online Broadcast?

If you work on a local area network or an intranet that has the Office Server Extensions installed on the server, you can use Online Collaboration to share a presentation with others. When you do this, you use NetMeeting, a component of the Internet Explorer suite of programs. Here are the steps:

1. From the Tools menu, choose Online Collaboration | Meet Now to open the Place A Call dialog box, shown next.

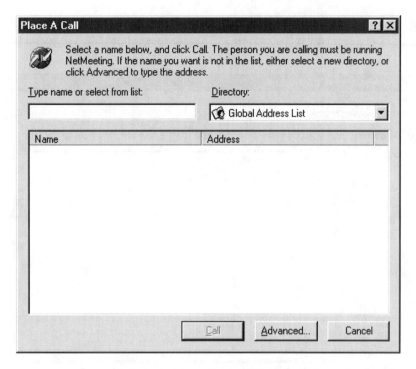

2. Enter a name or select it from a list. If necessary, click the Advanced button and type a computer name or network address of the person with whom you want to meet.

3. Click the Call button to place the call.

Note   *The other person must also be running NetMeeting for Online Collaboration to work. For more information about NetMeeting, see Chapter 25.*

You use Online Collaboration when you want to use the features of NetMeeting to collaborate on a document. For example, you can share PowerPoint with another person who can then edit your presentation. In an Online Broadcast, however, you simply broadcast your presentation over the web. You might want to do this if your enterprise has groups at remote sites, for example, or if you'd like a project team to review a presentation before you make it to the entire corporation. All your viewers need to see the presentation is a web browser.

To set up and schedule an Online Broadcast, follow these steps:

1. Open the presentation you want to broadcast, and choose Slide Show | Online Broadcast.

2. From the submenu, Choose Set Up and Schedule to open the Broadcast Schedule dialog box.

3. Be sure that the Set Up And Schedule A New Broadcast option button is selected, and click OK to open the Schedule A New Broadcast dialog box:

5. Select the Description tab, enter a title for your presentation in the Title box (if you want a title other than the filename), and enter a description and contact information. This information will appear in your Lobby Page. To see how your Lobby Page will be displayed in the browser, click Preview Lobby Page.

6. Select the Broadcast Settings tab. (Your webmaster or system administrator may have already set these options, or you may need to contact this person about how you set these options.)

7. Click the Server Options button to open the Server Options dialog box. Enter the path name of a folder on your network server. When you start your presentation, PowerPoint puts the broadcast-formatted presentation at that location. Click OK.

8. When all your options are set, click the Schedule Broadcast button to open your e-mail program.

The Lobby Page

The Lobby Page is the screen your viewers will see when they join the broadcast. In addition to displaying the information you enter on the Description tab, the Lobby Page notifies viewers about how much time is left before the broadcast begins. If the broadcast is delayed, the host of the presentation can display a message about the delay and indicate when the slide show will start.

9. Select recipients and compose your message. The URL of the broadcast will automatically be embedded in your message.

To start a presentation, follow these steps:

1. Open your presentation.
2. Choose Slide Show | Online Broadcast | Begin Broadcast. (Your presentation is saved in HTML on the server location you specified.)

To view a presentation, follow these steps:

1. Open the mail message that notified you of the broadcast.
2. Click the URL. The broadcast will begin automatically. If it is delayed, you can minimize the Lobby Page and continue working.

Web Publishing with Access

Web publishing in Access consists of creating a new type of Access object called a data access page. Data access pages are special types of web pages that people can use from within Internet Explorer 5 or newer to read and write data (if the page is designed to allow changes to the database) to a Microsoft Access or SQL Server database. Data access pages offer an excellent way to facilitate the browsing or changing of a database across an intranet or the Internet.

Creating Data Access Pages

To create a data access page, click the Pages button on the Objects bar, and then click New. Select Page Wizard from the list, choose what table or query you want your data access page to access, then click OK. Choose the table or query in the Tables/Queries box containing the fields you want to add to your page, and then double-click the fields you want to add in the Available Fields box (see Figure 6-26). Click Next, then create any grouping levels you want for the page and click Next again. Choose how you want records sorted, click Next, then enter a title for your page in the text box provided. If you want to format your page with one of Office's themes, select the Do You Want To Apply A Theme To Your Page check box. Click Finish.

 When you save a data access page, you save the page as an HTML file on your hard drive or web server instead of back into your Access database file. Access automatically creates a shortcut to this file, which you can access by clicking the Pages button on the Objects bar.

Modifying Data Access Pages

Once you've created a data access page, you may want to modify its design. If you've created any forms in Access before, you'll find that creating data access pages works basically the same (for more information on creating forms, see Chapter 26).

To add a field to your page, just drag it from the Field List to the appropriate place inside the form part of your data access page. Use the toolbox to add other controls you want. You can also add Microsoft Office Web Components by clicking the Office PivotTable, Office Chart, or Office Spreadsheet buttons on the toolbox, then clicking and dragging in your data access page to create a box for the component to be inserted in. (For more information on Microsoft Office Web Components, see Chapter 24.)

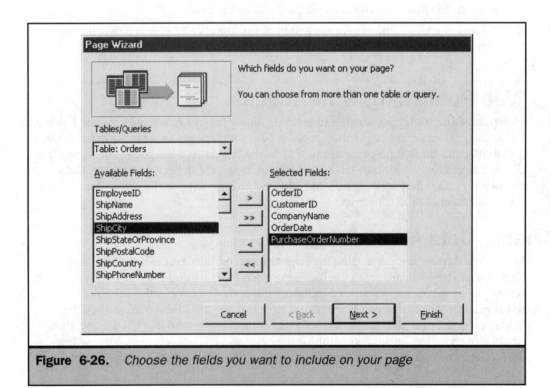

Figure 6-26.   *Choose the fields you want to include on your page*

Tip

To link a data source to a PivotTable, drag the table or query you want to use as your data source from the Field List to the PivotTable. Access will do the rest.

To modify text on the page surrounding the actual data access form, edit it as you would text in a word processor. To resize a portion of the data access form, click on the part of the form you want to resize, click a resizing handle, and drag the outline of the object until it is sized appropriately (see Figure 6-27).

Tip

Once you've finished setting up the actual data access form with Access, you can use another Microsoft Office 2000 program such as FrontPage to finish editing the page and make it more attractive before you publish it to your web site. You can safely use FrontPage or Word to edit your data access page without worrying about the form being broken.

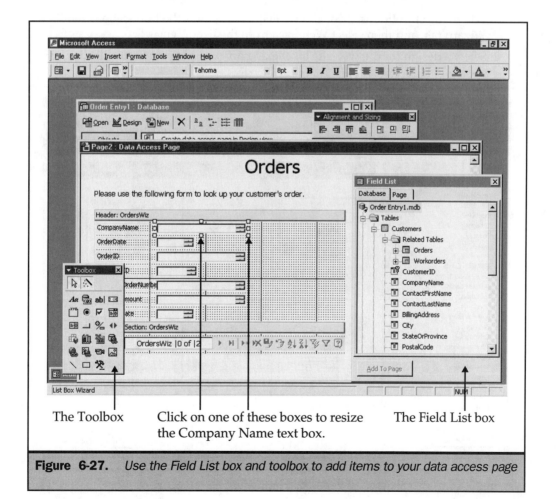

The Toolbox   Click on one of these boxes to resize   The Field List box
                     the Company Name text box.

Figure 6-27. *Use the Field List box and toolbox to add items to your data access page*

Web Publishing with Publisher

Publisher provides three ways in which you can create web pages: using the Web Site Wizard, using a blank web page template, or converting an existing Publisher document into a web page or web site. Publisher also provides a handful of extra tools available only for documents intended for web publication. This section describes the web publishing options available in Publisher.

Creating a Web Site

Publisher comes with a special wizard designed specifically for creating web sites. Using this wizard, you can select a web site template and easily add a handful of common web pages to the site. To create a web site using this wizard, follow these steps:

1. When you start Publisher or choose File | New, click the Publications By Wizard tab, and then select Web Sites from the list of wizards.

2. Select a design for the web site by clicking an example page in the list box, as shown in Figure 6-28.

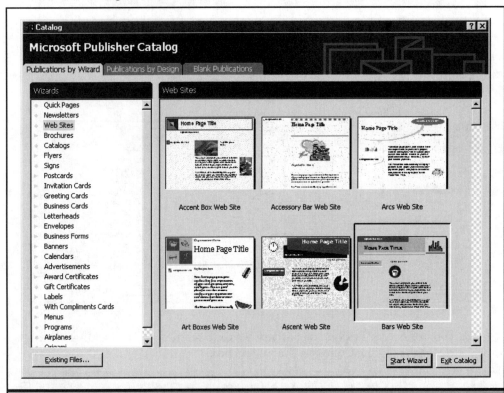

Figure 6-28. *Using a wizard to create a web site*

3. Click Start Wizard.

4. Click Next to begin the wizard.

5. Select a color scheme and click Next

6. Check the boxes next to the pages you want to include in the site, as shown in Figure 6-29. As you check the boxes, Publisher adds these pages to the web site. Click Next.

7. Select a form to add to the web site and click Next.

8. Select a format for the navigation bar used on the pages in the web site and click Next.

9. Tell the wizard whether you want to play sound on the home page and click Next.

10. Specify whether you want to use a textured background for the web site and click Next.

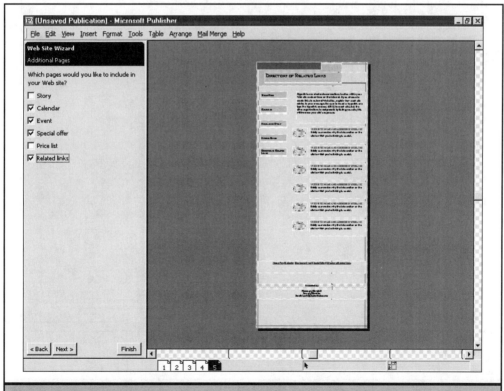

Figure 6-29. *Adding web pages to the site*

11. Specify which set of information you want to use in the web site. If necessary, click Update to review and edit the information.

12. Click Finish to begin working with the pages of the web site.

To convert a Publisher document intended for print into a web page, choose File | Create Web Site from Current Publication or if you're displaying the wizard, click the Convert To Web Site item in the wizard.

To create a web page or web site from scratch, click the Blank Publications tab in the Microsoft Publisher Catalog. Then select Web Page from the list of blank publications and click Create, as shown in Figure 6-30.

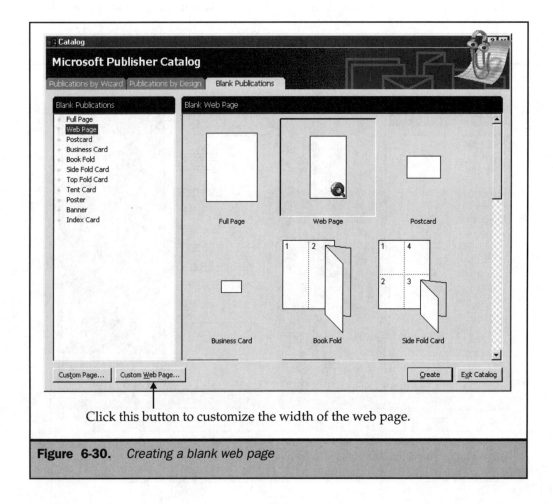

Click this button to customize the width of the web page.

Figure 6-30. *Creating a blank web page*

Adding Web Content

You add content to a web page in the same fashion you add content to other Publisher documents. However, Publisher provides three extra buttons on the Objects bar that are used specifically for web publishing:

- **Hot Spot Tool**   To create a hyperlink over a part of an image or a page, click the Hot Spot Tool button and drag across the area you want to link to another location. After you release the mouse button, Publisher displays the Hyperlink dialog box, which you use to specify the URL of the linked resource.

- **Form Control**   To add form fields to a web page, click the Form Control button, select the form field you want to add to the web page, and then drag the mouse across the area in which you want to place the field. To specify the properties of the field, right-click the field and choose the Properties command for the field you inserted. Then use the dialog box Publisher displays for the field to edit the field's properties.

- **HTML Code Fragment**   To insert pieces of HTML code in a web page, click the HTML Code Fragment button, drag the mouse across the area of the page in which you want to place the HTML code, and use the HTML Code Fragment Properties dialog box to enter the code. Click OK when you've finished.

Tip   *Note that every form needs a Submit button that viewers click to submit their answers. Before you can save a web site that includes a form, you need to specify the properties of the Submit button. To do so, right-click the button and choose Command Button Properties from the shortcut menu. Use the Command Button Properties dialog box to specify the data retrieval method and information.*

Using Web Design Gallery Objects

Most of Publisher's Design Gallery objects for the web have equivalents for printed documents. For example, the Web Mastheads item is equivalent to the regular Mastheads item for printed documents. And the same is true for Web Reply Forms, Web Sidebars, and Web Pull Quotes. However, the Design Gallery offers two extra objects not available for print documents: Web Navigation Bars and Web Buttons. When you insert a Navigation Bar, Publisher adds a bar of hyperlinks to each of the web pages in the site. When you add a Web Button, Publisher adds a button hyperlink. Right-click the button and choose the shortcut menu's Hyperlink command to specify the properties of the hyperlink. For example, if you add an E-Mail button, click the An Internet E-mail Address option button, specify the address, and click OK.

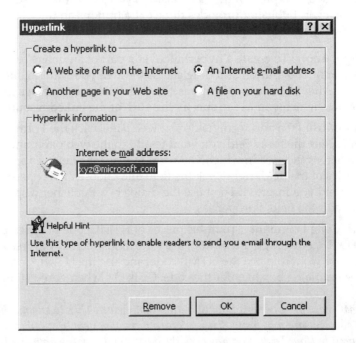

The Complete Reference

Office 2000

Part II

Microsoft Word

The Complete Reference

Office 2000

Chapter 7

Laying Out a Document

Oscar Wilde said, "Appearances are everything." In word processing, how a page looks isn't necessarily everything, but it counts for a lot. To make a good impression on readers, a well-written, well-thought-out, and to-the-point Word 2000 document should also look good on the page. This chapter, the first in Part II, explains how to lay out documents so that readers know they are looking at a document that was created by someone who really knows word processing.

This chapter explains how to hyphenate text, how to control where one page ends and another begins, and how to handle tricky punctuation such as em and en dashes. It describes how to indent text and create hanging indents and hanging headings, as well as how to create section breaks for drastic layout changes. This chapter also explains how to determine how much empty space appears between lines and between paragraphs. It shows you how to number a document's pages and include headers and footers in documents.

Laying Out the Text

In this part of the chapter, you learn how to tell Word 2000 exactly where and how text should fall on the page. These pages explain how to hyphenate text, break sentences and pages in the middle, and keep paragraphs together on a single page. This part of the chapter also describes how to handle unusual punctuation, including dashes, ellipses, and quotation marks. It also tells how to center, justify, right-align, or left-align text.

Hyphenating Text

One of the first things you should know about hyphenating text is that it may not be necessary. Text that hasn't been hyphenated is easier to read. Consider the pages of this book, for example. To make reading easier, words in this book aren't usually hyphenated on the right margin. In my opinion, it is only necessary to hyphenate text when you're creating formal documents, when you need to squeeze text into columns, and when text is justified, that is, aligned on both the left and right margins. Word 2000 offers several ways to hyphenate text. You can hyphenate a single word yourself by entering an optional hyphen, you can tell Word 2000 to hyphenate the words automatically, you can review words one at a time and tell Word 2000 where to hyphenate them, and you can even tell Word 2000 not to hyphenate a word or a paragraph. Read on for the glorious details.

"Comparing the Hyphenation Techniques" explains all the ways to hyphenate words, paragraphs, and documents. By the way, a hyphen is different from an em dash—a punctuation mark that is used to show an abrupt change of thought and that is normally the width of the capital letter *M* in the font you are using. It is also different from an en dash, a smaller dash that is used to show inclusive numbers or time periods and that is normally the width of the capital letter *N* in the font you are using. See "Handling Dashes and Quotation Marks" later in this chapter to learn how to use dashes correctly.

Tip *You can tell Word 2000 to hyphenate words as you enter them (by telling the program to hyphenate the document automatically), but doing so is a distraction. It hurts the eyes and makes the program run more slowly. I recommend typing the words first and then hyphenating them.*

Comparing the Hyphenation Techniques

Word 2000 offers no less than four ways to hyphenate (or not hyphenate) a word, paragraph, or document. Which technique works best depends on what you are trying to accomplish:

- **Automatic Hyphenation** With this technique, Word hyphenates the entire document quickly. Unfortunately, you can't tell Word not to hyphenate a single part of a document automatically. For example, you can't select a paragraph or two and hyphenate them automatically. You can, however, quickly remove hyphens that were made automatically.

- **Manual Hyphenation** With this technique, you review each place where Word suggests putting a hyphen, and you say Yes or No to each suggestion. It takes longer to go this route than it does to hyphenate a document automatically, and if you change your mind about hyphens that were inserted manually, you have to delete them one at a time with the BACKSPACE or DELETE key. On the other hand, you get to choose where hyphens fall and you can also hyphenate part of a document. All you have to do is select the part of the document that you want to hyphenate first.

- **Optional Hyphens** If a word is crying out to be hyphenated, you can insert a manual hyphen by pressing CTRL-- (hyphen) instead of going to the trouble of giving a hyphenation command.

- **Keeping Paragraphs from Being Hyphenated** You can prevent a paragraph from being hyphenated by choosing Format | Paragraph, clicking the Line and Page Breaks tab in the Paragraph dialog box, and clicking the Don't Hyphenate check box.

- **Keeping Hyphenated Words from Breaking Across Lines** Some words, such as "e-mail" and "X-Men," should not be broken across two different lines. To keep these words from being broken, press CTRL-SHIFT-- (hyphen) instead of entering a plain hyphen.

Hyphenating Text in a Document

Word 2000 offers two ways to hyphenate an entire document or many paragraphs at once—the automatic way and the manual way. In my experience, the best way to hyphenate an entire document is to hyphenate it automatically, review the paragraphs to see how Word 2000 hyphenated them, and then manually hyphenate the paragraphs you think Word 2000 didn't do a good job on. As the previous sidebar points out, you cannot automatically hyphenate a handful of paragraphs. When you opt for the automatic hyphenation technique, you have to go whole hog and hyphenate the entire document.

Automatic Hyphenation

All the text is hyphenated when you hyphenate automatically. To hyphenate a document automatically:

1. Put the cursor anywhere in the document.
2. Choose Tools | Language | Hyphenation. You see the Hyphenation dialog box shown in Figure 7-1.

Note   *If the Hyphenation feature was not installed when you installed Word, you'll see a message that you need to install it. You'll need to insert the installation disk in your CD drive.*

3. Click the Automatically Hyphenate Document check box.

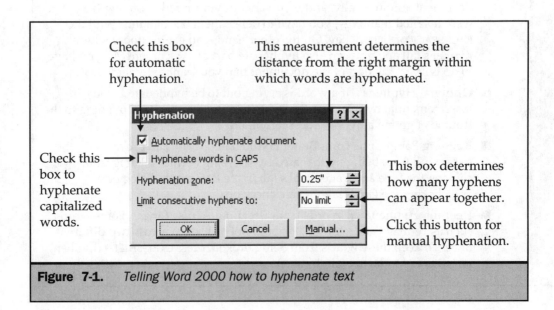

Figure 7-1.   *Telling Word 2000 how to hyphenate text*

4. Click Hyphenate Words In CAPS to remove the check mark if you want words in capital letters not to be hyphenated.

5. If you want, make an entry in the Hyphenation Zone box to say how large the hyphenation zone should be. Word 2000 tries to break words that cross into the hyphenation zone. With a large hyphenation zone, more words are hyphenated, but more white space appears between words. With a small hyphenation zone, fewer words are hyphenated but less white space appears between words. Figure 7-2 shows a paragraph that hasn't been hyphenated, the same paragraph with the hyphenation zone set to 0.2, and the paragraph yet again with the hyphenation zone set to 0.5.

Tip   *Small hyphenation zones work better with justified text. With text that hasn't been justified (when it is "ragged right"), use a large hyphenation zone.*

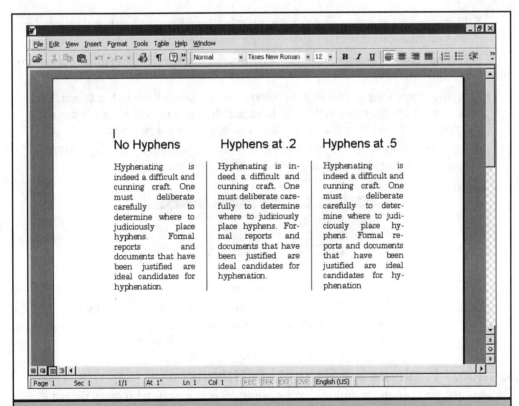

Figure 7-2.   *Comparing hyphenation settings: no hyphens (left); the hyphenation zone at 0.2 (middle); and the hyphenation zone at 0.5 (right)*

6. Make an entry in the Limit Consecutive Hyphens To box if you want no more than a certain number of hyphens to appear one after the other on the right side of a paragraph. In book publishing, the rule is to never allow more than two hyphens to appear together. In magazine or newspaper publishing, the sky is the limit when it comes to how many hyphens can appear together.

7. Click OK to close the Hyphenation dialog box.

LEARN BY EXAMPLE
If you care to experiment with hyphenating, open the Figure 7-2 (Hyphenation) file on the companion CD.

Hyphenating Text Manually

Follow these steps to review each hyphen that Word 2000 proposes to enter as it hyphenates a document:

1. Place the cursor where you want to start hyphenating. To hyphenate part of a document, select it.

2. Choose Tools | Language | Hyphenation. You see the Hyphenation dialog box (see Figure 7-1).

3. Follow steps 4 through 6 in the previous set of instructions to tell Word 2000 how to hyphenate words that are in capital letters, how often words are to be hyphenated, and how many hyphens can appear consecutively.

4. Click the Manual button. You see the Manual Hyphenation dialog box. The cursor blinks at the place where Word 2000 suggests putting a hyphen:

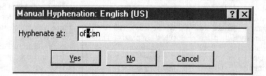

5. Click Yes or No to accept or reject the suggestion.

6. Keep clicking Yes or No until Word 2000 tells you that it has finished hyphenating the document or the paragraphs you selected.

7. Click OK.

Optional Hyphens for Fixing Line Breaks

Rather than go to all the trouble of hyphenating an entire document or section of a document, you can simply insert an optional hyphen to keep lines from straying too far into the right margin or too far toward the right side of a column. An optional hyphen breaks the words. To insert an optional hyphen, press CTRL-- (hyphen).

The following illustration shows two identical sentences. In the sentence on the right, I pressed CTRL-- after "tintinnab" to insert an optional hyphen and make the line break. Now the three lines look better on the page. If I entered another word at the start of the sentence, "tintinnabulation" would move to the following line, and the optional hyphen would disappear.

As he walked, he heard the tintinnabulation of the bells, which rang the hour, and he knew his time was up at last.

As he walked, he heard the tintinnab-ulation of the bells, which rang the hour, and he knew his time was up at last.

Whatever you do, don't enter a plain hyphen to solve a line-break problem. Your hyphen will remain in the text, even if half the words get pushed to the next line. Optional hyphens, on the other hand, disappear when they aren't breaking words in half on the right margin.

Keeping Compound Words from Breaking

Contrary to breaking lines with hyphens, sometimes it is better for a line not to break over a hyphenated word. Consider the hyphens in the following sentence. When Word 2000 encountered the hyphens in these compound words—"X-Men" and "e-mail"—it broke the lines where the hyphens appeared.

If what you say about my heroes the X-men is true, and they were nixed by the G-men, then you had better send me an e-mail message to say why.

But in cases like these, Word 2000 should not have broken the lines at the hyphens. To keep words like these from breaking at the end of a line, press CTRL-SHIFT-- (hyphen) instead of entering a hyphen when you type the word.

Removing the Hyphens from Text

Unfortunately, the only way to remove hyphens from text that has been hyphenated manually is to remove the hyphens one by one by pressing the BACKSPACE or DELETE key. What a drag! On the other hand, removing hyphens that were put in automatically is quite simple:

1. Put the cursor anywhere in the document.

2. Choose Tools | Language | Hyphenation. The Hyphenation dialog box appears (see Figure 7-1).

3. Click to remove the check mark from the Automatically Hyphenate Document check box.

4. Click OK.

Keeping Paragraphs from Being Hyphenated

Besides the myriad other ways to handle hyphens, Word 2000 offers one more hyphenation tidbit—a way to keep paragraphs from being hyphenated. This option is chiefly for use with styles, but you can also use it to tag individual paragraphs to keep them from being hyphenated. After you've marked the paragraphs that you don't want to be hyphenated, you can run a quick and dirty automatic hyphenation over the entire document and be done with it.

To keep a paragraph from being hyphenated:

1. Either click in the paragraph or select the paragraphs that are not to be hyphenated.

2. Choose Format | Paragraph.

3. Click the Line and Page Breaks tab. It is shown in Figure 7-3.

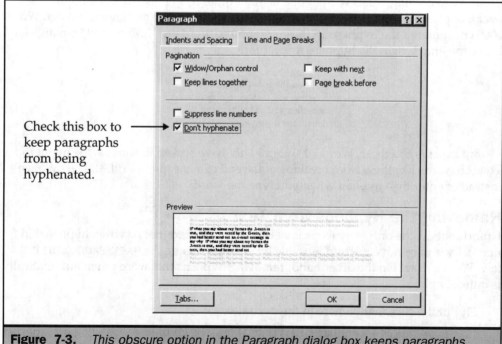

Figure 7-3. *This obscure option in the Paragraph dialog box keeps paragraphs from being hyphenated. Use it when you create styles*

4. Click the Don't Hyphenate check box.

5. Click OK.

 If you can't hyphenate a paragraph, it is probably because someone unintentionally checked the Don't Hyphenate check box.

Controlling Where Text Falls on the Page

This section explains some tried-and-true techniques for making sure that text appears exactly where you want it to appear on the page. Following are instructions for breaking a line in the middle (without pressing the ENTER key), ending a page before you've reached the bottom, making sure text appears at the top of a page, and keeping lines from being separated by a page break. You also learn to anchor a paragraph so it stays in one place and doesn't slide down the page if new text is placed above it.

Breaking a Sentence in the Middle

As you no doubt know, pressing the ENTER key starts a new paragraph and moves the cursor to the next line. But what if you want to move words to the following line without starting a new paragraph? In the following illustration, for example, the "We" at the end of the first line should probably move to the second line. That would plug the enormous hole that appears at the end of the second line. Typesetters and desktop publishers have to solve these kinds of problems all the time.

> "Let me be Frank," Frank said. "We are quite sad. We are thoroughly upset and unconditionally discombobulated. If the Los Angeles Dodgers dare to move back to Brooklyn, we will go berserk. Berserk I tell you!"

To move text to the following line without creating a new paragraph, press SHIFT-ENTER. For the following illustration, I placed the cursor before the *W* in "We" and pressed SHIFT-ENTER. Notice how the second line is filled up. Now the document is easier to read.

> "Let me be Frank," Frank said. "We are quite sad. We are thoroughly upset and unconditionally discombobulated. If the Los Angeles Dodgers dare to move back to Brooklyn, we will go berserk. Berserk I tell you!"

Unless you click the Show/Hide button, it is impossible to tell where a line was broken by pressing SHIFT-ENTER. If you find yourself fiddling with text and can't understand why a line has moved down the page, click the Show/Hide button and look for the leftward-pointing arrow symbol. That symbol means that you or someone else pressed SHIFT-ENTER.

Breaking a Page in the Middle

Word 2000 gives you a new page to write on when you fill up one page. But what if you want to start a new page right away? In that case, press CTRL-ENTER. In Print Layout view, you see the top of the new page you created. In Normal view, the words "Page Break" and a dotted line appear across the screen:

--Page Break--

To remove a page break, switch to Normal view, click on the words "Page Break," and press the DELETE key.

Incidentally, you can enter a page break before a heading if you want it always to be at the top of the page where everyone can see it.

Making Sure a Title or Heading Appears at the Top of a Page

To make sure that a chapter title or heading appears at the top of a page:

1. Click in the chapter title or heading that you want to appear at the top.
2. Choose Format | Paragraph.
3. In the Paragraph dialog box, click the Line and Page Breaks tab (see Figure 7-3).
4. Click the Page Break Before check box.
5. Click OK.

Keeping Lines Together on the Page

When the last line on the page is a heading, you have a problem. Readers expect text to fall directly beneath a heading. However, when you are working on a long document, sometimes headings get pushed to the bottom of the page. To solve this problem, Word 2000 offers two commands in the Paragraph dialog box for keeping lines of text together:

■ **Keep Lines Together** Keeps a paragraph from breaking across pages.

■ **Keep With Next** Keeps a paragraph or several paragraphs and the paragraph that follows from breaking across pages.

The commands for keeping text on the same page are chiefly for use with styles. Sometimes Word 2000 has to break a page early to make paragraphs and text stay together. As a result, empty, forlorn white space may appear at the bottom of pages.

To keep a heading and the paragraphs that follow it, two paragraphs, several lines, or a graphic and its caption from breaking across a page, do the following:

1. Select the stuff you want to keep on the same page. To keep paragraphs together, either place the cursor in the paragraph that you want to tie to the following paragraph, or select all the paragraphs to be kept together except the last one.

2. Choose Format | Paragraph.

3. Click the Line and Page Breaks tab. It is shown in Figure 7-4.

4. Under Pagination, click a check box:

   - **Keep Lines Together**   Keeps the lines you selected from being broken across two pages.

   - **Keep With Next**   Ties the paragraph or paragraphs to the paragraph that follows so that they all stay on the same page.

5. Click OK.

Word 2000 offers a special command for keeping captions on the same page as the figures, charts, graphs, or whatnot that they describe. See "Captions for Figures, Graphs, Tables, and What All" in Chapter 11.

Preventing Widows and Orphans

On the Line and Page Breaks tab of the Paragraph dialog box (see Figure 7-4) is a check box called Widow/Orphan Control. This check box is selected by default, and you should seldom have a reason for unselecting it. In typesetting terminology, a widow is the last line of a paragraph that appears at the top of a page. An orphan is the first line of a paragraph that appears at the bottom of a page. In the typesetting biz, widows and orphans are thought to be eyesores, but you can prevent orphans from appearing in your documents by never unchecking the Widow/Orphan Control check box.

Anchoring a Paragraph So It Stays in One Place

Suppose you are working on a company newsletter, and in the middle of the newsletter is an important announcement that has to stay smack-dab where it is.

Check this box to keep a single paragraph or group of paragraphs on the same page.

Check this box if your document has a heading and you want to keep a paragraph or group of paragraphs and the paragraph that follows on the same page.

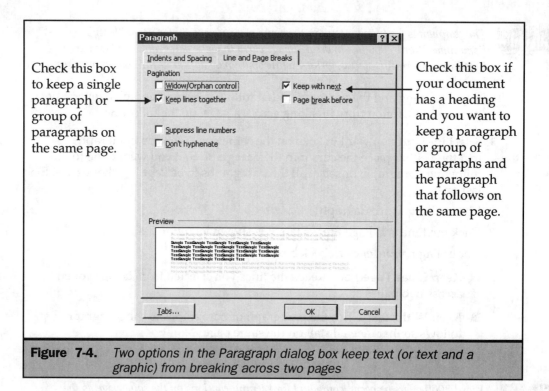

Figure 7-4.   *Two options in the Paragraph dialog box keep text (or text and a graphic) from breaking across two pages*

In other words, no matter how much company news gets inserted at the start of the newsletter, the announcement has to stay right in the middle of the page.

To keep a paragraph or graphic in one place, you can anchor it. After you drop anchor, text flows around the paragraph or graphic, and the paragraph or graphic never moves, no matter how many words or sentences you insert above it in the document.

Tip   *To anchor text, put it in a text box first. See "Text Boxes for Announcements and Headings" at the start of Chapter 10 if you need instructions for doing so.*

To anchor text or a graphic, you start by telling Word 2000 that you want to anchor it, and then you drag the text or graphic to the place where you want it to remain on the page. Follow these steps to anchor text or a graphic:

1. If you're not already there, switch to Print Layout view.

2. Click the Zoom drop-down list and choose Whole Page. When you are anchoring text or a graphic, it pays to shrink the document down so you can see most of the page.

3. Select the text box or graphic (if you are anchoring text, be sure to put it in a text box first (see Chapter 10 for information on text boxes). To select a text box or

graphic, click inside it. Square selection handles appear on the corners and sides, as shown in this illustration:

> The·Annual·Company·Tug-of-War·will·take·place·on·Friday·
> afternoon·at·4:30.·This·year,·Sales·and·Marketing·will·do·battle·
> with·Accounting·and·Administration.¶
> As·always,·only·the·winning·team·will·be·able·to·participate·in·
> the·company's·401(k)·plan.¶

4. Choose Format | Picture if you are anchoring a graphic or Format | Text Box if you are anchoring a text box. Either the Format Text Box or the Format Picture dialog box appears.

5. Click the Layout tab. Figure 7-5 shows the Layout tab of the Format Text Box dialog box. The options in the Format Picture dialog box are the same.

6. Select a layout and click the Advanced button to open the Advanced Layout dialog box, as shown in Figure 7-6.

7. Select the Picture Position tab, if necessary, and click the Lock Anchor check box.

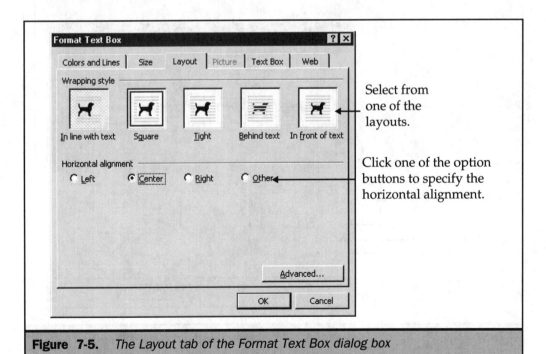

Figure 7-5. *The Layout tab of the Format Text Box dialog box*

8. Click the Move Object With Text check box to remove the check mark, and click Allow Overlap to remove the check mark. Notice that the Vertical Absolute Position Below setting has changed to Page.

9. Choose Page from the Horizontal Alignment Relative To drop-down menu.

Don't concern yourself with the Horizontal and Vertical settings on the Picture Position tab. When you return to the document, you drag the text box or graphic to establish its horizontal and vertical position.

10. Click OK to close the Advanced Layout dialog box.

11. Click OK to close the Format Text Box dialog box and return to the document.

After you anchor a text box or graphic, you likely have to click the Wrapping tab in the Format dialog box to tell Word 2000 how text should behave when it encounters the text box or graphic. See "Wrapping Text Around Graphics and Text Boxes" in Chapter 10.

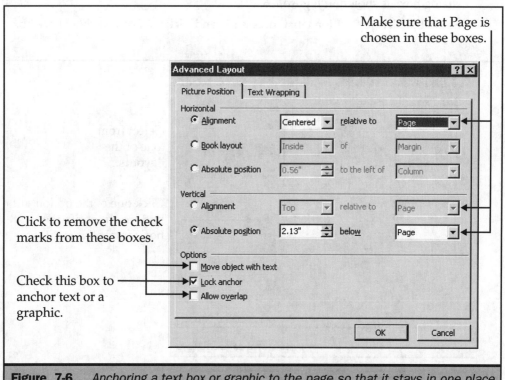

Figure 7-6. *Anchoring a text box or graphic to the page so that it stays in one place*

12. Move the pointer to the border, but not a handle of the graphic frame or text box. The pointer changes into a four-headed arrow.

13. Drag the text box or graphic where you want it to remain on the page.

Figure 7-7 shows a company newsletter with an anchored announcement and an anchored graphic. No matter how much new text goes into this document, the announcement and graphic will stay in the same place—prominently on page 1.

LEARN BY EXAMPLE
To experiment with how text behaves beside an anchored text box and graphic, open the Word 2000 document Figure 7-7 (Anchoring) on the companion CD.

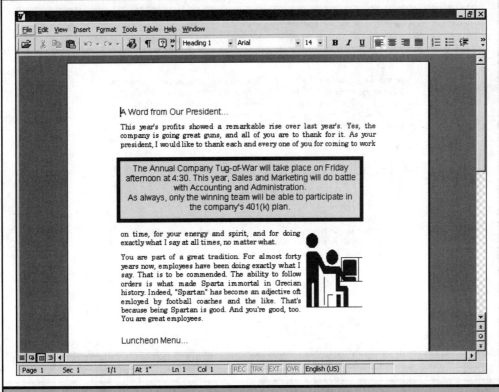

Figure 7-7. *The announcement and graphic in this newsletter have been anchored to the page and will not move with the text*

Aligning Text on the Page

When it comes to aligning text, Word 2000 makes a distinction between aligning text in paragraphs with respect to the margins and aligning all the text on the page with respect to the borders of the page. How to align text is the subject of this section.

Aligning Text with Respect to the Left and Right Margins

So important is aligning text with respect to the left and right margins, Word 2000 offers buttons on the Formatting toolbar for doing it: the Align Left, Center, Align Right, and Justify buttons. Each aligns text in a different way, as shown in Figure 7-8.

To align paragraph text in a document, follow these steps:

1. Select the paragraphs you want to align. If you are aligning a single paragraph, all you have to do is click it.

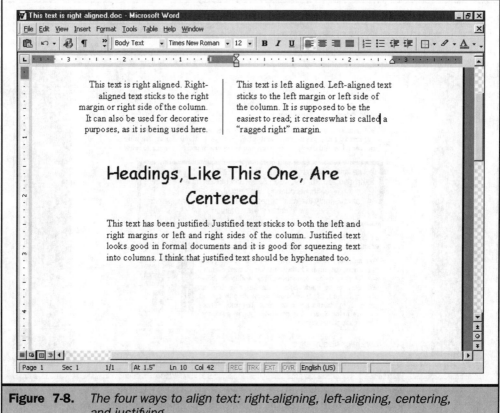

Figure 7-8. *The four ways to align text: right-aligning, left-aligning, centering, and justifying*

2. Click an alignment button on the Formatting toolbar:

- **Align Left**   Aligns text with the left margin or left side of the column.

- **Center**   Centers the text between the margins or between the column boundaries.

- **Align Right**   Aligns text with the right margin or right side of the column.

- **Justify**   Aligns text with both the left and right margins and left and right sides of the column.

It isn't necessary to select an entire paragraph when you want to align text or give any command that pertains to paragraphs, for that matter. All you have to do is put the cursor in the paragraph or, to select more than one paragraph, select part of each one.

You can also control text alignment by way of the Paragraph dialog box:

1. Choose Format | Paragraph.

2. On the Indents and Spacing tab of the Paragraph dialog box, click the Alignment down-arrow and choose an alignment option: Left, Center, Right, or Justify.

3. Click OK.

Aligning Text with Respect to the Top and Bottom Margins

Word 2000 also offers commands called Top, Center, and Justified in the Page Setup dialog box for aligning text with respect to the top and bottom margins of the page. The Justify setting only applies to pages that are filled up. When a page is only partly full, Word 2000 aligns it with the top margin. Figure 7-9 shows the three ways to align text with respect to the top and bottom margins of the page.

To change the alignment of text vis-à-vis the top and bottom margins, follow these steps:

1. Click at the top of the page that is to be aligned in a new way. If you are aligning all the pages in a document, it doesn't matter where the cursor is before you give the command. If you are aligning all the pages in a section, make sure the cursor is in the section.

2. Choose File | Page Setup.

3. Click the Layout tab in the Page Setup dialog box. The Layout tab is shown in Figure 7-10.

4. Under Vertical Alignment, choose Top, Center, or Justified.

5. Under Apply To, tell Word 2000 which pages in the document are to be aligned vertically: Whole Document applies to the entire document; This Point Forward

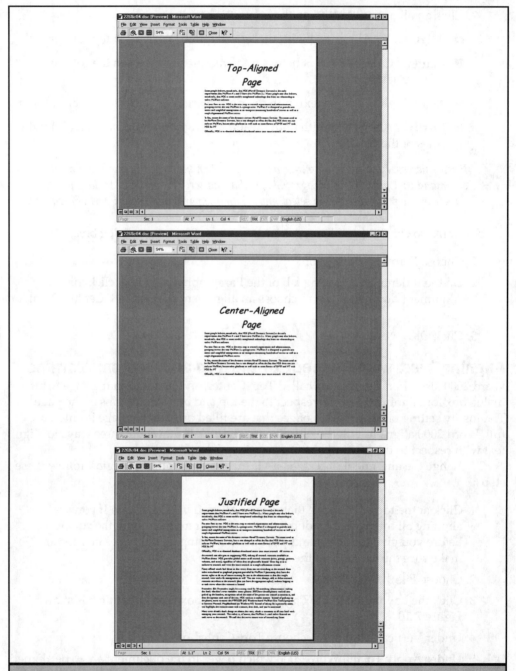

Figure 7-9. *From the Page Setup dialog box, you can tell Word 2000 how to align all the text on a page with respect to the top and bottom margins*

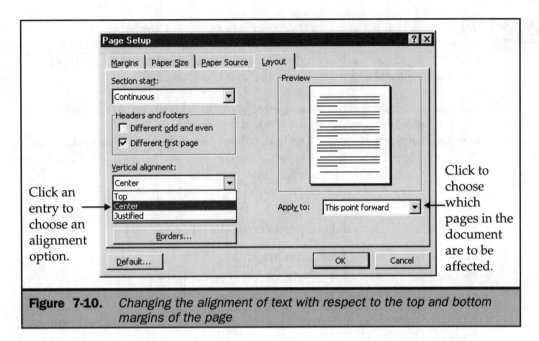

Click an entry to choose an alignment option.

Click to choose which pages in the document are to be affected.

WORD

Figure 7-10. *Changing the alignment of text with respect to the top and bottom margins of the page*

applies to all the pages from the cursor position to the end of the document; and This Section applies to all the pages in the section that the cursor is in.

6. Click OK.

Handling Dashes and Quotation Marks

This part of the chapter looks into a pesky aspect of Word 2000: how to handle punctuation marks. As you must have noticed by now, the program occasionally reaches over your shoulder and enters punctuation marks for you. For example, Word 2000 is geared for curly quotation marks and puts them in documents unless you tell it not to. And it enters ellipses (...) automatically as well. This part of the chapter explains how to usurp Word 2000 and take command of punctuation marks.

Inserting Em and En Dashes

Dashes are punctuation marks and are different from hyphens. An em dash shows an abrupt change of direction in the middle of a sentence—know what I mean? You can always spot an amateur desktop publisher because amateurs use dashes incorrectly. In the following illustration, the last sentence is the one with a proper em dash. The other em dashes were made by amateurs.

> An em dash looks like a hyphen-but it's wider.
> An em dash looks like a hyphen--but it's wider.
> An em dash looks like a hyphen – but it's wider.
> An em dash looks like a hyphen—but it's wider.

Unless you've changed Word 2000's default options, the program enters an em dash automatically when you type two hyphens in a row. If that isn't happening and you want it to happen, choose Tools | AutoCorrect, click the AutoFormat As You Type tab, and click the Symbol Characters (- -) With Symbols (—) check box.

Similar to an em dash, an en dash is used to show inclusive numbers or time periods. Amateurs let the hyphen do the work of the en dash. In the following illustration, en dashes appear in the first line, but hyphens appear in the second.

pp. 9–17   Aug.–Sept. 1999   Exodus 16:11–18

pp. 9-17   Aug.-Sept. 1999   Exodus 16:11-18

To include an em or en dash in a document, do the following:

1. Place the cursor where the dash is to appear.
2. Choose Insert | Symbol. The Symbol dialog box appears.
3. Click the Special Characters tab. It is shown in Figure 7-11.
4. Either click Em Dash at the top of the list, or click En Dash, the second item on the list.
5. Click the Insert button.
6. Click the Close button.

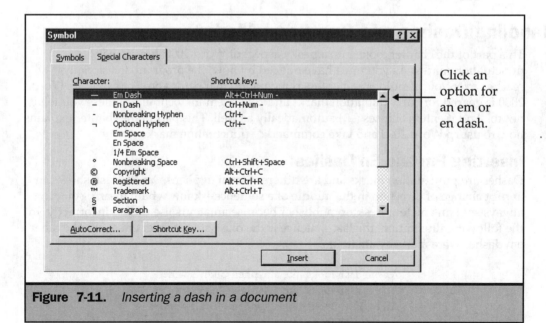

Figure 7-11. *Inserting a dash in a document*

Tip	*If you prefer pressing keys instead of clicking commands, you might prefer the keyboard shortcut for entering an em dash: Simultaneously press the* ALT *key, the* CTRL *key, and the minus key on the numeric keypad (the key in the upper-right corner of the keyboard). To enter an en dash, simultaneously press the* CTRL *key and the minus key on the numeric keypad.*

Using Curly or Straight Quotation Marks

Until you fiddle with the default options, Word 2000 puts curly quotes rather than straight quotes in documents. In the following illustration, curly quotes (also known as "smart quotes" because they know which way to turn on either side of text) appear in the first sentence and straight quotes appear in the second sentence:

"Frankly," Frank said, "this is what he told me: 'No.'"
"Frankly," Frank said, "this is what he told me: 'No.'"

The problem with curly quotes is that they don't look good in some fonts, especially monospace fonts like Courier. And some people prefer straight quotation marks to curly ones.

To tell Word 2000 to use straight quotes or curly ones, do the following:

1. Choose Tools | AutoCorrect to open the AutoCorrect dialog box.

2. Click the AutoFormat As You Type tab. It is shown in Figure 7-12.

3. To use curly quotes, make sure a check mark appears in the "Straight Quotes" With "Smart Quotes" check box.

4. Click OK.

Laying Out the Page

The second half of this chapter explores how to lay out the text in a Word 2000 document. If you were to take your nose out of the text and hold the page at arm's length, would the page itself look good? This section explains how to fashion an elegant layout. It describes how to indent text, how to create a section break when you want to change layouts in the middle of a document, how to adjust the spacing between lines and the spacing between paragraphs, how to number the pages in a document, and how to create a header or footer for document pages.

Tip	*By far the best way to handle fancy page layouts is to construct a style for each one you propose to put in your document. It takes time to lay out the different parts of a document. By creating styles, you only have to lay out a few representative paragraphs. After that, you can simply apply the styles you created to the different parts of the document. Styles are explained in Chapter 9.*

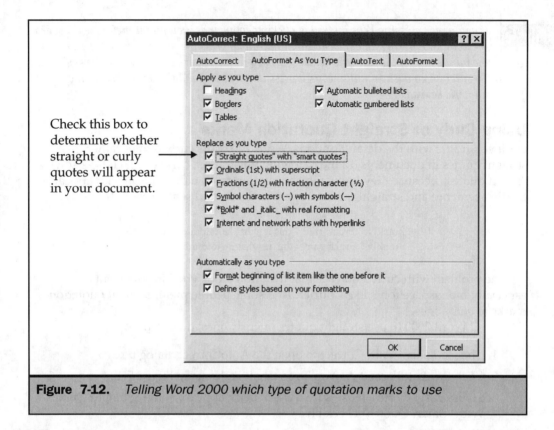

Check this box to determine whether straight or curly quotes will appear in your document.

Figure 7-12.   *Telling Word 2000 which type of quotation marks to use*

Indenting Text

The following pages explain how to indent text from the margin. The important thing to remember about indenting text is that text is indented with respect to the margins, not the edges of the page. In other words, if you indent a paragraph from the left margin by one inch and the left margin setting is one inch already, the text will fall two inches from the edge of the page. Margin settings are made from the edge of the page. Indentions are made from the margin.

Word 2000 offers no less than three ways to indent text. Moreover, when changing indentions, you can indent the first line of a paragraph, indent the entire paragraph, or create hanging headings. Better read on.

Indenting Text from the Margins

To indent text from the margins, you can drag markers on the ruler, click the Increase Indent and Decrease Indent buttons on the Formatting toolbar, or open the Paragraph dialog box and change indention settings.

If you are doing a quick-and-dirty job on a document that needs to get out the door fast, dragging the indent markers on the ruler is probably the way to go. However, to make sure that paragraphs are indented consistently from page to page, the best way to indent paragraphs is to use the Paragraph dialog box and enter exact measurements. In fact, the absolute best way is to create a style using the Paragraph dialog box. With the ruler, you have to "eyeball it" and hope for the best. With the buttons, you click away and watch the text get indented by one tab stop with each click of the mouse.

INDENTING TEXT WITH THE PARAGRAPH DIALOG BOX   Follow these steps to indent text with the Paragraph dialog box:

1. Select all or part of the paragraphs you want to indent. If you are indenting a single paragraph, simply click in it.

2. Choose Format | Paragraph. You see the Paragraph dialog box shown in Figure 7-13.

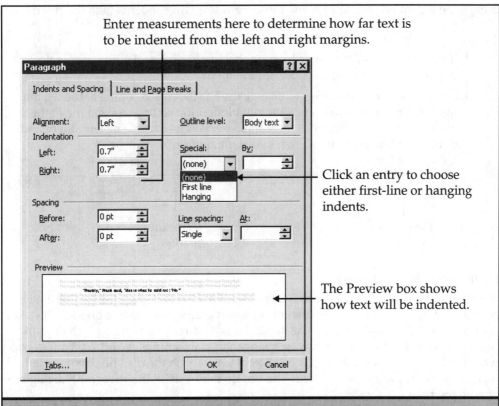

Figure 7-13. *Besides changing indentions, you can create hanging indents and first-line indents in the Paragraph dialog box*

3. Under Indentation, make entries in the Left and Right boxes to say how far text is to be indented from the left and right margins. As you make choices, watch the Preview box. It gives you an idea of what your choices mean in real terms.

4. Click OK.

INDENTING TEXT WITH THE INDENT BUTTONS   If you're in a hurry to change indentions, you might try clicking the Increase Indent or Decrease Indent buttons on the Formatting toolbar. These buttons move the text rightward to the next or previous tab stop (a half inch if you haven't changed the tab settings) and work only with respect to the left margin. In other words, if you click the Increase Indent button, the paragraph or paragraphs you selected move away from the left margin, but nothing happens on the right margin.

Click the Decrease Indent button if you clicked the Increase Indent button too many times and moved text too far from the left margin.

INDENTING TEXT WITH THE RULER   By dragging markers on the ruler, you can change the indention settings. Follow these steps to change indents with the ruler:

1. Choose View | Ruler if the ruler isn't onscreen.

2. If you are indenting a single paragraph, simply click in it. Otherwise, select all or part of the paragraphs you want to indent.

3. Drag the left indent marker to change the left indention setting and drag the right indent marker to change the right indention setting. As you move the pointer over a marker, a box appears to tell you its name. The left indent and right indent markers are shown in this illustration:

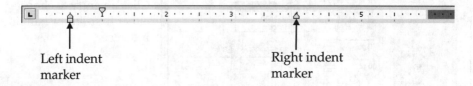

Left indent marker

Right indent marker

Indenting First Lines

In some kinds of documents, the first line is indented to mark the place where a new paragraph begins. To indent the first line of a paragraph most people press the TAB key once. In Word 2000, pressing the TAB key indents the first line by a half inch or to the first tab setting, if you or someone else changed the tab settings. Word 2000 offers two ways (three if you count pressing the TAB key) to establish the distance from the left margin that the first line is indented. You can do it by way of the Paragraph dialog box or with the ruler.

INDENTING THE FIRST LINE WITH THE PARAGRAPH DIALOG BOX   As you create a style, or if you merely intend to indent the first line of a paragraph or paragraphs, follow these steps to create a first-line indent:

1. Click in the paragraph or select all or part of the paragraphs whose first lines you want to indent.

2. Choose Format | Paragraph. You see the Paragraph dialog box (see Figure 7-12).

3. Click the Special drop-down list to open it and then choose First Line.

4. In the By box, enter the distance from the left margin that the first line is to be indented.

5. Click OK.

INDENTING THE FIRST LINE WITH THE RULER   To indent the first line with the ruler, follow these steps:

1. Choose View | Ruler if the ruler isn't onscreen.

2. Click in a paragraph or select all or part of the paragraphs whose first lines you want to indent.

3. On the ruler, drag the first-line indent marker to the right. When you move the pointer over the marker, a box appears and tells you which marker it is.

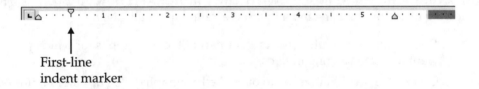

First-line
indent marker

Creating a Hanging Indent

A hanging indent is one in which the first line of the paragraph is closer to the left margin than the other lines in the paragraph are. Word 2000 creates hanging indents automatically for numbered and bulleted lists. In those cases, the first line of the paragraph—the one with the number or bullet in it—is closer to the left margin than the other lines are. Notice where the first-line indent marker is in the following illustration. In this numbered list, the left indent marker is directly on the left margin, but the second line in each paragraph is at the .25 inch mark:

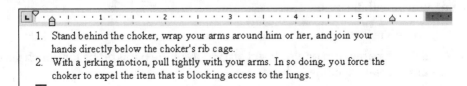

Hanging indents can be used for elegant effects in many ways. Notice where the first-line indent marker is in the following list, which leaves the names of four famous moptops hanging:

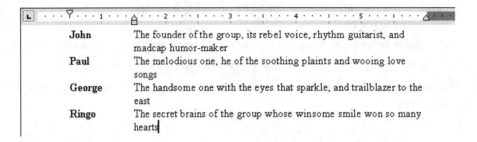

John	The founder of the group, its rebel voice, rhythm guitarist, and madcap humor-maker
Paul	The melodious one, he of the soothing plaints and wooing love songs
George	The handsome one with the eyes that sparkle, and trailblazer to the east
Ringo	The secret brains of the group whose winsome smile won so many hearts

To create a hanging indent, you can do so either by way of the Paragraph dialog box or the ruler.

LEARN BY EXAMPLE
To experiment with hanging indents, open the Word 2000 document Figure 7A (Hanging Indents) on the companion CD.

CREATING A HANGING INDENT WITH THE PARAGRAPH DIALOG BOX   Do the following to create a hanging indent with the Paragraph dialog box:

1. Click in the paragraph or select all or part of the paragraphs for which you want to create hanging indents.

2. Choose Format | Paragraph to open the Paragraph dialog box (see Figure 7-12).

3. Click the Special drop-down list and choose Hanging.

4. In the By box, enter the amount of space beyond the left indention setting by which all lines in the paragraph after the first line are to be indented. In other words, if the left indention setting is 0.5 inches and you enter 1 inch in the By box, the second and subsequent lines in the paragraph will be indented by 1.5 inches.

5. Click OK.

CREATING A HANGING INDENT WITH THE RULER   Follow these steps to create a hanging indent with the ruler:

1. Choose View | Ruler if the ruler isn't onscreen.

2. Click in a paragraph or else select all or part of the paragraphs for which you want to create hanging indents.

3. On the ruler, drag the hanging indent marker to the right. As you drag, the left indent marker moves as well.

Most likely, you'll have to pull and tug, pull and tug on the hanging indent marker several times until you get it right.

Creating a Hanging Heading

A hanging heading is one that lies closer to the left margin than the text that falls below it. Hanging headings are quite elegant and they make it easier for readers to look up information in a document. They make it easier because the headings stand out more and readers can find them more quickly. Figure 7-14 shows a document whose headings "hang."

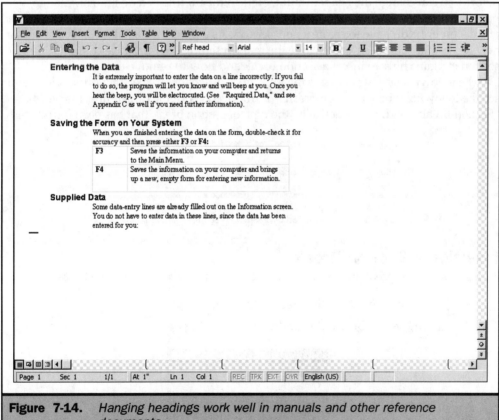

Figure 7-14. *Hanging headings work well in manuals and other reference documents*

As if you didn't expect it, Word 2000 offers two ways to create a hanging heading:

- **With the Paragraph Dialog Box** In the Special drop-down list, choose First Line. Then enter a negative number in the Left box in the Indentation section of the dialog box.

- **With the Ruler** Click in the heading and drag the First-line indent marker on the ruler to the left instead of to the right, as shown in Figure 7-14.

LEARN BY EXAMPLE
To try your hand at hanging headings, open the Figure 7-13 (Hanging Headings) file on the companion CD.

Section Breaks for Drastic Layout Changes

Before you can change the headers and footers in the middle of a document, change the page-numbering scheme or sequence, put text in columns, or change the margins for part of a document, you have to create a new section. As a matter of fact, Word 2000 creates a new section for you when you change the margin settings or introduce columns. This section explains how to insert a section break and how to remove one.

The following sidebar explains the four types of section breaks. In Normal view, you see the following when a section break is introduced: a double dotted line, the words "Section Break," and, parenthetically, the type of section break that has been introduced:

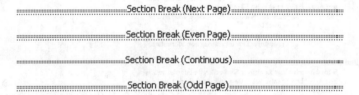

Inserting a Section Break

To insert a section break in a document and create a new section, do the following:

1. Place the cursor where the break is to occur.

2. Choose Insert | Break. You see the Break dialog box:

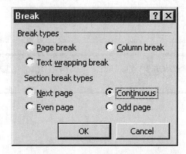

The Four Kinds of Section Breaks

In the Break dialog box (choose Insert | Break to get there), Word 2000 offers four kinds of section breaks:

- **Next Page**   Creates a section break and a page break at the same time.
- **Continuous**   Creates a section break in the middle of the page. This type of section break occurs, for example, between a heading and the two or three columns that appear below it in a newsletter. When margin settings are changed in the middle of a document, Word creates this kind of break.
- **Even Page**   Creates the section break on the next even-numbered page.
- **Odd Page**   Creates the section break on the next odd-numbered page. In conventional publishing, a new chapter always begins on an odd page. In a document with headers or footers that change from chapter to chapter, create an Odd Page section break to start subsequent chapters on odd pages, and you will be able to change headers or footers as well.

3. Under Section Break Types, click the kind of break you want.

4. Click OK.

Deleting a Section Break

To delete a section break, do the following:

1. Switch to Normal view if you are in another type of view. It's hard to find section breaks in Page Layout view, for example.

2. Click on the words that tell where the section break is.

3. Press the DELETE key.

Adjusting Space Between Lines and Paragraphs

This section has to do with space, not outer space, but the kinds of decisions regarding space that sometimes have to be made when you are laying out a document. The following pages explain how to adjust the amount of space between lines, adjust for space between paragraphs, and fix spacing problems between characters in headings.

Adjusting the Space Between Lines

Double-spacing and single-spacing the lines in a document are two of the most common chores word processors do, so Word 2000 offers special shortcuts for single- and double-spacing lines. The program offers many other line-spacing options as well. All line-spacing options are available in the Paragraph dialog box. Table 7-1 explains all of them.

Option	Keyboard Shortcut	Description
Single-Spacing	CTRL-1	Makes room for the tallest character in the line plus a small amount of extra space.
1.5 Line Spacing	CTRL-5	Puts one-and-a-half times the font size between lines. For example, if the characters are 12 points high, it puts 18 points between lines.
Double-Spacing	CTRL-2	Puts two times the font size between lines. If the characters are 12 points high, it puts 24 points between lines.
At Least		Normally, Word 2000 adds extra space between lines to accommodate tall characters. This option tells Word to adjust for tall characters, but only to a certain point—the point you specify with the At Least option.
Exactly		Puts a specific amount of space between lines, no ifs, ands, or buts. With this option, Word does not accommodate tall characters. Instead of increasing the amount of space, tall characters' heads are cut off.
Multiple		Works like double-spacing, only the Multiple option allows for triple-spacing, quadruple-spacing, and so on.

Table 7-1.   *Line Spacing Options*

Note   *When Word 2000 encounters a tall character or graphic that is too big to fit on a line, it automatically allows more space between lines to accommodate the tall character or graphic, except in the case of the Exactly option. When Exactly is chosen, the top of the tall character or graphic gets cut off by the line above.*

To tell Word 2000 how much space to put between lines in a document, do the following:

1. Select all or part of the paragraphs whose line spacing you wish to change. If you want to change line spacing in a single paragraph, click in it.

2. Choose Format | Paragraph. You see the Paragraph dialog box shown in Figure 7-15.

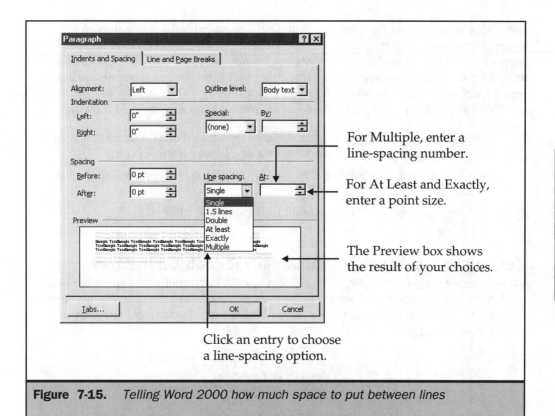

Figure 7-15. *Telling Word 2000 how much space to put between lines*

3. Open the Line Spacing drop-down list and choose an option (see Table 7-1).

4. If you chose At Least, Exactly, or Multiple, enter a number in the At box:

   ■ **At Least**   Enter, in points, the minimum distance that Word 2000 can increase line spacing to accommodate tall characters.

   ■ **Exactly**   Enter, in points, the exact amount of space that is to appear between lines.

   ■ **Multiple**   Enter a number that expresses how much space goes between lines. For example, if you enter 3, the lines will be triple-spaced.

5. Click OK.

Adjusting the Space Between Paragraphs

The Paragraph dialog box offers commands for telling Word 2000 how much space to put before each paragraph and after each paragraph. These commands are strictly for use with styles (Chapter 9 explains styles). Don't use them indiscriminately to put space before and after paragraphs because, used together, they can have unexpected consequences. For example, when a paragraph with such-and-such amount of space after it is followed by a paragraph with such-and-such amount of space before it, too much space may appear between the two paragraphs.

To tell Word 2000 to put space before and after a paragraph, do the following:

1. Select all or part of the paragraphs whose before and after space settings you want to change. If you are working on a single paragraph, click it.

2. Choose Format | Paragraph. The Paragraph dialog box appears (see Figure 7-15).

3. Under Spacing, enter an amount in the Before and After boxes.

4. Click OK.

Kerning to Fix Spacing Problems Between Characters

When letters are enlarged in headings, spacing problems sometimes appear between the letters. In the following illustration, for example, the *T* and the *w* in "Twins" appear to be too far apart, and the *r* and the *n* in "Born" appear to be too close together and almost look like an *m*:

Twins Born in Twin Cities

You can fix spacing problems like the ones in the illustration by adjusting the *kerning*, which refers to the space between individual letters.

 Only proportional-spaced fonts can be kerned.

Follow these steps to fix spacing problems between characters:

1. Select the two letters in question.

2. Choose Format | Font.

3. Click the Character Spacing tab. It is shown in Figure 7-16.

4. In the Spacing drop-down list, choose Expanded to put more space between the letters or Condensed to pack them closer together.

5. If you want, change the setting in the By box to make the letters closer together or farther apart. Word 2000 makes a suggestion automatically, but if the letters in the Preview box don't look right, you can improve on Word 2000's suggestion by making an entry of your own.

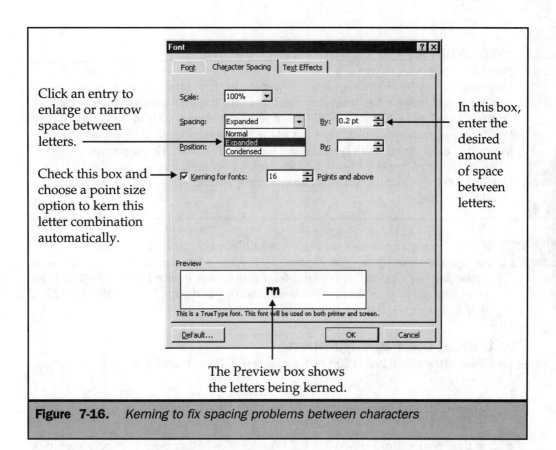

Click an entry to enlarge or narrow space between letters. ──►

Check this box and ──► choose a point size option to kern this letter combination automatically.

In this box, enter the desired amount of space between letters.

The Preview box shows the letters being kerned.

Figure 7-16. *Kerning to fix spacing problems between characters*

WORD

6. Click the Kerning For Fonts check box if you want Word 2000 to kern the letter combination you are working with automatically. In the Points And Above box, make an entry to tell Word 2000 at which point size to start kerning the letter combination.

7. Click OK.

Numbering a Document's Pages

It almost goes without saying, but long documents aren't worth much unless the pages are numbered. Readers want to know what page they are on and how many pages are in a document. And if the document is to have a table of contents or an index, pages absolutely must be numbered. This section explains how to number the pages of a document, how to position page numbers on the pages, and how to choose a numbering scheme other than standard Arabic numbers. It also explains how to start from a number other than one and how to include chapter numbers in page numbers (1-1, 1-2, 1-3, and so on). This section also explains how to remove page numbers from a document.

Page Numbers in Headers and Footers

Word 2000 offers two ways to number the pages of a document—with standard page numbers or by including page numbers in headers and footers. If your document will include headers and footers, put the page numbers there (and see "Putting Headers and Footers on Pages" a few pages hence to find out how). When an automatic page number such as the ones described in this section is inserted in a document with headers and footers, the automatic page number overlaps the header and footer. That looks ugly. You can put page numbers in headers and footers or use Word's automatic page numbering feature, but you shouldn't do both.

Tip *If your document includes what publishers call "front matter"—a title page, table of contents, introduction, or other elements that appear before the main text—create a new section for those elements and number them with Roman numerals. If you fail to take my advice and you number the entire document starting with page 1, your title page will start with page 1, and that will throw off the numbering scheme.*

Positioning the Page Numbers

Follow these steps to tell Word 2000 where page numbers should appear on the pages of a document:

1. Choose Insert | Page Numbers. You see the Page Numbers dialog box shown in Figure 7-17.

2. In the Position drop-down list, tell Word 2000 whether page numbers should be placed along the top or the bottom of the page.

3. In the Alignment drop-down list, tell Word 2000 if the page number should go on the left side, center, or right side of the bottom or top of the page. The Alignment drop-down list also offers options called Inside and Outside. These options are for double-sided documents in which text appears on both sides of the page. Inside puts the page numbers near the binding; Outside puts them away from the binding (Outside is highly recommended). Watch the Preview box to see the effects your choices have on the sample page or pages.

4. Click OK.

Taking the Number Off or Putting It On the First Page

In letters, informal documents, and notices, the standard practice is not to put page numbers on the first page. By default, Word 2000 puts a page number on the first page of a document or section, but that doesn't mean you can't remove it.

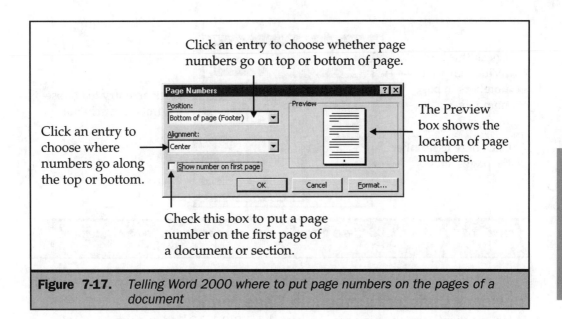

Figure 7-17. *Telling Word 2000 where to put page numbers on the pages of a document*

To remove a page number from the first page of a document or section, choose Insert | Page Numbers, and, in the Page Numbers dialog box (see Figure 7-17), make sure that no check mark appears in the Show Number On First Page check box.

Numbering with Roman Numerals and Letters

Arabic numerals are not the only ones that can be used to number the pages of a document. In the spirit of multiculturalism and cultural diversity, Word 2000 permits you to leave the Arabic world and return to Roman times, when computer documents were numbered with Roman numerals. The program offers other schemes for numbering pages as well.

To choose a numbering scheme for the pages of a document, follow these steps:

1. Choose Insert | Page Numbers. You see the Page Numbers dialog box (see Figure 7-17).

2. Click the Format button. The Page Number Format dialog box appears, as shown in Figure 7-18.

3. Click the Number Format drop-down list and choose a numbering scheme.

4. Click OK to close the Page Number Format dialog box.

5. Click OK in the Page Numbers dialog box.

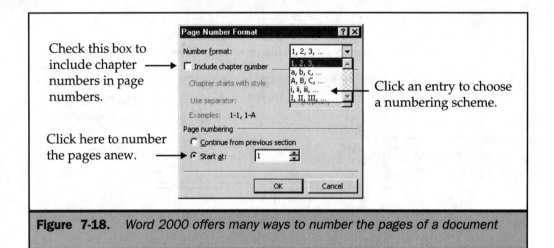

Figure 7-18.   *Word 2000 offers many ways to number the pages of a document*

Including Chapter Numbers in Page Numbers

To include chapter numbers in page numbers (1-1, 1-2, 2-1, 2-2, and so on), you must have assigned styles to the headings in your document (Chapter 9 explains styles). Truth be told, you must have diligently assigned the Heading 1 style to the first heading in each chapter. Not only that, but you must have chosen Format | Bullets and Numbering, clicked the Outline Numbered tab, and chosen an outline numbering scheme for the chapter titles. See "Numbering the Headings in a Document" in Chapter 11 for more instruction.

If you did all that, follow these steps to include chapter numbers in page numbers:

1. Choose Insert | Page Numbers. The Page Numbers dialog box appears (see Figure 7-17).

2. Choose where the page number is to go on the pages (turn backward to "Positioning the Page Numbers" if you need help).

3. Click the Format button. The Page Number Format dialog box appears (see Figure 7-18).

4. Click the Include Chapter Number check box.

5. If necessary, click the Chapter Starts With Style drop-down list and choose Heading 1 from the list.

6. By default, Word 2000 places a hyphen between the chapter number and the page number, but you can open the Use Separator drop-down list and choose another symbol if you want.

7. Click OK in the Page Number Format dialog box.

8. Click OK in the Page Numbers dialog box.

LEARN BY EXAMPLE
To experiment with chapter numbers in page numbers, open the Word 2000 document
Figure 7-18 (Page Numbers) on the companion CD.

Numbering the Pages Differently in the Middle of a Document

To start numbering the pages anew in a document, perhaps to choose a different numbering scheme or to start all over with page 1 in a new chapter, you must have divided the document into sections. Word 2000 cannot change numbering schemes unless you create a section for the pages that are to be numbered a different way.

Follow these steps to number the pages in part of a document differently:

1. Place the insertion point in the section of the document where you want to start a new numbering scheme.

2. Choose Insert | Page Numbers.

3. In the Page Numbers dialog box (see Figure 7-17), click the Format button. You see the Page Number Format dialog box (see Figure 7-18).

4. Click the Start At check box.

5. If the new set of pages is to start with a number other than 1, a, A, i, or I, enter the page number (or letter) in the box to the right of the Start At check box.

6. Click OK in the Page Number Format dialog box.

7. Click OK in the Page Numbers dialog box.

Removing Page Numbers

All right, you went to the trouble of numbering the pages in a document, and now you want to remove the page numbers. Follow these steps to remove them:

1. Choose View | Header and Footer. As shown in Figure 7-19, the Header and Footer toolbar appears. If your page numbers are along the top of the pages, you see a page number. If your page numbers are along the bottom of the pages, click the Switch Between Header and Footer button on the toolbar to see the footer at the bottom of the page along with the page number.

2. Click on the page number. A hashed border appears around the page number.

3. Move the pointer over the hash marks, and when the pointer changes into a four-headed arrow, click. As shown in Figure 7-19, black squares appear around the page number.

4. Press the DELETE key.

5. Click the Close button on the Header and Footer toolbar.

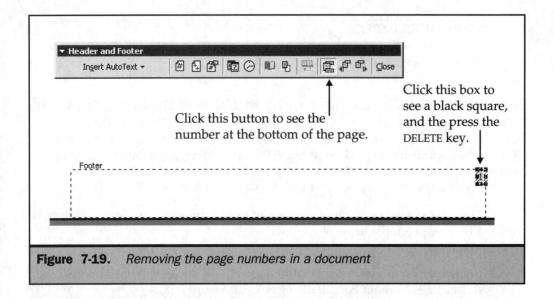

Click this button to see the
number at the bottom of the page.

Click this box to
see a black square,
and the press the
DELETE key.

Footer

Figure 7-19.   *Removing the page numbers in a document*

Putting Headers and Footers on Pages

A *header* is a bit of text along the top of a page that tells readers what's what in a document. Usually, the header includes the title of the document, the author's name, and a page number. *Footers* do the same things as headers, only they do it along the bottom of the page, as befits their name.

This section explains how to enter a header or footer; how to read and take advantage of the buttons on the Header and Footer toolbar; and how to include document information such as page numbers, dates, and times in headers. It describes how to create headers for odd and even pages and how to change the header in the middle of a document. It also explains how to remove a header or footer from the first page of a document.

ENTERING A HEADER AND FOOTER   Follow these steps to enter a header and footer in a document:

 1. Choose View | Header and Footer. The Header and Footer toolbar appears along with a rectangle and the word "Header."

> **Tip** *In Page Layout view, you can simply double-click a header or footer to make the Header or Footer rectangle appear.*

2. Type the header. As you do so, you can call on most of Word 2000's formatting commands. For example, you can choose a new typeface, or boldface or italicize the letters. You can even put graphics in headers and footers. The next section explains how to include document information in headers and footers with buttons on the Header and Footer toolbar.

3. Click the Switch Between Header and Footer button on the toolbar. Now you see a rectangle and the word "Footer." The Switch Between Header and Footer button takes you back and forth between the header and footer.

4. Enter the text of the footer.

5. Click the Close button on the right side of the Header and Footer toolbar.

Including Document Information in Headers and Footers

The Header and Footer toolbar offers several buttons for entering information about the document you are working on in a header and footer. Table 7-2 explains why and when to click those buttons.

Creating Different Headers and Footers for the First Page

To create a different header or footer for the first page of a document, or to remove a header and footer from the first page of a document, follow these steps:

1. Click the Page Setup button on the Header and Footer toolbar or choose File | Page Setup. The Page Setup dialog box appears.

2. Click the Layout tab. It is shown in Figure 7-20.

3. Click the Different First Page check box.

4. Click OK.

5. Go to the first page of the document or section—the one whose header or footer is to be different.

6. Choose View | Header and Footer. Now the header or footer box says "First Page Header" or "First Page Footer" to let you know that this header or footer can be different than the others in the section or the document:

First Page Header -Section 1-

7. Enter a header, a footer, or both. Or, leave the header and footer box blank if you don't want a header or footer on the first page.

Button	Button Name	What It Does
Insert AutoText ▾	Insert AutoText	Opens a drop-down list with options for inserting document information. For example, you can list when the document was last saved or printed, and the name of the person who created it.
📄	Insert Page Number	Lists the page number.
📄	Insert Number of Pages	Lists the total number of pages in the document. By typing **page**, clicking the Insert Page Number button, typing **of**, and clicking the Insert Number of Pages button, you can enter the following in a header or footer: **page 1 of 20**.
📄	Insert Date	Lists the date the document was printed (not today's date or the date the header or footer was created).
🕓	Insert Time	Lists the time the document was printed.

Table 7-2. *Header and Footer Functions*

Check this box to create different headers and footers for odd and even pages.

Check this box to have a different header and footer for the first page.

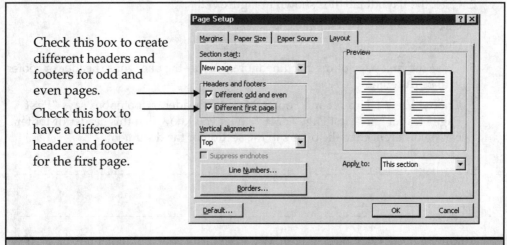

Figure 7-20. *From the Layout tab of the Page Setup dialog box, you can create headers and footers for first pages and odd and even pages*

8. Click the Close button on the Header and Footer toolbar.

Headers and Footers for Odd and Even Pages

In two-sided documents in which text is printed on both sides of the paper, sometimes the header and footer on the even page and the header and footer on the odd page are different. In the book you are holding in your hands, as a matter of fact, the headers on even pages tell you the title of the book, and the headers on odd pages tell you which chapter you are in.

You, too, can create different headers and footers for odd and even pages by following these steps:

1. Either click the Page Setup button on the Header and Footer toolbar or choose File | Page Setup. The Page Setup dialog box appears.

2. Click the Layout tab (see Figure 7-20).

3. Click the Different Odd And Even check box.

4. Click OK.

5. Move the cursor to an even page and choose View | Header and Footer. Now the Header and Footer boxes tell you that you are entering a header or footer that will appear only on even pages:

```
Even Page Header
```

6. Enter the header, the footer, or both for the even pages.

7. Move the cursor to an odd page and repeat steps 5 and 6.

8. Click the Close button on the Header and Footer toolbar.

Changing Headers or Footers in the Middle of a Document

To change headers or footers in the middle of a document, you must create a new section. When you create a new section, Word 2000 assumes you want to keep the same headers and footers throughout, and it runs the headers and footers from the previous section in the new section as well. However, suppose you want to create new headers and footers for the section you created. To do that, follow these steps:

1. Click in the section of the document in which you want to create new headers and footers.

2. Choose View | Header and Footer. The Header and Footer toolbar appears. This time, however, the Header (or Footer) box tells you which section you are in and that the header (or footer) is the same as that in the previous section as shown next.

```
Header -Section 2-                                              Same as Previous
Going Whole Hog: A Proposal for Excellence              Page 33
```

3. Click the Same as Previous button on the toolbar. Now the words "Same as Previous" disappear from the Header (or Footer) box and you can rest assured that the new header you type will be different from the old one.

4. Delete the header (or footer) contents and enter the new information.

5. Click the Close button on the Header and Footer toolbar.

 On the Header and Footer toolbar are buttons called Show Next and Show Previous. As you compose a new header (or footer), click these buttons to see what the header (or footer) in the next or previous section is.

Removing a Header or Footer

Removing a header or footer is pretty simple. All you have to do is put the header and footer onscreen either by choosing View | Headers and Footer or double-clicking the header or footer while the screen is in Page Layout view. Next, drag the pointer across the header or footer to select it. Then press DELETE.

The
Complete
Reference

Office
2000

Chapter 8

Working Faster
and Better

In my humble opinion, computers were invented not so you can marvel at how wonderful technology is, but so you can get your work done faster and better. In this chapter, you will find shortcuts, tips, and techniques designed to get you out of the office quicker. Or, if you work at home, the advice in this chapter will enable you to get away from your desk sooner so you can really start living.

This chapter provides instructions for moving around quickly in documents, viewing your work in different ways, and keeping errors to a minimum. You also learn how to select text, as well as two advanced techniques for copying text in Word 2000. This chapter also explains how to find and replace text and organize your documents better.

Moving Quickly in Documents

The more you work on a Word document, the longer it gets. And when documents start to get very long, it is difficult to move around in them quickly. How do you get to the last page of a document if you are on the first page? And if you are on page 37, how do you get quickly to the heading that you know is somewhere between page 14 and 19? This section explains techniques for getting there fast.

This section also explains keyboard and scrollbar techniques for moving around, how to use the Go To and Go Back command, and how to use the Select Browse Object button. You will also find instructions for moving around with the Document Map and for using bookmarks to mark the places you come back to often.

Keyboard and Scrollbar Techniques for Going Long Distances

When you have to get there in a hurry, the fastest way is to press either one of Word's keyboard shortcuts or use the scrollbars. The keyboard shortcuts are for people with nimble fingers; the scrollbars are for mouse mavens who prefer to click and drag. Both techniques are described in the following pages.

Getting Around by Pressing Shortcut Keys

Word offers a host of keyboard shortcuts for moving from place to place. Table 8-1 explains the most useful ones.

Tip	*Pressing* CTRL-PAGE UP *or* CTRL-PAGE DOWN *doesn't move the cursor to the top of the previous or following page if you or someone else clicked the Select Browse Object button at the bottom of the vertical scrollbar to move the cursor to the previous or next comment, heading, bookmark, or whatever. "Using the Select Browse Object Button to Get Around," the next topic in this chapter, explains how the Select Browse Object button works. Suffice it to say, if the arrows are blue on either side of the button, pressing* CTRL-PAGE UP *or* CTRL-PAGE DOWN *does not take you to the previous or following page.*

Key(s)	Where the Cursor Moves
CTRL-HOME	To the top of the document
CTRL-END	To the bottom of the document
CTRL-PAGE UP	To the top of the previous page
PAGE UP	Up the length of one screen
PAGE DOWN	Down the length of one screen
CTRL-PAGE DOWN	To the top of the following page

Table 8-1.   *Keyboard Shortcuts for Moving Around*

Getting Around with the Scrollbar

The other means of getting around quickly is to use the vertical scrollbar along the right side of the screen. Figure 8-1 labels the different parts of the vertical scrollbar. The following instructions explain how to use this valuable tool to get from place to place quickly:

To Move	Do This
Screen by screen	Click on the scrollbar but not on the scroll box or on the arrows.
Line by line	Click the single arrow at the top or bottom of the scrollbar.
Page by page	Click the double-arrows on either side of the Select Browse Object button. (Clicking the double-arrows when they are blue does not move the cursor page by page, but moves the cursor to the previous or next comment, heading, bookmark, or whatever.)
Very quickly up and down	Drag the scroll box, the square on the scrollbar, shown in Figure 8-1. As you drag, a box appears and tells you which page will be displayed.

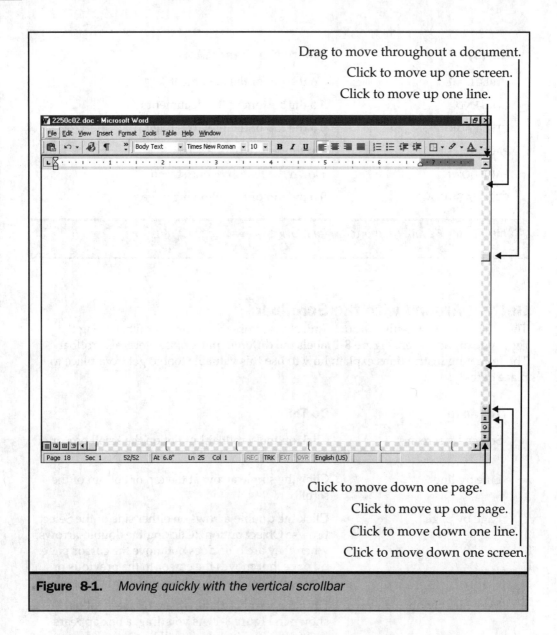

Drag to move throughout a document.
Click to move up one screen.
Click to move up one line.

Click to move down one page.
Click to move up one page.
Click to move down one line.
Click to move down one screen.

Figure 8-1. *Moving quickly with the vertical scrollbar*

If you have assigned heading styles to the headings in your document, heading names appear as well when you drag the scroll box, as shown in the following illustration.

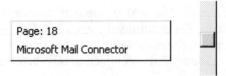

Page: 18
Microsoft Mail Connector

WORD

Tip *If the double-arrows on the bottom of the vertical scrollbar are blue but you want them to be black so you can move from page to page, click the Select Browse Object button and then click the Browse by Page button on the drop-down menu.*

By the way, a horizontal scroll bar lies along the bottom of the Word screen. Click its arrows or drag its scroll box to move a wide document from side to side onscreen so you can see either end of it.

LEARN BY EXAMPLE
The Figure 8-1 (Moving Around) file on the companion CD provides a long sample document in case you want to practice the keyboard and scrollbar techniques described here for moving around.

EXAMPLES

Using the Select Browse Object Button to Get Around

Another way to get from place to place quickly is to click the Select Browse Object button. This button, a round one, is in the lower-right corner of the screen. To begin with, the double-arrows on either side of it are black; if you click the double-arrows, the cursor moves either to the previous page or the next page. However, you can tell Word to move the cursor to other places by making a choice from the Select Browse Object menu.

Click the Select Browse Object button and you see a drop-down menu with buttons. Each button represents either a command or a different element that you can move the cursor to. For example, in the following illustration, the cursor is on the Browse by Heading button. If you click this button, Word moves the cursor to the next heading in the document:

After you click a button on the Select Browse Object menu, the double-arrows on either side of the button turn blue. Now when you click the double-arrows, the cursor moves either to the previous or the next example of the element you chose from the Select Browse Object menu. For example, if you choose Browse by Heading and then click the blue double-arrows, the cursor moves either to the previous or the next heading in the document, depending on which double-arrows you click.

 Choosing Browse by Page on the Select Browse Object menu tells Word to move the cursor from page to page. After this option is chosen, the double-arrows turn black.

The Select Browse Object button is excellent for moving quickly from element to element in a document. Instead of giving commands over and over again, all you have to do is click the blue double-arrows.

 The Find and Go To buttons on the Select Browse Object menu open, respectively, the Find tab and the Go To tab in the Find and Replace dialog box so you can give commands for finding text or moving the cursor to a specific part of a document. What's more, choosing Edit | Go To or Edit | Find from the menu bar and giving a command also turns the double-arrows beside the Select Browse Object button blue. After you give those commands, you can click the blue double-arrows to move around in a document.

 LEARN BY EXAMPLE
On the companion CD is a sample file called Figure 8-A (Browsing). It includes all the elements listed in the Select Browse Object menu. Use this sample file to experiment with the Select Browse Object button.

Using the Go To Command to Move to Numbered Pages and More

The Go To command can get you very quickly to numbered items in a document: page numbers, bookmark numbers, footnote numbers, and line numbers, for example. You can get there directly by telling Word the number of the item you want to get to, or you can click dialog box buttons to jump from item to item.

 "Numbers, Numbers, and More Numbers" in Chapter 11 explains how to number the lines and headings in a document.

Follow these steps to use the Go To command to get from place to place:

1. Choose Edit | Go To, press F5, or click the Select Browse Object button and choose Go To on the drop-down list. As shown in Figure 8-2, you see the Go To tab of the Find and Replace dialog box.

2. In the Go To What scroll list, choose the item you want to move the cursor to.

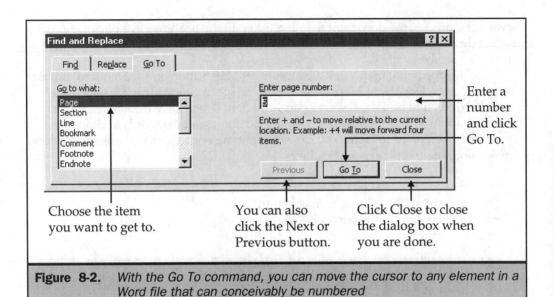

Figure 8-2.   With the Go To command, you can move the cursor to any element in a Word file that can conceivably be numbered

3. Choose how you want to get there:

- Click the Next or Previous button to go to the following or previous instance of the item you want to get to.

- Enter a number in the Enter Number box and click the Go To button to get there (the name of the box changes, depending on what you are trying to get to).

- Enter a plus or minus sign and a number to skip ahead or skip behind several instances of the item you want to get to.

4. Word takes you to the item, but the dialog box stays open in case you want to keep searching. You can click buttons all over again, or make a new entry in the Enter Number box if you want.

5. Click Close.

LEARN BY EXAMPLE
Check out the Figure 8-2 (Go To) file on the companion CD if you want to experiment with the Go To command.

Moving Around with the Document Map

As long as you applied heading styles to the headings in a document, you can get from place to place very quickly with the document map (Chapter 9 explains styles). As shown in Figure 8-3, the document map is a list of all the headings in a document. By scrolling down the list and clicking on the heading you want to move to, you can get there very quickly.

To see the document map, click the Document Map button on the Standard toolbar or choose View | Document Map. To move the cursor to a heading, click on it. You may have to scroll to find the heading you want first. If you have trouble reading a heading, point to it with the cursor. As Figure 8-3 shows, all the words in headings appear when you point to them. You can also drag the border of the headings window to make more room onscreen for headings.

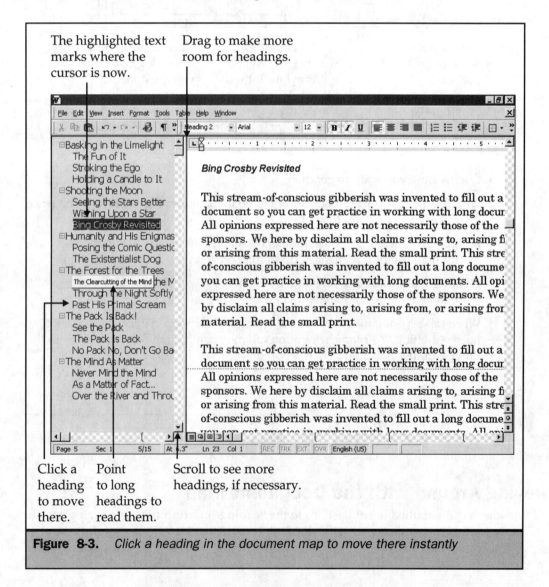

The highlighted text marks where the cursor is now.

Drag to make more room for headings.

Click a heading to move there.

Point to long headings to read them.

Scroll to see more headings, if necessary.

Figure 8-3. *Click a heading in the document map to move there instantly*

Click the Document Map button again or choose View | Document Map to leave Document Map view.

EXAMPLES

LEARN BY EXAMPLE
The Figure 8-3 (Document Map) file on the companion CD includes lots of headings in case you want to play around in Document Map view.

Using Bookmarks to Get from Place to Place

One way to get from place to place is to mark the places to which you will often return with bookmarks. Then, all you have to do to go to a place you've marked is choose Insert | Bookmark or use the Go To dialog box. As you will learn throughout this book, bookmarks have many uses. For example, in order to create a hyperlink or cross-reference to a sentence or paragraph in a document, you have to create a bookmark in the sentence or paragraph first.

To mark a place in a document with a bookmark, do the following:

1. Click where you want the bookmark to go.

2. Choose Insert | Bookmark. The Bookmark dialog box appears, as shown in Figure 8-4.

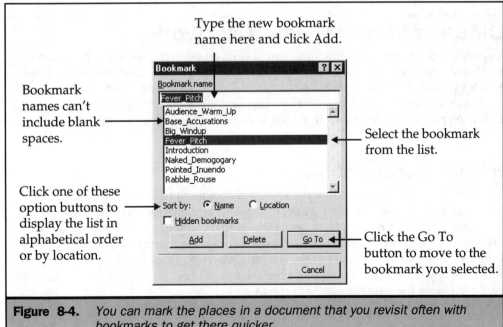

Figure 8-4. *You can mark the places in a document that you revisit often with bookmarks to get there quicker*

3. Type a name in the Bookmark Name box. Bookmark names can't include spaces, but you can get around that by typing underscores where spaces would go.

4. Click the Add button.

Follow these steps to move to a spot in a document that you've marked with a bookmark:

1. Choose Insert | Bookmark.

2. Either double-click the bookmark or click it and then click the Go To button. To help find the right bookmark, click the Name radio button to arrange the names on the list in alphabetical order, or click the Location radio button to arrange them by order in the document.

3. Click the Go To button.

To delete a bookmark, click its name in the Bookmark dialog box and then click the Delete button.

LEARN BY EXAMPLE
To try your hand at using bookmarks, open the Figure 8-4 (Bookmarks) file on the companion CD that comes with this book.

Different Ways to View Your Work

Depending on the kind of work you want to do, you might try viewing the screen in a different way. Normal view, for example, is good for writing first drafts, but when you want to focus on the layout, Print Layout view is best. Word offers six views in all. Each is explained in this section. And, in case you want to be in two places at once, the following pages also discuss how to split the screen and view more than one document at a time.

Word's Six Document Views

Figure 8-5 demonstrates the six ways to view a document in Word. Table 8-2, meanwhile, describes each view. Each view has its advantages and disadvantages, but the important thing for you to remember is that changing views is easy. You can change views either by choosing commands on the View menu or by clicking the View buttons in the lower-left corner of the screen. (One view, Print Preview, was designed for reviewing documents before you print them, but I find this view so valuable that I count it among the views that Word offers.)

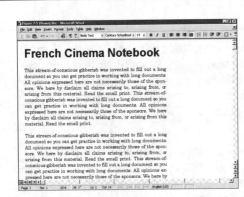

A. Normal view

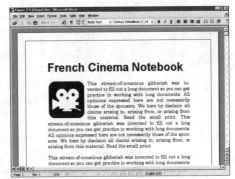

B. Print Layout view

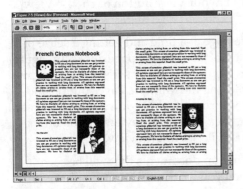

C. Print Preview view

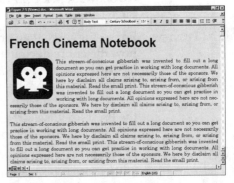

D. Web Layout view

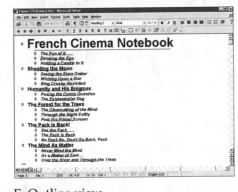

E. Outline view

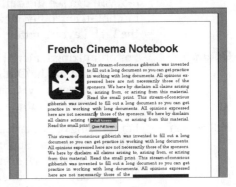

F. Full Screen view

Figure 8-5.   *The six ways to view a document in Word*

WORD

View	Description
Normal	For writing first drafts and doing basic editing work. In Normal view, you can concentrate on the words. Sophisticated layouts, including graphics, either do not appear in Normal view or appear in the wrong places, as Figure 8-5 demonstrates. Click the Normal View button or choose View | Normal to switch to Normal view.
Print Layout	For laying out documents. In Print Layout view, you can see precisely where columns begin and end, where the page's edges are, and where graphics and text boxes appear. In addition to graphics, page borders appear in Print Layout view, as Figure 8-5 shows. Click the Print Layout View button or choose View | Page Layout.
Print Preview	For seeing more than one page at a time and getting a sense of how the entire document, not just a single page, looks. In Figure 8-5, two pages appear on the Print Preview screen, but you can display many more by clicking the Multiple Pages button and selecting several page icons from the drop-down menu. To get to the Print Preview screen, click the Print Preview button on the Standard toolbar or choose File | Print Preview.
Web Layout	For laying out and dressing up documents that will be seen online. Use this view when you work on documents that won't be printed, but will be seen only on computer screens. In Figure 8-5, you can see the dark page background in Web Layout view, but not in any other view. Choose View | Web Layout or click the Web Layout button.
Outline	For organizing material into headings. In Figure 8-5, I clicked the 2 button on the Outline toolbar to display first and second level headings only. Chapter 11 describes Outline view in detail. Choose View | Outline or click the Outline View button.
Full Screen	For focusing on the task at hand. In Full Screen view, the menus, toolbars, status bar, and taskbar are stripped from the screen so you can see what the document will look like when it is printed. To give commands, either use keyboard shortcuts, right-click to see shortcut menus, or slide the pointer to the top of the screen, which makes the menu bar appear so you can choose commands. Choose View | Full screen to switch to Full Screen view. To leave Full Screen view, click the Close Full Screen button or press the ESC key.

Table 8-2.   *Word's Six Views*

LEARN BY EXAMPLE
If you would like to test-drive Word's different views, open the Figure 8-5 (Views) file on the companion CD.

Working in More Than One Place at a Time

Word offers commands for working on many documents at the same time and for working on different parts of the same document. I can think of hundreds of reasons for using these valuable commands. For example, you might open a second document so you can review it and perhaps copy text from it to the document you are working on. And when you are working on a long report, you might split the screen or open a second window so you can see two parts of the document at the same time and make sure that the work is well organized.

The following pages explain how to split the screen so you can see two different parts of the same document, put two different documents onscreen at the same time, and open a second (or third or fourth) window on the same document so you can work on several parts at the same time.

Splitting the Screen

Splitting the screen means placing one part of a document on the top half of the screen and another part on the bottom half. Split the screen when you want to compare parts of the same document or move text from one part to another. Figure 8-6 shows an example of a split screen.

Follow these steps to split the screen:

1. Choose Window | Split. A gray line appears across the middle of the screen. On the gray line is a cursor with two arrows that point north and south.

2. Move the cursor up or down to the place where the screen is to be split.

3. Click the mouse button.

After the screen has been split, a solid gray line appears across the screen and scrollbars appear on either side of the split. Use the scrollbars or press shortcut keys to move to new places in the document. To move from one half of the split to the other, click in the other half or press F6. You can adjust the split by dragging the gray line to a new location.

Choose Window | Remove Split to end the schizophrenic arrangement and get a single screen again.

You can also split the screen by clicking on the tiny box above the up arrow on the vertical scrollbar and dragging the gray line to the middle of the screen.

Opening Several Windows on a Document

Besides splitting the screen, another way to view more than one part of a document is to open more windows. With this technique, you open another window on the document.

Drag the gray line to adjust the split.

Choose Window | Remove Split to "unsplit" the screen.

Click the scrollbars to move around in either half of the screen.

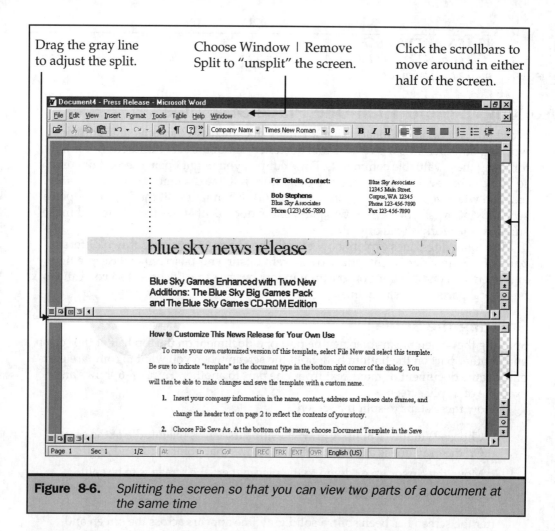

Figure 8-6. *Splitting the screen so that you can view two parts of a document at the same time*

Then, in the window you just opened, you scroll to an important place that you intend to visit often. After that, when you want to revisit that place, you choose it on the Window menu.

On the Window menu shown here are five different windows of the same document. Each view is numbered. The check mark tells which window is onscreen. To switch to another window, simply choose it on the menu, as shown next.

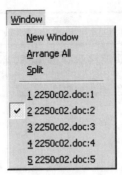

Follow these instructions to open and close new windows on a document:

- **Opening**   To open a new window on a document, choose Window | New Window.

- **Closing**   To close a window, click its Close button. The Close button is the × in the upper-right corner of the screen. Be sure to click the document window's Close button, not Word's Close button:

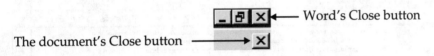

Note No matter how many windows of a single document are open, all work is saved to the same document file. You are working on a single document, not on several, when you choose Window | New Window and work in a second window on a document.

Viewing More Than One Document

Chapter 2 explained how to open several files at once and go from one file to the other by choosing its name on the Window menu. Another way to work on several files at once is to put them all onscreen. However, viewing several files at once is only good for comparing files and maybe copying or moving text from one file to another. When more than two files are onscreen, there isn't enough room to do any work.

To place several Word documents onscreen at the same time, follow these steps:

1. Open all the files that you want to see onscreen.

2. Choose Window | Arrange All. Word endeavors to squeeze all the files on the screen, as shown in Figure 8-7.

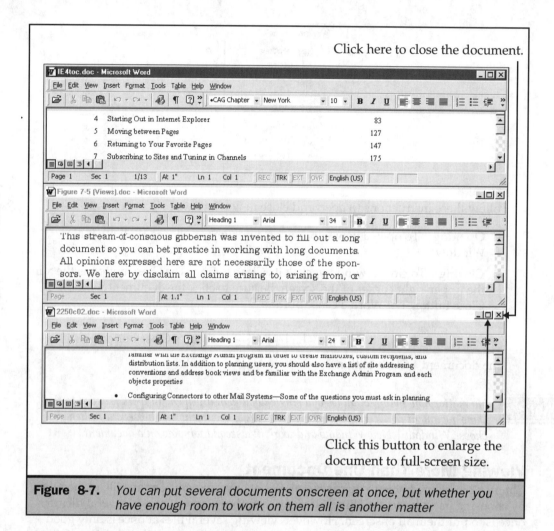

Click here to close the document.

Click this button to enlarge the document to full-screen size.

Figure 8-7. *You can put several documents onscreen at once, but whether you have enough room to work on them all is another matter*

After the documents are onscreen, click in the one you want to work on. To close a document, click its Close button (the ×). To enlarge a document so you can work on it, click its Maximize button. The document grows to full-screen size. You can shrink a document that is full-screen size by clicking its Restore button (the button shows two overlapping squares).

Techniques for Entering Text and Graphics Quickly

In your work, you no doubt enter certain things over and over again in Word documents. Your address, for example. Or the name of the company you work for.

Perhaps a logo or other graphic. The following pages offer techniques for entering text and graphics quickly without having to retype or re-enter them.

AutoText for Entering Text and Graphics

Word has a special feature called AutoText for entering the blurbs, salutations, and what-all that people enter time and time again as they write letters, construct headers and footers, and do other things besides. By creating an AutoText entry or choosing one from Word's list, you spare yourself the trouble of typing them yourself. And you can also insert a graphic as an AutoText entry and spare yourself the considerable trouble of importing it, resizing it, and perhaps changing its color or hue. This section explains how to insert an AutoText entry as well as devise AutoText entries of your own.

Inserting an AutoText Entry in a Document

Figure 8-8 shows the AutoText entries on the Closing submenu. Click one of these entries to close a letter and save yourself the trouble of typing "Love," "Respectfully

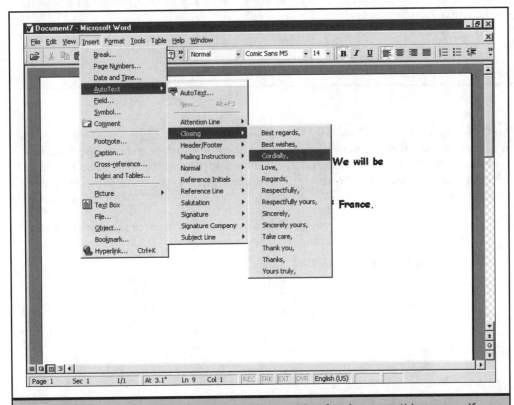

Figure 8-8. *AutoText entries save you the trouble of typing something yourself*

yours," "Yours truly," or another letter closing. To insert one of Word's AutoText entries, follow these steps:

1. Place the cursor where the words in the AutoText entry should go.
2. Choose Insert | AutoText.
3. On the submenu, click the name of the category in which the AutoText entry you want to make is found. In Figure 8-8, the category is "Closing." AutoText entries you create yourself appear on the Normal submenu.
4. On the submenu, click the word or words you want to insert.

"Automatic" AutoText Entries

AutoText entries on the Normal, Signature, and Signature Company submenus can be entered without choosing Insert | AutoText. To enter one of those AutoText entries, type the first four letters. After the fourth letter, a small box appears and lists the rest of the AutoText entry. Press the ENTER key or F3 at that point to insert the entire AutoText entry:

> The Flying Weverkas
>
> "Yes, ma'am, I'm a trapeze artist, a member of The F|

Creating Your Own AutoText Entries

Besides making use of the generic AutoText entries in Word, you can create AutoText entries of your own. Homemade AutoText entries appear on the Normal submenu (choose Insert | AutoText | Normal). Follow these steps to create an AutoText entry of your own:

1. Enter or create the address, graphic, slogan, motto, logo, or whatnot that you want to be an AutoText entry.
2. Select the item you just created.

3. Choose Insert | AutoText | New. You see the Create AutoText dialog box:

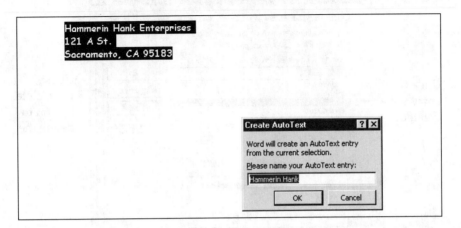

4. Word 2000 enters the first few words of the entry (if yours is a text entry), but you can enter a name of your own by typing it in the text box.

5. Click OK.

Deleting AutoText Entries

The AutoText submenus are crowded with AutoText entries, some of which you no doubt will never need or use. Therefore, you might consider pruning the list of AutoText entries to make the ones you do want easier to find. And if you change addresses or change names, you would have to delete a homemade AutoText entry, too.

Follow these steps to delete an AutoText entry:

1. Choose Insert | AutoText, and then click AutoText. As shown in Figure 8-9, you see the AutoText tab of the AutoCorrect dialog box.

2. Find and click the AutoText entry you want to delete. The entries are in alphabetical order below the Enter AutoText Entries Here box.

3. Click the Delete button.

4. Click the Close button.

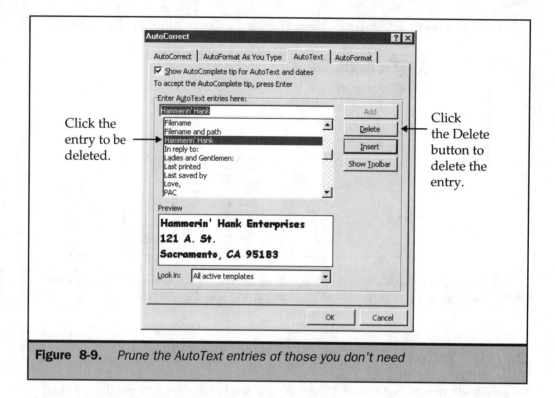

Click the entry to be deleted.

Click the Delete button to delete the entry.

Figure 8-9.   *Prune the AutoText entries of those you don't need*

Using the AutoCorrect Feature to Enter Text Quickly

Chapter 3 explains Office 2000's AutoCorrect mechanism. Even if you haven't read that chapter yet, you must have encountered AutoCorrect by now. When you start a sentence in Word with a lowercase letter, for example, Word automatically changes the lowercase letter to an uppercase letter. Try misspelling the word "weird" by typing it this way: **wierd**—Word immediately fixes the misspelling for you. With the AutoCorrect feature, you can tell Word 2000 to correct—I mean autocorrect—the spelling errors that you make over and over again.

Although it wasn't necessarily designed that way, you can also use the AutoCorrect feature to quickly enter text. For example, suppose you are writing the definitive work about the Scotsman Thomas of Erceldoune, also know as Thomas the Rhymer, the thirteenth-century poet and seer. Rather than type "Thomas of Erceldoune" over and over again in the course of the work, you could arrange things so that every time you type **Erc/**, Word spells out "Thomas of Erceldoune."

To use the AutoCorrect feature to enter text quickly, follow these steps:

1. Choose Tools | AutoCorrect. The AutoCorrect dialog box appears, as shown in Figure 8-10.

2. In the Replace box, enter a code for the long word or phrase that you intend to enter over and over again. For "Thomas of Erceldoune," for example, you could enter **Erc/**.

Caution   *Make sure that what you enter in the Replace box is not a real word. For example, if I enter "toe" for "Thomas of Erceldoune" and later try to write that word, the program will autocorrect the word "toe." "I stubbed my toe" would become "I stubbed my Thomas of Erceldoune."*

3. In the With box, enter the word or phrase.

4. Click the Add button.

Each time you need to enter the long word or phrase, type the three or four characters you entered in the Replace box; then press the SPACEBAR, press ENTER, press TAB, or type a punctuation mark. Word will automatically correct your entry.

Both AutoText and AutoCorrect work quickly to replace commonly used text. They both require you to take a moment to enter the word or phrase that you want Word to finish for you. The question you have to answer in deciding which to use is, do you want a little dialog box to appear or do you want Word to just finish the phrase for

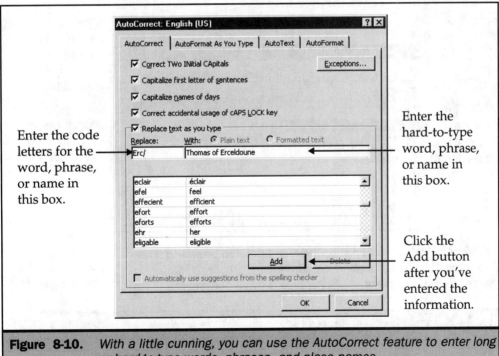

Enter the code letters for the word, phrase, or name in this box.

Enter the hard-to-type word, phrase, or name in this box.

Click the Add button after you've entered the information.

Figure 8-10.   *With a little cunning, you can use the AutoCorrect feature to enter long or hard-to-type words, phrases, and place names*

WORD

you? If your word or phrase could easily be mistaken for another word, it is best to use AutoText, if not, you may prefer to use AutoCorrect.

Searching for the Right Word with the Thesaurus

Choosing the right word—*le mot juste*—is so important in writing that the French invented a special phrase for it and Microsoft included a thesaurus with its word processor. As you write, use the thesaurus to find synonyms—words that have the same or a similar meaning. The thesaurus is invaluable.

To find a synonym for a word, follow these steps:

1. Click the word for which you want a synonym.

2. Press SHIFT-F7 or choose Tools | Language | Thesaurus. You see the Thesaurus dialog box shown in Figure 8-11.

3. Commence a search for the right word.

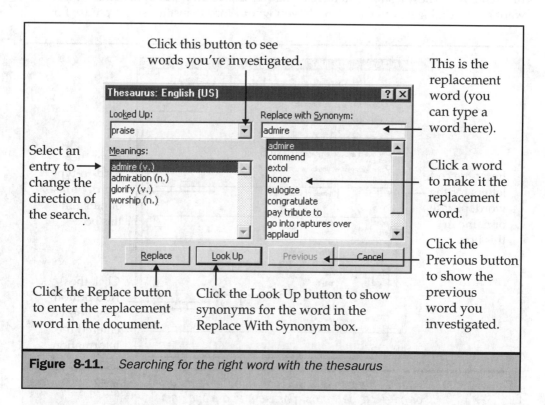

Click this button to see words you've investigated.

This is the replacement word (you can type a word here).

Select an entry to change the direction of the search.

Click a word to make it the replacement word.

Click the Previous button to show the previous word you investigated.

Click the Replace button to enter the replacement word in the document.

Click the Look Up button to show synonyms for the word in the Replace With Synonym box.

Figure 8-11. *Searching for the right word with the thesaurus*

4. Click the Replace button when you've found a good synonym and it appears in the Replace With Synonym box.

Word replaces the word you clicked in step 1 with the word in the Replace With Synonym box.

> **Tip** *If you can't quite think of the word you want but you know its antonym (its opposite), try opening the Thesaurus dialog box and seeing if the antonym has an antonym. The antonym of the antonym might be the synonym you are looking for. For example, if you need the word that means the opposite of "praise," try looking up "praise" in the thesaurus. If Antonyms appears in the Meanings box, click Antonyms and see if you can find the opposite of "praise" that way.*

Fast Ways to Select Text

Numerous word processing tasks require you to select text first. Before you can change fonts or point sizes, you have to select text. Before you can delete text, you have to select it. Before you can move or copy text, you have to select it. Learn the many ways to select text in Word, and you can become a much faster worker. The following pages explain speedy ways to select text.

Selecting Text with the Mouse

Table 8-3 describes techniques for selecting text with the mouse. To select some kinds of text, you click in the left margin. You can tell when the pointer is selecting an entire line of text because it points to the upper-right corner of the screen, not to the upper-left corner, as is usually the case.

> **Tip** *You can also select an entire document by choosing Edit | Select All or by pressing CTRL-A.*

"Extending" a Selection

Besides using the mouse, you can press F8 or double-click EXT (for "extend") on the status bar to select text. With this technique, you click where you want to start selecting text, press F8 or double-click EXT, and then click at the opposite side of the text you want to select. For example, to select the paragraph you are reading at this very moment, you would click at the start of the paragraph before the *B* in "Besides," press F8 or double-click EXT, and then click after the period at the end of this sentence.

By the way, all the keyboard shortcuts for moving the cursor also work for selecting text after you press F8 or double-click EXT. For example, press F8 and then press CTRL-END to select everything from the cursor to the end of the document. Or double-click EXT and press HOME to select to the start of the line.

To Select This	Do This
A word	Double-click the word.
A line	Click in the selection bar next to the line.
Several lines	Drag the mouse over the lines or down the selection bar. You can also click at the start of the text you want to select, hold down the SHIFT key, click at the end of the text, and release the SHIFT key.
A paragraph	Double-click in the selection bar next to the paragraph or triple-click in the paragraph.
A document	Press CTRL-A, triple-click in the selection bar, or CTRL-click in the selection bar.

Table 8-3.   *Selecting Text with the Mouse*

Watch Out for the Paragraph Symbol When You Select Text

When you select text, whether you select the paragraph symbol at the end of paragraphs means a lot (click the Show/Hide button to see the paragraph symbols that Word puts at the end of paragraphs). In effect, the paragraph symbol holds all the formatting for the paragraph. For example, if you select text that is indented by an inch and you select it along with its paragraph symbol, it will be indented by an inch in the new location to which you move or copy it. On the other hand, if you select the text without selecting the paragraph symbol, the paragraph will be indented however far other text is indented in the location to which you move or copy it.

To select paragraph symbols when you select text, click in the selection bar when you make the selection. For example, double-clicking in the selection bar to select a paragraph selects the paragraph symbol as well as the text, but dragging the cursor over all the text in the paragraph selects all the text in the paragraph, but not the paragraph symbol.

Tip   *If a bunch of highlighted text is onscreen and you want the highlight to go away but it won't (because you pressed F8 or double-clicked EXT to select it), double-click EXT again or press ESC.*

Advanced Techniques for Copying and Moving Text

It almost goes without saying, but copying and moving text are two of the most common word processing chores. Why enter text all over again when you can copy from a document or paragraph you've already written, or move it from another place in the document you are working on? The following pages explain advanced techniques for copying and moving text.

Copying Text Quickly

Word offers many ways to copy text from one place to another. By one place to another, I mean from one part of a document to another, from one document to another document, and even from one program to another program. What's more, you can copy a single character to a new place, copy several paragraphs at once, or even insert an entire document into the document you are working on.

The following pages describe advanced techniques for copying text. Table 8-4 describes ways to copy text in Word.

Copy Technique	How It Works
Choose Edit | Copy	After you choose the Copy command, give a Paste command to copy the text.
Press CTRL-C	This is the keyboard shortcut for copying text.
Click the Copy button	The Copy button, located on the Standard toolbar, also copies text to the Clipboard.
Right-click and choose Copy from the shortcut menu	Shortcut menus also offer commands for copying and pasting text.
Press SHIFT-F2	After you press SHIFT-F2, move the insertion point where you want to copy the text, and then press ENTER.
Choose Insert | File	Copies an entire file into a document.
Drag the text to the Windows desktop	Creates a document scrap—an icon you can drag into a document for copying purposes.
Select the text to be copied, then hold down the CTRL key as you drag the text to a new location	This is the drag-and-drop copying technique. Text is not copied to the Clipboard with this technique.

Table 8-4.   *Techniques for Copying Text*

Comparing the Copy Techniques

Which copy technique is best for you? It depends on how adept you are with the mouse and keyboard, how many documents you are working on, and how far you want to copy text.

The quickest way to copy text is to use the drag-and-drop method, but to use it you have to be good with the mouse, and both the text you are copying and the place where you want to copy it have to be onscreen at the same time.

By choosing Edit | Copy, pressing CTRL-C, or clicking the Copy button, you copy the text to the Clipboard. With that done, you can paste the text several pages back or forth in a document, in another document, in another window, or even in another Windows-based application. Copy text to the Clipboard when you want to copy it long distances or when you want to copy it several times into a document.

To copy text from many places, use document scraps, which are explained later in this chapter. You can insert document scraps in any order you wish.

Word offers two other techniques for copying text. You can link objects as described in Chapter 5, so that changes made to the original are made instantaneously to the copy. And with the AutoText feature, you can copy addresses, company names, quotations or anything else into a document by clicking a few buttons (AutoText is explained earlier in this chapter).

Copying Text with Drag-and-Drop

The fastest way to copy text is to "drag-and-drop" it. Use this technique to copy text to new locations on the screen. In theory, you can drag-and-drop text across a split window or from one open window to another, but that is more trouble than it's worth, because the screen has a habit of scrolling erratically when you drag text into a new window.

To copy text with the drag-and-drop method:

1. Select the text you want to copy.

2. Position the mouse over the text so the mouse pointer changes into an arrow.

3. Hold down the CTRL key, and then click and hold the mouse button down. A box appears below the pointer.

4. Drag the text to a new location.

5. Let up on the mouse button and release the CTRL key.

 Don't forget to hold the CTRL key down when you drag-and-drop the text. If you don't hold it down, you will move the text instead of copying it.

Besides being the fastest way to copy text, the drag-and-drop method has another advantage: It doesn't disturb what is on the Clipboard. If you've gone to the trouble of copying an ornate logo or long-winded passage to the Clipboard, you can keep it there and still copy text by using the drag-and-drop method.

Copying Text by Pressing SHIFT-F2

Word 2000 offers another way to copy text without disturbing the Clipboard. What's more, you can use this technique to copy text to parts of a document that aren't onscreen or to other documents. To use this technique:

1. Select the text you want to copy.

2. Press SHIFT-F2. The status bar reads, "Copy to where?"

3. Move the cursor where you want to copy the text. To get there, you can click on the scroll bar, press keys to move the cursor, switch to another document, or open another document.

4. Press ENTER.

Copying Scraps for a Document

Suppose you want to copy text from many places and assemble the text in a single document. That is hard to do with conventional copying techniques. You have to open one document, copy text, open another document, paste the text there, and start all over again. You could get a blister on your clicking finger that way.

Lucky for you, Word 2000 offers document scraps, a handy technique for copying text from many documents. With this technique, you drag the text you want to copy onto the Windows desktop. Then, with the text arranged neatly in "scraps" on the desktop, you drag the scraps into a document one at a time.

To copy text with the document scraps method:

1. Select the text you want to copy.

2. Click the Restore button in the upper-right corner of the Word 2000 window to make the window smaller onscreen. At this point, you should see a patch of naked desktop to the right of the Word 2000 window, as shown in Figure 8-12. Beginning with step 3, you will drag document scraps onto the desktop. If you intend to create several document scraps, you need room for all of them. Drag the Word window to the left side of the desktop by clicking and dragging its title bar. You might also shrink the window by dragging its borders.

3. Drag the text you selected onto the desktop to copy it there. You don't have to hold down the CTRL key to copy the text. Simply hold the mouse button on the text you selected in step 1, roll your mouse until the text is on the desktop, and then release the mouse.

   As Figure 8-12 shows, Word creates a document scrap—an icon that appears to be torn at the bottom. The document scrap has a name to help you identify it. The name comes from the first few words of the text you copied, but you can change the name by right-clicking, choosing Rename from the shortcut menu, and typing a new name. A document scrap is a mini-file. By right-clicking on it, you can do a number of things from the shortcut menu, including deleting the document scrap. You can also drag document scraps to new places on the desktop.

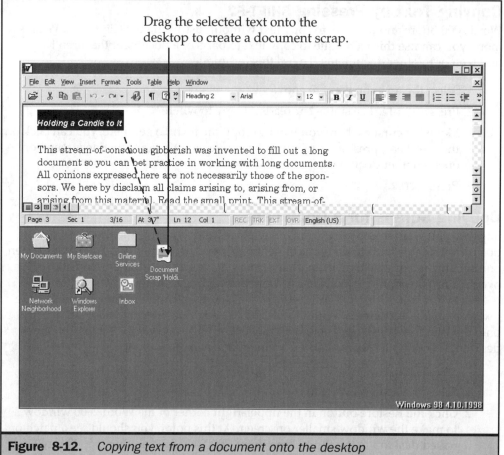

Drag the selected text onto the
desktop to create a document scrap.

Figure 8-12. *Copying text from a document onto the desktop*

Tip *If Windows is set up to "autoarrange" icons on the desktop, document scraps appear on the left side of the desktop when you copy them. To be able to drag document scraps on the desktop, you must tell Windows not to autoarrange the icons. To do that, right-click on the desktop, click Arrange Icons, and click Auto Arrange to remove the check mark from that option.*

4. Select more text from the document that is open, or else open another document and select text from it.

5. Drag the next document scrap onto the desktop. You can put as many scraps on the desktop as you wish, provided you make room for them and you can remember what all of them are. Figure 8-13 shows several scraps on the Windows 95 desktop.

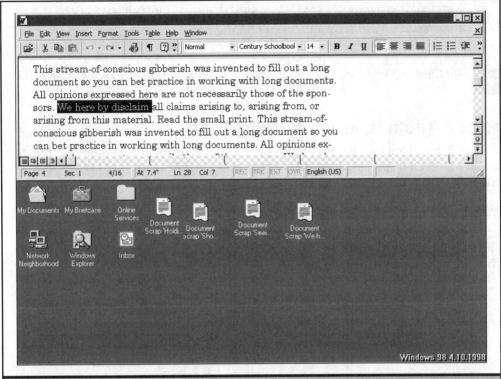

Figure 8-13.   *Paste scraps in a document by dragging them from the desktop to a Word 2000 document*

After you copy all the scraps to the desktop, you are ready to paste them one at a time in a Word 2000 document:

1. Open the document that is to receive all the scraps and scroll to the place where the first scrap is to be copied.

2. Click the Restore buttons so that you can see both your document and the scraps on the desktop.

3. Drag a scrap from the desktop to the document. As you drag, a dotted line shows you where the text will go when you release the mouse button.

4. One by one, copy each scrap into your document.

When you are done, the document scraps remain on the Windows desktop. To remove them, right-click each scrap and choose Delete from the shortcut menu. When Word asks if you are sure you want to delete the scraps, click Yes.

You can delete all the scraps at once by holding down the CTRL key and clicking on each one. When all have been selected, either right-click on a scrap and choose Delete from the shortcut menu or press the DELETE key. Word asks if you want to delete them all. Click Yes.

 See Chapter 3 for information about using the Clipboard toolbar to copy and paste.

Advanced Technique for Moving Text

Chapter 3 explained how to move text by cutting and pasting it elsewhere. Cutting text to and pasting it from the Clipboard is fine if you're not in a hurry, but Word also offers an advanced technique for moving text.

Moving Text with Drag-and-Drop

Use the drag-and-drop technique to move text from one onscreen location to another. This technique doesn't work unless the place the text comes from and the place it will go to both appear on screen. To move text with the drag-and-drop method:

1. Select the text.
2. Slide the mouse over the text until the mouse pointer changes into an arrow.
3. Click and hold the mouse button down. A box appears below the pointer.
4. Drag the text to move it to a new location.
5. Release the mouse button.

Finding and Replacing Text and Other Things

This section explains how to find text or formats in a document and how, if necessary, to replace them. Being able to find text or a format is important if you have to make a hasty, last-minute change. In any case, finding text or formats in a Word document takes but a few seconds and is far easier than reading a document to find whatever it is you are looking for. Finding and replacing text or formats is a great advantage, too. If you were writing the great American novel and you called the main character Jane but later decided to change her name to Jean, you could find Jane and replace her name with Jean throughout the hundreds of pages in your novel in about five seconds.

Finding Text and Text Formats in Documents

The following pages explain how to search for words, phrases, and formats in a document, as well as punctuation marks, section breaks, and other oddities.

Searching for Words and Phrases

To search for a word or phrase in a document, follow these steps:

1. Choose Edit | Find or press CTRL-F. You see the Find and Replace dialog box.

2. If necessary, click the Find tab. The Find tab is shown in Figure 8-14. (Figure 8-14 shows the Find and Replace dialog box after clicking the More button.)

3. Type the word or phrase you are looking for in the Find What box.

Tip   *The Find What drop-down box lists the words and phrases you looked for recently. Click the down-arrow and choose a word or phrase if you already looked for it once since the last time you opened Word 2000.*

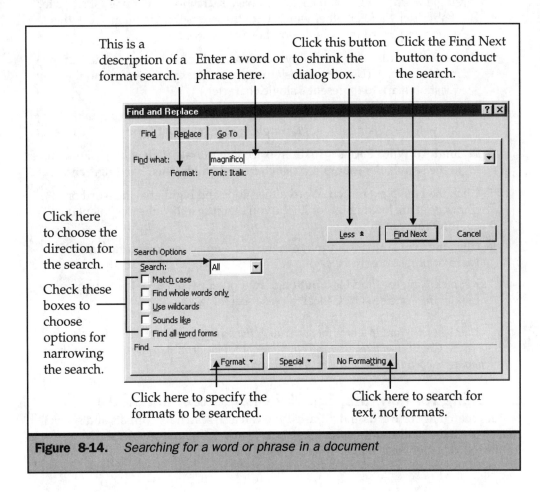

Figure 8-14.   *Searching for a word or phrase in a document*

4. To make the search go faster, you can click the More button and choose search options. When you click More, the dialog box grows larger and the following options appear:

- **Search** Tells Word in which direction to search. Up searches from the cursor position to the start of the document; Down searches from the cursor position to the end of the document.

- **Match Case** Finds words with upper- and lowercase letters that exactly match those of the word or phrase you entered in the Find What box. For example, a search for "sit" finds that word but not "Sit" or "SIT."

- **Find Whole Words Only** Be sure to click this box if you are looking for single words. Unless you click this box, a search for "sit" finds "sits," "site," "babysitter," and all other words with the letters "sit" in them. Click this option and Word finds "sit," not those other words.

- **Use Wildcards** Click here if you entered wildcards such as * and ? in the Find What box. (Use the asterisk to represent many characters and the question mark to represent a single character.)

- **Sounds Like** With this option, Word looks for words that sound like the one you are looking for. For example, a search for "sit" finds "set" as well.

- **Find All Word Forms** Takes into account plurals, verb endings, and tenses in the search. For example, a search for "sit" finds "sits," "sitting," and "sat."

5. Click the Find Next button. Word either finds and highlights the word or phrase you are looking for, or it tells you that it searched the document but couldn't find anything.

6. Click the Less button to shrink the Find and Replace dialog box and see the word or phrase onscreen.

7. Keep clicking the Find Next button to find other instances of the thing you are looking for, or else click Cancel to cease searching.

After you tell Word to search for something, the arrows on either side of the Select Browse Object turn blue. You can click one of the blue arrows to search again without having to open the Find and Replace dialog box.

Searching for Formats, Special Characters, and More

Besides searching for words and phrases, you can also search for formats and special characters in the Find and Replace dialog box. Figure 8-14, for example, shows a search for the word "magnifico" in italics, italics being the format.

SEARCHING FOR A FORMAT   To search for a format, follow these steps:

1. Choose Edit | Find or press CTRL-F to open the Find and Replace dialog box (see Figure 8-14).

2. If you are looking for a word or phrase that has been formatted a certain way, enter the word or phrase in the Find What box.

3. Click the More button, if necessary.

4. Click the Format button. You see the following menu:

5. Choose the type of format you are looking for. For example, to look for italicized text, click the Font option. When you click an option, the dialog box that was used to create the format opens.

6. In the dialog box, choose options to describe the format you are looking for. For example, to look for italicized text, choose Italic in the Font dialog box's Font Style combo box.

7. Click OK to close the dialog box. In the Find and Replace dialog box, a description of the format you are looking for appears beneath the Find What box.

8. Click the Find Next button.

 Click the No Formatting button in the Find and Replace dialog box when Word is set to search for formats but you no longer want to search for them.

SEARCHING FOR SPECIAL CHARACTERS AND PUNCTUATION   To search for special characters and punctuation, follow the instructions for conducting a search, and click the Special button in the Find and Replace dialog box. You see a long list of things you can search for. Make a choice from the list and then click the Find Next button.

Replacing Text with Text and Formats with Formats

It almost goes without saying, but Word's Replace command is valuable indeed. Instead of painstakingly going through a document to find errors you made and fixing them one error at a time, you can use the Replace command to get the job done very quickly.

The Replace command works similarly to the Find command. First you tell Word what you want to replace by choosing the very same options that you choose when you tell Word what to look for with the Find command. Then you enter the replacement text or, if you are replacing a format, you tell Word what format will replace the one you told Word to find.

The following pages explain how to replace text with text, replace formats with formats, and use the Clipboard to get around the Find and Replace dialog box's 255-character limitation. It might seem impossible to replace the word "resume" with the frenchified "résumé" in a document because the Find and Replace dialog box doesn't permit you to enter accented characters. *Au contraire!* These pages explain how to replace "resume" with "résumé."

Caution   *Always save a document before replacing text or formats. The Replace command is a powerful one indeed. It can wreak havoc on a document. For example, if you want to change all references to Chapter 3 to Chapter 4 and you choose to replace only the numbers, you'll get replacements for the number 3 in any context—dates, page numbers, and so on. By saving the document, you give yourself the opportunity to close it without saving your changes and thereby abandon all the mistakes that the Replace command introduced.*

Replacing Text with Text

Follow these steps to replace text with text:

1. Save the document.

2. Choose Edit | Replace or press CTRL-H. You see the Find and Replace dialog box.

3. Click the Replace tab, if necessary. It is shown in Figure 8-15. (Figure 8-15 shows the dialog box after the More button has been clicked.)

4. Click the More button. The dialog box gets larger, as shown in Figure 8-15.

5. In the Find What box, enter the text that is to be replaced.

6. Click the Find Whole Words Only check box.

Tip   *Always click the Find Whole Words Only check box when you replace text. By clicking it, you make sure that the command doesn't replace snippets of words inside other words. For example, replacing the word "fat" with "portly" is fine, but what happens when Word 2000 encounters the word "fatuous"? Unless you click the Find Whole Words Only check box, the Replace command changes "fat" to "portlyuous."*

Enter the word to
be found in this box.

This is the format
to be found.

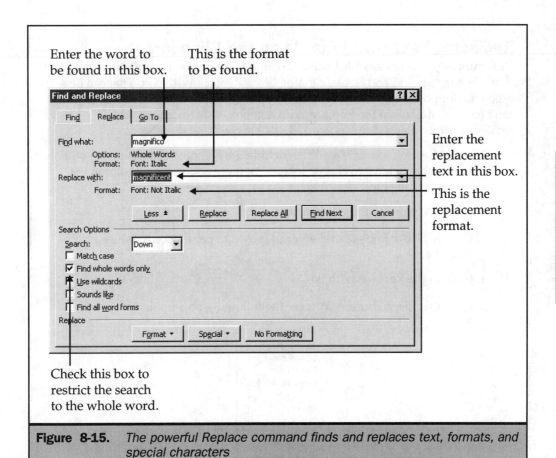

Enter the
replacement
text in this box.

This is the
replacement
format.

Check this box to
restrict the search
to the whole word.

Figure 8-15. *The powerful Replace command finds and replaces text, formats, and special characters*

7. Click the Find Next button. If Word finds the text you are seeking to replace, it highlights the text in the document.

8. Click the Find Next, Replace, or Replace All button:

■ **Find Next**   Bypasses the text that Word found and does not replace it with the Replace With text.

■ **Replace**   Replaces the text and highlights the next instance of the text in the document. Click this button to review each occasion in which Word wants to replace the text.

■ **Replace All**   Replaces the text throughout the document immediately. Click this button if you are holding four aces and are absolutely certain that the text Word has found is the text you want to replace throughout the document.

Replacing Text with What Is on the Clipboard

Unfortunately, it is impossible to enter accent marks, umlauts, and other strange characters in the Find and Replace dialog box's Replace With box. That can be a problem. Suppose you want to replace "cooperate" with "coöperate." Since you can't enter an umlaut in the Replace With text box, how do you make the replacement? By using the Clipboard, that's how. Follow these steps:

1. Type the replacement word. To include the accented characters or symbols, you probably have to choose Insert | Symbol and make a choice in the Symbol dialog box.

2. Copy the word to the Clipboard.

3. Choose Edit | Replace and enter the word to be replaced in the Find What box.

4. Click in the Replace With box.

5. Click the Special button. You see the following pop-up list:

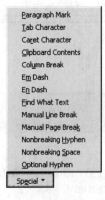

6. Choose Clipboard Contents. Word enters ^c in the Replace With box.

7. Click the Find Next button and start finding and replacing the text.

Reformatting Text with the Find and Replace Commands

Like the Find command, which offers a means of finding formats and finding words that were formatted a certain way, the Replace command can find formats and replace them with other formats. Turn back a few pages to "Searching for a Format" to find out how to tell Word which format to look for. The instructions for searching for a format also apply on the Replace tab of the Find and Replace dialog box.

After you have told Word which format to look for, use the same techniques to tell the program what the replacement format is. For example, click in the Replace With box, then click the Format button and choose Font to tell Word to replace italicized text with plain text. As shown in Figure 8-15, Word puts a description of the format you are seeking and the one that is to replace it underneath the Find What and Replace What text boxes.

Note   *You can also replace punctuation marks in the Find and Replace dialog box by clicking the Special button. If you entered em or en dashes incorrectly, for example, you can find and replace them by way of the Special button.*

Chapter 9

Styles for Consistent
and Easy Formatting

Y ou needn't bother learning how styles work or how to apply styles if you never create documents longer than one or two pages. But if you create complex documents with headings and paragraphs that are formatted in different ways, learning how to create and apply styles is well worth the effort. A *style* is a collection of fonts or paragraph formats to which a name has been given. Instead of going to the work of choosing fonts, line spacing options, indention settings, and what-all for each paragraph in a document, you can bundle the different formatting commands in a style and simply apply the style to each paragraph that is to be formatted the same way. Applying a style takes but a second. Formatting paragraphs and headings one at a time is a tedious activity and is strictly for the birds.

This important chapter delves into the details of how styles work. It starts by explaining what a style is, the difference between paragraph and character styles, and what a template is. It shows how to create, apply, and redefine a style. This chapter also tells how to copy styles between documents, delete and rename styles, and collect styles into a template so that you can use styles in more than one document.

How Styles Work

Styles are a bit confusing, even intimidating, at first. There are two kinds of styles: paragraph styles and character styles. And each Word document comes with a set of styles, but which styles it comes with depends on the template with which it was created. A *template* is a blueprint for a new document. Among other things, a template contains a collection of styles you can choose from to format documents. Word offers numerous templates, and you can create your own templates, too. The following pages explain everything you need to know to create and apply styles wisely.

What Is a Style, Anyway?

A style is a collection of formatting commands that have been assembled under one name. To create a style, you tell Word that you are creating it, give several formatting commands, and then name the style. Later, when you apply the style by choosing it from the Style list, you really choose several formatting commands at once. In effect, you choose all the formatting commands that you chose when you or someone else created and named the style.

Figure 9-1 shows a style called Salutation being chosen from the Style list. After the user clicks Salutation, all the commands that are bundled into that style are applied to the text that is highlighted in the document—in Figure 9-1, the salutation. The Salutation style calls for 11 points of empty space to appear above and below the paragraph; and for the text to be set in 10-point Times New Roman.

Why Styles Are Essential

By working with styles, you free yourself from having to visit and revisit numerous dialog boxes each time you want to format a paragraph or change the font and font size of text. After you create a style, you can simply choose it from the Style menu instead of giving formatting commands.

With styles, moreover, you can rest assured that headings and paragraphs throughout a document are consistent. All headings given the Heading 1 style look the same. Paragraphs given the Intro Para style also look alike. And if you decide, for example, that the Intro Para style doesn't look quite right, you can change it and thereby instantaneously change every single paragraph to which the Intro Para style has been assigned. Styles, besides making it easy to format paragraphs and headings, are a sort of insurance policy. If you change your mind about the look of a heading, all you have to do is redefine the style which you've assigned to it—and all headings that were given the same style are redefined as well.

In a business setting, styles are especially important. A company makes a good impression when the memos, faxes, and invoices that it sends to clients and customers have a similar look. You can give them a similar look by creating styles for faxes, memos, and invoices and saving them in a template. Creating styles for company correspondence also saves time. Instead of wrestling with Word's formatting commands, employees can simply choose styles from a menu as they create documents.

Some Word commands don't work unless the headings in the document have been assigned a style. For example, you can't automatically create a table of contents unless each heading in the document was assigned a heading style. Nor can you take advantage of Outline view and the commands on the Outline toolbar. And you can't cross-reference headings or number the headings in a document. To create a table of figures or illustrations, you must have tagged their captions with the Caption style. The advantages of using styles are many. Do yourself a big favor by learning how styles work and how to apply styles.

> **Tip**   *To see the formatting applied to text, choose Help | What's This?, and right-click the text.*

Imagine how much trouble formatting a salutation would be if you had to format it anew each time you wrote a letter, rather than just applying the Salutation style. You would have to do the following:

- Choose Format | Paragraph; under Spacing, enter **11** in the Before box and **11** in the After box; and click OK.
- Select the text in the salutation, choose Times New Roman from the Font menu, and choose 10 from the Font Size menu.

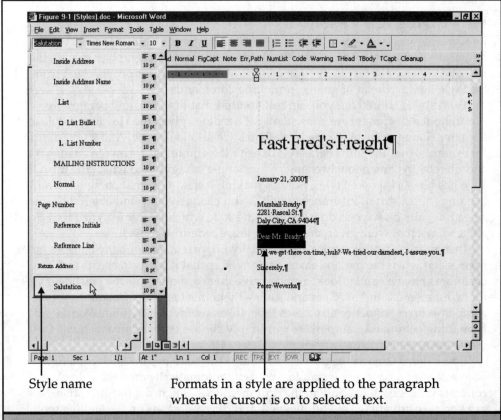

Style name   Formats in a style are applied to the paragraph
                              where the cursor is or to selected text.

Figure 9-1. *When you apply a style to text, you apply several formatting commands at once and spare yourself the trouble of visiting lots of different menus and dialog boxes*

EXAMPLES

LEARN BY EXAMPLE
The letter in Figure 9-1 was created with a Word template called Professional Letter. Open the Figure 9-1 (Styles) file on the companion CD if you want to experiment with the styles in the Professional Letter template.

TEMPLATES

HEADSTART
To experiment with styles, open a file based on one of the templates in the New dialog box. Choose File | New, click any tab besides General, click a template, and click OK. Then examine the styles on the Style list to get an idea of what styles are for.

Paragraph Styles and Character Styles

Word offers two kinds of styles: paragraph styles and character styles. By far the majority of styles are paragraph styles. Character styles merely apply to text, whereas paragraph styles apply to text as well as paragraphs:

- **Paragraph Style**   Create a paragraph style for indentions, line spacing, tab settings, and all else that falls in the "formatting" category. A paragraph style, like a character style, can also include font and font size settings. When you assign a paragraph style, its format and font settings apply to the text in the paragraph that the cursor is in (or to the text in several paragraphs if you selected all or part of several paragraphs).

- **Character Style**   Create a character style for text that is hard to lay out (such as small capitals), for combinations of font and font size commands that are too troublesome to apply in conventional ways, for shaded text or text that is surrounded by borders, or for foreign words that the spell checker and grammar checker are to skip. Before you assign a character style, select text in the document. Character styles apply to selected text, not to all the text in a paragraph.

On the Style menu, paragraph styles are marked with the paragraph symbol (¶) and character styles are marked with the letter *a*:

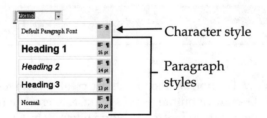

Commands That Can Be Bundled into a Style

To create a style, visit the dialog boxes you would visit if you were applying formatting commands. A paragraph style can include formats made with all the commands in Table 9-1. A character style can include formats made with the commands in the table that are marked with an asterisk.

Styles and Templates

A template is a special type of file that can be used as the starting point for creating other files. In each Word template are many predefined styles for formatting documents. How many predefined styles are available depends on the template you choose when you create the document.

Command	Formats for Styles
Font (on the Format menu)*	Fonts, font styles, font sizes, font color, text effects (such as small capitals and embossed text), character spacing, animation
Paragraph (on the Format menu)	Text alignment (Left, Center, and so on), indention, before and after paragraph spacing, line spacing, outline level, widow and orphan control and other pagination instructions, hyphenation, suppressing line numbers
Bullets and Numbering (on the Format menu)	Bulleted list formats, number schemes, outline numbering schemes
Borders and Shading (on the Format menu)*	Borderlines for paragraphs and pages, shading for paragraphs
Tabs (on the Format menu)	Tab stop settings, leader settings
Set Language (on the Tools menu's Language submenu)*	Language for the spelling and grammar checkers
*Also for creating character styles	

Table 9-1.   *Commands for Building Styles*

Whether you know it or not, all documents are created from templates. When you click the New Blank Document button or press CTRL-N to create a new document, Word opens a generic document created from the Normal template. Choose File | New and click a tab in the New dialog box, on the other hand, and Word presents many templates for creating new documents. Figure 9-2 shows the templates on the Letters & Faxes tab. Choose one of these templates, and you are presented with numerous predefined styles for laying out a fax or letter. (In Figure 9-1, you can see some of the styles that are available in the Professional Letter template.)

Besides creating files from the templates that Word provides, you can create your own templates and then create files from them. In fact, if you've gone to the trouble of creating elaborate styles for a document, you might as well save them in a template so you can make use of them again. The last third of this chapter explains how to create a template, copy styles to and from different templates, apply the styles in a template to a document you've already created, and turn a document into a template.

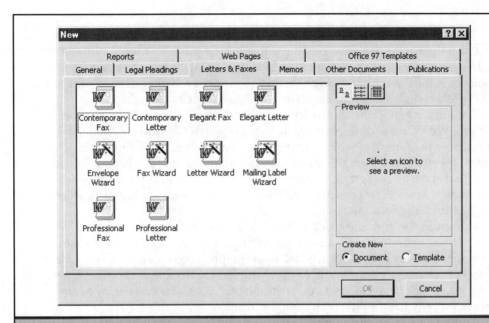

Figure 9-2. *Create a document from a template and you get many predefined styles to help with the layout*

Creating Styles

To create a paragraph style, either build it from the ground up by choosing Format | Style and working inside the Style dialog box, or format a paragraph in a document and tell Word to make it a prototype for the style you want to create. To create a character style, you must choose Format | Style and work inside the Style dialog box. Each method is explained in the following pages.

What Is the Best Way to Create a Style?

Word offers two ways to create a style: the prototype method and the building-block method. Which is better?

The prototype method has the advantage of letting you see exactly what the style looks like onscreen. With the prototype method, you format a paragraph, stare at it, change its formats if necessary, make sure it is just-so, type a style name in the Style list box on the Formatting toolbar, and press the ENTER key. When you assign the style you created to a paragraph, the paragraph looks exactly like the paragraph you used as a prototype.

Creating a style with the building-block method takes longer, and you don't see what the style looks like onscreen, but you get to be more thorough. With the building-block method, you start from the Style dialog box and visit the Font dialog box, the Paragraph dialog box, and any number of dialog boxes, where you tell Word precisely how the new style is going to format a paragraph.

The building-block method offers several advantages over the prototype method. With the building-block method, you can tell Word to redefine a style each time a paragraph to which the style has been assigned is changed. In other words, if you make a formatting change to a paragraph that has been assigned the Bold Text style, all paragraphs assigned the Bold Text style in the document are reformatted as well. You can also add the styles you create to a template when you use the building-block method.

Moreover, the building-block method gives you the opportunity to tell Word to always follow one style with another style. Suppose the Chapter Title style in a document is always to be followed by a paragraph tagged with the Chapter Intro style. For consistency's sake, and to save yourself the trouble of choosing a new style from the Style menu after you write chapter titles, you can tell Word to always follow Chapter Title with Chapter Intro.

Anyhow, most people aren't lucky enough or wise enough to create a perfect style the first time around. Maybe the best way to create a style is to go at it both ways, through the Style dialog box and with the prototype method. Later in this chapter, the section "Redefining a Style" explains how to fine-tune a style. You can do that with the Style dialog box or the prototype method.

Creating a Style from a Prototype Paragraph

To create a style from a prototype paragraph, you start with a model paragraph whose formats are exactly the ones that the new style is supposed to embody. Follow these steps to create a style from a prototype paragraph:

1. Either find or create a model paragraph in your document.

2. Click in the paragraph.

Note *In Word, a paragraph is simply what you type onscreen before you press the ENTER key. Therefore, a heading is a paragraph. To create a heading style with the prototype method, click in a heading.*

3. Click the Style menu box. The words in the Style box are highlighted:

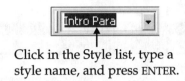

Click in the Style list, type a
style name, and press ENTER.

4. Type a name for the new style.

5. Press the ENTER key.

Choosing a Style Name

Choosing a meaningful style name that is nonetheless short enough to keep the Style menu from stretching out and covering half the document window is a real challenge. Style names can be 255 characters long, but only a prankster would choose a name longer than 20 or so characters. Consider the following Style list, whose names are too long. Working with this Style list would be well-nigh impossible.

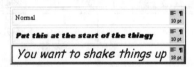

Creating a Style from the Ground Up

To create a style from the ground up, the building-block method, follow these steps:

1. Click the paragraph or heading for which you want to create a new paragraph style, or select the text for which you want to create a character style.

2. Choose Format | Style. You see the Style dialog box.

3. Click the New button. The New Style dialog box appears, as shown in Figure 9-3.

4. Enter a name for the style in the Name box. The name you enter will appear on the Style drop-down list.

5. In the Style Type drop-down list, choose Character if you are creating a character style. Otherwise, let the Paragraph option stand.

6. Select the following options and check boxes as you deem fit:

■ **Based On**   Choose a style from the drop-down list to tie the style you are creating to another style. For example, by choosing the Default Paragraph

Enter a style name.

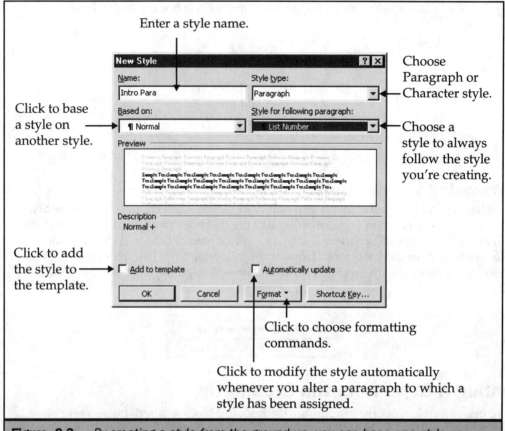

Choose Paragraph or Character style.

Click to base a style on another style.

Choose a style to always follow the style you're creating.

Click to add the style to the template.

Click to choose formatting commands.

Click to modify the style automatically whenever you alter a paragraph to which a style has been assigned.

Figure 9-3. *By creating a style from the ground up, you can base one style on another or designate a style that is always to follow the style you are creating*

Font style, you tell Word to always display text in the Default Paragraph Font, whatever that font happens to be. If you change the default style, styles based on that style will change as well. The style you are creating will inherit formats from the style that is chosen in the Based On drop-down list.

Caution   *When you choose a style from the Based On drop-down list, either choose a bare-bones style like Normal or Default Paragraph Font or choose (no style). If you choose an elaborate style from the drop-down list and you or someone else changes that style at a later day, changes to the elaborate style will be inherited by the new style. That can have bad consequences. But by sticking to a bare-bones style or no style at all, you can rest assured that changes to the based-on style won't have negative repercussions on the style you are creating.*

- **Style For Following Paragraph**   If you want, choose a style from this drop-down list if the style you're creating is always to be followed by an existing style.

- **Add To Template**   Click this check box if you want to add the style you are creating to the template with which you created the document. New styles are available only in the document for which they were created, unless this box is checked. Clicking this box saves the style you create in the document and in the template. A user who creates a file with the template can draw upon the style you create if this box is checked.

- **Automatically Update**   Normally, when a formatting change is made to a paragraph, the style assigned to the paragraph does not change at all. Checking this box tells Word to redefine the style each time a paragraph to which the style has been assigned is reformatted. With this box checked, all paragraphs in the document that were assigned the style are reformatted automatically each time you reformat a single paragraph that was assigned the style.

Tip   *If you are the type who likes to press keys to give commands, including style commands, click the Shortcut Key button. The Customize Keyboard dialog box appears. See "Assigning a New Keyboard Shortcut" in Chapter 4 to learn how to assign a keyboard shortcut to a style or command.*

7. Click the Format button. You see a menu of formatting choices (Table 9-1 lists the command equivalents of these options):

8. Choose an option to open a dialog box and give formatting commands. For example, choosing Paragraph opens the Paragraph dialog box.

9. In the dialog box, choose formatting options for the new style and then click OK.

10. Repeat steps 7 through 9 as many times as necessary to create the style.

11. Click OK to close the New Style dialog box.

12. Click Apply to format the paragraph or selected text with the new style.

Redefining a Style

It's not easy to create the perfect style the first time around. Very likely, you have to tinker with styles to make them come out right. Redefining a style, like creating a style, can be done two ways: with the prototype method or the Modify Style dialog box.

 You can replace one style with another with the Edit menu's Replace command. Choose Edit | Replace, click the More button, click the Formats button, and choose Style. For details, see "Finding and Replacing Text and Other Things" in Chapter 8.

Redefining Styles with the Prototype Method

To redefine a style with the prototype method, follow these steps:

1. Click in a paragraph to which you've applied the style that you want to redefine.

2. Reformat the paragraph, and select it.

3. Click in the Style menu. The letters of the style name are highlighted.

4. Press the ENTER key. You see the Modify Style dialog box:

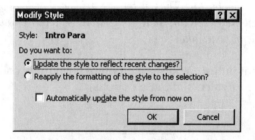

5. Make sure the Update The Style To Reflect Recent Changes? check box is checked.

6. Click OK.

 The Automatically Update The Style From Now On check box is the equivalent of the New Style dialog box's Automatically Update check box (see Figure 9-3). Click this check box and all the paragraphs in the document that were assigned the style are reformatted each time you reformat a single paragraph that was assigned the style.

Redefining Styles with the Modify Style Dialog Box

The other way to modify a style is to use the Modify Style dialog box:

1. Click a paragraph whose style you want to redefine (or select the text if you are modifying a character style).

2. Choose Format | Style to open the Style dialog box.

3. Click the Modify button. You see the Modify Style dialog box. If it looks frightfully familiar that is because its options, check boxes, and buttons work exactly like those in the New Style dialog box (see Figure 9-3). See "Creating a Style from the Ground Up," earlier in this chapter, if you need instructions for filling in the Modify Style dialog box.

4. Modify the style in the Modify Style dialog box.

5. Click OK.

6. Click the Apply button to apply the new formats to all paragraphs or text in the document that were assigned the style you modified.

Applying a Style in a Document

After you have gone to the work of creating and redefining a style, applying it is easy. All you have to do is click in the paragraph to which you want to apply a style (or select the text if you are applying a character style) and then choose a style from the Style drop-down list. Or, to apply a style to several paragraphs, select all or part of all the paragraphs first. Figure 9-4 shows a style called Message Header First being chosen from the Style drop-down list. Sometimes you have to scroll to the bottom of the Style list to find the style you are after.

Notice that the Style list hints at what paragraphs will look like after a style has been chosen. Letters in the style names are shown in the same font as letters in the style itself. To the right of each style name is a box that tells how text is aligned, whether the style is a paragraph or a character style, and how many points high the letters in the style are.

EXAMPLES

LEARN BY EXAMPLE

The memo in Figure 9-4 was created with a Word template called Professional Memo. Open the Figure 9-4 (Styles) file on the companion CD if you want to experiment with the styles in the Professional Memo template.

Working with Styles

This section explains the ins and outs of working with styles. It tells how to delete a style, rename a style, and copy styles to and from documents. The following pages offer a couple of tricks for finding out precisely which styles are which in a document and what to do if the modifications you make to a style keep fading out and disappearing. It happens.

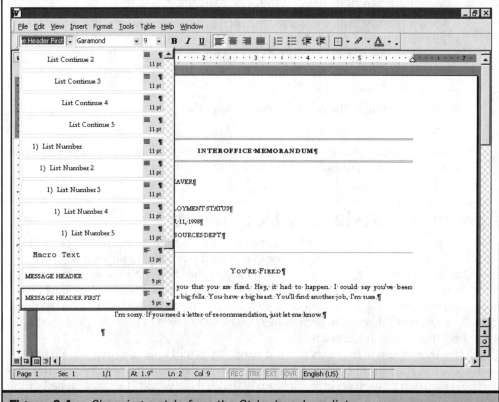

Figure 9-4. *Choosing a style from the Style drop-down list*

Seeing Which Styles Are in Use

In complex documents with many styles, it is sometimes hard to tell which style is which. And it is also hard to remember what each style's formats are. Fortunately, you can rely on a special command in the Options dialog box to see exactly which styles are in use in a document. You can also use the Help menu's What's This? command to see how each style formats text and paragraphs.

The easiest way to tell which styles are in use is to make Word display style names along the left side of the document window, as shown in Figure 9-5. In the figure are styles named Message Header First, Message Header, Message Header Last, and so on. With style names displayed this way, it is easy to see which style has been applied to which paragraph and what each style does in the way of formatting.

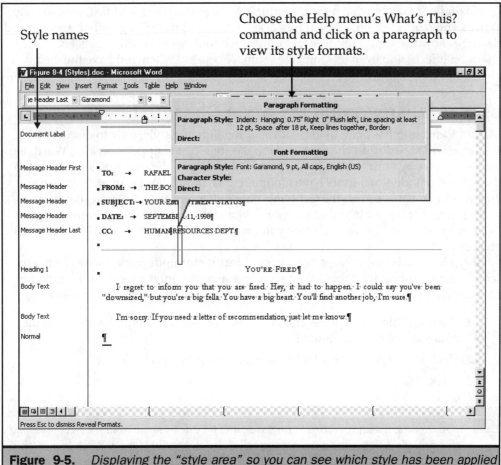

Figure 9-5. *Displaying the "style area" so you can see which style has been applied to each paragraph*

To display style names on the left side of the document window (Word calls it the *style area*), follow these steps:

1. Choose Tools | Options to open the Options dialog box.

2. Click the View tab, if necessary.

3. Go to the Style Area Width scroll box in the lower-left corner of the View tab and click the up arrow button to enlarge the style area to 0.5 or 0.7 inches.

4. Click OK.

To remove the style names, repeat these steps, but shrink the style area to 0.0 inches.

To find out exactly what a style's formats do to a paragraph and text, choose Help | What's This? and click on a paragraph. As shown in Figure 9-5, a gray box appears and describes how the paragraph was laid out, which fonts were applied to its text, its character effects, and even its language setting. Press ESC when you have finished examining the gray box.

Help! Word Disregarded My Style Changes!

Many a Word user has gone to the trouble of redefining a style, only to discover later that Word disregarded all changes made to the style. That happens because Word offers a feature by which styles in a document conform to the template's styles, not to the styles that individual users have modified or changed. For example, suppose you create a document based on the Contemporary Letter template, but you change one of the styles that is built into that template. When you close the file and open it again, Word may disregard the style change you made and reimpose the template's original style instead.

It can happen because Word has a special feature for updating all styles from the template and reimposing those styles each time a document is reopened. To turn that feature off and keep styles from being updated from the template, do the following:

1. Choose Tools | Templates and Add-Ins. You see the Templates and Add-ins dialog box shown in Figure 9-6.

2. Uncheck the Automatically Update Document Styles check box.

3. Click OK.

> **Tip**   *Sometimes users get the mistaken impression that Word is fooling with their styles because the automatic updating feature is turned on and they don't know it. In the New Style and Modify Style dialog boxes is a check box called Automatically Update. When that check box is selected, changes made to the formatting of individual paragraphs are made to the style itself, so all paragraphs in the document that have been assigned the same style are changed each time an individual paragraph's formats are changed. Redefine the style and uncheck the Automatically Update check box to keep that from happening.*

Deleting and Renaming Styles

Long Style lists are a drag because they make it harder to find and apply styles. To keep Style lists from growing too long, Word gives you the opportunity to delete the styles you don't need to format documents. You can also rename styles. You might do this to give a style a more suitable name or to copy a style to another document. As the next section explains, it is impossible to copy a style from one document to another if a style in the receiving document has the same name as the style being copied. Following are instructions for deleting and renaming styles.

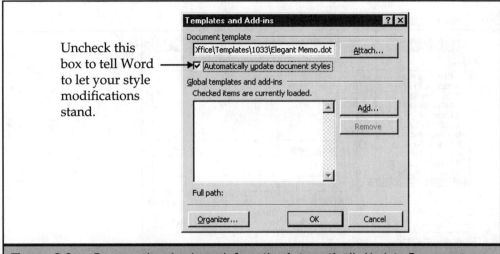

Uncheck this box to tell Word to let your style modifications stand.

Figure 9-6. *Remove the check mark from the Automatically Update Document Styles check box to keep styles from being updated from the template on which the document is based*

Deleting a Style

When you delete a style, paragraphs to which the style was assigned are assigned the Normal style instead. Word doesn't let you delete the built-in styles that come with every Word document (Normal and the Heading styles, for example), but you can delete styles you fashioned yourself and the many extraneous styles that come with the templates. Follow these steps to delete a style:

1. Choose Format | Style. The Style dialog box shown in Figure 9-7 appears.

2. Click the List drop-down menu and choose User-Defined Styles or Styles In Use. By doing so, you trim the list of files in the Styles list and make it easier to find the style you want to delete.

3. In the Styles list, click the style you want to delete.

4. Click the Delete button.

5. Click Yes when Word asks if you really want to delete the style.

6. Click Close to close the Style dialog box.

Renaming a Style

It almost goes without saying, but you can't give a style a name that is claimed already by another style. Other than that caveat, renaming a style is similar to modifying a

Click the style to be deleted.

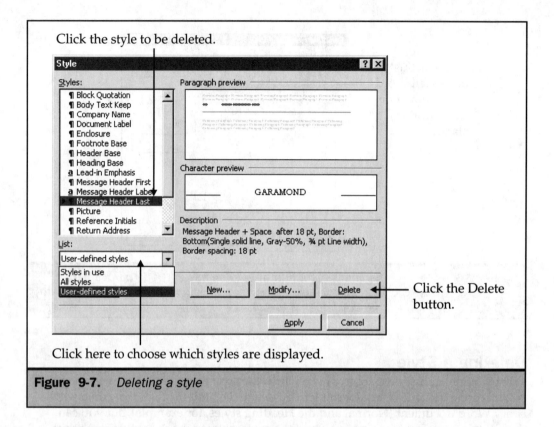

Click the Delete button.

Click here to choose which styles are displayed.

Figure 9-7.   *Deleting a style*

style. Choose Format | Style to open the Style dialog box. In the Styles list, click on the style you want to rename, and then click the Modify button. In the Modify Style dialog box, click in the Name field and type a new name. Then click OK. If you want to apply the style to the current paragraph or selection, click Apply. Otherwise, click the Close button.

Copying Styles Between Documents

To copy a style from one document and make it available in another, all you have to do is copy a paragraph to which you've assigned the style from the first document to the second. As long as you copy an entire paragraph (including the paragraph symbol at the end of the paragraph), the style in the first document will land safely in the second and be available there as well. After you copy the paragraph, delete the text. Although the text has been deleted, the style it was assigned stays in the document and is available on the Style drop-down list.

To copy a style, its name must be different from all the style names already present in the document that is receiving the copy. Rename the style being copied, if necessary.

By the way, the reason you have to copy an entire paragraph (by double-clicking in the left margin) is because Word formats—including styles—for each paragraph are stored in the paragraph symbol at the end of the paragraph. You can see this symbol by clicking the Show/Hide button. By copying the entire paragraph, you copy the paragraph symbol as well.

 You can also use the Organizer to copy styles from one document to another. See "Assembling Styles for a Template," a bit later in this chapter. The same techniques for assembling styles for a template work for copying styles between documents.

Constructing Word Templates

So far in this chapter you have learned to create styles and save them in a document. But suppose you go to all the trouble of creating intricate, elegant styles for a document and you want to use the styles over again for other documents. You could copy the styles one at a time, as the previous section explained, but that would be a chore. It would be easier to create a new template for the new styles you created. That way, all you have to do to make use of the styles you so carefully crafted is choose File | New and choose the template you created in the New dialog box.

The following pages explain how to assemble styles into a template, copy styles between templates, and choose a new template for a document.

Creating a Template for the Styles You Created

The fastest way to create a template for styles you created is to open the document for which you created the styles, save the document as a template, then open the template and delete the text. After you delete the text, the styles remain in the template and can be applied by anyone who uses the template to create a document.

To create a template for the styles you created in a document, follow these steps:

1. Open the document.
2. Choose File | Save As. The Save As dialog box appears.
3. Click the Save As Type drop-down list and choose Document Template. The Templates folder appears in the Save In list at the top of the dialog box. This is where Word stores templates that appear on the General tab of the Templates dialog box. If you want the template to reside in a different category, double-click the folder representing the template category you want.

4. Type a descriptive name in the File Name box.

5. Click Save to complete the operation and close the Save As dialog box.

6. Delete all the text in the template.

7. Click the Save button to save your changes to the template.

8. Choose File | Close to close the template.

As Figure 9-8 shows, templates you store in the Templates folder appear beside the Blank Document template on the General tab of the New dialog box. To create a document with the template you created, choose File | New; click the General tab of the New dialog box, if necessary; click the template you created; and click OK.

Assembling Styles for a Template

Another way to create a template is to collect styles from different templates and documents and assemble them in a single template. Word offers a special tool called the Organizer for doing just that. Besides copying styles between documents and templates, you can copy macros, AutoText entries, and toolbars with the Organizer.

To create a template with the Organizer, you either create a brand-new template or open a template that you want to add styles to. Then you open the Organizer and start copying styles (and macros, AutoText entries, and toolbars, too, if you want) from other templates and documents to the template you created or opened.

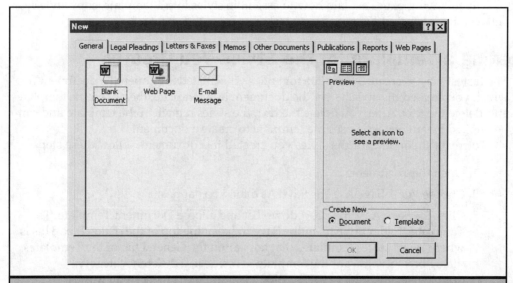

Figure 9-8.   *To create a document from a template you created, choose File | New and click the category tab that corresponds to the name of the folder in which you stored the template*

Follow these steps to copy styles from templates and documents to a template:

1. Either create a brand-new template or open the template that you want to copy styles to:

   ■ **Create a Template** Choose File | New. In the New dialog box, click the Template radio button in the lower-right corner. Then click OK. When the new template opens, click the Save button and save and name your new template.

   ■ **Open a Template** Choose File | Open. In the Open dialog box, click the Files Of Type drop-down list and choose Document Templates. Find the folder with the template you want to copy styles to, click the template's name, and click the Open button. Click Enable Macros if Word asks how to open the template.

2. Choose Format | Style. The Style dialog box opens.

3. Click the Organizer button. You see the Organizer dialog box shown in Figure 9-9 (if necessary, click the Styles tab). For now, don't worry that the arrows on the Copy button are pointing in the wrong direction. In the next five steps, you

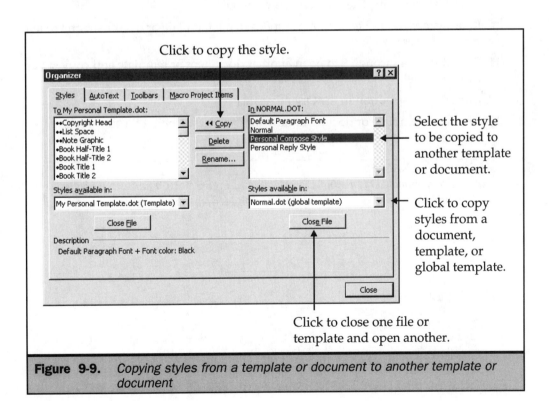

Figure 9-9. *Copying styles from a template or document to another template or document*

will open a template or document on the right side of the dialog box, click the name of a style you want to copy, and thereby change the direction of the arrows on the Copy button.

4. Click the Close File button on the right side of the dialog box. The button changes its name to Open File.

5. Click the Open File button. You see the Open dialog box.

6. In the Open dialog box, click the name of the template or document you want to copy files from and click Open. The styles in the template or document appear in the box on the right side of the screen.

7. If necessary, open the Styles Available In drop-down list on the right side of the dialog box and choose either the current file or the Normal template to change which styles appear in the list of styles on the right side of the dialog box.

8. On the right side of the dialog box, click the name of a style you want to copy to your template or document on the left side of the dialog box. As soon as you click, the arrows on the Copy button point to the left. Notice the description of the style at the bottom of the Organizer dialog box.

9. Click the Copy button. The name of the style now appears in the box on the left as well as the right. The style has been copied.

10. Repeat steps 8 and 9 to copy more styles to the template or document on the left side of the screen.

11. Repeat steps 4 through 9 to open another document or template and copy styles from it as well.

12. Click the Close button in the Organizer.

13. Save your template or document now that you have copied the new styles.

EXAMPLES

LEARN BY EXAMPLE

On the companion CD is a sample template called Figure 9-9 (Organizer). If you feel like experimenting, be my guest and use it to copy styles from other templates and documents.

When Style Names Collide

Do not copy styles with the same name from one template or document to the next. Word assumes that the style being copied takes precedence over the style that is already there, so you lose a style in the "copied to" document or template when you copy identically named styles.

To keep from losing a style, rename the style in the "copied to" template or document. To do that, click it and click the Organizer's Rename button. Type a new name in the Rename dialog box and click OK.

Choosing a Different Template for a Document

As you know, Word gives you the opportunity to create a style from a template. By choosing File | New and selecting a template in the New dialog box, you can create a document with ready-made styles. But suppose you chose the wrong template. For example, suppose you chose the Contemporary Letter template for a letter, but after some thought, you realize that you should have chosen the Elegant Letter template. Oh my, feeling more elegant than contemporary these days, are we? Fortunately, you can always change horses in the middle of the stream and choose a new template for a document, even if you already created and formatted it.

Follow these steps to choose a different template for a document you have created:

1. Open the document.
2. Choose Tools | Template and Add-Ins. You see the Templates and Add-ins dialog box shown in Figure 9-10. The template you used to create the document is listed in the Document Template box.
3. Click the Attach button. The Attach Template dialog box appears.
4. Find and click the name of the template you want for the document, and then click the Open button. Back in the Templates and Add-ins dialog box, the name of the new template is listed in the Document Template box.
5. Click the Automatically Update Document Styles check box.
6. Click OK.

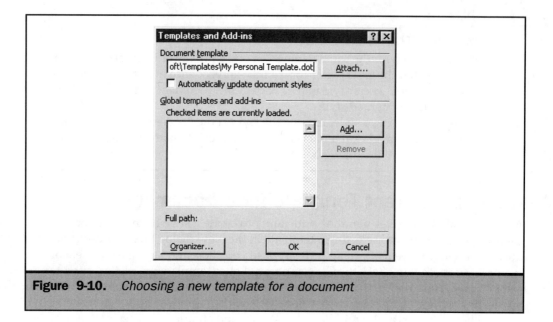

Figure 9-10. *Choosing a new template for a document*

Tip *By default, templates are stored in the Templates folder in C:\Windows\Application Data\Microsoft. To delete a template, choose File | Open, browse to the Templates folder, select the template you want to delete, and click the Delete button.*

The
Complete
Reference

Office
2000

Chapter 10

Desktop Publishing with Word

Although you probably want to use a desktop publishing program such as Publisher to create documents that require a more complex layout and design, Word offers several desktop publishing features you can use if you don't have Publisher or if the publication you want to create doesn't require all the tools of a full-fledged desktop publishing program. You can lay out and present text and graphics in many interesting ways with Word; some publishers even use Word to lay out entire books. This chapter describes Word's desktop publishing features. It explains how to put text in a text box, shade a text box, and put borders around text boxes. It tells how to wrap text around graphics and text boxes in attractive, elegant ways. This chapter also explains how to arrange text in columns, create headers, and format and lay out a table.

Text Boxes for Announcements and Headings

Text boxes are handy tools to use when you want to format and move around floating blocks of text. To put an announcement in the middle of a page, create a text box for the announcement. To put borders around text, shade it, or give it a color background, create a text box. If you are working on a newsletter and you want the story on page 1 to be continued on page 3, create two text boxes and link them together so that text from the text box on page 1 goes automatically to the second text box on page 3.

The following pages explain how to create a text box, change its size and shape, position it on the page, and remove the text box. They also explain how to flip and rotate text in a text box. See these parts of Chapter 10 to learn more about text boxes:

- "All About Borders, Shading, and Color" explains how to change the border and put a color or gray shade background in a text box.

- "Wrapping Text Around Graphics and Text Boxes" explains how to tell Word how text should wind its way around a text box in a document.

- "Arranging Text in Newspaper-Style Columns" explains how to make text "float" from one text box to another.

Inserting a Text Box

The techniques for inserting and changing the size of text boxes are the same as those for inserting and changing the size of graphics. The only trick with text boxes is telling Word whether they should be attached to a paragraph and therefore move with that paragraph when it moves or not be attached so that they stay in one place.

Tip   *If you've already entered the text, you can select it and then give commands for putting a text box around it. You end up with a text box with your text inside it. However, creating a text box by selecting text first wreaks havoc with the position settings of the new text box. It is much easier to create the text box first and then copy text into it.*

To begin with, don't worry about whether the text box is the right size or where it belongs on the page. You can handle that stuff after you have followed these steps to insert a text box in a document:

1. Scroll to the page where you want to insert the text box.

2. Choose Insert | Text Box. The pointer changes into a cross and Word switches to Page Layout view, if you are not already there.

3. Click in what is to be the upper-left corner of the text box and drag the pointer across the page to what is to be the opposite corner. Lines appear to show where the borders of the text box are.

4. Release the mouse button. Square sizing handles and hash marks appear around the text box:

Your Text Here

5. Click in the text box and start typing. You can format text in the text box by calling on most of Word's formatting commands, including the Align buttons and font settings.

Changing the Size and Shape of a Text Box

By far, the easiest way to manipulate text boxes is to drag a sizing handle. Sizing handles are the hollow squares that appear on the corners and sides of text boxes. To change the size and shape of a text box, follow these steps:

1. Click in the text box to select it. Sizing handles and hash marks appear around the box.

2. Move the pointer over a sizing handle. When you do so, the pointer changes into a two-headed arrow. In the next step, you will drag a selection handle, but whether you drag a handle in a corner or on a side determines whether the text box keeps its proportions when you change its size:

   ■ **Changing Size and Proportions** Hold down the CTRL key and drag a sizing handle on a side of the text box. As the text box on the right side of Figure 10-1 shows, the text box changes shape.

   ■ **Changing Size But Keeping Proportions** Drag a selection handle in the corner of the text box. As the text box in the middle of Figure 10-1 shows, the text box keeps its original shape but gets larger or smaller.

3. Drag a sizing handle on a corner or a side of the text box. A dotted line shows how the text box is being changed.

4. Release the mouse button.

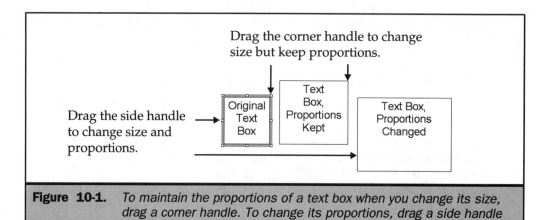

Figure 10-1.   *To maintain the proportions of a text box when you change its size, drag a corner handle. To change its proportions, drag a side handle*

LEARN BY EXAMPLE
Open the Figure 10-1 (Text Boxes) file on the companion CD if you'd like to experiment with changing the size and shape of text boxes.

Word offers a second way to change the shape and size of text boxes: Choose Format | Text Box, click the Size tab in the Format Text Box dialog box, and change the settings in the Height and Width boxes. Use this technique to create square text boxes and symmetrical text boxes.

Tip   *To create text boxes of the same size, copy the prototype text box, paste in the copy, remove the text, and enter new text. Before you can copy a text box, you have to select it. Do that by clicking on the perimeter of the box, not on the inside. If you click correctly, you see dots around the border of the text box instead of just the usual hash marks.*

Positioning a Text Box on the Page

To position a text box on the page, drag it to a new location. Follow these steps:

1. Move the pointer over the perimeter of the text box, but not over a sizing handle. The pointer changes into a four-headed arrow.

2. Drag the text box to a new location. Dotted lines show where you are moving the text box.

3. Release the mouse button.

Positioning a Text Box Relative to the Column, Margin, or Page

Besides changing the position of a text box by dragging it, you can change positions in the Advanced Layout dialog box shown in Figure 10-2. Choose Format | Text Box, select the Layout tab in the dialog box, click the Advanced button, select the Picture Position tab, and change the Horizontal and Vertical settings. Go this route if you are working with several text boxes and you want each to be in the same position relative to the column, paragraph, or page. Or, as explained in "Anchoring a Paragraph So It Stays in One Place" in Chapter 7, go this route if you want to lock the text box in one place and keep it from moving when text is inserted before it in a document.

On the Picture Position tab are settings to tell Word where to position the left edge and top of a text box with respect to the margin, page, or paragraph in which the text box lies. Use the Absolute Position settings to enter the space settings.

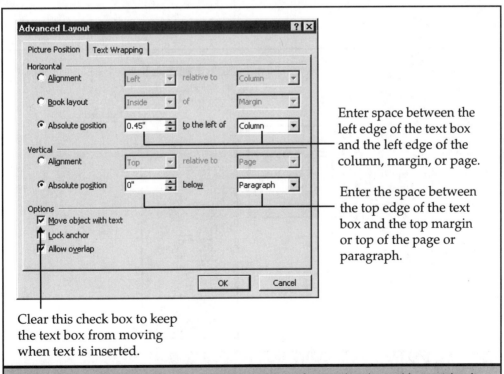

Enter space between the left edge of the text box and the left edge of the column, margin, or page.

Enter the space between the top edge of the text box and the top margin or top of the page or paragraph.

Clear this check box to keep the text box from moving when text is inserted.

Figure 10-2.   *You can also change the position of a text box by making entries in the Advanced Layout dialog box*

Flipping and Rotating Text in a Text Box

On the Text Box toolbar is a neat button for turning the text in a text box on its ear. After you turn text on its side, you usually have to change the size of the text box to make all the text appear onscreen. To flip or rotate text in a text box, follow these steps:

1. Click in the text box.

2. Right-click on a toolbar and choose Text Box to bring the Text Box toolbar onscreen, if necessary. It is shown in Figure 10-3.

3. Click the Change Text Direction button, the rightmost button on the toolbar, as many times as necessary to flip the text.

LEARN BY EXAMPLE
Check out the Figure 10-3 (Text Boxes) file on the companion CD. It offers text boxes whose text you can flip and rotate to your heart's content.

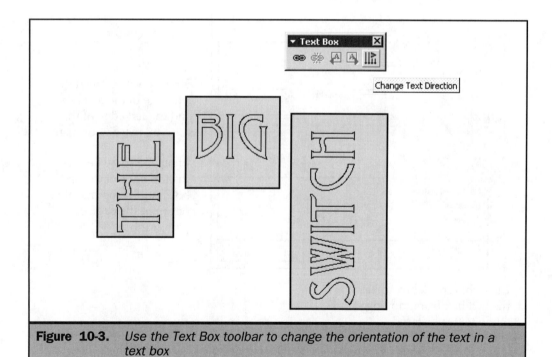

Figure 10-3.   *Use the Text Box toolbar to change the orientation of the text in a text box*

Removing a Text Box

All you have to do to remove a text box is select it by clicking on its perimeter, and then press the DELETE key. To select a text box correctly, click when you see a four-headed arrow. Text inside the text box is, alas, removed along with the text box, so if you still need the text, copy the text elsewhere before you delete the text box.

All About Borders, Shading, and Color

One way to dress up graphics and text boxes is to put borders around them, fill them with color, or fill them with gray shades. You can create fanciful artwork this way. In Figure 10-4, different borders and gray shades appear around and in three text boxes and three graphics. The result is a little Mexican pastiche.

The following pages explain how to put different kinds of borders on graphics, text boxes, and whole pages. They also describe how to "fill" a graphic or text box with color or a gray shade.

EXAMPLES

LEARN BY EXAMPLE
Open the Figure 10-4 (Borders) file on the companion CD to experiment with borders, gray shades, and colors for text boxes and graphics.

Figure 10-4. *By experimenting with borders, gray shades, and color, you can create fanciful artwork around text boxes and graphics*

Drawing Borders Around Text Boxes and Graphics

Word puts a border around text boxes when you create them, but you can change the width and style of borders and even remove them. As for graphics, some have borders already. When you add a border to a graphic that already has a border, the graphic, in effect, gets two borders and grows thicker.

   Borders make graphics and text boxes wider and taller. That becomes a consideration when you line up text boxes or graphics in a row or line them up one below the other. Unless the borders on the text boxes and graphics are the same width, the text boxes and graphics do not line up with one another.

Drawing a Border

Follow these steps to create a border around a text box or graphic:

1. Click the text box or graphic to select it.

2. Choose Format | Text Box or Format | Picture. The Format Text Box or Format Picture dialog box appears.

3. Click the Colors and Lines tab, which is shown in Figure 10-5. The options for creating borders around text boxes and pictures are the same.

4. In the Line settings, click the Color drop-down menu and choose a color for the border, if necessary.

5. If you want, click the down arrow on the Dashed drop-down list and choose a dashed line. Don't bother with this drop-down list if you want an unbroken line for the border.

6. Open the Style drop-down list and choose the type of line you want.

7. Enter how many points wide the line is to be in the Weight box.

8. Click OK.

Removing a Border

Follow these steps to remove the border around a text box or graphic.

1. Click the text box or graphic to select it.

2. Choose Format | Text Box or Format | Picture.

3. Click the Colors and Lines tab, if necessary (see Figure 10-5).

4. In the Line section, open the Color drop-down list and choose No Line.

5. Click OK.

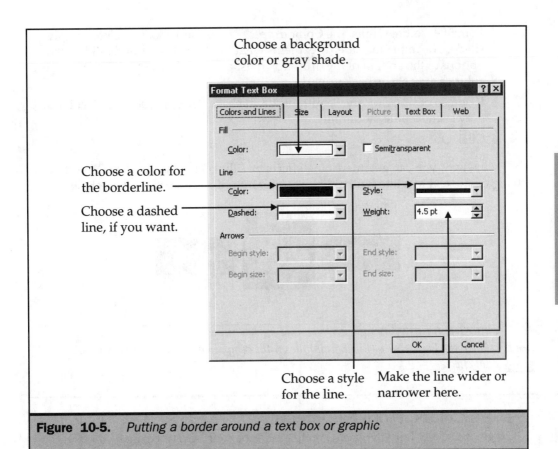

Choose a background
color or gray shade.

Choose a color for
the borderline.

Choose a dashed
line, if you want.

Choose a style
for the line.

Make the line wider or
narrower here.

Figure 10-5. *Putting a border around a text box or graphic*

Shading and "Colorizing" Text Boxes and Graphics

Another way to embellish a text box or graphic is to fill it with color or a gray shade.
Announcements stand out when they are given a color or gray-shade background. By
playing with the background of a clip art image, you can come up with interesting
variations.

Follow these steps to give color or a gray shade to a text box or graphic:

1. Click the text box or graphic to select it.

2. Choose Format | Text Box or Format | Picture. You see the Format Text Box or
   Format Picture dialog box.

3. Click the Colors and Lines tab, if necessary (see Figure 10-5).

4. In the Fill settings, open the Color drop-down list and choose a color or gray shade. The following sidebar explains what the More Colors and Fill Effects options at the bottom of the drop-down list are for. Choose No Fill to remove a color or gray shade background.

5. If you so desire, click the Semitransparent check box to render the fill color or gray shade a little bit dimmer.

6. Click OK.

By the way, you can get interesting effects by filling a text box with black and changing the text to white (with the Font Color button), as this illustration shows:

LEARN BY EXAMPLE
Open the Figure 10-6 (Fill Effects) file on the companion CD to experiment with fill effects.

More Colors, More Fill Effects

To get especially fancy, you can create a color of your own or create a "fill effect" for a graphic or text box. To do that, choose More Colors or Fill Effects from the Color drop-down list on the Colors and Lines tab:

- ■ **More Colors**   To select a color apart from those on the Colors and Lines tab, click the More Colors option. You see the Color dialog box. On the Standard tab, click a color in the rainbow assortment of colors. On the Custom tab, either click a color in the rainbow assortment or enter hue, saturation, and luminance percentages, or red, green, and blue percentages to create a color. The New box in the lower-right corner shows precisely what color you are creating.

- ■ **Fill Effects**   When you choose Fill Effects at the bottom of the Color drop-down list, you see the Fill Effects dialog box with its four tabs: Gradient, Texture, Pattern, and Picture. The kinds of fill effects you can get by clicking one of the tabs and playing with the options are shown in Figure 10-6. To make a picture the background in a text box, you must either have installed the Clip Art Gallery or have clip art of your own on disk.

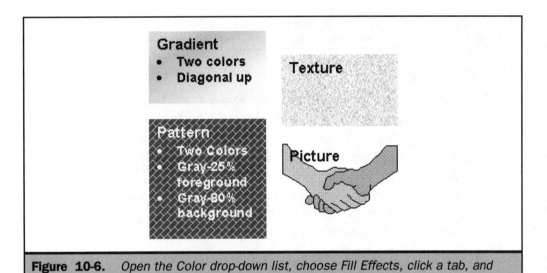

Figure 10-6. *Open the Color drop-down list, choose Fill Effects, click a tab, and start experimenting to create text boxes like these*

Drawing a Border Around a Page

Besides drawing a border around text boxes and graphics, you can draw a border around one, two, three, or all four sides of a page. Borders can go around all the pages in a document or a select few. Some of the borders that Word offers are quite playful. This illustration shows a page border surrounding a salad menu:

The following steps explain how to put a border around all the pages in a document, some of the pages, or a single page. To put a border around a single page or a handful of pages in the middle of a document, create a section for those pages before following these steps:

1. Click on the page that you want to put a border around.

2. Choose Format | Borders and Shading. You see the Borders and Shading dialog box.

3. Click on the Page Border tab. It is shown in Figure 10-7.

4. Under Setting, click the type of border you want. The None setting is for removing page borders. Click the Custom setting if you want to put borders on one, two, or three sides of the page or pages.

5. Under Style, click the type of line you want for the borders.

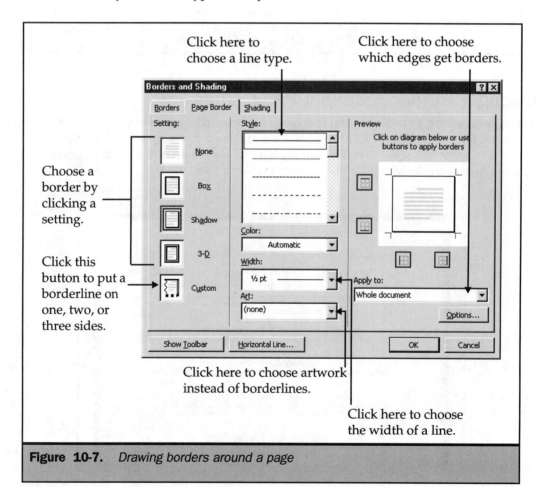

Figure 10-7.   *Drawing borders around a page*

6. If you want, choose a color for the borderlines on the Color drop-down list.

7. Open the Width drop-down list and choose a point setting to tell Word how wide the borderlines should be.

8. If you want artwork instead of lines around the border, click the Art drop-down list and choose pieces of cake, umbrellas, or whatever tickles your fancy.

9. If you chose the Custom setting in step 4, either click one of the four buttons or click in the diagram in the Preview area to tell Word which side or sides to draw borders on.

10. If you want to draw borders around some, but not all, of the pages in the document, click the Apply To drop-down menu and make a choice to tell Word which pages in the document to put borders around.

11. Click OK.

If you want to get specific about how close the borderlines can come to the edge of the page or pages, click the Options button and make choices in the Border and Shading Options dialog box.

Wrapping Text Around Graphics and Text Boxes

In word processing terms, *wrapping* means to make text wind around the side or sides of a text box or graphic. Don't confuse "wrapping" with "rapping," which means to make words fly around the sides of a boom box or topic. Wrapping text is one of the easiest ways to create an elegant layout and impress your impressionable friends and employers.

Tip *To make the most of text wrapping, hyphenate and justify the text that is being wrapped. That way, the text can get closer to the graphic or text box. For more information about setting hyphenation options in Word, see Chapter 7.*

Figure 10-8 illustrates several ways to wrap text. When you wrap text, you choose a wrapping style and tell Word along which side or sides of the text box or graphic to wrap the text:

- **Wrapping Styles** The style choices are Square, Tight, Through, Top And Bottom, Behind Text, In Front Of Text, and In Line With Text. When you choose Through, you can pull text as close to a text box or graphic as you want it to go. You can even make text overlap a text box or graphic.

- **Wrap To** The choices are Both Sides, Left Only, Right Only, and Largest Only. As Figure 10-8 shows, the Largest Only choice wraps the text around the side of the graphic that allows the most room for wrapping, and it leaves empty space next to the narrow side of the graphic.

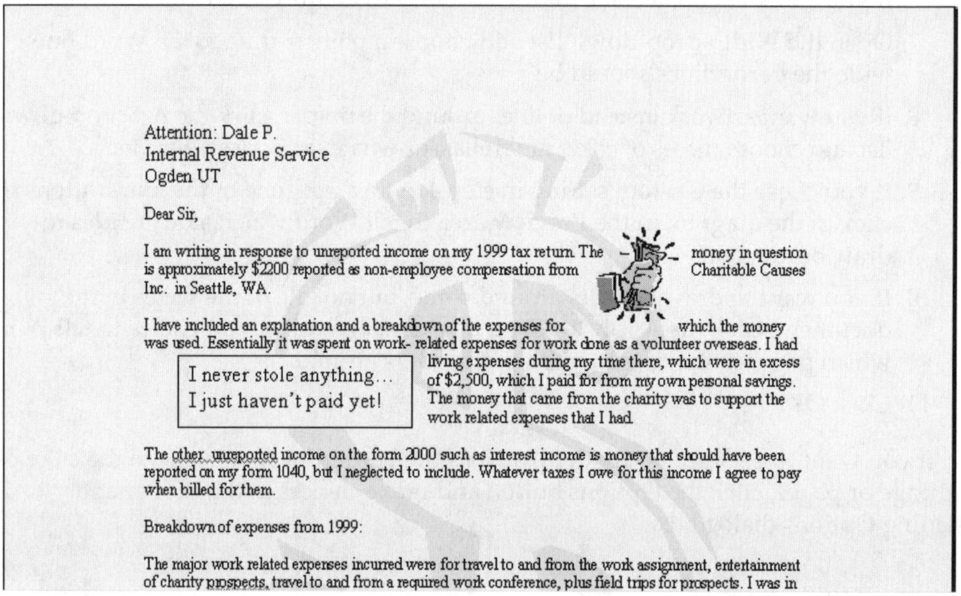

Attention: Dale P.
Internal Revenue Service
Ogden UT

Dear Sir,

I am writing in response to unreported income on my 1999 tax return. The money in question is approximately $2200 reported as non-employee compensation from Charitable Causes Inc. in Seattle, WA.

I have included an explanation and a breakdown of the expenses for which the money was used. Essentially it was spent on work- related expenses for work done as a volunteer overseas. I had living expenses during my time there, which were in excess of $2,500, which I paid for from my own personal savings. The money that came from the charity was to support the work related expenses that I had.

> I never stole anything...
> I just haven't paid yet!

The other unreported income on the form 2000 such as interest income is money that should have been reported on my form 1040, but I neglected to include. Whatever taxes I owe for this income I agree to pay when billed for them.

Breakdown of expenses from 1999:

The major work related expenses incurred were for travel to and from the work assignment, entertainment of charity prospects, travel to and from a required work conference, plus field trips for prospects. I was in

Figure 10-8.   *Word offers many elegant ways to wrap text around a text box or graphic*

To wrap text around a text box or graphic, follow these steps:

1. Click the text box or graphic to select it.

2. Choose Format | Text Box or Format | Picture. The Format Text Box or Format Picture dialog box appears.

3. Click the Layout tab, click the Advanced button, and in the Advanced Layout dialog box, click the Text Wrapping tab. It is shown in Figure 10-9.

4. Under Wrapping Styles, click a box to tell Word how to wrap text around the text box or graphic.

5. Under Wrap Text, click a box to tell Word which side or sides of the text box or graphic to wrap the text around.

6. If you want to be specific about how close text can come to the graphic or text box, choose settings under Distance From Text.

7. Click OK twice.

EXAMPLES

LEARN BY EXAMPLE
Open the Figure 10-A (Wrapping) file on the companion CD if you want to try your hand at different wrapping styles and methods.

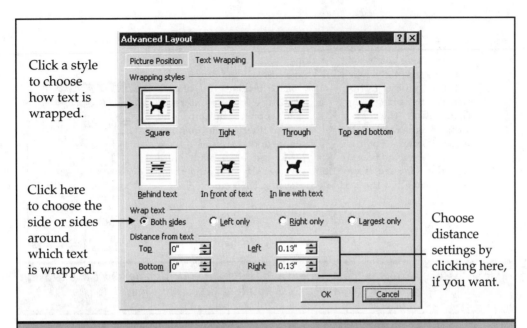

Click a style to choose how text is wrapped.

Click here to choose the side or sides around which text is wrapped.

Choose distance settings by clicking here, if you want.

WORD

Figure 10-9. *Telling Word how to wrap text and in which direction to wrap it*

Wrapping "Through" a Graphic

The Through wrapping style in the Advanced Layout dialog box is for making text wrap very, very close to a graphic or for making text overlap part of a graphic. After you choose the Through option and place the graphic in the text, you can make the text come closer by following these steps:

1. Click the graphic to select it.

2. Right-click on a toolbar and choose Picture to bring the Picture toolbar onscreen.

3. Click the Text Wrapping button and choose Edit Wrap Points from the shortcut menu, as shown in Figure 10-10. Black wrap points—small squares—appear on the graphic. You can see them in the figure.

4. Click and drag the wrap points inward to make text come closer to the graphic.

5. Click on the text when you are done.

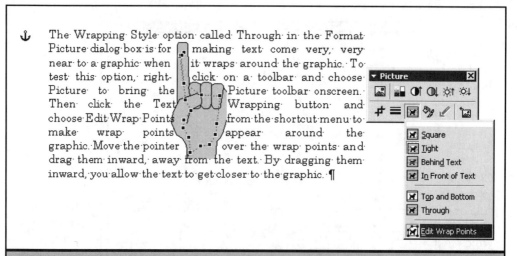

Figure 10-10. *Wrap points are the black squares that determine how close text can come to a graphic. Click and drag wrap points inward to make text come closer*

LEARN BY EXAMPLE

To doodle around with the Through option and see how wrap points work, open the Figure 10-10 (Through Wrap) file on the companion CD.

Creating a Drop Cap

A *drop cap*, also known as a *drop capital*, is a letter that falls two, three, four, or more lines into the text. Figure 10-11 shows examples of drop caps. In Victorian times, it was considered very stylish to begin each chapter in a book with a drop cap, but drop caps can be used for other purposes, as the figure demonstrates.

Follow these steps to create a drop cap:

1. Click anywhere in the paragraph whose first letter is to be the drop cap.

2. Choose Format | Drop Cap. The Drop Cap dialog box appears, as shown in Figure 10-12.

3. Choose Dropped or In Margin (the None setting is for removing drop caps):

■ **Dropped** Wraps text around the drop cap.

■ **In Margin** Places the drop cap in the margin beside the text. You cannot use this setting with text that has been laid out in columns.

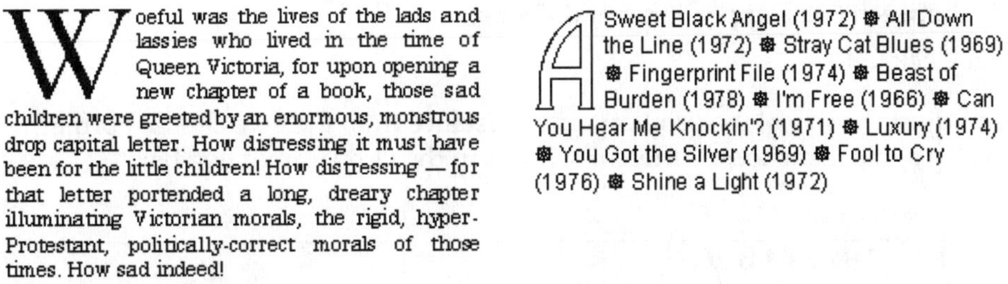

oeful was the lives of the lads and lassies who lived in the time of Queen Victoria, for upon opening a new chapter of a book, those sad children were greeted by an enormous, monstrous drop capital letter. How distressing it must have been for the little children! How distressing — for that letter portended a long, dreary chapter illuminating Victorian morals, the rigid, hyper-Protestant, politically-correct morals of those times. How sad indeed!

Sweet Black Angel (1972) ✹ All Down the Line (1972) ✹ Stray Cat Blues (1969) ✹ Fingerprint File (1974) ✹ Beast of Burden (1978) ✹ I'm Free (1966) ✹ Can You Hear Me Knockin'? (1971) ✹ Luxury (1974) ✹ You Got the Silver (1969) ✹ Fool to Cry (1976) ✹ Shine a Light (1972)

Figure 10-11.   *The uses of drop caps at the start of an essay (left) and to mark the A side of a homemade cassette tape (right)*

4. Click the Font menu and choose a font for the drop capital letter. Choose a font that is different from the text in the paragraph that the letter is being "dropped in."

5. In the Lines To Drop box, enter how many lines the letter is to drop. In Figure 10-11, for example, each drop cap drops four lines into the text.

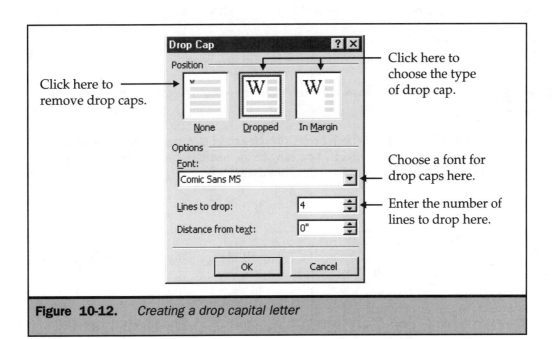

Click here to remove drop caps.

Click here to choose the type of drop cap.

Choose a font for drop caps here.

Enter the number of lines to drop here.

Figure 10-12.   *Creating a drop capital letter*

6. In the Distance From Text box, enter a number, if necessary, to put more space between the dropped letter and the text.

7. Click OK.

To adjust the size of the drop cap or its distance from the text, choose Format | Drop Cap again and choose different settings in the Drop Cap dialog box.

EXAMPLES

LEARN BY EXAMPLE
Open the Figure 10-11 (Drop Caps) file on the companion CD if you want to play around with drop capital letters.

Using One of Word's "Text Effects"

In the Font dialog box are a number of "text effects" that you can use to embellish text in various ways. Use the text effects along with boldface, italics, and underlining to draw readers' attention to headings and announcements in documents. The four most artful text effects—outlining, embossing, engraving, and shadowing—are shown in Figure 10-13. Some of the text effects look better on dark or black backgrounds.

Follow these steps to apply one of Word's "text effects" to a document:

1. Select the text.

2. Choose Format | Font. You see the Font dialog box.

Tip *Most of the text effects work better when the text being "effected" has been boldfaced.*

3. Under Effects, click a check box. Don't be afraid to experiment and to choose combinations of text effects. You can see the results of your experiments in the Preview box at the bottom of the Font dialog box.

4. Click OK.

EXAMPLES

LEARN BY EXAMPLE
On the companion CD is a file called Figure 10-13 (Text Effects). Open it if you would like to experiment with Word's text effects.

Arranging Text in Newspaper-Style Columns

Text looks great when it is laid out in newspaper-style columns. In columns, you can pack more text on the page. And you can put two or three stories on a page and give

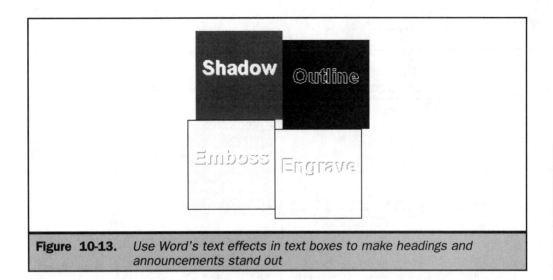

Figure 10-13. *Use Word's text effects in text boxes to make headings and announcements stand out*

readers a choice as to which story they read first. This part of the chapter explains how to create newspaper-style columns in Word like the columns shown in Figure 10-14. It tells how to adjust the width of columns, break columns in the middle, create a heading that straddles columns, and make text in columns float to different pages.

However, before you take the plunge and create columns, I strongly recommend getting out a piece of scratch paper and designing your little newsletter. Decide how wide to make the columns, how much space to put between columns, how many columns you want, and how tall to make the headings. While you're at it, choose File | Page Setup and tell Word how wide to make the margins. You usually don't need wide margins, headers, or footers in a newsletter. Word gives you lots of opportunities to tinker with columns and column sizes after you lay them out, but it takes a lot of time and shilly-shallying to do that. Better to get it right from the start and know precisely what you want to do.

 You can only work with column properties and formatting in Page Layout view.

Creating and Adjusting Columns

The Columns button on the Standard toolbar offers a fast but dicey way to create columns, but I think you should be thorough about it. The Columns button simply throws out a number of columns and says, "Hello, I'm done." But columns are a tricky affair. It's hard to get them right the first time.

When you create columns, Word asks what part of the document to "columnize," so where the cursor is matters a lot when you give the command to create columns. You can columnize an entire document, everything past the position of the cursor, an

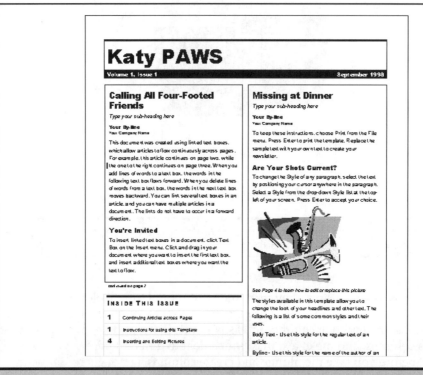

Figure 10-14.   *You can create handsome column layouts with Word*

Should You Be Using a Table?

Some people create a two- or three-column document when they should be creating a table instead. Résumés, for example, are usually laid out in two columns (one for job titles, for example, and one for job descriptions), but you would be foolish to use Word's Column command to lay out a résumé. Why? Because when you enter text at the top of the first column, text gets bumped downward to the bottom of the first column and into the second column. With Word's Column command, text "snakes" from one column to the next whenever you enter new text. If you were trying to create a résumé or other document in which the text in one column has to refer to the text in the next column (Job Title to Job Description, for example), you would go through hell trying to line up text in the two columns. Each time you made an edit or entered a word or two, text would start snaking and everything would turn into chaos.

For résumés, schedules, and other two-column documents in which one column refers to the other, create a two-column table. Then optionally remove the table borders. See "Working with Tables in Word," later in this chapter.

entire section, or selected text. Word creates a new section when you create columns in the middle of a document.

Following are instructions for creating columns and for adjusting columns after you have created them:

1. If you are creating columns, place the cursor in a section you want to columnize, select the text you want to columnize, or place the cursor at the position where columns are to begin appearing. If you are adjusting a column layout, click in a column.

2. Choose Format | Columns. You see the Columns dialog box shown in Figure 10-15.

3. Click a Presets box to choose a predesigned column layout of one, two, or three columns; or, if you want more than three columns, enter the number of columns you want in the Number Of Columns box.

4. Click the Line Between check box if you want Word to draw lines between columns.

Caution

You can't have it both ways. If you click the Line Between check box, lines appear between all the columns. You can't tell Word to place lines between one or two columns but not the others.

5. If you want to, tell Word how wide each column should be and how much space to put between columns in the Width And Spacing area. Watch the Preview box to see the effects of your choices. As you make entries in the Width and Spacing boxes, Word adjusts width and spacing settings so that all the columns can fit across the page. Be prepared to wrestle with these option boxes:

   ■ **Width**   For each column, enter a number to tell Word how wide to make the column. Click the down arrow on the scroll bar, if necessary, to get to the fourth, fifth, or sixth column. (Make sure the Equal Column Width check box is cleared if you want columns of unequal size.)

   ■ **Spacing**   For each column, enter a number to tell Word how much space to put between it and the column to its right.

6. In the Apply To drop-down list, tell Word to "columnize" the section that the cursor is in, the remainder of the document, the entire document, or text you selected.

7. Click OK.

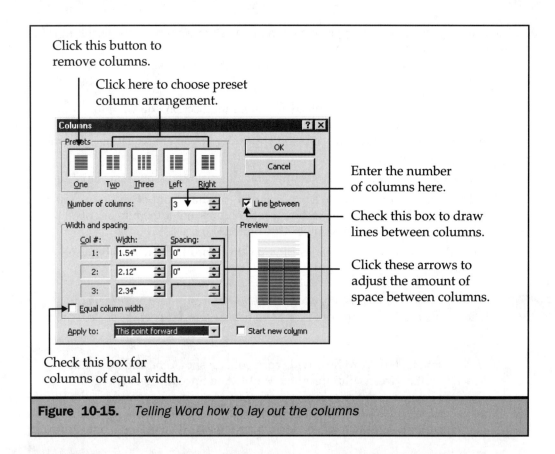

Click this button to remove columns.

Click here to choose preset column arrangement.

Enter the number of columns here.

Check this box to draw lines between columns.

Click these arrows to adjust the amount of space between columns.

Check this box for columns of equal width.

Figure 10-15. *Telling Word how to lay out the columns*

Breaking a Column for Empty Space, a Text Box, or a Graphic

Suppose you want to break a column in the middle in order to insert a graphic, insert a text box, or merely to put some empty white space in the bottom of a column. Following are instructions for breaking a column.

Creating White Space at the Bottom of a Column

To empty out the bottom of a column, click at the end of what is to be the last line in the column and either press CTRL-SHIFT-ENTER or choose Insert | Break and click the Column break option button. Word breaks the column, and text that was at the bottom of the column is pushed into the next column, as shown in Figure 10-16.

WORD

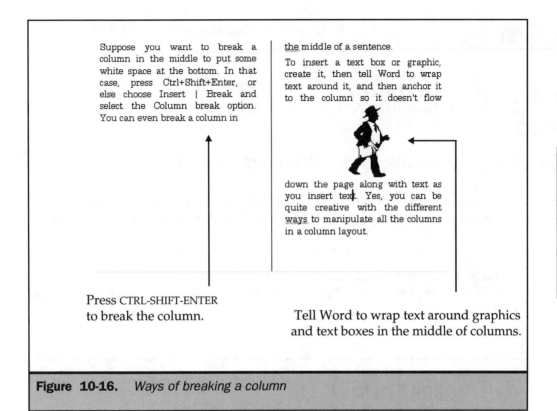

Suppose you want to break a column in the middle to put some white space at the bottom. In that case, press Ctrl+Shift+Enter, or else choose Insert | Break and select the Column break option. You can even break a column in the middle of a sentence.

To insert a text box or graphic, create it, then tell Word to wrap text around it, and then anchor it to the column so it doesn't flow down the page along with text as you insert text. Yes, you can be quite creative with the different ways to manipulate all the columns in a column layout.

Press CTRL-SHIFT-ENTER to break the column.

Tell Word to wrap text around graphics and text boxes in the middle of columns.

Figure 10-16.   *Ways of breaking a column*

Breaking a Column with a Text Box or Graphic

To break a column with a text box or graphic, create a text box or import a graphic and tell Word to wrap the text around the graphic or text box. After you have imported the graphic or text box and positioned it roughly where it is to go, follow these steps:

1. Click the graphic or text box and choose Format | Picture or Format | Text Box.

2. In the Format dialog box, click the Layout tab, click the Advanced button, select the Text Wrapping tab, and choose Top & Bottom as the wrapping style.

Note *You can also wrap text around the sides of a graphic. See "Wrapping Text Around Graphics and Text Boxes," earlier in this chapter.*

3. Click the Picture Position tab and uncheck the Move Object With Text check box.

4. Click OK twice.

5. Drag the graphic or text box to locate it correctly in the column.

Tip   *To find out where a column break was inserted and perhaps delete it, click the Show/Hide button on the Standard toolbar.*

LEARN BY EXAMPLE
Open the Figure 10-16 (Column Break) file on the companion CD if you want to experiment with column breaks.

Creating a Heading That Straddles Columns

Creating a heading that straddles columns, like the heading in Figure 10-17, is similar to inserting a text box in the middle of a single column. All you have to do is create the text box and fill it with the heading. Then you anchor the heading to the page and tell Word to wrap text around the heading.

Follow these steps to create a heading that straddles columns:

1. Create the text box and type the heading inside it. Format the letters in the heading. Be sure to make the text box as small as is necessary to hold the heading.

2. Click the text box and choose Format | Text Box. You see the Format Text Box dialog box.

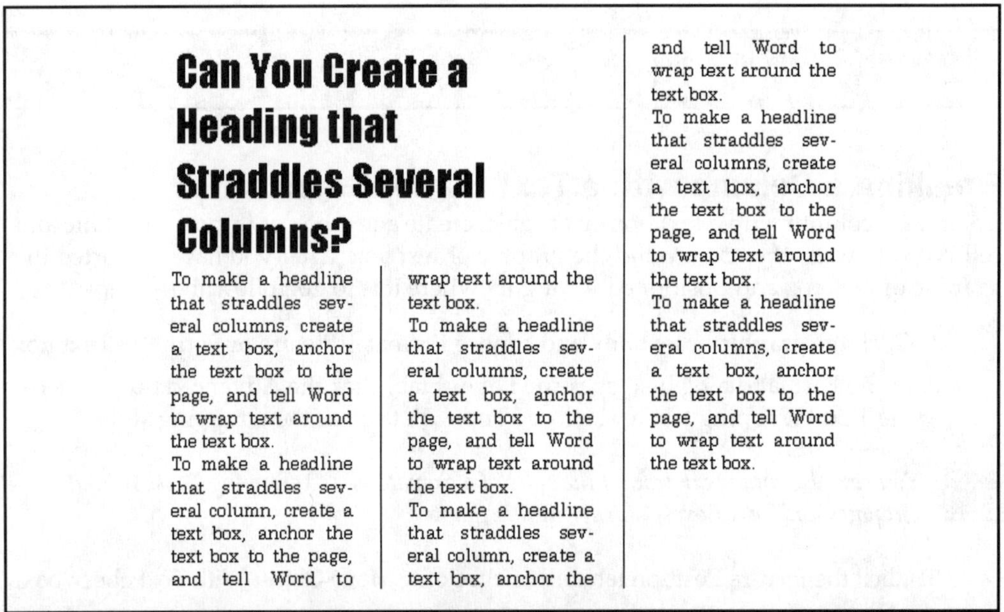

Can You Create a Heading that Straddles Several Columns?

To make a headline that straddles several columns, create a text box, anchor the text box to the page, and tell Word to wrap text around the text box.

To make a headline that straddles several column, create a text box, anchor the text box to the page, and tell Word to

wrap text around the text box.

To make a headline that straddles several columns, create a text box, anchor the text box to the page, and tell Word to wrap text around the text box.

To make a headline that straddles several column, create a text box, anchor the

and tell Word to wrap text around the text box.

To make a headline that straddles several columns, create a text box, anchor the text box to the page, and tell Word to wrap text around the text box.

To make a headline that straddles several columns, create a text box, anchor the text box to the page, and tell Word to wrap text around the text box.

Figure 10-17.   *Create a text box to lay out a heading that straddles, or crosses, several columns*

3. Click the Colors and Lines tab and, under Line, choose No Line on the Color drop-down menu.

4. Click the Layout tab, click the Advanced button, select the Picture Position tab, and anchor the text box to the page. To do that, uncheck the Move Object With Text check box, click to put a check mark in the Lock Anchor check box, and choose Page in the Horizontal drop-down menu.

5. Click the Text Wrapping tab and choose Top & Bottom as the wrapping style.

6. Click OK twice.

LEARN BY EXAMPLE
On the companion CD is a sample file called Figure 10-17 (Heading Straddle) that demonstrates a heading that straddles columns.

Making Text in Columns "Float" to Different Pages

Word's Format | Columns command is fine and good for laying out newsletters, but suppose a story begins on page 1 and resumes on page 3. What do you do then? In the Columns dialog box, Word offers no way to make text go from the front page to page 3 as the front page fills up. However, by tweaking Word, you can make linked text boxes so that text flows automatically from one page to the next when a story needs to be broken in the middle of the page. Doing so requires a little planning and forethought, but it can be done.

Note   *Publisher allows you to more easily work with floating text boxes (which it calls frames) to create publications such as newsletters. If you have Publisher, you probably want to use it to save yourself time and trouble when creating such documents. Chapter 30 describes how to use Publisher to lay out a publication.*

To make it work, you ignore the Format | Columns command and create columns with text boxes. On the Text Box toolbar is a button for establishing a link between two text boxes so that text from the first goes automatically to the second when the first fills up. After you've linked all the text boxes, you paste text in the start of the first box and it flows into all the text boxes in the chain.

Tip   *Click the Next Text Box or Previous Text Box button on the Text Box toolbar to go from text box to text box in a chain.*

For this technique of linking text boxes to work, you have to very carefully lay out the text boxes first. Word doesn't allow you to link text boxes in which text has already been put, so you have to plan carefully where the text boxes go. And you have to write all the text first and then be prepared to copy it in one shot into the text boxes. Follow these general steps to lay out and link the text boxes:

1. Create a text box for each column, as well as one for each heading and each "continued on" slug (the slug at the bottom of the column that says "Cont'd on page 2," for example). All of the text boxes need not be columns. On page 2, for example, you could create large boxes, for the spillover text from page 1.

2. After you have created the text boxes, right-click on a toolbar and choose Text Box, if necessary, to see the Text Box toolbar.

3. Click the first text box in the chain of text boxes that text is supposed to pass to and from.

4. Click the Create Text Box Link button. The cursor changes into an odd-looking shape, something like a pitcher:

Create Text Box Link button

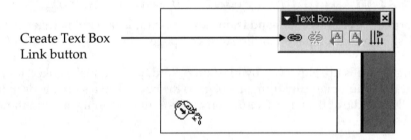

5. Move the pointer to the next text box in the chain and click it.

6. Copy the text you want to paste into the newsletter.

7. Click at the top of the first text box and give the Paste command. Text flows from the first text box into the next one.

8. Click in the second text box, if necessary, and repeat steps 4 and 5 to keep the text flowing to a third text box. You can link as many text boxes as is necessary this way.

Also on the Text Box toolbar is the Break Forward Link button for breaking the relationship between text boxes that are linked together. Click the text box that is to be the last in the chain and then click the Break Forward Link button to break a link.

LEARN BY EXAMPLE
Open the Figure 10-B (Text Float) file on the companion CD if you would like to experiment with using text boxes in a newsletter to make text float from place to place. At the bottom of the document is some text. Copy it to the Clipboard, then follow the instructions above for linking text boxes in a chain.

Removing the Columns

To remove columns, click anywhere in the columns and choose Format | Columns. You see the Columns dialog box (see Figure 10-15). Under Presets, click One and then click OK.

Working with Tables in Word

Tables are an important part of any report or other kind of document that presents figures, so this part of the chapter explains how to create, enter numbers in, edit, change the layout of, and create header rows in a table.

Tip *Work on tables in Page Layout view. That way, you know precisely how close text comes to the margins. One of the biggest difficulties of working with tables is making all the data fit. One way to get around that problem is to print the page with the table on it in Landscape orientation.*

Creating a Table

The best way to work on a table is to create a simple table, enter the data, and then worry about formats and layouts. Don't concern yourself with what the table looks like until you've entered all the text. That way, you can focus on the data itself and make sure it is accurate.

To create a table, click the Insert Table button on the Standard toolbar. When you click the button, a 4 × 5 grid appears. Move the pointer over the grid and then click to tell Word how many columns and rows you want. To create a table bigger than four rows and five columns, hold down the mouse button as you move the mouse. This expands the grid. Release the mouse button when the table shows the number of rows and columns you want. In this illustration, clicking would create a table that is six rows long and seven columns wide.

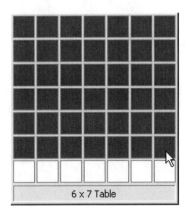
6 x 7 Table

Don't bother choosing the right number of rows and columns for now. As the following pages explain, it is easy to add and delete rows and columns.

 A fast way to create a table is to do it with the Draw Table tool. Right-click on a toolbar and choose Tables and Borders. Then click the Draw Table tool and draw your table.

Entering and Editing Table Data

After you have created the rows and columns, you can start entering the data. These instructions explain how to move from cell to cell to enter data, as well as how to move long distances in a table. You also find out how to delete and insert columns and rows and how to select them. You can't insert or delete columns or rows without selecting them first.

Moving Around in a Table

As you enter data, you can press the arrow keys or click in cells to move from place to place. Use the following shortcut keys to go long distances:

Press	To Move Here
TAB	Next cell in row
SHIFT-TAB	Previous cell in a row
ALT-END	End of the row
ALT-HOME	Start of the row
ALT-PAGE DOWN	Bottom of the column
ALT-PAGE UP	Top of the column

 A cell is the place where a row and column intersect. Each cell holds one data item.

Deleting Rows and Columns

To delete a row or column, follow these steps:

1. Click a cell in a row or column that you want to delete.
2. Click the Table menu, click Delete, and click the item that corresponds to what you want to delete.

Inserting Rows and Columns

To insert a row or column, follow these steps:

1. Click a cell in a row or column where you want to insert.

2. Click the Table menu, click Insert, and then select the item that corresponds to what you want to insert.

 To insert a new last row in a table, click in the last column of the last row and press the TAB key.

Formatting a Table

Word offers about a billion commands for formatting tables. However, unless you are the type who enjoys tinkering with table borders, shading, and other table formats, your best bet is to let Word do the work with the AutoFormat command. The following pages explain how to select rows and column, how to use the AutoFormat command, how to align text in columns and rows, and how to change the width of columns and the height of rows.

Selecting Rows and Columns

Before you can format rows and columns, you have to select them:

- **Columns**   To select a column, move the pointer to the top of the column. When the pointer changes into a black arrow that points down, click. To select several columns at once, continue to hold down the mouse button and drag the mouse to the right or left after you have selected the first column. Another way to select columns is to hold down the ALT key and click anywhere in the column. To select adjacent columns with this technique, continue to hold down the ALT key and drag across the desired columns.

- **Rows**   To select a row, move the pointer to the left side of the row you want to select. When the pointer points to the upper-right corner of the screen, click. To select several rows, continue to hold down the mouse button and drag the mouse up or down.

- **Entire Table**   To select an entire table, either choose Table | Select Table or hold down the ALT key and double-click in the table.

Changing the Look of a Table

After the table has been "autoformatted," you can tweak it here and there to make it look better. First, however, let Word's AutoFormat command do the bulk of the work by following these steps:

1. Click in the table.

2. Choose Table | Table AutoFormat. You see the Table AutoFormat dialog box shown in Figure 10-18.

3. In the Formats box, click the names of formats to find the one you like best. The Preview box shows what the formats look like.

4. Experiment with the Formats To Apply and Apply Special Formats To check boxes to see how checking and unchecking the options affects the look of the table. Keep your eye on the Preview box as you do so.

5. Click OK when the table looks tip-top.

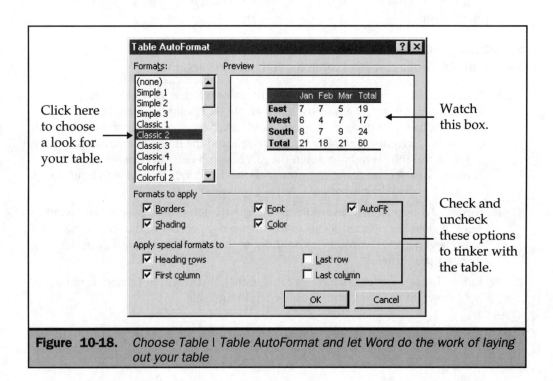

Figure 10-18. Choose Table | Table AutoFormat and let Word do the work of laying out your table

Aligning Text in Table Columns and Rows

Word provides nine ways to align text. After you select what you want to align, right-click on it, place the cursor on Cell Alignment from the shortcut menu, and then make a selection from the submenu:

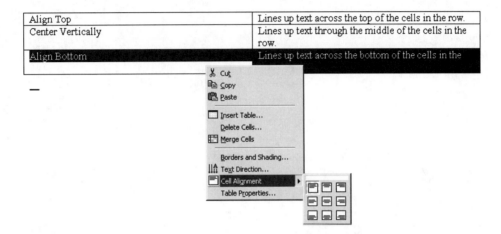

Align Top	Lines up text across the top of the cells in the row.
Center Vertically	Lines up text through the middle of the cells in the row.
Align Bottom	Lines up text across the bottom of the cells in the

Changing the Width of Columns and the Height of Rows

In Page Layout view, drag column bars and row bars to change the width of columns and the height of rows. This illustration shows the row bars and column bars:

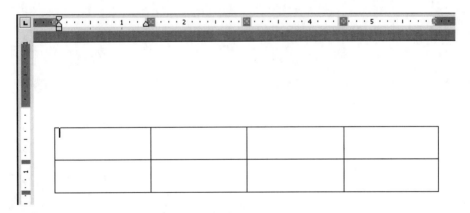

To make the rows in a table the same height or columns the same width, select the rows or columns, right-click, choose Table | AutoFit, and then choose Distribute Rows Evenly or Distribute Columns Evenly.

The
Complete
Reference

Office
2000

Chapter 11

Writing Reports and Scholarly Papers

In this chapter, you will find advice and instructions for working on long documents such as reports, manuals, and scholarly papers. You will be glad to learn that Word has taken much of the drudgery out of writing long documents.

To help keep organized, you can work in Outline view or gather documents into a master document. That way, you always know where the various and sundry parts of your report or manual are and whether you need to rearrange things. Of course, no report or manual is complete without lots of lists and tables, so this chapter explains how to create numbered and bulleted lists, as well as how to create tables of contents and tables of figures, among other kinds of tables.

This chapter includes instructions for numbering the lines on a page and numbering the headings in a document. It tells how to create indexes and cross-references, as well as automatic captions for figures, graphs, and tables. Because footnotes and endnotes are such a chore, this chapter explains how to create them with Word's very excellent Insert menu's Footnote command.

When I went to college during the Mesozoic era, students used typewriters to enter footnotes, figure tables, and the like. Perhaps this, and not disco culture, explains why I have never been nostalgic for those years.

Organizing Your Work

This section delves into two techniques for making sure that a long report, manual, or whatnot is well organized. It describes how to switch to Outline view to get a read on whether the work is organized well and how to rearrange documents in Outline view. The following pages also explain how to create a master document—a collection of subdocuments that, together, make up a single work. Create a master document for very, very big jobs.

LEARN BY EXAMPLE
Open the Figure 11-1 (Outline) file on the companion CD if you want to test-drive Word's Outline view options.

Organizing Your Work with Outlines

If your report or manual is a long one with many different headings in it, you can do yourself a big favor by assigning styles to the headings and taking advantage of Outline view. In Outline view, you can glance at a single page and see how the different parts of a document fit together. And if they don't fit together correctly, you can rearrange headings and the text that comes below them. This section explains how to do that, and it also explains how to edit headings, arrange headings in alphabetic order, and print an outline.

Styles are explained in Chapter 9. You can't see headings in Outline view unless the correct styles have been assigned to the headings.

Viewing the Outline of a Document

To see a document in Outline view, either click the Outline View button in the lower-left corner of the screen or choose View | Outline. The Outlining toolbar appears. To begin with, all headings and body text appear in the document window. However, by clicking buttons on the Outlining toolbar, you can tell Word how much or how little of the document to show onscreen.

For Figure 11-1, I clicked the 4 button on the toolbar to tell Word to display headings to which I assigned the Heading 1, Heading 2, Heading 3, and Heading 4

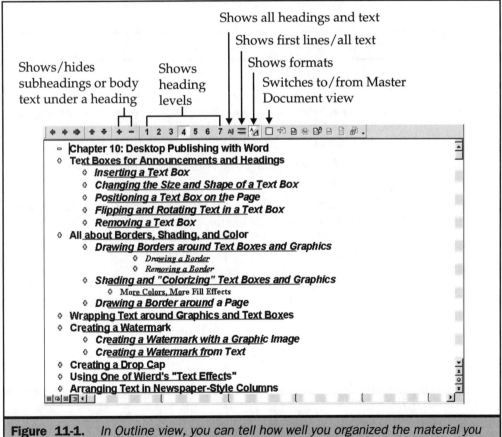

Figure 11-1. *In Outline view, you can tell how well you organized the material you want to present*

WORD

styles. Now I can read the headings in the document and tell if I am presenting the material in the right way. You can tell which are the Heading 4 styles in the figure because they are indented farthest from the left side of the screen.

After a document is in Outline view, click buttons on the right side of the Outlining toolbar to view the outline in different ways. Table 11-1 explains the buttons on the Outlining toolbar.

Editing Text in Outline View

Yes indeed, you can edit text in Outline view as though you were editing it in Normal or Print Layout view. In fact, editing headings in Outline view is the best way to see many headings at once and make sure that they all have the same tone and are presented in an organized fashion in your scholarly report or chapter.

Button	What It Does
Expand	Shows the subheadings and subordinate text under a heading. Click on a heading and click this button to display its subheadings.
Collapse	Shows the heading only. Click this button after you click the Expand button.
1–7	Shows different heading levels in a document. Click the 1 button to see only the headings to which the Heading 1 style has been applied; click the 7 button to see headings to which the Heading 1, 2, 3, 4, 5, 6, and 7 styles have been applied.
All	Shows all the headings in the document.
Show First Line Only	Shows the headings and the first line in each paragraph of subordinate text. When this button is not clicked—when it is not "pressed down"—all the text is shown.
Show Formatting	Shows the font and type size of the text.

Table 11-1.   *The Outlining Toolbar Buttons*

Rearranging a Document in Outline View

With a document in Outline view, you can do many things that would take far, far longer to do in Normal or Print Layout view. For example, you can promote or demote headings very easily. And if a heading and the text underneath it are in the wrong place, you can click toolbar buttons to move them—you don't have to visit the Cut and Paste commands.

The following pages explain how to promote and demote headings in Outline view and how to move headings forward or backward in a document. I've thrown in a neat trick for alphabetizing all the Heading 1s in a document, too.

 When you promote a heading, you make it a higher level. For example, promoting a level 4 heading makes it a level 3. When you demote a heading, you make it a level lower.

PROMOTING AND DEMOTING HEADINGS   Suppose, after looking over a document in Outline view, you decide that a heading needs to be promoted or demoted or that a heading shouldn't be a heading at all, but should be turned into text. For example, if a Heading 3 should be a Heading 4 or should be turned into plain text, you can make it so by clicking one of the three buttons on the left side of the Outlining toolbar. Notice that each button has an arrow on it. Click a button to promote or demote a heading and thereby move in the direction of or away from the left side of the screen.

Click the heading and then click one of the buttons on the Outlining toolbar to promote and demote headings. Table 11-2 explains the buttons on the toolbar.

Button	What It Does
Promote	Click this button once, twice, or as many times as necessary to move a heading up the ladder. For example, pressing the Promote button while the cursor is in a Heading 3 heading turns the heading into a Heading 2 heading.
Demote	Click this button to bust a heading down a rank.
Demote to Body Text	Click this button to make a heading into text. Headings are assigned the Normal style when you click this button.

Table 11-2.   *More Buttons on the Outlining Toolbar*

To promote or demote several headings at once, select them first by dragging the pointer across the headings you want to select.

MOVING HEADINGS (AND THE TEXT UNDERNEATH THEM) IN A DOCUMENT

Also on the left side of the Outlining toolbar are two buttons, Move Up and Move Down, for moving headings and the text underneath them to new places in a document. Being able to move text in Outline view is convenient indeed. Instead of cutting the heading and text and pasting it elsewhere, you can simply move it in Outline view.

When you move a heading in Outline view, the text underneath the heading moves along with the heading. Whether subheadings underneath the heading move as well depends on whether the subheadings are displayed on screen:

- ■ If no subheadings are displayed beneath the heading when you move the heading, the subheadings move along with the heading.

- ■ If subheadings are displayed beneath the heading, only the heading and its associated text moves.

To see how this works, look at Figure 11-2. If I click the fourth heading, "Arranging Text in Newspaper-Style Columns," and click the Move Up button, it will become the third heading in the document, but "Creating and Adjusting Columns"" will remain the fifth heading. It won't move along with its parent heading because I can see it onscreen. On the other hand, if I click "Arranging Text in Newspaper-Style Columns," then click the Collapse button to make the four subheadings below disappear, then click the Move Up button, "Arranging Text in Newspaper-Style Columns" and all

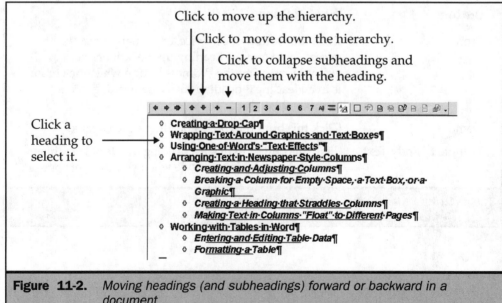

Figure 11-2. *Moving headings (and subheadings) forward or backward in a document*

its subheadings will become the third, fourth, fifth, sixth, and seventh headings in the document.

Follow these steps to move a heading forward or backward in a document:

1. Click the heading you want to move.

2. Tell Word whether you want to move subheadings (if there are any) below the heading:

   ■ To move the subheadings as well, click the Collapse button to fold the subheadings into the heading.

   ■ To move the heading independently of its subheadings, click the Expand button to display the subheadings in the window.

3. Click the Move Up or Move Down button as many times as necessary to land the heading in the right place.

Arranging Headings in Alphabetical Order

To arrange the Heading 1 headings in a document in alphabetic order, follow these steps:

1. Switch to Outline view.

2. Click the 1 button on the Outlining toolbar.

3. Choose Table | Sort. The Sort Text dialog box appears. For this task, you needn't worry about the options in this dialog box.

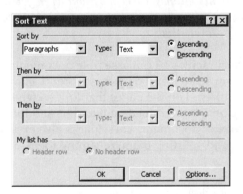

4. Click OK.

Text underneath the headings, and subheadings as well, are moved right along with the headings themselves.

Printing an Outline

When you print an outline, Word gives you whatever is onscreen in Outline view. In other words, to print the Heading 1s, Heading 2s, and Heading 3s, switch to Outline view and click the 3 button on the Outlining toolbar. Expand or collapse subheadings by clicking the Expand or Collapse button.

When exactly what you want to print is onscreen, click the Print button on the Standard toolbar. What you see is what you get.

Master Documents for Organizing Big Jobs

Word offers a special feature called a master document for working on book-length projects. If you were writing a 500-page Maileresque tome about the state of America and your ego, it would be a mistake to put all 500 pages in a single document. Imagine trying to find a paragraph or heading in such a long work. No, instead of hacking away at 500 pages at once, you could create a master document, a collection of subdocuments that are organized into one entity.

After the work has been organized into subdocuments, all you have to do is open a subdocument and start working on it. Changes made to the subdocument are all recorded in the master document. And when you work in the master document, changes made there are recorded in the subdocument as well.

Everything that can be done in Outline view can be done to a master document, but you can do it all at once to two, three, five, seven, or seventeen subdocuments. In other words, you can see whether the work is organized well, and move headings and text from subdocument to subdocument, if necessary. So master documents, besides making it easier to work on long documents, offer all the advantages of Outline view.

Knowing how to work in Outline view is important when you work with master documents. Don't create a master document unless you know how to use and operate all the buttons on the Outlining toolbar.

To create a master document, you can assemble documents you've been working on for a while or start from scratch and devise a master document for a new project. Advice for doing both is offered on the pages that follow, where you will also find instructions for working on a master document and its subdocument and removing subdocuments from a master document. These pages also explain moving subdocuments, merging and splitting them, renaming them, and locking them so that no one can change them.

Be sure to back up your documents frequently when using the Master Document feature; also disable the Fast Save feature. Choose Tools | Options, select the Save tab, and clear the Allow Fast Saves check box.

Creating a Master Document

Depending on where you start from, the techniques for creating a master document are different. Following are instructions for creating a master document from scratch and assembling documents for a master document.

To keep things simple and moving smoothly, keep all subdocuments in the same folder. Moreover, Word gets very confused when subdocuments are created with different templates, so make sure that all the documents in the master document are founded on the same template.

LEARN BY EXAMPLE
To try your hand at creating a master document, open the Figure 11-3 (Master Document) file from the companion CD.

CREATING A MASTER DOCUMENT FOR A NEW PROJECT   Follow these steps to create a master document from scratch:

1. Create a folder for the master document.

2. Create a new document.

3. Save the document in the folder you created in step 1. Congratulations. You just created the master document.

4. Choose View | Outline. As shown in Figure 11-3, the Master Document toolbar appears along with the Outlining toolbar.

5. Enter the headings in the document. In other words, draw up an outline for your masterpiece. As you enter the headings, assign each one a heading style. In steps 6 and 7, you will divide the outline into sample documents, so be sure to assign the Heading 1 style to what will be the first heading in each subdocument.

6. Select the headings for the first subdocument. To do that, click the plus symbol beside a heading to which the Heading 1 style has been applied.

7. Click the Create Subdocument button on the Master Document toolbar. As shown in Figure 11-3, a gray box appears around the headings in the subdocument. Meanwhile, a subdocument icon appears in the upper-left corner of the box.

You can click the cross next to a Heading 1 heading to select it and all its subheadings.

WORD

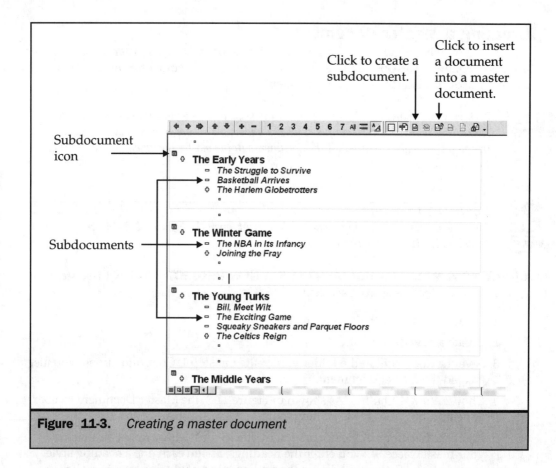

Click to create a subdocument.

Click to insert a document into a master document.

Subdocument icon

Subdocuments

The Early Years
The Struggle to Survive
Basketball Arrives
The Harlem Globetrotters

The Winter Game
The NBA in Its Infancy
Joining the Fray

The Young Turks
Bill, Meet Wilt
The Exciting Game
Squeaky Sneakers and Parquet Floors
The Celtics Reign

The Middle Years

Figure 11-3. *Creating a master document*

8. Select the next batch of headings and click the Create Subdocument button again. Keep doing this until you have created all the subdocuments.

9. Save the master document.

When you save a master document, Word saves its subdocuments as well. Word gets subdocument names from each subdocument's first heading.

ASSEMBLING DOCUMENTS FOR A MASTER DOCUMENT If your masterpiece is half completed and comprises many documents in many folders, you can still assemble the documents into a master document by following these steps:

1. Create a folder for the master document.

2. Create a new document.

WORD

3. Save the document in the folder you just created. You just created a master document.

4. Choose View | Outline. The Master Document toolbar appears (see Figure 11-3).

5. Click the Insert Subdocument button. You see the Insert Subdocument dialog box.

6. Find and click the first file that you want to be part of the master document, then click Open.

7. Click the 1 or 2 button on the Master Document toolbar. It's easier to work in Master Document view with only one or two headings showing.

8. Go to the bottom of the master document and repeat steps 5 and 6 as many times as necessary to insert all the subdocuments.

Existing documents keep their original names when they are inserted into a master document.

Working on a Master Document and Its Subdocuments

To work on a master document or one of its subdocuments, you can either start from the master document or a subdocument. If you open a subdocument, all is well. You can open a subdocument, work on it, save it, and close it without ever knowing that it is part of a master document.

Open the master, however, and you see a document that looks something like Figure 11-4. Those underlined characters are hyperlinks. Notice that each lists the path to a subdocument. By clicking a hyperlink, you can open a subdocument and start working. (Chapter 23 explains hyperlinks in great detail.)

Or, if you are so inclined, you can work directly in the master document by clicking the Expand Subdocuments button. Do that and you see the master document in Outline view. Scroll to the part of the master document you want to work on and then click the Normal or Print Layout button to start working.

 You can open a subdocument in Master Document view. To do so, double-click a subdocument icon.

Reorganizing, Caring for, and Maintaining Master Documents

After you have created the master document, you can take advantage of all the buttons on the Outlining toolbar to move headings and subheadings from place to place and to change the status of headings inside each subdocument. The previous section of this chapter explains how. For example, to move a heading to a new position inside a subdocument, click it, click the Collapse button if necessary, and then click the Move Up or Move Down button.

Suppose, however, that you want to rearrange the subdocuments inside a master document. Or you want to split a subdocument in two or merge two subdocuments.

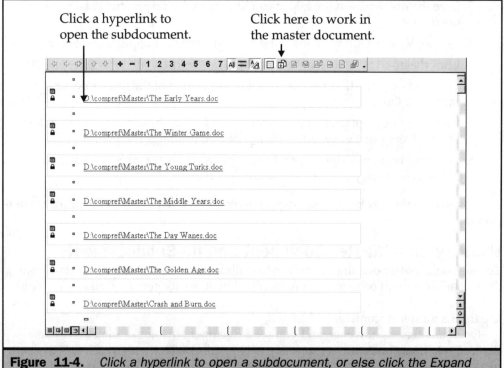

Figure 11-4. *Click a hyperlink to open a subdocument, or else click the Expand Subdocuments button to work inside the master document*

The following pages explain how to maintain, care for, and feed subdocuments in a master document.

Except when splitting subdocuments, click the 1 button on the Master Document toolbar so you see only the first-level headings in the document. That makes it easier to move, merge, and remove subdocuments.

REMOVING A SUBDOCUMENT   To remove a subdocument, click its subdocument icon and then click the Remove Subdocument button, as shown in Figure 11-5. When you delete a subdocument this way, the document is not erased from the hard disk. It is simply removed from the master document.

DIVIDING A SUBDOCUMENT IN TWO   To divide a subdocument into two subdocuments, click the first heading in the subdocument and then click the Expand button. Next, click the heading that is to be the first heading in the new subdocument and click the Split Subdocument button.

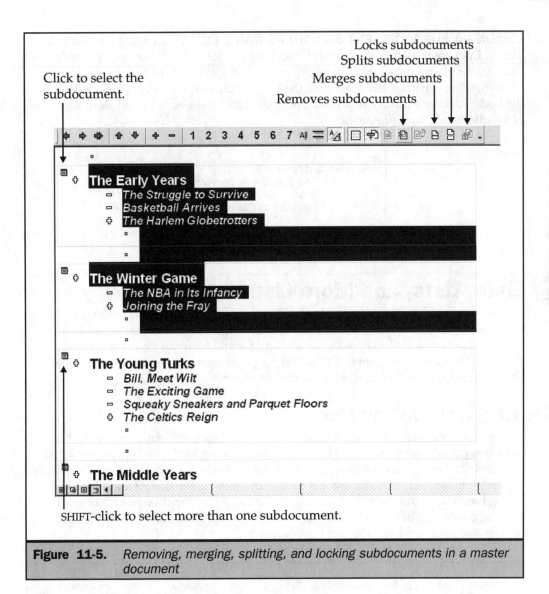

Figure 11-5. *Removing, merging, splitting, and locking subdocuments in a master document*

MERGING SUBDOCUMENTS   To merge subdocuments, move the subdocuments so that they appear one below the other in the master document. Next, select the subdocuments. To do so, click the first subdocument's icon, then hold down the SHIFT key and click the subdocument icon of each subdocument you want to merge (see Figure 11-5). With that done, click the Merge Subdocument button.

MOVING SUBDOCUMENTS   I've found that the best way to move subdocuments is to remove them and then reinsert them. See "Removing a Subdocument" and "Assembling Documents for a Master Document" for more information.

LOCKING A SUBDOCUMENT SO OTHERS CAN'T EDIT IT On the tail end of the Master Document toolbar is a button for locking subdocuments. Locking means to mark the subdocument so that others can read it but not alter it. To lock a subdocument, click anywhere inside it and then click the Lock Document button. To unlock it, click the Lock Document button again. Subdocuments that have been locked show a picture of a padlock next to their names:

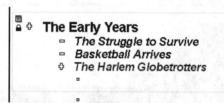

Lists, Lists, and More Lists

This section explains how to create bulleted lists, numbered lists, and numbering schemes for headings. Word offers some very convenient ways to handle lists. And if Word's numbers or bullets aren't good enough for you, you can invent numbering schemes or bullets of your own. The following pages explain how to create numbered lists, bulleted lists, and numbers for chapter headings.

Creating a Numbered List

Figure 11-6 shows a sample of the types of numbered lists you can create with Word. How fancy you want your lists to be is up to you. On the left is the list you get when you click the Numbering button on the Formatting toolbar. The two lists in the middle are preformatted lists that you can get simply by opening the Bullets and Numbering dialog box. The list on the right is a customized list. Although it takes a bit of work, you can create number formats on your own. This section explains how. It also tells how to start, stop, and resume lists in documents.

1.	Abbot and Costello	I.	Abbot and Costello	a)	Abbot and Costello	A.	Abbot and Costello
2.	Laurel and Hardy	II.	Laurel and Hardy	b)	Laurel and Hardy	B.	Laurel and Hardy
3.	The Marx Brothers	III.	The Marx Brothers	c)	The Marx Brothers	C.	The Marx Brothers
4.	The Three Stooges	IV.	The Three Stooges	d)	The Three Stooges	D.	The Three Stooges

Figure 11-6. *A sampling of Word's numbered list formats*

Keeping Numbered Lists from Appearing Automatically

Word creates numbered lists automatically whether you like it or not when you type 1, A., or i; then enter a blank space or press TAB; type some text; and then press the ENTER key. Yours truly finds that extremely annoying. Perhaps you do, too. Follow these steps to tell Word not to create numbered lists automatically:

1. Choose Insert | AutoText | AutoText. You see the AutoCorrect dialog box.

2. Click the AutoFormat As You Type tab. It is shown in Figure 11-7.

3. Click the Automatic Numbered Lists check box to remove the check mark.

4. Click OK.

WORD

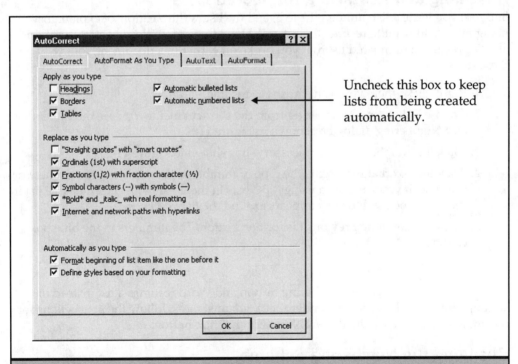

Uncheck this box to keep lists from being created automatically.

Figure 11-7.   *Telling Word not to create numbered lists automatically*

LEARN BY EXAMPLE
To experiment with the many options for numbering lists, open the Figure 11-A
(Numbered List) file on the companion CD.

Creating a List

To create a simple list that isn't broken in the middle and doesn't require fancy
formatting, type the items one at a time without any concern for numbers. Press ENTER
after you have typed each item. When the list is done, select it and click the Numbering
button on the Formatting toolbar.

The other way to create a simple list is to click the Numbering button and start
typing. Each time you press ENTER, Word adds a new number to the list. When you are
finished typing your list, press the ENTER key and then click the Numbering button to
remove the last number.

Resuming and Restarting Numbered Lists

Suppose you write a list numbered 1 to 6, end the list, write a couple of explanatory
paragraphs, and want to resume the list at 7. How do you tell Word to start numbering
at 7? To resume a numbered list that you broke off earlier in a document, follow
these steps:

1. Right-click where you want the list to resume.

2. Choose Bullets and Numbering from the shortcut menu. You see the Bullets
   and Numbering dialog box shown in Figure 11-8.

3. Click the Numbered tab, if necessary. It is shown in Figure 11-8.

4. Click the box that represents the type of numbered list you want to resume. For
   example, if you have been using ABC lists in the document, click the ABC list in
   the dialog box. A blue box appears around the list you chose.

5. Click the Continue Previous List option button. The numbers in the blue box
   change.

6. Click OK.

Sometimes you click the Numbering button and Word resumes a list instead of
starting one anew. To start a list under those circumstances, follow the instructions for
resuming a list, but click the Restart Numbering option button.

Changing the Numbering Scheme

Word offers seven numbering schemes in the Bullets and Numbering dialog box.
Follow these steps to choose one of Word's numbering schemes:

1. Select the items to be included in the list; or, if you've already created the list
   and want to change its numbering scheme, select the list.

2. Right-click and choose Bullets and Numbering from the shortcut menu. You see the Numbered tab of the Bullets and Numbering dialog box (see Figure 11-8).

3. Click the type of list you want. A blue box appears around the list.

4. Click OK.

Note

After you choose a new numbering scheme in the Bullets and Numbering dialog box, it becomes the default scheme for the document you are working on. After you chose Roman numerals or letters, for example, you get Roman numbers or letters when you click the Numbering button on the Formatting toolbar.

Creating Your Own Format for Numbered Lists

If none of Word's formats do the trick, you can format the numbers on your own. You can choose a font for numbers and decide which punctuation mark follows the number. To be adventurous, you can tell Word how to align numbers and how far from the left margin to indent the text that follows the numbers.

Follow these steps to design a number format of your own:

1. Either select the items in the numbered list, or, if you haven't entered the items yet, place the insertion point where the list is to start.

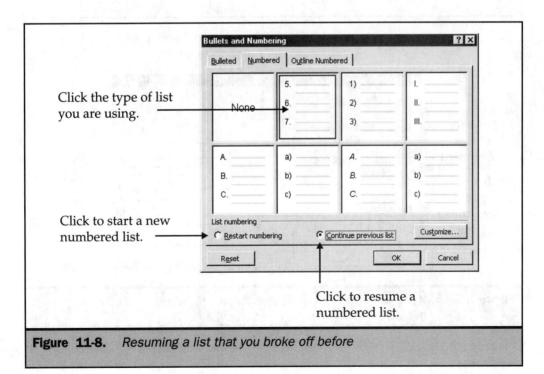

Figure 11-8. *Resuming a list that you broke off before*

2. Right-click and choose Bullets and Numbering. You see the Bullets and Numbering dialog box.

3. Click the Numbered tab (see Figure 11-8), if necessary.

4. Click the numbered list that most resembles the one you want to create on your own.

5. Click the Customize button. You see the Customize Numbered List dialog box shown in Figure 11-9.

6. If you want, change the punctuation mark that is to follow the numbers or letters in the list by clicking in the Number Format box, erasing the period, and entering a new punctuation mark. For example, you could enter a colon (:) or hyphen (-).

7. Click the Font button to choose a new font and font size for the numbers or letters. The Font dialog box appears. Choose a new font and font size, and then click OK.

Tip *Besides choosing fonts, you can choose special effects and even animate the numbers or letters by choosing options in the Font dialog box. To animate text, select the Text Effects tab and select from the Animations list.*

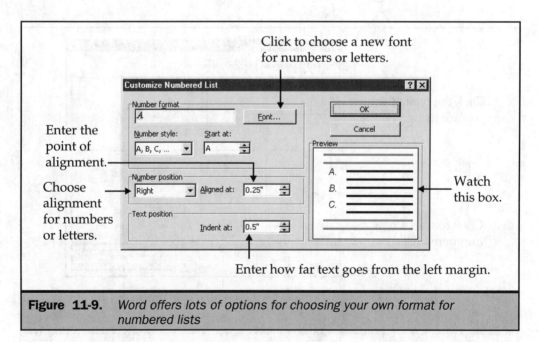

Figure 11-9. *Word offers lots of options for choosing your own format for numbered lists*

8. In the Number Position box, choose Left, Center, or Right to tell Word how the numbers or letters in the list are to be aligned with one another. The Preview box shows precisely what your choices amount to.

9. In the Aligned At box, enter a number to tell Word at what point with respect to the left margin to align the numbers or letters. For example, if you enter **0.5"** and the numbers or letters are left-aligned, all numbers or letters will appear directly to the right of the 0.5-inch mark. If you enter **0.5"** and the numbers or letters are centered, all numbers or letters will be centered on the 0.5-inch mark on the horizontal ruler.

10. In the Indent At box, tell Word how far from the left margin to indent the text, not the numbers or letters, in the list. A large number puts a lot of space between the numbers or letters and the text; a small number puts little space.

11. Click OK to close the Customize Numbered List dialog box.

Note

After you create your own format for numbered lists, Word applies it to the document you are working on when you click the Numbering button on the Formatting toolbar. Moreover, the format you created becomes an option in the Bullets and Numbering dialog box. It replaces the option you started with (in step 4 of the previous set of instructions) when you created your own number format. To get Word's old number format back, click the format you tampered with in the Bullets and Numbering dialog box, and then click the Reset button.

Working with Bulleted Lists

A bullet is a black, filled-in circle or other character that marks an item on a list. When you click the Bullets button, Word puts a bullet at the start of the paragraph. Besides the standard bullet, you can use symbols as bullets. Figure 11-10 shows several ways to present a bulleted list. The following pages explain how to create a bulleted list, use unusual characters as bullets, and format a bulleted list on your own.

	Abbot and Costello	❑	Abbot and Costello	♦	Abbot and Costello	⚿	Abbot and Costello
•	Laurel and Hardy	❑	Laurel and Hardy	♦	Laurel and Hardy	⚿	Laurel and Hardy
•	The Marx Brothers	❑	The Marx Brothers	♦	The Marx Brothers	⚿	The Marx Brothers
•	The Three Stooges	❑	The Three Stooges	♦	The Three Stooges	⚿	The Three Stooges

Figure 11-10.   *In bulleted lists, you can use almost any symbol you care to use*

LEARN BY EXAMPLE
To futz around with bulleted lists, open the Figure 11-10 (Bulleted List) file on the CD that comes with this book.

Creating a Bulleted List

To create a bulleted list, enter the items for the list, select the list, and then click the Bullets button on the Formatting toolbar. Or, to create the list as you type it, click the Bullets button and start typing.

Removing bullets from a list is easy: select the list and click the Bullets button.

Choosing a Bullet Character

If the standard round bullet that Word provides doesn't do it for you, you can use another symbol for the bullets in your list. Word offers seven kinds of bullets in the Bullets and Numbering dialog box, and if they don't do the job, you can use any symbol from the Symbol dialog box.

USING ONE OF WORD'S SYMBOLS FOR BULLETS   Follow these steps to use any one of Word seven bullet characters to mark items in a list:

1. Select the list if you've already entered it, or else place the cursor where the list is to begin.

2. Right-click and choose Bullets and Numbering.

3. If necessary, click the Bulleted tab. It is shown in Figure 11-11.

4. Click one of the eight boxes to choose a new symbol for the list.

5. Click OK.

Tip   *After you choose a new character for bulleted lists, it becomes the default bullet character. Click the Bullets button and you get the symbol you chose, not the standard round bullet. To get the standard bullet again, open the Bullets and Numbering dialog box and choose it on the Bulleted tab.*

CHOOSING YOUR OWN SYMBOL FOR BULLETS   To use a character for lists apart from the seven on the Bulleted tab of the Bullets and Numbering dialog box, follow these steps:

1. Right-click and choose Bullets and Numbering.

2. If necessary, click the Bulleted tab (see Figure 11-11).

3. Click the box that holds the bullets you are least likely to need. Take this step because, when you are done choosing a new character for bulleted lists, it will appear on the Bulleted tab and take the place of the box you click in this step. Therefore, click a box whose bullets you don't care for.

WORD

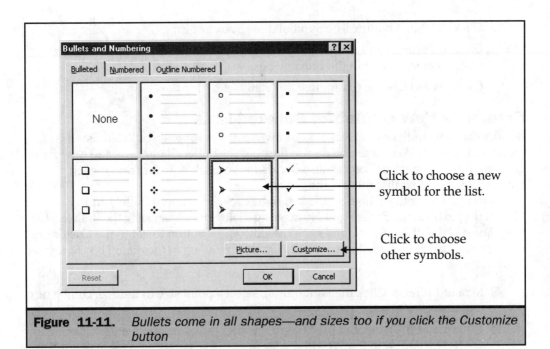

Figure 11-11.   *Bullets come in all shapes—and sizes too if you click the Customize button*

4. Click the Customize button. You see the Customize Bulleted List dialog box shown in Figure 11-12.

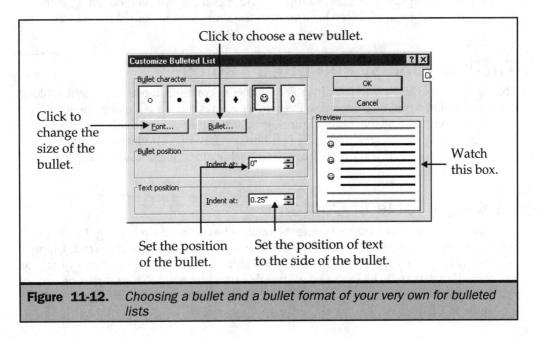

Figure 11-12.   *Choosing a bullet and a bullet format of your very own for bulleted lists*

5. Click the Bullet button. The Symbol dialog box appears.

6. Choose a symbol and click OK. The symbol you chose appears in the gallery of bullet characters and in the Preview box.

7. Click OK to close the Customize Bulleted List dialog box.

Creating a New Format for Bulleted Lists

Besides choosing bullet characters of your own, you can format a bulleted list to your own specifications. Word lets you decide how big the bullet character is and how far it goes from the left margin. You can also decide for yourself how far from the left margin to put the text that follows the bullet.

To format a bulleted list, select the list, right-click, and choose Bullets and Numbering to open the Bullets and Numbering dialog box. Then click the Bulleted tab (see Figure 11-11), if necessary, and click the Customize button to get to the Customize Bulleted List dialog box (see Figure 11-12). Do the following in the dialog box to format bullet lists:

- **Size of Bullets**   Click the Font button, select a point size in the Size combo box, and then click OK.

- **Distance of Bullet from Left Margin**   Under Bullet position, enter a setting in the Indent At box to tell Word how far from the left margin to place the bullets in the list. Keep your eyes on the Preview box to see what your choices mean in real terms.

- **Distance of List from Left Margin**   Under Text position, enter a setting in the Indent At box to tell Word how far from the left margin to place the text in the list.

Tables, Tables, and More Tables

This section explains how to handle tables—tables of contents; tables of figures, tables, and graphs; and tables of authorities. Everybody knows what a table of contents is. In Word, you can create a table of the figures, graphics, equations, and other things in a document. You can also create a table of authorities. Lawyers and legal secretaries know what those are. If you don't know what a table of authorities is, count yourself among the blessed.

Generating a Table of Contents

Unless a long work has a table of contents, readers have a hard time using it as a reference. This section explains how to generate a table of contents with Word. Doing so is pretty darn simple as long as you applied styles to the headings and other parts of the document that are to be included in the table of contents (TOC). Any part of a document that has been assigned a style can be included in the TOC (styles are explained in Chapter 9).

Following are instructions for generating a TOC, telling Word what to put in the TOC, and choosing a format for it.

LEARN BY EXAMPLE
On the companion CD is a file called Figure 11-13 (TOC). Open that file if you would like to test out the TOC instructions in this book.

Generating a Simple Table of Contents

To generate a simple table of contents with only the headings in a document, follow these steps:

1. At or near the start of the document, type **Table of Contents** and press ENTER once or twice.

2. Choose Insert | Index and Tables.

3. Click the Table of Contents tab in the Index and Tables dialog box. It is shown in Figure 11-13.

4. In the Formats box, choose a format for the table of contents. As you click formats, watch the Preview boxes. They show what the formats look like in print and on the web.

5. In the Show Levels box, enter a number to say which headings should appear in the TOC. Entering **1**, for example, puts only the Heading 1 headings in the TOC. Entering **3** puts Heading 1, Heading 2, and Heading 3 headings in the TOC.

Some Advice About TOCs

Before you create a table of contents, create a new section in which to put it and number the TOC pages with Roman numerals. If you don't create a new section, the TOC will start on the first page and occupy the first handful of pages in the document. The first heading in the document, instead of appearing on page 1, will appear on page 2 or 3 or 4, because the TOC will push it there. It doesn't do to have a TOC whose first entry cites a heading on page 2 or 3 or 4.

TOCs should only include the first one, two, and at most three levels of headings. If your document goes seven headings deep, do not under any circumstances put all seven levels of headings in the TOC. That creates a long TOC that readers have to wade through to find what they are looking for. The object of a TOC is to help people find information. Having to read through many pages to find what you are looking for defeats the purpose of having a TOC.

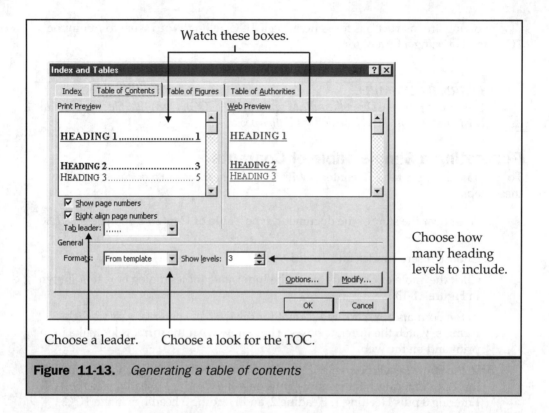

Watch these boxes.

Choose how many heading levels to include.

Choose a leader.   Choose a look for the TOC.

Figure 11-13.   *Generating a table of contents*

6. Depending on the format you chose for your TOC, you might be able to tinker with it by choosing options at the bottom of the Table of Contents tab:

■ **Show Page Numbers**   The TOC includes page numbers unless you click to remove the check mark from this check box.

■ **Right Align Page Numbers**   Page numbers are right-aligned so that the 1s and 10s line up underneath each other, but you can left-align them by clicking this check box and removing the check mark.

■ **Tab Leader**   A leader is a punctuation mark that steers the reader's eye in the TOC from the heading to the page number that the heading is on. Choose a leader from the drop-down list. If you choose not to show page numbers, the Tab Leader box is grayed out, which effectively means no leaders.

7. Click OK.

Tip   *If you're creating a TOC or any other table for a web page, you'll probably want to uncheck the Show Page Numbers box.*

Including Tables, Captions, and More in the TOC

Besides heading styles, you can include any part of a document to which you have assigned a style in a TOC. Captions, paragraphs, and announcements for which you created a special style, for example, can be included in a TOC. As a matter of fact, you can exclude headings from a TOC as well.

To choose exactly what goes into a TOC, choose Insert | Index and Tables and click the Table of Contents tab in the Index and Tables dialog box (see Figure 11-13). Choose the kind of TOC you want, how many level of headings to include in the TOC, and so on, and then follow these steps:

1. Click the Options button. You see the Table of Contents Options dialog box shown in Figure 11-14.

2. In the TOC Level box beside each style name, enter a level number to tell Word which level the style is to appear on in the TOC. In Figure 11-14, for example, headings assigned the Digression style will be formatted like and indented as far as headings assigned the Heading 3 style, because a **3** is entered in the TOC Level box beside both style names.

3. Click OK to close the Table of Contents Options dialog box.

4. Click OK in the Index and Tables dialog box.

Updating a TOC

Suppose you add one or two parts to your document, and each part has a heading. Meanwhile, you remove one or two other parts and their headings. Now the TOC you generated isn't accurate and up to date. To update the TOC, click it so it turns gray,

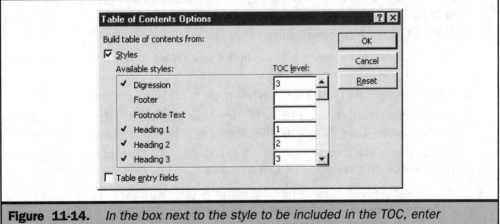

Figure 11-14.   *In the box next to the style to be included in the TOC, enter a number*

press F9, and in the Update Table of Contents dialog box, indicate whether to update only page numbers or to update the entire TOC. That's all there is to it.

Tables for Figures, Graphs, Tables, and What All

Sometimes reports and scholarly works, besides a table of contents, include other tables that list figures, graphs, and illustrations. Word can generate these kinds of tables as easily as it can generate a table of contents. For Word to generate the table, however, you must have used the Insert menu's Caption command to put captions on figures, graphs, and so on, or you must have devised a style for the parts of a document that you want to compile into a table.

The following pages explain how to compile a table of figures, graphs, tables, equations, listings, or program lines that were given captions with the Insert menu's Caption command. It also explains how to compile a table of all the parts of a document that were given the same style.

Generating a Table from Captions

Later in this chapter, "Captions for Figures, Graphs, Tables, and What All" explains how to use the Insert menu's Caption command to put captions on figures, graphs, tables, equations, listings, and program lines. As long as you use the Insert menu's Caption command to put captions on those things, you can generate a table with all the captions you wrote. For example, a report about agricultural production in Transylvania with graphs showing sorghum, soybean, and radish production could include a "Table of Graphs in This Report." The table would steer Transylvania scholars to the pages where the all-important agricultural data is given.

Follow these steps to generate a table of the figures, graphs, and what all that have been captioned with the Caption command:

1. Enter a title for the table near the start of the document and press ENTER once or twice.

2. Choose Insert | Index and Tables.

3. Click the Table of Figures tab in the Index and Tables dialog box. It is shown in Figure 11-15.

4. In the Caption Label box, choose which type of table to generate.

5. In the Formats box, choose a format for the table. As you click formats, watch the Preview boxes. They show what the formats look like in print and on the web.

6. Depending on the format you chose for the table, you can fool with the options at the bottom to change the look of the table:

   ■ **Show Page Numbers** The table includes page numbers unless you click to remove the check mark from this check box.

   ■ **Right Align Page Numbers** Page numbers are right-aligned so that the 1s and 10s line up underneath each other, but you can left-align them by clicking this check box and removing the check mark.

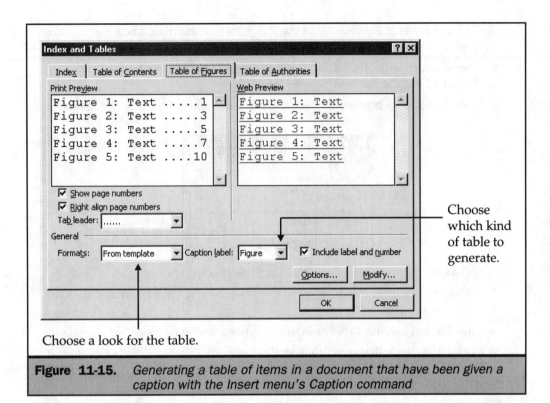

Choose which kind of table to generate.

Choose a look for the table.

Figure 11-15. *Generating a table of items in a document that have been given a caption with the Insert menu's Caption command*

- ■ **Include Label And Number** Click this box and remove the check mark to keep labels and numbers from appearing in the table. For example, entries in a table of figures would list the captions only. The word "Figure" and the figure number would not appear with each caption.

- ■ **Tab Leader** A leader is a punctuation mark that steers the reader's eye in the table to page numbers in the table. In Figure 11-15, a period is used as the leader. Choose a leader from the drop-down list.

   7. Click OK.

Generating a Table from Styles

As long as you thoughtfully applied a style to each sidebar heading, joke box, or whatever that you want to compile in a table, you can compile a "Table of Sidebars" or "Joke Boxes" at the start of a document. To do so, follow these steps:

   1. Enter a title for the table near the start of the document, and press ENTER once or twice.

   2. Choose Insert | Index and Tables.

3. Click the Table of Figures tab in the Index and Tables dialog box (see Figure 11-15).

4. Choose a format for the table. ("Generating a Table from Captions" explains how to fill out the Table of Figures tab.)

5. Click the Options button. You see the Table of Figures Options dialog box:

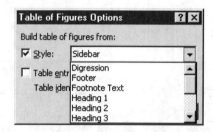

6. Make sure there is a check mark in the Style check box.

7. Click the Style drop-down menu and choose the style whose entries are to be compiled in a table.

8. Click OK to close the Table of Figures Options dialog box.

9. Click OK in the Index and Tables dialog box.

Updating the Table

To update a table of figures, graphs, or whatnot, all you have to do is click it, wait till it turns gray, and then press F9. If you add more figures, graphs, or whatnot, or remove some of them from a document, simply click the table, press F9, and in the Update Table of Contents dialog box, indicate whether to update only page numbers or to update the entire table. Users who are averse to pressing F9 can right-click on the table and choose Update Field from the shortcut menu.

Creating a Table of Authorities

As every legal secretary and lawyer knows, a table of authorities is a list of the rules, cases, statues, regulations, and so on, cited in a legal document. Word makes it fairly easy to create these tables. The following pages explain how to enter citations for a table of authorities and how to generate the table itself.

Entering the Citations

Follow these steps to enter the citations in a table of authorities:

1. Go to the first citation and select it.

2. Press ALT-SHIFT-I. The Mark Citation dialog box appears, as shown in Figure 11-16. Your selection is listed in the Selected Text and Short Citation text boxes.

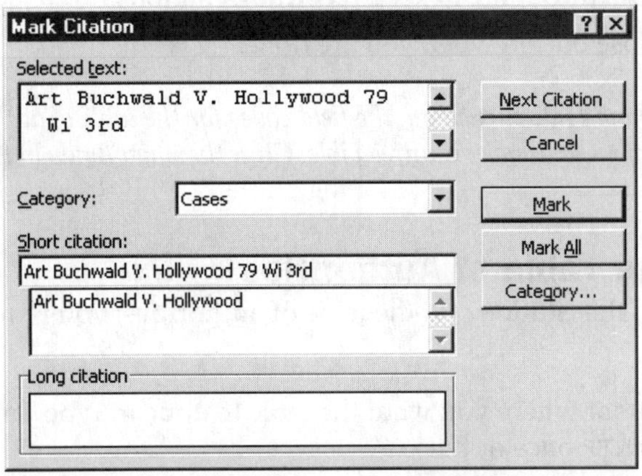

Mark Citation   ? X

Selected text:

Art Buchwald V. Hollywood 79
  Wi 3rd

Next Citation

Cancel

Category: Cases

Mark

Short citation:

Art Buchwald V. Hollywood 79 Wi 3rd

Mark All

Art Buchwald V. Hollywood

Category...

Long citation

Figure 11-16. *Marking the citations for a table of authorities*

3. In the Selected Text box, edit the citation so that it looks like you want it to look in the table of authorities.

4. Choose a category from the Category drop-down list.

Tip   *If none of the categories in the Category list suits you, click the Category button to open the Edit Category dialog box. From there, either choose a category from the Category list or create a new category by entering it in the Replace With box and clicking the Replace button. Click OK when you are done.*

5. In the Short Citation box, edit the citation for brevity. What you enter here determines what the citation looks like in the Mark Citation dialog box if you need to select it again.

6. Click the Mark button so that the citation appears in the table of authorities when you generate it. If other instances of this citation appear in your document, you can place them all in the table of authorities by clicking the Mark All button.

7. Click the Next Citation button. Word searches for other citations. To do so, it looks for cryptic examples of legalese such as *V* and *in re*. When Word finds another citation, the *V* or *in re* or whatever and the text that surrounds it appears in the Selected Text box.

8. Click outside the dialog box and select the citation as you did in step 1. You may have to move the Mark Citation dialog box aside to do so. Click in the dialog box after you select the citation.

WORD

9. Repeat steps 2 through 7 to keep recording citations.

10. Click the Close button when you are done.

If you have Show/Hide turned on, the field codes for the table of authorities now appear in your document and make it unreadable. Click the Show/Hide button to wipe the codes off the screen.

Generating the Table of Authorities

After you record all the citations for the table of authorities, you're ready to generate the table itself:

1. Place the cursor where you want the table to appear, type **Table of Authorities**, and press ENTER once or twice.

2. Choose Insert | Index and Tables.

3. Click the Table of Authorities tab. It is shown in Figure 11-17.

4. Choose a format from the Formats list. The Preview boxes show what the different formats look like. You can scroll down the Preview boxes.

5. In the Category box, choose which categories to include in the table.

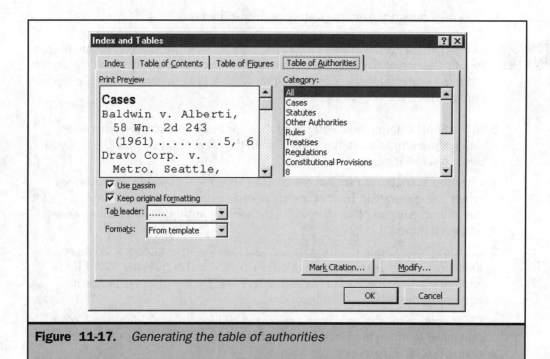

Figure 11-17. *Generating the table of authorities*

6. If you leave the Use Passim box checked, more than five references to the same citation are cited with the word "passim" instead of a page number. "Passim" means "scattered" in Latin. The word is used to refer to citations that appear throughout a legal document. Similarly, when possums are scattered throughout a meadow, they are said to be "passim possums."

7. The Keep Original Formatting text box retains the original formatting of long citations in the table. Uncheck this box if you want the table of authorities only to show short citations.

8. Choose a tab leader from the Tab Leader drop-down list if you want something other than periods to appear between the citation and the page number in the table.

9. Click OK to generate the table of authorities.

Updating a Table of Authorities

To update a table of authorities after you have made changes to the citations in a legal document, either click the table and press F9 or right-click the table and choose Update Fields from the shortcut menu.

Numbers, Numbers, and More Numbers

The following pages explain how to number the lines in a document and how to number the headings. Lines in some kinds of legal documents have to be numbered. Passages in poems and religious texts are sometimes numbered as well to make it easier for scholars to cite specific lines. In scholarly papers and formal documents, headings are often numbered to make cross-referencing easier.

 If you came here to learn how to number the pages in a document, you came to the wrong place. Numbering pages is explained in Chapter 7.

Numbering the Lines on Pages

Line numbers appear in the left margin. Follow these steps to number the lines in a document:

1. To number all the lines in a document, place the insertion point at the start of the document. Otherwise, place the insertion point at the start of a section to number all the lines in a section, or place the insertion point where you want to start numbering lines.

2. Choose File | Page Setup. You see the Page Setup dialog box.

3. Click the Layout tab.

4. Click the Line Numbers button. The Line Numbers dialog box appears, as shown in Figure 11-18.

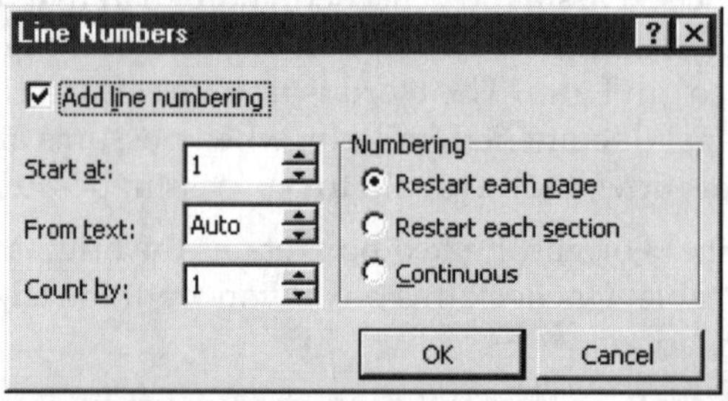

Figure 11-18. *Click the Add Line Numbering check box to number the lines in a document*

5. Click the Add Line Numbering check box.

6. Tell Word how the lines are to be numbered:

■ **Start At**   To begin counting with a number other than 1, enter it.

■ **From Text**   The number in this box determines how far numbers are from the text. The larger the number, the further numbers are from the text and the closer the numbers are to the left side of the page.

■ **Count By**   Choose a number here to make numbers appear at intervals. For example, entering **10** makes intervals of ten (10, 20, and so on) appear.

■ **Numbering**   The numbers can begin anew on each page or at the start of each section. Choose Continuous to number all the lines consecutively.

7. Click OK to close the Line Numbers dialog box. You return to the Layout tab of the Page Setup dialog box.

8. Choose an Apply To option to tell Word which part of the document to number.

9. Click OK to close the Page Setup dialog box.

Line numbers can only be seen in Print Layout view. Since they appear in the margin, you likely have to scroll to the left side of the page to see them:

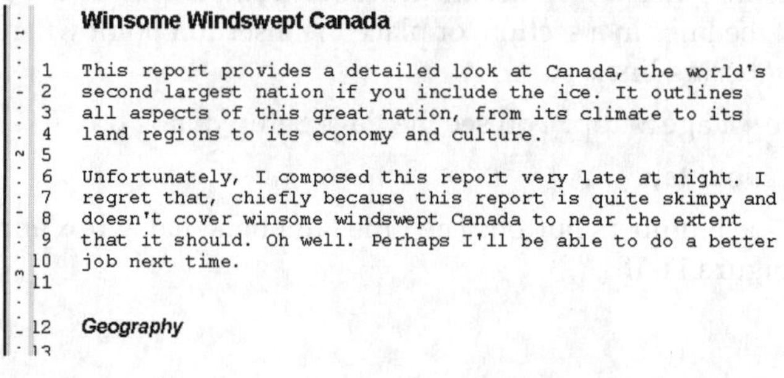

If you regret numbering the lines and want to remove the numbers, choose File │ Page Setup, click the Layout tab, and click the Line Numbers button. In the Line Numbers dialog box (see Figure 11-18), click the Add Line Numbering check box to remove the check mark, and then click OK twice.

LEARN BY EXAMPLE
To experiment with line numbers, open the Figure 11-18 (Line Numbers) file on the companion CD and give it a try.

Numbering the Headings in a Document

As long as you applied Heading styles to the headings in a document, you can number the headings automatically with the Format menu's Bullets and Numbering command. After the headings have been numbered, they are renumbered automatically when you remove or add a heading. So you can rest assured that all headings are numbered in sequence when you number the headings automatically.

Word offers a lot of ways to number the headings. And you can also make words such as "Chapter," "Article," and "Section" appear in front of heading numbers automatically. Follow these steps to number the headings in a document:

1. Switch to Outline view. You get a better look at what you are doing from there.

2. Select the headings you want to number. To number all the headings, select the entire document.

3. Choose Format │ Bullets and Numbering. You see the Bullets and Numbering dialog box.

4. Click the Outline Numbered tab. It is shown in Figure 11-19.

5. Choose a numbering scheme by clicking on it. Notice the numbering schemes in the second row. The one on the left puts the word "Article" in front of Heading 1 headings and the word "Section" in front of Heading 2 headings. The one on the right puts the word "Chapter" in front of Heading 1 headings but does not number the headings below Heading 1.

6. Click OK.

To remove the numbers from headings, select the headings, open the Bullets and Numbering dialog box, select the Outline Numbered tab, click the None choice, and click OK.

LEARN BY EXAMPLE
Open the Figure 11-19 (Heading Numbers) file on the companion CD if you care to experiment with heading numbers.

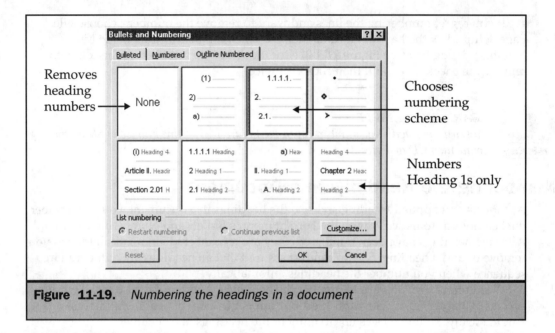

Figure 11-19. *Numbering the headings in a document*

Indexing a Document

A long document that readers will refer to often to get information is not complete without an index. Besides looking in the table of contents, looking in the index is the surest way to find out where information is. Unfortunately, writing an index is not easy, because Word cannot write the index entries for you, and writing a good index entry is certainly as hard as writing a good, descriptive heading.

Writing an index is not easy, but marking index entries and compiling an index is. The following pages explain how to do that.

Marking the Index Entries

To mark index entries, open the Mark Index Entry dialog box. After the box is open, you can tuck it in a corner, scroll through a document, and mark entries as you go along. Follow these steps to mark the index entries so you can compile them into an index later on:

1. Go to the first place where you want to make an index entry. If a word or phrase in the text can be included in the entry, select the word or phrase. You can save a little time that way.

2. Press ALT-SHIFT-X. You see the Mark Index Entry dialog box shown in Figure 11-20.

Ways of Handling Index Entries

An index entry can be a cross-reference, a main entry, a subentry, or a sub-subentry. Moreover, index entries can refer to a single page or a page range. The following illustration shows the different types of index entries you can make with Word:

```
                    calcium, 58
                    California, 147-170
                        economy, 162
                            agriculture, 163
                            farming, 162
                            industry, 165
                        geography, 148
                        history, 154
                    coconut oil See tanning oil
                    Cuthbertson, Joanne, 111-122
```

As you mark index entries, Word asks which type of entry you are marking. The Mark Index Entry dialog box offers option buttons and text boxes for entering the following types of entries in an index:

- **Cross-reference**   A cross-reference refers the reader to another entry in the index. Make sure, when you enter a cross-reference, that the thing being referred to is really in the index.

- **Subentry**   A subentry is subordinate to a main entry in the index. It offers specific information about a general topic listed in the index.

- **Sub-subentry**   A sub-subentry is subordinate to a subentry (and the subentry's main entry, too). It offers very specific information about a sub-entry.

- **Page Range**   Besides referring to a single page, an index entry can refer to two or more pages. To make a page-range index entry, you must enter a bookmark that includes all the text in the page range. To create such a bookmark, select all text on the pages in question before you give the Insert menu's Bookmark command.

As you mark index entries, ask yourself how you would search for information in an index and mark entries accordingly. Others will use your index to get information. Make sure your index entries don't lead them on a wild goose chase.

WORD

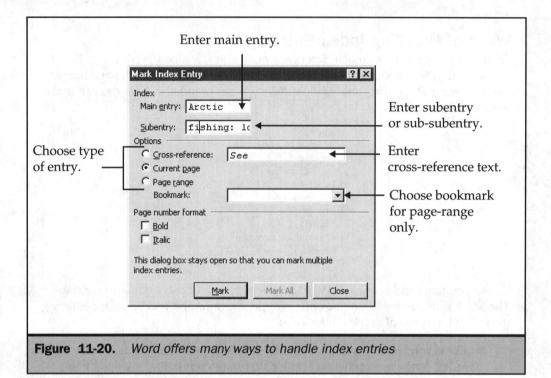

Figure 11-20. *Word offers many ways to handle index entries*

3. Tell Word how to handle the index entry:

- **Main Entry**   Enter the main entry here. If you selected a word or phrase in step 1, it appears in the Main Entry box. Either edit the word or phrase or keep it. The word or phrase you enter in this box will appear in the index.

- **Subentry**   Enter subentry or sub-subentry text in this box. Leave it blank if the index entry does not have a subentry. To enter a sub-subentry, type a colon (:) and then type the sub-subentry, as shown in Figure 11-20. What you type in this box will appear in the index.

4. Tell Word how to handle the page reference in the entry:

- **Cross-reference**   To refer the reader to a main entry in the index, type the main entry's name in this box after the word "See." What you type in this box appears in the index.

For cross-reference entries, be sure to refer the reader to a main entry that is really in the index. Word cannot double-check what you enter. You have to do that yourself and make sure that the cross-reference is accurate.

- **Current Page**   Click to create an index reference to a single page in the document.

- **Page Range**   Click to create a reference to a range of pages. In order to create a page-range entry, you must create a bookmark that encompasses the page range. You can do that by clicking outside the Mark Index Entry dialog box, selecting all the text in the page range, choosing Insert | Bookmark, typing a name in the Bookmark Name text box, and clicking Add. Then, in the Mark Entry dialog box, click the down arrow in the Page Range option button, and choose the bookmark from the drop-down list.

5. Click the Bold or Italic check box to tell Word if you want to boldface or italicize the page number or page range in the index entry. In some indexes, the page or page range where the topic is explained in the most depth is italicized or boldfaced so readers can go there first, if they want to.

6. Click the Mark or Mark All button:

   - **Mark Button**   Enters the entry in the index.

   - **Mark All Button**   As long as you selected a word in step 1, you may click Mark All to tell Word to mark all words in the document that are identical to the word in the Main Entry box.

7. Click outside the dialog box and find the next word or phrase for the index, and then repeat steps 2 through 6 to mark more index entries.

8. Click Close when you're done to close the Mark Index Entry dialog box.

When you're done, you see field codes in your document. That's distracting, but you can hide the field codes by clicking the Show/Hide button.

Generating the Index

After you have marked all the index entries, it is time to generate the index. Follow these steps to generate an index:

1. Go to the end of the document, insert a page break, type the word **Index**, and press ENTER a couple of times.

2. Choose Insert | Index and Tables to open the Index and Tables dialog box.

3. Click the Index tab, if necessary. It is shown in Figure 11-21.

Tip   *Watch the Preview box as you make choices. It shows very plainly what the options you choose in the Index and Tables dialog box amount to.*

4. Under Type, choose Run-in instead of Indented if you want subentries and sub-subentries to fall directly below main entries. With the Indented option, subentries and sub-subentries are indented, as shown in the Preview box in Figure 11-21.

5. Click a format in the Formats drop-down box. Experiment at will, but keep your eyes on the Preview box.

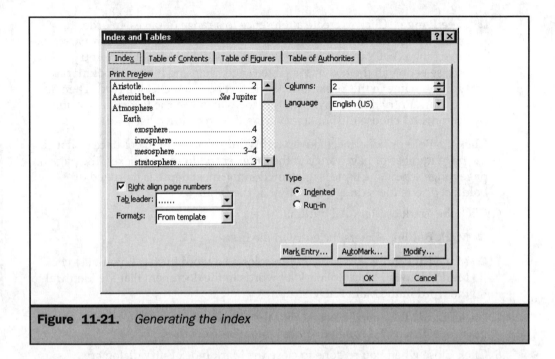

Figure 11-21.   *Generating the index*

6. Choose options in the bottom of the dialog box to get very specific about what the index should look like:

   ■ **Right Align Page Numbers**   Page numbers appear right after entries, unless you click this check box, in which case page numbers appear right below one another.

   ■ **Columns**   If you can fit more than two columns on the page or want only one, make an entry in the Columns box. Indexes with sub-subentries cannot fit more than two columns on a page.

   ■ **Tab Leader**   A leader is a series of punctuation marks. Choose a leader of your own to go between the index entry and the page number, if you want and if the index format you chose in step 5 calls for leaders.

7. Click OK to close the Index and Tables dialog box.

LEARN BY EXAMPLE
Open the Figure 11-21 (Index) file on the companion CD to try your hand at forging an index.

Editing and Updating an Index

After you have generated the index, read it carefully. Make sure that all the entries are useful to readers. If you notice an unsuitable entry, find it in the document and either erase or edit the index field code. And be sure to update the index after you have finished editing it. The following pages explain how.

Editing Index Entries

Follow these steps to find and edit an index entry in a document:

1. If you cannot see the field codes and index entries in the text, click the Show/Hide button on the Standard toolbar.

2. Either scan the document for the entry or choose Edit | Find, and in the Find and Replace dialog box, enter the entry you are looking for and then click the Find Next button. Enter the index entry verbatim. The Find command finds index entries as well as words—as long as you click the Show/Hide button.

3. If you decided to use the Find feature to locate the index entry, when Word finds the entry, click Cancel to close the Find and Replace dialog box. Index entries are enclosed in braces and quotation marks and are preceded by the letters *XE*, like so:

   Manufacturing{ XE:"economy:manufacturing"·}¶

4. Either edit the index entry by clicking between the quotation marks and deleting and entering letters, or delete the entry by selecting it and pressing the DELETE key.

Updating an Index

To update an index after you have edited it or added entries to it, either right-click it and choose Update Field from the shortcut menu, or click it and press F9.

Captions for Figures, Graphs, Tables, and What All

Word offers a special command for putting captions on figures, graphs, tables, equations, listings, and program lines. The command makes creating captions a little bit easier, but the chief advantage of the command is being able to number the captions automatically. When you add a caption or delete one, the other captions are automatically renumbered. What's more, the captions can be compiled in a table. "Tables for Figures, Graphs, Tables, and What All," earlier in this chapter, explains how to compile captions into a table so that readers can find out right away what page a certain graph or equation is on, for example.

To enter a caption, start by selecting the thing that is to be captioned. In the case of figures, graphs, tables, and equations, all you have to do is click on them. By clicking, you select them. But to put a caption on a list or series of program lines, select all the lines first. Follow these steps to caption a figure, graph, or what all automatically:

1. Select the thing that is to be captioned.

2. Choose Insert | Caption. You see the Caption dialog box shown in Figure 11-22.

3. In the Caption box, enter the caption. As Figure 11-22 shows, you have to enter the punctuation mark after the figure number yourself. Usually, a colon (:) or a period follows the figure number.

4. If necessary, click the Label drop-down list and tell Word what it is you are labeling in the caption.

You can create a label for an item that isn't on the Label drop-down list. To do so, click the New Label button, type a label in the Label box, and click OK.

5. Click the Position drop-down list and choose Above Selected Item or Below Selected Item to tell Word where the caption goes.

6. Click OK.

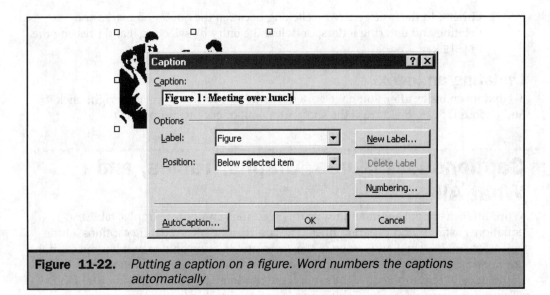

Figure 11-22. *Putting a caption on a figure. Word numbers the captions automatically*

LEARN BY EXAMPLE
To try your hand at captions, open the Figure 11-22 (Captions) file on the companion CD that comes with this book.

Managing Footnotes and Endnotes

Footnotes, the references, explanations, or comments that appear along the bottom of a page, are a chore, but at least Word relieves you of having to worry about numbering and formatting them. Yes, you still have to list authors, their works, and the dates their works were published correctly, but you don't have to worry whether a footnote is out of sequence or whether it fits on the page. Word takes care of all that. It also handles endnotes, which do exactly what footnotes do but do it at the end of the chapter or document.

Unless you fiddle with default options, footnotes go in the bottom margin of the page and endnotes go at the end of the document. Footnotes go directly above the footer, on the bottom of the page, unless you tell Word to put them directly below the text. A document can have both footnotes and endnotes. Word numbers footnotes with Arabic numerals and endnotes with Roman numerals.

This part of Chapter 11 explains how to enter a footnote or endnote, change the position of notes, change their numbering scheme, as well as move, delete, and edit notes.

LEARN BY EXAMPLE
Open the Figure 11-23 (Foot and Endnotes) file on the companion CD if you want to experiment with footnotes and endnotes.

Inserting a Footnote or Endnote

To insert a footnote or endnote, follow these steps:

1. Place the cursor where the note citation is to go. In other words, place the cursor where you want the number or symbol that marks the footnote or endnote reference to be.

2. Choose Insert | Footnote. You see the Footnote and Endnote dialog box shown in Figure 11-23.

3. Under Insert, click Footnote to enter a footnote or Endnote to enter an endnote.

4. Under Numbering, tell Word whether the citation is to be a number or a symbol:

   ■ **AutoNumber**   Click AutoNumber to make Word number the notes automatically.

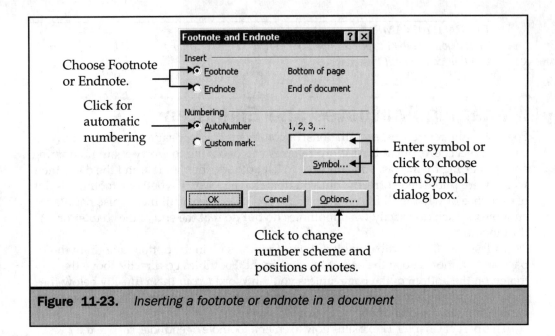

Choose Footnote or Endnote.

Click for automatic numbering

Enter symbol or click to choose from Symbol dialog box.

Click to change number scheme and positions of notes.

Figure 11-23.   *Inserting a footnote or endnote in a document*

■ **Custom Mark**   Click Custom Mark to mark the note with a symbol. To choose the symbol, either enter it yourself in the text box or click the Symbol button and choose a symbol from the Symbol dialog box.

5. Click OK. If you are in Print Layout view, Word takes you to the bottom of the page or the end of the document or section, where, beside the symbol or number, you can type the footnote or endnote. In Normal view, a notes box opens:

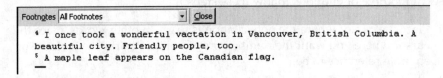

6. Type the footnote or endnote.

7. Click Close if you are in Normal view to leave the notes box. In Print Layout view, scroll up the page.

Changing the Numbering Scheme and Position of Notes

By clicking the Options button in the Footnote and Endnote dialog box (see Figure 11-23), you can change the position or numbering scheme of footnotes and endnotes. Follow these steps to do so:

1. Choose Insert | Footnote.

2. Click the Options button. You see the Note Options dialog box shown in Figure 11-24. The figure shows the options for footnotes on the All Footnotes tab. The options for endnotes on the All Endnotes tab are nearly the same.

3. Click the All Footnotes or All Endnotes tab and choose options:

   ■ **Place At**   Puts footnotes at the bottom of the page, but you can choose Beneath Text to put footnotes below the last text line on the page, even if it appears in the middle of the page. For endnotes, either choose End Of Section (if the document is divided into sections) to make endnotes appear at the back of sections, or choose End Of Document to put the endnotes at the end of the document.

   ■ **Number Format**   Choose a numbering scheme. Choose symbols if you want to use symbols.

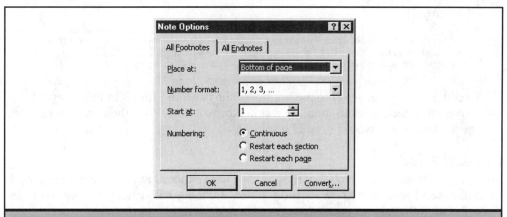

Figure 11-24.   *Changing the position and numbering scheme of footnotes. The options on the All Endnotes tab are nearly the same as those on the All Footnotes tab*

WORD

■ **Start At**   Enter a number or letter to start numbering the notes at a place other than 1, A, or i.

■ **Numbering**   The Continuous option numbers the notes continuously from the start of the document to the end; the Restart Each Section option starts numbering anew at each section in the document. For footnotes, Restart Each Page begins numbering anew on each page.

■ **Convert**   Choose this option to change all endnotes into footnotes, and all footnotes into endnotes.

4. Click OK to close the Notes Options dialog box.

5. Click OK in the Footnote and Endnote dialog box.

Editing, Moving, and Deleting Footnotes and Endnotes

Editing, moving, and deleting footnotes and endnotes is easy, I am happy to report. Following are instructions that explain how easy it is.

Editing a Note

You can read footnotes and endnotes simply by placing the pointer on the note citation. When you do so, a box appears with the footnote or endnote text:

Economy

Canada is rich in natural resources and mineral we boasts many fine universities and has a well-educa populace. By any standard, Canada is a prosperous country.[4]

> I once took a wonderful vactation in Vancouver, British Columbia. A beautiful city. Friendly people, too.

To edit a note, either scroll to the bottom of the page and find it in Print Layout view, or double-click its citation in the text in Normal view. With the note onscreen, change the text as you would normal text.

Moving a Note

To move a note, select its symbol or number and then either drag it where it is supposed to go or cut and paste it to a new location. When you move a note, all the other notes are renumbered, if that proves necessary.

Deleting a Note

To delete a note, select its symbol or number and press the DELETE key. Notes are renumbered when you delete one.

Including Cross-References in Documents

Word's cross-reference feature is mighty handy indeed. With it, you can refer readers to specific pages or to headings in a document (provided the headings have been assigned a style). Best of all, Word double-checks the references to make sure that all are accurate. If you refer to a page or a heading that isn't there, Word alerts you to the fact. And you can even include a hypertext link in a cross-reference (Chapter 23 explains hypertext links in detail).

The following pages explain how to insert cross-references, fix errant cross-references, and update the cross-references in a document.

Inserting a Cross-Reference

Follow these steps to insert a cross-reference:

1. Type the cross-reference text:

   ■ **To a Page Number**   If your reference is to a page number, type something like this: **To learn more about the Canadian wilderness, turn to page**. Enter a blank space after the word "page." A page number will appear after the blank space.

   ■ **To a Heading**   If your reference is to a heading, type something like this: **To learn more about our windswept northern neighbor, see "**. The heading will come directly after the quotation mark, so don't enter a blank space after the quotation mark.

2. Choose Insert | Cross-reference. You see the Cross-reference dialog box shown in Figure 11-25.

3. In the Reference Type drop-down list, choose what the cross-reference refers to. Except for bookmarks, you must have assigned a style or caption to all the options listed in the drop-down list if you want to refer to them. Bookmarks are

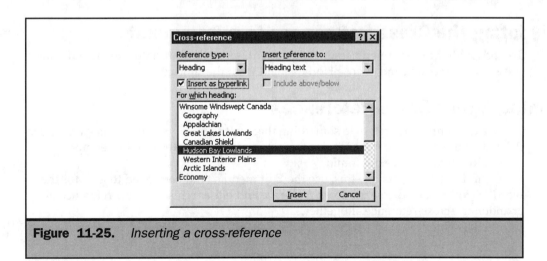

Figure 11-25.   *Inserting a cross-reference*

for referring to page numbers in cross-references. To refer to the page a paragraph is on, click outside the dialog box, scroll to the paragraph, and put a bookmark there with the Insert menu's Bookmark command.

4. In the Insert Reference To drop-down list, what you chose in step 3 determines whether the reference is to a numbered item, text such as a heading, or a page number. Make the appropriate choice in the Insert Reference To drop-down list. Do the following to make the cross-reference to text or a number, or a page number:

   ■ **Text**   Choose this option (Heading text, Bookmark text, and so on) to include text in the cross-reference.

   ■ **Number**   Choose this option to refer to a paragraph to which a bookmark has been applied.

5. Click to remove the check mark from the Insert As Hyperlink check box if you don't want to create a hyperlink as part of the cross-reference. Chapter 23 explains hyperlinks. By clicking a hyperlink, online users can go directly to the thing being cross-referenced.

6. You can add the word "above" or "below" to the cross-reference by clicking the Include Above/Below check box. (The check box is available with some Reference Type options).

7. In the For Which Heading box, click on the thing that the cross-reference refers to, be it a heading, bookmark, footnote, or whatever.

8. Click the Insert button.

9. Click the Close button.

10. Finish writing the cross-reference text in the document.

Updating the Cross-References in a Document

To update all the cross-references in a document, select the entire document and either press F9 or right-click and choose Update Field from the shortcut menu.

Fixing Errant Cross-References

When a cross-reference refers to something that isn't there anymore because it has been deleted, you see an error message like this when you update the cross-references: "Error! Reference source not found."

To find and fix errors like this, use the Edit menu's Find command to look for the word "Error!". Then delete the cross-reference and either reinsert a new reference or abandon the cross-reference altogether.

The
Complete
Reference

Office 2000

Part III

Microsoft Excel

The
Complete
Reference

Office 2000

Chapter 12

Excel Basics

T his chapter describes the basic construction techniques you'll use to build Excel workbooks. With the information that this chapter and the next chapter provide, in fact, you should be able to build almost any type of Excel workbook.

Touring the Excel Program Window

The first time you see Excel's program window and the workbook program window inside the program, they can inspire a certain amount of stress. Cryptic codes and pseudo-hieroglyphics appear scattered all over the program window. Clickable boxes and buttons abound, and a status bar along the bottom edge of the window displays all sorts of strange messages.

Despite all the seeming confusion, however, Excel's program window, which is shown in Figure 12-1, is actually pretty well organized. And once you've had each of its components identified and described, you should find it easy to understand and use each of the parts of the window.

The topmost row of the program window is the program window title bar. It names the program and supplies a program control menu icon, which you'll probably never use (because it's largely redundant), as well as the program window buttons, which let you minimize, maximize/restore, and close the program window. The Minimize button shrinks the program window into a button that appears on the taskbar. The Maximize/Restore button alternative increases the size of the program window so it fills the screen or restores it to its original, unenlarged size. The Close button closes, or stops, the Excel program.

Beneath the title bar are the menu bar and the Standard and Formatting toolbars. The menu bar contains the menus of commands you'll sometimes use to perform tasks in the Excel program. The Standard and Formatting toolbars provide clickable buttons and boxes you can also use to issue commands to the Excel program. (Chapter 3 identifies and describes the tools on the Standard and Formatting toolbars.)

The area beneath the toolbar provides a Name box and the Formula bar. The Name box provides the cell address or name of the active, or selected, cell. The Formula bar displays the contents of the active cell. You'll learn more about both of these items in the paragraphs that follow.

The major portion of the Excel program window shows the workbook window described in detail in the next section.

At the bottom of the program window is the status bar. It provides a message area, the AutoCalculate area, and the keyboard indicator. Excel uses the message area to send you messages. For example, if Excel is ready to receive a command, the message area shows the one-word message, "Ready." If Excel is busy recalculating the formulas you've placed in a worksheet, it will display the message "Calculating cells," followed by the percentage of cells it's calculated. The AutoCalculate area calculates the values in the selected cells using the function you specify—Sum, Average, Count, Count Nums, Min, or Max. Finally, the keyboard indicator just tells you whether you've

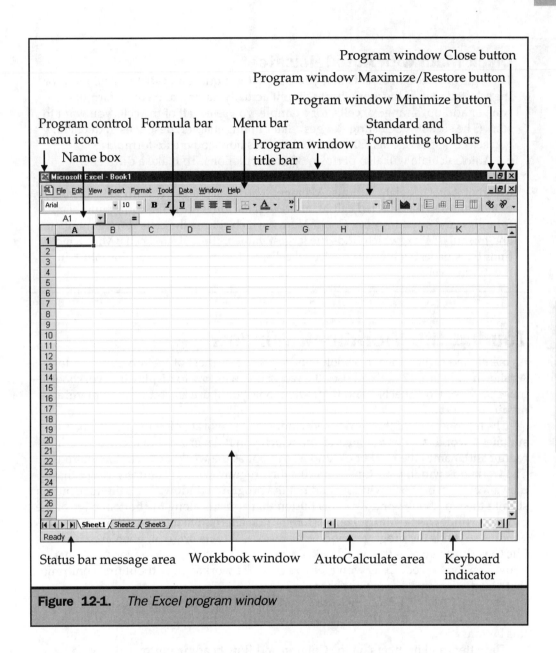

Program window Close button
Program window Maximize/Restore button
Program window Minimize button
Program control menu icon
Formula bar
Menu bar
Standard and Formatting toolbars
Name box
Program window title bar

Status bar message area   Workbook window   AutoCalculate area   Keyboard indicator

Figure 12-1. *The Excel program window*

EXCEL

turned on any of your keyboard's toggle switches: the CAPS LOCK key (sometimes identified with the abbreviation CAPS), the NUM LOCK key (identified with the abbreviation NUM), the INSERT, or over-type, key (identified with the abbreviation OVR), and so forth.

Quick Math with AutoCalculate

The logic of AutoCalculate is that you can perform quick-and-dirty calculations on the selected area of the worksheet without actually having to create a formula. To sum, or add up, a range of cells, for example, you select all of the cells you want to sum. (The section, "Selecting Ranges," later in this chapter, describes in detail how you select ranges of cells. Chapter 13 describes how you create formulas.)

AutoCalculate will also perform other calculations. To make a different calculation, right-click the AutoCalculate area. Excel displays a menu listing different AutoCalculate options: Average, which calculates the arithmetic mean of the values in the selected cells; Count, which counts the cells storing numbers, formulas, and anything else; Count Nums, which counts the cells storing numbers and formulas; Max, which finds the largest value in the selected cells; Min, which finds the smallest value in the selected cells; and Sum, which sums the values in the selected cells.

Touring the Workbook Window

As mentioned earlier, the workbook window occupies most of the program window. As shown in Figure 12-2, Excel uses the workbook window to display the workbooks—those stacks of worksheets—and to provide tools you'll use as you view, explore, and modify a workbook.

The topmost row of the workbook window is the workbook window title bar. It supplies a workbook control menu icon, which you'll never need to use (because it's redundant), names the workbook, and also supplies the workbook window buttons. The workbook window buttons work like the program window buttons except that they affect the workbook window and not the program window. The Minimize button shrinks the workbook window into a button that appears along the bottom edge of the program window. The Maximize/Restore button alternative increases the workbook window so it fills the program window or restores it to its original, unenlarged size. The Close button closes the workbook. (If you've made changes to a workbook that you haven't yet saved, Excel won't let you close the workbook without first confirming that you don't want to save your changes.)

The Select All box selects the entire worksheet. You might want to do this if you are making a change that affects the whole worksheet. But in practice, you'll rarely use this button.

The letters and numbers on the Column and Row heading buttons identify a worksheet's columns and rows and also identify the cells, or column-row intersections, that make up the worksheet. For example, the cell at the intersection of column B and row 2 is cell B2.

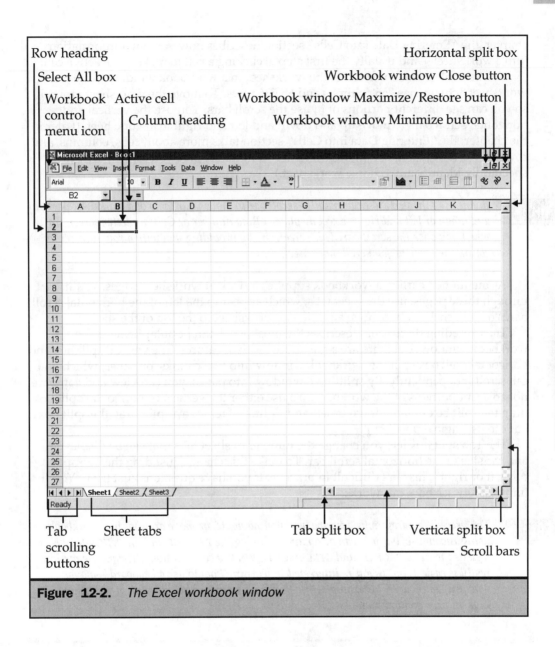

Row heading

Select All box

Workbook control menu icon

Active cell

Column heading

Horizontal split box

Workbook window Close button

Workbook window Maximize/Restore button

Workbook window Minimize button

Tab scrolling buttons

Sheet tabs

Tab split box

Vertical split box

Scroll bars

Figure 12-2. *The Excel workbook window*

In Figure 12-2, by the way, cell B2 is the active cell. You can tell it's the active cell both because Excel places a dark border around the cell and because the Name box gives its cell address. Knowing which cell is the active one is important. Later in the chapter, the "Entering Data into Cells" section describes how you enter information into a worksheet—and usually the first step is clicking a cell to make it the active cell.

You see only a small portion of the worksheet in a workbook window. An Excel worksheet actually has 256 columns and 65,536 rows. To move the worksheet around so you can see different portions of it, use the scroll bars. You use the vertical and horizontal scroll bars to move up and down and left and right in a worksheet. (Later in the chapter, the "Entering Data into Cells" section talks more about cells, columns, and rows, so for now just note that these letters and numbers give you an easy way to specifically identify any cell in a worksheet.)

Note   *If you drag the vertical or horizontal scroll bar to move your view of a worksheet page up and down or left and right, Excel displays a Row number or Column letter screen tip when you click the scroll bar. This screen tip, by providing you with a row number or column letter, lets you scroll more precisely.*

As mentioned earlier, a workbook supplies a stack of worksheet pages. To flip through these pages, use the sheet tabs, which appear to the left of the horizontal scroll bar. You just click a tab to move a particular worksheet to the top of the stack.

The preceding discussion describes the most usual and popular items in the workbook window, but there are a few more hidden features. The vertical split box and horizontal split box split the workbook window into two chunks, or panes, which you can scroll independently. By splitting a window into panes, you can view and compare nonadjacent portions of the workbook. To use either the vertical or horizontal split box, drag the split box up and down or left and right. (To remove a split, drag the split box back to its original position.)

The Tab split box lets you change the number of sheet tabs that can be displayed and the size of the horizontal scroll bar. To make this change, just drag the Tab split box left or right. This isn't difficult in practice. If you have questions, just try it. You'll immediately see how this works.

Note   *The preceding paragraphs describe how you navigate, or move around, in a workbook using the mouse, but you can also navigate using the PAGE UP and PAGE DOWN keys, as well as the CTRL-PAGE UP and CTRL-PAGE DOWN key combinations. The mouse method really is easiest, but if you're interested in learning how to use a keyboard—maybe you're a laptop user, for example—just open a workbook and experiment with these keys and key combinations.*

Entering Data into Cells

Excel's basic building blocks are its worksheet pages, which are simply tables, or grids, you use for storing information you want to manipulate—usually in calculations. For this reason, you'll want to learn as much as you can about entering data into a worksheet.

To enter some bit of information into a cell—which is really just a text box—simply click the cell using the mouse and begin typing. When you press ENTER or click the Formula bar's Enter button, Excel places whatever you type into the cell. (If you don't see the Enter, Cancel, and Edit Formula buttons, click the Formula bar to display them. They are also displayed after you enter something in a cell.)

The Cancel button   The Edit Formula button

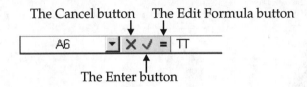

The Enter button

If you begin typing an entry and then realize that you don't want your entry placed into a cell, press ESC or click the Formula bar's Cancel button. Figure 12-3 shows an example Excel workbook with a bit of information.

For purposes of the discussion that follows, this book assumes you are proficient both in entering data into a text box and in editing data already in a text box. If you don't already possess this knowledge, you'll benefit greatly by first acquiring it. You should be able to get this information from just about any good introductory Windows 95/98 or Windows NT tutorial.

LEARN BY EXAMPLE
If you want to follow along with our discussion here, you can open the example Excel workbook in the Figure 12-3 (simple Excel workbook) file from the companion CD.

Editing and Erasing Data

When you want to change a cell's information, you have two choices. You can replace the cell's existing contents by typing over them. For example, you can click the cell, type your new entry, and press ENTER. Or you can edit the existing entry.

To edit a cell's contents, double-click the cell. Excel turns the cell into an editable text box. You can then edit the cell's contents in the same manner that you edit the contents of any text box. To place the edited cell contents back into the cell, press ENTER or click the Formula bar's Enter button. To erase the contents of a cell, select the cell and press the DELETE key.

To enter this information, click cell A1 and type the word **Sales**.

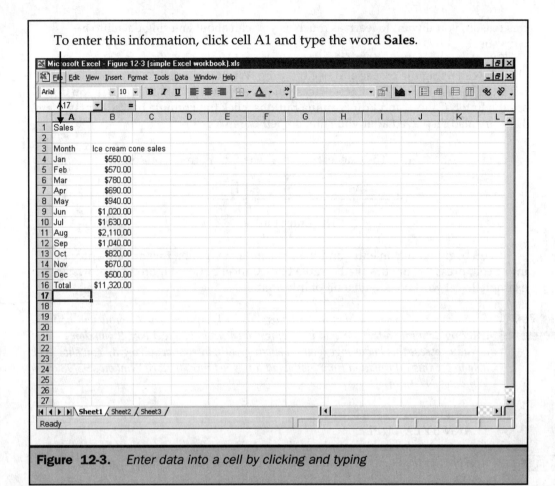

Figure 12-3. *Enter data into a cell by clicking and typing*

Tip *You can't erase the cell data by clicking on a cell and pressing the SPACEBAR. While this technique appears to work, it really doesn't because all you're really doing is replacing the cell's current contents with a space character. This can cause problems later if the cell is included in calculations.*

Types of Cell Data

You can enter three types of data into the cells of a worksheet: labels, values, and formulas. *Labels* are text used to describe areas of the worksheet. *Values* are the data you want to use in a calculation. *Formulas* are the instructions that tell Excel what and how to calculate.

Note | *In Figure 12-3, cells A1 through A16 and cell B3 hold labels. Cells B4 through B15 hold values. Cell B16 holds a formula.*

Labels

As just mentioned, a label is a chunk of alphanumeric text. The main differentiating characteristic of a label is that the label isn't used in calculations. Typically, you use labels to describe the values you do want to use in calculations. In Figure 12-3, for example, all the cell entries in column A are labels.

As a practical matter, you can enter labels that are as long as you need. But if you type in a label that's wider than the column you're placing it in, you'll often need to adjust the column width. Here's the reason: Although Excel will let a long label spill over into the adjacent cell or cells if they are empty, it displays only the portion of the label that fits in its own cell if the adjacent cell or cells store data. This sounds complicated, but really it's not. Take a look at the worksheet shown in Figure 12-4. Notice that the long labels in cells A1 through A5 spill over across cells B1 through B5. This is because cells B1 through B5 are empty.

Note | *Technically, there is a limit to label length: You can't enter a label of more than 32,000 characters. Be careful, though; only 1,024 characters in a cell can be printed.*

EXAMPLES

LEARN BY EXAMPLE
To follow along with the discussion here, open the example Excel workbook in the Figure 12-4 (incomplete income statement) file on the companion CD.

However, as soon as you enter another label or value into the adjacent cell, Excel truncates the long label. Figure 12-5 shows what happens when you do this.

The labels in cells A1 through A5 are too long to fit within their cells.

	A	B	C
1	Sales revenue		
2	Cost of goods sold		
3	Gross margin		
4	Operating expenses		
5	Profit before income taxes		

Figure 12-4. *Long labels spill over into adjacent cells—if there is room*

EXCEL

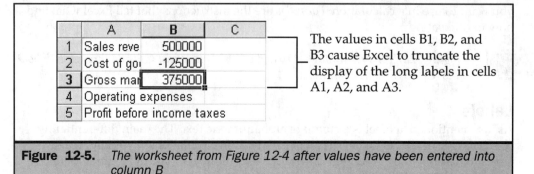

The values in cells B1, B2, and B3 cause Excel to truncate the display of the long labels in cells A1, A2, and A3.

Figure 12-5. *The worksheet from Figure 12-4 after values have been entered into column B*

EXAMPLES

LEARN BY EXAMPLE
To follow along with the discussion here, open the example Excel workbook in the Figure 12-5 (almost complete income statement) file on the companion CD.

When a label's display does get cut off because it can't spill over into adjacent cells or you don't want a label spilling over into adjacent cells, you just need to adjust the column width. There are a couple of quick ways to do this. If you want to make a column as wide as the widest piece of data it holds—a label or a value—you can double-click the right border of the column heading button. Alternatively, you can drag the right border of the column heading button using the mouse. Figure 12-6 shows the income statement worksheet after the column widths have been adjusted.

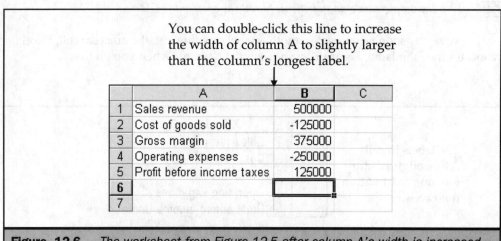

You can double-click this line to increase the width of column A to slightly larger than the column's longest label.

Figure 12-6. *The worksheet from Figure 12-5 after column A's width is increased*

You can change the heights of rows using the same basic mechanics: You can double-click the bottom border of the row heading button or you can drag the bottom border of the row heading button.

LEARN BY EXAMPLE

To follow along with the discussion here, open the example Excel workbook in the Figure 12-6 (complete income statement) file on the companion CD.

Label Entry Tools

Excel provides two handy tools that make data entry of labels easier—AutoComplete and Pick From List. AutoComplete works like this: When you begin entering a label in a column, Excel looks at each of the other entries in the column to see if it looks like your entry might just match one of those. If Excel finds that the first few characters of your entry match the first few characters of another entry, it automatically completes, or "AutoCompletes," your entry so it matches the earlier entry. This sounds kooky, perhaps, but let's take a quick look at a worksheet in which this AutoComplete tool would be really handy. Say you're building a list of customer names and addresses and you're using columns to store the individual fields of customer information. (See Figure 12-7.)

Take a close look at the entry started in row 5. When one begins typing the first part of the customer's city, *S*, there's a pretty good chance that one should finish the entry by typing "eattle." In other words, it's very likely that some of the customers are located in the same town. So Excel finishes the city entry by typing out "eattle." If you were doing this and you did want to enter that customer's city as Seattle, you press ENTER or click the formula bar's Enter button. If you want to enter something else, you just keep typing. Excel replaces "eattle" with whatever else you type. For example, if the customer described in row 5 really does business in San Francisco, when you type the next letters of the city name, Excel replaces "eattle" with your entry—in this case "an Francisco."

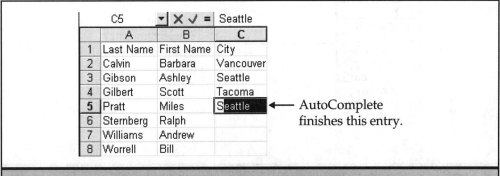

Figure 12-7. *A simple customer list illustrates the usefulness of AutoComplete*

LEARN BY EXAMPLE
You can open the example Excel workbook in the Figure 12-7 (customer list) file on the companion CD if you want to follow along with the discussion here.

You don't have to do anything to turn on the AutoComplete feature. It's automatically turned on when you install Excel. If you find the AutoComplete feature irritating—and some users will—you can turn it off. To do so, choose Tools | Options, click the Edit tab, and then uncheck the Enable AutoComplete For Cell Values box. (The check box is the last one shown on the Edit tab of options.)

The Pick From List feature also works to make data entry of labels easier. If you right-click a cell and choose the shortcut menu's Pick From List command, Excel displays a list of all the labels you've already entered in the column. (See Figure 12-8.) To enter one of the listed labels into the active cell, you just select it from the list.

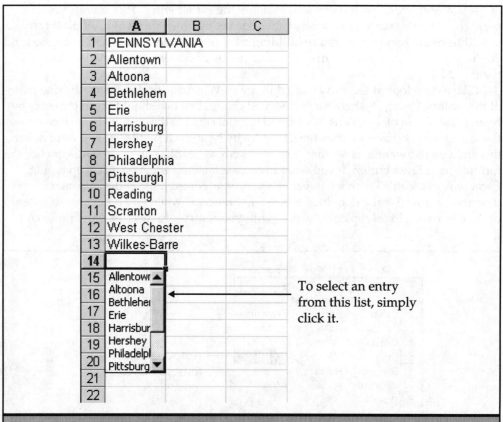

Figure 12-8. *The Pick From List command displays a list of entries you've already made in a column*

LEARN BY EXAMPLE
To follow along with the discussion here, open the example Excel workbook in the Figure
12-8 (pick from list example) file on the companion CD.

Values

You use values in calculations. If you were building a worksheet that tallied the cost of
an extended business trip to Europe, for example, you might build a worksheet like
that shown in Figure 12-9. Notice that column A holds labels that describe the values
and that column B holds the values—the estimated costs of the trip.

Basic Values

A few observations about cell values need to be made here. First, you typically don't
type dollar signs, commas, and so forth. You usually add these symbols to the values
by applying number formatting. You do need to include a decimal point if a value
includes decimal values. In cell B4, for example, the cost of transportation is given as
839.86. To show the price in both dollars and cents, therefore, you use the decimal
place between the dollars and the cents.

Formatting is discussed further in Chapter 3.

Figure 12-9 doesn't show any negative values, but worksheet cells accept negative
values. To enter a negative value, just precede the number with the minus symbol. If
you wanted to enter a "minus 200" into some cell, for example, you enter **–200.**

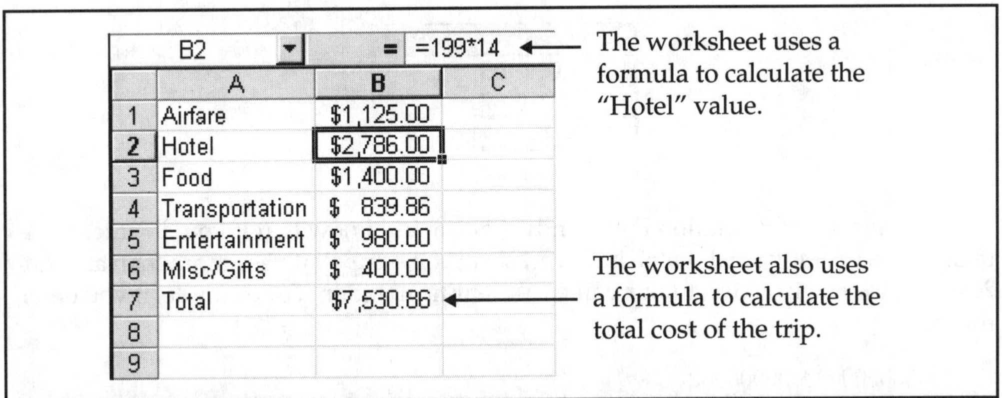

	B2	▼	=	=199*14	◄──	The worksheet uses a

	A	B	C
1	Airfare	$1,125.00	
2	Hotel	$2,786.00	
3	Food	$1,400.00	
4	Transportation	$ 839.86	
5	Entertainment	$ 980.00	
6	Misc/Gifts	$ 400.00	
7	Total	$7,530.86	
8			
9			

The worksheet uses a
formula to calculate the
"Hotel" value.

The worksheet also uses
a formula to calculate the
total cost of the trip.

Figure 12-9.   *This worksheet tallies the estimated costs of a lengthy business trip*
to Europe

Special Values

Most of the time you will enter values like those shown in Figure 12-9. You should know, however, that Excel accepts values that look or work differently. (Remember that a value is just data you want to later use in a calculation.) For example, you can use scientific notation, date and time values, percentages, and fractions.

SCIENTIFIC NOTATION   Scientific notation amounts to a shorthand system for efficiently expressing very large or very small values. Using scientific notation, you express a value (sometimes only approximately) by multiplying a decimal value by ten, raised or lowered to a specified power. For example, you might express the value 1,500,000 as the decimal value 1.5 multiplied by 106. (10^6 equals 1,000,000). Because 1.5 × 1,000,000 equals 1,500,000, the value 1,500,000 and the scientific notation value 1.5 × 10^6 are equivalent. In similar fashion, you might express the value 0.000000123 as the decimal value 1.23 multiplied by 10^{-7} (10^{-7} equals 0.0000001). Because 1.23 × 0.0000001 equals 0.000000123, the value 0.0000001232 and the scientific notation value .123 × 10^{-7} are equivalent.

You may already know this, but 10^6 equals 10 × 10 × 10 × 10 × 10 × 10, or 1,000,000.
10^{-7} equals 1/10 × 1/10 × 1/10 × 1/10 × 1/10 × 1/10 × 1/10, or 0.0000001.

You'll notice that as the power of ten increases, the number of zeros increases, and as the negative power of ten increases, the number of decimal places increases. And this is what makes scientific notation so useful. It's much easier, for example, to write 10^{100} than it is to write one with one hundred zeros after it. Values written using scientific notation take up less space because you use a special kind of shorthand to express them. In scientific notation, a decimal value, 1.23 × 10^{-7} is written as 1.23E-07. In other words, in place of the "× 10" portion of the traditional notation, you just use an E.

	A	B
1	1.00E+20	
2	1.23E-07	
3		
4		

Because scientific notation is so handy, you should know that if you do enter a really large or really small value in a worksheet cell—one that uses more than around 20 digits, Excel will convert your value to scientific notation. For example, if you enter the value:

100000000000000000000

Excel stores the following value in the cell:

10E+20

How Precise Is Excel?

Excel is more precise than most users will need. But you should know that Excel only uses the first 15 digits of a value. For example, if you enter the following 20-digit value:

12345678901234567890

Excel won't store this value in the cell. Rather, it will store the following 20-digit value:

12345678901234500000

Do you see what happens? Excel, in effect, loses the last five digits of this 20-digit number by converting them to zeros. Note, too, that Excel hasn't done any rounding. So, what's really happened is that Excel has just dropped 67,890 from the value.

This same sort of lost-number problem occurs on the other side of the decimal place. If you entered the decimal value

.12345678901234567890

Excel would actually place the following value into the cell:

0.123456789012345

While these dropped numbers sound terrible, it turns out that for most users, they don't really matter. If you were calibrating dollars, for example, how significant would roughly a $70,000 error be if you're talking about 12 million trillion? Not very.

DATE AND TIME VALUES   Excel considers dates and times to be values, too. This sounds weird when you first hear it, but treating dates and times as values means you can perform date and time arithmetic. You can easily calculate, for example, by which day you're supposed to pay an invoice due 45 days from today. And you can easily calculate how many hours you work if you start at 6:30 A.M., take a 45-minute lunch, and then continue working until 4:00 P.M.

To enter a date or time value, you just enter a value that looks like a date. Any of the following entries for February 8, 1999, looks like a date to Excel:

February 8, 1999	02-08-99
Feb 8, 1999	2/8/99
8-Feb-99	02/08/99
2-8-99	

Note   *Interestingly, as long as you haven't applied any specific cell formatting, if you enter a date value using either the first or second entry shown in the preceding list, Excel converts your entry to the third entry listed and also displays it this way. Similarly, if you enter a date value using the fourth entry shown in the preceding list, Excel converts your entry to the fifth entry listed and also displays it this way. Although these conversions may seem strange, what's really happening is this: Excel recognizes that your entry is a date value, sees it has been entered incorrectly, and then converts it to an accepted date value syntax.*

Time values work in a fashion that is similar to date values. If you enter into a cell something that looks like a time, for example:

1:00
2:30 A.M.
5:00:01 P.M.
16:45

Excel treats your entry as a time value. (Excel considers the entry 1:00 to be 1:00 A.M., by the way.) If you enter something that resembles a time value, but doesn't actually use the correct syntax—"1:00 p" for example—Excel edits your entry so it does use the correct syntax.

Here's another weird little twist on date and time values. Although you can enter date and time values in the way just described—as little snippets of characters that look like a date or time—you can also enter them as regular values and then later format them to look like dates or times. According to Excel, for example, the integer 1, represents January 1, 1900. The integer 2 represents January 2, 1900. And the integer 3 represents January 3, 1900. And so on.

	A	B	C
1	225	August 12,1900	
2	5490	January 11, 1915	
3	6704	May 9, 1918	
4	21070	September 7, 1957	
5	32111	November 30, 1987	
6			

Tip   *When you enter date or time values that look like date or time values, you're actually including formatting with the value. In other words, you're simultaneously entering a value into a cell and also telling Excel how to display, or format, the cell.*

Excel uses decimal values to represent time values. The decimal value 0.00, for example, represents 12:00:00 A.M. The decimal value 0.25 represents 6:00:00 A.M. The decimal value 0.5 represents 12:00:00 P.M., and so on. This business about time values being decimal values should make sense if you think about it for a minute. If Excel uses the whole number 1 to represent an entire day, then values less than one—in other words, decimal values—must be used to represent units of time less than a day: seconds, minutes, hours, and so forth.

	A	B
1	0.05	1:12 AM
2	0.32	7:40 AM
3	0.47	11:16 AM
4	0.75	6:00 PM
5	0.89	9:21 PM
6		

Excel also lets you combine integers and decimal values to create date-and-time value combinations. For example, the value 1.0 represents January 1, 1900, 12:00:00 A.M. The value 2.25 represents January 2, 1900, 6:00:00 A.M. The value 3.5 represents January 3, 1900, 12:00:00 P.M.

Working with values that you enter as values is usually too confusing. You won't know that the value 36,502.2 represents 4:48 A.M., December 8, 1999, until you format it. And, in fact, if you did enter the value 36,502.2 and then formatted it as a date, Excel would replace your entry (36,502.2) with the date value 12/8/1999 4:48 A.M.

Note *For more information about formatting values, refer to Chapter 3.*

But you should still remember something about all this: Each day's date value is one more than the previous day's date value. If you remember this, you'll be able to easily construct formulas that manipulate date values by adding values to date values. For example, if you want to know the precise date that falls 45 days after the date January 25, 1997, you can add the value 45 to the date value 1/25/1997. (The next chapter talks more about how you construct formulas.)

PERCENTAGES AND FRACTIONS   You can enter percent values into worksheet cells by following the value with a percent symbol. Excel enters the decimal equivalent for the percent value into the cell, but displays the value as a percentage. Does that make sense? In other words, if you enter **75%** into a cell, Excel stores the decimal value 0.75 in the cell, but displays it as 75%.

You can also enter fractional values into worksheet cells as long as Excel understands that what you're entering is a fraction. If you enter **1 2/5** into a cell, for example, Excel figures that you're probably trying to enter a fraction. So it plops the

Splitting Hairs About Time Values

Some big Office books also like to tell you that the value 0.041666667 represents one hour, that the value 0.000694444444444444 represents one minute, and that the value 1.15741E-05 represents one second. The authors of this book don't think this information all that useful, however. If you remember that there are 24 hours in a day, 60 minutes in an hour, and 60 seconds in a minute, you can easily construct formulas that calculate the exact decimal values for any time value. The value 1 divided by 24 returns the decimal value for an hour. The decimal value for an hour divided by 60 returns the decimal value for a minute. And the decimal value for a minute divided by 60 returns the decimal value for a second.

value 1.4 into the cell, formatting it to look like a fraction. Note that the way you enter this is by typing the integer first (1), then a space, then the numerator (2), then a slash, and then the denominator (5).

Note   *The preceding paragraph's information about fractions illustrates again an important point mentioned earlier. What a cell holds isn't necessarily the same thing as what a cell displays. For example, if you enter 1 2/5 into a cell, the worksheet cell displays this fraction. But the cell actually holds the value 1.4. (You can confirm this by entering such a fraction into a worksheet cell and then comparing what the cell displays with what the formula bar shows as the cell's contents.)*

   If you want to enter a fraction that doesn't contain a whole number and that could be misinterpreted by Excel as a date (for example, is the entry 2/5 a date value for February 5 or a fraction?) just enter the fraction as **0 2/5**.

Wide Values

There's one final point you'll want to know concerning the values you enter into the cells of a worksheet: It's very likely that you'll want to enter values into cells that are wider than the column. But that's actually not a problem. If you enter a value with more digits than will fit into the width of a column, Excel does one of two things. If you haven't directly or indirectly told Excel to use special formatting for the cell, Excel displays the value using scientific notation, as cell B1 shows:

	A	B
1		3.58E+11
2		
3		

If you have told Excel to use special formatting, Excel either attempts to widen the column when the number is entered or displays pound signs instead of the value as cell B1 shows:

To make a column wide enough to display the value the way you want, double-click the right border of the column letter box. Alternatively, you can drag the right border of the column using the mouse. (These are the same techniques for changing column widths as mentioned earlier in the chapter in the discussion of wide labels.)

Formulas

The next chapter talks about formulas in detail. Before you finish reading this discussion of values, however, you should know that there's actually a final type of value called a *formula*. By entering a formula, you simply tell Excel to calculate a return using values that the formula either supplies or references. For example, if you enter the formula **=2+2** into a cell, you tell Excel to add two and two together and display the result (which is four, of course). And if you enter the formula **=A1+A2** into a cell, you tell Excel to add the value in cell A1 to the value in cell A2 and then display the result. This comment is relevant here because much of what you have read about values also applies to formulas. For example,

- Formula returns can be used in other formulas.
- Formulas can use and may display their results using scientific notation.
- Formulas are only precise to the 15 most significant digits.
- Formula results may be too wide to be displayed in a standard-width column.

Don't get hung up on this formula business. The next chapter explains everything. Do remember, however, that formulas are just another type of value.

Annotating Cells with Comments

Most people—at least when they're first working with Excel—enter data only into a worksheet's cells. But a worksheet's cells aren't the only place to enter and store information. You can also attach comments—electronic sticky notes, in effect—to cells. Why you do this is probably obvious: You can further document the contents of a cell without cluttering up the worksheet.

To attach a comment to a cell, follow these steps:

1. Click the cell to which you want to attach the note.

2. Choose Insert | Comment. Excel displays a comment pop-up box.

	A	B	C	D	E
1	Airfare	$1,125.00			
2	Hotel	$2,786.00			
3	Food	$1,400.00			
4	Transportation	$ 839.86			
5	Entertainment	$ 980.00	Patricia A. Coleman:		
6	Misc/Gifts	$ 400.00	Try to keep these costs down!		
7	Total	$7,530.86			
8					
9					
10					

3. Enter the cell note into the pop-up box.

4. Click outside of the comment box when you're finished.

Once you've attached a comment to a cell, Excel places a small red triangle in the upper-right corner of the cell to show you that the cell has a comment. To later read the comment, place the mouse pointer over the center of the cell. Excel displays the comment in a small pop-up box, as shown in Figure 12-10. You can also later read all comments by all choosing View | Comment.

TEMPLATES

HEADSTART
The companion CD includes the retirement planner worksheet shown in Figure 12-10 (retire.xls) as a Headstart template. The retirement planner worksheet uses cell comments to describe the input you supply to the Headstart template and to explain the template's output.

Working with Ranges

In the preceding pages of this chapter, the assumption is that you enter data into a worksheet one cell at a time. Your simplest approach to do this is just to click the cell

The comment pop-up box

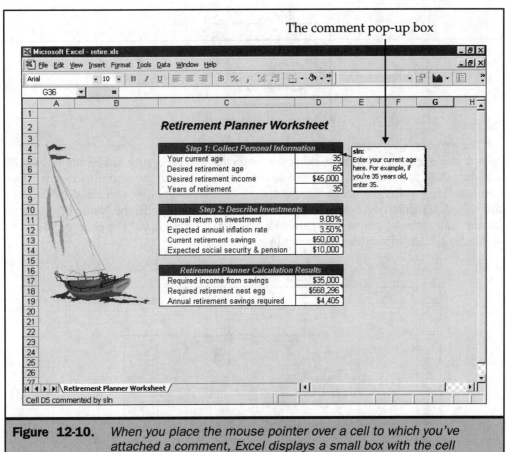

Figure 12-10. *When you place the mouse pointer over a cell to which you've attached a comment, Excel displays a small box with the cell comment*

and then type your entry. You can, however, select more than one cell at a time and enter data into more than one cell at a time. So, let's talk about this for a minute.

Selecting Ranges

To enter data into more than one cell at a time, you first need to know how to select a range of cells. Before you learn about range selection mechanics, however, let's quickly review how you select a single cell: You click the cell or move the cell selector to the cell using the arrow keys. When you do, Excel identifies your selection by placing a dark border around the cell. It also uses the Name box to give the selected cell's address, as shown in the following illustration.

The process is very similar to this when you select a group, or range, of adjacent cells. Instead of simply clicking, however, you click on one corner of a rectangle of cells and then drag the mouse to the opposite corner, as shown in the next illustration. (If you're following along in front of your computer, make sure that you can duplicate this selection using the mouse.) When you select a range of cells, the Name box doesn't identify the entire selection—only the active cell in the selection. (The chapter talks about the significance of the active cell in a minute.)

You describe a contiguous range selection by giving the cell address of the top-left corner of the range and the cell address of the bottom-right corner of the range, separating the two addresses with a colon. For example, the range shown in the preceding illustration is B3:E8. You'll need to remember this bit of information because you'll often use range addresses in Excel dialog boxes and in constructing formulas.

Note   *You can also use the keyboard to select a range of cells. To do this, first select one corner of the range using the arrow keys. Then, while holding down the SHIFT key, use the arrow keys to increase the size of the selection. If this doesn't make sense to you—and it is hard to explain—just try it on your computer. You'll immediately see how it works.*

A range can also be composed of nonadjacent cells. You can also select more than one range of cells using the mouse. To do so, select the group of cells, hold down the

CTRL key, and then select the second and any subsequent groups of cells. The range address for the cells selected in the next illustration is B1:B2,B4:B6,B8,B12:B13,B15,B17.

	A	B
1	Algeria	213
2	Belize	501
3	Chile	56
4	Croatia	385
5	Equador	593
6	Ethiopia	251
7	France	33
8	Guatemala	502
9	Hungary	36
10	Iran	98
11	Japan	81
12	Libya	218
13	Morocco	212
14	Netherlands	31
15	Panama	507
16	Sri Lanka	94
17	Tunisia	216
18	United Kingdom	44
19	Vietnam	84
20		

To select a three-dimensional range—in other words, to select the same group of cells on more than one sheet of a workbook—first group the worksheets. If all of the worksheet tabs are located next to each other, start by selecting the first worksheet tab and then holding down the SHIFT key as you select the last worksheet tab. If the tabs for worksheets to be grouped are not next to each other, start by selecting the first worksheet tab, then hold down the CTRL key as you click on each additional worksheet tab. Then, select the range on the active worksheet. You might want to select a three-dimensional range to quickly format more than one sheet at a time or if you are creating a formula that references the selected range on the selected sheets.

To select a column or row with the mouse, simply click the Column heading button that displays the column's letter or the Row heading button that displays the row's number. Excel selects the entire column or row.

To select a column or row with the keyboard, make sure the active cell is within the column or row you wish to select, then press CTRL-SPACEBAR to select the column or SHIFT-SPACEBAR to select the row.

Once you select a range of cells, you can begin to enter data into the range. You can do this either manually or by using a command.

Entering Data into a Selected Range Manually

The white cell in a range selection is called the *active cell*, and it is into this cell that what you type gets placed. For example, if you select the range shown in the illustration below, type the word **Mississippi**, and then press ENTER, Excel places your entry into cell C19.

	A	B	C	D	E
1					
2					
3					
4					
5					
6					
7					
8					
9					
10					
11					
12			Delaware	321	
13			Hawaii	907	
14			Iowa	880	
15			Lousiana	450	
16			Maine	567	
17			Michigan	220	
18			Minnesota	567	
19					
20					

When you do select a range or multiple ranges, Excel lets you use the ENTER and TAB keys as well as the SHIFT-ENTER and SHIFT-TAB key combinations to easily place whatever you've typed into the active cell and to then change the active cell of the current range selection. Pressing ENTER and SHIFT-ENTER moves the active cell down and up the cells of the selected column. Pressing TAB and SHIFT-TAB moves the active cell right and left within the selected row.

At this point in a discussion of range selection mechanics, I could describe in a few paragraphs what happens when you get to the end of a column or row or rectangle and then again press ENTER, TAB, SHIFT-ENTER, or SHIFT-TAB. Instead, just try this out for yourself by selecting a few ranges on a worksheet, and then experiment with the keys and key combinations described here. You'll immediately see—and more important, remember—how these keys move the active cell around a worksheet's selected ranges.

One other thing you should know, however, concerns three-dimensional ranges. When you make one of these selections and then start entering data into the selection, what you enter on one worksheet of the selection gets automatically entered into the other worksheet's ranges. For example, if you select the range shown in the illustration that follows on the worksheets Sheet1, Sheet2, and Sheet3, and then enter the values shown, whatever you enter into the range B2:D4 of Sheet1 also gets placed into range B2:D4 of Sheet2 and range B2:D4 of Sheet3. If this seems confusing, select the range B2:D4 in Sheet1, hold down the SHIFT key, and click the Sheet3 tab, and then enter the values shown in the illustration. When you're done, browse through Sheet1, Sheet2, and Sheet3, and you'll see exactly what happens.

	A	B	C	D
1		January	February	March
2	Sales	15000	20000	10000
3	Expense	12000	12000	12000
4	Profit	3000	8000	-2000
5				

Manually entering data into a range selection may not seem like all that neat a data-entry technique. But it actually is. If you're entering a large quantity of data, you'll find it usually saves you time to select the worksheet range into which you want to enter the data first—and then later concentrate simply on entering the data, pressing ENTER, entering more data, pressing ENTER again, and so on. This will be especially true if you're a touch typist.

Copying and Moving Worksheet Ranges

Once you know how to select a worksheet range, you can easily copy or move a worksheet range. To move the selected worksheet range, just drag the border of the selected range using the mouse. To copy the selected worksheet range, hold down the CTRL key, and then drag the border of the selected worksheet range using the mouse. As you drag the border of a selected range you're copying or moving, Excel displays an outline of the range to show you where the range is copied or moved to.

When you copy or move a range, you replace the contents of the destination range.

Using the Fill Series Command

Range selection is useful to know about if you want to enter, copy, or move data in a worksheet, but it's also useful if you're going to use Excel's Fill Series command, which is a terribly handy tool for quickly entering values that fit an easily identifiable pattern. For example, if you want to build a worksheet that describes how a loan balance is repaid over, say, 30 years with monthly payments, you might want to number and date the 360 monthly payment dates, as shown in the partially completed worksheet in Figure 12-11.

LEARN BY EXAMPLE

To follow along with the discussion here, open the example Excel workbook in the, Figure 12-11 (loan amortization schedule) file on the companion CD.

EXAMPLES

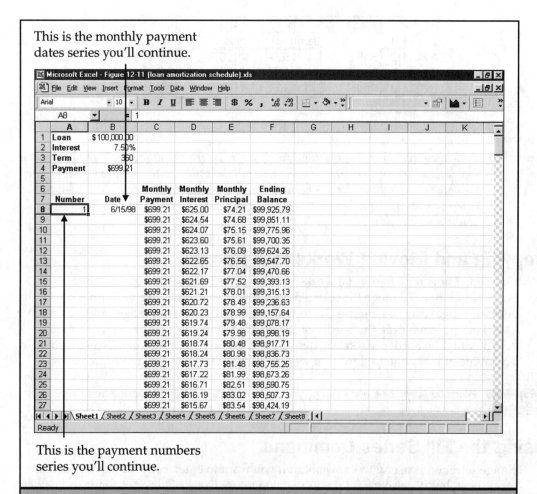

Figure 12-11. *You can use the Edit menu's Fill Series command to enter the payment numbers and monthly payment dates into this worksheet*

Rather than manually entering this series of payment number and date values, you can use the Edit menu's Fill Series command. You might also want to number the monthly payments made on such a loan: 1, 2, 3, and so on all the way to the 360th payment. Again, rather than manually entering this series of values, you can use the Edit menu's Fill Series command. To do this, follow these steps:

1. Enter the starting value for the pattern you're creating into the first cell of the range you'll select. In Figure 12-11, for example, you would enter the value **1** into cell A8 and the date value for the first monthly payment date, **6/15/98**, in cell B8.

2. Select the range you want to fill. In Figure 12-11, for example, to fill the range A9:A367 with payment numbers, you select the range A8:A367. To fill the range B9:B367 with monthly payment dates, you select the range B8:B367.

3. Choose Edit | Fill | Series. Excel displays the Series dialog box.

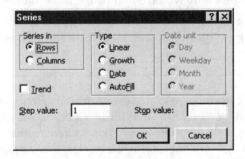

4. Use the Step Value text box to describe how the first cell's value changes as it's adjusted and placed into subsequent cells. (Optionally, you can enter the value that ends the pattern using the Stop Value text box.)

5. Use the Series In buttons to indicate whether you want the range selection filled row by row or column by column. In the case where you're filling column A with payment numbers or column B with monthly payment dates, you mark the Series In Columns option button.

6. Use the Type buttons to indicate how the start value is adjusted using the Step Value. The default pattern is for a Linear pattern, which simply means that the step value is added to the previous cell's value to get the current cell's value. (You would mark this option button to fill in the payment number series.) The Growth pattern means the Step Value is multiplied by the previous cell's value to get the current cell's value. The Date pattern tells Excel the series should follow the pattern you describe using the Date Unit buttons. (You would mark the Month option button to fill in the monthly payment date series.) The AutoFill pattern tells Excel to look at the values you've already entered into the range (if you've done this) and then continue that pattern.

7. If you indicate you want to use a date series—you would do this by marking the Type Date option button in step 6—you need to specify which date units you'll use to describe the series. You do this using the Date Unit option buttons: Day, Weekday, Month, or Year. In the case of the monthly loan amortization schedule, for example, you would click the Month option button.

8. Enter the value which Excel should add to the first value in the series into the Step Value text box. In the case of the payment number series, you would enter **1** since the next payment number should be created by adding one to the previous payment number. In the case of the monthly payment date series, you would also enter **1** since the next monthly payment date value should be created by adding one month to the previous monthly payment date.

9. Optionally, if you know the last value of the series, enter it into the Stop Value text box. In the case of the payment number series, for example, you could enter **360** since there are only 360 payments in a 30-year mortgage with monthly payments. (You probably wouldn't know the last monthly payment date value.)

10. When the Series dialog box correctly describes the series, click OK. Excel fills the selected range with a data series like the one you describe.

TEMPLATES

HEADSTART

The companion CD includes several loan amortization Headstart templates you can use: a 30-year fixed rate mortgage loan amortization schedule (30yrloan.xls), which actually shows how Figure 12-11 looks after the payment numbers and monthly payment dates have been entered; a 30-year adjustable rate mortgage loan amortization schedule (30yr-adj.xls); a 15-year fixed rate loan amortization schedule (15yrloan.xls); a 15-year adjustable rate loan amortization schedule (15yr-adj.xls); a 60-month fixed rate loan amortization schedule (60moloan.xls), such as might be used for a 60-month fixed-rate car loan; and a 60-month adjustable rate loan amortization schedule (60mo-adj.xls).

Using AutoFill with a Mouse

AutoFill, as mentioned earlier, refers to Excel's ability to identify a pattern from the values you've already entered and then continue the pattern. Although you can choose Edit | Fill | Series to use AutoFill, you'll more often want to use the mouse. It's easier.

To AutoFill a range selection using the mouse, first enter the first few values of the pattern—just enough to clearly show the pattern. Then, select the range that holds those values. In Figure 12-12, for example, you would select the range A8:B9.

To continue the pattern, you drag the fill handle, which appears as a square with cross-hairs in the lower-right corner of the range selection, into the range of cells that you want to fill. Actually using AutoFill is the best way to learn and appreciate its power. So do try it. Enter the date values shown in Figure 12-12, select the range holding the payment numbers and date values (A8:B9), and then drag the selected range's fill handle down several rows.

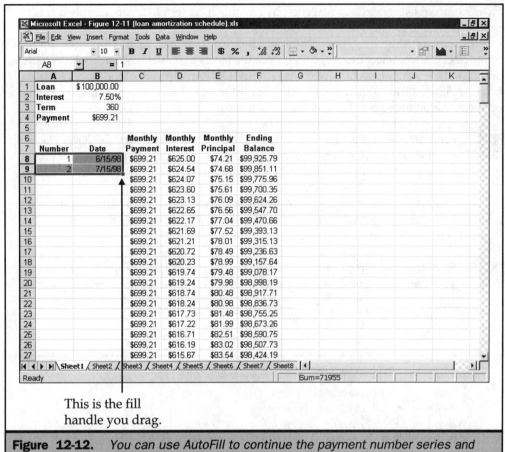

This is the fill
handle you drag.

Figure 12-12. *You can use AutoFill to continue the payment number series and monthly payment date series already shown in A8:B9*

Tip   *You can also use AutoFill to copy the contents of single cell into a range. To do this, enter a label or value into a cell, select the cell, and then drag the cell's fill handle.*

Using a Custom List

AutoFill is a very powerful tool because Excel can identify almost any pattern you concoct: odd numbers, even numbers, a growth rate of 10%, days of the week, months of the year, and so on. There will, however, be patterns you'll enter that will be unique to your work. For example, you might have a list of employee names you enter frequently. Or a list of department names. Or product numbers. Anytime you start such a list, you actually know you are beginning a recognizable pattern. But the problem is that only you know the pattern. Excel doesn't. And this knowledge gap on the part of Excel is what

Excel's custom lists address. In essence, by creating a custom list, you identify a special, unique pattern that Excel can use to AutoFill.

To create a custom list, first enter the labels or values that make up the list someplace in a worksheet. Then, select the range that holds the labels or values, choose Tools | Options, and click the Custom Lists tab. Excel displays the Custom Lists tab of the Options dialog box (see Figure 12-13). When you click the Import button, Excel creates a custom list based on the entries in the selected range. Click OK to close the Options dialog box.

Note   *To edit the entries in a custom list, choose Tools | Options and click the Custom Lists tab. Select the list you want to change from the Custom Lists box. Then, make your changes using the List Entries box. When you finish editing the list entries, click the OK button.*

Once you define a custom list, AutoFill recognizes a custom list entry as the start of a pattern. To use a custom list, therefore, all you have to do is enter the custom list's first entry in a cell. Then you drag that cell's fill handle.

Note   *This chapter only briefly covered the topics of cell formulas—perhaps the most important type of entry you'll make in your worksheets. To learn more about formulas, you may want to turn to the next chapter. It describes in detail how formulas and a special formula tool, called functions, work.*

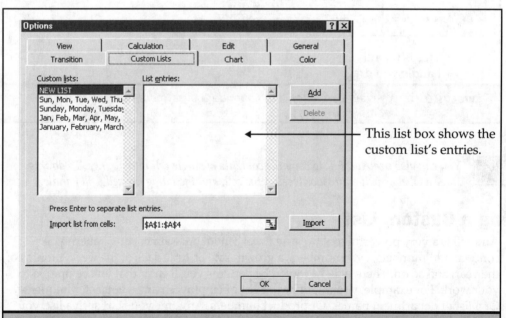

Figure 12-13.   *You use the Options dialog box's Custom Lists tab to create and modify custom lists*

The Complete Reference

Office 2000

Chapter 13

Excel Formulas and Functions

If you read the last chapter, you already know in general terms that Excel's cells also accept formulas. What you may not yet know is how powerful these formulas are. Excel lets you easily construct formulas that make complicated and cumbersome calculations. Excel even lets you create formulas that, instead of mathematically manipulating values, manipulate chunks of text. In this chapter, you'll learn how to use Excel's formulas to turn your Excel worksheets into powerful analytical tools.

Formula Basics

A *formula* simply takes input values, mathematically manipulates them, and then returns a result. All the following are, for example, formulas:

```
2+2
991
5*5000+2*5000
```

Formulas may not seem like something you should get excited about, but they actually represent the foundation of Excel's power. Why? Because Excel lets you enter formulas into worksheet cells, and then it instantaneously calculates and displays the formula result.

Entering a Formula into a Worksheet Cell

Entering a formula into a worksheet cell is easy. You simply follow these steps:

1. Select the cell you want to place the formula into.

2. Type the equal sign (=) to tell Excel that you're about to enter a formula.

3. Enter the formula using any input values and the appropriate mathematical operators that make up your formula.

The table that follows describes the five basic operators and provides examples of simple formulas that show how they're used.

Operator	Description	Example	Result
+	Addition	=2+2	4
−	Subtraction	=4–2	2
*	Multiplication	=4*2	8
/	Division	=12/4	3
^	Exponentiation	=4^2	16

Although the formulas in the preceding table can be useful ones to calculate, the neat part of Excel's formulas is that you don't have to include the actual values in the formula. In fact, you usually don't. You can typically reference the cells that hold the values. For example, let's say you want to calculate the monthly interest on a $100,000 loan that will charge 7 percent interest annually. To make this calculation, you could construct a formula that looks like what follows:

=100000*7.5%/12

An easier method (because it lets you quickly change formula input values later) is to construct a simple worksheet that stores the loan values and then references these values in the actual formula. Figure 13-1 shows just such a worksheet. To construct it, enter the labels and values shown in the range A1:B2 as well as the label shown in cell A3. Then enter the formula **=B1*B2/12** into cell B3.

LEARN BY EXAMPLE
To follow along with the discussion here, open the example Excel workbook in the Figure 13-1 (loan interest calculation) file on the companion CD.

When you enter the formula into cell B3, you tell Excel to multiply the value in cell B1 by the value in cell B2 and to then divide that result by 12. (Notice that because cell B3 is the selected cell in Figure 13-1, its contents show on the formula bar.)

The neat thing about the formula in Figure 13-1 is that, by using cell references in the formula rather than actual values, it's easy to recalculate the formula using

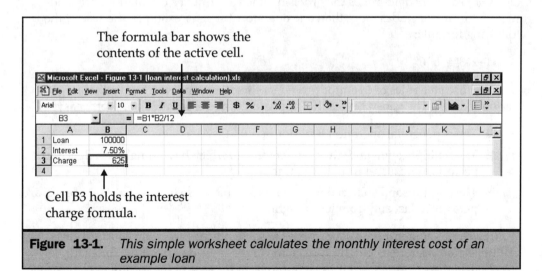

Figure 13-1. *This simple worksheet calculates the monthly interest cost of an example loan*

different inputs. If interest rates pop up to, say, 9.75 percent, you can recalculate the monthly interest charge simply by replacing the existing value in cell B2, 7.5%, with the new value, 9.75%.

	A	B	C
1	Loan	100000	
2	Interest	9.75%	
3	Charge	812.5	
4			

The values 9.5 and 9.75 percent, by the way, are equivalent to the decimal values 0.095 and 0.0975.

While you can type out the cell addresses of all the cell references you want to use in a formula, it's often just as easy and usually more accurate to type the operators and then click the cells. For example, to create the formula =B1*B2/12, rather than typing =B1*B2/12, you could type =, click cell B1, type *, click cell B2, and then finally type /12. The reason this works is that if you've already told Excel that you're entering a formula—which you do when you type the first equal sign (=)—Excel assumes that any of the subsequent cells you click should be included in the formula.

Operator Precedence

You need to keep in mind the issue of operator precedence as you write formulas. *Operator precedence* determines the order in which a formula's calculations are made when a formula includes more than one operator. Take, for example, the case of the following formula:

=1+2–3*4/5^6

Excel uses the rules of operator precedence to determine which calculations get performed first. The general rules that apply to the above formula are pretty easy:

■ The exponential operation is performed first.

■ The multiplication and division operations, which have equal precedence, are performed next and from left to right.

■ The addition and subtraction operations, which also have equal precedence, are performed last and from left to right.

If two operators in a formula possess the same precedence—say a formula uses two multiplication operations or a multiplication and a division operation, for example—Excel calculates operators in left-to-right order. In the case of the formula given earlier, therefore, Excel first makes the exponential calculation, then does multiplication, then the division, then the addition, and finally the subtraction.

 To verify that you understand how this works, try to calculate the above formula with a calculator and scratch pad and then test your result by entering the formula into an empty worksheet cell.

To change the order in which Excel calculates a formula's operators, enclose the operator and its operands (the values it uses in its calculation) in parentheses. If you want to change the order of another additional formula operator, repeat the process: Enclose the operator and its operands (which may actually include a calculation result) in parentheses. For example, suppose that you want to use the formula =1+2–3*4/5^6 in some worksheet cell, but also want the operators used in exactly the opposite order that Excel would typically use them. In other words, rather than calculating the operators in the default order—exponentiation, multiplication, division, addition, and subtraction—you want them calculated in this order: subtraction, addition, division, multiplication, and finally, exponentiation. Here's how you would place your parenthesis marks:

=((1+(2–3))*(4/5))^6

You calculate the above formula by working from the innermost set of parentheses outward. After the first level of calculation is completed, the result is (0*0.262144)^6. The next level of calculation would be 0^6. The final result, then, is zero. If you had not changed the order of calculation by using parentheses, the result would have been 2.999232.

If you find this operator precedence business confusing—and it sometimes can be—your best bet is to keep your formulas simple. Don't construct lengthy formulas that use a bunch of different operators. If you can, substitute a function. (This chapter describes functions a bit later in the section, "Using Functions.") Or, alternatively, break a long formula into several shorter formulas, placing these shorter formulas into separate cells.

Boolean Logic Operators

Excel supports another category of arithmetic operators called *Boolean logic operators*. These operators have lower precedence than any of the other five operators discussed up to this point. In other words, in any formula that includes them, the Boolean operations would be the last operations performed.

In effect, Boolean logic operators let you compare two values or labels by asking a question, such as "Is the value in cell A1 equal to the value in cell B1?" If the answer to the comparison question is yes, the operator returns a 1. If the answer to the comparison question is no, the operator returns a 0. The table that follows identifies, illustrates, and describes the Boolean operators that Excel provides.

Operator	Example	Comparison Made
=	A1=5	Is the value in cell A1 equal to 5?
>	A1>5	Is the value in cell A1 greater than 5?
<	A1<5	Is the value in cell A1 less than 5?
<>	A1<>5	Is the value in cell A1 not equal to 5?
=>	A1=>5	Is the value in cell A1 greater than or equal to 5?
=<	A1=<5	Is the value in cell A1 less than or equal to 5?

Boolean logic operators can seem sort of funny, but they actually become quite handy when you're using logical functions that return a value or label based on a result of the comparison test that a Boolean logic operator can make—for example, "If the student's test result is less than 60, return his letter grade as 'F'."

Interpreting Error Values

You can create formulas that don't make sense because they aren't possible. For example, you can't divide a value by zero. That mathematical operation is undefined. So, if you enter a formula such as =1/0 into a cell, Excel can't calculate it. Instead, what Excel displays as the result of the formula calculation is an error, #DIV/0?. This error value tells you, first, that Excel can't calculate the formula, and, second, why Excel can't calculate it. In this case, it is because you're attempting to divide some value by zero, which is nonsensical. (In essence, you can think of division by zero as saying, "what formula result do I get if I don't divide some value?"). The following table provides a complete list of the error values that Excel can return when a formula calculation can't be made. Some of these won't make sense until you finish reading this chapter. But you'll want to have a complete list of error values some place—and it makes more sense to do it here, rather than at the very end of the chapter or in some easy-to-miss appendix.

Error Value	Description
#DIV/0!	Formula attempts to divide some value by zero, which is an undefined mathematical operation.

Error Value	Description
#N/A	Formula references a cell that supplies the "Not Available" error value. A cell supplies this error value by using the =NA( ) function.
#NAME?	Formula uses a cell or range name that hasn't been defined, or the function name has been misspelled, or a text string is not enclosed in quotation marks.
#NULL!	Formula references a cell as the intersection of two ranges—except there is no intersection of the two ranges.
#NUM!	An invalid argument has been supplied for the function, where the function expects a numeric argument, or the result is either too large or too small to be represented in Excel.
#REF!	Formula references cells that no longer exist because you deleted them.
#VALUE!	Formula attempts to use the wrong argument or operand—for example, a chunk of text in a mathematical operation, which, of course, makes no sense.

If you do create a formula that returns an error value, use the error value to identify the type of error. (You can use the preceding table of error values to help you do this.) Then, if the error isn't temporary—perhaps a result of the fact that your worksheet still isn't complete—you'll need to correct the problem or problems that produce the error value.

How Excel Recalculates Formulas

Excel calculates the formulas you enter in the order they need to be calculated. For example, it first calculates any formulas that are independent of any other formulas. (These might be formulas that use only values and cell references, or they might be formulas that reference only cells that hold values and not other formulas.) After Excel has calculated these independent formulas, it begins calculating the dependent formulas, working its way from your least dependent formulas to your most dependent formulas. (A "dependent" formula needs other formulas' results in order to be calculated.)

Note   *Excel calculates a worksheet's formula any time a formula's input changes. On a fast computer or in a workbook that doesn't have a great number of complicated formulas, the recalculation usually happens so fast that you don't ever know it has occurred.*

Most of the time this calculating happens automatically. You don't need to think about it. You don't need to worry about it. However, you can create something called a "circular reference," and that typically creates problems.

A *circular reference* is a formula that either directly or indirectly depends on itself. With a circular reference formula, you can't calculate the formula because to calculate the formula you first need to calculate the formula. Although that description sounds like gobbledy-gook, it's more common in real life than you might think. (Pension fund calculations, for example, are often circular.) Say you were building a budgeting worksheet and that one of your formulas calculated an employee bonus that equaled, say, 10 percent of the profits after deducting the bonus. To calculate the bonus, you need to know the profits. But to calculate the profits, you need to know the bonus. You see the circular nature of this. Figure 13-2 shows an example workbook that makes just this calculation.

LEARN BY EXAMPLE

To follow along with the discussion here, open the example Excel workbook in the Figure 13-2 (circular reference example) file on the companion CD.

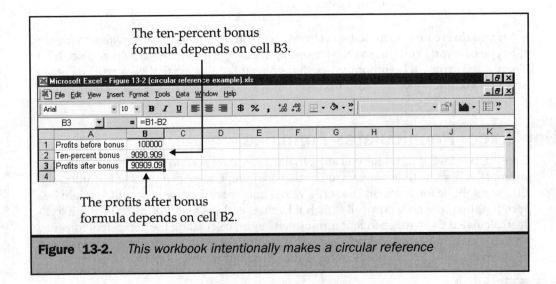

Figure 13-2.   *This workbook intentionally makes a circular reference*

If you build a worksheet that makes a circular reference, Excel initially assumes you've made an error and displays the message shown here:

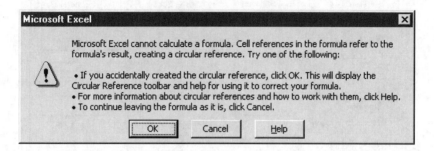

After you click the OK button in the alert box, Excel uses the status bar to identify the cell with the formula creating the circular reference. (The message says "Circular:" followed by the cell address with the circular reference formula.)

If you know you've made an error, click OK; Excel displays the Circular Reference toolbar, shown next. You can use its drop-down list box to display a list of the cell references that make up the circular reference and to move to any of these cell references. (The idea here, perhaps obviously, is that you move through each of the cells that make up the circular reference, looking for the formula that erroneously creates the circularity.)

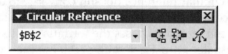

 You can also display the Circular Reference toolbar by choosing View | Toolbars | Circular Reference.

If you build a worksheet that intentionally uses a circular reference, Excel may be able to iteratively solve the circular reference. It turns out that some circular references—like the one about an employee bonus equaling 10 percent of the profits after the bonus—converge to a single solution. All Excel has to do is repeatedly recalculate the worksheet. To tell Excel that you want it to repeatedly calculate a worksheet in an attempt to resolve a circular reference, choose Tools | Options, select the Calculation tab, and then mark the Iteration check box.

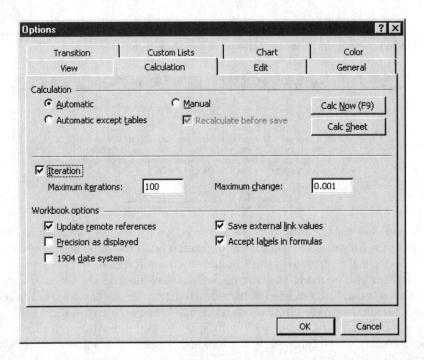

Note, however, that some circular references can't be solved. In this case, the formula that creates the circular reference doesn't converge to a single, correct solution. Sometimes, this lack of convergence causes formula results to jump around wildly. Other times, the lack of convergence causes the formula results either to continue to grow or decline—and usually at an accelerating rate. In practice, circular references that don't converge to a single solution are erroneous formulas. You've either made an error entering the formula—perhaps you referenced an incorrect cell or the cell itself with the formula. Or you've constructed a large, complex workbook—and your modeling logic has broken down someplace.

Excel doesn't alert you to circular references if you've already told it you want it to make iterative, or repeated, workbook recalculations. Excel figures that if you've told it to do this, you know you've got circular references that you're trying to solve through convergence.

Creating Linking Formulas

Most of the formulas you create will reference other cells on the same worksheet. You aren't limited to doing this, however. You can pull values from cells located on other worksheets and even from cells in other workbooks.

The easiest way to do this, by the way, is to create the formula by typing the operators and then clicking the cells whose contents you want to use in the formula you're building. If you remember that you can display another worksheet page by clicking its sheet tab and you can display another workbook either by opening it or choosing it from the Window menu, then you can display the cell you want to use and click it.

You can also type out a formula that links to, or uses, cells on other worksheets or cells in a different workbook. To create a formula that uses a cell on another worksheet, just precede the cell address with the sheet name and an exclamation point. For example, to create a formula that multiplies the value in cell B2 on Sheet5 by 25, you use the following formula:

=Sheet5!B2*25

To create a formula that uses a cell in another workbook, precede the cell address with a single quote mark, the workbook name in brackets, the sheet name, a single quote mark, and an exclamation point. For example, to create a formula that multiplies the value in cell B2 on Sheet5 of the workbook named Budget by 25, you use the following formula:

='[Budget]Sheet5'!B2*25

By the way, if you change the name of a workbook—say from Budget to Budget 1999—Excel updates any linking formulas for you as long as the both the workbook you're renaming and the workbook that uses the linking formulas are open.

EXCEL

Using Arrays

An array is simply a string of values. For example, the following set of values is an array: 1, 2, 3, 4, and 5. The reason arrays are interesting—at least to Excel users—is that you can use arrays in formulas to create still other arrays. For example, you could add the following two arrays to create a third array:

	Array 1:	1	2	3	4	5
+	Array 2:	2	4	6	8	10
=	Result:	3	6	9	12	15

Do you see what's happened? When you add two five-value arrays together, you create a third five-value array. In the resulting array, the first value is calculated as the first value from array 1 (1) plus the first value from array 2 (2). The second value is calculated as the second value from array 1 (2) plus the second value from array 2 (4). The third value in the resulting array is calculated by adding the third values in array 1 and array 2, and so on.

Creating Array Formulas

Although arrays may not seem all that useful, they can be very powerful in Excel worksheets—and once you see the actual mechanics, you'll understand why. Let's say you're creating a simple project time budget, in hours, that just coincidentally uses the same values as the array example (see Figure 13-3).

LEARN BY EXAMPLE
To follow along with the discussion here, open the example Excel workbook in the Figure 13-3 (project hours before array formula) file on the companion CD.

To create an array for the total values in row 4, first select the range B4:F4, type an equal sign (=), select the range B2:F2, type a plus sign (+), select the range B3:F3, and then press CTRL-SHIFT-ENTER. (You press these three keys simultaneously.) When you do this, Excel enters the array formula {=B2:F2+B3:F3} into each of the cells in the range B4:F4. (Note that you don't enter the curly brackets; Excel adds these when you press CTRL-SHIFT-ENTER.) Figure 13-4 shows the workbook from Figure 13-3 after adding an array formula.

Let's quickly review what's happening with this array formula to make sure that you understand how it works. In cell B4, the formula {=B2:F2+B3:F3} tells Excel to calculate its result by adding the values in B2 and B3. In cell C4, the formula tells Excel to add the values in C2 and C3. In cells D4, E4, and F4, the same basic mechanics apply: Excel calculates the correct column's total by adding the values in row 2 and row 3 of that column. You see how this works, right?

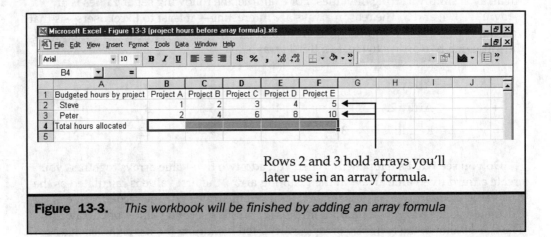

Rows 2 and 3 hold arrays you'll later use in an array formula.

Figure 13-3. *This workbook will be finished by adding an array formula*

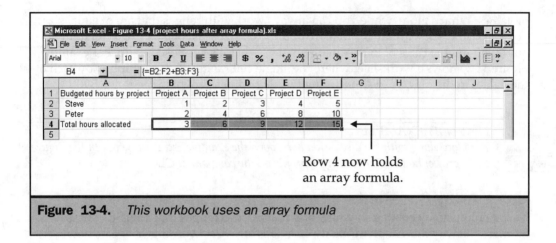

Row 4 now holds
an array formula.

Figure 13-4. *This workbook uses an array formula*

LEARN BY EXAMPLE
To follow along with the discussion here, open the example Excel workbook in the Figure 13-4 (project hours after array formula) file on the companion CD.

The array formula illustrated in Figure 13-4 provides a single-dimension array. You can create two-dimensional array formulas, however. To do this, you just need to select a two-dimensional range for the array formula and use a two-dimensional range in the formula itself.

Now that you understand how array formulas work, you'll also understand why they are so powerful: You only have to enter a single formula to make several calculations. Excel takes your single formula and stores it in the cells that hold the result array's values. But you've still only entered a single formula. That makes for less work, obviously. But there's a more important benefit when you're creating and working with large or complex workbooks: You'll have fewer formulas, which means you'll have fewer formulas to error-check and fewer formulas that may be incorrectly constructed and, therefore, returning erroneous results. Restated more simply: Array formulas simplify your workbooks by reducing the number of formulas. And that almost always reduces the number of errors, or bugs, in your workbooks.

Using Arrays As an Extension of Matrix Mathematics

In effect, what array formulas do is apply something you may remember as matrix mathematics from your school days. Using matrix mathematics, you simultaneously add, subtract, multiply, or divide matrices of values, thereby producing a new matrix of values. What's more, while you can always work with ranges that are of equal size, you can also work with ranges that are of unequal size—as long as Excel can figure out (applying the rules of matrix mathematics) what it's supposed to do. For example, Figure 13-5 shows a worksheet where the single cell range, B6, is multiplied by each of the values in the range B2:F4, returning the new values shown in the range B9:F11.

LEARN BY EXAMPLE
To follow along with the discussion here, open the example Excel workbook in the Figure 13-5 (project hours after contingency) file on the companion CD.

Using Array Constants

You should usually create array formulas that refer to ranges that contain your arrays. So that's the way this chapter initially describes arrays as working. You can, however, create array formulas in which the formulas themselves hold the array values. For example, to add the array 1, 2, 3, 4, and 5 to the array 2, 4, 6, 8, and 10, and place the results in a worksheet range, you probably should follow the approach shown in Figure 13-4. You could also enter the following formula into the range B4:F4:

$$=\{1,2,3,4,5\}+\{2,4,6,8,10\}$$

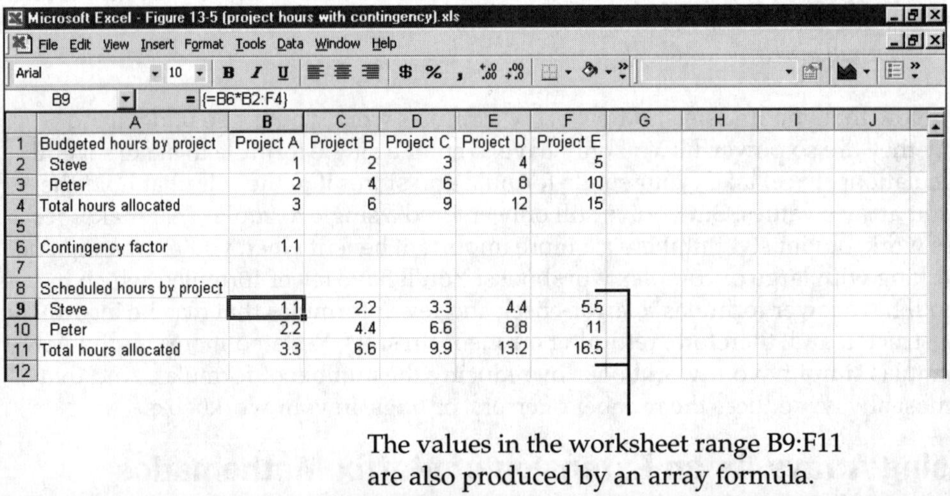

	A	B	C	D	E	F
	B9	= {=B6*B2:F4}				
1	Budgeted hours by project	Project A	Project B	Project C	Project D	Project E
2	Steve	1	2	3	4	5
3	Peter	2	4	6	8	10
4	Total hours allocated	3	6	9	12	15
5						
6	Contingency factor	1.1				
7						
8	Scheduled hours by project					
9	Steve	1.1	2.2	3.3	4.4	5.5
10	Peter	2.2	4.4	6.6	8.8	11
11	Total hours allocated	3.3	6.6	9.9	13.2	16.5
12						

The values in the worksheet range B9:F11 are also produced by an array formula.

Figure 13-5.   *Array formulas also let you use matrix mathematics in your worksheets*

When you press CTRL-SHIFT-ENTER, Excel places the following formula into the selected range:

{={1,2,3,4,5}+{2,4,6,8,10}}

 Notice that you would include the curly brackets when you type the array formula that includes the constants. Notice also that Excel adds its own set of curly brackets when you press CTRL-SHIFT-ENTER.

Figure 13-6 shows an example Excel workbook that uses an array formula that uses constants.

LEARN BY EXAMPLE
To follow along with the discussion here, open the example Excel workbook in the Figure 13-6 (project hours using constant array formula) file on the companion CD.

Editing Array Formulas

You edit array formulas in almost the same way as you edit other formulas. Double-click the cell with the formula you want to edit. Then, when Excel displays the formula in an editable text box, make your changes. The one thing you need to remember is that when you finish making your changes, you must press CTRL-SHIFT-ENTER to update the array formula in all the cells holding the formula.

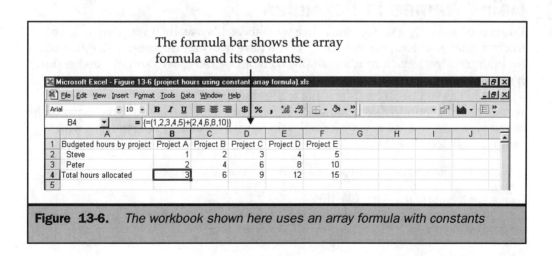

Figure 13-6.   *The workbook shown here uses an array formula with constants*

Excel makes you press CTRL-SHIFT-ENTER to finish your editing. Excel won't let you break the array formula by mucking about with only one of the cells in which the array formula returns its results.

Using Text Formulas

Although most formulas only mathematically manipulate values, it turns out that you can also have text formulas. Obviously, you can't add two pieces of text together. But what you can do is concatenate, or moosh together, two or more pieces of text. To do this, you use the concatenation operator, &. This chapter won't spend much time on this concatenation business because it's pretty simple. Just take a look at the next table, which illustrates how the concatenation operator works:

Text Formula	What It Returns
="White"&"house"	Whitehouse
=A1&A2	Whitehouse (if cell A1 holds the label "White" and cell A2 holds the label "house")
="Agatha"&" "&"Christie"	Agatha Christie

Notice, by the way, that the third text formula actually concatenates three chunks of text: the name "Agatha," a space enclosed in quotation marks, and the name "Christie."

Using Names in Formulas

When you have only a few formulas in a worksheet, it's usually pretty easy to keep track of what your formulas are doing. If you have to do a little research to figure out, for example, why some formula multiplies cell B81 by cell Z7, it's sort of a bother. But it's not an unbearable burden.

As soon as you begin creating some really substantial workbooks, however—workbooks with hundreds or thousands of formulas—you'll want to name many of the cells and ranges you use in your formulas. In this way, you'll be able to work with formulas that look like this:

=Interest_Rate*Loan_Balance

instead of formulas that look like this:

=B81*Z7

Naming Cells and Ranges

Excel provides probably a half-dozen ways to name cells and ranges. But the easiest and usually the fastest way to name a cell or range is simply by using the Name box. The Name box is the box that shows the active cell's address; it appears at the left end of the formula bar, just below the Formatting toolbar.

To name a cell or range, follow these steps:

1. Select the cell or range.

2. Click the Name box. Excel turns it into an editable text box and highlights the cell address (which is the cell address of the active cell).

3. Type the name you want to use for the selected cell or range. You can use numbers, letters, and the period (.), backslash (\), and underscore (_) symbols in your names, but you can't create cell or range names that resemble cell addresses.

Units		=	20000

	A	B	C
1	Units	20000	
2	Price	10	
3	Sales	20000	
4			

When you want to use the name in a formula, you can simply type it in place of the cell address. Or, if you're building formulas by clicking cell addresses, activate the Name box and choose the name from it.

To have Excel automatically update your worksheet formulas to use the new names you create in place of the equivalent cell or range references, choose Insert | Name | Apply. When Excel displays the Apply Names dialog box, select the name or names you want to substitute for cell or range addresses in your worksheet's formulas. Then click OK.

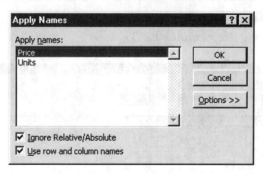

To later change the name of a cell or range or to change the cell or range a name refers to, choose Insert | Name | Define. When Excel displays the Define Name dialog box, select the named cell or range from the Names In Workbook list box. Then, make changes to the name using the Names In Workbook text box and make any changes to the cell or range address using the Refers To text box. Then click OK.

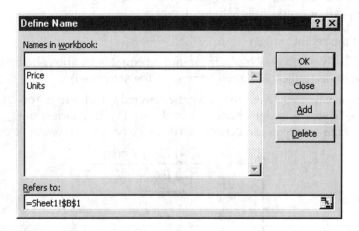

Natural-Language Formulas

Excel supports natural-language formulas. Natural-language formulas let you write formulas that use label descriptions rather than cell references. As a result, you (and other people) can more easily read the formulas. For example, take a look at Figure 13-7. If you build this worksheet in the usual way, you might calculate the interest using the formula =B2*B3.

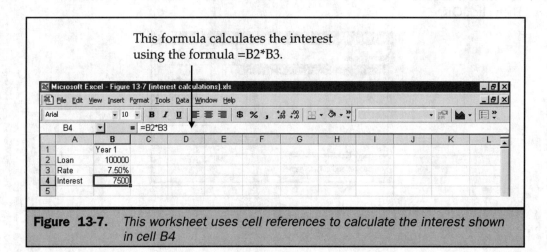

Figure 13-7.   *This worksheet uses cell references to calculate the interest shown in cell B4*

LEARN BY EXAMPLE
To follow along with the discussion here, open the example Excel workbook in the Figure 13-7 (interest calculations) file on the companion CD.

You can, however, rewrite the formula in cell B4 as =Loan*Rate, as shown in Figure 13-8.

LEARN BY EXAMPLE
To follow along with the discussion here, open the example Excel workbook in the Figure 13-8 (interest calculations using natural-language formulas) file on the companion CD.

If you had a worksheet like the one shown in Figure 13-9, you could write the interest formula in cell B4 as =Year 1 Loan*Year 1 Rate. In this case, you could also write the interest formula in cell C4 as =Year 2 Loan*Year 2 Rate, and the interest formula in cell D4 as =Year 3 Loan*Year 3 Rate. (Notice that you put a space between the column heading and the row heading.)

LEARN BY EXAMPLE
To follow along with the discussion here, open the example Excel workbook in the Figure 13-9 (interest calculations using other natural-language formulas) file on the companion CD.

*You could also calculate the interest amounts in cells B4, C4, and D4 by using the same formula in all three cells, =Loan*Rate.*

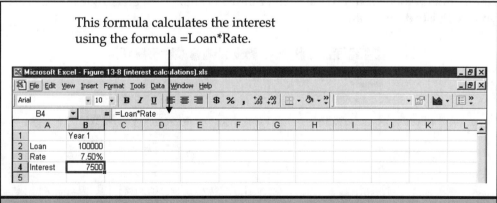

Figure 13-8.   *This worksheet uses a natural-language formula to calculate the interest shown in cell B4*

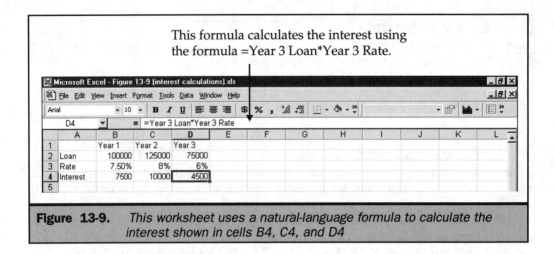

This formula calculates the interest using
the formula =Year 3 Loan*Year 3 Rate.

Figure 13-9. *This worksheet uses a natural-language formula to calculate the interest shown in cells B4, C4, and D4*

The only trick to writing a natural-language formula is to have your formula use the same labels that your worksheet uses to identify some cell holding an input value.

Naming Constants

You can create named constant values and use these in worksheet formulas, too. If you were continually using, for example, a 4 percent inflation estimate in some large budgeting workbook, you could just name the constant, 0.04, as Inflation. This would deliver a couple of benefits in your modeling: Your formulas would be more legible, and you would only have to change the constant in one place.

To name a constant, choose Insert | Name | Define. When Excel displays the Define Name dialog box, enter the name you want to use to refer to the constant in the Names In Workbook text box. Then, enter the constant in the Refers To text box. When you are finished, click OK.

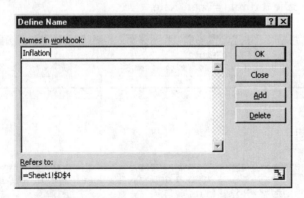

If you sometime later want to change the value of the named constant, once again choose Insert | Name | Define. Then, when Excel displays the Define Name dialog box, select the constant from the Names In Workbook list box and edit the value shown in the Refers To text box. (A quick note, however: If you've got a constant you're occasionally changing, it isn't really a constant at all. So, it really belongs in a cell in your worksheet.)

Copying Formulas

Chapter 3 describes how you can use the Copy and Paste buttons to copy information in an Office document file. So you won't be surprised to learn that you can copy formulas, too. What may surprise you, however, is that Excel is smarter than you might at first think about the way it copies formulas. Specifically, Excel edits the formulas as it copies them so the formulas still make sense in their new location.

To demonstrate this, let's say, for example, that you are creating the worksheet shown in Figure 13-10 and that you enter the formula **=B2+B3+B4** into cell B5 to total the Western Region's expenses. Notice that Figure 13-10 shows how the worksheet looks after you enter this formula. The formula bar shows the cell's formula.

Clearly, you would want to enter an equivalent formula into cells C4, D4, and E4. However, the formula in cell B6 wouldn't work for cell B13, right? The formula in cell B5 sums the values in the cells B2, B3, and B4. So, what do you do? Do you just enter another formula into cell C5? No. It turns out that you can copy the formula in cell B5 to cell C5:E5 because Excel edits the formula so it works in its new location. For example, if you copy the formula in cell B5 into cell C5, Excel places the formula =C2+C3+C4 into cell C5. If you copy the formula in cell B5 into cell D5, Excel places

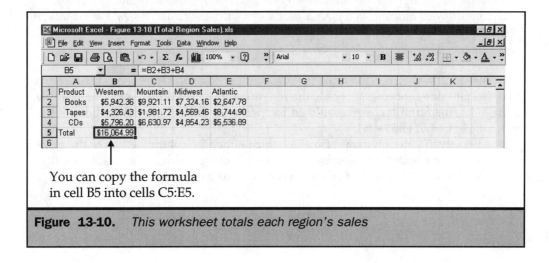

You can copy the formula
in cell B5 into cells C5:E5.

Figure 13-10.   *This worksheet totals each region's sales*

the formula =D2+D3+D4 into cell D5. And if you copy the formula in cell B5 into cell E5, Excel places the formula =E2+E3+E4 into cell E5. In other words, Excel correctly adjusts the copied formula as it pastes it into its new locations.

Note   *Copying a formula works in much the same way as copying a label or value. Just select the cell or range holding the formula or formulas that you want to copy. Then, while holding down the CTRL key, drag the border of the selection to the new location. Or, if you want to copy a formula across a continuous range, select the cell holding the formula and drag that cell's selection handle across the range.*

The reason that Excel adjusts the cell references used in the formula is because Excel considers your cell references to be relative. In other words, while you might read the formula =B2+B3+B4 as saying "Sum the values in cells B2, B3, and B4," Excel reads it a bit differently. If, as in the worksheet shown in Figure 13-10, the formula appears in cell B5, Excel reads the formula =B2+B3+B4 as saying "Sum the values in the three cells directly above the cell with the formula." Do you see the difference? Excel figures, then, that when you copy the formula in cell B5 to its new location, it's still supposed to sum the three cells directly above the cell with the formula.

How Excel handles this formula-editing business is really pretty simple. If you copy a formula, say, seven rows down, Excel adjusts all the row numbers in your cell references by seven rows. If you copy a formula four columns left, Excel adjusts the column letters in your row numbers by four columns.

Note   *The fact that Excel automatically edits formulas as you copy them is usually exactly what you want. You should know, however, that you can stop Excel from performing this formula editing by writing your cell references in a slightly different way. If you don't want Excel to adjust the column letter of a cell reference as the formula is copied into different columns, you precede the column letter with a dollar sign. For example, in the following formula, Excel would edit as necessary the row numbers but not the column reference: =$B2+$B3+$B4.*

If you don't want Excel to adjust the row number of a cell reference as the formula is copied into different rows, precede the row number with a dollar sign. For example, in the following formula, Excel would edit as necessary the column letters but not the row numbers: =B$2+B$3+B$4.

Predictably, if you don't want Excel to adjust either the column letters or the row numbers, precede both these elements of the cell reference with dollar signs, like this: =$B$2+$B$3+$B$4. This type of cell reference is called an *absolute reference*.

Tip

Although you typically type the dollar signs used to convert a relative cell reference to an absolute cell reference, you can also use the F4 key. If you are entering or editing a cell reference, repeatedly pressing the F4 key cycles through the different ways you can write the cell reference. For example if you have just entered the cell reference B2 or you were editing a formula and the insertion point rested on the cell reference B2, pressing F4 repeatedly would rewrite the reference as $B$2, then B$2, then $B2, and finally B2.

You can also rewrite range addresses so that they aren't edited in the usual way. For example, you could rewrite the formula =SUM(B2:B5) as =SUM($B$2:$B$5). And if you did, Excel wouldn't adjust the range address as you copy the formula.

Note

The next section, "Using Functions," describes what functions are and how you use them.

A practical warning is in order here, however: If you start rewriting range addresses so some portions of the range address are adjusted while other portions aren't, you'll find it very difficult to monitor and error-check the formula editing that Excel is performing. Remember that a range address uses the cell addresses of the range's opposite corners. So, if you rewrite the formula =SUM(G20:G25) as =SUM($G$20:G25), you've fixed one corner of the range but not the other. In this case, Excel won't adjust the $G$20 corner of the range address as the formula is copied, but it will adjust the G25 corner of the range address. Unfortunately, this partial adjustment of the formula gets very confusing. If you copy your formula down rows or right across columns, for example, your range address actually grows larger and larger. But if you copy your formula up rows or left across columns, your range address first shrinks in size and then begins to grow. If you rewrite the formula =SUM($G20:G25), so Excel won't adjust the column of the first corner but will adjust the row, the formula adjustment gets even more confusing to monitor.

Note

It's important to note that Excel has no problem correctly adjusting the copied formulas. The problem is just that this sort of adjustment is difficult for you to monitor and error-check. For this reason, you may want to avoid constructing formulas that use partially fixed, or mixed-range, references. You'll keep your worksheets much simpler and easier to error-check by doing so.

Using Functions

Using the formula operators described thus far in the chapter, you can create formulas that make almost any calculation. But as a practical matter, some of your formulas—

supposing you did do everything from scratch—would be very complicated. To make your formulas easier, Excel supplies predefined formulas called *functions*. One advantage of functions, then, is that they save you the time and trouble of building your own, more complicated formulas. But there's another advantage of functions, too. They are usually very clever and efficient about the way they accept and handle any inputs to the formula. If you're going to do any serious work with Excel, therefore, you'll want to know how to use Excel's functions.

Understanding How a Function Works

The best way to explain how a function works is to show you how they actually work in a workbook. Take a look at the worksheet shown in Figure 13-11. It supplies the sales orders booked by an imaginary team of sales people.

Let's suppose, for the sake of illustration, that you want to calculate the average sales orders of team members and place this value in cell B11. To do this, you could construct a formula like the one shown next and then enter it in your worksheet:

=(B2+B3+B4+B5+B6+B7+B8+B9+B10)/9

But an easier approach would be to use a prebuilt function that calculates the average of a set of values stored in the range B2:B10. To do this, you would enter the following formula into your worksheet:

=AVERAGE(B2:B10)

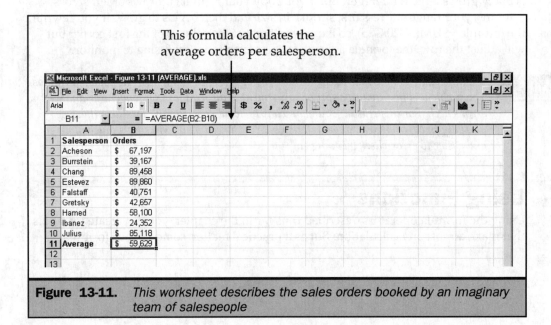

Figure 13-11. *This worksheet describes the sales orders booked by an imaginary team of salespeople*

Clearly, using the AVERAGE function is easier even in this simple example. And you can imagine how much easier the function makes your calculations in the case where you might be calculating, say, the average orders of all the salespeople in a 100-person or 1,000-person sales organization.

To create a function-based formula, you follow these steps:

1. Type the equal sign (=). (This is the way all formulas begin, of course.)

2. Type the function name followed by the open parenthesis mark.

3. Enter the input values, or arguments, that the function needs or uses to make its calculation. The example AVERAGE calculation includes one argument, the range B2:B10. Many times, however, functions accept or expect more than one argument, and in that case, you separate the arguments with commas. For example, it wouldn't make much sense—because all you would be doing is increasing your work—but you could rewrite the AVERAGE function given earlier as:

   =AVERAGE(B2,B3,B4,B5,B6,B7,B8,B9,B10)

4. Type the close parenthesis mark and then press ENTER.

Note *Not all functions require arguments. For example, Excel supplies a function that returns the mathematical constant for pi and it requires no arguments. In the case of functions that don't require arguments, you still follow the function name with the parenthesis marks, but you enclose nothing in between the parentheses. For example, the function-based formula to return the constant pi would look like this: =PI()*

While a function's arguments are often cell references, you can also use named constants, cells or ranges, actual values, and even other functions. For example, if you name the range B2:B10 as Salespeople's orders, you can calculate the average orders per salesperson using the following formula:

   =AVERAGE(Salespeople's orders)

Or, you could use the actual Salespeople's orders' values in the formula:

   =AVERAGE(67197,39167,89458,89860,40751,42657,58100,24352,85118)

And you can use as arguments the results of still other functions. You get the basic idea: If a function wants a value as an argument, you can supply that value in a variety of ways.

Note *Some functions expect labels or text strings as arguments. To supply one of these text functions with an argument, you can also use cell and range addresses (as long as the cell or range holds the necessary label or labels), named cells or ranges, and even the actual text strings themselves. If you do include the actual text string as an argument, you need to enclose it in quotation marks.*

Using the Paste Function Command

As a practical matter, while functions are terribly useful, they present a couple of problems to users. The first problem is that it's usually tough to know whether Excel supplies a function that calculates a particular formula. You've already read earlier in this chapter that Excel provides a long list of functions. But you don't really know whether Excel supplies functions to calculate things like loan payments or logarithms or whatever else you want to calculate. And even if this chapter told you about each and every function, you wouldn't retain that knowledge for very long. (There are roughly 350 functions if you include those supplied by the Analysis ToolPak add-in, which you'll find on the Office 2000 CD.)

The second practical problem with functions is that you'll find it nearly impossible to remember which arguments a function needs and in which order you're supposed to supply them. For example, the function for calculating a loan payment needs three arguments: the loan balance, the interest rate, and the number of payments. But you've got to enter these arguments in the right order, or the function can't make its calculations.

Fortunately, Excel provides something called the Paste Function command that cleverly addresses and almost entirely solves these two problems. The Paste Function command first helps you find the function (if any) that makes a particular calculation. Then, it explains which arguments you need to supply to the function and helps you to enter them in the right order.

To illustrate how all this works, suppose that you were considering the purchase of a new car and wanted to know what your monthly principal and interest payment would equal. As a practical matter, it would be a chore for you to construct a formula, from scratch, that made this calculation. So, you might decide to look for a function. And assuming you found such a function, of course, you would use it to make the calculation. Here's how you would use the Paste Function command to accomplish all these things:

1. Click the Paste Function button on the Standard toolbar or choose Insert | Function. When you do, Excel displays the Paste Function dialog box:

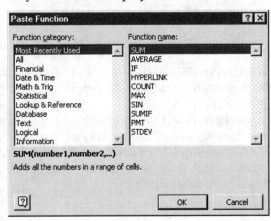

2. Use the Function Category list box to select the category into which a function calculation falls. In the case of a loan payment calculation, for example, you would select Financial. When you do, Excel displays a list of the functions in the selected category using the Function Name list box.

3. Select the appropriate function in the Function Name list box. If you're not sure—and you won't be until you've used a function a few times—just click the function to select it and then read the description of the function that appears at the bottom of the dialog box. (If you still have questions about a function, you can click the Office Assistant button, click the Help With This Feature button, and then click the Help On Selected Function button. Excel then displays the Help window with a complete and detailed description of the function.) Once you've selected the function you want—the PMT function in the case of a loan payment calculation—click OK. Excel displays the Formula Palette—in the area just below the formula bar:

PMT		
Rate		= number
Nper		= number
Pv		= number
Fv		= number
Type		= number
		=
Calculates the payment for a loan based on constant payments and a constant interest rate.		
Rate is the interest rate per period for the loan.		
Formula result =	OK	Cancel

4. Supply the arguments by filling in the text boxes. You can enter values, cell addresses, or formulas into these text boxes. As you select an argument's text box, Excel describes what the argument should look like. Notice that to the right of each argument's text box, there's a Collapse Dialog button. You can click this if you need to temporarily resize the dialog box so you can select cells on the worksheet. If you have additional questions about a particular argument, click the Office Assistant button. As soon as you've supplied the last needed argument, Excel calculates the function result and displays this value in the lower-left corner of the dialog box.

5. Click the OK button when you've finished supplying the arguments. Excel closes the Formula Palette and places the function into the active cell. Figure 13-12 shows a car loan payment worksheet constructed in just this way.

EXAMPLES

LEARN BY EXAMPLE
To follow along with the discussion here, open the example Excel workbook in the Figure 13-12 (car loan payment) file on the companion CD.

Divide the annual interest rate percentage by
12 to get the computed monthly interest rate.

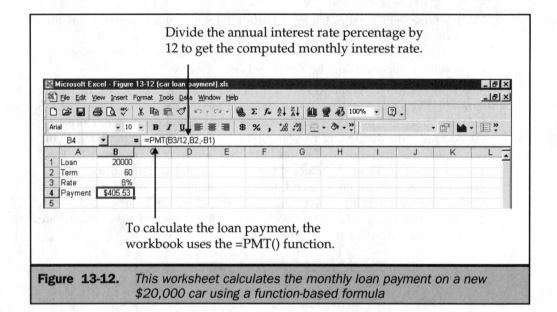

To calculate the loan payment, the
workbook uses the =PMT() function.

Figure 13-12.   *This worksheet calculates the monthly loan payment on a new
$20,000 car using a function-based formula*

TEMPLATES

HEADSTART
*The companion CD includes two Headstart templates you can use for calculating loan
payments in 60-month car loans: 60 mo-adj.xls, which calculates the payments and
builds an amortization schedule for a 60-month, adjustable-interest-rate loan, and
60 moloan.xls, which calculates the payments and builds an amortization schedule
for a 60-month, fixed-interest-rate loan.*

Using the AutoSum Tool

Most of the time you'll either want to use the Paste Function button to enter
function-based formulas into your worksheets or you'll just enter a function by typing it
in. (Once you've used a function several dozen times, you may know its arguments well
enough to enter them from memory.) But there is one function that is so commonly used,
Excel's Standard toolbar provides a special tool, the AutoSum button, for it. That function
is the SUM function.

To understand how the AutoSum button works, first know that the SUM function
simply sums, or adds up, its arguments. That's all. While that doesn't sound very
powerful, it turns out that this is something you'll be doing all the time. And so, the
SUM function is one you'll use over and over again.

To use the AutoSum button, you first enter the labels and values shown in Figure
13-13. Next, you select the range B2:F6 and then click the AutoSum button. Excel adds
SUM functions to the range B6:E6 and F2:F6 to total the expenses by quarter and by
expense category.

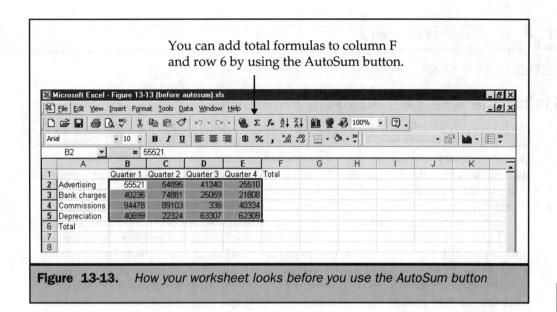

Figure 13-13. *How your worksheet looks before you use the AutoSum button*

If you take a look at the worksheet shown in Figure 13-14, both the total values shown in column F and the total values shown in row 6 get calculated by SUM functions.

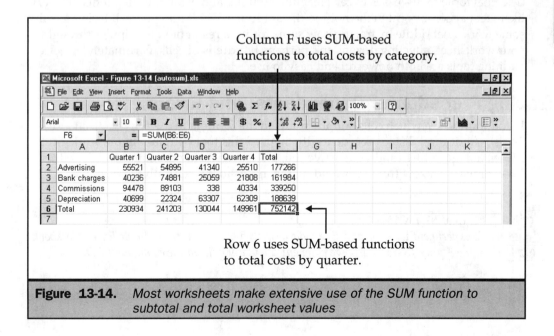

Figure 13-14. *Most worksheets make extensive use of the SUM function to subtotal and total worksheet values*

LEARN BY EXAMPLE
To follow along with the discussion here, open the example Excel workbook in the Figure 13-14 (budget before autosum) file on the companion CD.

Using the Analysis ToolPak Functions

As it's usually installed, Excel comes with roughly 200 functions. For most users, this function set is more than adequate. You'll rarely use more than a handful of functions. Some users, however, are going to need richer function sets. If you're a financial analyst, for example, Excel's basic financial functions may prove insufficient if you want to, say, calculate bond durations or yields to maturity. And statisticians, quantitative researchers, and engineers may find themselves in the same boat.

Fortunately, there's an easy way to expand the set of functions that Excel supplies. You can install the Analysis ToolPak, which supplies (roughly) another 150 functions to complement the (roughly) 200 functions that Excel initially supplies. To install the Analysis ToolPak, choose Tools | Add-Ins. Then, when Excel displays the Add-Ins dialog box, mark the Analysis ToolPak entry in the Add-Ins Available list box, and click OK. (If the Analysis ToolPak entry is already marked, you or someone else has already installed this add-in.)

Auditing and Error-Checking Formulas

One final topic to discuss is Excel's formula auditing and error-checking tools. It's very likely that at some point in the not-too-distant future you'll find yourself trying to solve some worksheet riddle by tracing how some formula result or value ripples through your worksheet, affecting dozens and perhaps hundreds of cells. Fortunately, Excel's auditing tools are both powerful and easy to use.

Tracing Precedents, Dependents, and Errors

If you want to see which cells supply inputs to the formula in the active cell, choose Tools | Auditing | Trace Precedents. If you used this tool with the simple worksheet shown in Figure 13-15 and your active cell, prior to choosing the command, is cell B5, Excel draws an arrow from cells holding the inputs to the cell with the formula.

LEARN BY EXAMPLE
To experiment with the auditing tools described here, open the example Excel Workbook in the Figure 13-15 (mortgage payment calculator) file on the companion CD.

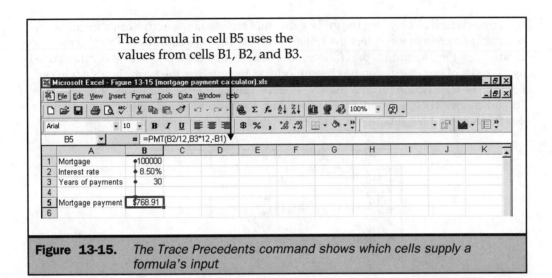

The formula in cell B5 uses the
values from cells B1, B2, and B3.

Figure 13-15.   *The Trace Precedents command shows which cells supply a
formula's input*

Note   *Excel provides another way to visually see which cells supply input to a formula. If you
double-click a cell containing a formula, Excel colors the cell references supplying input
and then draws a border around referenced cells using the same color. For example, in
the example Excel workbook shown in Figure 13-15, the formula in cell B5 calculates the
mortgage. This formula is =PMT(B2/12,B3*12,-B1). If you double-click cell B5—the cell
with the formula—Excel colors the cell reference B2 in blue and draws a blue border
around cell B2. Excel colors the cell reference B3 green and draws a green border around
cell B3. Finally, Excel colors the cell reference B1 purple and then draws a purple border
around cell B1. If the preceding description sounds confusing, just open the Learn by
Example sample document for Figure 13-15 and then double-click cell B5.*

If you want to see which cells rely on a particular cell's value or calculation result,
select the cell and choose Tools I Auditing I Trace Dependents. If you used this tool with
the simple worksheet shown in Figure 13-15 and your active cell, prior to choosing the
command, is cell B3, Excel draws an arrow that points from cell B3 to cell B5:

	A	B	C
1	Mortgage	100000	
2	Interest rate	8.50%	
3	Years of payments	◆ 30	
4			
5	Mortgage payment	$768.91	
6			

To see which cell returns the error value that results in the active cell's formula returning an error value, select the cell and choose Tools | Auditing | Trace Error. For example, in the illustration that follows, the simple mortgage payment worksheet used as the basis of our discussion has been modified by entering the formula =NA() in cell B3. (The NA() function returns the #N/A error value.) If after doing this, you select cell B5 and choose Tools | Auditing | Trace Error, Excel draws a red arrow from cell B3 to cell B5 showing how this error value ripples through the worksheet.

	A	B	C
1	Mortgage	100000	
2	Interest rate	8.50%	
3	Years of payments	#N/A	
4			
5	Mortgage payment	#N/A	
6			

If you've been following along at your computer or you've at least looked at the Auditing submenu, you can guess how you get rid of the arrows that the Trace Precedents, Trace Dependents, and Trace Error commands draw. You choose the Remove All Arrows command.

The Auditing submenu also provides a Show Auditing Toolbar command. You can choose this command to display a toolbar with buttons you can click in place of choosing commands from the Auditing submenu. The toolbar includes buttons for tracing precedents, dependents, and errors, for removing tracing arrows, for attaching cell comments, and circling and uncircling invalid data. (You define valid and invalid data for a cell by choosing Data | Validation.)

Using the Go To and Info Boxes

If you choose Edit | Go To, Excel displays the Go To dialog box, shown in the following illustration. More than ten years ago, now, this command was included in the original version of Excel as a quick and easy way to move around a worksheet. You can still use the Go To command and its dialog box this way. Simply choose the command and then, when Excel displays the Go To dialog box, enter the name or address of the cell or range to which you want to move and click OK. (If you select a range, the Go To command only searches that range. If you don't select a range, then the Go To command searches the entire worksheet.)

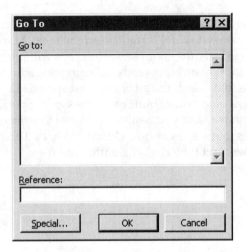

The Go To command has become more and more powerful over time, however. It now lets you move to or locate cells having specified attributes. To use the Go To command and dialog box in this manner, choose the command and then click its Special command button. Excel displays the Go To Special dialog box:

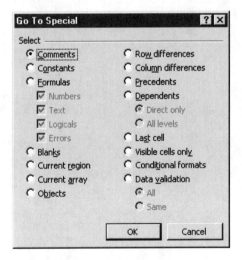

To use the Go To Special dialog box, use its buttons to describe the attributes of the cells you're looking for. Mark the Comments button, for example, to have the command select cells with comments. Mark the Constants button to have the command select cells with labels or number values (but not formulas or functions). Mark the Formulas button and use its check boxes to have the command select cells with formulas having specified characteristics, and so on. When you're ready to begin your search, click the OK button. Excel selects those cells that match the attributes you specified.

By the way, there are many other buttons on the Go To Special dialog box, as the preceding illustration shows. But you really don't have to worry about these. If you have a question about some button or box, click the What's This? button (in the dialog box's upper-right corner) and then click the button or box.

The
Complete
Reference

Office
2000

Chapter 14

Using the Chart Wizard

Although tabular presentations of data are very useful, it's also often handy to both present and analyze your worksheet data visually—in other words, in a chart. This chapter prepares you to do this by first explaining how chart data is organized and by then showing how you create, use, and customize your Excel charts.

You can easily use Excel charts in Word documents and PowerPoint presentations. In fact, this book assumes that you don't use the Microsoft Graph tool to create charts for Word or PowerPoint and do use Excel's Chart Wizard (because the Excel Chart Wizard is easier to use and more powerful).

Understanding Data Series and Data Categories

You need to understand what data series and data categories are—and how to arrange your worksheet data so that Excel easily identifies your data series and data categories—before you begin working with Excel's charting feature.

A *data* series is a set of values you plot in a chart. If you plot sales revenues over, say, the last ten years, the set of sales revenue values is a data series. If you plot expenses over, say, the same ten-year time frame, the set of expense values is another data series. The key thing to remember is that, fundamentally, data series are what you plot with charts.

Figure 14-1, for example, shows a chart with two data series: sales revenues and expenses.

LEARN BY EXAMPLE
To follow along with the discussion here, open the example chart in the Figure 14-1 (simple chart) file on the companion CD.

Note that on a chart that already exists, you can identify data series by looking at the *data markers*, which are the graphical objects that the chart uses to show the plotted values. The data markers for a data series are usually visually connected in some way. In Figure 14-1, for example, Excel plots each data series using a separate line. In a bar chart—which we'll discuss a little later—the bars for a particular data series chart are all the same color. The same thing is true for a column chart. You get the idea.

Data categories, the other charting term you must understand, organize the data points—the individual values—within a data series. For example, in any chart that shows how a value changes over time—what's called a *time-series chart*—time is the data category. In a time-series chart, you use units of time—years, months, days, or whatever—to organize the individual data points within a data series. In Figure 14-1, for example, the data categories are years. You can, however, use data categories other than time to organize the data points in a data series. Take a look at Figure 14-2, for example. Note how I've substituted the names of fictional corporations for the years. So

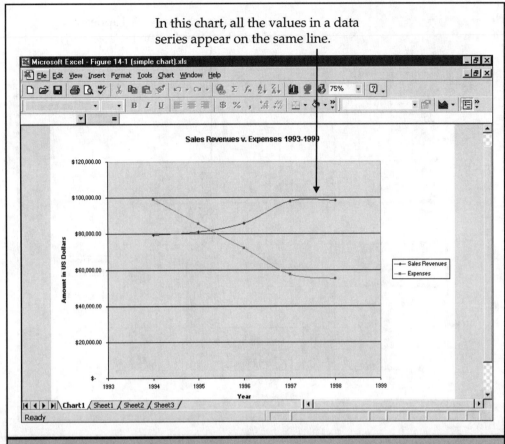

In this chart, all the values in a data
series appear on the same line.

Figure 14-1. *You plot data series—such as the sales revenues and expenses
shown here—with a chart*

these fictional companies have become the data categories that organize the data points
in a data series. Note, too, that fundamentally the chart still plots sales revenue and
expense information. The two data series are still sales revenues and expenses.

LEARN BY EXAMPLE
*To follow along with the discussion here, open the example Excel chart in the Figure
14-2 (chart with company names as data categories) file on the companion CD.*

Once you understand what data series and data categories are, you will understand
how Excel organizes your to-be-charted data. With this information, you'll find it easy

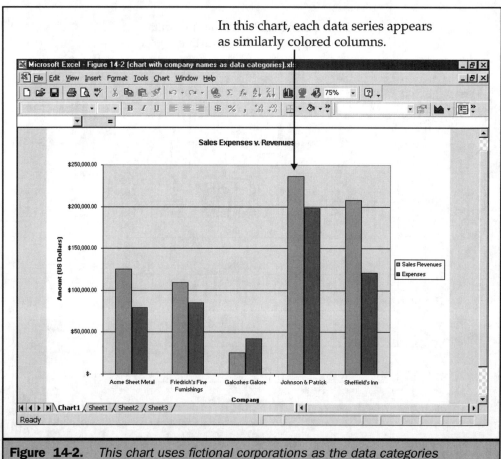

Figure 14-2.   *This chart uses fictional corporations as the data categories*

to first collect chart data using a worksheet and then to later plot the data using Excel's Chart Wizard.

Collecting the Data You Want to Chart

Once you know which data series you want to plot and what your categories are, you're ready to enter your data into a worksheet. You can organize your data series into either rows or columns, as long as each data series has no more than 4,000 data points. (If data series do have more than 4,000 data points, you need to use separate columns for each data series—otherwise, you won't have room in a row for all of a data series' data points.)

> **Note** *A chart can't show more than 255 data series. Each data series can't include more than 4,000 data points. A chart in total can't include more than 32,000 data points. But these limits are probably way beyond any you'll ever need.*

To collect the data you will plot in a chart, follow these steps:

1. Enter the data series names and values into the worksheet using a separate row or column for each data series. (The actual data points must be values, of course.) Figure 14-3 uses row 2 for the first data series, Sales, and row 3 for the second data series, Profits. It could just as well have organized the data as shown in Figure 14-4, however, with the data categories organized by column.

LEARN BY EXAMPLE
To follow along with the discussion here, open the example worksheets: Figure 14-3 (data series in rows) and Figure 14-4 (data series in columns) on the companion CD.

> **Note** *Take a minute and look at both Figures 14-3 and 14-4 until you clearly see that they show the same information. The only difference is that Figure 14-3 organizes the data series by row, while Figure 14-4 organizes the data series by column.*

> **Tip** *You can provide the data points of a series by entering actual, numeric values into the cells or by supplying formulas that calculate the values.*

2. Enter values or labels that identify the data categories. In Figure 14-3, the data categories are described by the contents of the range B1:F1. In Figure 14-4, the data categories are described by the contents of the range A2:A6. Note the placement of the data category information: In Figure 14-3, which organizes the data series by row, the data category information appears in the row above the rows with the data series. In Figure 14-4, which organizes the data series by column, the data category information appears in the column to the left of the columns with the data series.

> **Note** *You don't have to enter or collect the data you'll plot into a contiguous worksheet range, as shown in Figure 14-3 or Figure 14-4. Doing so, however, makes it much easier to plot the data.*

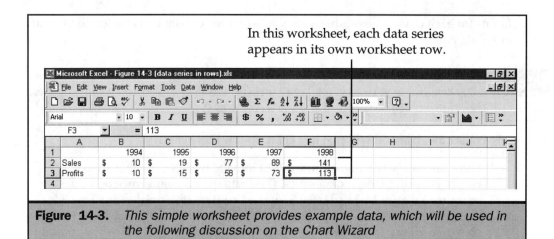

Figure 14-3. *This simple worksheet provides example data, which will be used in the following discussion on the Chart Wizard*

Using the Chart Wizard

Once you've collected the data you want to plot, you're ready to use the Chart Wizard. To use the Chart Wizard, follow these steps:

1. Select the range that holds the data series and the data categories information. If you were plotting the sales and profit information shown in Figure 14-3, for example, you should select A1:F3.

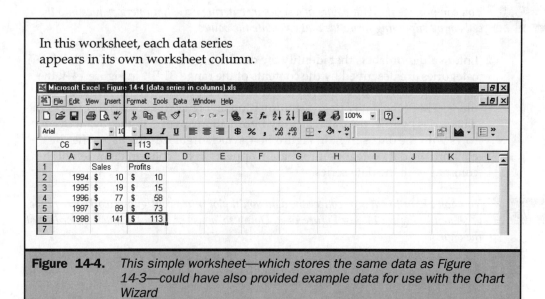

Figure 14-4. *This simple worksheet—which stores the same data as Figure 14-3—could have also provided example data for use with the Chart Wizard*

2. Choose Insert | Chart or click the Chart Wizard tool, which appears on the Standard toolbar. Once you do this, Excel starts the Chart Wizard. The Chart Wizard steps you through a series of four dialog boxes that ask, in essence, what you want your chart to look like.

3. When the first Chart Wizard dialog box asks which type of chart you want, select an entry from the Chart Type list box. In Figure 14-5, the Column type is selected. Then select one of the chart's subtypes by clicking the button that shows a picture of the chart. In Figure 14-5, the Clustered Column subtype is selected. (A little later in the chapter, by the way, I describe all 14 of the standard Excel chart types and why you typically use each.) After you pick the chart type and subtype, click Next to continue.

4. When the second Chart Wizard dialog box asks you to confirm the worksheet range you selected before starting the Chart Wizard, as shown in Figure 14-6, verify that the range shown in the Data Range text box is correct. (This range will be correct if you selected the worksheet range before clicking the Chart

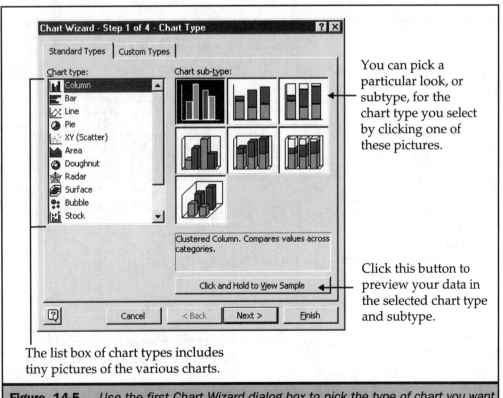

You can pick a particular look, or subtype, for the chart type you select by clicking one of these pictures.

Click this button to preview your data in the selected chart type and subtype.

The list box of chart types includes tiny pictures of the various charts.

Figure 14-5. *Use the first Chart Wizard dialog box to pick the type of chart you want*

EXCEL

Wizard tool.) The second Chart Wizard dialog box also asks how you've organized your worksheet data. Use the Series In option buttons to tell Excel how you've organized your worksheet data. (Excel assumes that you'll have more data categories than you'll have data series, and marks either the Rows or Columns option button to show this assumption.) After you complete the second Chart Wizard dialog box, click Next.

5. When Excel displays the third Chart Wizard dialog box, shown in Figure 14-7, use its text boxes to add titles to the chart. To add a title to the chart, enter whatever you want to use for the title in the Chart Title text box. Typically, people either use the name of the organization being described in the chart, or they summarize the chart's message. As shown in Figure 14-7, for example, you might give the name of the organization for which sales and profit data are plotted—Acme Trading Corporation. Or, if you were trying to use the chart to make a point such as "Sales and profits continue to grow," you might use that message as the chart title.

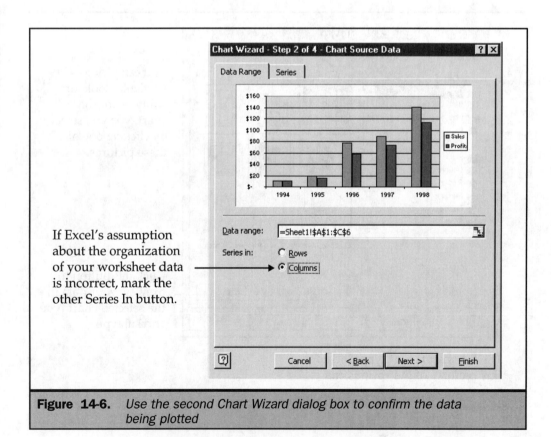

If Excel's assumption about the organization of your worksheet data is incorrect, mark the other Series In button.

Figure 14-6.   *Use the second Chart Wizard dialog box to confirm the data being plotted*

The chart title ⟶

The category
axis title ⟶

The value axis title ⟶

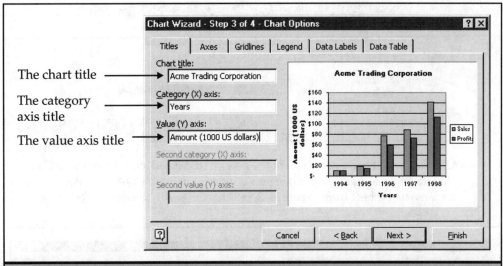

Figure 14-7.   *Use the third Chart Wizard dialog box to add a chart title, a title for the chart axis that identifies your data categories, and a title for the chart axis that calibrates your data series values*

Tip   *You can use the other tabs in the Chart Wizard dialog box shown in Figure 14-7 to make additional changes to the chart, as described later in this chapter in the section "Customizing Charts."*

The axis title text boxes let you add titles to the axis that shows the categories (in Figure 14-7, the horizontal axis) and to the axis that calibrates the data series' data points (in Figure 14-7, the vertical axis). If what the categories show and how the data series' points are calibrated are obvious, you don't need to include these extra chunks of text. However, if the categories aren't clear or the data series values aren't adequately calibrated, you can often use the axis titles to mitigate confusion. For example, if the values plotted as data points are actually thousands—in other words, you've omitted the zeros—you could and probably should use an axis title to make this clear. After you finish specifying whether you want a legend and adding any chart titles you want, click the Next button.

6. When the Chart Wizard displays the fourth and final Chart Wizard dialog box, use it to indicate where you want the new chart placed: on a new page, or sheet, of the workbook or as an embedded object floating over the top of an existing worksheet page. If you choose the As Object In option button, as shown next, Excel embeds a chart object on the current worksheet. If you choose the As New Sheet option button, Excel adds a new chart sheet page to the worksheet and places your chart there.

EXCEL

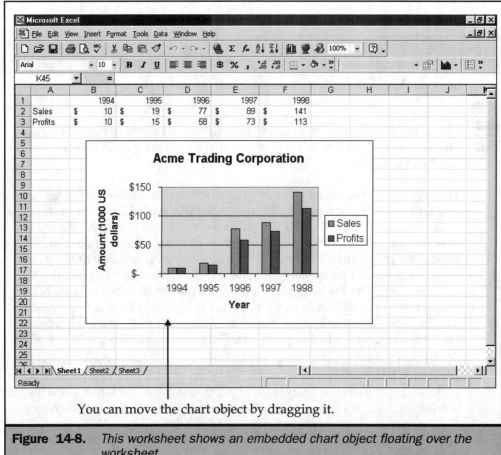

7. After you specify where you want the new chart created, click Finish. The Chart Wizard draws a chart like the one you've specified. Figure 14-8, for example, shows the same worksheet from Figure 14-3, but this time with the embedded chart.

Figure 14-8. *This worksheet shows an embedded chart object floating over the worksheet*

EXAMPLES

LEARN BY EXAMPLE
To follow along with the discussion here, open the example worksheet in the Figure 14-8 (embedded chart) file on the companion CD.

As mentioned earlier, charts can either be embedded as objects that float on top of a regular worksheet or they can appear on their own chart sheets. (Figure 14-8 shows an embedded chart.) If in step 6 you had chosen the As New Sheet option button instead of the As Object In option button, the Chart Wizard would have added a separate sheet to the workbook, named Chart1 if this were the first chart sheet you'd added, and placed the chart there. To expand the chart so it fills the screen, choose View | Sized with Window.

Picking a Chart Type

You can pick a particular chart type either as part of using the Chart Wizard or, later on, after you've actually created the chart. If you pick the chart type as you're creating the chart with the Chart Wizard, you simply select your chart type using the first dialog box that the Chart Wizard displays, as shown in Figure 14-5.

If you change your mind about the chart type you want after creating the chart, Excel provides several ways to change the chart type. The easiest method for changing the chart type is by using the Chart menu's Chart Type command. And this raises an important distinction: Excel supplies a menu bar, but you use a different menu bar for working with charts. So, before you can use the Chart menu's Chart Type command, you need to tell Excel that it should swap the chart menu bar for the standard, worksheet menu bar. How you do this depends on whether you want to work with an embedded chart (one that appears on a worksheet page) or with a chart that appears on its own chart sheet page. If the chart is embedded, you simply click it. Excel adds sizing handles to the chart to show it's selected, and replaces the standard worksheet menu bar with the chart menu bar. If the chart appears on its own chart sheet page, Excel actually swaps the menu bars when you display the page. In other words, if you display the chart sheet page, Excel knows that if you need any menu commands, they'll be the ones from the chart menu bar—and not the ones from the worksheet menu bar.

Tip   *To unselect a chart object so that you work with the worksheet, click somewhere outside the chart.*

When you choose Chart | Chart Type, Excel displays the Chart Type dialog box, shown in Figure 14-9, which lets you pick both a chart type and a subtype for the chart type. If you remember much about the Chart Wizard's operation, you might recall that this is what you do in step 1 of the four-step chart-building process that the Chart Wizard steps you through.

EXCEL

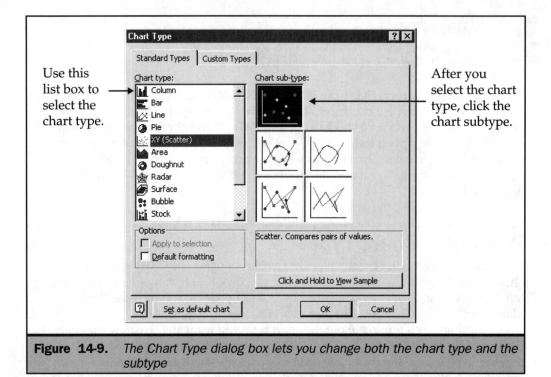

Use this
list box to
select the
chart type.

After you
select the chart
type, click the
chart subtype.

Figure 14-9.   *The Chart Type dialog box lets you change both the chart type and the subtype*

Initially, the Chart Type dialog box shows the subtypes available for the existing chart type. These subtypes, as mentioned earlier, are simply variations, or styles, of a particular chart type. To select another chart type, however, all you have to do is select the chart type from the Chart Type list box. When you do, Excel displays pictures of the subtypes available for that chart type. You then select the subtype you want by clicking its picture. After you choose the chart type and subtype, click OK. Excel redraws your chart so it reflects your changes. It's that easy.

Reviewing the Chart Types

You can easily choose or change the chart type and subtype, but knowing *why* you change or choose a chart type and subtype is probably more important than knowing *how* you change or choose a chart type and subtype. For this reason, the next section describes what each of the chart types does, points out some of the more unique subtypes, and gives you some hints as to when you might want to use particular chart types and subtypes.

Area Charts

The various area chart subtypes, as shown in Figure 14-10, plot your data series as colored areas. The unique thing about area charts is that Excel stacks these colored areas on top of each other. Excel creates the first data series' area by first drawing a line plotting the series' data point values and then coloring, or shading, this area. Excel creates the second data series' area, however, by drawing a line that plots the sum of the first and second data series' values and then coloring this new area. In essence, stacking the first second area on top of the second first area. Subsequent data series are plotted in the same way: Excel creates the third data series' area by drawing a line that plots the sum of the first, second, and third data series' values and then coloring this new area, stacking the representative area on top of the others.

Area charts, then, do two things really well. Best of all, they show how the data category totals of your plotted data change over time. For example, if you were plotting the sales revenues of all the major competitors in a particular industry, an area chart would emphasize how total industry revenues are changing over time. (The second and fourth subtypes let you make this visual analysis.) Another thing that area charts

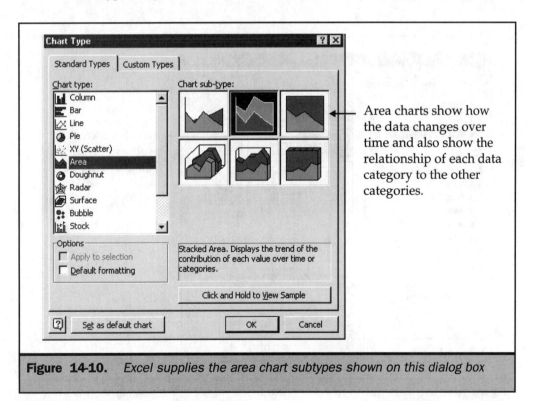

Area charts show how the data changes over time and also show the relationship of each data category to the other categories.

Figure 14-10.   *Excel supplies the area chart subtypes shown on this dialog box*

do, albeit not as well, is show you how the proportion of an individual data series changes over time relative to the total of all the data series' value. (The third and sixth subtypes let you make this visual analysis.) Take the example of an area chart that plots the sales revenues of all the major competitors in an industry. You might be able to use such an area chart to identify a trend, like "Competitor A is still growing, but they're becoming a less significant presence in the total market."

 A basic rule of charting is that your chart shouldn't have more dimensions than your data. As such, many of the chart subtypes that Excel provides don't use the third dimension of depth to organize your data.

Bar Charts

Bar charts plot your data points as horizontal, individual bars, as shown in Figure 14-11. Because bar charts use individual data markers for each data point, they emphasize and let chart viewers compare the individual values. This is particularly true of the first and fourth subtypes (although this isn't as true of the other bar chart subtypes, which stack

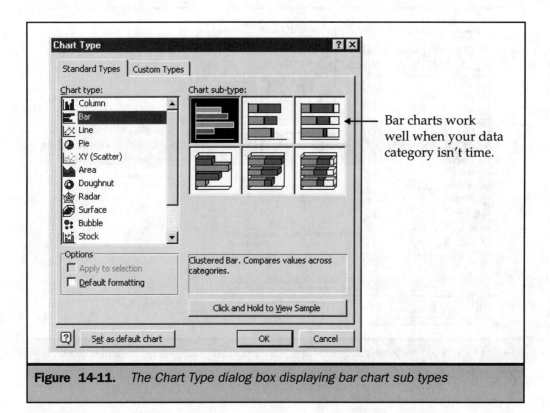

Figure 14-11. *The Chart Type dialog box displaying bar chart sub types*

the bar data markers). In comparison, note that the area charts described in the previous section tend to emphasize changes in data point values rather than the actual data point values themselves.

One other important consideration with regard to the bar chart subtypes is that because the category axis is vertical rather than horizontal, the bar chart type often works well when your data category isn't time. The reason this is so is that most people are accustomed to using horizontal data category axes as chronological time lines. Therefore, if you use a vertical data category axis, the chart reader is less likely to mistakenly interpret your data category as a time unit.

Column Charts

Column charts work exactly like bar charts—and almost look like bar charts—except that they plot your data points using vertical rather than horizontal bars, as shown Figure 14-12. Like the bar charts they resemble, column charts use individual data markers for each data point. In this manner, they emphasize and let chart viewers

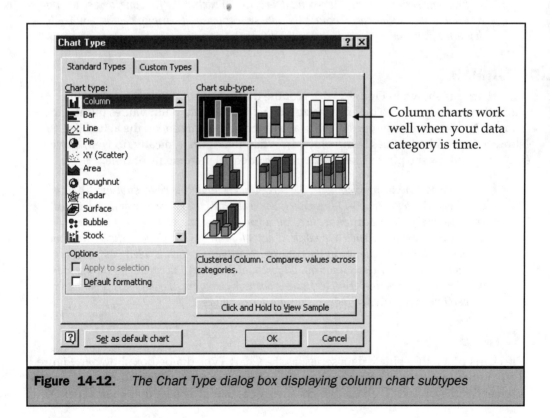

Column charts work well when your data category is time.

Figure 14-12. *The Chart Type dialog box displaying column chart subtypes*

compare the individual values. Because the column chart uses a horizontal category axis, column charts work particularly well for comparing individual values over time.

Note   *The ability to compare individual values over time is particularly true of the first, fourth, and seventh column subtypes. The other column chart subtypes, in comparison, stack the data markers in a manner very similar to the way that the area chart types stack the areas they plot, so they work better for comparing the relationship among the data category totals over time.*

Caution   *Despite the extra visual interest that the third dimension adds to a bar or column chart, it's rarely a good idea to use a third dimension when you choose either of these chart types. And here's why this is the case: The reason for choosing a bar data marker—and this could be in either a bar or column chart—is to compare the individual values within and between data series. However, that extra dimension of depth that Excel provides by showing you the "top" of the bar makes it more difficult to do this. By adding a "top" to a very short bar, for example, you can dramatically increase its visual presence—even though it may still be immaterial. If you use the extra dimension of depth to organize your data series by putting the first data series in front, the second data series in back of the first one, and so on, things get even worse. In this case, because the data series appear at varying depths, you really shouldn't make comparisons between the different data series.*

Line Charts

Line charts, as shown in Figure 14-13, plot the data points of a data series in a line. As such, they usually tend to de-emphasize the individual data point values (although some of the line chart subtypes include additional data markers on the actual line to show the individual values being plotted). What line charts typically do well, however, is show you how the plotted values change over equal increments of time.

There's also a subtle problem with the three-dimensional line chart subtype. To give the illusion of depth to a 3-D line chart, Excel elevates the far corner of the plot area. Unfortunately, this elevation reduces the apparent positive slope of the line. And while that may not seem like such a big deal, it actually can be. The slope of the plotted line or lines indicates the change in the data series' values—which is what you're trying to show with the line chart anyway. Unfortunately, when Excel reduces the apparent positive slope of the line, it understates a positive change in the data series values or it overstates a negative change in the data series values.

Pie Charts

Pie charts plot only a single data series, as the Chart Type dialog box shown in Figure 14-14 indicates. In a pie chart, each data point shows as a proportional slice of the pie (a segment of the circle). Pie charts typically aren't as useful as the other chart types. You

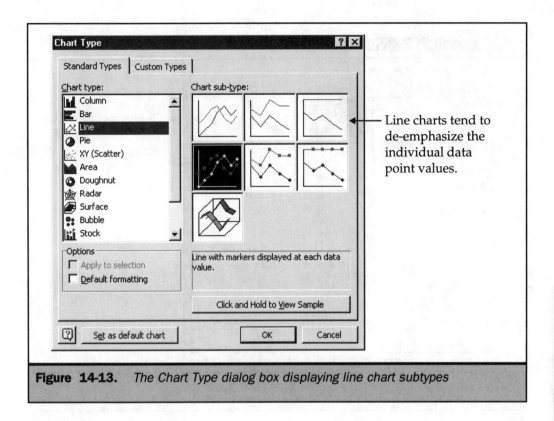

Line charts tend to de-emphasize the individual data point values.

Figure 14-13.   *The Chart Type dialog box displaying line chart subtypes*

typically can't plot more than a handful of data points in a pie chart because otherwise the slices of the pie get too small.

The fact that 3-D pie charts exaggerate the size of slices shown in the foreground and minimize the size of slices shown in the background is often used to strengthen, dishonestly, a chart's message. Take a look, for example, at the next 3-D pie chart you see in a magazine or newspaper. You may see that if the newspaper or magazine wants to convince you that a certain pie slice is large, it will appear in the foreground. And you may see that if a newspaper or magazine wants to convince you that a certain pie slice is small, it will appear in the background.

Why You Probably Shouldn't Use Pie Charts

Because pie charts only show a single data series and because they limit you, practically speaking, to a handful of data points, you shouldn't use them very much—and maybe you shouldn't use them at all. As a practical matter, you'll usually present your

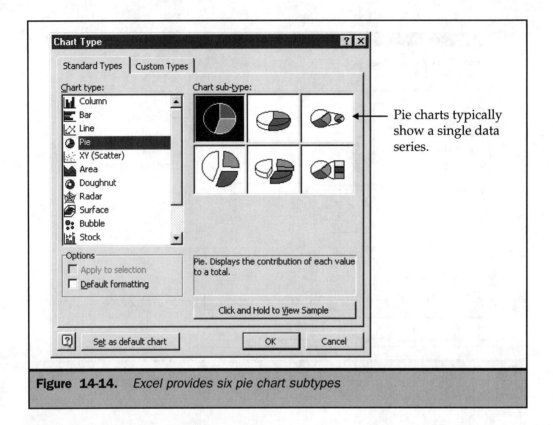

Pie charts typically show a single data series.

Figure 14-14.   *Excel provides six pie chart subtypes*

information in a much cleaner and more meaningful way by just using a tabular format—in other words, a regular worksheet range.

Note, however, that there is one time when pie charts do seem to be very effective: They tend to be wonderful tools—because they are so simplistic—for explaining to children what charts do. Even very young children can see that larger pie slices indicate relatively larger values.

Doughnut Charts

Doughnut charts resemble pie charts, but they allow you to show more than a single data series by plotting the multiple data series as concentric circles. Each data point is represented by a segment (or bite) of the doughnut. Although doughnut charts are popular in some cultures, you probably want to think carefully about their usefulness in your situation. A segment that represents the very same value will appear larger the farther away its concentric ring is from the center of the circle. What that means is that you can't compare values in different data series. And then that, of course, begs the question as to why you're plotting the multiple data series together in the first place. (If you did want to compare both the relative proportions of data series' values and values from different data series, a better option would be to use stacked bar or column chart subtypes.)

Radar Charts

Radar charts plot data points as radial points from a central origin, as shown in Figure 4-15. Each data series' points are connected in a line, and the radar chart uses as many radial axes as there are data points in your series. Although radar charts can be a little confusing at first, they can be very useful. Radar charts allow you to more precisely calibrate each data series' points because each data point appears directly on an axis. The one other advantage of a radar chart is that it lets you compare the aggregate values—the totals of all of a data series' values.

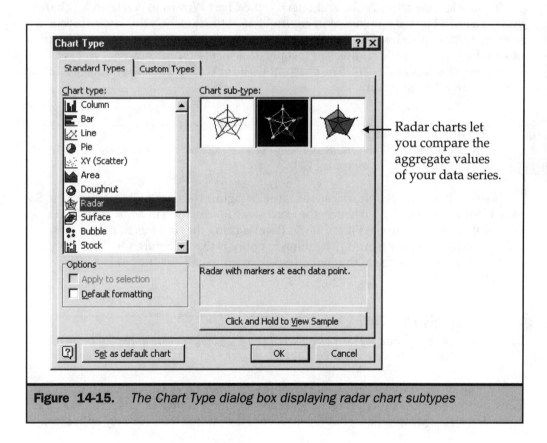

Radar charts let you compare the aggregate values of your data series.

Figure 14-15.   *The Chart Type dialog box displaying radar chart subtypes*

XY (Scatter) Charts

The XY, or scatter, chart type is Excel's most useful chart type. It allows you visually to explore the relationship between two or more data series: an independent data series, which replaces the data categories that other charts use, and one or more dependent data series. Because this represents a change from the way that Excel's other chart types work, you'll probably benefit from knowing in detail how to actually use an XY chart.

Your first step is to create a worksheet range that shows at least two data series that you think may have a cause-and-effect relationship. You may not know the exact nature of the relationship, but that's what you want to explore by creating an XY chart.

You can easily sort your data in ascending or descending order by selecting the range that holds both the independent data series and the dependent data series and then clicking the Standard toolbar's Sort Ascending or Sort Descending tool.

If you select the range A1:B5 and then use the Chart Wizard to create an XY chart, you get a chart like the one shown in Figure 14-16. At first glance, this doesn't seem very interesting, perhaps. But it is. What the chart in Figure 14-16 shows you, among other things, is that while adding salespeople does increase your revenue, you get diminishing returns as a result. The chart shows this because the slope of the line in Figure 14-16 is flattening out.

LEARN BY EXAMPLE
To follow along with the discussion here, open the example chart in the Figure 14-16 (XY chart) file on the companion CD.

If you're like most people, the significance of Figure 14-16 isn't all that apparent. So take a look at Figure 14-17. It shows the exact same information in a line chart. (You can tell this is so, because in Figure 14-17, Excel is using the contents of the range A2:A5 for data category names.) The thing to notice is that in Figure 14-17 the diminishing returns of the additional salespeople isn't at all obvious. In fact, it's basically hidden.

LEARN BY EXAMPLE
To follow along with the discussion here, open the example chart in the Figure 14-17 (line chart) file on the companion CD.

Various chart subtypes are available for the XY chart type. Most of the differences between the available subtypes relate to cosmetics: Some subtypes have gridlines, and some don't, for example. Some subtypes smooth the plotted lines (so they appear less

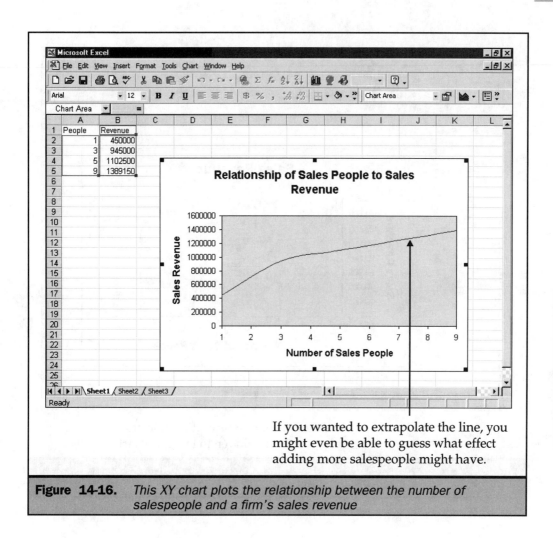

Figure 14-16.   *This XY chart plots the relationship between the number of salespeople and a firm's sales revenue*

jagged). And some use individual data markers for the dependent data series values and a line, while others don't.

Surface

Surface charts are probably Excel's most interesting and perhaps most useful three-dimensional chart type. What they let you do is plot a data set using a three-dimensional surface, as shown in Figure 14-18. By drawing a three-dimensional surface, a 3-D surface chart lets you explore relationships that exist both within a data series and with a data category. In fact, one indication of a data set that may be usefully

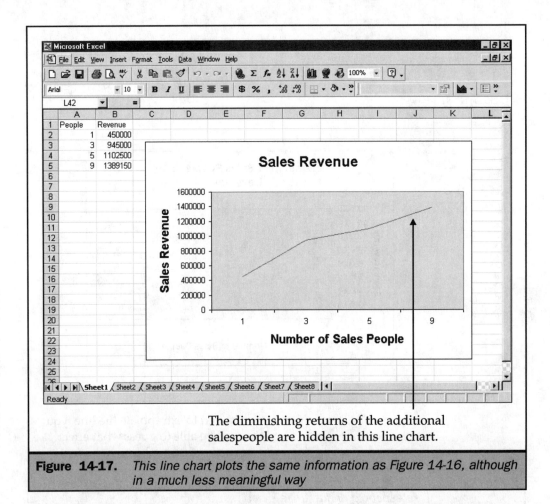

The diminishing returns of the additional salespeople are hidden in this line chart.

Figure 14-17.   *This line chart plots the same information as Figure 14-16, although in a much less meaningful way*

plotted as a 3-D surface chart is when, even though you truly understand the difference between data categories and data series, you still have trouble defining which is which.

Bubble Charts

Bubble charts amount to a variant of Excel's XY scatter chart. Like an XY scatter chart, a bubble chart plots an independent and dependent data series, thereby allowing you to visually explore correlation between the data series. A bubble chart adds a new wrinkle to the standard XY scatter chart, however, by allowing you to include a third data

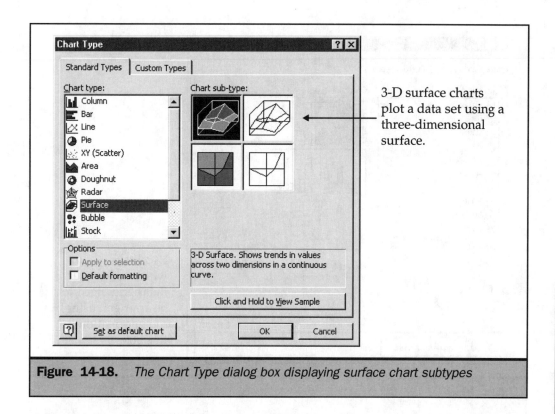

3-D surface charts plot a data set using a three-dimensional surface.

Figure 14-18.   *The Chart Type dialog box displaying surface chart subtypes*

series. Excel uses the third data series' values to size bubble data markers. Excel has two bubble chart subtypes.

Stock Charts

Stock charts let you plot daily opening, high, low, and closing stock prices in a special variety of bar chart used by technical security analysts. (Two varieties of the stock chart also let you include a second values axis, which can be used to plot shares-traded volume.) Figure 14-19 shows what the four stock chart subtypes look like. The lower two subtypes shown plot volume using columns.

Cylinder, Cone, and Pyramid Charts

Cylinder, cone, and pyramid charts work like and resemble bar and column charts. The difference is that, rather than use a rectangular data marker, these chart types use three-dimensional cylinders, cones, or pyramids. For example, Figure 14-20 shows

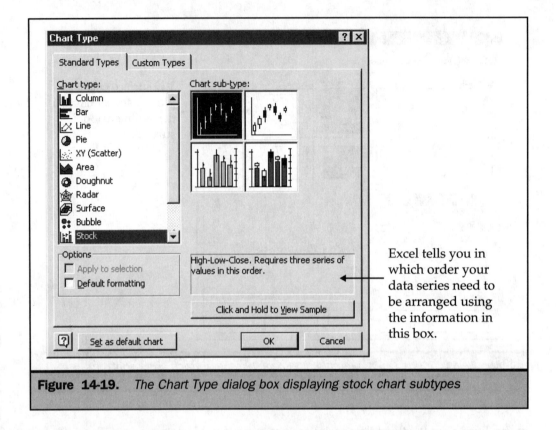

Excel tells you in which order your data series need to be arranged using the information in this box.

Figure 14-19. *The Chart Type dialog box displaying stock chart subtypes*

how some of the cylinder chart subtypes resemble bar charts while others resemble column charts.

Despite the fact that cylinder, cone, and pyramid charts look different, however, they should generally be used in the same manner as bar and column charts. For example, those chart subtypes that use a horizontal values axis are useful for comparing data point values when the data category isn't time. Those chart types that use a vertical values axis are useful for comparing data point values when the data category is time.

Custom Logarithmic Charts

As you may have noticed, the Chart Type dialog box also includes a Custom Types tab. If you click this tab, Excel displays a lengthy list of more specialized and unusual-looking chart types. The most interesting Custom Type is the logarithmic chart, because it uses logarithmic scaling of the values axis. Logarithmic scaling lets

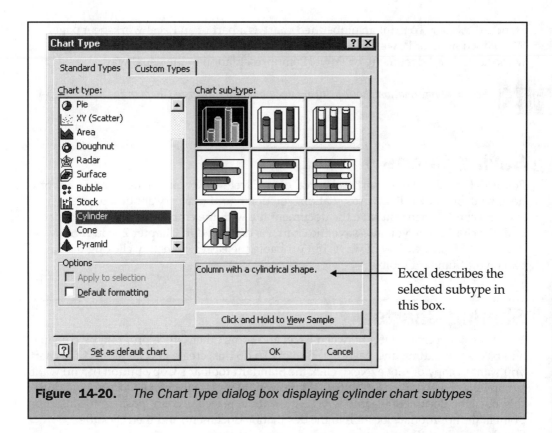

Excel describes the
selected subtype in
this box.

Figure 14-20.   *The Chart Type dialog box displaying cylinder chart subtypes*

you plot the range of change in a data series. This may seem too technical or esoteric to be of interest, but it's probably not. If you don't believe this statement and you have the time, create a line chart that plots the revenues of two companies: a $500 million company growing at five percent annually over ten years and a $1 million company growing at 50 percent annually over ten years. Then flip-flop back and forth between a regular line chart subtype (which doesn't use logarithmic scaling) and the logarithmic chart type, which does. What you'll notice is that the significantly faster growth rate enjoyed by the smaller company doesn't even show up on a line chart. It does show up, however, on the logarithmic chart that uses logarithmic scaling.

Printing Charts

Printing a chart isn't difficult. To print an embedded chart but not any of the worksheet page in which it's embedded, simply click the chart, and then click the Print tool on the

Standard toolbar. To print an embedded chart as a part of an Excel worksheet page, Word document, or PowerPoint presentation in which it's embedded, print the worksheet, Word document, or PowerPoint presentation in the usual way.

Note   *For more information about printing document files, refer to Chapter 2.*

Saving Charts

Because charts are always part and parcel of an Excel workbook (the usual case), a Word document, or a PowerPoint presentation, you don't need to worry about separately saving a chart. When you save the document file with the embedded chart object or with the chart sheet, you also save the chart. As discussed in Chapter 2, you can save a document file in a variety of ways, but probably the easiest is just by clicking the Save tool on the Standard toolbar.

Sharing Charts

You can share a chart object between Excel and some other Office program by copying and pasting or cutting and pasting the chart. To do this, create and then select the chart you want to copy or move. Next, click the Standard toolbar's Copy button (if you want to copy the chart) or the Cut button (if you want to move the chart). Once you've done this, open the document file into which you want to place the chart, position the insertion point in the appropriate location in the destination document, and then click the Standard toolbar's Paste button.

Note   *For more information on sharing objects between Office programs, refer to Chapter 5.*

Customizing Charts

You can customize just about any aspect of a chart. You can add text that describes the chart or some element of the chart. You can add items such as gridlines or axes—or modify these items—to better calibrate the plotted data series for chart viewers. You can change the appearance of any of the parts of a chart. And you can even use special tools such as trend lines and error bars. The best part of all this is that none of this customization is difficult. As long as you understand how to create charts using Excel's Chart Wizard—which you already know how to do if you've read the previous portions of this chapter—you'll have no trouble customizing those charts.

Adding and Editing Titles, Legends, and Data Labels

To annotate the data your charts plot or to emphasize their messages, Excel lets you add chart and axis titles, legends, and data labels to existing charts. Typically, you add titles and legends when you create the chart, of course; but you can add these later on, as well as data labels.

Adding Chart and Axis Titles

To add titles to an existing chart, you first need to display the chart's chart sheet if it's on its own chart sheet, or click the chart if it's embedded in a worksheet. When you do this, Excel replaces the worksheet menu bar with the chart menu bar.

To add a title to the chart or its axis, choose Chart | Chart Options. When Excel displays the Chart Options dialog box, click the Titles tab, enter titles into the text boxes as shown in the illustration that follows, and then click OK.

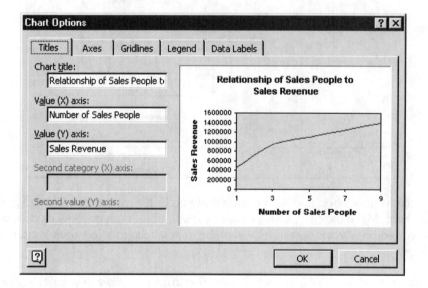

Editing Chart and Axis Titles

To edit a chart or an axis title, click the title to select it. Then click the mouse to position the insertion point inside the title text box. Once you've done this, you can edit the chart title in the way you edit the contents of any text box. If you want to remove a title, click it and then press the DELETE key.

To separate your title on different lines, click a chart title you've already added. (You can click on the chart sheet or the embedded chart.) Position the insertion point at the exact spot where you want to break the title into two lines of text, and then press CTRL-ENTER to end a line.

Using Data Labels

Data labels annotate your data markers either by displaying the data point value (its relative percent of the data category total) or by displaying the data category name next to or above the marker. Many of the subtypes—particularly those supplied for the pie and doughnut chart types—initially supply data labels. You can add and remove data labels to or from any chart, however, by choosing Chart | Chart Options and then clicking the Data Labels tab. When Excel displays the Data Labels tab of the Chart Options dialog box, you use its option buttons to indicate which type of data label you want.

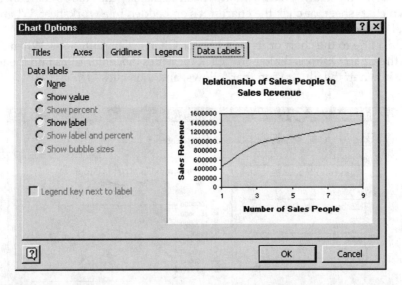

If you add data labels and then decide that you don't want them, you can easily remove them. Make the chart active either by displaying its chart sheet or clicking it (if it's embedded on a worksheet). Then click the data labels (to select them) and press the DELETE key.

Note   *To format a data label in the active chart, first display its chart sheet page or click it (if it's an embedded chart) to make it active. Click the data label you want to format and then right-click the data label so Excel displays the shortcut menu. Choose the Format Data Labels command. When Excel displays the Format Data Labels dialog box, use the options that its four different tabs supply—Patterns, Font, Number, and Alignment—to specify exactly how you want the label displayed.*

Using Chart Legends

A chart legend simply names the data series. You have the choice of specifying that you want a legend when you create a chart with the Chart Wizard. Or, you can add one later by choosing Chart | Chart Options, clicking the Legend tab, and then checking the Show Legend box. You can also control the placement of the legend in the same dialog box.

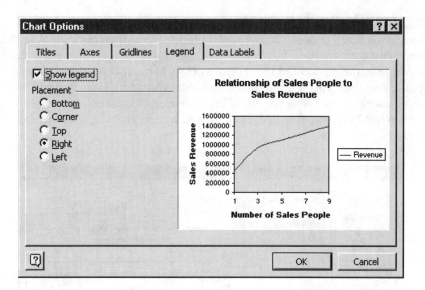

Tip   *To add a meaningful legend, you must include the data series names in the initial worksheet range you select to plot. Otherwise, Excel uses the rather meaningless series names—Series 1, Series 2, Series 3, and so on.*

You can move a legend anywhere in the chart area by clicking the legend and then dragging it. You can also resize the legend (and thereby change the way it arranges the key information) by clicking the legend box and then dragging the sizing handles. (The sizing handles are those little black squares that appear on the corners and edges of a selected object—such as a selected legend.) You can remove a legend by clicking it and pressing the DELETE key. Finally, you can change the foreground and background pattern, the font, and the legend placement by right-clicking the legend to display the shortcut menu, and choosing the Format Legend command. When Excel displays the Format Legend dialog box, you can use its Patterns, Font, and Placement tabs to change the appearance and position of the legend box. The Patterns and Font tabs work in exactly the same way that these tabs work for formatting other objects. The Placement tab provides option buttons you can click to move the legend around the chart area.

Calibrating and Organizing the Data Markers

Excel provides two visual tools to make it easier for chart readers to better calibrate and organize a chart's data markers: axes and gridlines. Although many of the subtypes use these tools, you can, of course, fine-tune the way Excel draws and uses chart axes and gridlines.

Adding and Removing Axes

To add axes to a chart, choose Chart | Chart Options, and then click the Axes tab. (For the Chart menu commands to be available, as mentioned earlier, either the chart sheet must be active or the embedded chart on a worksheet must be selected.) When Excel displays the Axes tab, you can indicate which axes you want Excel to draw on the chart by marking check boxes. Or, if you want to remove an axis, of course, you can clear a check box. When you have finished, click the OK button and Excel will update the axes on your chart.

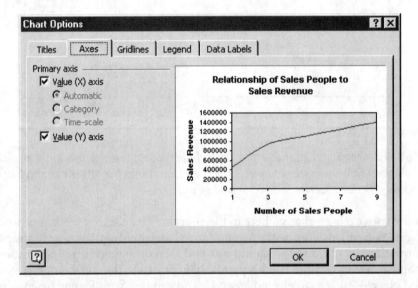

When Excel displays the Gridlines tab, shown next, you can indicate whether you want it to draw vertical and horizontal gridlines. Simply mark its check boxes to indicate whether you want major gridlines extending from an axis's major tick marks and minor gridlines extending from an axis's minor tick marks. (Gridlines aren't usually difficult to understand or use, so if you have questions, just experiment.)

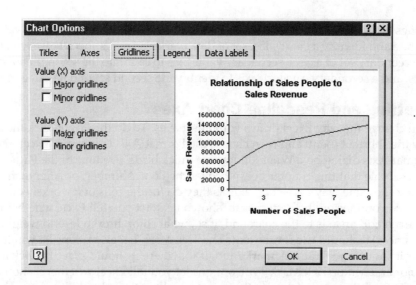

> **Tip**
>
> *To better understand these options, your best bet is to just create an example chart or open a Learn By Example workbook and experiment with the Axes and Gridlines tabs' options.*

The only thing that's tricky about this axes business is that a chart can actually have as many as three primary axes and two secondary axes. For any chart type but the pie chart and doughnut chart—which don't use axes—you can supply a value axis to calibrate the data markers, and you can supply a category axis to identify the data categories. For some of the three-dimensional chart subtypes, you can also supply a series axis to identify the data series. These axes, when they exist, represent the chart's primary axes.

> **Note**
>
> *If you add a series axis to a three-dimensional chart, you don't need a legend. Series axes and legends do the same thing: They name and identify the plotted data series. Therefore, you only need one or the other. Because series axes are easier for the chart reader to use—they place the series names right alongside the series' data markers—you should usually employ them, when available, rather than legends. Note that series axes aren't available, however, for all of the three-dimensional chart types—only those that use the extra dimension of depth to organize, or segregate, the data series.*

EXCEL

Things get just a bit more complex in the case of a chart that uses a second value axis to calibrate and identify a chart's last set of data markers. In this special case, you also have a secondary set of axes: a secondary value axis to calibrate the second set of data markers, and a secondary category axis to identify the second set of data categories.

Formatting and Rescaling Chart Axes

You can change the way Excel draws your chart axes. To do this, right-click the axis to display the shortcut menu and then choose the Format Axis command. Excel displays the Format Axis dialog box. What follows is a quick birds' eye tour of the Patterns and Scale tabs. Note that this chapter doesn't cover the Font, Number, or Alignment tabs; they work the same way for a chart axis as they do for the cells of a worksheet.

The Axis options on the Patterns tab, shown next, let you tell Excel whether it should even add an axis to the chart and, if so, what color, line style, and weight (or line thickness) it should use for the axis. The Tick Mark Labels options let you tell Excel whether it should label the tick marks and, if so, where it should place the tick marks. The Major and Minor Tick Mark Type options let you tell Excel whether it should add tick marks, or little crosshatches, to the axis, and where they should be placed. You could spend several paragraphs reading in detail exactly how these options effect your charts. The best way for you to learn what they do, however, is to simply experiment with an existing chart.

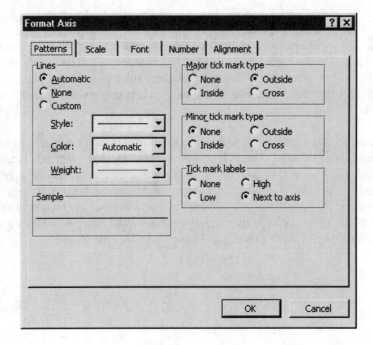

The Format Axis dialog box's Scale tab, shown next, lets you control how Excel scales a value or category axis and how often it displays tick marks and tick-mark labels. The illustration that follows shows the Scale tab for a value axis. The Auto check boxes, if marked, tell Excel to scale the value axis by choosing where the value scale starts (its minimum value), where the value scale ends (its maximum value), which units of measurement should be used for the major and minor tick marks, and where the category axis should intersect, or cross, the value axis. If you don't want Excel to automatically calculate these settings, you can uncheck the check boxes and enter your own values into the text boxes. The Logarithmic Scale check box tells Excel to use a logarithmically scaled value axis. (As noted in earlier in the chapter in the "Reviewing the Chart Types" section's discussion of the line chart subtypes, logarithmically scaled value axes can be a wonderful tool for showing the rate of change in the plotted data series' values.) The Values In Reverse Order check box tells Excel to flip-flop the standard order of the value axis, so everything looks upside down. Finally, the Value (X) Axis Crosses At Maximum Value check box tells Excel to draw the axis so, as the option label indicates, it intersects the value axis at the point of the largest plotted value.

If you take a quick look at the illustration that follows, you see that the Scale tab for a category axis looks quite a bit different from the Scale tab for a value axis. The dialog box provides three text boxes with self-explanatory labels: Value (Y) Axis Crosses At Category Number, Number Of Categories Between Tick-Mark Labels, and Number Of Categories Between Tick Marks. In addition, the dialog box provides three check boxes. The Value (Y) Axis Crosses Between Categories check box tells Excel to draw the intersection of the value and category axes so that the lines cross some place other than where a data marker is. The Categories In Reverse Order check box tells Excel to plot the categories in right-to-left order rather than in the usual left-to-right order. And the Value (Y) Axis Crosses At Maximum Category check box tells Excel to place the value axis after the last data category instead of before the first data category.

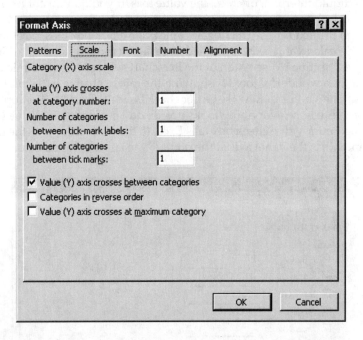

Note   *The Scale tab for a series axis provides a subset of the options available for a category axis.*

Adding a Data Table to a Chart

You can add a data table to a chart by selecting the chart and choosing Chart | Chart Options. The Chart Options dialog box, shown in Figure 14-21, opens on top of the chart. A data table simply shows the chart's data point values plotted in a table that appears beneath the chart. This is especially useful if you've created your chart on a separate chart sheet and then find that you need to include the source data in your printout. To display the chart data, click the Show Data Table check box to select it and click OK.

Working with the Data Markers

Excel also lets you customize the data markers. You won't be surprised to hear that you can change their color and shape, of course. But you may be surprised to learn about

The Perils of Automatic Axes Scaling

Most of the time, you will want Excel to automatically scale your value axis by automatically selecting the axis minimum and maximum, as well as the units used to scale the axis. You should, however, verify that the way Excel has scaled an axis is reasonable and relevant. Excel tends to scale an axis in a way that emphasizes the differences in the plotted data points' values. Yet, if the differences in the plotted data points are insignificant, this probably doesn't make sense. (For a really good example of this sort of kooky value axis scaling, look at the way they plot the Dow Jones stock average the next time you watch the nightly news. What you'll see is that every single trading day of the year, the differences in the plotted data points' values show up as visually significant because the value axis maximum equals the daily high of the average and the value axis minimum equals the daily low of the average.)

One other time you'll want to consider overriding Excel's automatic scaling is when you're presenting several charts to viewers in one sitting. In this case, you should probably scale each of the charts using the same value axis so that viewers can make comparisons between the charts.

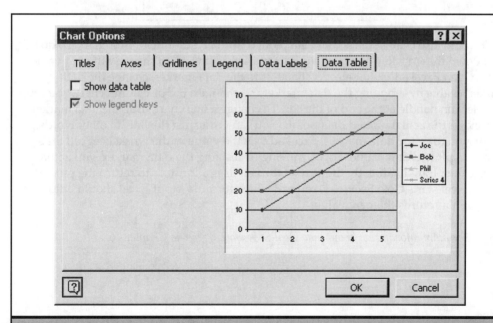

Figure 14-21.   *The Data Table tab of the Chart Options dialog box*

some of the other changes you can make. You can, for example, use clip art pictures in place of Excel's data markers. And you can add trend lines and error bars.

Changing the Plotted Data

Excel lets you make a couple of changes to the actual data plotted in a chart. You can add a new data series to a chart, and you can adjust the actual data point value. Most people—and this probably includes you—aren't going to want to mess around with these sorts of changes. But just in case you want to do this, I'll quickly describe how you make these changes.

To add another data series to a chart, display the chart sheet or, if the chart is embedded in a worksheet, click it. Then choose Chart | Add Data. When Excel displays the Add Data dialog box, click the Range text box and then select the worksheet range that holds the data series you want to add to the chart:

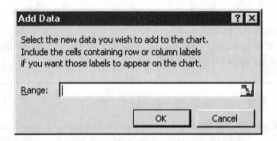

You can also change the actual data plotted in a bar, column, or line chart. To do this, hold down the CTRL key and click the data marker you want to show a different value. Then, when Excel adds the selection handles to the data marker, change the data marker's value by dragging the data marker. To change a bar or column chart, you drag the selection handle at the end of the bar. To change a line chart, drag the data marker that shows the actual plotted data point. (You can't drag just the line, in other words.)

As you drag the data marker, Excel adjusts the value in the worksheet cell that holds the plotted data value. So, by moving or resizing the data marker, you actually change the plotted value. By the way, if the cell uses a formula to return the plotted value, Excel starts Goal Seek so it can ask which formula input Excel should adjust so the formula returns the new value.

Note *For more information about how Goal Seek works, refer to Chapter 16.*

Formatting the Data Markers

Mechanically, you can probably already guess how to format the data markers for a series. Click the marker to select the complete set of data markers for the data series. Then, right-click any of the selected data markers to display the shortcut menu and choose the Format Data Series command. Excel displays the Format Data Series dialog box, shown in the illustration that follows:

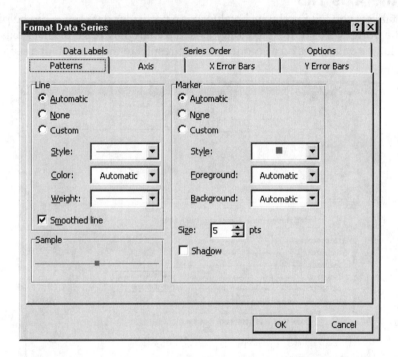

To reformat an individual data marker, click once on the marker to select the entire series, then click once again to select the individual data marker (the sizing handles will move to the data marker). Then, double-click the data marker to display the Format Data Point dialog box.

Using the Patterns Tab

The preceding illustration shows the Patterns tab for a line, but the Patterns tab looks different depending on the type of data marker you select. You actually make the same sorts of changes no matter which data marker type you're customizing, however. You can change the line that Excel uses to draw the data marker or its border. You can also change the color and pattern of the data marker or its interior. And, in some cases, you can make other changes to the data marker's pattern, too. For line and XY scatter charts, for example, Excel provides a Smoothed Line option. It tells Excel to smooth out, or soften, the plotted line's jaggedness.

Using the Axis Tab

The Axis tab lets you tell Excel which value axis a particular data series can be plotted against: the primary axis or the secondary axis. If a chart only has a primary axis, telling Excel to plot the data series on a second axis also results in the creation of a second axis.

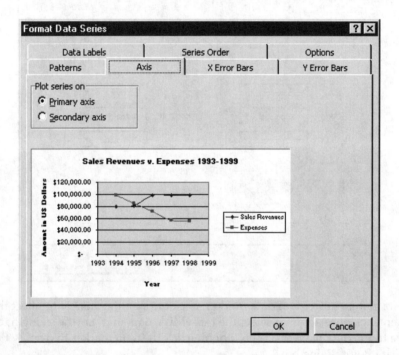

Using the Error Bars Tabs

To visually show that imprecision exists in your plotted data, you can add error bars. Error bars, in effect, show the chart reader that the plotted value isn't precise, but instead falls within an error range. To add error bars to the plotted data series, you use the X Error Bars tab or the Y Error Bars tab, shown next.

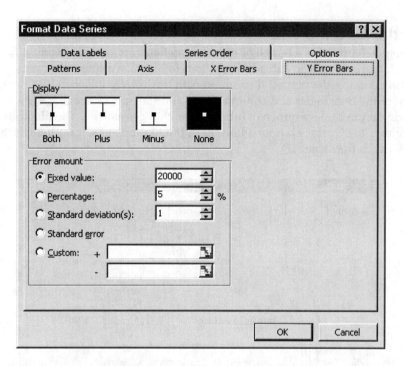

Use the Display options to specify whether Excel should display plus or minus error bars, or both. Use the Error Amount options to specify how Excel calculates the error range: as a fixed amount added to and subtracted from the plotted value, as a percentage of the plotted value, as a specified number of standard deviation from the mean of the plotted value, as a standard error, or as some other amount you specify.

Note *The Data Labels tab lets you add data labels to the selected data series. For information about how the Data Labels tab works, refer to the earlier chapter section, "Using Data Labels."*

Using the Series Order Tab

The Series Order tab lets you choose the order in which Excel plots the different data series. It provides one list box and a couple of command buttons, Move Up and Move Down. To change the order of a particular series, select it from the list box and then, as you've guessed, click either the Move Up or Move Down button. To show you what effect your reordering has on the chart, Excel updates a preview of the chart within the dialog box.

Using the Options Tab

The Options tab provides a bunch of rather miscellaneous settings for modifying the group of data markers. You can add drop lines to line charts and area charts. (Drop lines simply connect the plotted data markers to the horizontal axis.) You can control the width of the bars in bar and column charts and the gap, or spacing, between the bars. And you can make a bunch of other minor changes as well. The illustration that follows shows the Options tab for a line chart, but Options tabs for other charts look and work much the same.

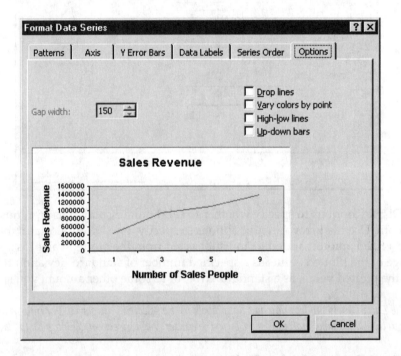

 You can replace Excel's standard data markers with pictures—such as a clip art image, or a drawing object—to make your charts more interesting or unusual. To do this, first copy or cut the picture or image by selecting it and then clicking the Standard toolbar button's Copy or Cut button. Next, click the data marker you want to replace with the picture or image and then click the Standard toolbar's Paste button.

Working with Trend Lines

Trend lines represent the final customization opportunity you have with regards to data markers. Trend lines, however, don't actually change the way data markers look or how they're calibrated. What they instead do is show you the trend of a data series' values by calculating and then drawing with a trend or regression line. To add a trend line, click the data series for which you want to add a trend line, and then right-click it and choose the Add Trendline command from the shortcut menu. When Excel displays the Trendline dialog box (shown next), use the Type tab to pick the type of trend line you want. Most people will probably want either the linear trend line (which simply plots the trend in a straight line) or a logarithmic trend line (which plots the trend as a rate of change). If you want to perform more sophisticated trend analysis, you can use the Polynomial, Power, Exponential, or Moving Average options.

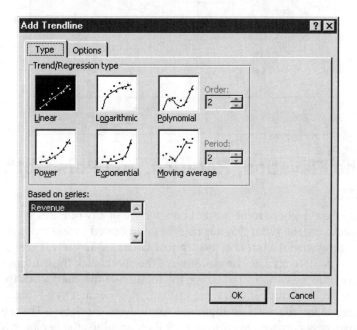

The Options tab of the Trendline dialog box lets you name the trend line. (In essence, the trend line is almost like another data series.) You can specify how far forward into the future or back into the past the trend line should continue. (You make these specifications using the Forecast options.) Use the check boxes at the bottom of the Options tab, shown next, to tell Excel where the trend line should intercept the value axis, to provide the line's equation next to the line, and to display the R-squared value on the chart.

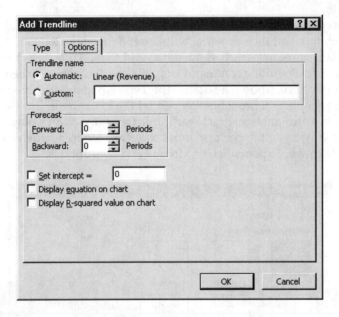

Adjusting the Elevation, Rotation, and Perspective of 3-D Charts

You can adjust the elevation, rotation, and perspective of any of Excel's three-dimensional charts. What this means is best illustrated by example. If you quickly create a three-dimensional chart and then choose Chart | 3-D View, Excel displays the 3-D View dialog box. To change the elevation of the chart, click the buttons with the large arrows that point up and down. To change the rotation of the chart, click the buttons that show an arrow circling a line. If you want to change the perspective— basically, the perceived depth of the chart—clear the Right Angle Axes check box. Then, when Excel displays the two, new perspective buttons, click these to adjust the perspective. As you make changes to the elevation, rotation, or perspective, Excel updates the picture of the chart shown in the dialog box so you know the effect of your changes.

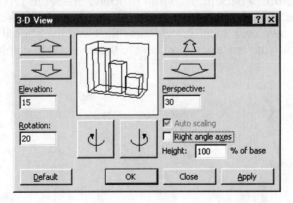

The Complete Reference

Office 2000

Chapter 15

Working with PivotTables

PivotTables organize, analyze, and present information from worksheet lists. You can take a long, unwieldy list and reorganize it into a more compact and readable table. In the process, you transform some former list columns into PivotTable rows, and others into PivotTable columns. Then, if you want, you can "pivot" the table, exchanging, for instance, a row heading for a column heading, turning the table on its side, or inside out. That's what gives PivotTables their flexibility—they easily display the same information in a number of ways, depending on what aspect you'd like to focus upon.

Excel provides a handy PivotTable Wizard to make it easy for you to create and modify PivotTables. In this chapter, you'll learn how to use the wizard and how to use PivotTables to analyze information, create charts, consolidate several tables into one, and more.

Working with Lists

PivotTables work with worksheet lists, which this book doesn't talk about—or at least talk about much. So a brief overview is in order. In essence, lists are databases that you create in an Excel worksheet. A database is simply a list of records, with each record containing a set of fields. The worksheet shown in Figure 15-1 is one example of a list: The worksheet lists records that describe a company's sales by region, quarter, product (flavor), units, and revenue. Another common example of a list might be a collection of records that describe each of your customers' names and addresses.

Although lists and list management are an important feature of Excel, this book will only talk about them in passing and in the context of PivotTables. The reason for this limited coverage is simple: Access database tables are a vastly superior replacement for Excel lists in almost all cases. Therefore, it doesn't really make sense to waste your reading time learning about an inferior information management tool.

Using the PivotTable Wizard

The list shown in Figure 15-1 contains two years' sales data for a company that makes ice cream and sells it nationwide. For each of the seven flavors it sells, the ice cream company has recorded sales by region for each quarter in the years 2000 and 2001. The sales report gives both unit sales and equivalent dollar amounts. The information shown in Figure 15-1 is exactly the sort of information that lends itself well to analysis with a PivotTable.

LEARN BY EXAMPLE
To follow along with the discussion here, open the sample worksheet in the Figure 15-1 (simple list for PivotTable) file on the companion CD.

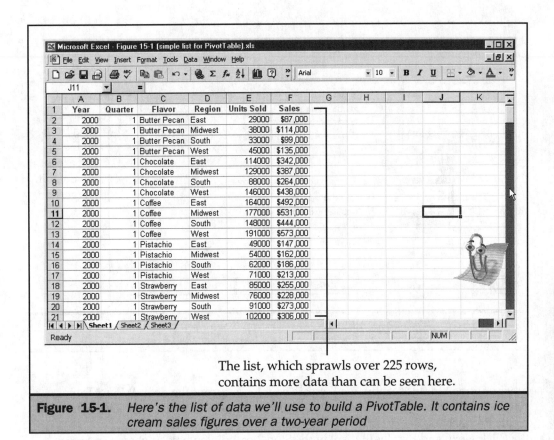

The list, which sprawls over 225 rows, contains more data than can be seen here.

Figure 15-1.   *Here's the list of data we'll use to build a PivotTable. It contains ice cream sales figures over a two-year period*

Notice, by the way, that the data shown in Figure 15-1, while very detailed, doesn't provide much general information. You can't, for example, easily discern trends in sales from one year to the next or from one quarter to the next. You can't, without a great deal of effort, see in which region sales are strongest or which flavors sell best. You can get this information, however, by creating a PivotTable from the list shown in Figure 15-1.

Invoking the PivotTable Wizard

Once you've created a list with the information you want to analyze, click any cell in the list, and then choose Data | PivotTable and PivotChart Report.

Excel displays the first dialog box of the PivotTable and PivotChart Wizard, as shown in Figure 15-2. The wizard asks you the location from which to take data for the PivotTable and whether you want to create a table or a chart. If a list is on an Excel worksheet, accept the default option, Microsoft Excel List Or Database. (Later in this chapter, the section entitled "Importing Data into a PivotTable" examines some of the

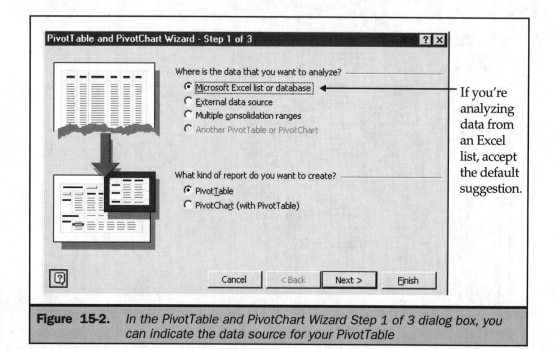

Figure 15-2. In the PivotTable and PivotChart Wizard Step 1 of 3 dialog box, you can indicate the data source for your PivotTable

other options.) In this section, we'll create a table, so accept the default PivotTable option. In the later section, "Using PivotTables to Create Charts," we'll look at how to create PivotCharts.

Click Next, and Excel will display the Step 2 of 3 dialog box, as shown in Figure 15-3. The list range will appear automatically in the Range text box. If the range selection is incorrect, you can re-enter the correct range here. (You can simply type in the range reference or select the list.)

Laying Out a PivotTable

When you've identified the range, click on Next again to move to the Step 3 of 3 dialog box, shown in Figure 15-4. It's in this dialog box that you specify the nuts and bolts of your PivotTable. PivotTables make extensive use of Windows' drag-and-drop feature,

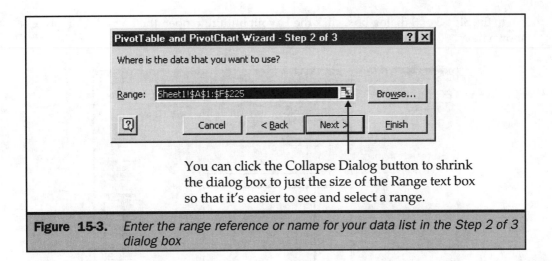

You can click the Collapse Dialog button to shrink
the dialog box to just the size of the Range text box
so that it's easier to see and select a range.

Figure 15-3.   *Enter the range reference or name for your data list in the Step 2 of 3
dialog box*

which you can use to set up the row and column headings and data fields of your table
now, and which you'll use to modify your table later.

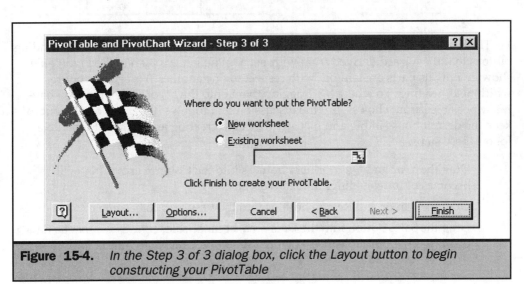

Figure 15-4.   *In the Step 3 of 3 dialog box, click the Layout button to begin
constructing your PivotTable*

In the Step 3 of 3 dialog box, click the Layout button to open the Layout dialog box, shown next:

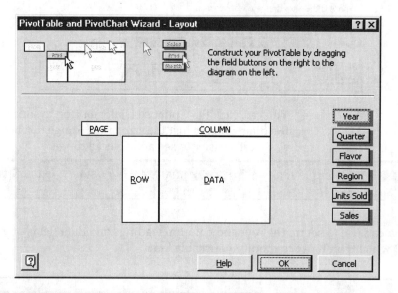

The Layout dialog box has two main areas. On the right are a series of field heading buttons that the wizard derived from your list. On the left is a plan of the PivotTable, showing how its parts are laid out with respect to one another. You get to choose which field headings go where by dragging them onto the PivotTable plan. You have many possible layout choices, but the discussion that follows illustrates one layout to keep the descriptions simple and focused. To begin creating an example PivotTable follow these steps:

1. Drag the Year and Quarter field buttons into the Column area. They will become column headings in the PivotTable.

2. Drag the Flavor and Region buttons into the Row area to become row headings.

3. Drag the Sales button into the Data area, because sales figures will be the data displayed in your table. (Don't worry about the Units Sold button for now—

you can add that information to your table later.) The dialog box should appear as shown below:

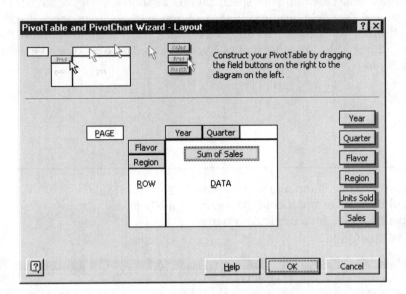

You'll notice that when you drag the sales heading into the Data area, the PivotTable Wizard renames it Sum of Sales. That's because the wizard assumes you'll want to add up sales figures to arrive at subtotals and totals. By default, the wizard will sum any numeric values and count any text entries you drag into the Data area.

You can override the defaults and apply different functions to field headings that you drag into the Data area. Double-click a heading in the data area to open the PivotTable Field dialog box, and you can see some of the other functions available. See "Using PivotTable Functions," later in the chapter, for more information.

4. Click on OK to move back to the Step 3 of 3 dialog box, shown in Figure 15-4.

5. Click the New Worksheet option button, if necessary, and then click Finish. The wizard goes to work creating your table, and soon displays it in the location you selected. The PivotTable toolbar is also displayed.

Taking a Closer Look at a PivotTable

Excel creates a table based on your specifications, as shown in Figure 15-5. If you put the Quarter and Year field headings in the Column area as shown above, Excel creates a column heading for each quarter and one for each year's total. In addition, there is a column heading for the grand total of two years' sales. These headings are said to be along the column axis of the table.

At each row and column intersection you can find the sales of a particular flavor, in a particular region for a particular quarter, in a particular year.

The PivotTable toolbar

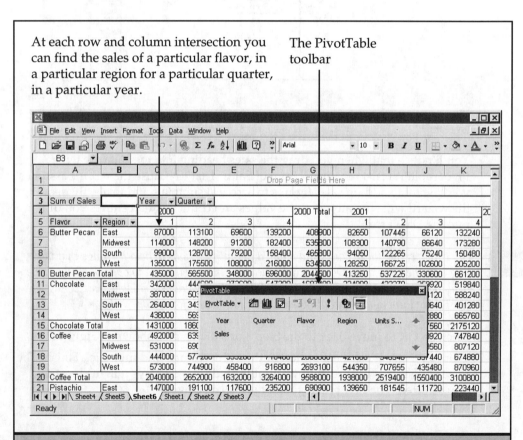

Figure 15-5. *Using the example data and the preceding step-by-step instructions, the PivotTable and PivotChart Wizard would create this PivotTable*

LEARN BY EXAMPLE
To follow along with the discussion here, open the PivotTable in the Figure 15-5 (simple PivotTable) file on the companion CD.

Along the row axis of the table are headings corresponding to the field headings you dragged to the row area in Figure 15-4: Flavor and Region. Within each of the four regions, each flavor has its own row. Because you dragged the Sales button into the Data area, sales figures appear in the body of the table.

Excel also adds rows showing regional subtotals and national grand totals for each quarter and year. Because these totals represent the sum of the Sales figures, Excel places the title Sum of Sales at the top of the table.

When you create a PivotTable, Excel displays the PivotTable toolbar, which contains several buttons useful for working with PivotTables. Later in the chapter, I'll talk more about the individual buttons as I discuss various aspects of working with PivotTables.

Refreshing PivotTables

As the data changes in the list upon which the PivotTable is based, you need to refresh the PivotTable because, although a PivotTable is linked to its source data, that link is not automatically updated. You can refresh a PivotTable in either of two ways: by choosing Data | Refresh Data, or by clicking on the Refresh Data button on the PivotTable toolbar.

The Refresh Data toolbar button is the one that shows an exclamation point. Remember, too, that you can point to any toolbar button to display the button's name in a ScreenTip.

Modifying PivotTables

What distinguishes PivotTables from other kinds of tables is the ease with which you can rearrange, or "pivot," them. For example, you can reshape a table by moving column headings to the row axis and row headings to the column axis. You can simplify a table by moving either row or column headings to the page axis. And you can change the emphasis of a PivotTable by changing the order in which headings and totals are displayed.

Pivoting PivotTables

Pivoting refers specifically to switching headings from the column axis to the row axis and vice versa. A couple of examples easily illustrate this. In Figure 15-6, you can see that the Flavor heading has been moved from the row axis to the column axis. Doing so

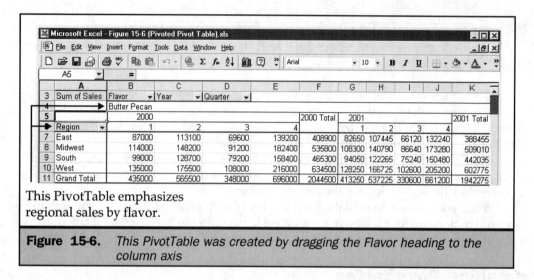

This PivotTable emphasizes
regional sales by flavor.

Figure 15-6.   *This PivotTable was created by dragging the Flavor heading to the column axis*

produces quite a different-looking table. The new table is 53 columns wide, but only 9 rows high. Now each flavor seems to have its own "mini-table," showing quarterly and yearly totals by region. Regional grand totals are displayed at the extreme right edge of the table. It's important to emphasize that pivoting the table hasn't changed the information displayed—just how it's displayed.

LEARN BY EXAMPLE
To follow along with the discussion here, open the PivotTable in the Figure 15-6 (pivoted PivotTable) file on the companion CD.

In Figure 15-7, the Flavor heading has been dragged back to the row axis, and the Year heading has been dragged to the row axis as well. Now each year appears to have its own table, one on top of the other, and quarterly grand totals are displayed at the bottom of the table.

LEARN BY EXAMPLE
To follow along with the discussion here, open the sample PivotTable in the Figure 15-7 (PivotTable emphasizing yearly sales) file on the companion CD.

Reordering Fields

PivotTables have a hierarchy of fields, depending on how you place their headings in the table. On the row axis, for example, the field you place to the outside (to the left) is the outer field, while the one to the inside (to the right) is the inner field. The outer field is higher in the hierarchy: All inner field items are repeated for each outer field item.

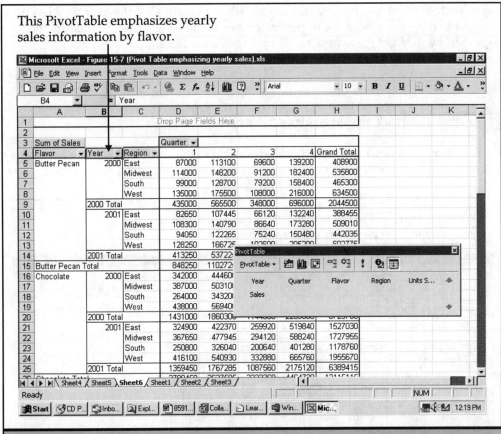

This PivotTable emphasizes yearly sales information by flavor.

Figure 15-7. *This PivotTable was created by dragging the Year heading to the row axis, displaying the same data in a very different fashion*

For example, if Flavor is an inner field and Region is an outer field, each region is broken down by flavor. You can easily reverse their positions, so that each flavor is broken down by region. To do this, you would just drag the Flavor heading from the PivotTable to the left of the Region heading.

Creating Page Fields

In the table shown in Figure 15-7, data for one year seems to be stacked upon data for the other. It's useful to view the data by year, but the resulting table is cumbersome. Luckily, there's a better way to view sales figures for each year—using the page axis. When you move a field to the page axis, you divide that field into a series of separate pages, each of which can be viewed individually. In Figure 15-8, the Year field has been dragged to the page axis, in the upper-left corner of the table. (You can identify the page axis, by the light gray caption, "Drop Page Fields Here.")

LEARN BY EXAMPLE

To follow along with the discussion here, open the sample PivotTable in the Figure 15-8 (PivotTable with page fields) file on the companion CD.

By clicking the downward-pointing arrow next to the Year heading you can display a drop-down menu, where you can choose to view figures for 2000, 2001, or both years

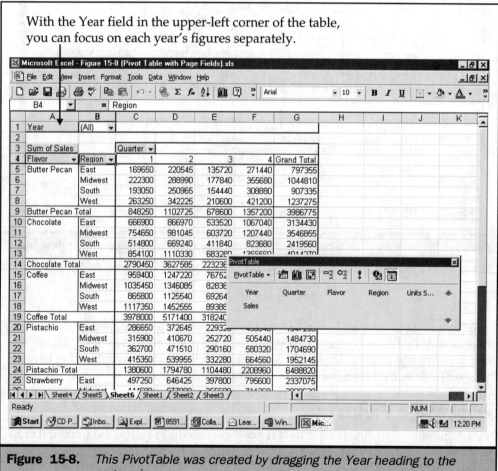

Figure 15-8. *This PivotTable was created by dragging the Year heading to the page axis*

combined (All). In a like manner, you can drag any of the other headings to the page axis to divide them into a series of pages. To narrow your focus even more, you can drag more than one heading to the page axis.

Displaying Pages on Separate Worksheets

By clicking on the PivotTable drop-down menu on the PivotTable toolbar and then clicking the Show Pages button when you use page fields, you can create a separate worksheet for each page in the field. When you click the Show Pages button, Excel displays the Show Pages dialog box:

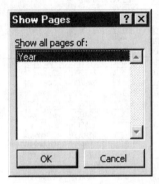

Select a page field, click OK, and Excel creates a page worksheet for each item in that field. For example, if you select the Year field, Excel creates separate worksheets for 2000 and 2001. Excel places each of the worksheets adjacent to the PivotTable worksheet, and names each of the new sheets appropriately for the page item it displays, as shown in Figure 15-9.

LEARN BY EXAMPLE
To follow along with the discussion here, open the sample worksheet in the Figure 15-9 (PivotTable with added sheets) file on the companion CD.

Adding New Fields and Deleting Existing Fields

To add a new field or delete an existing field, select any cell in the table. Click the PivotTable Wizard button on the PivotTable toolbar.

When Excel displays the PivotTable Wizard Step 3 of 3 dialog box, click the Layout button to open the Layout dialog box, which looks the way you last left it. Make changes to the table layout by dragging fields in and out of the table. Note that you can display more than one set of data in the Data area of the table. To add the Units Sold field to the table, for example, drag it into the Data area, click OK, and then click Finish. Figure 15-10 shows the PivotTable after the Units Sold field has been added.

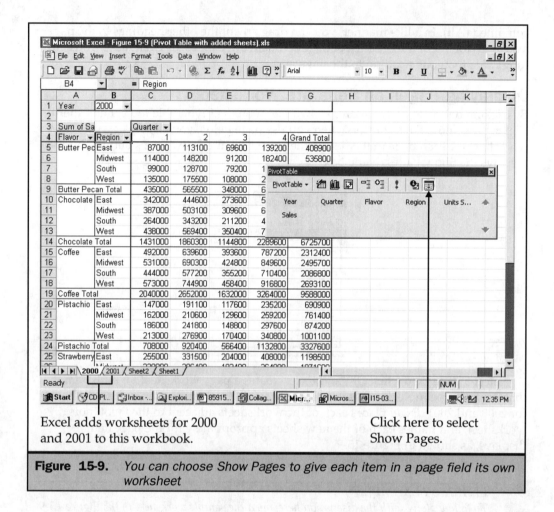

Excel adds worksheets for 2000 and 2001 to this workbook.

Click here to select Show Pages.

Figure 15-9.   *You can choose Show Pages to give each item in a page field its own worksheet*

In order to display the additional data effectively, Excel adds another heading named Data to the table. Each data category, Sales and Units Sold, is displayed on separate rows, and subtotals are given for both categories.

To rename a field heading, simply select the heading and edit it in the formula bar. If you change a heading name, the change affects all instances of the name in the table, including in subtotals and totals.

Showing and Hiding Fields

You can hide any of the items in a field to narrow the focus of a PivotTable. Suppose, for example, you'd like to concentrate on only four of the seven flavors in the Flavor

This row shows sales
revenue data in dollars.

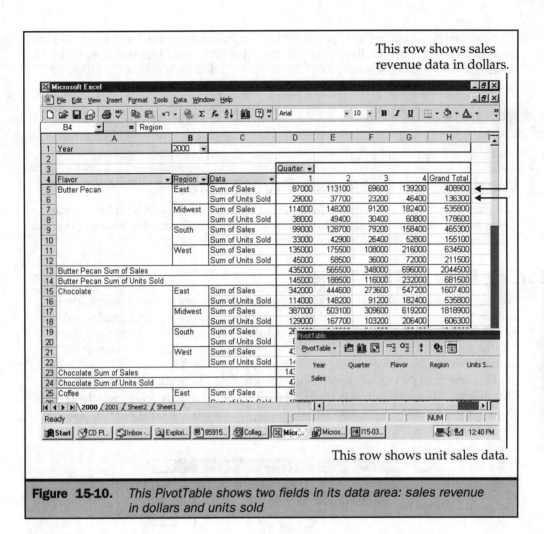

This row shows unit sales data.

Figure 15-10. *This PivotTable shows two fields in its data area: sales revenue in dollars and units sold*

field. To filter your data in this manner, click on the Flavor field drop-down arrow to display the list of flavors:

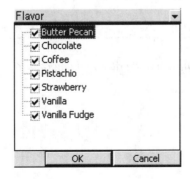

Now, simply click the items you want to hide (which removes the check marks by those items), and click OK. Excel displays the PivotTable and hides the items you selected. (When you hide items, those items are excluded from subtotals and grand totals as well.) Repeat this procedure to redisplay the data.

To hide an entire column, select the column, right-click, and choose Hide.

Working with Data in PivotTables

You can manipulate PivotTable data in various ways. You can sort data in ascending or descending order, group and ungroup data items, and perform calculations upon data. In addition, you can change how totals and subtotals are displayed.

Sorting Data in PivotTables

You can sort data field items in ascending or descending order. You can sort labels alphabetically, and you can sort values numerically. When Excel first creates your PivotTable, it sorts field items in ascending order. In Figure 15-5, for example, Excel lists the regions in alphabetic order, starting with East; it lists flavors, starting with Butter Pecan; and it lists quarters, starting with 1.

To change the sort order, select an item in the field you want to sort and choose Data | Sort. When Excel displays the Sort dialog box, as shown below, select either the Descending or Ascending option and click OK. Excel resorts the list information in the specified order.

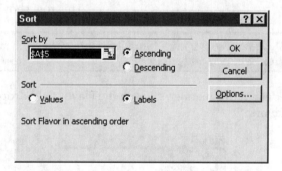

You can sort labels in alphabetical order, and you can sort values in numeric order.

Grouping Data in PivotTables

To make your PivotTables easier to read and understand or to provide different perspectives on the same data, you can create custom groupings of field items. Suppose that you really were working with a list like the one shown in Figure 15-1 and that you wanted to see how well flavors containing either vanilla or chocolate fared compared with the other flavors. You can create a special Vanilla-Chocolate group, and group the rest of the flavors together as Other.

To create a group, select all the flavors you want to place in the group. (If you press the CTRL key, you can select items that aren't adjacent to one another.) When you've selected all the items in the first group, select Data | Group and Outline | Group.

Excel names the groups using the generic description Group1 and creates a new column with the heading Flavor2. (To rename a group or a heading, select it and type in a new name.)

You can further improve the table's appearance and readability by hiding the individual flavor names. You can accomplish that simply by double-clicking the names of the new groups you've created. Your PivotTable will look like the one in Figure 15-11. (In Figure 15-11, I've also dragged the Flavor heading off the table and renamed the new heading "Flavor Groups.")

EXAMPLES

LEARN BY EXAMPLE
To follow along with the discussion here, open the sample worksheet in the Figure 15-11 (PivotTable with grouped data) file on the companion CD.

Grouping Numeric Items

If you have a long list of numeric items such as ZIP codes that you want to group, you often don't have to select them all individually. You may be able to specify a range of items to group. To group numeric items instead of labels, try the following method: Instead of selecting all the items you want to group, just select one. Next, choose Data | Group and Outline | Group.

In the Grouping dialog box, shown next, enter the number of the first and last items you want to group together, and an interval between items. Click OK. If you leave the Auto option selected, Excel will fill in the values for you.

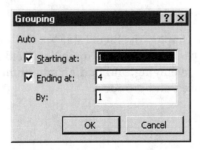

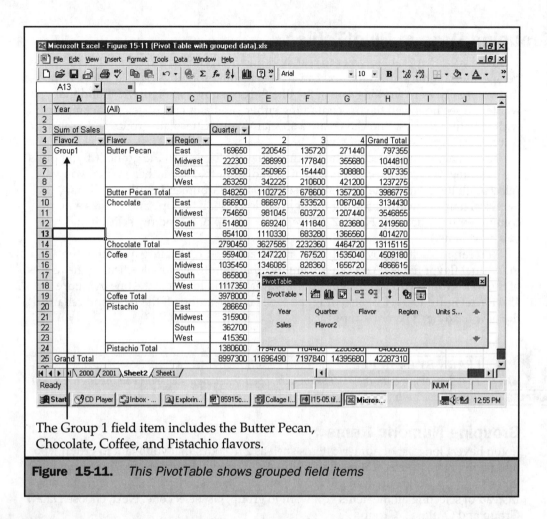

The Group 1 field item includes the Butter Pecan,
Chocolate, Coffee, and Pistachio flavors.

Figure 15-11. *This PivotTable shows grouped field items*

To ungroup items and return the table to its former appearance, select the item you want to ungroup and choose Data | Group and Outline | Ungroup.

Using PivotTable Functions

As mentioned earlier in the chapter, the PivotTable Wizard provides other functions besides summing that you can use to operate upon data field items. Those other functions include counting; averaging; and finding minimum and maximum values, standard deviations, variances, and products.

To specify which function you want the PivotTable to use, click the PivotTable Wizard button to display the PivotTable Wizard if it isn't already displayed, click the Layout button, and then double-click the data heading button once you've moved it to the data area:

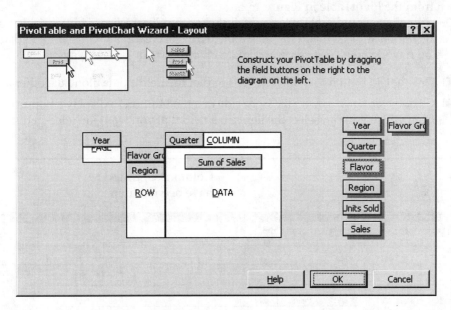

Once you do this, the PivotTable Wizard displays the PivotTable Field dialog box. To specify which calculation you want, select an entry from the Summarize By list box:

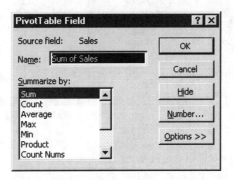

When you drag the heading of a text field into the data area, the wizard automatically applies the COUNT function to that field.

Using PivotTables to Create Charts

Creating a chart from a PivotTable is easy. First, hide any columns in the PivotTable that you don't want to include in the chart. Figure 15-12 shows columns G, L, and M hidden from the PivotTable in Figure 15-5.

Once you have your PivotTable ready, just click the Chart Wizard button (either on the Personal toolbar or on the PivotTable toolbar). Excel creates a PivotChart and places it on its own worksheet. You can manipulate PivotCharts in several ways:

- Drag a field button to a different axis to plot the field's data along the other axis.

- Click the down arrow on the right side of a field button to display a pop-up box from which you can select the items in a field that you want included in the chart.

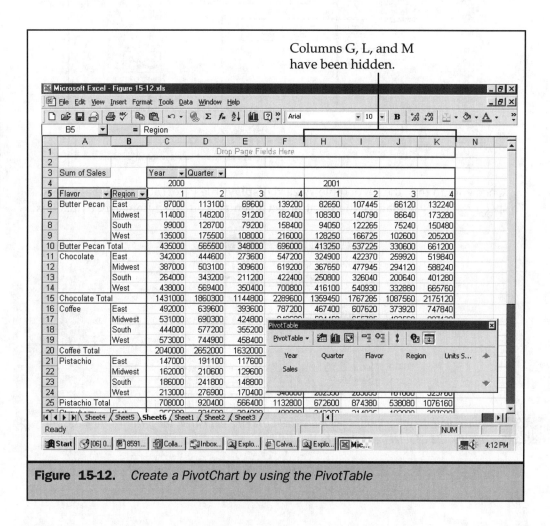

Figure 15-12. *Create a PivotChart by using the PivotTable*

- Choose Chart | Chart Type to change the PivotChart type.
- Click the PivotChart button on the PivotTable toolbar to display a menu of commands for working with PivotCharts—including commands for hiding and displaying the field buttons and removing fields from the PivotChart.

Figure 15-13 shows the chart I created based upon the data from Figure 15-12 and then manipulated to show only sales of Pistachio ice cream.

Tip   *For more information about creating charts, refer to Chapter 14.*

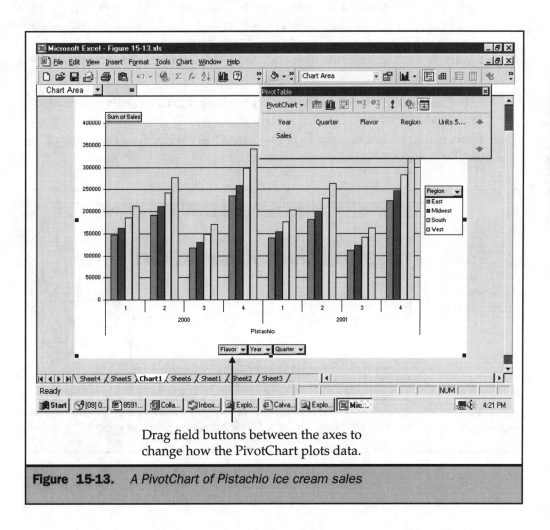

Drag field buttons between the axes to
change how the PivotChart plots data.

Figure 15-13.   *A PivotChart of Pistachio ice cream sales*

Importing Data into a PivotTable

If you want to create a PivotTable based on data in a database or other external application, you can select the External Data Source option in the first PivotTable Wizard dialog box.

When you take on this task, use the Query Wizard to get the data you want. In step 2 of the PivotTable Wizard, click the Get Data button. This starts the Query Wizard. To use the Query Wizard to import a database, follow these steps:

1. In the Choose Data Source dialog box, make sure that the Use The Query Wizard To Create/Edit Queries box is checked, as shown in Figure 15-14. Choose from the list of databases and queries, on the Databases and Queries, tabs. If the data source you want is not listed, or if no databases are defined, click New Data Source in the list box on the Databases tab and click OK.

2. If you create a new data source, the Query Wizard asks you to name the source and select the driver as shown in Figure 15-15. You might also need to install the driver if it hasn't already been installed. Click Connect when you are done.

3. Select the database or query you want to import.

4. In the first Query Wizard dialog box, choose the columns or fields you want to include and click Next.

5. (Optional) In the last two dialog boxes of the Query Wizard, you can filter or sort the order of your fields.

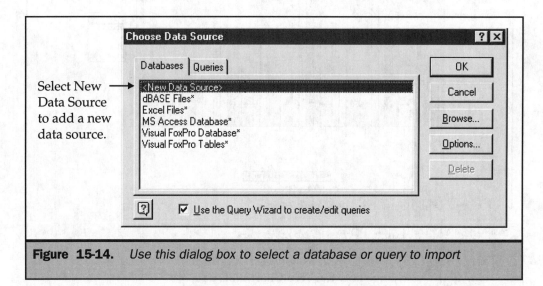

Figure 15-14.   *Use this dialog box to select a database or query to import*

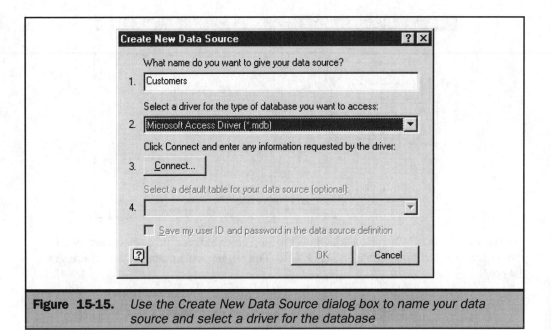

Figure 15-15.   *Use the Create New Data Source dialog box to name your data source and select a driver for the database*

EXCEL

6. When you are done, click Finish to return to the PivotTable Wizard.

7. Click Next to proceed through the PivotTable Wizard.

8. Select the location where you want the PivotTable to go and click Finish.

Should you ever wish to modify the query the table is based upon, you need to click the PivotTable Wizard button to restart the PivotTable Wizard and then go back through the wizard to reopen the query and make any changes to it.

Combining Worksheets in PivotTables

You can consolidate, or combine, data from separate Excel worksheets into a single PivotTable. Then, using the drop-down list of the page axis, you can still display separately data that originated in each worksheet. You can also use the same procedure to combine data from several ranges in the same worksheet.

To generate the consolidated table, select the Multiple Consolidation Ranges option in the first PivotTable Wizard dialog box, and click Next. In the Step 2a of 3 dialog box, select the Create A Single Page Field For Me option (which is the default).

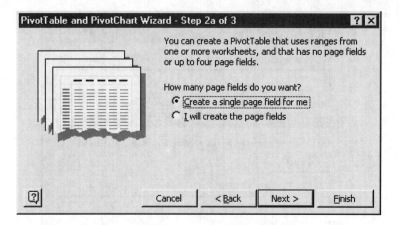

Then, click Next. When Excel displays the Step 2b of 3 dialog box, select each of the ranges you want to consolidate and click Add. The ranges will appear in the All Ranges list box.

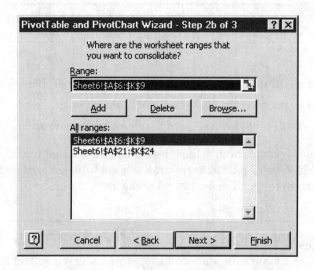

Click Next, and Excel displays the Step 3 of 3 dialog box, which will be familiar to you. Complete the rest of the PivotTable creation process as before.

Chapter 16

Advanced Modeling
Techniques

xcel provides a rich set of advanced modeling tools that you can use to examine, manipulate, and even create data. These analytical tools, which are described in this chapter, aren't going to be tools you employ all the time. But they do dramatically enhance your ability to perform real-life, complicated modeling. With the Data menu's Table command and the Scenario Manager, for example, you quickly simulate the effect of changing input variables. With the Goal Seek command, you can work backward from the formula results you want to the input values you need. With the Data menu's Consolidate command, you get an easy yet powerful way to combine and mathematically manipulate data from multiple worksheet ranges. Finally, by using the Solver add-in, you can perform sophisticated optimization modeling.

Note   *Excel's PivotTable feature is described in Chapter 15.*

Using Data Tables

Data tables let you show how a formula result changes as you supply different input values. While this may sound simple, data tables are extremely useful for performing what-if analyses. For example, if you want to estimate the future value of a retirement savings account based on $2,000-a-year contributions and a 10 percent annual rate of return after 10, 20, and 30 years, data tables provide the easiest means for performing this analysis. (In this example, the input values that you supply are the different forecasting horizons of 10, 20, and 30 years, and the formula result is the future value of the retirement savings account.) If you want to experiment with the gross income delivered by selling a consulting service at $80 an hour, $100 an hour, and $120 an hour, data tables again provide the easiest means for performing this analysis. (In this example, the input values are the different hourly billing rates and the formula result is the gross income.)

Two varieties of data tables exist: one-variable data tables (which accept only one input variable but allow you to calculate more than one formula result) and two-variable data tables (which predictably accept two input variables but only allow you to calculate a single formula result). But that's enough background information about data tables. The best way to understand what they do and when you'll want to use them is to see exactly how they work and exactly how you build them.

Creating a One-Variable Data Table

To make this example more concrete, let's suppose that you really did want to estimate the future value of a $2,000-a-year retirement savings program based on a 10 percent and a 12 percent annual return. In this case, as shown in Figure 16-1, you might enter the input values into the range B4:B7. In constructing a one-variable data table, then, you first enter the input values you want to supply to a formula into a range of cells in a single column.

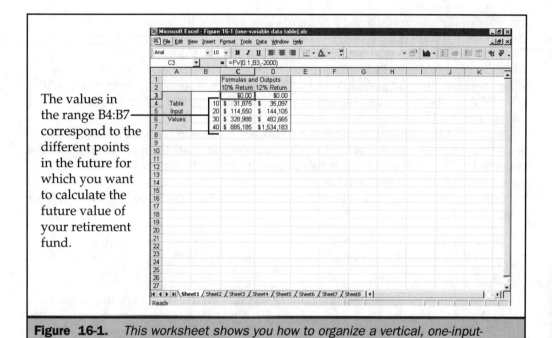

The values in the range B4:B7 correspond to the different points in the future for which you want to calculate the future value of your retirement fund.

Figure 16-1. *This worksheet shows you how to organize a vertical, one-input-variable data table*

Note *You can organize one-variable data tables in two ways—either vertically, with the input values and formula results stored in columns, or horizontally, with the input values and formula results stored in rows. This chapter only shows you how to organize a vertical one-variable table here, however. Both tables do the same work for you. And it gets unnecessarily confusing to flip-flop table orientation.*

The only trick in building this one-variable worksheet is to make sure that there's an extra, empty row above the row in which you begin storing your input values. In other words, in Figure 16-1, row 3 of column B needs to be empty when you start building your data table.

LEARN BY EXAMPLE
You can open the example Excel workbook in the Figure 16-1 (one-variable data table) file on the companion CD if you want to follow along with the discussion here.

Your next step is to enter the formulas you want to calculate into the subsequent columns—except that you need to enter the formula or formulas into the empty row that's above the row in which the first input value appears. In Figure 16-1, for example, there are two formulas: one for cell C3 and one for cell D3. These are the formulas that Excel will repeatedly recalculate using each of the input values supplied by the range B4:B7. The formula in cell C3, =FV(0.1,B3,−2000), estimates the future value of the $2,000-a-year retirement savings using a 10 percent rate of return. The formula in cell D3, =FV(0.12,B3,−2000), estimates the future value of the $2,000-a-year retirement savings using a 12 percent rate of return.

Notice that both formulas refer to the empty cell B3. In effect, what a data table does is use this cell, called the column input cell, to temporarily store the input values from the range B4:B7. Excel will calculate the formula using each of the inputs. Excel then stores the formula results in the same rows as the input values producing the results.

Once you've got your input values and your formulas entered, follow these steps to create your data table:

1. Select the range that includes both the input values and the formulas. In Figure 16-1, for example, this range would be B3:D7.

2. Choose Data | Table.

3. When Excel displays the Table dialog box (see Figure 16-2), click the Column Input Cell text box and then click cell B3. This tells Excel that for your vertically organized one-variable table, your formulas use cell B3 as the input cell.

4. Click OK.

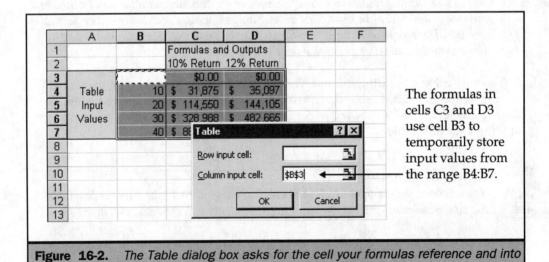

The formulas in cells C3 and D3 use cell B3 to temporarily store input values from the range B4:B7.

Figure 16-2. *The Table dialog box asks for the cell your formulas reference and into which Excel should temporarily store information*

After you click OK, Excel places a special formula based on the =TABLE() function into the ranges C4:C7 and D4:D7. This formula calculates the estimated future value of your retirement savings at various points in the future. For example, in cell C5, the formula returns $114,550, suggesting that you'll accumulate this amount if you save $2,000 a year for 20 years and earn 10 percent annually. And in cell D7, the formula returns $1,534,183, suggesting that you'll accumulate this amount if you save $2,000 a year for 40 years and earn 12 percent annually.

Note *In a horizontally organized one-variable table, you don't use the Column input cell text box. You use the Row input cell text box.*

One-variable data tables are neat for a couple of reasons. One is that the table only uses one =TABLE() formula for calculating its outputs. Each of the cells in the range C4:D7, for example, holds the same formula, ={TABLE(,B3)}. The benefit of this single-formula approach is probably obvious: the fewer formulas you use, the fewer formula errors your worksheets will contain.

The other neat thing about these data tables is that you can easily change a table's results simply by supplying new inputs. You can do this either by entering new values into the input value range (B4:B7 in the example) or by editing the formulas used to return the future value amounts. Figure 16-3 shows another version of the same data table shown in Figure 16-1 with only a few minor differences. Figure 16-3 uses a different set of forecasting periods: 10 years, 15 years, 20 years, and 25 years. And Figure 16-3 uses different annual return percentages—8 percent and 10 percent—in the two future-value

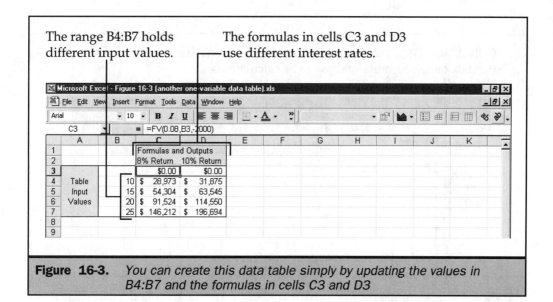

Figure 16-3. *You can create this data table simply by updating the values in B4:B7 and the formulas in cells C3 and D3*

formulas in cells C3 and D3. (Figure 16-3 also, of course, shows different labels in cells C2 and D2 so the data table correctly describes the annual returns used in those two columns' calculations.)

LEARN BY EXAMPLE
You can open the example Excel workbook in the Figure 16-3 (another one-variable data table) file on the companion CD if you want to see a completed version of the one-variable data table worksheet after changing the input values and editing the formulas.

Creating a Two-Variable Data Table

Two-variable data tables allow you to experiment with how changing two values affects a single formula's result. In constructing a two-variable table, you enter one set of input values into a range of cells in a single column and another set of input values into a range of cells in a single row. To make this discussion more concrete, however, let's suppose that you want to further analyze the future value of retirement savings, but this time you want to experiment with the effect of varying both the annual contribution amount and the annual return, while keeping the number of years until retirement constant. In this case, as shown in Figure 16-4, you might enter the varying contribution amount input values into the range B3:B6. And you might enter the fluctuating annual return percentages into the range C2:E2.

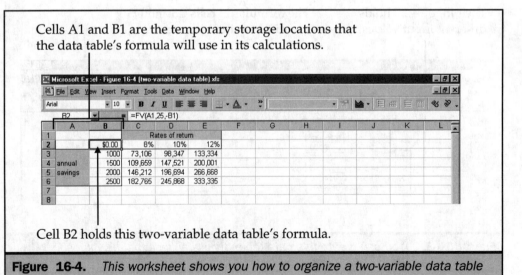

Cells A1 and B1 are the temporary storage locations that the data table's formula will use in its calculations.

Cell B2 holds this two-variable data table's formula.

Figure 16-4. *This worksheet shows you how to organize a two-variable data table*

You enter the formula that you want the data table to repeatedly recalculate into the cell that represents the intersection of the input value's row and column. In Figure 16-4, for example, that means the formula goes into cell B2. The tricky part of entering this formula, however, isn't simply clicking the correct cell. Rather, it's the fact that the formula needs to reference two empty cells, which the Data menu's Table command will use as temporary storage locations for each of the input values you supply. In Figure 16-4, the formula =FV(A1,25,–B1) calculates the formula result shown in cell B2. Notice that cells A1 and B1 are both empty. These then are the temporary storage locations just mentioned.

LEARN BY EXAMPLE
You can open the example Excel workbook in the Figure 16-4 (two-variable data table) file on the companion CD if you want to see a completed version of the two-variable data table worksheet discussed here.

HEADSTART
The companion CD includes a headstart template (retire.xls) that you can use for retirement savings calculations. The companion CD also includes a headstart template (savings.xls) that you can use for making general savings calculations.

Once you enter the input values and the formula, you're ready to build the data table. To do this, follow these steps:

1. Select the range that includes both sets of the input values and the formula. In Figure 16-4, for example, you would select the range B2:E6.

2. Choose Data | Table.

3. When Excel displays the Table dialog box, click the Row Input Cell text box and then click the cell that you want Excel to use for temporarily storing the input values from the range C2:E2. (In Figure 16-4, you would click cell A1.)

4. Click the Column Input Cell text box and then click the cell that you want Excel to use for temporarily storing the input values from the range B3:B6. (In Figure 16-4, you would click cell B1.)

5. Click OK.

After you click OK, Excel places the special formula based on the =TABLE() function into the range C3:E6. This formula calculates the estimated future value of your retirement savings after 25 years on the basis of varying contribution amounts and different annual returns. For example, in cell C4, the formula returns 109,659, suggesting that you'll accumulate this amount if you save $1,500 a year and earn 8 percent annually. In cell D6, the formula returns 245,868, suggesting that you'll accumulate this amount if you save $2,500 a year and earn 10 percent annually.

The only trick to using a two-variable data table is that you need to be sure, in the process of supplying the input values to the formula that the =TABLE() function uses in its calculations, that you don't get the input values mixed up. For example, in Figure 16-4, the real formula that keeps getting recalculated is =FV(A1,25,–B1). According to the =FV() function, this means cell A1 is supposed to supply the annual return percentage and that cell B1 is supposed to supply the annual savings amount. (This annual savings amount gets included as a negative amount because it represents a cash outflow.) When you choose Data | Table to display the Table dialog box, therefore, you need to enter **$A$1** into the Row Input Cell text box and **$B$1** into the Column Input Cell text box. If you get your Row Input Cell text box and Column Input Cell text box entries mixed up and criss-crossed, your formula won't return the correct results.

Using Goal Seek for Simple What-If Analysis

While typically you calculate formulas by supplying the input values and then asking Excel to calculate the formula's result, or output, you can work the other way. In other words, you can supply a formula, the result you want it to return, and then all of the input values except for the one Excel calculates for you. In effect then, Excel works backward from the calculation result to get one of your inputs.

To illustrate how Excel does this, suppose that you had calculated the monthly payment required for a home you want to purchase, as shown in Figure 16-5. As this simple worksheet shows, with a $100,000 loan balance, an 8 percent annual interest rate, and 360 months (30 years) of payments, your monthly principal and interest payment equals –$733.76. (The loan payment amount is a negative value because you'll pay out the money.)

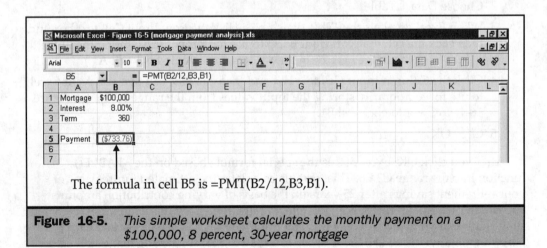

The formula in cell B5 is =PMT(B2/12,B3,B1).

Figure 16-5. *This simple worksheet calculates the monthly payment on a $100,000, 8 percent, 30-year mortgage*

Note *The formula in cell B5 divides the annual interest rate in cell B2 by 12 to convert it to a monthly interest rate so you can calculate your monthly payment.*

EXAMPLES

LEARN BY EXAMPLE
You can open the example Excel workbook in the Figure 16-5 (mortgage payment analysis) file on the companion CD if you want to see a completed version of the worksheet described here.

Now, for the sake of our illustration, assume that the largest monthly principal and interest payment you can possibly afford is $700. Rather than build new formulas that, for example, calculate the interest rate needed for a $700 payment, you can tell Excel to work backward by using the Tools menu's Goal Seek command.

TEMPLATES

HEADSTART
The companion CD includes a headstart template (homebuy.xls) that you can use for making mortgage qualification and home affordability calculations.

Here's how this would work in the case of the $700 mortgage payment example we're talking about here:

1. Click the cell with the formula that you want to return a specified result. (In Figure 16-5, for example, you would click B5.)

2. Choose Tools | Goal Seek. Excel displays the Goal Seek dialog box. Note that Excel enters an absolute address for the cell with the formula into the Set Cell text box.

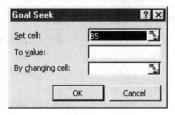

3. Specify the value you want the formula to return using the To Value text box. For this example, the value in the To Value text box is –700 because you want your monthly principal and interest payment to equal $700. (Notice that, because it's a cash outflow—an amount you pay out—the payment amount needs to be specified as a negative value.)

4. Click the By Changing Cell text box.

5. Click the cell that holds the input value you want Excel to adjust so the formula returns the result you want. If you want to calculate which interest rate is necessary in order for you to enjoy a $700 mortgage payment on a 30-year, $100,000 mortgage, simply click cell B2. Excel enters the absolute address for the cell, $B$2, into the By Changing Cell text box.

6. Click OK. Excel begins its calculations. If, by working backward, it can find an input value that causes the formula to return the specified result, it replaces the input value and it displays a dialog box that tells you it has done so:

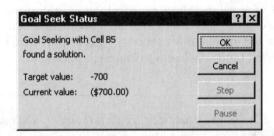

If you click OK, Excel updates the worksheet so the formula returns the result you want:

	A	B	C
1	Mortgage	$100,000	
2	Interest	7.51%	
3	Term	360	
4			
5	Payment	($700.00)	
6			

Using the Scenario Manager

As mentioned in the first part of this chapter, Excel's data tables let you experiment with the effect of changing one or two variables at a time. That's handy, to be sure. But, in reality, you're much more likely to consider changes that involve many more variables at a time. And this modeling reality is what the Scenario Manager addresses. Using the Scenario Manager, you can change as many as 32 variables at a time. You can also store (and easily retrieve) sets of input values.

Although the Scenario Manager isn't difficult to use, you'll find it much easier to follow the discussion here with a concrete example. Let's suppose, for the sake of illustration, that you're working with a worksheet like the one shown in Figure 16-6.

Each of the cells holding values is named.

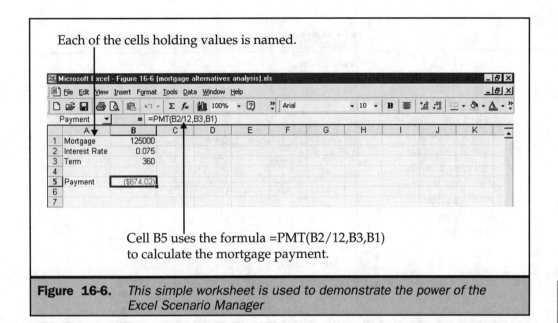

Cell B5 uses the formula =PMT(B2/12,B3,B1)
to calculate the mortgage payment.

Figure 16-6. *This simple worksheet is used to demonstrate the power of the Excel Scenario Manager*

To name the cells in the range B1:B3, select the range A1:B3, choose Insert | Name | Create, and then click OK. To name cell B5, select the range A5:B5, choose Insert | Name | Create, and then click OK again.

LEARN BY EXAMPLE
You can open the example Excel workbook in the Figure 16-6 (mortgage alternatives analysis) file on the companion CD if you want to see a completed version of the worksheet described here.

Creating a Scenario

Once you have a worksheet that you want to use in your what-if analysis, you're ready to begin creating your scenarios. To do this, follow these steps:

1. Choose Tools | Scenarios.

2. When Excel displays the Scenario Manager dialog box, click the Add button.

3. When Excel displays the Add Scenario dialog box, shown in Figure 16-7, name or describe the scenario using the Scenario Name text box.

Select the range B1:B3, because in this example this range holds the input values that describe a mortgage alternative.

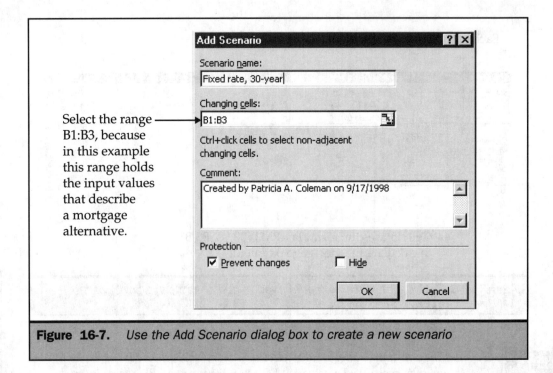

Figure 16-7. *Use the Add Scenario dialog box to create a new scenario*

4. Click the Changing Cells text box and then, using the mouse, select each of the cells or ranges into which you want the Scenario Manager to place values. In Figure 16-7, for example, you would select the range B1:B3. Remember that you can select multiple ranges or cells by holding down the CTRL key as you click and drag.

> **Note** *You can protect scenarios (in a manner very much like you protect cells and sheets) so other users can't change or modify the scenario. To protect or hide a scenario, first mark the Prevent Changes and Hide check boxes that appear at the bottom of the Add Scenario and Edit Scenario dialog boxes. Then, to turn on sheet protection, you choose Tools | Protection | Protect Sheet.*

5. After you identify the cells the Scenario Manager can change, click OK.

6. When the Scenario Manager next displays the Scenario Values dialog box (see Figure 16-8), you can provide the values you want the Scenario Manager to place into the cells. To enter a value, click the text box and enter the value. Notice in Figure 16-8 that the Scenario Manager uses the cell names to identify the cells. If you don't name the cells before you add the scenario, Scenario Manager just uses the cell addresses—which makes it a lot harder to keep your input values straight.

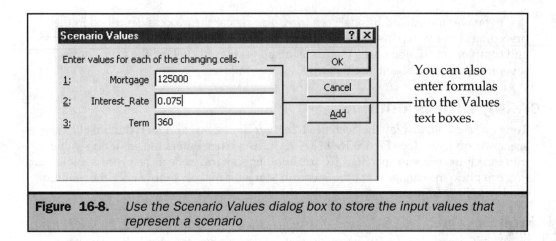

You can also enter formulas into the Values text boxes.

Figure 16-8. *Use the Scenario Values dialog box to store the input values that represent a scenario*

7. Click OK. Excel adds your scenario to its list of scenarios and returns you to the Scenario Manager dialog box (see Figure 16-9). It now lists your new scenario.

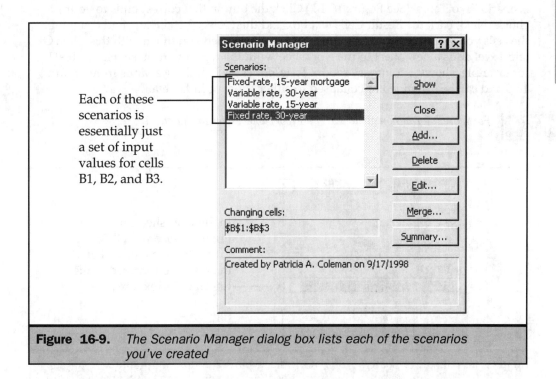

Each of these scenarios is essentially just a set of input values for cells B1, B2, and B3.

Figure 16-9. *The Scenario Manager dialog box lists each of the scenarios you've created*

EXCEL

If you want to add additional scenarios, you repeat the process described in the preceding step-by-step instructions: you can click the Scenario Manager's Add button and complete the dialog boxes that Excel displays. Figure 16-9, by the way, shows several scenarios added in just this way.

Working with Scenarios

To use a scenario, display the Scenario Manager dialog box and then double-click the scenario you want. (See Figure 16-9.) That's it. Excel then enters the scenario's values into the input cells you specified. To use another scenario, repeat the process. Note that you can undo the changes that the Scenario Manager makes: simply click the Standard toolbar's Undo button.

When the Scenario Manager enters input values into the specified cells, it replaces those cell's current contents. This means that it's possible to inadvertently lose data if you're not careful. For example, the Scenario Manager can replace a formula with a constant value.

To prepare a report that summarizes all of your scenarios, display the Scenario Manager dialog box and then click the Summary button. Excel displays the Scenario Summary dialog box that asks whether you want to prepare a Scenario Summary or a Scenario PivotTable. (See Figure 16-10.) Click the button that corresponds to your choice. Next, click the Result Cells text box and then select, by clicking and dragging, the cells you want to view on the summary report. When you finish with this, click OK and Excel adds a new sheet to the worksheet with the report you chose. Figure 16-11, for example, shows a summary report. It describes each of the scenarios from Figure 16-9 and can be expanded or collapsed to either show or hide detail.

Note   *For more information about Excel's PivotTables, refer to Chapter 15.*

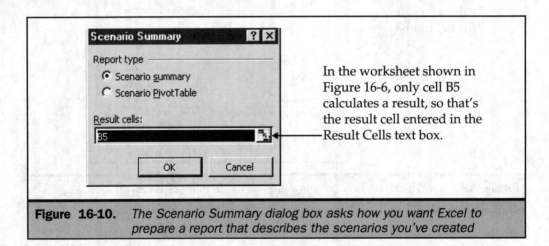

In the worksheet shown in Figure 16-6, only cell B5 calculates a result, so that's the result cell entered in the Result Cells text box.

Figure 16-10.   *The Scenario Summary dialog box asks how you want Excel to prepare a report that describes the scenarios you've created*

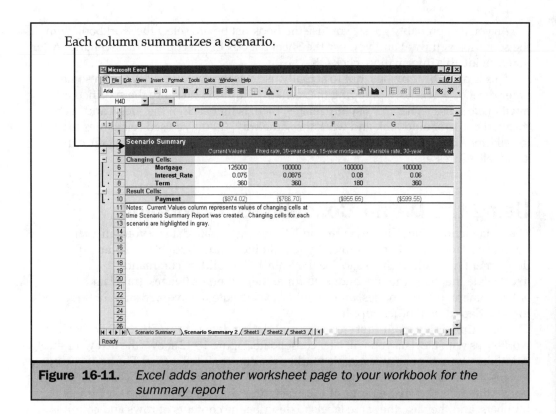

Each column summarizes a scenario.

Figure 16-11.   *Excel adds another worksheet page to your workbook for the summary report*

Merging Scenarios from Other Sheets and Workbooks

Scenarios are stored with specific worksheets and, therefore, get stored with Excel workbooks. You can retrieve scenarios you or someone else has created in another worksheet or workbook, however, by opening the workbook and then using the Scenario Manager's Merge button. When you click this button, Excel displays a dialog box that asks for the name of the workbook and the name of the worksheet from which you want to view and possibly retrieve scenarios, as shown in the following illustration:

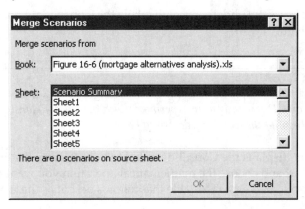

As you can probably guess, you use the Book list box to select the workbook with the scenarios you want and you use the Sheet list box to select the actual scenario. After you provide this information, click OK.

This is probably obvious, but to actually use a scenario you retrieve from some other sheet or worksheet, plopping the scenario's input values into the specified cells must make sense. What this usually means, then, is that each of the sheets and each of the workbooks should look and work the same way. If you've used cell names to refer to cells, for example, the scenarios should all use the same names and reference the same cell addresses.

Using the Data | Consolidate Command

The Data menu's Consolidate command lets you aggregate data so you can analyze the consolidated data. For example, if you built individual budgets by company department, you might choose to use the Data | Consolidate command to calculate the total amounts budgeted for all departments (wages, travel and entertainment, office supplies, and so on) or to calculate the average amount budgeted for, say, department office supplies.

Not surprisingly, your first step in consolidating data is to create the workbook or workbooks with the data you will later consolidate. Figure 16-12 shows the first worksheet, Administration, of such an example workbook. You can't tell it from Figure 16-12, but for this workbook, both the second and third worksheet pages, Research and Marketing, mirror the first. They use a range of the exact same dimensions to store the budget numbers, and they use the same labels to describe the contents of rows and columns. Only the sheet names and data are different.

Once you set up a workbook with the ranges you want to consolidate and then collect the data in those ranges, you're ready to use the Data | Consolidate command. To do this, follow these steps:

1. Select the top-left corner of the worksheet range into which you want to place the consolidated data. (You'll often want to set up this consolidation range on a separate worksheet.)

2. Choose Data | Consolidate. Excel displays the Consolidate dialog box, as shown in Figure 16-13.

EXAMPLES

LEARN BY EXAMPLE
You can open the example Excel workbook in the Figure 16-12 (pre-consolidation) file on the companion CD if you want to experiment with the Data | Consolidate command but don't want to build the workbook described here.

3. When Excel displays the Consolidate dialog box, activate the Function drop-down list box and choose the mathematical operation you want Excel to perform on the consolidated data. The table that follows describes these operations.

Function	What It Does
Sum	Sums the values in the consolidation ranges
Count	Counts the number of cells that aren't empty
Average	Calculates the average of the values
Max	Finds the largest value in each cell of the consolidation ranges
Min	Finds the smallest value in each cell of the consolidation ranges
Product	Multiplies the values in the consolidation ranges
CountNums	Counts the number of cells that hold values
StdDev	Calculates the sample standard deviation of the values
StdDevp	Calculates the population standard deviation of the values
Var	Calculates the sample variance of the values
Varp	Calculates the population variance of the values

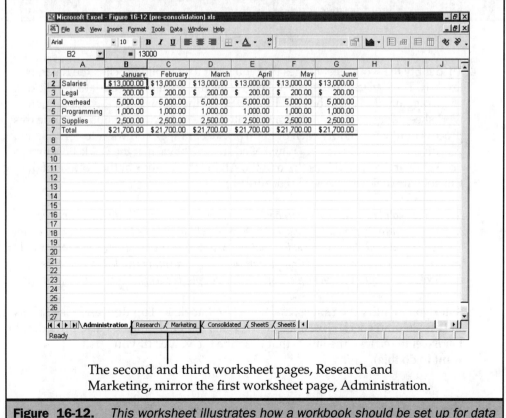

The second and third worksheet pages, Research and
Marketing, mirror the first worksheet page, Administration.

Figure 16-12.   *This worksheet illustrates how a workbook should be set up for data
consolidation to work*

Choose the mathematical operation you want Excel to perform on the consolidated data.

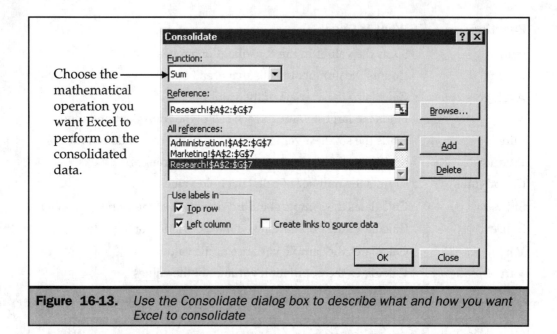

Figure 16-13. *Use the Consolidate dialog box to describe what and how you want Excel to consolidate*

4. To identify the worksheet ranges that you want to consolidate, click the Reference text box. Then select the first worksheet range you want to consolidate (by clicking and dragging) and click the Add button. Select the second and any subsequent worksheet ranges you want to consolidate in the same manner and continue this process until you identify each of the worksheet ranges you want to consolidate. As you do this, Excel creates a range of addresses for each of the worksheet ranges you select and add and lists them in the All References box at the bottom of the Consolidate dialog box. (See Figure 16-13.)

Note   *You can consolidate data from workbooks that aren't open, too. To do this, click the Browse button to display a Browse dialog box, which works like the regular Open dialog box. When you find the workbook file that you want to reference using the Browse dialog box, click OK. Excel writes the first part of the linking formula needed to reference the workbook. Note, however, that you will need to supply the worksheet name and range.*

5. After you identify the ranges, mark the Use Labels In Top Row and Use Labels In Left Column check boxes, which the Consolidate dialog box also provides, to tell Excel to retrieve the labels that describe the values (if you want to do this).

6. If you want Excel to update the information shown in the consolidation range any time data in the source worksheet ranges change, mark the Create Links To Source Data check box. This tells Excel to create linking formulas that calculate the values for the consolidation range rather than simply plopping constant values into this range. It also tells Excel to create the consolidation as an outline so you can show or hide item detail.

7. When you finish describing how and what you want Excel to consolidate, click OK. Excel consolidates the data in the ranges you specified. Figure 16-14, for example, shows the simple budgeting worksheet from Figure 16-12. It shows the company-wide budget amounts by summarizing the individual budgets for the three departments: Administrative, Marketing, and Research.

EXAMPLES

LEARN BY EXAMPLE
You can open the example Excel workbook in the Figure 16-14 (post-consolidation) file on the companion CD if you want to see a consolidated workbook.

Optimization Modeling with Solver

Optimization modeling is a sophisticated tool. What it does, in brief, is optimize a certain function subject to specified constraints. Unfortunately, the mechanics of optimization modeling are daunting to solve manually. And that's where Excel comes in: Using Excel, you can rather easily and very quickly solve optimization modeling problems.

This cell totals the values from the January Salaries budget amounts from the Administration, Research, and Marketing worksheets.

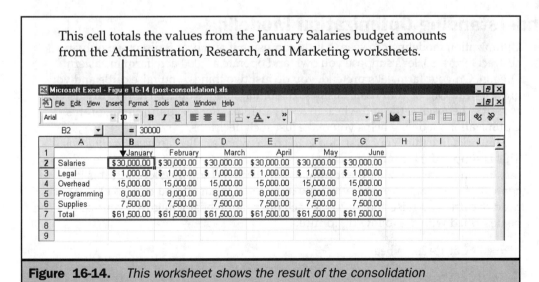

Figure 16-14. *This worksheet shows the result of the consolidation*

EXCEL

Consolidating by Position vs. Consolidating by Category

You can actually have Excel consolidate data in two ways: by position or by category. *By position* just means that you work with ranges that are all exactly the same size. *By category* means that you use the same labels to identify the rows and columns. The workbook that you see in Figure 16-12 (and again in Figure 16-14) can be consolidated either by position or by category because the source ranges are all the same size and because the labels that identify the contents of the worksheets' rows and columns are identical. But you should know that consolidating by category is usually preferable.

Category-based consolidation is more powerful because it lets you consolidate sets of data that aren't identical. In the case of the workbook shown in Figure 16-12, for example, if you budgeted a particular expense—say, legal fees—only for the Administration department and then budgeted another expense—say, programming—only for the Research department, you could still consolidate the department budgets. The consolidated data would show company-wide budgeted expenses for all the departments: both those expenses that are common across all your departments and those expenses that are unique to departments.

The trick in category-based consolidation is to use the exact same labels. If you use "Salaries" to describe the salaries expense in one department, for example, and then use "Salaries & Wages" to describe the salaries expense in another department, you'll see both expenses in the consolidated data range: "Salaries" and "Salaries & Wages."

Understanding Optimization Modeling

Optimization modeling can seem a little confusing if you hear it discussed only in abstract terms. So, let's suppose you own and operate a 5,000-acre farm in eastern Oregon. On your farm, let's pretend, you do just two things: you raise cattle and you grow wheat. One of your basic business dilemmas, then, would be how to divide your resources between cattle and wheat in a way that maximizes your farming profits. Optimization modeling helps you make just such decisions.

It works like this. Your first step is to create what's called an *objective function*. This is simply the formula that calculates some value you want to optimize either by maximizing or minimizing the formula's calculation result. But let's put this in the context of the imaginary farm you now own and operate. If you make $400 for each head of cattle you raise and $2.20 for each bushel of wheat you grow, your profits can be described with the following formula:

=400*Cattle+2.2*Wheat

So this formula is the objective function. And what you want to do, of course, is maximize your profits by raising as many head of cattle and by growing as many bushels of wheat as you can.

But, of course, there are limits to the number of cattle you can raise and the bushels of wheat you can grow. Optimization modeling incorporates these limits by way of *constraints*, which are simply formulas that describe the limits. For example, in the case of your farm, you are limited by your farm's acreage. If each head of cattle requires ten acres of land and each bushel of wheat requires at least 1/50 of an acre, ten times the number of cattle and 1/50 times the number of bushels of wheat must be less than or equal to the number of acres you farm. You can describe this constraint using the following formula:

10*Cattle+1/50*Wheat<=5000

Similarly, if you're limited to 5,000,000 gallons of water a year and each cow requires 1,500 gallons of water a year while each bushel of wheat requires 25 gallons of water, the water limit is another constraint. It can be quantified this way:

+1500*Cattle+25*Wheat<=5000000

And just for fun, let's say you have a couple of other constraints, too. For example, it may be that you must raise at least 50 head of cattle for your own needs—perhaps you have a big barbecue every Labor Day. And maybe you need to grow at least 1,000 bushels of wheat because you've contracted to supply that much to a local bakery. These limits would set other constraints on the objective function, as quantified this way:

+Cattle>=50
+Wheat>=1000

To summarize, what you really want to do is make as much money farming as you possibly can, except you can't farm more than 5,000 acres, you can't use more than 5,000,000 gallons of water, and you have to raise at least 50 head of cattle and grow at least 1,000 bushels of wheat.

You probably see the problem. Short of trial-and-error experimentation, there's no easy way to figure out the number of cattle you should raise and the bushels of wheat you should grow to make the maximum amount of profit. And that's where Solver comes in. By creating a formula that describes the objective function and formulas that quantify the constraints, Solver will tell you how to optimize the objective function. Or, restated in terms of your farm, it will tell you exactly how many head of cattle to raise and how much wheat to grow.

Using Solver

Once you understand the sorts of optimization modeling problems that Solver addresses, you'll often find it surprisingly easy to use Solver in modeling. You set up a worksheet that describes the particular optimization modeling problem you want to solve. Next, you describe to Solver how it finds the information it needs to begin its calculations. Finally, you review Solver's calculation results and, optionally, Solver's special reports.

Creating the Solver Worksheet

To use the Solver tool, your first step is to create a worksheet that names the variables of your objective function, describes the objective function, and then describes the constraints. Figure 16-15 shows a worksheet that does these three things for the example farming problem described in the preceding section. To review, that problem's objective function, which simply says your profits equal $400 times the head of cattle you raise and $2.20 times the bushels of wheat you grow, is

Profits=$400*Cattle+$2.2*Wheat

The following constraints, however, limit this objective function:

10 acres * Cattle + 1/50 acre * Wheat <= 5000 acres
1500 gallons * Cattle + 25 gallons * Wheat <= 5000000 gallons
Cattle >= 50
Wheat >= 1000

Note *Constraint formulas can be a little difficult to interpret the first time you encounter them, so a quick description is probably in order. The first constraint says that you can't farm more than 5,000 acres since that's the size of your farm. The second constraint says you can't use more than 5,000,000 gallons of water. The third constraint says you need to raise at least 50 head of cattle. And the fourth constraint says you need to grow at least 1,000 bushels of wheat.*

You'll need a worksheet like the one shown in Figure 16-15 to provide the information that the Solver needs. If you want to build the worksheet yourself, enter the labels shown in the range A1:A11. Next, enter the values shown in cells B2 and B3. (To start, it really doesn't matter which values you enter here. Typically, however, these represent your best guesses as to which modeling variable values are optimal.) Next, name cell B2 Cattle and cell B3 Wheat.

Tip *The easiest way to name the cells is to select the range A2:B3, choose Insert | Name | Create and then click OK.*

To describe the objective function, enter the formula **=400*Cattle+2.2*Wheat** into cell B5. Excel's Solver will look for the modeling variable values that optimize—in this case, maximize—the calculation result this formula returns.

EXAMPLES

LEARN BY EXAMPLE

You can open the example Excel workbook in the Figure 16-15 (pre-optimization) file on the companion CD if you want to perform optimization modeling without actually constructing the workbook shown in Figure 16-15 yourself.

Your next step is to describe the constraints that limit the number of cattle you raise and the amount of wheat you grow. To describe the acreage constraint, for example, enter the following formula into cell B8:

=10*Cattle+1/50*Wheat

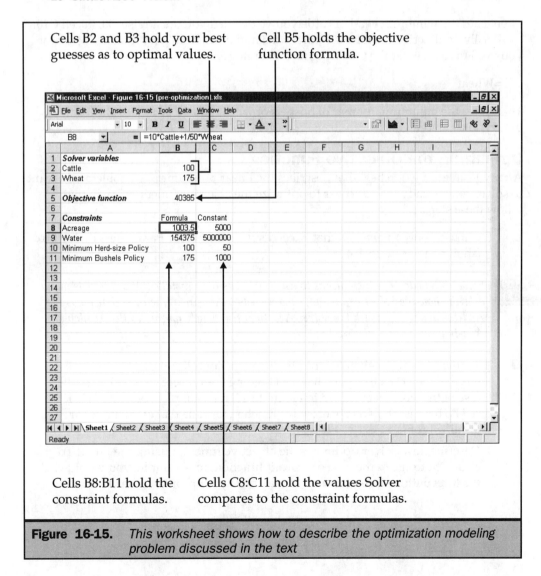

Cells B2 and B3 hold your best guesses as to optimal values.

Cell B5 holds the objective function formula.

Cells B8:B11 hold the constraint formulas.

Cells C8:C11 hold the values Solver compares to the constraint formulas.

Figure 16-15. *This worksheet shows how to describe the optimization modeling problem discussed in the text*

Then enter the number of acres, **5000**, into cell C8.

To describe the formula part of the water constraint, enter the following formula into cell B9:

=1500*Cattle+25*Wheat

Then enter the gallons of water, **5000000**, into cell C9.

To describe the formula part of the minimum-herd-size constraint, enter the following formula in cell B10:

=Cattle

Then enter the minimum head of cattle you've decided you must raise, **50**, in cell C10.

Finally, to describe the formula part of the minimum number of bushels of wheat you need to raise, enter the following formula into cell B11:

=Wheat

Then enter the minimum number of bushels of wheat you've promised the local bakery, **1000**, in cell C11.

Optimizing the Objective Function

After you create a worksheet that describes the linear programming problem you want to solve, you're ready to use Solver to optimize the objective function. To do this, follow these steps:

1. Choose Tools | Solver so that Excel displays the Solver Parameters dialog box (shown in Figure 16-16).

Note   *Solver is an add-in, which means to use it, it needs to be installed. If your Tools menu doesn't show the Solver command, choose Tools | Add-Ins. When Excel displays the Add-Ins dialog box, mark the Solver Add-In entry, which appears in the Available Add-Ins box. Then click OK.*

2. To identify which cell holds the objective function, click the Set Target Cell box and then click the worksheet cell holding your objective function. In the case of the worksheet shown in Figure 16-15, for example, you would click cell B5 because it holds the objective function formula that calculates your farming profits.

3. Describe how Solver optimizes the objective function using the Equal To option buttons. In the case of a profit function, for example, you would click the Max button since you want to maximize your profits. If the objective

Use the Equal To option buttons set to describe how you want to optimize the objective function. ——————

The Set Target Cell text box identifies which cell holds the objective function.

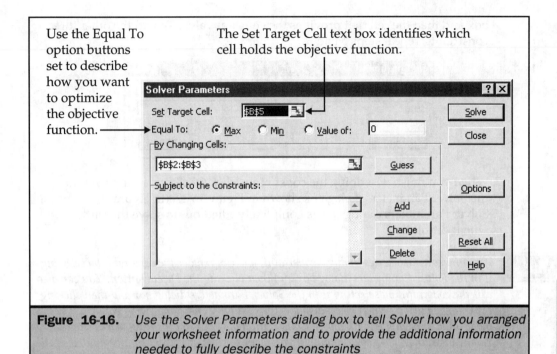

Figure 16-16.   *Use the Solver Parameters dialog box to tell Solver how you arranged your worksheet information and to provide the additional information needed to fully describe the constraints*

function instead described costs you wanted to minimize, you would mark the Min button. And if your objective function needs to return a specific value, mark the Value Of button and then enter the value using the Value Of box.

4. Identify the cells Solver should adjust to optimize the objective function. (In the discussion that follows, these are called the *adjustable cells*.) In the case of the cattle vs. wheat problem described in this chapter, you need to identify which adjustable cell holds the number of cattle you're supposed to be raising and which adjustable cell holds the bushels of wheat you're supposed to be growing. To do this, click the By Changing Cells text box and click each of the adjustable cells. (In Figure 16-15, for example, you would click cells B2 and B3.)

5. Click the Add button to begin identifying the constraints.

6. When Excel displays the Add Constraint dialog box (shown next), first click the Cell Reference box and then click the cell holding the formula part of a constraint. Next, use the Constraint drop-down list box to select the comparison operator that compares the formula to the constant value. Finally, click the Constraint

box and then the cell that provides the constant value. To add the other three constraints, repeat steps 5 and 6.

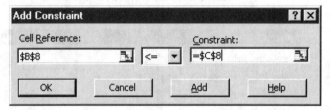

7. When you finish describing the constraints, click OK. Excel returns you to the Solver Parameters dialog box shown in Figure 16-17. (In Figure 16-17, the Solver Parameters dialog box is completely filled out to solve the cattle vs. wheat problem.)

Note   *If you make a mistake describing a constraint, you can remove the constraint by selecting it in the Solver Parameters dialog box and then clicking the Delete button. You can also edit the constraint by selecting it in the Solver Parameters dialog box and then clicking the Change button. When Excel displays the Change Constraint dialog box, you use it to modify the constraint. The Change Constraint dialog box, by the way, works like the Add Constraint dialog box. Finally, if you want to start over from scratch and erase all of your inputs—the Set Target Cell and By Changing Cells settings, and the constraints—click the Reset All button.*

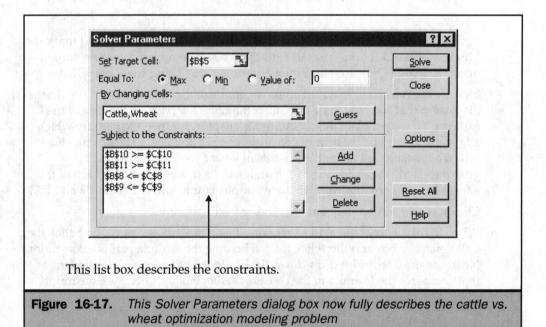

This list box describes the constraints.

Figure 16-17.   *This Solver Parameters dialog box now fully describes the cattle vs. wheat optimization modeling problem*

8. After you specify your constraints, click Solve. Excel attempts to optimize the objective function. If it can, it displays the Solver Results dialog box shown here. It gives you the option of replacing the original values in the adjustable cells with the optimal values that Excel calculates. Or you can restore the original values you entered into the adjustable cells.

Click this button to have Solver replace the current contents of the adjustable cells.

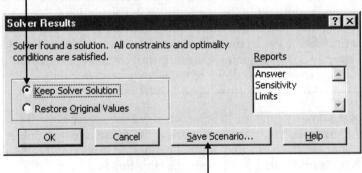

Click this button to create a scenario for the optimal values.

9. When you click OK, Solver replaces the values you originally used as the starting variable values.

Figure 16-18 shows the solution to the cattle vs. wheat problem. Cell B2 holds the value 113.6364, indicating the optimal number of cattle to raise is between 113 and 114. Cell B3 holds the value 193181.9, indicating that the optimal bushels of wheat to raise is roughly 193,182. If you really were a farmer, you would presumably convert this bushels-of-wheat figure into an acres-planted-in-wheat figure. This means that you would plant 3,864 acres of wheat since, according to our worksheet model, you get 50 bushels of wheat per acre.

EXAMPLES

LEARN BY EXAMPLE
You can open the example Excel workbook in the Figure 16-18 (post-optimization) file on the companion CD if you want to see an optimized workbook.

Using Solver's Reports

Knowing which combination of adjustable cell values causes your objective function to return its optimal value is interesting. But if you begin to use the Solver tool, you'll quickly find yourself interested in digging deeper into the details of the optimal solution.

Using Integer Constraints

It may be that as another constraint you want the objective function to return integers (whole numbers) to the adjustable cells. In the case of the cattle vs. wheat problem, for example, you might want to verify that Solver returns the optimal number of cattle and the optimal bushels of wheat as integer values. To make this specification, you create an integer constraint using "int" as the constraint operator and "integer" as the constraint formula result.

Although integer constraints make theoretical sense in many cases, they also make it much more difficult for Solver to finish its calculations. For this reason, you may choose to accept noninteger values in the adjustable cells—even though they don't make practical sense. In the case of the cattle vs. wheat problem, for example, you might happily accept a noninteger number of cattle as part of your optimal solution and then round up or down to the next, nearest integer.

You may want to know by how much Solver changed the adjustable cell values you started with, for example. You may want to know the extent to which Solver improved the result that your objective function originally returned. And you'll certainly want to know which constraints limit, or bind, your objective function.

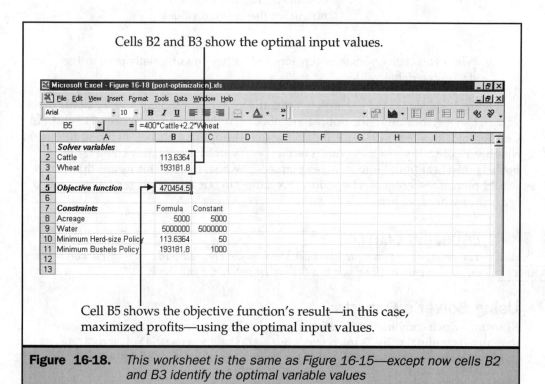

Cells B2 and B3 show the optimal input values.

Cell B5 shows the objective function's result—in this case, maximized profits—using the optimal input values.

Figure 16-18.   *This worksheet is the same as Figure 16-15—except now cells B2 and B3 identify the optimal variable values*

To gain these insights, you can tell Solver to prepare special reports that provide this information. To do this, use the Solver Results dialog box shown previously. Simply click the reports you want in the Reports box. When you click OK to close the Solver Results dialog box, Excel not only updates the values in the adjustable cells, it also adds new worksheet pages to your workbook. Figure 16-19 shows the Answer Report, which is probably the most useful report that Solver prepares.

At the top of the Answer Report, for example, Solver shows the values the target cell returned before and after Solver optimized the objective function. If the initial values in the adjustable cells reflect your plans before running Solver, this change in the target value information lets you see what improvement, if any, Solver has been able to suggest. Solver also reports on how the values in the adjustable cells changed after you used Solver to optimize the function.

You can tell by how much Solver improved your objective function by comparing cells D8 and E8.

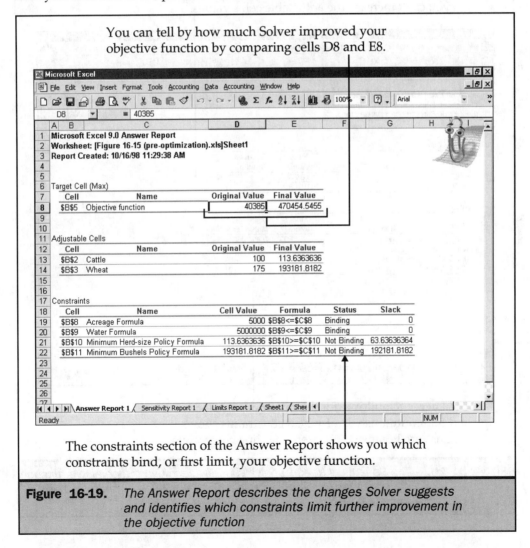

The constraints section of the Answer Report shows you which constraints bind, or first limit, your objective function.

Figure 16-19.   *The Answer Report describes the changes Solver suggests and identifies which constraints limit further improvement in the objective function*

At the bottom of the Answer Report, Solver identifies those that have no effect on the objective function as "nonbinding" and those that have an effect as "binding." In Figure 16-19, for example, both the acreage and the water constraints limit the objective function. (What this means, practically speaking, is that if you wanted in this example to increase your profits, you would need both more water and more land first.)

Figure 16-20 shows another of Solver's reports, the Sensitivity Report. For the adjustable cells, it shows the final, optimal values and something called the reduced gradient. The *reduced gradient* shows you how much the objective function's result would change if the adjustable cell's value increased by one. (In the cattle vs. wheat

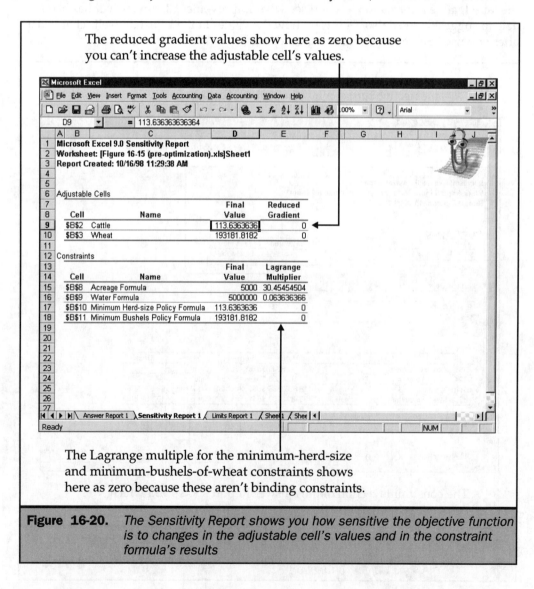

 The reduced gradient values show here as zero because you can't increase the adjustable cell's values.

The Lagrange multiple for the minimum-herd-size and minimum-bushels-of-wheat constraints shows here as zero because these aren't binding constraints.

Figure 16-20.   *The Sensitivity Report shows you how sensitive the objective function is to changes in the adjustable cell's values and in the constraint formula's results*

problem, for example, it shows how much your farming profit increases if you raise one more cow or grow one more bushel of wheat.) For the constraints, the Sensitivity Report shows the final values of the constraint formulas and something called the Lagrange multiple. The *Lagrange multiple* shows you how much the objective function's result would change if the constraint formula's result increased by one. (In the cattle vs. wheat problem, for example, it shows how much your farming profit changes if you have one more acre of land, one more gallon or water, and so forth.)

The Limits Report, shown in Figure 16-21, is the final report. It shows you how much the values in your adjustable cells can change without bumping up against your constraints.

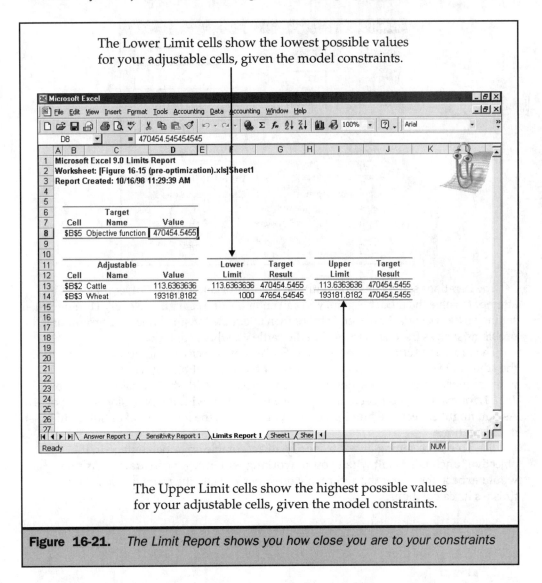

The Lower Limit cells show the lowest possible values for your adjustable cells, given the model constraints.

The Upper Limit cells show the highest possible values for your adjustable cells, given the model constraints.

Figure 16-21. *The Limit Report shows you how close you are to your constraints*

Fine-Tuning Solver's Operation

If you take a peek back at Figure 16-17, you'll notice that the Solver Parameters dialog box provides an Options button. You can click this button to display the Solver Options dialog box, shown here. It lets you fine-tune the way Solver works. For example, the Max Time setting lets you place a limit on the time Solver takes to solve some problem.

The initial Max Time setting is 100 seconds, but you can set a Max Time value up to 32,767 seconds (which is slightly more than nine hours).

```
Solver Options                                    ? X

Max Time:        100      seconds       OK

Iterations:      100                     Cancel

Precision:       0.000001               Load Model...

Tolerance:       5          %           Save Model...

Convergence:     0.001                  Help

    Assume Linear Model         Use Automatic Scaling
    Assume Non-Negative         Show Iteration Results
   Estimates          Derivatives         Search
    Tangent            Forward            Newton
    Quadratic          Central            Conjugate
```

The Iterations setting lets you limit the number of calculations Solver makes in its attempt to solve the model. Again, you can enter a value as high as 32,767. The suggested setting of 100 seconds, however, is more than adequate for small linear programming problems such as the one discussed in the cattle vs. wheat scenario.

The Precision setting, of course, tells Solver how precise it should be in calculating the adjustable cell values. You can specify a precision setting anywhere from 0 to 1, with smaller values representing increased precision. With the precision setting of .00001, for example, you get a more precise result than with the precision setting of .01. As you might expect, the more precision you require, the longer it takes Solver to finish its calculations.

The Tolerance setting lets you specify an acceptable error percentage in the objective function's result when you're working with integer constraints. As you would expect, the larger the acceptable error percentage, the more quickly Solver finishes its calculations.

In addition to those settings already discussed, Solver provides several other options you can use to exert even more control over the way Solver works and to solve more complex and much larger optimization modeling problems: Assume Linear Model, Use Automatic Scaling, Assume Non-Negative, Show Iteration Results, Estimates, Derivatives, and Search. Discussion of these options reaches far beyond the scope of this book. (If you want to learn more about linear programming, consult an upper-division or graduate-level operations research text such as *Operations Research, Applications, and Algorithms,* by Wayne L. Winston (Boston: PWS-Kent Publishing Co., 1991).

EXCEL

The Complete Reference

Office 2000

Part IV

Microsoft PowerPoint

Chapter 17

Creating a PowerPoint Presentation

This chapter is the first in Part IV, which explains how to use Microsoft PowerPoint, Office 2000's presentation program. To borrow a term from the classroom, PowerPoint is an audiovisual program. Use it to present ideas, sales pitches, budgets, plans—you name it—to groups of people.

In PowerPoint, you create what the program calls *slides*, but don't be confused by that term. A slide is simply an image. Yes, you can take the files you create with PowerPoint to the local graphics shop and turn them into slides or overhead transparencies, but that isn't absolutely necessary because PowerPoint slides can be shown on computer screens.

This chapter starts by explaining how to create what PowerPoint calls a presentation. A *presentation* is a series of slides whose goal is to dazzle or persuade an audience. As you will see shortly, PowerPoint offers many predesigned presentations. You don't have to be an artist to create a professional-looking presentation with this program. If you are not the adventurous kind or if you are in a hurry, you can create a "paint by numbers" presentation in a matter of minutes.

Besides showing you how to create a presentation, this chapter explores different ways of viewing your work, and explains how to enter and format text on the slides.

Creating a Presentation

PowerPoint offers no less than three ways to create a presentation: from a template, with the AutoContent Wizard, or from scratch. All three techniques are described on the following pages.

When you use a template or design a presentation with the AutoContent Wizard, you end up with a generic presentation complete with headings, text, and a full-fledged design. All you have to do is replace the generic headings and text with headings and text of your own. And you might have to remove or add a slide or two, of course.

What Is the Best Way to Create a Presentation?

All the techniques for creating a presentation have advantages and disadvantages. With the AutoContent Wizard, you get PowerPoint's help in deciding which design is the best for you—but you don't see the design until the presentation has been created. With a template, on the other hand, you get to see the design from the get-go—but PowerPoint offers no advice about which design is best. Both AutoContent and template presentations come with generic text and titles that you can use as a starting point for your own text and titles.

Whatever you do, don't worry about creating a perfect presentation the first time around. PowerPoint gives you ample opportunities to change a presentation's design, as well as add and remove slides.

Figure 17-1 shows the dialog box you see when you start PowerPoint. From here, you can create a presentation or open a presentation you have already created. Read on for the dirty details.

Creating a Template with the AutoContent Wizard

The quickest way to create a presentation, especially for new users and users in a hurry, is to use the AutoContent Wizard. The AutoContent Wizard asks a series of questions about the purpose of your presentation, what you want to communicate, and by what means you will present it. On the basis of the answers you give, it chooses a design for the slides and provides generic headings and text.

Follow these steps to create a PowerPoint presentation with the AutoContent Wizard:

1. From the PowerPoint dialog box (see Figure 17-1), click the AutoContent Wizard option button, if necessary, and then click OK. You see the following dialog box. In the course of choosing a presentation with the AutoContent Wizard, you will be asked questions about the presentation type, presentation style, and presentation options.

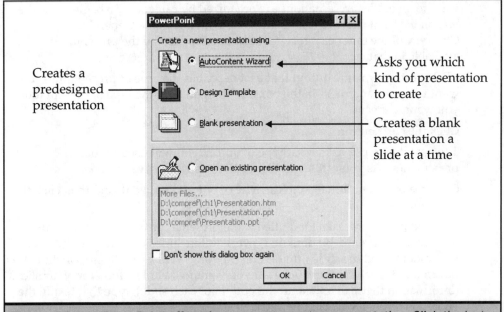

Figure 17-1.   *PowerPoint offers three ways to create a presentation. Click the last radio button or choose File | Open to open a presentation on which you have been working*

POWERPOINT

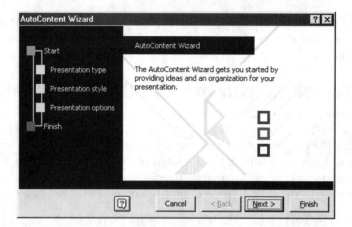

    If the PowerPoint dialog box isn't onscreen, you can still create a presentation with the AutoContent Wizard by choosing File | New, clicking the General tab in the New Presentation dialog box, and double-clicking the AutoContent Wizard icon.

2. Click the Next button. The next dialog box asks what kind of presentation you want to give. The presentations are organized by category. To begin with, the box on the right shows the presentations available in the General category. Click any of the other category name buttons to display the presentations available in that category.

3. Click a category name button that best describes the type of presentation you want to create, and then, in the box on the right, click the type of presentation you want to create.

4. Click the Next button.

   The next dialog box asks what type of output you will use for your presentation. As you can see in Figure 17-2, you have five options.

5. Click the option button next to the type of output you want, and then click the Next button.

6. The next dialog box asks for a title for the presentation and what you want to include on each slide. By default, PowerPoint includes the date the slide was last updated and the slide number. If you don't want your slides to include this information, uncheck these boxes. If you want to include a footer in your slides (information that will appear at the bottom of each slide), type that text in the Footer box. When you're done, click Next.

7. Click Finish to display the first slide that you and the AutoContent Wizard have just created.

8. Choose File | Save or click the Save button to save the new presentation.

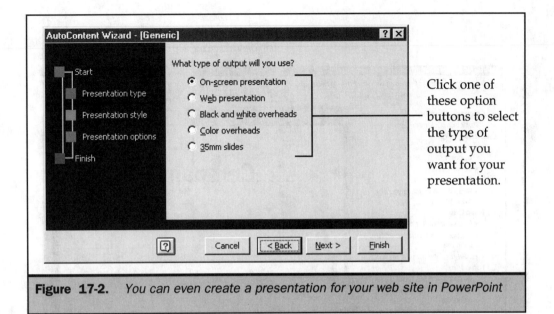

Figure 17-2.   *You can even create a presentation for your web site in PowerPoint*

Figure 17-3 shows the new presentation in Normal view. You can also display the presentation in four other views, and we'll look at all of them in detail in the section "Ways of Viewing and Working on Slides." To add content to your presentation slide by slide, click on a topic on the left to display that slide, and then enter your information in the slide on the right.

Creating a Presentation with a Template

A template does what the AutoContent Wizard does, only it does it in a shorter time. When you create a presentation with a template, you end up with a predesigned bunch of slides and generic text like that in Figure 17-3. The difference is, the presentation is created very quickly. PowerPoint doesn't query you to find out what kind of presentation you want to create. All you do is review choices on the Presentations tab of the New Presentations dialog box, click the presentation you want, and click OK.

HEADSTART
On the companion CD that comes with this book are about two dozen templates for creating PowerPoint presentations. Besides the templates that come with Office 2000, you can use these templates, as well. See Appendix E for information.

POWERPOINT

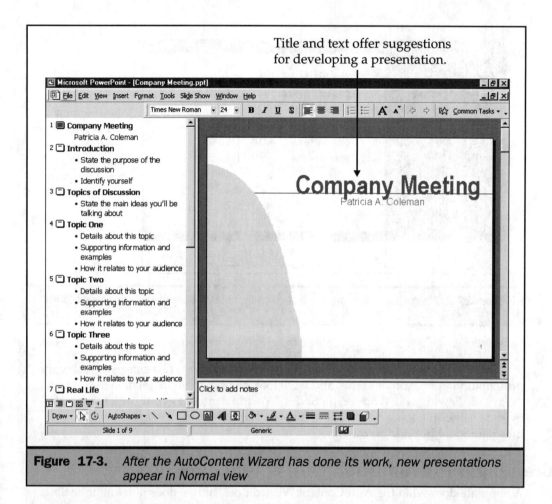

Figure 17-3.   *After the AutoContent Wizard has done its work, new presentations appear in Normal view*

To create a PowerPoint presentation from a template, follow these steps:

1. In the PowerPoint dialog box that you see when you start the program, click the Design Template option button and then click OK. You see the New Presentation dialog box.

Tip   *You can create a presentation from a template without starting from the PowerPoint dialog box. To do so, choose File | New. Click the Presentations tab. It is shown in Figure 17-4.*

2. Read the names of the icons to find the one that best describes the kind of presentation you want to create, then click the icon and look in the Preview box.

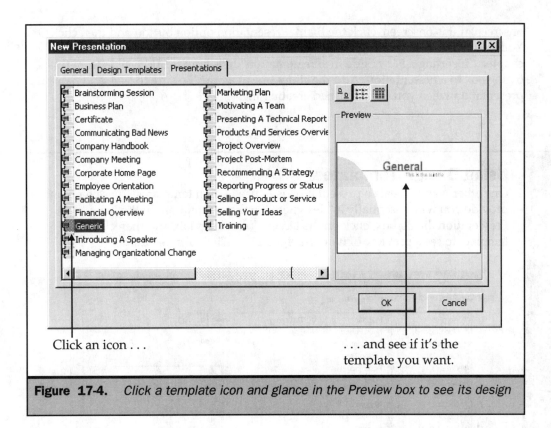

Click an icon . . .   . . . and see if it's the
                                                        template you want.

Figure 17-4.   *Click a template icon and glance in the Preview box to see its design*

Click as many icons as you like until you find one that does the job. Click OK
when you've found a suitable presentation. The title slide of the presentation
appears onscreen. Your presentation will look something like Figure 17-3.

3. Save and name your presentation.

See "Ways of Viewing and Working on Slides," later in this chapter, to learn
how to enter your own text in place of the generic headings and text that appear in
the presentation. Notice that the generic text offers suggestions for developing a
presentation.

Creating a Presentation from Scratch

Yet another way to create a presentation is to create it from the ground up. With this
technique, you add one slide at a time to the presentation.

To create a slide presentation without any help from a template or the AutoContent
Wizard, click the New button if the PowerPoint dialog box (see Figure 17-1) is not

POWERPOINT

onscreen; if it is onscreen, click the Blank Presentation option button and then click OK. You see the New Slide dialog box with its 12 so-called AutoLayouts. Later in this chapter, "Inserting a New Slide in a Presentation" tells how to add a slide from this dialog box to a presentation. Add the slides one at a time. Be sure to save and name the presentation when you have finished creating it.

Using Design Templates

One other way to create a presentation is to use Design templates. These templates provide you with essentially a "designer" blank presentation. In the New Presentation dialog box, click on the Design Templates tab, and then click a template to see a preview of it on the right. Dads Tie looks like this:

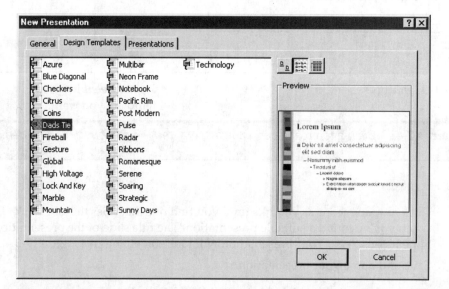

Not all these templates are installed when you install Office 2000. If you click a template that is not installed, simply select it and click OK to install it. (You'll need to insert your Office 2000 CD.)

When you find a template you like, click OK. You'll see the same New Slide dialog box and its layout options that you see when creating a blank presentation. Select a layout and click OK to display your "designer" blank presentation.

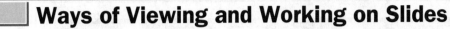

Ways of Viewing and Working on Slides

One of the hardest things to do when you create a presentation is get a fix on how it is taking shape. When you concentrate on the slides' appearance, it is easy to lose sight of a spelling or grammar error. And when you concentrate on the text, it is easy to lose sight of the slides' appearance. For that reason, PowerPoint offers a number of different ways to view the slides in a presentation. You can view them one at a time, view several at once, view one in excruciating detail, or focus on the text in the presentation.

Figure 17-5 shows the five views of a presentation: Normal view, Outline view, Slide view, Slide Sorter view, and Slide Show view. To change views, either click one of the view button in the lower-left corner of the screen or choose an option from the View menu (press ESC to leave Slide Show view). Table 17-1 compares and contrasts the different ways of viewing slides.

LEARN BY EXAMPLE
To explore the different ways of viewing PowerPoint presentations, open the Figure 17-5 (views) file on the companion CD.

View	Description
Normal	Shows all aspects of your presentation. From this view, you can work on content and appearance. To adjust the size of the panes, drag their borders.
Outline	Shows the text in the presentation. From this view, you can focus on the presentation's content. Good for entering and editing text.
Slide	Shows a single slide. Good for laying out text and importing clip art images.
Slide Sorter	Shows several slides at once (to see more or fewer slides, choose View | Zoom and select a percentage). Good for moving and deleting slides.
Slide Show	Shows a single slide that fills the entire screen. This is what the slide looks like in a presentation. Good for dress-rehearsing a presentation.

Table 17-1. *Ways of Viewing a Presentation*

POWERPOINT

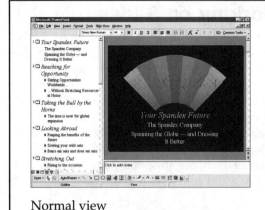

Normal view

Outline view

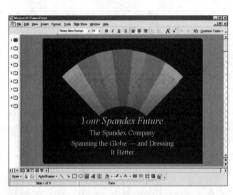

Slide view

Slide Sorter view

Slide Show view

Figure 17-5.   *The five presentation views*

Inserting, Deleting, Rearranging, and Copying Slides

At some point or other, as your presentation takes shape and you sculpt it into a masterpiece, you have to add and remove slides. When you add a slide, you have the choice of adding one of PowerPoint's 12 preformatted slides, called AutoLayouts. You can save a lot of work by choosing a preformatted slide. PowerPoint offers preformatted charts and organization charts, preformatted bulleted lists, boxes for importing clip art, and preformatted tables.

LEARN BY EXAMPLE
To practice inserting and deleting slides, open the Figure 17-A (add and remove) file on the companion CD.

Inserting a New Slide in a Presentation

Follow these steps to insert a slide in a presentation:

1. Switch to Slide Sorter view by clicking the Slide Sorter View button in the lower-left corner of the screen or by choosing View | Slide Sorter.

2. Click where the new slide is to go in the presentation. If you've noticed, slides are numbered in Slide Sorter view. Click to the right of slide 4, for example, to place a new slide between slides 4 and 5. To get to the slides at the end of a presentation, click the down arrow on the scroll bar.

3. Click the Common Tasks button and choose New Slide, press CTRL-M, or choose Insert | New Slide. You see the New Slide dialog box shown in Figure 17-6.

4. Click the kind of slide you want to insert. The box in the lower-right corner of the dialog box describes the slide that has been selected. The slide in the lower-right corner is a blank slide.

5. Click OK.

Deleting a Slide from a Presentation

To delete a slide, do it from Slide Sorter, Outline, or Normal view:

■ **In Slide Sorter View**   Click the slide. A black box appears around the slide to show it has been selected. Press the DELETE key.

To select more than one slide in Slide Sorter view, hold down the SHIFT key and start clicking on the slides you want to select.

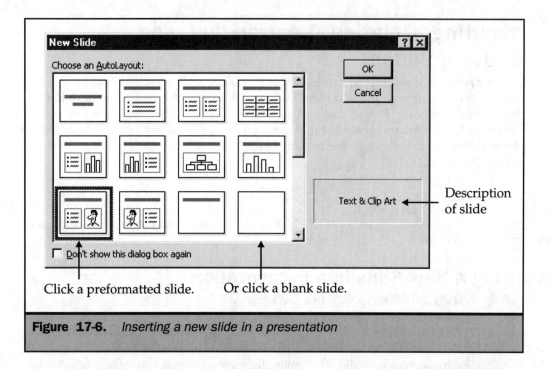

Click a preformatted slide.   Or click a blank slide.

Figure 17-6.   *Inserting a new slide in a presentation*

■ **In Outline View or Normal View**   Click on a slide icon, the small square to the left of the slide. When you do so, all the text in the slide is highlighted, as the following illustration shows. Next, press the DELETE key. (If clip art images or note pages are attached to the slide, PowerPoint informs you by way of a message box that you are about to delete them as well. Click OK.)

Rearranging the Slides

To move a slide to a new place in a presentation, you can start from Slide Sorter view, Outline view, or Normal view:

- **In Slide Sorter View**   Click the slide you want to move and start dragging. A vertical line appears to show where the slide will land when you release the mouse button. Release the mouse button when the slide is where you want it to be.

- **In Outline View or Normal View**   As shown in Figure 17-7, click the Collapse All button on the Outlining toolbar to see only the title for each slide. Next, click on the icon of the slide you want to move. The title is highlighted to show that the slide has been selected. Click the Move Up or Move Down button on the Outline toolbar.

 To display the Outlining toolbar, choose View | Toolbars, and check Outlining.

Copying a Slide

Follow these steps to copy a slide:

1. Switch to Slide Sorter view.

2. Right-click on the slide you want to copy and choose Copy from the shortcut menu.

3. Click between slides in the presentation where the copy of the slide is to go.

4. Right-click and choose Paste from the shortcut menu.

POWERPOINT

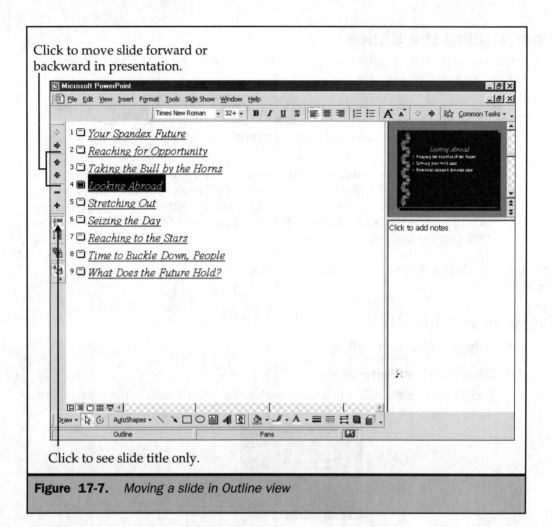

Figure 17-7.   *Moving a slide in Outline view*

Entering and Formatting the Text

Besides the standard Font and Font Size commands that can be found in all Office 2000 programs, PowerPoint offers a couple of amenities of its own for formatting text. This section explains how to enter, edit, and format text. It explains how to align text on slides and control the amount of space between lines. And you also find instructions for moving from slide to slide in the different views and importing text from a Word document.

Writing the Words on the Slides

With PowerPoint, you can fool your colleagues and business associates into thinking that you are a layout artist. The program offers many easy-to-use tools for doing that, and you can select a presentation template to help you with the content. The following pages offer advice for entering the text. They also explain how to keep speaker's notes for each slide so that you remember what to say at presentations as each slide appears onscreen. And you will also find a neat trick for using the headings in a Word document for the titles and text in a PowerPoint presentation.

Words on the slides in a presentation are like headings in a document—they announce the topic, they don't explain it in detail. You, as the speaker, fill in the details. Slides with a lot of text on them annoy the audience. Text on slides should be short, sweet, and to the point.

LEARN BY EXAMPLE
To practice entering the text for a presentation, open the Figure 17-8 (enter text) file on the companion CD.

Entering the Text in Normal and Outline Views

To enter text in Normal view or Outline view, choose the appropriate command from the View menu or click the appropriate View button in the lower-left corner of the screen. If you used a template or the AutoContent Wizard to create your presentation, replace the text that is already there with text of your own. If you are working with a blank slide, simply type the text you want to appear on the slide. To help you stay focused, display the Outlining toolbar on the left side of the screen. It offers a number of handy buttons. The buttons are explained in Table 17-2 and labeled in Figure 17-8. To display the Outlining toolbar, right-click a toolbar, and choose Outlining from the shortcut menu.

Which Is the Best Way to Enter the Text?

The best way to enter text depends on how you created your presentation. If you used a template or the AutoContent Wizard, PowerPoint has provided "placeholder text" and all you have to do is switch to Outline view or Normal view and replace PowerPoint's text with your own. You can enter text easily in either Normal view or Outline view.

In both views, you can read the headings and text on slides. And the Outlining toolbar offers several buttons to help with entering text. Another way to enter the text is to get it from a Word document. PowerPoint offers a special command for importing the headings from a Word document and using them for the slide titles and text in a PowerPoint presentation. Read on for the details.

POWERPOINT

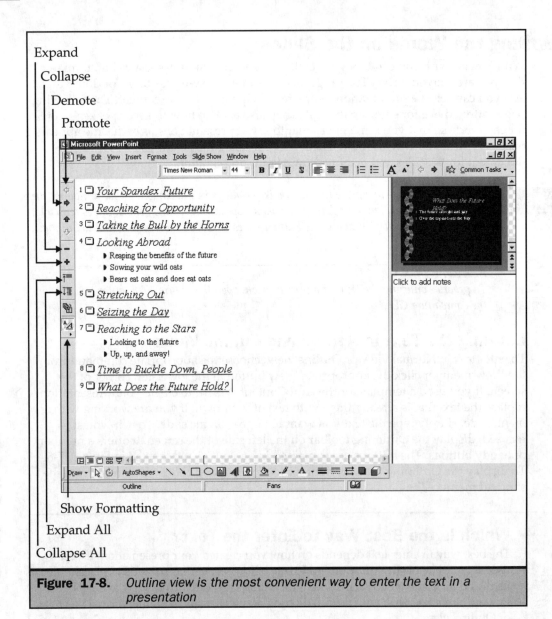

Figure 17-8. Outline view is the most convenient way to enter the text in a presentation

Button	What It Does
Promote	Moves a subheading or bulleted point in a slide up one heading level. For example, if you click on a subheading below the first heading on a slide and then click the Promote button, the subheading becomes a first heading and therefore becomes the first heading in a brand-new slide.
Demote	Moves a title, subheading, or bulleted point down one heading level in the hierarchy.
Move Up	Moves a selected heading or subheading up a line in the outline.
Move Down	Moves a selected heading or subheading down a line in the outline.
Collapse	Shows only the first heading in a slide. Click on a first heading and then click this button if you only want to see the first heading.
Expand	Shows all the subheadings under the first heading in a slide.
Collapse All	Shows only the first heading of each slide in the entire presentation.
Expand All	Shows all the text in all the slides in the presentation.
Summary Slide	Creates a new slide from selected titles, placing them in a bulleted list, and inserts the slide before the first selected slide.
Show Formatting	Shows/hides the font formatting when working in Outline view.

Table 17-2. *The Outlining Toolbar Buttons*

POWERPOINT

Entering Text—and Text Boxes—in Slide View

When you insert a new slide in a presentation and choose an AutoLayout for the new slide (see "Inserting a New Slide in a Presentation," earlier in this chapter), PowerPoint provides text boxes for entering the text. As Figure 17-9 shows, all you have to do is switch to Slide view, click in a text box, and start typing to enter a title or text for the new slide.

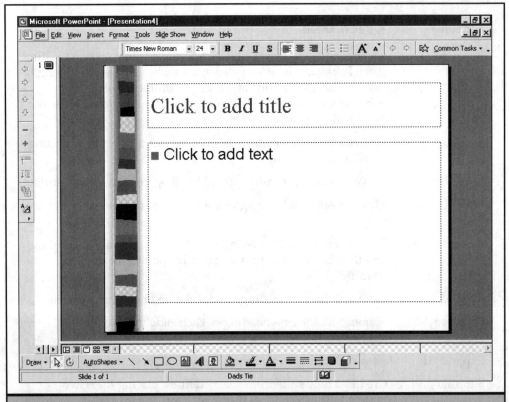

Figure 17-9. *To enter a title or text on the next slide, click the text and then type*

For blank slides, however, you have to create a text box yourself before you can enter the text if you want to work in Slide view. Follow these steps to create a text box and enter text inside it:

1. Switch to Slide view.

 It's better to work in Outline view on a blank slide. That way, you don't have to go through the trouble of creating a text box.

2. Choose Insert | Text Box. The pointer changes into an arrow that points down.

3. Click in what is to be one corner of the text box, and then drag across the slide. A box appears to show roughly how big the text box will be when you release the mouse button.

4. Release the mouse button when the text box is the right size.

5. Enter the text. As Figure 17-10 shows, the text box gets larger to accommodate the text you enter.

 Tip   *To reposition a text box, move the pointer over the perimeter. When the pointer changes into a four-headed arrow, click and drag the text box to a new location.*

Importing the Text from a Word Document

Personally, I think the easiest way to enter the text for a slide presentation is to simply get it from a Word 2000 document. PowerPoint offers a special command for doing just that: the Insert menu's Slides from Outline command. If you think about it, headings in a Word document are very much like text in a presentation—headings hit the high points and announce the topic that is under review.

To insert headings from a Word document, you must have assigned styles to the headings (styles are explained in Chapter 9). As Figure 17-11 shows, headings assigned

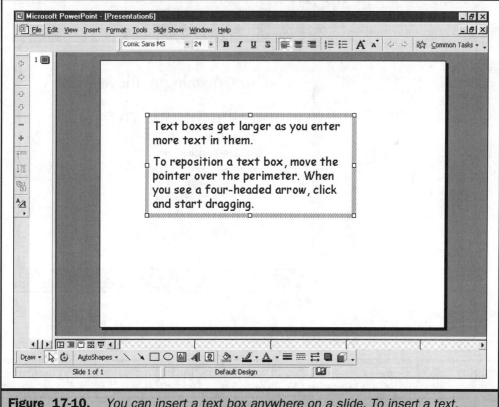

Figure 17-10.   *You can insert a text box anywhere on a slide. To insert a text, choose Insert | Text Box*

the Heading 1 style become slide titles in a presentation; all headings beyond Heading 2 headings are put in bulleted lists, with each kind of heading—Heading 3, 4, and so on—indented farther form the left margin. PowerPoint ignores text that wasn't assigned a heading style and does not bring it into the presentation along with the headings. In Figure 17-11, the Word document is shown in Outline view. You can see what happened to the headings when they were turned into a PowerPoint slide by looking on the right side of the figure. PowerPoint creates one slide for each Heading 1 in the Word document.

Follow these steps to use the headings from a Word document in a PowerPoint presentation:

1. Either create a new Word document and write the headings or open the Word document whose headings you want for a PowerPoint presentation.

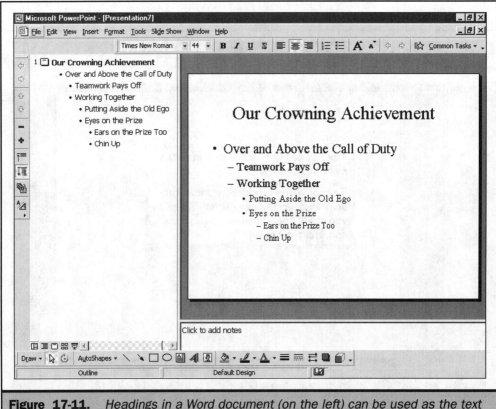

Figure 17-11. *Headings in a Word document (on the left) can be used as the text in a PowerPoint slide (on the right)*

2. Choose View | Outline to see the headings only.

3. If necessary, write or edit the headings. Be sure to assign a heading style to each one.

4. Save the document.

5. Switch to PowerPoint and either create a new presentation or place the cursor at the point in a presentation where you want to import headings from the Word document.

6. Choose Insert | Slides from Outline. You see the Insert Outline dialog box.

7. Find and click on the Word document whose headings you want to import.

8. Click the Insert button.

Note   *The first time you insert a Word document into a PowerPoint slide, PowerPoint will need to install a converter so that it can convert the file to a format that PowerPoint can use. You'll be asked to insert your Office 2000 CD.*

Writing the Words You Will Speak at the Presentation

Nobody wants to commit a gaffe during a presentation, so PowerPoint gives you the opportunity to write note pages. Note pages are notes on the slides, or the text of a presentation, or whatever will help you most when it comes time to deliver your little masterpiece. Viewers of the presentation don't see the note pages.

As Figure 17-12 shows, the note page for each slide is saved with an image of the slide itself. You can print note pages and read from them or refer to them during presentations. Be sure to be clear and grammatical if you intend to print and distribute your note pages. Don't embarrass yourself by subjecting others to a poorly written collection of sorry notes.

Follow these steps to record notes about a slide:

1. Select the slide in whatever view you happen to be in.

2. Choose View | Notes Page. You see the slide and, below it, a blank page.

3. Choose View | Zoom, and choose 66% or 100% to see what you type more clearly.

4. Click in the text box at the bottom of the page and type your notes. You can call on all the text-formatting commands as you do so.

Tip   *Use the scroll bar to get from slide to slide in Notes Page view.*

POWERPOINT

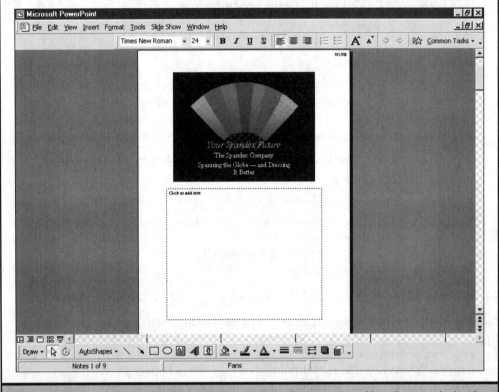

Figure 17-12. *Viewers can't see notes pages—but you can. Use them to help give the presentation*

Formatting the Text on Slides

Most of the common Office tools described in Part I of this book also work for formatting text on a slide. The techniques for choosing a font are the same in Word as PowerPoint, for example. Both programs have a Bullets button. The Align buttons work the same as the Align buttons in Excel.

More so than the other programs in Office 2000, however, PowerPoint presentations are meant to be seen and not read. Therefore, the program offers buttons that you can click to change font sizes and line spacing by increments and "eyeball" the text to make sure it looks right. As shown in Figure 17-13, select the text whose font size or line spacing you want to change and then click these buttons:

- Increase Paragraph Spacing or Decrease Paragraph Spacing to increase or decrease the amount of space that appears between lines. These buttons are not

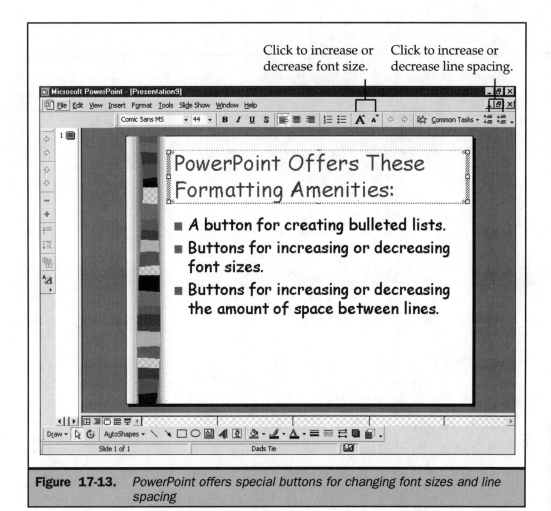

Figure 17-13.   *PowerPoint offers special buttons for changing font sizes and line spacing*

on the default toolbar, but you can add them using the techniques explained earlier in this book.

■ Increase Font Size or Decrease Font Size to enlarge or shrink the size of letters.

Chapter 18

Customizing Your Presentation

This chapter picks up where the last chapter left off and explains how to put the finishing touches on a slide presentation. It explains how to change the layout of a slide, choose a background for the slides in a presentation, or choose one of PowerPoint's designs. It describes how to control the transition between slides or "build" slides onscreen one line at a time. In this chapter, you learn how to make the slides in a presentation consistent with one another by using the so-called slide master. You also learn how to include graphs, charts, and tables on slides, and how to create a "multimedia" presentation with animation, sound, and video clips.

Deciding on the Look of Slides

This section explains the basics of choosing what slides look like. PowerPoint makes it pretty easy to experiment with slides' appearance, and you are hereby invited to toy with all the techniques described in the following pages until you find a look that will catch the eye of your audience.

Following are instructions for choosing a new layout for slides, choosing one of PowerPoint's designs, and creating a design of your own. To make sure that all slides in a presentation are consistent with one another—that slide titles and bulleted text are the same font and same font size—PowerPoint has a thing called a *master slide*. Master slide settings apply to all the slides in a presentation. The following pages explain how master slides work and how to include footers on slides.

LEARN BY EXAMPLE
To try out the techniques described in the following pages, open the Figure 18-A (Look of Slides) file on the companion CD.

Choosing a Different Layout for a Slide

"Inserting a New Slide in a Presentation" in Chapter 17 explained how to create a new slide with one of PowerPoint's preformatted layouts. You can save yourself a lot of work by choosing a preformatted slide. Suppose, however, that you choose the wrong format. Does PowerPoint in its benevolence let you apply a new format to a slide you already created? Indeed it does. Follow these steps to apply a new format to an old slide:

1. In Slide view, display the slide that is to be given a new layout.
2. Click the Common Tasks button and choose Slide Layout, or choose Format | Slide Layout. You see the Slide Layout dialog box shown in Figure 18-1. The layout in the blue box is the one that has been selected for the slide.
3. Click a new layout in the Slide Layout dialog box.
4. Click the Apply button.

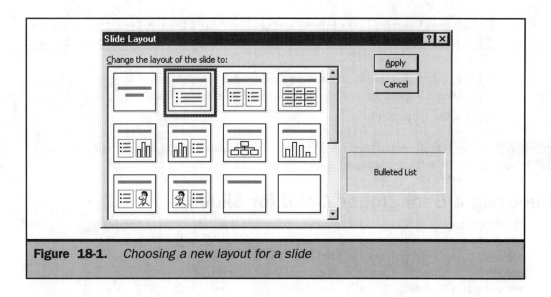

Figure 18-1. *Choosing a new layout for a slide*

You likely have to do a bit of reformatting after a slide is given a new layout. To do that, use the tools on the Formatting toolbar.

If you regret the formatting changes you make to a slide, you can get the original format back. To do so, click the Slide Layout button, click the Reapply button in the Slide Layout dialog box, and click OK.

Applying a New Design to a Presentation

As you know if you created your presentation with a template or the AutoContent Wizard, PowerPoint offers many designs for slide presentations. You can choose one of PowerPoint's designs and apply it to a finished presentation in about a second flat. And PowerPoint gives you the opportunity to look over the designs before you choose one.

HEADSTART
You can also use a PowerPoint template from the CD that comes with this book to change the design of a presentation. See Appendix E.

Follow these steps to choose one of PowerPoint's designs for all the slides in a presentation:

1. Open one of the slides in a presentation in Slide view.

POWERPOINT

2. Click the Common Tasks button and choose Apply Design Template, or choose Format | Apply Design Template. You see the Apply Design Template dialog box shown in Figure 18-2.

3. Click a design name in the box on the left and then glance at the preview box. Keep clicking design names until you find a suitable design.

4. Click the Apply button.

 To see that the new design has been applied to each slide in the presentation, click the Slide Sorter View button.

Choosing a Background Color for Slides

When it comes to choosing a background color for one slide or all the slides in a presentation, you have the option of putting a single color in the background or putting different colors behind titles, bulleted lists, and the rest of the slide. The following pages describe how to apply a single background color or a motley collection of colors to the various parts of slides.

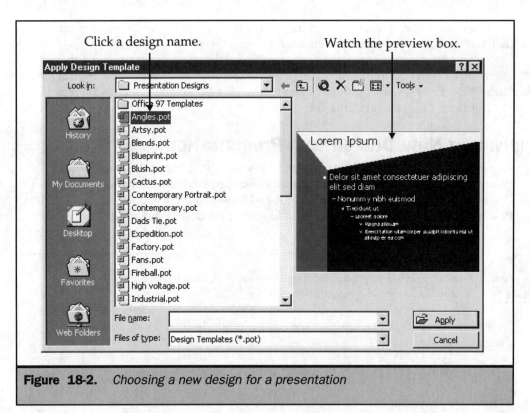

Figure 18-2. *Choosing a new design for a presentation*

A light background looks best on overhead transparencies. Use a dark background for 35mm slides and onscreen presentations.

Applying a Single Background Color to Slides

To apply a single background color to all the slides in a presentation, it doesn't matter where you start. But if you want to apply a single background color to one or a handful of slides, you have to select them first. To select a slide or slides, switch to Slide Sorter view and either click on a single slide or hold down the SHIFT key and click on the handful of slides you want to select.

 On a pre-designed slide like the one shown in Figure 18-3, the background color need not be the predominant one. In pre-designed slides, the background color is the one that is behind the others. Unless you are working with single-color slides, it is sometimes hard to tell which color is actually the "background."

Follow these steps to apply a background color to all the slides or to slides you selected:

1. Choose Format | Background. You see the Background dialog box shown in Figure 18-3.

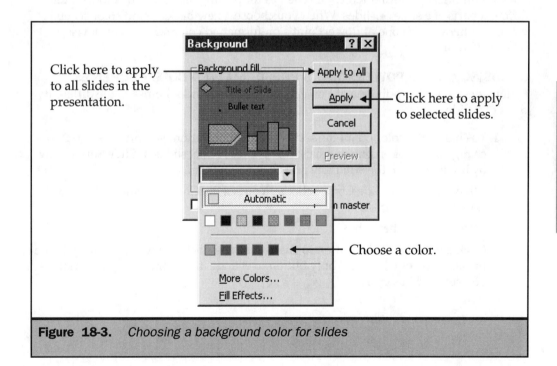

Figure 18-3. *Choosing a background color for slides*

POWERPOINT

2. Click the arrow to open the drop-down list and then choose a color:

■ **Predefined Colors**   Click a square on the drop-down menu to choose a predefined color.

■ **More Colors**   Click this button and you see the Color dialog box. On the Standard tab, click a color in the rainbow assortment of colors. On the Custom tab, either click a color in the rainbow assortment or enter hue, saturation, and brightness percentages or red, green, and blue percentages to create a color. The New box in the lower-right corner of each tab shows precisely what color you are creating.

■ **Fill Effects**   You see the Fill Effects dialog box with its four tabs—Gradient, Texture, Pattern, and Picture—from which you can devise a color or pattern or import a picture for the background.

3. Click the Apply To All button to give all the slides in the presentation the same color, or click the Apply button to apply the background color to the slides you selected.

Applying Your Own Background Color to Various Parts of Slides

PowerPoint offers preformatted color schemes for putting background colors on the different parts of a slide or slides. When you choose a new background color scheme, you can either go with one of PowerPoint's preformatted color schemes or devise a scheme of your own.

CHOOSING ONE OF POWERPOINT'S PREFORMATTED COLOR SCHEMES

Follow these steps to apply one of PowerPoint's background schemes to the different parts of a slide:

1. To change the color on all the slides in the presentation, you are all set; but to change the color on one or a handful of slides, select slides in Slide Sorter view by holding down the SHIFT key and clicking on them.

2. Choose Format | Slide Color Scheme. You see the Color Scheme dialog box shown in Figure 18-4.

3. Click a Color Scheme box.

4. Click the Apply To All button to change the color scheme of all the slides in the presentation or click the Apply button to change the color scheme of the slides you selected in step 1.

Click a background
color scheme.

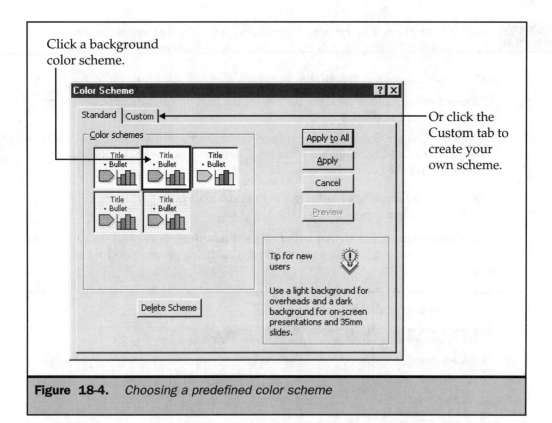

Or click the
Custom tab to
create your
own scheme.

Figure 18-4. *Choosing a predefined color scheme*

CREATING A COLOR SCHEME OF YOUR OWN   Follow these steps to apply your
own colors to different parts of a slide:

1. To change the background colors on several slides, select them in Slide Sorter
   view by holding down the SHIFT key and clicking on them. To change the color
   scheme of all the slides in the presentation, you don't have to select any slides.

2. Choose Format | Slide Color Scheme. The Standard tab of the Color Scheme
   dialog box appears (see Figure 18-4).

3. Click the color scheme box that most resembles the background color scheme
   you want to create.

After you create a new background color scheme, you can make it appear on the Standard tab by clicking the Add As Standard Scheme button on the Custom tab.

4. Click the Custom tab. It is shown in Figure 18-5.

5. Under Scheme Colors, click the option for the part of the slide or slides whose color you want to change.

6. Click the Change Color button. You see the Background Color dialog box with its Standard and Custom tabs. From here, you have two ways to designate a new color for the color scheme:

   ■ **Standard tab**   Click a color in the rainbow assortment of colors. Click OK when you are done.

   ■ **Custom tab**   Click a color in the rainbow assortment or enter hue, saturation, and brightness percentages or red, green, and blue percentages to create a

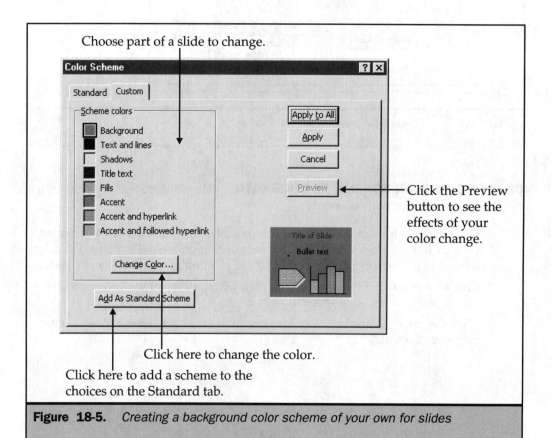

Figure 18-5.   *Creating a background color scheme of your own for slides*

color. The New box in the lower-right corner of each tab shows precisely what color you are creating. Click OK when you have chosen a color.

7. Click the Preview button. The slide or slides onscreen change to show what the color you added to the scheme looks like (you may have to drag the Color Scheme box out of the way to see the slide below it).

8. Repeat steps 5 through 7 to create more colors for your homegrown color scheme.

9. Click the Apply To All button to change the color scheme of all the slides in the presentation or the Apply button to change the color scheme of the slides you selected in step 1.

Master Slides for a Consistent, Professional Look

The surest way to create a professional-looking presentation is to make sure that the slides are consistent with one another. All the slide titles should be the same font and font size, as should the text in bulleted lists. If the same graphic appears on every slide, it should be the same size and appear in the same location from slide to slide. Footers on slides need to appear in the same places.

To be absolutely certain that all the slides are consistent with one another, you can do the formatting in what PowerPoint calls a *master slide*. Each presentation has two master slides, one for the title slide or slides, called the *title master*, and one for all other slides, called the *slide master*. The title master and slide master are representative slides. Format changes made on the title master are made on all title slides in the presentation; format changes made on the slide master are made to all slides in the presentation except title slides.

Usually, the first slide in a presentation is the title slide, but you can insert a title slide wherever you wish. In the Slide Layout dialog box (see Figure 18-1), which is used for inserting new slides in a presentation, the title slide is the one in the upper-left corner.

The following pages explain how to format text on the slide master so that text is the same font and font size from slide to slide. You also learn how to put the same text box or graphic image on each slide in a presentation and how to format text on the title master.

LEARN BY EXAMPLE
To experiment with the slide master and title master, open the Figure 18-6 (Slide Master) file on the companion CD.

The Slide Master for Consistent Text Formatting

Figure 18-6 shows the slide master slide. After you change the formats on this slide, your new formats set the standard for all the slides in the presentation except title slides. Follow these steps to apply the same formats across the length and breadth of a presentation:

1. Choose View | Master | Slide Master. You see the slide master shown in Figure 18-6.

2. Click in the Title Area For AutoLayouts box and choose a different font and font size from the Font and Font Size menus. Click the Boldface button or format the text in other ways. For example, you can choose a font color or align the text in different ways.

Note *Don't bother changing the text on the slide master. All that matters is changing the text's appearance. Text on the slide master is only there for identification purposes.*

3. Click in the Object Area For AutoLayouts box and, one by one, change the font and font size of master text styles, second level text, third level text, and so on.

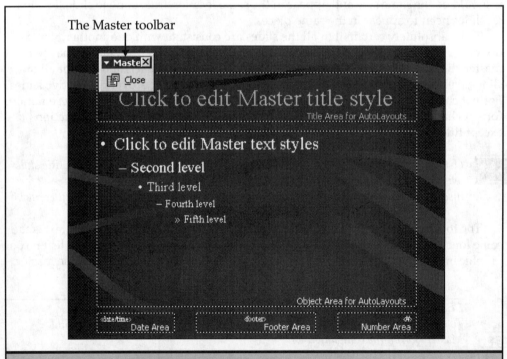

Figure 18-6. *Text formats in the slide master set the standard for formats throughout the presentation*

Simply click in the text whose formats you want to change and then choose new settings from the Font and Font Size menus.

4. Click in the Date Area, Footer Area, and Number Area boxes at the bottom of the slide master and change fonts and font sizes there as well, if you want. These three boxes constitute the footer.

Note *Later in this chapter, "Including Footers on Slides" explains how to put footers on all the slides in a presentation.*

5. Click the Close button in the Master toolbar.

Formatting the Title Master for Consistent Title Slides

The title master works exactly like the slide master, only the text formats made on the title master apply to title slides only. Most presentations have but one title slide. If yours has two or three, perhaps because you will cover two or three topics in the course of the presentation, you ought to go to the trouble of formatting text on the title slide to make sure your title slides are consistent with one another.

To format text on the title slide, choose View | Master | Title Master, click in the area that you want to change on the title master slide, reformat the text, and then click the Close button on the Master toolbar.

Putting the Same Image or Text on Each Slide

Figure 18-7 shows two slides with the same graphic and text on each one. Company logos, mottoes, and the like are candidates for inclusion on each slide in a presentation. To put the same graphic or text box on each slide, choose View | Master | Slide Master to see the slide master for your presentation. A graphic or text box placed on the slide master appears on all slides:

- ■ **Graphic** See "Inserting Clip Art into a Document File" in Chapter 3 if you need help placing a clip art image.

- ■ **Text box** See "Writing the Words on the Slides" in Chapter 17 if you need help inserting a text box.

Including Footers on Slides

In the case of slides, a footer is a bit of text that appears along the bottom. If you tell it to do so, PowerPoint puts the date and time in the footer, text of your choice such as a company name or slogan, and a slide number on all or some of the slides in a

POWERPOINT

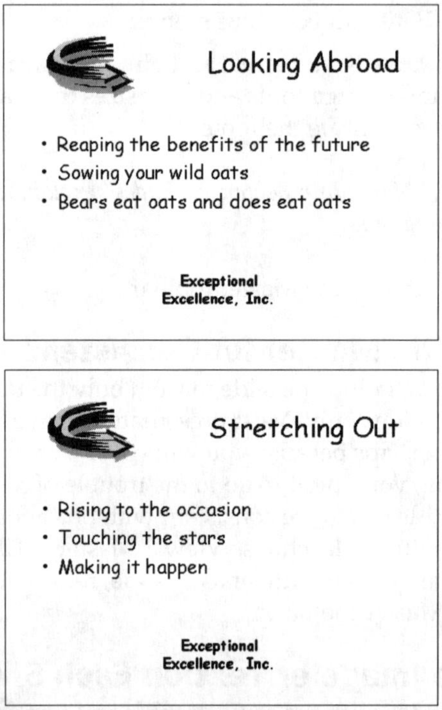

Figure 18-7. *Include the same graphics and text boxes on all slides in a presentation by inserting them into the slide master*

presentation. The footer in the following illustration lists the date, the title of the presentation, and the slide number.

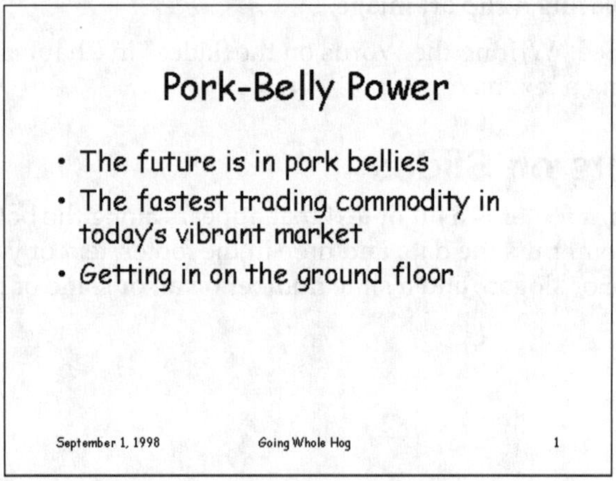

To include a footer on slides, follow these steps:

1. To tell PowerPoint which slides need footers, hold down the SHIFT key and click slides in Slide Sorter view. Don't bother selecting slides if you want all the slides or all except the title slide to have footers.

2. Choose View | Header and Footer. You see the Header and Footer dialog box shown in Figure 18-8.

3. If necessary, click the Date And Time check box to include the date or the date and the time in the footer.

4. Click one of the option buttons to tell PowerPoint how to display the date and time:

   ■ **Update Automatically**   Click this option button and then click the down arrow and choose a date or a date and time format from the drop-down list. With this option, the date or the date and time will always be current. A viewer watching the presentation on April 1, 1999 at 11:30 will be reminded throughout the presentation what day and time it is—the footer in each slide will say so.

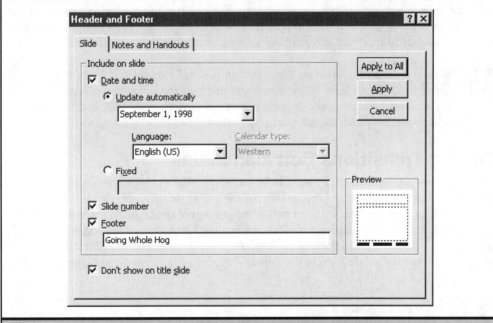

Figure 18-8.   *Including a footer on the slides in a presentation*

- **Fixed**   Click this option button and enter a date in the text box. The date you enter will appear in the footers, no ifs, ands, or buts.

5. Click the Slide Number check box to include the slide number in the lower-right corner of the slides.

6. Click the Footer check box and enter a title, company name, aphorism, or whatever you deem important in the text box. The text you enter appears in the middle of the footer.

7. To prevent the footer information from appearing on the title slide, click to enter a check mark in the Don't Show On Title Slide check box.

8. Click the Apply To All button to put the footer on all the slides in the presentation or the Apply button to put footers only on the slides you selected in step 1.

Giving an "Animated" Slide Presentation

People love to see images move—how else do you account for the success of television? The makers of PowerPoint, well aware that moving images catch the eye, have included a number of features for making text and graphics move on a slide. The following pages explain how to make slides not simply appear onscreen, but appear from one side or appear in an interesting way. They also explain how to make items in bulleted lists appear one at a time and parts of a slide—the title, for example—appear from one side, drop in, or do any number of interesting but possibly distracting things.

The techniques on the following pages for "animating" parts of a slide are dangerous. A slide presentation with too many animations distracts the audience and keeps it from focusing on the real purpose of a presentation—to communicate ideas and plans. Use animation techniques well and sparingly.

Controlling Transitions Between Slides

At the movies you must have noticed how sometimes the camera goes from a soft focus to a sharp focus. Blurred images turn slowly into images you can see and understand. In PowerPoint, you can make images arrive onscreen in a similar fashion. Instead of just appearing, slides can float in from the right side of the screen, for example, or "explode" onto the screen. *Transition* is the term PowerPoint uses to describe the way that slides arrive onscreen. The program offers 42 transitions in all.

LEARN BY EXAMPLE
To see examples of slide transitions, open the Figure 18-9 (Transitions) file on the companion CD.

When you assign transitions to slides, you can assign the same transition to all the slides at once or assign different transitions to different slides. Don't worry about the strange names that PowerPoint gives transitions. As you choose one, you get a chance to preview it and see precisely what it does. Follow these steps to choose a transition for slides:

1. In Slide Sorter view, select the slide or slides to which you want to assign a transition. To select more than one slide, hold down the SHIFT key as you click each one. If you want to assign the same transition to all the slides in the presentation, it doesn't matter how you start.

2. Either choose Slide Show | Slide Transition or right-click and choose Slide Transition from the shortcut menu. You see the Slide Transition dialog box shown in Figure 18-9.

3. Click the Effect drop-down list and choose a transition. As soon as you do so, the little doggy in the window disappears and a key appears in its place. Look closely at how the key appears in the dialog box—that is how the slide will appear onscreen if you keep the transition you chose in the Effect drop-down list. To choose a different transition, select it from the drop-down list and watch the dog and key show. Keep going until you find a transition that tickles your fancy.

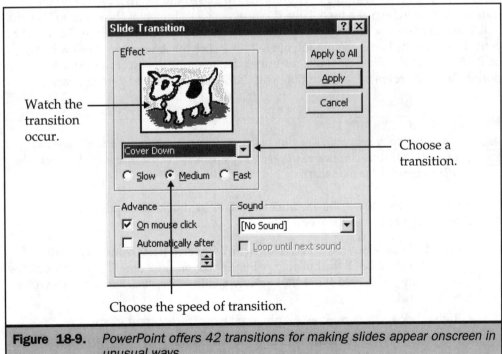

Figure 18-9. *PowerPoint offers 42 transitions for making slides appear onscreen in unusual ways*

You can also select a transition from the Slide Transition Effects drop-down list on the Slide Sorter toolbar. To activate the Slide Sorter toolbar, select a slide in Slide Sorter view.

4. Click the Slow, Medium, or Fast option button to tell PowerPoint how fast or slow to make the transition occur. Again, the dog jumps and the key lands so you can see what the slow, medium, and fast speeds are.

5. Click the Apply To All button to assign the transition to all the slides in the presentation, or click the Apply button to assign the transition to the slides you selected in step 1.

To remove a transition, open the Slide Transition dialog box and choose No Transition on the Effects drop-down list.

At the end of this chapter, "Including Sounds as Part of a Slide Transition" explains how to make sounds as well as sights a feature of slide transitions.

Making Bulleted Lists on Slides Appear One Bullet at a Time

Another way to keep the audience enthralled is to make bulleted lists appear on the slides one bulleted item at a time. PowerPoint gives you a bunch of choices as to how the bullets arrive onscreen. They can drop from the sky, flash, or simply appear. To see what your choices on the Preset Animation menu mean, click the Animation Preview button on the Slide Sorter toolbar. To make the bulleted items appear, you click the mouse during the slide presentation. Each time you click, another bulleted item appears.

LEARN BY EXAMPLE
To see and experiment with shooting bullets in PowerPoint presentations, open the Figure 18-B (Preset Animation) file on the companion CD. Be sure to click to make the bullets appear in the slide show.

Follow these steps to emphasize bulleted points in slide presentations by making the bulleted items appear one by one:

1. In Slide Sorter view, select each slide with a bulleted list in your presentation if you want to make all the bulleted points appear one at a time. To select the slides, click them as you hold the SHIFT key down. Otherwise, click a single slide with a bulleted list.

2. Right-click and choose Preset Animation from the shortcut menu.

3. Choose an animation technique from the submenu.

You can also apply text animation effects from the Preset Animation drop-down list on the Slide Sorter toolbar.

Animating Different Parts of a Slide

The previous handful of pages explained how to make a whole slide or the bulleted items on a slide drop onto the screen, fly in from the left, or do any number of acrobatic tricks. You can make different parts of a slide—the heading, the entire bulleted list (not just each bullet), a graphic, or a text box—perform acrobatic tricks as well. What's more, if more than one part of a slide is to perform acrobatically, you can determine which part performs first and which part performs last.

 Unless you're going for laughs, do not animate more than two—or at the very most, three—parts of a slide. Animation can be very, very distracting.

Follow these steps to animate different parts of a slide:

1. Find the inanimate slide that you want to animate, select it, and switch to Slide view.

2. Right-click a text box or graphic on the slide, and then choose Custom Animation. You see the Custom Animation dialog box shown in Figure 18-10.

3. Under Entry Animation And Sound, click to open the first drop-down list, and choose an animation effect. Then click the second drop-down list to choose a direction.

4. If you want and if your system is capable of producing sounds, click the second drop-down list and choose a sound to announce the arrival of the part of the slide onscreen.

5. Click to open the After Animation drop-down list and tell PowerPoint what the object you are animating is supposed to do after it lands onscreen:

   - **Color Palette**   Applies a color you select to the animation.

   - **More Colors**   Opens the Colors dialog box so that you can select from a wider choice of colors or create your own.

   - **Don't Dim**   Lets the object stay onscreen.

   - **Hide After Animation**   Makes the object disappear after it arrives onscreen.

   - **Hide On Next Mouse Click**   Makes the object disappear when you next click the mouse to bring something else onscreen.

6. If the part of the slide you are dealing with concerns text, choose from the following options:

   - **Introduce Text**   Tells PowerPoint to make the text appear all at once, a word at a time, or a letter at a time.

   - **Grouped By**   For text boxes in which more than one level of text appears, makes the text in the level you choose from the drop-down list appear first.

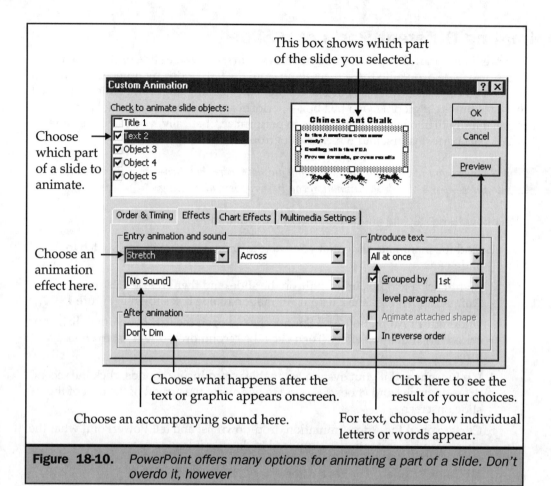

This box shows which part
of the slide you selected.

Choose
which part
of a slide to
animate.

Choose an
animation
effect here.

Choose what happens after the
text or graphic appears onscreen.

Click here to see the
result of your choices.

Choose an accompanying sound here.

For text, choose how individual
letters or words appear.

Figure 18-10. *PowerPoint offers many options for animating a part of a slide. Don't overdo it, however*

■ **In Reverse Order** Makes lists appear backward. In a numbered list, for
example, step 5 appears first and step 1 appears last.

7. Click the Preview button to get a look at what your many choices do. The
sample slide "animates" and does what the slide will do when you actually
show it. You can click the Stop button (it appears where the Preview button
used to be) if the performance takes too long and you want to halt it.

8. Repeat steps 2 through 7 for any other objects on the slide that you want to
animate.

9. To control the order in which animated objects will appear on the slide, select
the Order & Timing tab and click the part of the slide you want to control in the

Animation Order box. In the preview box, a box appears around the part of the slide you selected.

10. Click the up or down arrow to the right of the Animation Order box to tell PowerPoint when the item you selected in step 9 is to appear. The item at the top of the list appears first.

11. Click OK.

In Slide view, you can "animate" a slide by choosing Slide Show | Animation Preview.

LEARN BY EXAMPLE
To try your hand at animating the different parts of a slide, open the Figure 18-10 (Animation) file on the companion CD.

The Fast but Dicey Way to Animate Slides

Instead of fishing around in the Slide Transition or Custom Animation dialog boxes (see Figures 18-9 and 18-10), you can animate slides very quickly in Slide Sorter view. To do so, follow these steps:

1. In Slide Sorter view, select a slide or slides.

2. Right-click and from the shortcut menu, choose Preset Animation.

3. Choose an animation option for the main text on the slide (the text directly below the title).

In Slide Sorter view, icons appear below slides to which animation effects have been assigned. The icon is shown here:

This is an animation

Including Graphs, Charts, Tables, and Columns in Slides

This section explains how to include specialty items on slides—graphs, charts, tables, and two-column text. As shown in Figure 18-11, PowerPoint gives you an opportunity to insert preformatted slides—some of which are preformatted for charts, tables, and clip art—when you insert a new slide in a presentation. By all means, choose a preformatted slide. Those slides make it very easy to import graphs, charts, and clip art images, as the following pages demonstrate.

Creating an Organization Chart Slide

To include an organization chart on a slide, start by selecting the organization chart slide from the New Slide dialog box (see Figure 18-11) and clicking OK. Then, on the slide, enter a title for the chart and double-click in the Double Click To Add Org Chart box. The Organization Chart window appears, as shown in Figure 18-12.

Although you can enter a title for the chart at the top of the screen, it's not necessary since you've already titled your slide. Now, click in each box, delete the

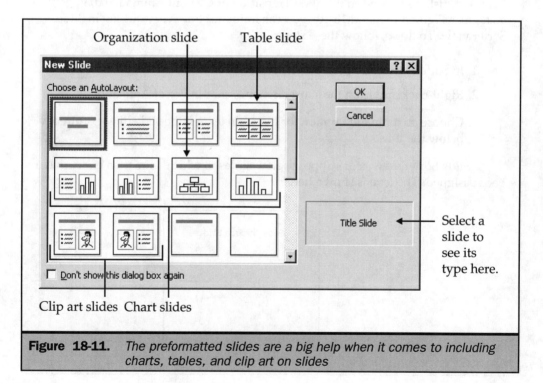

Figure 18-11.   *The preformatted slides are a big help when it comes to including charts, tables, and clip art on slides*

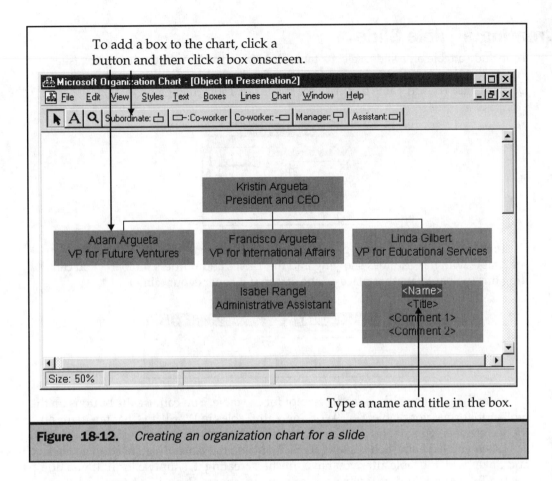

To add a box to the chart, click a
button and then click a box onscreen.

Type a name and title in the box.

Figure 18-12. *Creating an organization chart for a slide*

placeholder text, and type the names and titles of the people over whom you crack the
whip or under whom you bend when the whip is cracked. The boxes get larger and
smaller to accommodate the names and titles. To add a new box to the chart, click one
of the five buttons along the top of the screen—Subordinate, Co-worker, and so on—
and then click the box on the screen to which you need to attach the subordinate,
co-worker, and so on.

When you are done, choose File | Update Presentation, and click the Close button
to display your organization chart slide. To return to the Organization Chart window
and continue to fiddle with the chart, double-click the organization chart.

 Don't forget to save your presentation.

Creating a Table Slide

To include a table on a slide, select a table slide from the New Slide dialog box (see Figure 18-11) and click OK. Then enter a title for the table and double-click in the Double Click To Add Table box. You see the Insert Table dialog box:

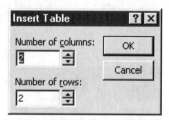

Tell PowerPoint how many rows and columns you want, and then click OK. You see a table with the gridlines showing and the Tables and Borders toolbar. (You can drag this toolbar to another place on the screen if it covers your table.)

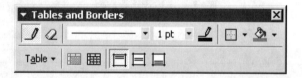

Enter the numbers, labels, and whatnot for the table. You can use the buttons on the toolbar to format your table. See "Working with Tables in Word" in Chapter 10 for all the secrets of creating tables.

When you have finished creating it, click outside the table. If you need to go back and tinker with the table after you have finished creating it, simply click it. If you don't see the Tables and Borders toolbar on your screen, choose View | Toolbars and choose Tables and Borders.

Another way to enter a table on a slide is to import it from Word, Excel, or Access. Make sure the table will fit on the slide, copy it to the Clipboard, and then paste it in the slide.

Creating a Chart Slide

PowerPoint offers no less than three preformatted slides for charts. To include a chart on a slide, choose one of the three preformatted slides in the New Slide dialog box (see Figure 18-11) and click OK. Then, enter a title for the slide and double-click in the Double Click To Add Chart box. You see a datasheet and prototype chart like the ones in the following illustration. Chapter 14 explains how to fashion a chart. If you are not up for making the trip to Chapter 14, simply replace the data in the datasheet with data of your own.

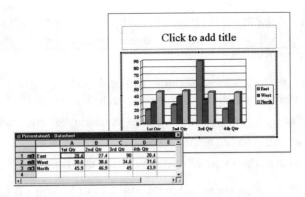

When you are done creating your chart, click on the slide. The datasheet disappears and you see the chart in all its glory. To see the datasheet again and re-enter numbers or labels for the chart, double-click the chart.

Creating Two Columns on a Slide

Here's a little trick for creating two columns on a slide: Choose the two-column text slide in the New Slide dialog box (see Figure 18-11). PowerPoint gives you two bulleted lists, but you can make those lists into ordinary columns by selecting them and clicking the Bullets button. After that, you get normal, all-American columns. By the way, the columns are not newspaper-style columns—text does not spill over from one column to the next.

Getting Fancy with Sound and Video

Provided your system is set up to handle it, you can include motion clips and sound recordings in a PowerPoint presentation. (Office 2000 uses the term *motion clips* to refer to video.) When a motion clip or sound is attached to a slide, it appears as an icon. You can either double-click the icon to play the motion clip or sound, or you can arrange for PowerPoint to play it automatically when the slide appears onscreen.

  Sound and video take up a lot of disk space. Moreover, if you intend to include sound and video sequences in your slide presentation, be sure to test the presentation on the computer on which the presentation will be run. That way, you can see if the sound and video play at acceptable speeds. It is embarrassing to have to wait two minutes for a video sequence to start running during a presentation.

Inserting a Motion Clip

When you insert a motion clip, you can use either one of your own or one from the Microsoft Clip Gallery. To insert a clip of your own, choose Insert | Movies and

Sounds, click Movie from File, find the motion-clip file in the Insert Movie dialog box, and click Insert Clip. Follow these steps to insert a motion clip from the Microsoft Clip Gallery in a slide presentation:

1. Choose Insert | Movies and Sounds, and then click Movie from Gallery to open the other Insert Movie dialog box, as shown in Figure 18-13.

2. Click a category to find a clip that piques your interest and then click on it.

3. Click Preview Clip to see what it does.

4. Click Insert Clip when you've found a motion clip that you like.

The following illustration shows what the clip looks like when it lands on the slide. You can drag the clip to a new location on a side. Double-click a motion clip to play it during a presentation. To play it when the slide appears onscreen, right-click the clip,

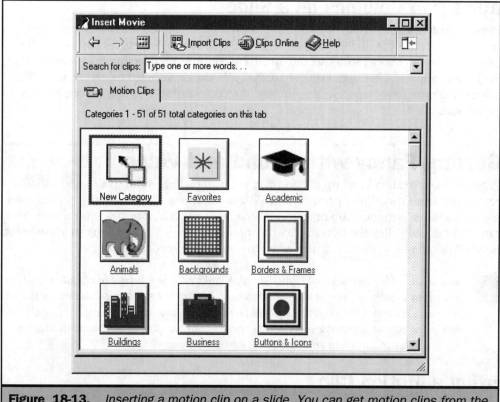

Figure 18-13.   *Inserting a motion clip on a slide. You can get motion clips from the Microsoft Clip Gallery*

choose Custom Animation from the shortcut menu, and turn a few pages back to "Animating Different Parts of a Slide" and Figure 18-10 for all the details.

LEARN BY EXAMPLE
To see firsthand how video clips on slides work, open the Figure 18-13 (Video Clip) file on the companion CD.

Including Sounds in Slides

PowerPoint offers three ways to attach sounds to a slide: by importing a sound file from the Microsoft Clip Gallery, by importing a sound file of your own, or by including sound as part of a slide transition. To import your own sound file, choose Insert | Movies and Sound, click Sound from File, find the sound file in the Insert Sound dialog box, and click OK. The other two techniques for inserting a sound file are described on the following pages.

Inserting a Sound from the Clip Gallery

Follow these steps to insert a sound from the Microsoft Clip Gallery:

1. Choose Insert | Movies and Sound, and click Sound from Gallery. You see the other Insert Sound dialog box.

2. Click a category until you find the sound of your choice, click Play Clip, and listen carefully.

3. Click Insert Clip when you've found the sound you want.

A very small icon—it looks like a speaker—appears on the slide. By double-clicking the icon during a presentation, you can play the sound:

> **Is that the sound of
> little corporate feet?** ◀»

Drag sound icons to the lower-right corner of slides. That way, you always know where they are. You can enlarge a sound icon by dragging one of its corners.

Including Sounds as Part of a Slide Transition

Another way to include sound in a slide show is to include a sound as part of a slide transition. "Controlling Transitions Between Slides," earlier in this chapter, gave the lowdown on slide transitions. Follow these steps to make sounds a part of slide transitions:

1. In Slide Sorter view, select the slide or slides to which you want to assign a sound transition. To select more than one slide, hold down the SHIFT key as you click each one. If you want to assign the same sound to all the slides in the presentation, it doesn't matter how you start.

2. Choose Slide Show | Slide Transition. You see the Slide Transition dialog box shown in Figure 18-14.

3. On the Sound drop-down menu, choose a sound to accompany the transition.

4. Click the Loop Until Next Sound check box if you want the sound to play continuously while the slide is onscreen.

5. Click the Apply To All button to assign the sound to all the slides in the presentation, or click the Apply button to assign the sound to the slides you selected in step 1.

Tip   *To remove a sound, open the Slide Transition dialog box and choose No Sound on the Sound drop-down menu.*

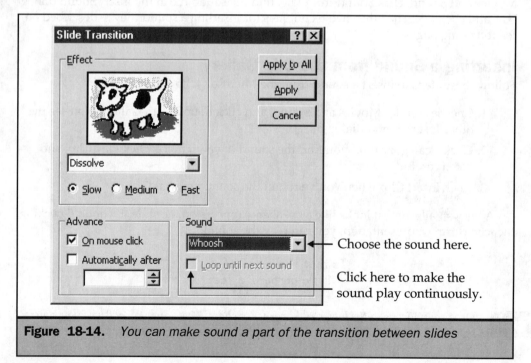

Figure 18-14.   *You can make sound a part of the transition between slides*

Chapter 19

Showing a Presentation

The previous two chapters explained how to prepare a slide presentation. In this short chapter, you learn to give a show, make it lively, and print a presentation so that the audience can take it home, ponder it, and marvel at how satisfying and enriching it was.

This chapter explains how to run a presentation and designate some slides as "hidden" so that you have the option of displaying them or not displaying them during the show. It explains how to start a presentation and move from slide to slide. You don't have to show the slides in order if you decide not to. You will learn two or three tricks for adding a little drama to the show. You also will learn how to draw onscreen during a show and how to black out the screen. If you have ever wanted to create a kiosk presentation that repeats itself until the cows come home, or learn how to take notes during a presentation (and include the notes as part of the handout that the audience receives after the show), read on.

This chapter also reviews how to print transparencies, slide transparencies, slides on paper, speakers notes, and handouts for the audience.

Dress-Rehearsing a Presentation

Before you give a presentation, be sure to dress-rehearse it two or three times. And as you dress-rehearse, try timing the presentation to see how long it takes. That way, you will know how long to book the conference room and whether your presentation is too long or too short. In case your presentation falls short of its allotted time, you can create two or three hidden slides and show them only if you have the time.

 You should dress-rehearse the presentation on the computer that you will use for the genuine presentation.

The following pages explain how to time a presentation and how to create and show hidden slides.

 LEARN BY EXAMPLE
To practice timing a presentation, open the Figure 19-A (Timing) file on the companion CD.

Timing a Presentation

These instructions explain how to dress-rehearse a slide show and find out how long each slide stayed onscreen and how long the entire show lasted. When you are done timing the presentation, PowerPoint will ask if you want to be able to see how long you lingered with each slide and whether you want each slide to advance automatically after a certain amount of time. If you answer yes, the number of seconds each slide was presented will appear below each slide in Slide Sorter view and slides will advance after the number of seconds has passed. Follow these steps to find out how long it takes to give your presentation:

1. Switch to Slide Sorter view.

2. Either click the Rehearse Timings button on the Slide Sorter toolbar or choose Slide Show | Rehearse Timings. The first slide fills the entire screen. In the upper-left corner of the slide, the Rehearsal dialog box tells how long the first slide in the presentation has been onscreen and how long the slide show has taken so far:

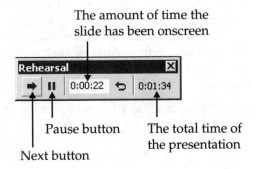

The amount of time the slide has been onscreen

Next button

Pause button

The total time of the presentation

3. Pretend that you are giving the presentation and discuss the first slide. Say everything that you intend to say about this slide. The clock in the center of the Rehearsal dialog box records how long the slide has been onscreen. If you think your slide will engender a discussion, take that into account, too, and leave the slide onscreen longer.

Note

Later in this chapter, "Printing the Speaker's Notes Along with Slide Images" explains how to print the speaker's notes, if you jotted down any. You might print the speaker's notes and read them as you time your presentation.

4. Click the Next button to go to the next slide and pretend that you are showing it to an audience, too. The clock in the center of the Rehearsal dialog box is reset to 00:00:00, but the clock on the right, which records the entire presentation, not each slide's stay onscreen, continues to tick.

Tip

Click the Pause button to stop the clocks from running if your dress-rehearsal is interrupted by a phone call, a hungry cat, or some other distraction. To start all over and "show" a slide from the beginning, click the Repeat button.

5. When you click the Next button after showing the last slide, you see a message box like the one in the next illustration. It tells how long the presentation took

POWERPOINT

to show in toto, and asks if you want to record "the new slide timings" and use them to view the slide show.

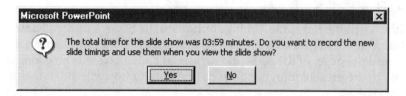

By "use them," PowerPoint is referring to the fact that you can make slides advance automatically during a show after a certain number of seconds. If you click the Yes button in this dialog box, slides will appear onscreen during the show for the same amount of time you allowed them to stay onscreen during the rehearsal and you won't have to press N or PAGE DOWN or click to advance the slides.

6. Click Yes or No. If you click Yes, listings appear below each slide in Slide Sorter view to show how long it will stay onscreen:

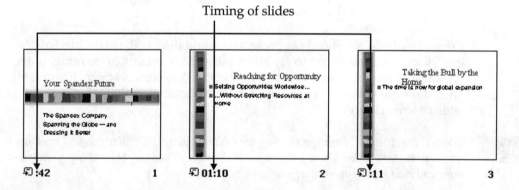

| Note | *Advancing slides automatically after a certain amount of time is useful in kiosk presentations. "Showing a Timed Kiosk Presentation," later in this chapter, gives all the details of creating a presentation that loops and loops and repeats itself until you or someone else tells it to stop. You probably don't want to do this when giving a live presentation, however. It's very easy to become distracted and lose control.* |

Designating Some Slides as "Hidden"

A hidden slide is like an insurance policy in case a presentation falls short of the time you allotted for it. Rather than stare at the audience and ad-lib for ten minutes, you can create two, three, four, or any number of hidden slides. If you come to the end of a show a few minutes early, simply show a hidden slide and discuss it. The following pages explain how to "hide" a slide and how to show a hidden slide during a presentation.

LEARN BY EXAMPLE
To practice hiding slides and showing them during presentations, open the Figure 19-1 (Hide Slide) file on the companion CD.

Telling PowerPoint to Hide a Slide

Follow these steps to "hide" a slide:

1. Create a few slides you can call on in case of an emergency.

> **Tip** *A quick way to create a gratuitous hidden slide is to select all the slides in the presentation except the first one in Slide Sorter or Outline view and then click the Summary Slide button. PowerPoint creates a summary slide with all the titles of the slides you selected in a bulleted list. Move the new summary slide to the end of the presentation.*

2. Switch to Slide Sorter view.
3. Select the slide or slides that you want to hide. To select more than one, hold down the SHIFT key and click on slides.
4. Click the Hide Slide button or choose Slide Show | Hide Slide. A slash appears across the slide number to show that the slide has been hidden:

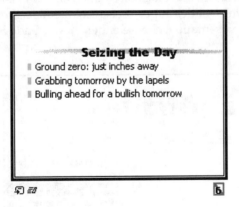

To "unhide" a slide, select it in Slide Sorter view and click the Hide Slide button (again).

> **Tip** *Put hidden slides at the end of the presentation. That way, you always know where they are.*

Showing a Hidden Slide in a Presentation

Unless you happen to have created the presentation and know where the hidden slides are, you can show an entire presentation without encountering them. PowerPoint bypasses hidden slides unless you tell it specifically to display them. Follow these steps to show a hidden slide during a presentation:

1. While presenting a slide show, right-click anywhere on a slide.
2. Click the Go command on the shortcut menu.
3. Choose By Title on the submenu. You see a list of all the slides in the presentation. Parentheses appear around the numbers of the slides that have been hidden. In Figure 19-1, slides 6, 7, and 8 are hidden slides.
4. Click the hidden slide that you want to display.

If you know that the next slide in a presentation is a hidden slide and you want to show the it, press H. The computer beeps if the next slide is not a hidden one.

Giving a Presentation

You will be pleasantly surprised to find out how easy it is to give a presentation. After you have gone to all the trouble of creating it, giving it is, by contrast, a piece of cake. The following pages explain how to give a presentation from first slide to last and how to jump around in a presentation and show the slides out of sequence. These pages also explain how to draw on slides and black out the screen. You also learn how to create a kiosk presentation in which slides appear onscreen after specific time intervals.

To start showing a presentation, choose either View | Slide Show or Slide Show | View Show.

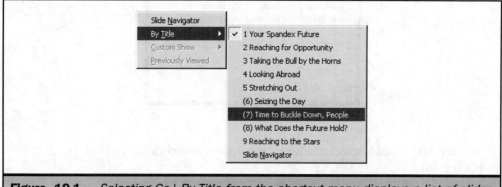

Figure 19-1.   *Selecting Go | By Title from the shortcut menu displays a list of slides. The slide numbers in parentheses are the hidden slides*

Moving from Slide to Slide

When you show slides, you can do so by going from the first to the last, or you can jump from place to place. Following are instructions for doing both.

LEARN BY EXAMPLE
To try your hand at giving a presentation, open the Figure 19-2 (Present) file on the companion CD.

Viewing the Slides in Order

To give a slide show from first slide to last slide, choose either View | Slide Show or Slide Show | View Show. You see the first slide onscreen. PowerPoint offers no less than five ways to see the next and subsequent slides:

- Click with the mouse.
- Press N (for next).
- Press the PAGE DOWN key.
- Right-click and choose Next from the shortcut menu.
- Click the button in the lower-left corner of the screen and choose Next from the shortcut menu.

When the presentation is over, the screen returns to whichever view it was in when you started the presentation. Press ESC to end a presentation before it reaches the end.

"Giving an 'Animated' Slide Presentation" in Chapter 18 explained how to make parts of a slide appear one at a time. If you told PowerPoint to make parts of a slide appear that way, clicking, pressing N, pressing the PAGE DOWN key, and all the other means of going from slide to slide instead make the different parts of a slide appear. Only after the entire slide arrives onscreen does clicking, pressing N, and so on advance the presentation to the next slide.

Viewing Slides Anywhere in a Slide Show

Suppose an attentive busybody asks a question in the middle of a slide presentation, and to answer it you have to go back to a slide that you showed already or go forward to a slide near the end of the presentation. PowerPoint offers a bunch of ways to skip around to different slides.

To go backward slide by slide in a presentation, do the following:

- Press P (for previous).
- Press the PAGE UP key.

■ Right-click and choose Previous from the shortcut menu.

■ Click the button in the lower-left corner of the screen and choose Previous from the shortcut menu.

To go backward or forward anywhere you wish in a presentation, follow these steps:

1. Either click on the button in the lower-left corner of the window or right-click anywhere on the screen.

2. As shown in Figure 19-2, choose Go from the shortcut menu.

3. Choose By Title from the submenu.

4. Click the title of the slide you want to see onscreen.

Techniques for Making a Show Livelier

To add a bit of spice to a show, you might try drawing on the screen or blacking out the screen. In Figure 19-3, the presenter has placed check marks next to the first three items. Presumably, the presenter did this as part of the talk to keep the audience focused on the screen and to help them follow along with each point of the

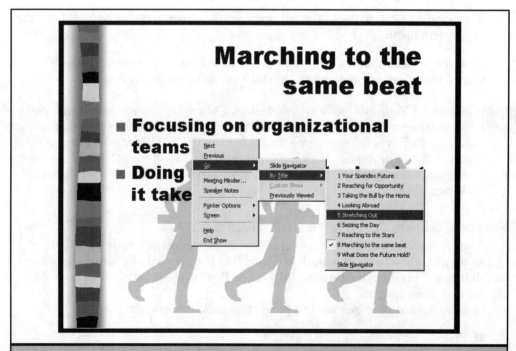

Figure 19-2. *You can go to any slide in a slide show by choosing Go | By Title*

presentation. In the course of a presentation, you might black out the screen when the members of the audience start discussing a topic among themselves and no longer need to focus on a slide.

The following pages explain how to use the pen, change the color of the pen, and black out the screen.

Using the Pen for Emphasis

How to choose a color for the pen is explained shortly. Meanwhile, read on to learn how to draw with the pen.

DRAWING WITH THE PEN   To draw with the pen during a presentation, follow these steps:

1. Right-click, choose Pointer Options from the shortcut menu, and then choose Pen. The pointer changes into a pen.

2. Drag the pointer and then click and drag to draw lines and shapes onscreen.

3. Press ESC when you have finished using the pen.

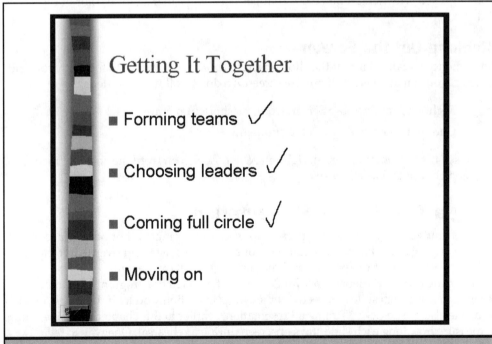

Figure 19-3.   *Draw on the screen to highlight important parts of a presentation*

Hold down the SHIFT key as you drag the mouse if you want to draw a straight vertical or horizontal line.

Pen marks are not permanent. They are much easier to erase than graffiti. As soon as you move to the next slide, the pen marks are wiped clean. Return to the slide again and you see that all the pen marks are gone. However, if you must remove pen marks right away, right-click, choose Screen, and then choose Erase Pen.

  Be careful not to press ESC twice when you have finished using the pen. Pressing it once removes the pen; pressing it once again ends the slide presentation.

CHOOSING A COLOR FOR THE PEN   To choose a color for the pen, follow these steps:

1. Right-click and choose Pointer Options from the shortcut menu.
2. Choose Pen Color on the submenu.
3. Choose a new color.

To get the default ink color back, right-click and choose Pointer Options | Pen Color | Reset. (The default pen color changes—it always matches the color of the slide text.)

Blacking Out the Screen

An audience usually stares at the slide onscreen, but if you want it to focus on you, the speaker, you can always black out the screen. To do so, follow these steps:

1. Right-click and choose Screen from the shortcut menu.
2. Choose Black Screen from the submenu.

To see the presentation again, right-click, choose Screen from the shortcut menu, and then choose Unblack Screen.

Showing a Timed Kiosk Presentation

Perhaps you've seen a kiosk-style presentation at a shopping mall or other place where people congregate. A kiosk presentation is one that plays over and over. After the last slide appears, the first re-appears, and the saga begins all over again.

To create a kiosk presentation with PowerPoint, you tell the program how many seconds to leave each slide onscreen, set the works in motion, and let it run until you or someone else presses ESC. "Timing a Presentation," earlier in this chapter, explained how to measure how long each slide stays onscreen during a rehearsal. One way to tell

PowerPoint how long to leave each slide onscreen during a kiosk presentation is to time the presentation and tell PowerPoint to record the settings. This way, PowerPoint leaves each slide onscreen the same amount of time it stayed onscreen during the rehearsal.

See "Timing a Presentation," earlier in this chapter, if you want to use the rehearsal method to determine how long to leave each slide onscreen. The other way to handle a kiosk presentation is to simply tell PowerPoint how long to leave each slide onscreen. Follow these steps to do so:

1. In Slide Sorter view, click on a single slide if you want it to stay onscreen a certain amount of time. Otherwise, to tell PowerPoint to leave all the slides onscreen the same amount of time, you don't have to select any slides.

2. Choose Slide Show I Slide Transition. You see the Slide Transition dialog box shown in Figure 19-4.

3. Clear the check mark from the On Mouse Click check box.

4. Click the Automatically After check box.

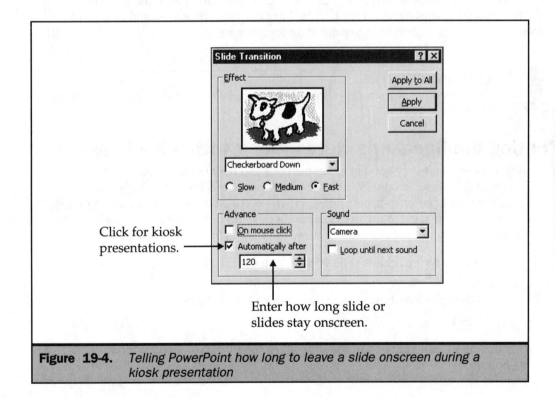

Click for kiosk presentations.

Enter how long slide or slides stay onscreen.

Figure 19-4. Telling PowerPoint how long to leave a slide onscreen during a kiosk presentation

POWERPOINT

5. In the seconds box, enter how many seconds the slide or slides should stay onscreen before the following slide appears automatically.

6. Click the Apply To All button to make all the slides in the presentation appear onscreen for the same amount of time, or click the Apply button to make only the slides you selected in step 1 appear onscreen for the same amount of time.

7. Choose Slide Show | Set Up Show.

8. Click the Loop Continuously Until 'Esc' check box.

9. Click OK.

Printing a Presentation

Giving a presentation on a computer screen, by way of a slide projector, and in overhead transparencies are not the only ways to present your masterpiece. You can also print it. In fact, printing it in the form of a handout is a good idea, because it gives the audience a chance to look over the slide presentation after it is over.

You can print the slides, or you can print the slides along with the speaker's notes. The following pages explain how to print hard copies of the slides and the speaker's notes. They also explain how to print slide transparencies.

EXAMPLES

LEARN BY EXAMPLE
To get some practice printing slides and speaker's notes, open the Figure 19-5 (Printing) file on the companion CD.

Printing the Speaker's Notes Along with Slide Images

Most people aren't very good at extemporizing , so they need speaker's notes to read from during a presentation. "Writing the Words on the Slides," in Chapter 17, describes how to enter speaker's notes. When you print the speaker's notes, you get one page for each slide in the presentation. At the top of the page is an image of the slide; at the bottom are your notes. Follow these steps to print the speaker's notes:

1. From any view, choose File | Print. You see the Print dialog box shown in Figure 19-5.

2. In the Print What drop-down list, choose Notes Pages.

3. Click OK.

PowerPoint prints a copy of the slide at the top of the page and your notes at the bottom.

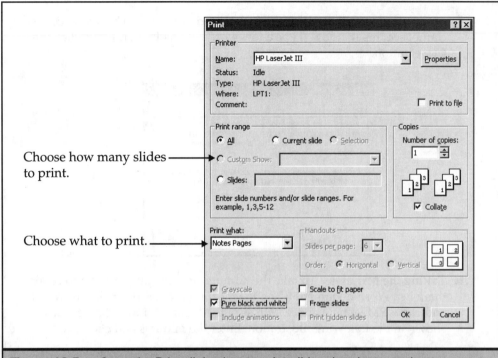

Choose how many slides to print.

Choose what to print.

Figure 19-5. Open the Print dialog box to print slides, handouts, and notes pages (speaker's notes)

Note Chapter 2 explains all the details of printing in an Office 2000 program.

Taking the Minutes of the Meeting

During a presentation, you can add to the speaker's notes that pertain to a slide, take minutes, or jot down what PowerPoint calls "action items"—a better word is "work assignments"—and display all the action items you jotted down on a slide that appears at the end of the presentation.

■ **Adding to Speaker's Notes** To add to or create new speaker's notes while a presentation is in progress, right-click on a slide and choose Speaker Notes. As shown in the following illustration, a window appears with the

POWERPOINT

notes you already jotted down, if you jotted down any. The audience cannot see this window. Type a few words of wisdom and then click the Close button.

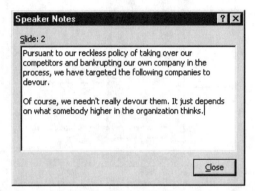

■ **Taking the Minutes**   To take the minutes of a meeting in order to collect them in a Word document when the meeting is over, right-click on a slide and choose Meeting Minder. You see the Meeting Minder dialog box shown in the following illustration. Enter the minutes and click OK.

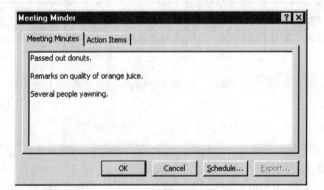

When the presentation is over, you can assemble all the minutes you took throughout the slide presentation into a single Word document. To do so, save the PowerPoint presentation and choose View | Slide Show. Then right-click on a slide; choose Meeting Minder; click the Meeting Minutes tab, if necessary; and click the Export button. A dialog box asks if you want to send the meeting minutes and action items to Microsoft Word. Click the check box, if necessary, and then click the Export Now button. If Word isn't running already, it starts running. You see a new document with your minutes in it. Name and save the document.

■ **Jotting Down "Action Items" for the Last Slide**   To record work
assignments—or "action items," as Microsoft so cavalierly calls them—as
you present each slide, right-click on a slide, choose Meeting Minder from
the shortcut menu, and click the Action Items tab. Then enter a description
of the task in the Description box, the person to whom the task is assigned,
and the date it is supposed to be done, as shown in the following
illustration. Then click Add. Enter as many assignments as you want at one
time. All action items entered on the Action Items tab appear in an
action-packed slide that PowerPoint creates and puts at the end of
the presentation.

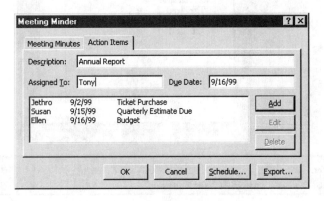

Making the Notes Pages Presentable

If you intend to hand out the speaker's notes along with slide images to the audience,
you ought to make the notes presentable. In other words, you ought to format the text,
and perhaps include a header or footer on the pages. All that can be done from a thing
that PowerPoint calls the *notes master*.

Follow these steps to lay out the notes pages so that they look good to the audience
who will receive them:

1. Choose View | Master | Notes Master. You see the notes master shown in
   Figure 19-6.

2. Click in the Notes Body Area box and choose a different font and font size from
   the Font and Font Size menus for each level of text you've included in your
   notes. Titles are first-level text, text goes on the second level, and bulleted lists
   go on the third level. Click the Boldface button or format the text in other ways.
   For example, you can align the text in different ways. Don't bother changing the
   text on the notes master. All that matters is changing the text's appearance. Text
   on the notes master is only there for identification purposes.

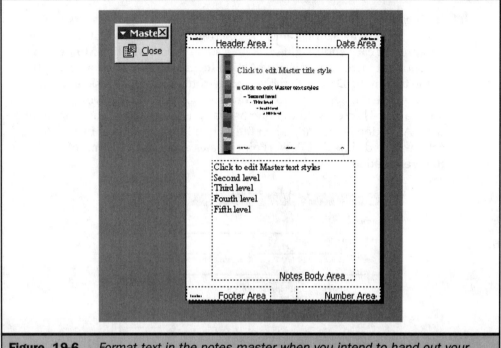

Figure 19-6. *Format text in the notes master when you intend to hand out your speaker's notes to the audience*

3. In the Date Area and Number Area, click in the text and change the text formatting.

4. Click in the Header Area and Footer Area and change the text formatting there as well. To enter text for a header or footer, choose View | Zoom, click a percentage to see what you are doing, and click OK. Then scroll to the header and footer respectively, select the text between the angle brackets (< >), delete the text, and enter text of your own. The text you enter between the brackets will appear in the header and footer on all the pages you print.

5. Click the Close button on the Master toolbar.

Printing Handouts of Slides

Besides printing speaker's notes and slides, you can print only the slides. PowerPoint calls a sheet with slides on it a *handout*. You can print two, three, or six slides per page.

Follow these steps to print the slides in a presentation so the audience can take the slides away when the presentation is over:

1. Choose File | Print. You see the Print dialog box shown in Figure 19-7.

2. In the Print What drop-down list, choose the Handout option and then tell PowerPoint how many slides to print on each page by selecting a number from the Slides per page drop-down list.

3. Click the check boxes at the bottom of the dialog box to tell PowerPoint how the slides should look.

   ■ **Grayscale**   Converts colors to gray shades.

   ■ **Pure Black and White**   Does not allow gray shades, but displays images in black and white only.

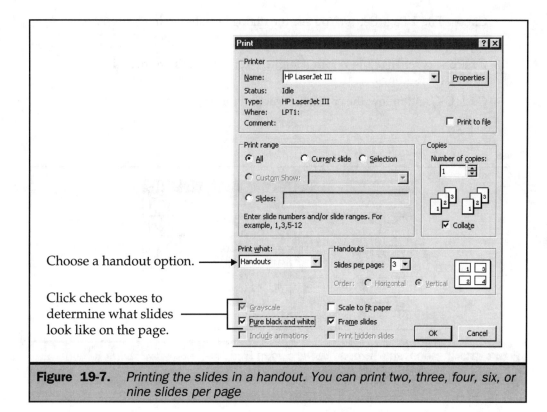

Figure 19-7.   *Printing the slides in a handout. You can print two, three, four, six, or nine slides per page*

- **Scale To Fit Paper** Makes slides larger or smaller so they fit across the page.

- **Frame Slides** Draws a thin line around the border of slides.

4. Click OK.

  To print the slides in color, remove the check mark from the Grayscale check box.

Printing Transparencies

To print transparencies, start by loading your printer tray with transparencies. You might have to consult the dreary manual that came with your printer to find out if it can handle transparencies and which kind of transparencies to use. Follow these steps to tell PowerPoint that you want to print transparencies:

1. Choose File | Page Setup. You see the dialog box shown in Figure 19-8.

2. In the Slides Sized For drop-down list, choose Overhead.

3. If necessary, change the Width, Height, Number Slides From, and Orientation settings.

4. Click OK, and follow the earlier instruction for printing.

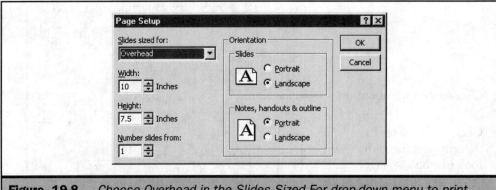

Figure 19-8. *Choose Overhead in the Slides Sized For drop-down menu to print slide transparencies*

The Complete Reference

Office 2000

Part V

Microsoft Outlook

The Complete Reference

Office 2000

Chapter 20

Using Outlook
for E-Mail

This chapter, the first in Part V, explains how to use Outlook to communicate with coworkers, friends, and colleagues by way of a network or the Internet. Besides helping you send and receive e-mail, the program is also what software marketers call a "personal information manager." That means you can use it to keep address lists, schedule meetings, and organize work schedules. Chapter 21 explains the personal information manager side of Outlook.

In this chapter, you familiarize yourself with Outlook and learn how to get from place to place. Then you learn how to send, forward, and receive e-mail messages. Unfortunately, e-mail has become a way for people in crowded offices to document their every decision, action, and thought. Thus, many Outlook users receive hundreds of e-mail messages a week. This chapter explains how to organize those messages in folders so you can keep track of them. It also explains how to delete messages, flag urgent messages, request replies for messages, and send files along with e-mail messages.

A Quick Geography Lesson

The primary difference between Outlook and the other Office 2000 programs is that in Outlook you start from a different folder, depending on what you want to do. For example, to open incoming e-mail messages, you go to the Inbox folder. To find a colleague or friend's address, you go to the Contacts folder.

> **Tip** *The first time you run Outlook you are presented with the Outlook Startup Wizard, which will help you set up Outlook to handle your e-mail account(s). For more information on running the Outlook Startup Wizard, see Appendix A, "Installing Microsoft Office 2000."*

Figure 20-1 shows the Inbox folder, the one that you spend most of your time in when using e-mail. On the left side of this screen is something called the Outlook bar. Notice the shortcut icons and the three group buttons—Outlook Shortcuts, My Shortcuts, and Other Shortcuts—in the Outlook bar:

- **Group** Click a group button and you see a new set of shortcuts in the Outlook bar.

- **Shortcut** Click a shortcut to go to that folder. To get to some shortcuts, you may have to click the down arrow at the bottom of the Outlook bar.

> **Tip** *Besides the Outlook bar, Outlook offers two other ways to move to a different folder: either click the down arrow beside the folder name and choose an item from the drop-down menu, or choose a folder from the Go menu.*

Click a shortcut to go to a different folder.

This is the folder name. Click the name and choose a folder.

Click on a message to display it in the preview pane.

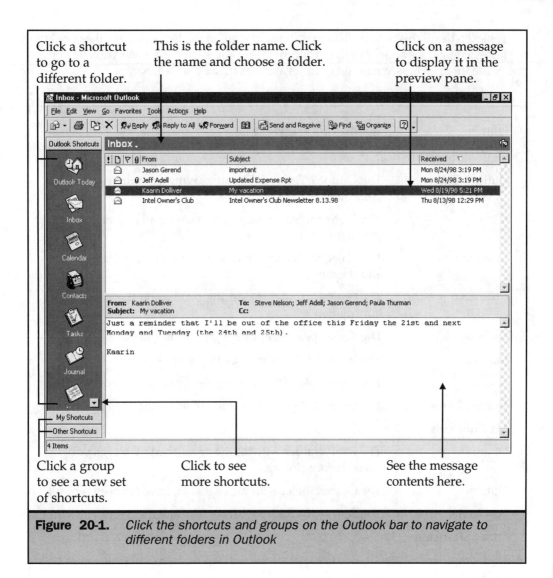

Click a group to see a new set of shortcuts.

Click to see more shortcuts.

See the message contents here.

Figure 20-1. *Click the shortcuts and groups on the Outlook bar to navigate to different folders in Outlook*

Tip   *You can perform almost any action you need by choosing the command from the Actions menu. This menu changes, depending on which folder you're in, to show you only those actions you can perform in your current folder.*

Table 20-1 explains where clicking a shortcut icon on the Outlook bar takes you. In the table, icon names appear under group names. That is because when you click on one of the three groups, a new set of icons appears in the Outlook bar.

Icon	Opens This Folder
Outlook Shortcuts	
Outlook Today	The Outlook Today folder displaying a summary view of your other folders and items
Inbox	The Inbox folder where you work with all of your received messages
Calendar	The Calendar folder for scheduling your appointments and meetings
Contacts	The Contacts folder for storing people and their contact information
Tasks	The Tasks folder for planning projects and tasks
Journal	The Journal folder for recording work activity
Notes	The Notes folder for creating electronic sticky notes
Deleted Items	The Deleted Items folder with all items that you deleted
My Shortcuts	
Drafts	The Drafts folder with all the unfinished messages you saved before closing
Outbox	The Outbox folder with messages that have not been sent yet
Sent Items	The Sent Items folder with copies of all messages you sent
Other Shortcuts	
My Computer	The My Computer folder with the contents of your computer
My Documents	The My Documents folder with all documents you saved to the My Documents folder
Favorites	The Favorites folder with shortcuts for viewing web pages, folders, and files

Table 20-1.   *Groups and Shortcuts on the Outlook Bar*

E-Mail Format Compatibility

Outlook sends e-mail messages in one of three formats: HTML, Microsoft Outlook Rich Text, and Plain Text. Almost all modern e-mail programs support HTML mail, but many users, especially students and teachers, still use text-only e-mail systems that choke on anything more complex than Plain Text. It's generally best to send messages in Plain Text format unless you're sure that your recipient is equipped to read HTML or Rich Text. You should always send in Plain Text format when you're sending to a mailing list.

To make Plain Text your default message format, choose Tools | Options. Click the Mail Format tab and then choose Plain Text from the Send In This Message Format drop-down list box. To change an individual message to HTML or Outlook Rich Text (which can be useful for sending forms to people on your Exchange Server network), in the New Message window choose the desired format from the Format menu.

Tip   *The Outlook Today folder, or more accurately your Personal Folder file, is like the root directory on your hard drive—it contains all of your other folders. To make Outlook open to a different folder, choose Tools | Options, click the Other tab, then click the Advanced Options button. Choose a new folder from the Startup In This Folder drop-down menu.*

Composing E-Mail Messages

This section explains how to send e-mail messages with Outlook. It tells how to compose a message, give Outlook the recipient's e-mail address, and send your message across the Internet—or a Local Area Network, if your computer happens to be connected to one of those. Before you attempt to send or receive e-mail with Outlook, you need to know which services the program works with, so that is covered in the following pages as well. You also learn how to flag messages in different ways and send a file along with your message.

Composing a Message

This section gives bare-bones instructions for composing and sending an e-mail message. Later on, you will find out how to flag messages to be followed up, attach files to messages, and send copies of messages. The techniques that follow are techniques you will use each time you send an e-mail message with Outlook.

OUTLOOK

Click to select Click to send   Enter the subject   Type the
the recipient. a message.   of the message.   message.

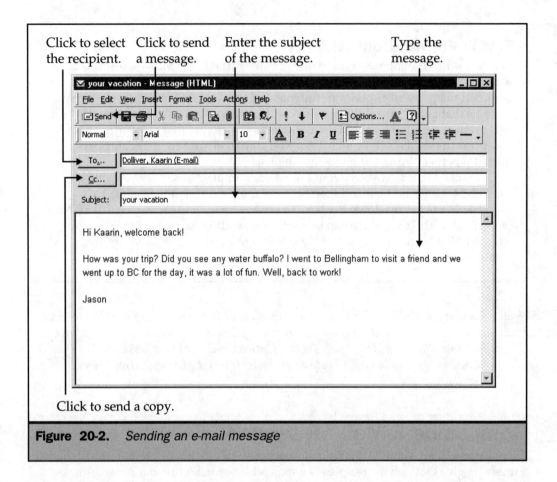

Click to send a copy.

Figure 20-2. *Sending an e-mail message*

Follow these steps to send an e-mail message with Outlook:

1. From either the Outlook Today folder or the Inbox folder (see Figure 20-1), click the New Mail Message button. You see a Message window like the one in Figure 20-2.

2. Type the name or e-mail address of the recipient or click the To button. If you clicked the To button, you see the Select Names dialog box shown in Figure 20-3.

3. In the Show Names From The drop-down list, click the name of the list where the e-mail address is stored. In Figure 20-3, the Contacts list has been chosen.

4. In the list of names on the left, click the name of the person you want to send a message to. To send the message to more than one person, hold down the CTRL key and click each name.

Click or CTRL-click recipients' names.

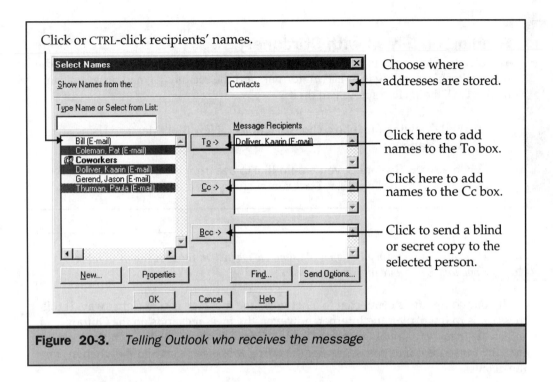

Choose where addresses are stored.

Click here to add names to the To box.

Click here to add names to the Cc box.

Click to send a blind or secret copy to the selected person.

Figure 20-3.   *Telling Outlook who receives the message*

5. Click the To button. The name or names appear to the right of the To button in the Message Recipients box.

6. Click OK. You return to the Message window (see Figure 20-2).

7. Optionally, type a name in the Cc box, or click the Cc button to send a copy of the message to someone.

8. In the Subject line, enter a subject for the message. Be sure to enter descriptive words on the Subject line. If the person to whom you send this message receives lots of e-mail, they need to know how important this message is and whether to answer it today or a fortnight from now. By entering a descriptive subject, you help the recipient prioritize your message.

9. In the box on the bottom half of the window, type your message.

10. Click the Send button. Outlook closes the Message window and you see the Inbox screen again.

Tip   *If Outlook can't find the address of the person you're e-mailing, you will see a screen telling you to choose between any close matches found or create a new address for the individual. You can also click the Show More Names button to view your address book.*

Sending an E-Mail with Stationery

You can use Stationery to add colorful backgrounds to your messages provided the message you're sending is in HTML format, and the recipient's mail program can read HTML mail. Here's how you do it:

1. While viewing the Inbox, choose Actions | New Mail Message Using... | More Stationery.

2. Choose the Stationery you would like to use from the Select A Stationery window, then click OK to start composing your e-mail.

HEADSTART

There are a number of additional Stationeries located on the companion CD. See Appendix E for more information.

If your computer is connected to a network, the message is sent right away. If this message is to travel over the Internet, however, the message lands on the Outbox screen. It stays there until you choose Tools | Check for New Mail. As Outlook collects mail, it also sends e-mail messages. See "Sending Messages," later in this chapter, for the details.

If you are in the middle of composing a message and decide you want to continue working on it later, click the Save button to save the message to the Drafts folder, where you can retrieve it later.

Is Word Your E-Mail Editor?

When you install Office, Word may be set up automatically to be your e-mail editor. If it isn't, don't worry—you can still make Word your e-mail editor by following these steps:

1. Choose Tools | Options. You see the Options dialog box.

2. Click the Mail Format tab.

3. Click the Use Microsoft Word To Edit E-mail Messages check box.

4. Click OK.

Making Word your e-mail editor offers many advantages. You have access to Word's powerful Spelling and Grammar checkers, as well as its formatting tools such as Tables and Columns.

Replying to and Forwarding Messages

Outlook makes it pretty easy to reply to and forward messages. To reply to a message, all you have to do is click one of the two buttons on the left side of the Message window—Reply or Reply to All—and enter the text of a reply. To forward a message, all you have to do is click the Forward message and give Outlook the name and addresses of the parties to whom the message will be forwarded. The following pages explain how to reply to and forward messages.

Replying to a Message

When you reply to a message, you don't have to know the e-mail address of the person to whom you are replying. Outlook keeps that information for you. All you have to do is click the Reply or Reply to All button and enter the text of your reply. Follow these steps to reply to a message:

1. Click the Reply or Reply to All button:

   - **Reply**   Click this button to reply to the person who sent you the message.

   - **Reply to All**   Click this button to reply to the person who sent you the message, as well as all the people to whom copies of the message were sent. As shown in Figure 20-4, the names of people who received copies appear next to the Cc: button in the RE: Message window.

   After you click a button, you see the RE: Message window, as shown in Figure 20-4. What Outlook calls the "memo header"—the name of the person the message is from, when the message was sent, who it was sent to, the names of people who received copies (if any), and the subject of the message—appears in the text box along with the text of the message.

2. Click above the message and write your reply. If you're replying to a HTML or Rich Text formatted message, the words you type appear in blue. If you want, you can delete the memo header and all or as much of the original message as you like. You needn't include all of it in the reply.

To turn off the automatic quoting of original messages when replying, choose Tools | Options, then click the E-mail Options button. From the When Replying To A Message drop-down list box, choose Do Not Include Original Message.

3. Click the Send button.

In your reply, you can call on all the techniques described in "Composing E-Mail Messages," earlier in this chapter, to flag the message, attach a file, or send your reply to others besides those people listed on the To: and Cc: lines of the memo header.

Forwarding a Message

To forward a message, all you have to do is click the Forward button in the Message window. A "memo header" with the author's name, the names of the people to whom

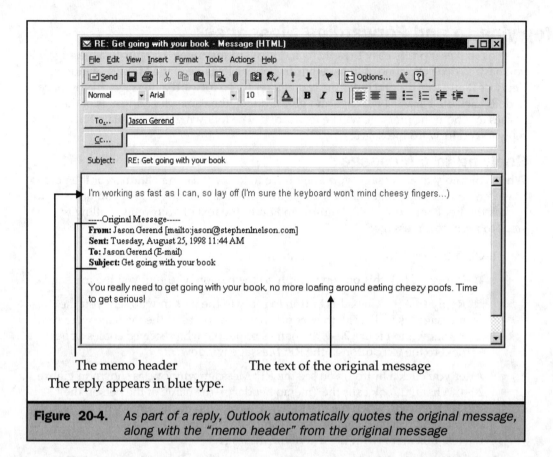

The memo header   The text of the original message
The reply appears in blue type.

Figure 20-4. *As part of a reply, Outlook automatically quotes the original message, along with the "memo header" from the original message*

Finding Out Someone's E-Mail Address

When you reply to a message, you don't need to know the e-mail address of the person you are replying to. But suppose you want to know it? Suppose you want to tell somebody else the address.

You can get another person's e-mail address by opening the message and looking in the From field. If the e-mail address isn't displayed, right-click on the name and choose the Properties command from the shortcut menu to show the sender's information.

the message and copies of the message were sent, and the subject of the message, appears at the top of the FW: Message window, as shown in this illustration:

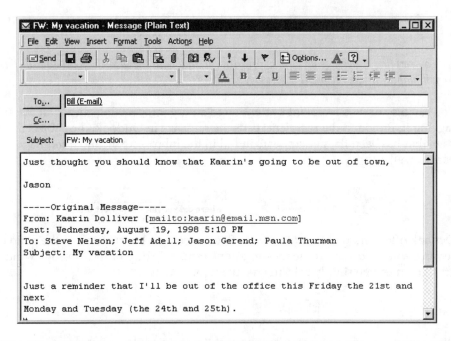

Click the To button and tell Outlook who the message is to be forwarded to in the Select Names dialog box. See "Composing a Message," near the start of this chapter, if you aren't sure how the Select Names dialog box works.

Calling Recipients' Attention to Urgent Messages

Outlook offers two ways to tell others that the messages you sent are urgent and need immediate attention. The first is to click the Importance: High button (the exclamation point) on the Standard toolbar in the Message window. (See the section on personalized toolbars in Chapter 3 if you don't see the button.) Provided that the person who receives the message receives it with a modern e-mail program, the recipient will see a red exclamation point or some other symbol beside the message in the Inbox screen:

And when the recipient opens the message, he or she sees the following words near the top of the Message window if the recipient is using Outlook:

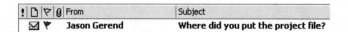

This message was sent with High importance.

Note   *You can flag a message as well as prioritize it, and both the priority level and the flag will appear in the recipient's Message window.*

You can also draw a recipient's attention to an urgent, pressing, and vital message by flagging it. Provided the recipient reads the message in Outlook, the subject line of a message that has been flagged appears in red in the Inbox screen, and a red flag appears as well:

!	☐	⊽	𝟢	From	Subject
	✉	❮		**Jason Gerend**	**Where did you put the project file?**

Outlook offers many different ways to flag a message. Instructions to the recipient concerning what to do about the message appear near the top of the Message window. This flagged message simply asks the recipient for a reply:

Reply

When you flag a message, you can request the recipient to respond by a certain date. If the recipient fails to do so, an Overdue dialog box like the one in the following illustration appears in the middle of the screen. The recipient can click the Dismiss button to make the dialog box disappear, click Open to open the message, or click Snooze and choose how long to procrastinate by choosing an option from the Click Snooze To Be Reminded Again drop-down list.

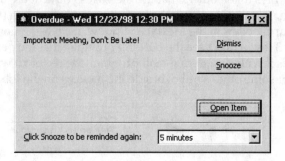

Creating a Distinctive Signature

A Signature is a name, a name and address, or perhaps a pithy saying with which a user of Outlook always ends his or her messages. I knew somebody who always ended his e-mail messages with a Signature calling for the goddess Vishnu the Destroyer to ascend to earth and simultaneously destroy and rejuvenate, but that's another story.

To create a Signature and tell Outlook to append it automatically to the end of all your e-mail messages, follow these steps:

1. Choose Tools | Options.

2. Click the Mail Format tab, and then click the Signature Picker button.

3. Click the New button to create a new Signature.

4. Type a name for your signature, then choose whether to start from scratch or use an existing signature or file as a template.

5. In the Edit Signature window, type your signature, then click OK.

The following sections contain instructions for flagging e-mail messages in different ways.

6. In the Signature Picker window, make sure the desired signature is selected and then click OK.

Next time you create a new e-mail message or reply to a message that someone has sent you, you will see your Signature as soon as the Message window opens. You can delete it if you decide not to use it in a particular message.

High- and Low-Priority Messages

Prioritizing a message is easy. In the Message window, as you compose the message, either click the Importance: High or Importance: Low button on the Standard toolbar. The buttons appear next to one another on the toolbar. The High button is a red exclamation point; the Low button is a red arrow that points down.

Flagging a Message

To flag a message, follow these steps:

1. In the Message window, click the Flag Message button on the Standard toolbar. The Flag Message dialog box appears:

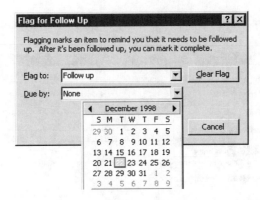

2. From the Flag To drop-down menu, choose how you want to label your message. Among the choices are Follow Up, Review, No Response Necessary, and Call.

3. If you want the recipient to reply by a certain date, click the Due By drop-down arrow and select a date from the calendar. Click the arrows at the top of the Calendar to go backward or forward in time.

4. Click OK.

A notice appears in the Message window. The choices in the Flag Message dialog box shown in step 1 yield the following message, which the recipient of the message will also see:

> ⬥ Follow up by Tuesday, March 02, 1999 4:30 PM.

 To remove a flag from a message, click the Flag button and then click Clear Flag in the Flag Message dialog box.

Private, Personal, and Confidential Messages

Another way to flag a message is to post the word "Private," "Personal," or "Confidential" near the top of the message window. Of course, you could always tell the recipient in the message that the words you are sending are confidential, private, or personal, but stamping one of the three words on a message may make it seem more official.

To stamp the word "Private," "Personal," or "Confidential" on a message, follow these steps:

1. In the Message window where you compose the message, click the Options button.

OUTLOOK

2. Click the down arrow on the Sensitivity drop-down menu and choose an option:

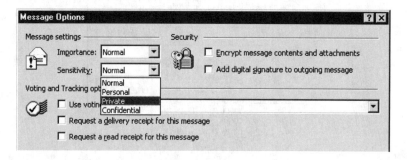

3. Click Close to get back to writing your message.

When the message is received, the recipient will see, near the top of the Message window, a yellow sign with an exclamation point, the words "Please treat this as," and the word "Private," "Personal," or "Confidential." Not only is this message private, it has been given a high-importance rating:

> **!** Please treat this as Private.

Sending Files Along with Messages

Outlook makes it pretty easy to send a file along with a message. As shown in Figure 20-5, all you have to do is click the Insert File button (the paper clip) on the Standard toolbar. You see the Insert File dialog box. Find and click the file you want to send along with your message, and then click OK. As the figure shows, a file icon appears in the Message window. You can send as many files as you want this way. When you send the e-mail message, the file is sent right along with it.

You can't send a file if you move it to a different folder after you insert it in a message. If you move the file, Outlook won't know where to find it when it comes time to deliver the message.

Later in this chapter, "Opening and Storing a File That Someone Sent You" explains how to open and store a file that has been sent to you.

Sending Messages

Having explained everything there is to know about messages except how to send them, this section explains how to send the messages you so thoughtfully composed, arranged to send copies of, added your signature to, flagged, stamped as confidential,

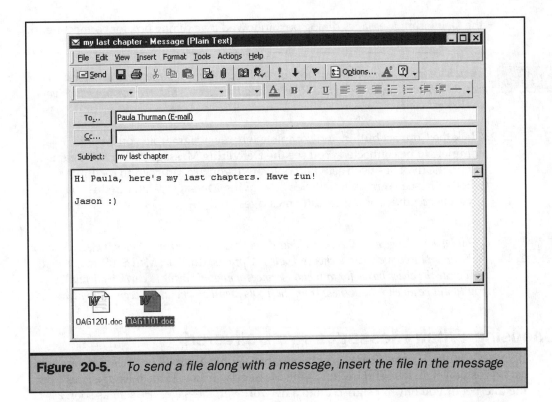

Figure 20-5. *To send a file along with a message, insert the file in the message*

and attached files to. The following pages explain how to send files over a network and the Internet. They also explain how to tell Outlook when to deliver messages, how to find out when a message arrived, and how to change or delete a message before you send it.

Sending Messages Over a Network or the Internet

When you click the Send button in the Message window, your e-mail message is sent right away if your computer is directly connected to the network you want to send the message over. If you are sending a message to someone else on your local network, or if you are sending Internet e-mail across your direct connection to the Internet, Outlook sends the message immediately. However, if the message is to travel over the Internet and you haven't connected to the Internet yet, or you are not connected to your local network, you have to tell Outlook to send the message.

Follow these steps to send a message you have composed if it was not sent automatically:

1. From the Inbox screen, click the Send and Receive button. When Outlook checks for new mail, it collects mail that has been sent to you as well. You see

the Delivering Messages dialog box, followed by a dialog box for connecting to the service from which you collect mail.

| Note |

If you have more than one e-mail account and you wish to only retrieve mail for a certain account, choose Tools | Send and Receive, and then choose the service from which you want to get mail.

2. Click the Connect button and complete whatever rigmarole you have to complete to be connected. You see the Delivering Message dialog box again. When the mail has been sent and delivered, you are returned to the Inbox, where you see your new mail. See "Receiving Messages," later in this chapter, if you need advice about reading messages.

| Tip |

If you have multiple e-mail accounts but do not want to check all of them when you click the Send and Receive button, choose Tools | Options. Click the Mail Services tab, and then clear the check boxes for any mail services you don't want to check by default. You'll still be able to check them from the Tools menu's Send and Receive submenu.

Choosing When Messages Are Delivered

If your computer is connected to a network and you have signed on, messages are sent as soon as you click the Send button in the Message window. If the message goes over the Internet or you haven't signed on to a network yet, messages are sent as soon as you click the Send and Receive button. Suppose, however, that you want to wait a few days before sending a message. You can tell Outlook when to send a message by following these steps:

1. Compose the message in the Message window.

2. Click the Options button to open the Message Options window, shown in Figure 20-6.

3. Under Delivery options, click the Do Not Deliver Before down arrow and click the date on the calendar before which the message is not to be delivered. Outlook will not deliver the message before 5:00 P.M. on the date you choose. To choose a date, click on it. To go from month to month, click the arrow on either side of the month name.

4. Click the Expires After down arrow and choose an expiration date, if you want. If you do not connect to a network or the Internet between the delivery date and the expiration date, the message is not sent.

5. Click the Send button.

Using Outlook on a Local Network

You can use Outlook to send e-mail as well as files to other local area network users as long as your computer is connected to a local area network that includes an Exchange server, or other mail server. Moreover, the Exchange or other mail server administrator must have set up an account for you. If you have an Exchange account and if the other users on the network make use of the Calendar in Outlook, you may even be able to use Outlook to schedule group meetings. Exchange server, by the way, runs on a Windows NT server and is part of the Microsoft BackOffice. However, how the Exchange server works shouldn't be of any concern to you—worrying about the Exchange server is the network administrator's business. If you have questions about your mail server, talk to your network administrator.

Except for a few minor differences, Outlook works the same on a local network as it does on an online service. If you are using Outlook on a network, take note of the following differences:

- On a local network, you usually don't do anything special to send or retrieve messages. When you click the Send button in the Message window, Outlook immediately and automatically sends the message to the Exchange server. Meanwhile, the Exchange server also automatically delivers e-mail messages that others sent you. If your network provides you a direct connection to the Internet, sending and receiving Internet mail works the same too.

- Your Address Book includes another set of people, called the Global Address List. The Global Address List names and identifies the local area network users to whom you can send e-mail. (To see the Global Address List, click the Address Book button and select Global Address List from the Show Names From list box.)

- Provided that others on the network are using Outlook and the Exchange administrator has set up the network correctly, network users can schedule meetings with others on the network. For this to work, the Exchange administrator must have set up Exchange so that one Outlook user can view another's Outlook Calendar. Moreover—and this is important—other Outlook users must be using the Calendar as their scheduling tool.

You can use Outlook as an e-mail client both with an Internet Service Provider and on a local area network that includes an Exchange server. It's also possible to use Outlook as an e-mail client with online services such as The Microsoft Network and CompuServe if you or the network administrator installs what's called a *connector*. For more information about all this, consult your network administrator or the online service's technical support staff.

OUTLOOK

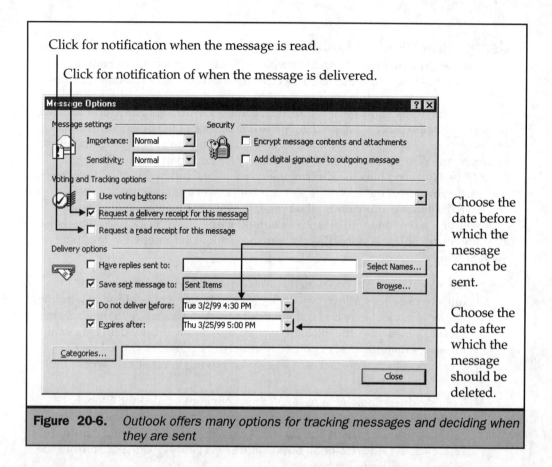

Click for notification when the message is read.

Click for notification of when the message is delivered.

Choose the date before which the message cannot be sent.

Choose the date after which the message should be deleted.

Figure 20-6. *Outlook offers many options for tracking messages and deciding when they are sent*

Getting Notification When Messages Are Delivered and Read

Also on the Options tab in the Message window (see Figure 20-6) are check boxes for being informed when messages are delivered and when they are read. Read Receipts work only over local networks running an Exchange server while Delivery Receipts can work over the Internet if the recipient's software supports it.

Follow these steps to receive notification when a message is read or delivered:

1. Compose the message in the Message window.

2. Click the Options button.

3. Click the Request A Delivery Receipt For This Message check box.

4. Click the Request A Read Receipt For This Message check box.

5. Click the Send button.

If you want, you can be informed when all of your messages are delivered and read without having to visit the Message Options window. Choose Tools | Options; click the E-mail Options button. Click the Tracking Options button, then check the Request A Read Receipt For All Messages I Send and the Request A Delivery Receipt For All Messages That I Send check boxes.

Changing and Recalling Messages

Suppose you compose a message to somebody, click the Send button in the Message window, and regret sending the message. Can you recall the message? Can you head it off at the pass before it is sent? It depends on whether you are connected to a network. Network users connected to an Exchange server can recall messages. As for people using Outlook over the Internet, the only way to recall a message is to go to the Outbox screen, hope the message has not been sent yet, and either change or delete the message there.

 Messages sent by way of the Internet cannot be recalled after they are sent.

Changing or Deleting Messages That Haven't Been Sent

If the message hasn't been sent yet, you can find and open it or else delete it in the Outbox screen. Follow these steps to do so:

1. Click the My Shortcuts group in the Outlook bar.

2. Click the Outbox icon. You see the Outbox folder shown in Figure 20-7.

3. Click the message you want to delete or change.

4. Either delete or change the message:

   ■ **Deleting**   Click the Delete button to delete the message.

   ■ **Changing**   Double-click the message. The Message window opens. Change the text of the message, the address, the delivery settings, or whatever else needs changing. Then click the Send button.

Recalling a Message That Has Been Sent

Follow these steps to recall an embarrassing or inaccurate message that you sent over a network or intranet:

1. Click the My Shortcuts group in the Outlook bar.

2. Click the Sent Items shortcut. You see the Sent Items folder with copies of all the messages you sent.

3. Open the message you want to recall.

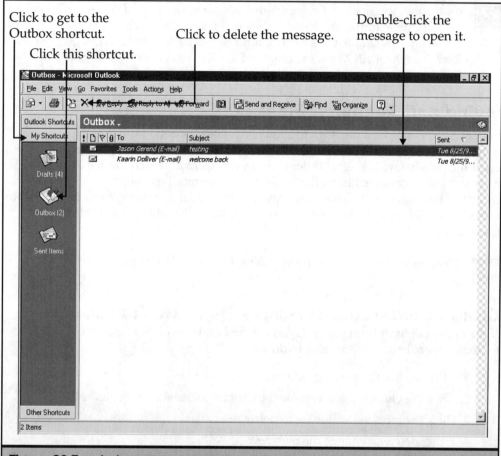

Figure 20-7.   *As long as a message hasn't been sent yet, you can change or delete it on the Outbox screen*

4. Choose Actions | Recall This Message.

5. Click the Delete Unread Copies Of This Message check box.

Caution   *It isn't always possible to recall messages that have been sent.*

Where Outlook Stores Copies of Sent Messages

Copies of the messages you send are kept on the Sent Items screen. Click the My Shortcuts group and then the Sent Items shortcut in the Outlook bar to open the Sent Items screen. With that done, double-click a message to open and read it.

After a while, the number of sent items gets large and takes up valuable disk space. Outlook takes care of this by automatically archiving sent messages older than two months. To access these settings, right click on the Sent Items shortcut in the Outlook Bar and choose the Properties command, then click the AutoArchive tab.

Receiving Messages

The button for receiving e-mail messages is the same as the button for sending them: the Send and Receive button. The following pages explain the ins and outs of retrieving mail. They also explain how to preview messages after they arrive, read messages, delete messages, and arrange messages on the Inbox screen. You will also find instructions here for replying to and forwarding messages.

Collecting and Reading Your E-Mail

Collecting e-mail messages is as easy as choosing Tools | Check for New Mail and, in the case of the Internet, following your standard procedure to connect to the Internet.

If you use more than one Internet provider, or if your computer is connected to both a network and the Internet, clicking the Send and Receive button checks for new mail on all of your e-mail accounts. To check a specific account, choose the account from the Tools menu's Send and Receive submenu.

Mail arrives in the Inbox, as shown in Figure 20-8. A closed envelope appears next to messages that haven't been read yet, and the first few lines of text are displayed underneath it. Select a message to view its contents in the preview pane. Messages that have been read show an open envelope. The lower-left corner of the Inbox screen tells how many messages are in the Inbox and how many remain unread. In Figure 20-8 you see exclamation points, flags, and paper clip icons next to some of the messages. The first part of this chapter explains what those icons mean.

Tip *If for some reason you want to indicate that you haven't read a message, perhaps to remind yourself to return to it again, select the message and choose Edit | Mark As Unread.*

OUTLOOK

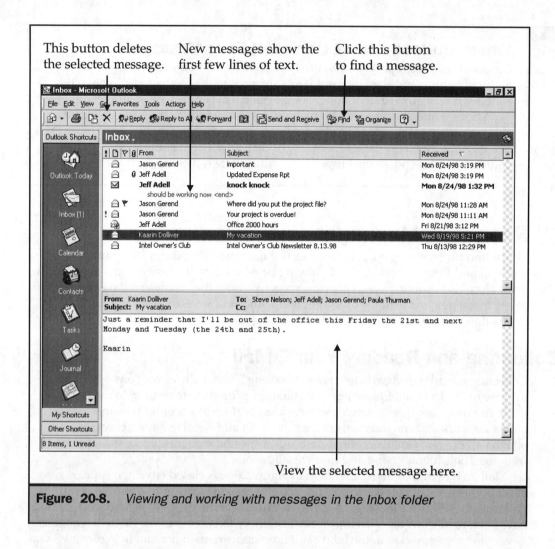

This button deletes the selected message.

New messages show the first few lines of text.

Click this button to find a message.

View the selected message here.

Figure 20-8. *Viewing and working with messages in the Inbox folder*

To open a message in the Inbox folder, double-click it. You see a message like the one in the next illustration.

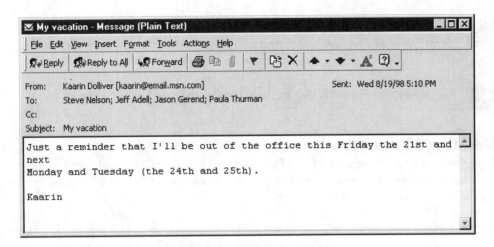

Hiding the Message Header makes it easier to read long messages. To do this, choose View | Message Header. When you choose this command the Cc and Subject fields are removed from the top of the Message window.

After you have read the message, either choose File | Close or click the Close button in the Message window to return to the Inbox screen.

Speed Techniques for Reading and Handling Messages

Some poor souls receive hundreds and hundreds of e-mail messages a week. Rather than slog through all those messages one at a time, you can take advantage of the power Outlook has to handle messages quickly. Following are techniques for reading e-mail as fast as possible.

Previewing the Messages

You can preview messages two ways in Outlook; using AutoPreview and using the Preview Pane (see Figure 20-9). As shown in the figure, AutoPreview displays the first two lines of all new messages, and is handy for quickly determining whether or not you would like to read a message. The Preview Pane displays the contents of the currently selected message in a resizable pane at the bottom of your screen. If a message is too big to efficiently read in the Preview Pane, you can always double click the message to open it in a message window.

To toggle the AutoPreview or Preview Pane on or off, choose the View menu's AutoPreview or Preview Pane command. To change the Preview Pane's options, choose Tools | Options, click the Other tab, then click the Preview Pane button.

  Hit the spacebar to quickly display the next message in the Preview Pane.

Deleting Messages

When you delete a message with the Delete button in a Message window, Outlook immediately opens the previous message in the Inbox screen. You don't go back to the Inbox folder to choose another message to open.

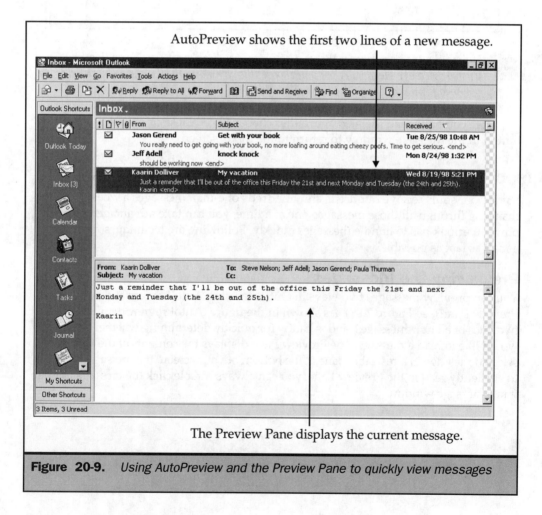

Figure 20-9.   *Using AutoPreview and the Preview Pane to quickly view messages*

Jumping to Different Messages

After you have opened a message, you needn't return to the Inbox screen to open another one. To go to the previous or next message in the Inbox screen, click the Previous Item or Next Item button. The next or previous message, whether you've already read it or not, is opened and the message you were looking at is closed.

Moreover, if you click the drop-down menu attached to either of these buttons, you see a list of items you can go to, as the following illustration shows. For example, click Item from Sender to open the previous or next item in the Inbox from the person who sent you the message you are looking at. Click Flagged Message to see the next or previous flagged message you were sent.

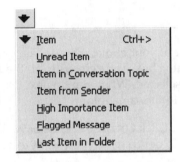

Deleting a Message

Outlook gives you lots of opportunities for deleting messages. Wherever you see the Delete button, all you have to do to delete a message is select it and click the Delete button. The Delete button, an X, is located on the Standard toolbar in every Outlook screen.

When you delete a message, it doesn't disappear for good. Deleted messages land in the Deleted Items screen. This screen works like the Windows Recycle Bin. If you regret deleting a message, you can click the Outlook Shortcuts group in the Outlook bar and then click the Deleted Items shortcut to open the Deleted Items folder. From there, you can resuscitate the message by copying it to a different folder.

However, letting deleted messages languish in the Deleted Items folder takes up disk space. Periodically open the Deleted Items folder, hold down the CTRL key and click on the messages that need deleting, and then click the Delete button.

 To delete all the messages in the Deleted Items folder, choose Tools | Empty Deleted Items.

Opening and Storing a File That Someone Sent You

As shown in the following illustration, files appear as icons in the message window when someone sends you a file. To open a file, double-click on it.

OUTLOOK

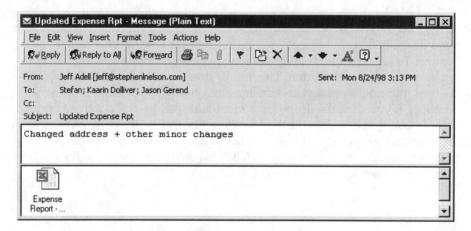

To save a file in the folder of your choice, choose File | Save Attachments. You see the Save All Attachments dialog box. To begin with, all the files that were sent along with the e-mail message are selected. What you do next depends on whether or not you want to save all the files to the same folder:

- **Files to Same Folder** Click OK. You see the Save All Attachments dialog box. Find and click on the folder to which you want to save the files, and then click the Save button.

- **Files to Different Folders** Click some of the files to deselect them, and then click OK. In the Save All Attachments dialog box, find and click on the folder in which the files are to be saved, and then click the Save button. Back in the Save All Attachments dialog box, start all over again to save the other files.

Storing and Organizing Messages

If you are one of those important personages who gets lots and lots of e-mail, you can do yourself a big favor by storing e-mail messages in different folders. For example, you might create a folder for each project, plan, scheme, or undertaking in which you are involved. Then, as e-mail messages come flooding in, you can store each one in the appropriate folder and find and read it when the right time comes. Following are instructions for creating folders and for storing messages in the folders you have created.

Creating a Folder for Messages

Follow these steps to create a folder for storing messages:

1. Choose File | New | Folder.
2. Type a name for the folder in the Create New Folder window shown in Figure 20-10.

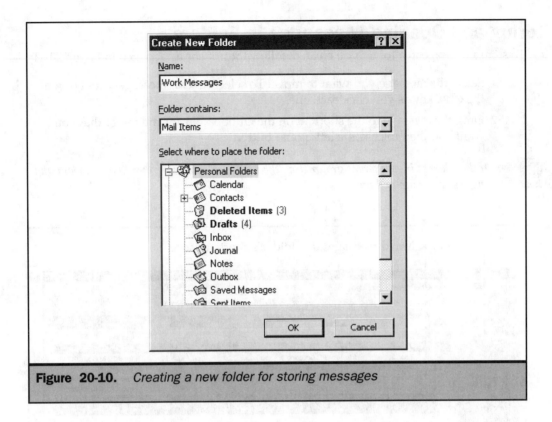

Figure 20-10.   *Creating a new folder for storing messages*

3. Select the Personal Folders folder or whatever folder you want to store the new folder in.

4. Click OK, then click Yes to place a shortcut to the folder on your Outlook Bar, or No to skip this.

To delete or rename a folder you created, click View | Folder List and then find and right-click on the folder in question. Next, choose the Delete or Rename commands from the pop-up menu.

You can rearrange the shortcuts on the Outlook Bar simply by clicking and dragging them to the desired location on the Outlook Bar. Drag them to a group name to open that group.

You can create a new group for shortcuts on the Outlook Bar by right-clicking on the Outlook Bar and choosing the Add New Group command.

OUTLOOK

Storing and Opening Messages in Folders

To store a message in a folder you created, follow these steps as depicted in Figure 20-11:

1. Select the message you want to move. To select several messages, hold down the CTRL key as you click each one.

2. Drag the message to the shortcut on the Outlook Bar for the folder that you want and then release the left mouse button.

 If the folder is in a different group, drag the messages onto the group that you want and the desired group will open.

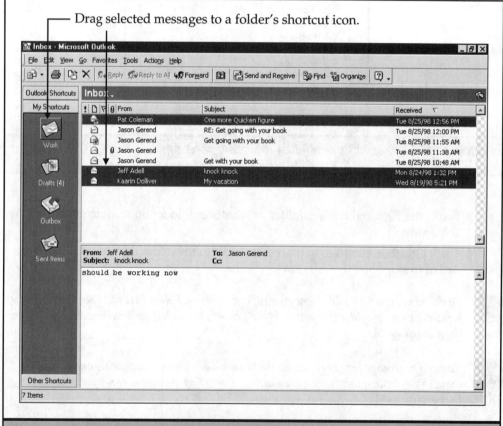

Figure 20-11. *To move messages from one folder to another, drag the messages to the shortcut for the destination folder on the Outlook Bar*

Note *If the folder you want doesn't have a shortcut on the Outlook Bar, choose View | Folder List to open a list of your Outlook folders that you can drag and drop to.*

Organizing Messages in a Folder

To organize items in a message folder, follow these steps:

1. While viewing the folder you wish to organize, click the Organize button. Outlook displays the Organize Pane as shown in Figure 20-12.

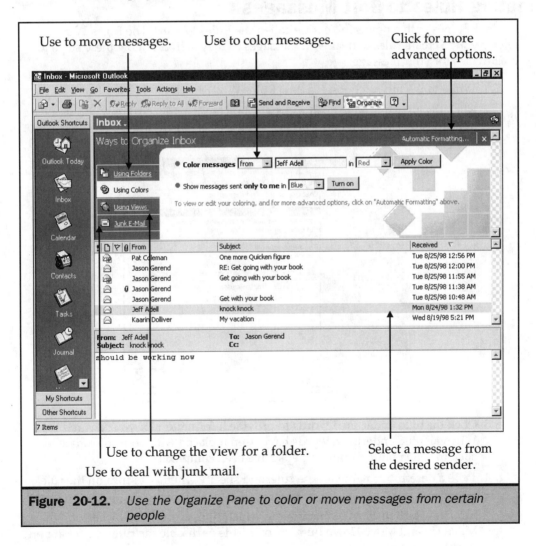

Figure 20-12. *Use the Organize Pane to color or move messages from certain people*

2. To color messages, click the Using Colors tab. Select a message from the person you wish to color messages from, choose your desired color, then click the Apply Color button. To color messages sent only to you, pick a color, then click the Turn On button.

3. To color or move junk mail messages, click the Junk E-mail tab. Choose whether to color or move Junk and Adult Content messages, and what color or folder to use, then click the Turn On button.

Creating Rules to Sort Messages

Outlook comes with a powerful feature called the Rules Wizard. The Rules Wizard allows you to create rules to deal with messages as they arrive. Follow these steps to create rules for your message:

1. While in the Inbox, choose Tools | Rules Wizard.

2. Click the New button to create a new rule. The Rules Wizard now shows a list of actions that you can perform, as shown in this illustration:

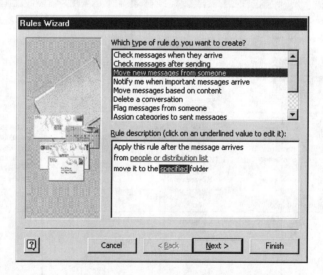

3. Click the blue underlined words to provide information for your desired rule. When all blue underlined words have been replaced with your information, click the Next button until all steps have been completed.

4. Type a descriptive name for the rule, and specify whether to turn on the rule.

5. Once you're done, you can apply it to messages already received by clicking the Run Now button, change the order in which rules are applied by clicking the Move Up and Move Down buttons, or enable or disable the rule by clicking on the box next to the rule.

Chapter 21

Using Outlook as a Personal Information Manager

This chapter explains the personal information manager side of Outlook. If you peered into the last chapter, you know that Outlook can be used to send and receive e-mail. This chapter explains how to use the program to bring order to the chaos of your life.

On the personal information manager side of Outlook are five folders:

Folder	What It Is For
Calendar	Scheduling appointments, meetings, and events, and seeing where you are supposed to be on a daily, weekly, or monthly basis.
Contacts	Keeping detailed information about the addresses, phone numbers, and e-mail addresses of your friends, colleagues, and clients.
Tasks	Juggling work assignments. Tasks appear in both the Tasks folder and Calendar folder.
Journal	Keeping track of the files you work on, how long you work on each one, and who you send e-mail to and receive e-mail from.
Notes	A place for jotting down reminder notes.

The following pages explain how to organize yourself with these folders.

 "A Quick Geography Lesson," at the start of Chapter 20, explains how to open the different screens in Outlook.

Keeping a List of Contacts

As you know if you read the last chapter, Outlook gets e-mail addresses from the Contacts folder. Besides e-mail addresses, you can keep street addresses, web page addresses, phone numbers of all types and varieties (including pager numbers and fax numbers), and even miscellaneous information such as birthdays on the Contacts List. Outlook calls a person's information a *contact*.

Read on to learn how to enter a new contact on the list, find a contact on the list, tell Outlook to dial a contact's phone number, and map a contact's address or send a contact an e-mail message.

Entering Contacts on the List

To enter a contact on the Contacts List (click the Contacts shortcut in the Outlook bar to get there), start by clicking the New Contact button. You see the Contact dialog box shown in Figure 21-1. On this screen are five tabs: General, Details, Activities, Certificates, and All Fields. Only the General tab needs filling out, but you can fill in the other four, too, if you want to keep dossiers on your friends, colleagues, and clients.

When you are done filling out the Contact dialog box, click the Save and Close button. Following are the details about filling in these tabs.

> **Tip** *If the contact whose data you want to enter works for the same company as a contact whose data you have entered already, you can get a head start entering the data. In the Contacts List, click the name of the contact whose data you have already entered in the Contacts List. Then, instead of clicking the New Contact button to enter contact information, choose Actions | New Contact from Same Company.*

> **Tip** *You can import address information from another program by choosing File | Import and Export, and then choosing the Import Internet Mail And Addresses or Import From Another Program Or File option and clicking Next. Use the next screens to select the application you want to import from, find the file, and specify how to deal with duplicate items.*

General Tab

The General tab is for entering names, addresses, e-mail addresses, web page addresses, phone numbers, and all-purpose descriptions of the person in question.

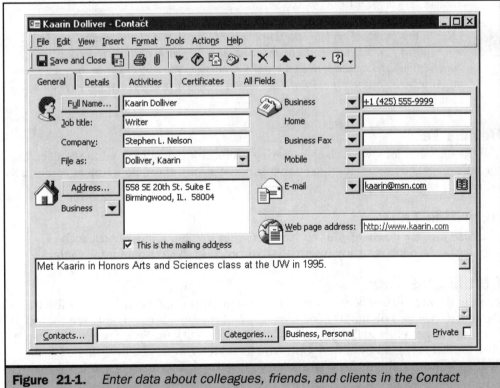

Figure 21-1. *Enter data about colleagues, friends, and clients in the Contact dialog box*

How to enter information on this tab is fairly self-explanatory. Click the Full Name button and Address button to enter the name and address one part at a time. By default, the name you enter appears in the Contacts List last name first, followed by first name, followed by middle initial, but you can make it appear any number of ways by making a choice from the File As drop-down menu or typing in how you want it to appear:

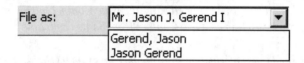

By choosing from drop-down menus, you can enter as many as three addresses and three e-mail addresses, and as many as 18 different types of phone numbers, ranging from Business to Mobile to Teletype. Notice the text box for entering a web page address, too.

 The bottom of the Contact dialog box is for jotting down a few words about the colleague, client, or friend. If your Contacts List is a long one, be sure to enter descriptions so that when the time comes to weed names from the list, you will be able to tell who is who and whether each name needs weeding.

 Later in this chapter I explain how you can get Outlook to dial phone numbers. Don't worry about punctuation marks in phone numbers, because Outlook ignores punctuation marks when it dials numbers. Moreover, you don't have to enter a 1 to use the AutoDialer because the AutoDialer does it for you when you dial numbers outside your area code.

Details Tab

The Details tab is for—what else?—entering excruciating details about the contact. On the tab are text boxes for entering anniversary dates, birthdays, department names, and other such arcana.

Activities Tab

The Activities tab is where you can view activities involving the contact, such as appointments, notes, and any information recorded in the Journal for the contact.

Certificates Tab

The Certificates tab is where you can view and manage digital certificates or IDs from the contact. Using a digital ID allows you to send encrypted messages to the contact. If you want to get a digital ID, choose Tools | Options, click the Security tab, and then click the Get A Digital ID button. Once you have an ID, you need to click the Change Settings button on the Security tab, name your settings, and then click OK.

All Fields Tab

The All Fields tab is simply a shortcut for viewing data about the client. At the top of the tab is the Select From drop-down menu. By making a choice from this menu, you can see quickly what it is you want to know about the contact.

Finding a Contact in the Contacts List

Your Contacts List can get very long, so Outlook offers a number of different ways to find a contact. Figure 21-2 outlines the several different ways. The following list spells out the details:

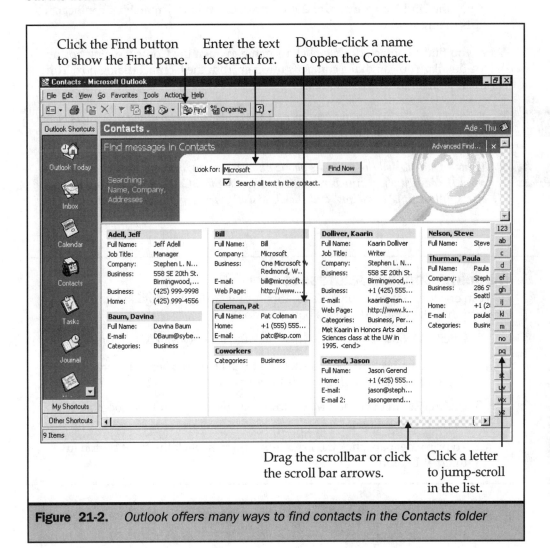

Figure 21-2.   *Outlook offers many ways to find contacts in the Contacts folder*

- **Click a Letter Button**   Click a letter button and Outlook takes you down the list to entries that are filed under the letter you clicked.

- **Use the Scroll Bar**   Either click arrows on the scroll bar at the bottom of the screen or drag the scroll box to move through the list.

- **Change the View**   Make a choice from the Current View drop-down list to display more or fewer contacts onscreen.

- **Click the Find Items Button**   You can search for any text in a contact entry by clicking the Find button and, in the Look For text box, entering the company name, street name, or any other text you remember entering in the contact item. Click the Find Now button, and if Outlook can find any matching contacts, it lists them for you.

After you find a contact, double-click its name to open the Contact dialog box and see all the details. You can dial a contact's number from the Contact dialog box. You can also send e-mail messages and faxes.

You can e-mail or fax a contact by opening the contact and choosing the Actions menu's New Message or New Fax command.

To have Outlook dial the contact's phone number for you, click the AutoDialer button, select the desired phone number, and then click the Start Call button. Pick up the phone after Outlook finishes dialing, and click End Call when you're ready to hang up.

Mapping Contact Addresses

You can create a map of a contact's location using Outlook (provided you have a connection to the Internet). Here's how you do it:

1. Open the contact entry, and then click the Display Map Of Address button.

2. Outlook connects to the Internet and opens Expedia Maps in Internet Explorer as shown in Figure 21-3.

3. Use the Zoom Level and Map Mover buttons to control the zoom and position of your map.

4. To print the map, click the Print link, and then click the Print button in Internet Explorer.

Figure 21-3. *Expedia Maps' Address Finder*

Scheduling Appointments, Meetings, and Events with the Calendar

Outlook offers the Calendar folder for making sure you don't miss activities you have scheduled for yourself. After you schedule an activity, it appears in the Calendar folder, where you can see daily appointments (in Day view), appointments for an entire week (in Work Week and Week views), or appointments for an entire month (in Month view). Figure 21-4 shows the Calendar screen in Day view. The Calendar was devised to tell you at a glance where you are expected to be and what you are expected to do each day, week, and month.

As Figure 21-4 shows, Outlook makes a somewhat arbitrary distinction between appointments, meetings, and events when it comes to scheduling. Following is an explanation of appointments, meetings, and events.

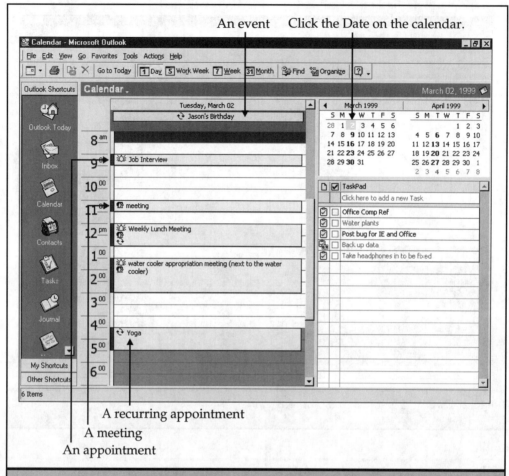

Figure 21-4. *In the Calendar folder, you can schedule one-time and recurring events, meetings, and appointments*

Appointments

An *appointment* is an activity that occupies a specific time period. For example, the job interview that takes place between 9:00 and 9:30 in Figure 21-4 is an appointment. The yoga appointment that takes place between 4:30 and 5:30 is a recurring appointment—it happens every Tuesday. The alarm bell icons you see in Figure 21-4 mean that Outlook will make the computer chime before the appointment or meeting takes place.

Meetings

A *meeting*, like an appointment, occupies a specific time period, but it involves other people besides yourself. If you are using Outlook at home, the difference between an appointment and a meeting doesn't matter at all; but if your computer is connected to a network and the network uses Microsoft Exchange Server, you can send invitations to others on the network at the same time as you schedule a meeting.

In Figure 21-4, a meeting takes place between 1:30 and 3:00, and a recurring meeting takes place between 12:00 and 1:00. Notice the two small heads in the 12:00 and 1:30 time slots—those heads tell you that a meeting has been scheduled. The revolving arrows mark recurring meetings or recurring appointments.

Events

An *event* is an activity that occupies at least 24 hours of time. The classic example of an event is a birthday. Schedule a birthday so as not to forget a loved one's or boss's special day. An all-day trade show, for example, would also be scheduled as an event. Events appear at the top of the window on the Calendar screen. In Figure 21-4, the user has recorded a birthday.

The following pages explain how to schedule one-time and recurring appointments, meetings, and events, as well as how to view your schedule in different ways and delete, edit, and reschedule activities.

 "A Quick Geography Lesson," at the start of Chapter 20, explains how to open the Calendar folder and other Outlook folders.

Scheduling One-Time Appointments, Meetings, and Events

To schedule a one-time appointment, meeting, or event, follow these steps:

1. Switch to Day view, if necessary, by clicking the Day button or choosing View | Day.

2. In the calendars on the right side of the Day or Week view, click the day when the activity is to take place. If the month in which the activity is to take place is not in view, click the arrow to the left or right of the month names to see different months.

 To go quickly to a date far in the future or past, click CTRL-G or choose Go | Go to Date, then enter the desired date and click OK.

3. Click on the hour in the day when the activity is to start and type in a brief title for your activity. To create an event, click the desired date and type in your desired Event title.

4. To lengthen the duration of the activity, click and drag the lower edge of the activity to the desired ending time.

5. To set a reminder, invite attendees, specify a location, or other details, double-click on the activity to open it in a window, as shown in Figure 21-5.

6. Fill out the desired field, then click Save and Close when finished.

Note *The Private and Show Time As fields are really only relevant when publishing your schedule on a network or to a web site as an iCalendar file.*

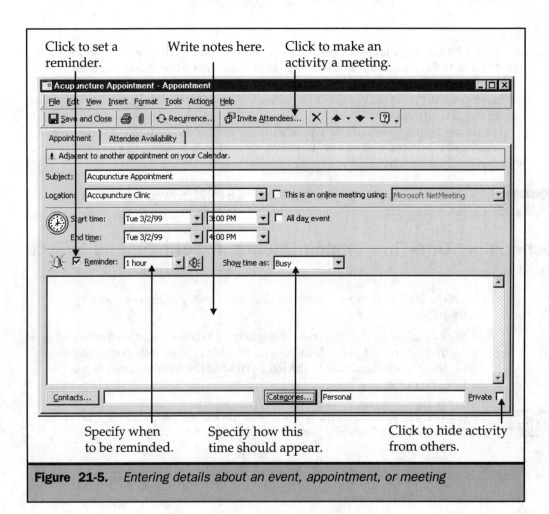

Figure 21-5. *Entering details about an event, appointment, or meeting*

Planning an Online Meeting

With Outlook, there are several ways that you can plan a meeting with someone not connected to your local Exchange Server. You can send someone an e-mail with your meeting attached as an iCalendar file, you can browse to someone's schedule that has been published to the Internet as an iCalendar file, or you can publish your own Free and Busy information to the Internet as an iCalendar file.

To send a message with an attached iCalendar, select the meeting or appointment in your Calendar folder and choose Actions | Forward as iCalendar. Outlook creates a new e-mail message with an iCalendar attachment. Compose and send the e-mail normally. If the recipients are using a calendar program compatible with iCalendar, they will be able to open the activity and save it to their own calendar.

To browse someone's iCalendar on the Internet, while viewing the Calendar folder, choose Actions | Plan a Meeting. Click the Invite Others button, then type in the URL of the iCalendar of the person whom you wish to invite. After connecting to the Internet and downloading the information, click OK, and then click Make a Meeting. Fill out the information for the meeting, then click the Send button.

To publish your own iCalendar to the Internet for anyone with an iCalendar-compatible calendar program (such as Outlook 2000 and the latest version of Lotus Organizer and Notes), choose Tools | Options, click the Calendar Options button, and then click the Free/Busy Options button. Select the Publish My Free/Busy Information check box, type the URL for your web site and the filename you want, and then click OK. Choose Tools | Send and Receive | Free/Busy Information to launch the Web Publishing Wizard and post your calendar information to your web site.

Scheduling Recurring Appointments, Meetings, and Events

Follow these steps to schedule a recurring appointment, meeting, or event:

1. On one of the calendars in the upper-right corner of the Calendar screen, click on the first day on which the recurring activity is to take place.

2. Click the hour in the day at which the recurring activity takes place.

| Tip | *To turn a one-time activity into a recurring activity, open it in the Calendar window and, when you see the Appointment, Meeting, or Event dialog box, click the Recurrence button. To open an activity in the Calendar window, double-click on it.* |

3. Choose an option from the Actions menu: New Recurring Appointment, or New Recurring Meeting. You see the Appointment Recurrence dialog box shown in Figure 21-6.

4. Under Appointment Time, make choices from the drop-down lists to tell Outlook how long the activity lasts.

OUTLOOK

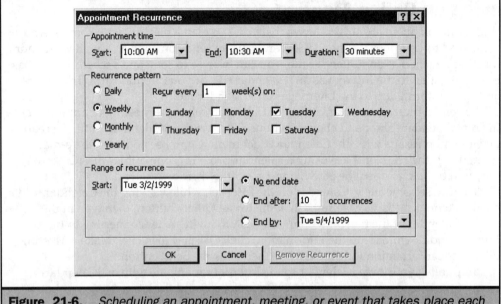

Figure 21-6. *Scheduling an appointment, meeting, or event that takes place each day, week, month, or year*

5. Under Recurrence Pattern, click the Daily, Weekly, Monthly, or Yearly option button. Depending on which button you click, you see a different array of choices to the right of the option buttons. If necessary, use the drop-down lists to more adequately tell Outlook when the meeting takes place.

6. Under Range Of Recurrence, click an option from the drop-down menus or click radio buttons to tell Outlook how far into the future these meetings will "recur."

7. Click OK. You see an Appointment, Meeting, or Event dialog box similar to the one in Figure 21-5.

8. Fill out the subject field and any other desired fields, then click Save and Close when finished.

Getting a Look at Your Schedule

After you have scheduled a bunch of activities, how can you find out what you are supposed to do and where you are supposed to be? Outlook offers several different ways to look at your schedule, as shown in Figure 21-7. The following list explains them in detail:

■ **Changing Views** To see daily appointments, weekly appointments, or monthly appointments, either click the Day, Work Week, Week, or Month

Choose a view or customize   Choose your view.
your current view.

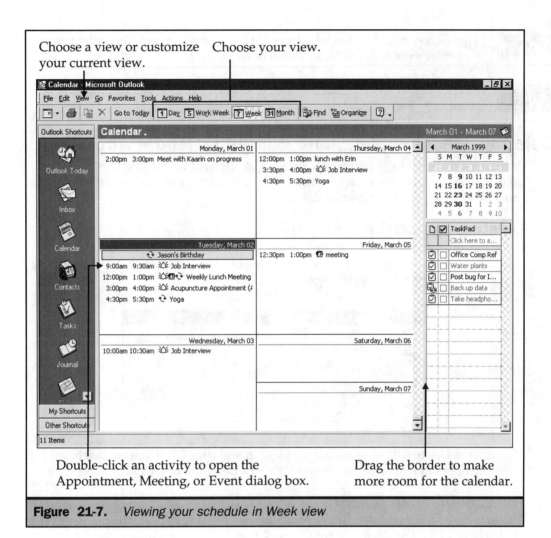

Double-click an activity to open the   Drag the border to make
Appointment, Meeting, or Event dialog box.   more room for the calendar.

Figure 21-7.   *Viewing your schedule in Week view*

button on the toolbar or choose the View menu's Day, Work Week, Week, or Month command. Figure 21-7 shows the Calendar folder in Week view. (Figure 21-4 shows it in Day view.)

■ **Seeing Specific Types of Activities**   By making a selection from the View menu's Current View submenu, you can see only active appointments, events, annual events, recurring appointments, or certain categories of events.

■ **Seeing a Single Activity**   To open the Appointment, Meeting, or Event dialog box and get all the details about an appointment, move the pointer across the activity and double-click.

To get more room to see calendar dates on the Calendar screen, drag the border between the calendar dates and TaskPad, as shown in Figure 21-7.

 Wherever you are on the Calendar screen, you can always click the Go To Today button to view today's activities.

Deleting, Rescheduling, and Editing Calendar Activities

Activities often need to be postponed, delayed, shelved, or rescheduled, so Outlook gives you the opportunity to delete, move, and edit calendar activities on the Calendar screen. Following are directions for doing so.

Deleting an Activity

If you cancel an appointment, meeting, or event, you can delete it from the Calendar screen by clicking on it and then clicking the Delete button. If the activity is a recurring activity, you see the following dialog box:

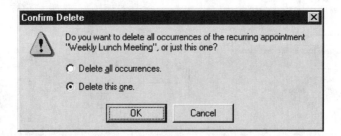

Click the Delete All Occurrences radio button and click OK if you are deleting a recurring appointment, meeting, or event. Otherwise, simply click OK.

Rescheduling an Activity

To reschedule an activity, drag it to a new location. To do that, move the pointer over the left edge of the activity you want to reschedule. When you see a four-headed arrow, click and drag the activity either to a new time or new day. You can reschedule an activity a couple months in advance by displaying the calendar month to which the activity will be rescheduled in the upper-right corner of the Calendar screen and then dragging the activity to a day on the calendar.

Editing an Activity

To edit a calendar activity, click to select it on the Calendar folder, and then double-click the item. You see the Activity, Meeting, or Event dialog box, where you can choose new options or enter new text.

Managing Your Time Better with the Tasks Folder

It's not easy to juggle several different tasks at once, but to help you become a better juggler, Outlook offers the Tasks folder. As Figure 21-8 shows, the Tasks folder tells you which tasks need doing, how urgent each one is, when tasks need to be completed, and whether a task is overdue.

The due date of each task appears on the Tasks folder. Overdue tasks appear in red. Tasks that have been completed are crossed off. Outlook offers many ways to view the Tasks screen. As shown in Figure 21-8, Detailed List view shows each task's status; how close you are to completing each task; whether the task has been given a high

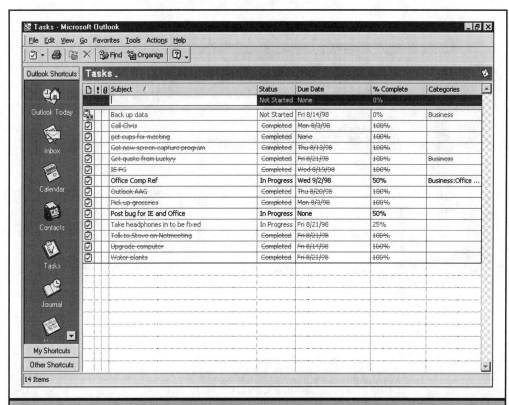

Figure 21-8.   *The Tasks folder shows how far along each task is, when it is due, and whether it is overdue. This figure shows the Tasks folder in Detailed List view*

OUTLOOK

priority or not; and which category, if any, each task falls in. Because tasks often have to be juggled along with meetings and appointments, tasks also appear on the Calendar folder on what Microsoft calls the "TaskPad" (never confuse the TaskPad with what hippies used to call the "crash pad"). Compare Figure 21-8 to Figure 21-9, which shows tasks on the TaskPad.

The following pages explain how to enter tasks in the Tasks folder, view tasks in different ways, update tasks, delete tasks, and assign a task to someone else.

Entering Tasks in the Tasks Folder

To create a new task in the Tasks Folder, click near the top of the screen where it says "Click here to add a new Task." After you click, enter a few words to describe the task.

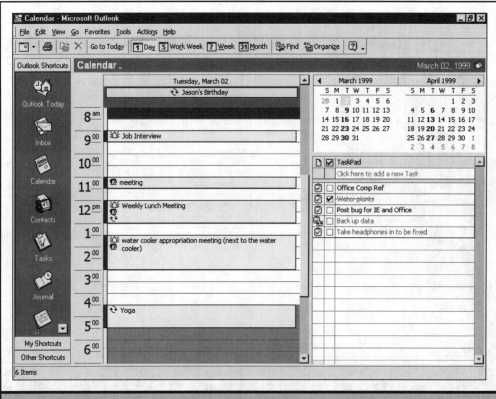

Figure 21-9. *The TaskPad as it appears on Outlook's calendar screen*

To assign a due date, click the down arrow under Due Date, as shown next, choose a date from the calendar, and press the ENTER key:

If you want to edit a task, say to prioritize tasks, track how close or far they are from completion, be reminded when they are due to be finished, keep notes about them, or even track things such as mileage or how many hours you worked on a task, you need to follow these steps:

1. Click the New Tasks button or press CTRL-N. You see the Task dialog box shown in Figure 21-10.

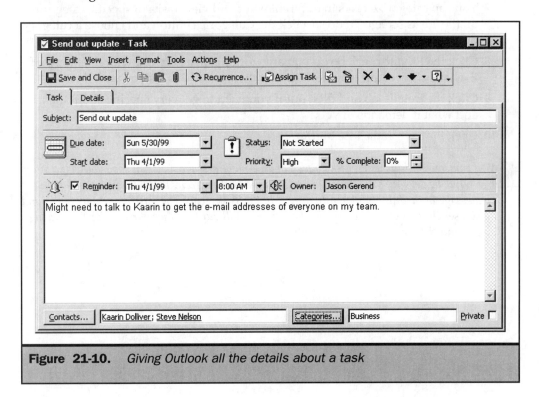

Figure 21-10.   *Giving Outlook all the details about a task*

2. In the Subject text box, enter a description of the task. What you enter appears in the Tasks folder and the TaskPad of the Calendar folder.

3. If the task is to be completed by a certain day, click the Due Date drop-down arrow and choose the day from the mini-calendar. If you started the task already, open the Start Date drop-down list and tell Outlook when you started this task.

4. Under Status, click the drop-down arrow and choose a status demarcation that best describes the task; prioritize the task with the Priority drop-down list; and tell Outlook how complete the task is by clicking arrows in the % Complete box.

5. To be reminded when the task falls due, click the Reminder check box and then choose when you want to be reminded by making a choice in the drop-down menu. Reminders come in the form of a customizable sound that Outlook plays over the speaker in your computer.

Tip *Click the Speaker icon next to the Reminder time box to specify a different sound file to be played when the task is due.*

6. Enter a few words in the text box to describe the task.

7. You can categorize tasks in different ways and view tasks in specific categories on the Tasks screen. To do so, click the Categories button and choose a category or two.

8. Click the Private check box if you are working on a network with the Microsoft Exchange Server and you don't want others to see this task on your Tasks list.

9. Click the Details tab and fill it out if you want to get very specific about the task and what it demands of you.

10. Click the Save and Close button.

Tip *If someone assigns you a task by way of an e-mail message, you can save yourself a bit of trouble by dragging the e-mail message to the Tasks screen. To do so, click the e-mail message in the Inbox and gently drag it to the Tasks icon. The Task dialog box opens and you see the text of the message in the text box. Fill out the other parts of the Task dialog box and click the Save and Close button.*

Seeing the Tasks That Need to Be Done

After you have entered the numerous tasks that you are expected to do, how can you get a fix on all the tasks and tell which one to tackle first? To do that, choose View | Current View and choose one of the ten views:

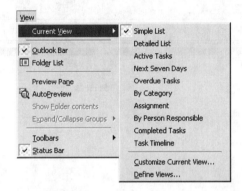

A new set of tasks appears in the view, depending on which view you chose. All views except Simple List tell you the task's status, how near it is to completion, and which category it was filed under, if any.

Choose Task Timeline view and click the Week or Month button on the toolbar to see a timeline that shows when tasks are due and when you are supposed to be working on them. Timelines appear for tasks for which you have designated a start date and due date. For tasks to which only a due date is assigned, a box with a check mark appears on the due date. As Figure 21-11 shows, if you have tasks shown in Task Timeline view and the text isn't shown in, you can move the mouse pointer on top of the tasks icon to see which task it represents.

Updating and Deleting Tasks on the Tasks Screen

Following are instructions for keeping the Tasks screen up to date and deleting tasks in the Task screen.

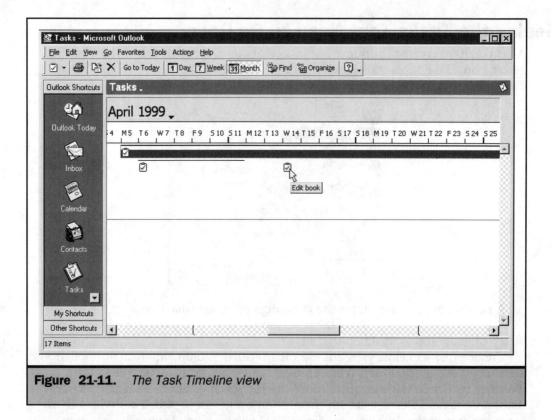

Figure 21-11. *The Task Timeline view*

Updating the Tasks Screen

To tell Outlook that a task has been completed, that a due date needs changing, that a task needs to be prioritized in a different way, or do whatever it takes to update a task, double-click it in the Tasks folder. The Task dialog box opens (see Figure 21-10). From there, you can choose options to your heart's content.

A faster but not as thorough way to update a task is to simply delete characters and enter new ones on the Tasks screen. Some views offer drop-down menus in the Status and View Date columns for changing the status of a task or the day it is due:

In Simple List view, simply click the empty box next to a task to show that it has been completed.

Assigning a Task to Someone Else

As long as your computer is connected to a network that uses the Microsoft Exchange Server, you can hand off a task to someone else. Follow these steps to do so:

1. Choose File | New | Task Request. You see a Task dialog box similar to the one in Figure 21-10, but this Task dialog box also has a To button.

2. Fill in the Task dialog box (see "Entering Tasks in the Tasks Folder," earlier in this chapter, if you need help).

3. Click the To button and tell Outlook to whom you want to assign the task.

4. Click the Send button.

In due time you receive a notice in your Inbox from the other person about whether or not they care to do the task you assigned.

Deleting a Task

After you have completed a task, you can take great pleasure in removing it from the Tasks screen. To do that, simply click a task to select it and then click the Delete button.

Recording Day-to-Day Events in the Journal

The Journal is an electronic log of the files you work on and the e-mail messages you receive and send to others. The program is set up to record the sending of e-mail messages and work done to Access, Excel, PowerPoint, and Word files. For Figure 21-12, I asked the Journal to show me the Word files that I worked on during the day of August 27, 1998. By double-clicking a Word file, I can find out how long I worked on the file and even open the Word file directly from the Journal screen.

The following pages explain how to record entries in the Journal folder, how to view the entries in different ways, how to open files, and how to delete entries.

Recording Entries in the Journal

Outlook can record certain kinds of events automatically on the Journal screen. E-mail transmissions, meeting requests, and work done to files that were created with one of the programs in the Office 2000 suite can be recorded automatically if you so choose. UFO sightings, United States World Cup championships, and other extraordinary events have to be recorded manually. Following are instructions for making automatic and manual entries in the Journal folder.

OUTLOOK

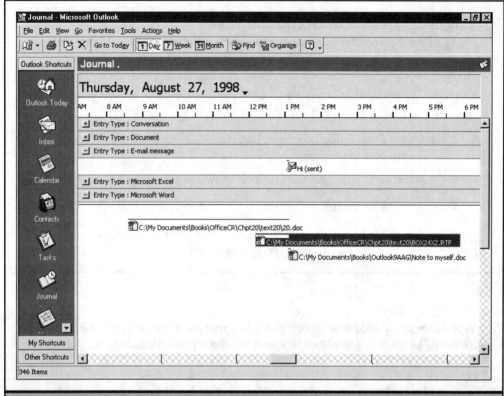

Figure 21-12. *From the Journal screen, you can track how you spent your time in Office 2000. You can open files from the Journal screen as well*

Automatic Journal Entries

To begin with, Outlook is set up to record work done in Access, Excel, PowerPoint, and Word automatically. But you can decide for yourself what is recorded on the Journal screen by following these steps:

1. Choose Tools | Options to open the Options dialog box.

2. Click the Journal Options button to open the Journal Options window. It is shown in Figure 21-13. The top half of window is for telling Outlook what type of activities to record and with whom to record them. The bottom half of the tab is for telling Outlook to record activities performed in Microsoft Office computer programs.

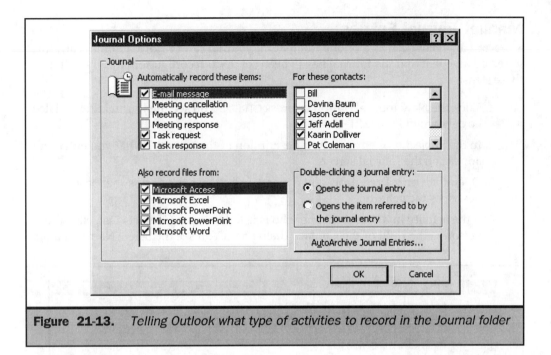

Figure 21-13. *Telling Outlook what type of activities to record in the Journal folder*

3. Under Automatically Record These Items, click next to the activities you want to record in the Journal.

4. Under For These Contacts, click beside the names of the people who are important enough to be included in Journal entries.

5. Under Also Record Files From, click to remove the check mark beside the names of the Office programs you do not care to track with Outlook. To begin with, the Journal tracks activity in all the Office programs.

Tip *Normally, when you double-click an entry on the Journal screen, you see a dialog box that says how long you worked on the file or message and offers other details as well. However, if you want to double-click to open messages and files instead, click the Opens The Item Referred To By The Journal Entry option button on the Journal tab. This option button is for people who want to make the Journal the starting point for doing their work. You can also open messages and files by right-clicking on the Journal entry and choosing the Open Item Referred To command.*

6. Click OK twice to get back to the Journal folder.

OUTLOOK

Manual Journal Entries

To record an event such as a phone call that the Journal can't record automatically, or to record an event that the Journal hasn't been set up to record automatically, follow these steps:

1. Click the New Journal button or press CTRL-N. You see the Journal Entry dialog box shown in Figure 21-14.

2. In the Subject box, enter a short description of the activity. What you enter will appear on the Journal screen.

3. Open the Entry Type drop-down menu and choose the option that best describes the activity.

4. If the activity involves someone who is listed on your Contacts List, click the button to the right of the Contact dialog box. You see the Select Names dialog

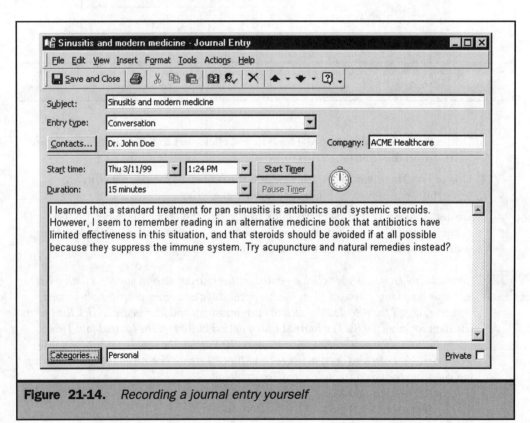

Figure 21-14. *Recording a journal entry yourself*

box. Click a contact name, click the Add button, and click OK. Back in the Journal Entry dialog box, you can enter a company name in the Company box if one isn't entered automatically.

5. Under Start Time, change the start date and time, if necessary. If this is an activity whose duration you can record, you can click the Start Timer button to move the clock and find out how long the activity lasts.

6. Enter a few words in the text box to describe the activity.

7. If you want to, click the Categories button and choose categories that describe this activity. You can display journal entries in the Journal folder by category.

8. Click the Private button if your computer is connected to a network that uses the Microsoft Exchange Server and you don't want others nosing around in your Journal folder.

9. Click the Save and Close button.

Looking at Your Journal Entries

Figure 21-15 outlines the ways to view entries in the Journal folder. Following are instructions for looking at your Journal entries and perhaps opening a file from the Journal folder:

- **Choosing Which Type of Entries to Display** Click the plus sign next to an entry type to display its entries onscreen. In Figure 21-15, the plus sign beside Entry Type: Microsoft Word has been clicked and the screen shows which Word files were worked on. To hide entries, click the minus sign beside an entry type.

- **Choosing How Entries Are Displayed** Open the View menu's Current View submenu to change the way entries are displayed. To see phone call entries, choose Phone Calls, the bottom-most option on the drop-down menu.

- **Choosing a Time Period** Click the Day, Week, or Month button on the toolbar to tell Outlook to display a day's worth, a week's worth, or a month's worth of entries. Use the scroll bar on the bottom of the screen to move backward or forward in time. (This option is only available when the Current View is set to By Type, By Contact, or By Category.)

- **Viewing the Details of an Entry** Right-click an entry, and then choose Open Journal Entry to open the Journal Entry dialog box (see Figure 21-14) and learn more about the entry. The Journal Entry dialog box tells, among other things, when and how long you worked on the file or message.

OUTLOOK

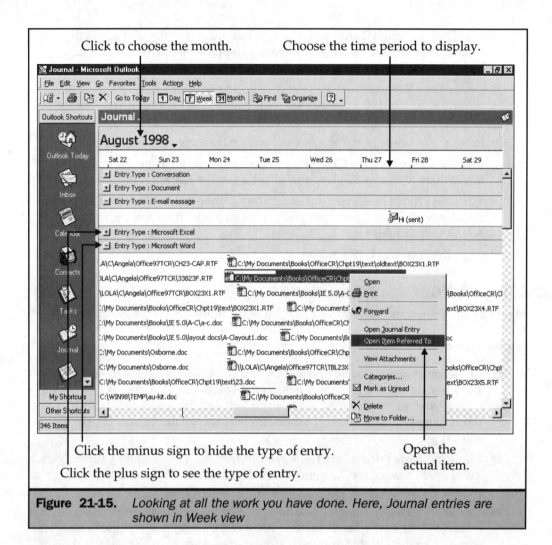

Figure 21-15. *Looking at all the work you have done. Here, Journal entries are shown in Week view*

Caution *The time listing in the Journal Entry dialog box isn't necessarily accurate. The Journal only measures how many hours and minutes you actually worked on the file, not how many hours and minutes the file was open. For example, if you open two Word files simultaneously and work with each for an hour, the Journal only records one hour each for both files, not two hours total. The clock ticks only when the file is open and active.*

■ **Opening a Message or File** To open a message or file, select an entry, right-click, and choose Open Item Referred To on the shortcut menu.

Tip   *To delete an entry in the Journal folder, select it and either click the Delete button or right-click and choose Delete from the shortcut menu.*

Jotting Down Reminders in the Notes Folder

The Notes screen is the computer equivalent of a refrigerator door. As Figure 21-16 shows, you can jot down reminder notes to yourself and keep them on the Notes

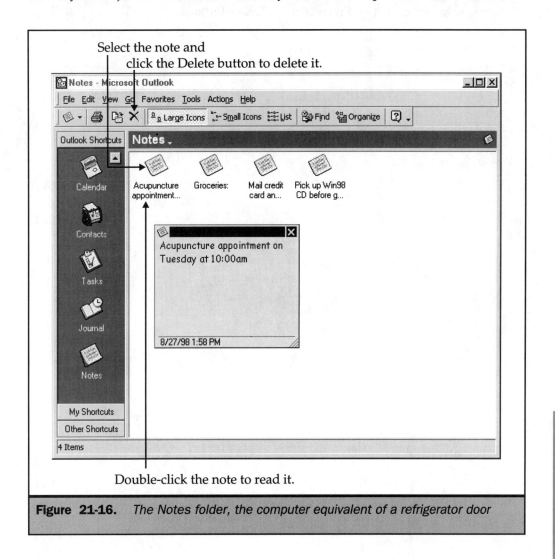

Figure 21-16.   *The Notes folder, the computer equivalent of a refrigerator door*

screen. The notes look like the yellow "sticky" notes that are always falling off refrigerator doors and landing in the trash.

To write a note to yourself, start by clicking the Notes icon on the Outlook bar, and then click the New Note button. A Note box appears onscreen. Type the note. When you are done, click the Close button (the ×) in the upper-right corner of the note. The note gets pasted onscreen beside the other notes you have written.

If you can't read a note onscreen, double-click it. The Note box appears. Drag the lower-right corner of the Note box if you can't read the note in its entirety.

To delete a note, click it and then click the Delete button.

The
Complete
Reference

Office 2000

Chapter 22

Working with
Newsgroups

This chapter explains how you can use Outlook Express, the newsreader program for Outlook and Internet Explorer, to work with newsgroups. If you've used Outlook for sending and receiving e-mail, you'll feel right at home working with newsgroups in Outlook Express. Outlook Express lets you subscribe to newsgroups, download messages, and post messages just as easily as you send and receive e-mail.

Note   *For information about using Outlook Express for e-mail, see Chapter 25.*

Getting Around in Outlook Express

Outlook Express looks and works very much like Outlook, with a few minor differences. To launch Outlook Express from Outlook, choose View | Go To and then choose News. When you launch Outlook Express, you see a page very similar to Outlook Today, except instead of displaying frequently used folders, this page displays common tasks (see Figure 22-1). However, most of the time it's easier just to use the folder pane on the left to switch between newsgroups and folders.

Tip   *Outlook Express maintains its own folders, which you can't access from Outlook.*

Note   *Depending on whether you chose to import settings from a different newsreader when setting up Outlook Express, your screen may look a little different from the one shown in Figure 22-1.*

Finding and Subscribing to Newsgroups

There are thousands of newsgroups on the Internet, and many contain an enormous amount of information. Since you can't (and surely wouldn't want to) personally read every message posted to each and every newsgroup, you need to locate the specific newsgroups that interest you, then keep them easily accessible. In other words, you need to learn how to find and subscribe to newsgroups.

Viewing a List of All Newsgroups

To view a list of newsgroups available on your server, either click the name of a news server in the folder pane, or on the Outlook Express page click the Subscribe to Newsgroups hyperlink. Then click the Newsgroups button. Outlook Express displays the Newsgroup Subscriptions dialog box, as shown in Figure 22-2.

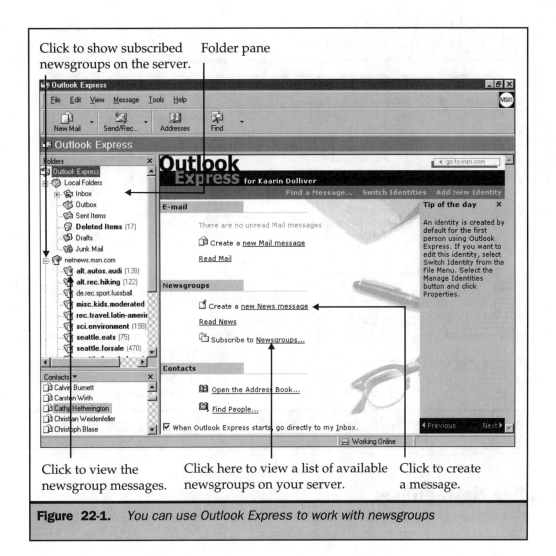

Click to show subscribed newsgroups on the server.   Folder pane

Click to view the newsgroup messages.   Click here to view a list of available newsgroups on your server.   Click to create a message.

Figure 22-1.   *You can use Outlook Express to work with newsgroups*

Note   *If you didn't set up a news server when setting up your Internet connection, you need to do so before you can browse newsgroups. To set up a news server, choose Tools | Accounts. Then click the Add button and choose News. This starts the Internet Connection Wizard, which asks you to enter your e-mail address as you want it to appear in messages you post and to enter your NNTP server. If you don't know the NNTP server's URL, contact your ISP or network administrator.*

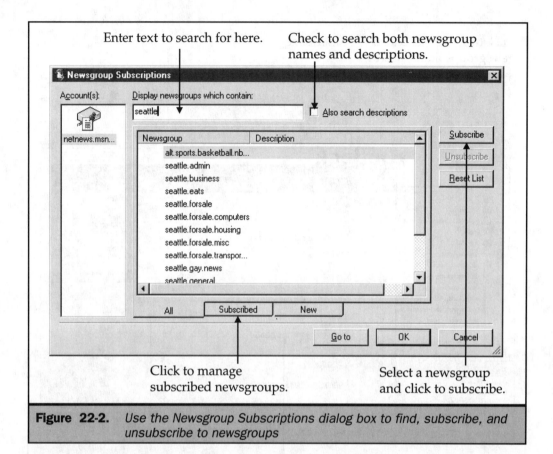

Enter text to search for here.

Check to search both newsgroup names and descriptions.

Click to manage subscribed newsgroups.

Select a newsgroup and click to subscribe.

Figure 22-2. *Use the Newsgroup Subscriptions dialog box to find, subscribe, and unsubscribe to newsgroups*

Finding Newsgroups

To find a newsgroup about a topic that interests you, type a word or two that might be in the title of a newsgroup on your topic (see Figure 22-2). For example, if you wanted to see what newsgroups were about Seattle area topics, you'd type **seattle** in the text box.

*Finding newsgroups is hard, especially since newsgroups names are sometimes cryptic. DejaNews (**http://www.dejanews.com**) offers an excellent directory service for finding the right newsgroup. It also provides a search engine you can use to search for a topic across all newsgroups.*

Opening and Subscribing to Newsgroups

Once you've found the newsgroup you want to read, just double-click it to open it and start reading messages. If you know you want to subscribe to the newsgroup, select it and click Subscribe. The newsgroup will appear under your news server in the folder pane as shown in this illustration. Click on it to start viewing messages.

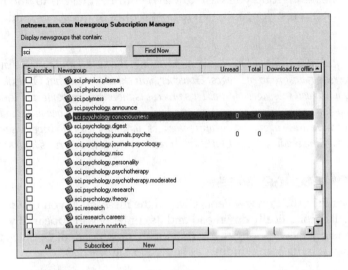

Newsgroup Names

In order to figure out which newsgroups might interest you, it helps to understand what the newsgroup prefixes mean. To get a list of newsgroup prefixes and what they stand for, go to news.answers and search for the Master List of Newsgroup Hierarchies or go to **http://www.magmacom.com/~leisen/master_list.html**. Here are a few of the more popular ones to get you started:

Prefix	Description
alt	alternative newsgroup; anything goes
bionet	biology-related newsgroup
biz	business-related newsgroup
comp	computer-related newsgroup
k12	school-related newsgroup
rec	recreation-related newsgroup
sci	science-related newsgroup
soc	society and culture-related newsgroup

Working with Newsgroup Messages

After opening the newsgroup you wish to view, your next task is to find and download the messages that interest you, and then to post replies or questions, and open message attachments.

Note   *This chapter talks about online newsgroup reading, the fastest and easiest way for most people to read newsgroup messages. However, you should know that Outlook Express also allows you to read messages offline. This process is more cumbersome and time-consuming, but if you have a very slow connection or a limited usage dial-up account, and are only interested in reading a few newsgroup messages, you may want to investigate Outlook Express's offline reading tools. Outlook Express' online help describes how to use them.*

Viewing and Opening Messages

To view a message in the Preview Pane, click on the message. If you're working online, the message will automatically download and its contents will appear. If you're working offline, you can only view messages you previously downloaded. Double-click a message to open it in its own window, as shown in Figure 22-3.

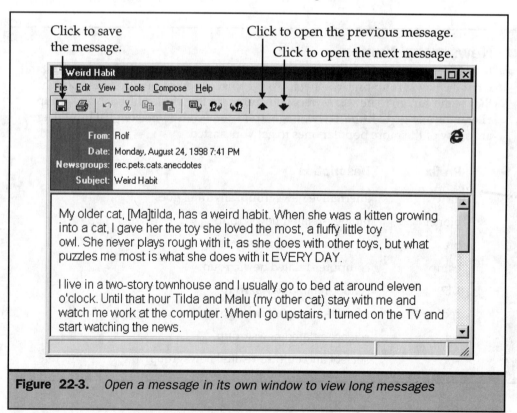

Figure 22-3.   *Open a message in its own window to view long messages*

If you're working online, the first 100 headers are downloaded automatically when you first open a newsgroup. To download more headers, choose Tools | Get Next 100 Headers. You can tell Outlook Express to download more than 100 at a time by choosing Tools | Options and clicking the Read tab. Then adjust the number in the Get Headers At A Time box.

Saving Messages

Saving newsgroup messages with Outlook Express is a little different than saving mail messages in Outlook. Instead of your saved messages being stored in your Personal Folder file like they are in Outlook, Outlook Express saves each message as an individual file that you can place anywhere on your computer.

To save a newsgroup message, open the message in its own window, then choose File | Save As. In the Save Message As dialog box, choose where you want to store your message, and whether you wish to save it as a news file or as a plain text file that can be opened by any word processor.

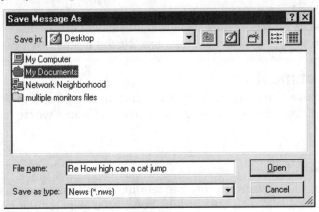

 It's a good idea to save all of your documents and files you care about in the My Documents folder. Doing this makes it easier for you to find your files, as well as making it simple to back up all of your important files at once.

Working with Attachments

Often times, messages will have files such as pictures or programs attached to them. You work with attachments to news messages just as you would attachments in e-mail messages. You know a message has an attachment when you see a paperclip in the upper-right corner of the Preview Pane, or a file listed in the Attach part of a message window.

 Even messages that seem innocuous can contain image attachments that you may find objectionable or that may be inappropriate to view in your computing environment. Be cautious as you display messages in the Preview Pane.

OUTLOOK

Opening Attachments

To open an attachment from a message window, double-click on a file listed in the Attach part of the message window, or from the Preview Pane click the paperclip and select the attachment as shown in the following illustration:

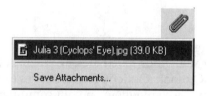

Outlook Express will probably ask whether you want to save or open the file. Click the Open It option and click OK.

 Files found on newsgroups can contain viruses. Image files are often safe, but any sort of program found on a newsgroup should be run through a virus checker before opening. If your virus checker doesn't show up next to the Save or Open command in Outlook, save the file to your hard drive and use your virus checker to scan that file.

Saving Attachments

To save an attachment you wish to keep, right-click on the desired attachment in a message window, then choose the Save As command. Choose where to save the file, then click Save.

Posting Messages

Posting messages to a newsgroup, just like sending e-mail messages, is really easy. However, it's advisable to do a little lurking before you leap; regular newsgroup followers get tired of new users asking the same questions over and over again, especially if the answers are in an FAQ (a compilation of the newsgroup's frequently asked questions). You can browse newsgroup FAQs on the web by going to **www.faqs.org**.

To post a new message, follow these steps:

1. While viewing the newsgroup to which you want to post, click the New Message button to open a new message window.

2. To post to a different newsgroup or more than one newsgroup, click Newsgroups in the message window to open the Pick Newsgroups dialog box. Select the desired newsgroups and click the Add button, as shown in the following illustration. Click OK when finished.

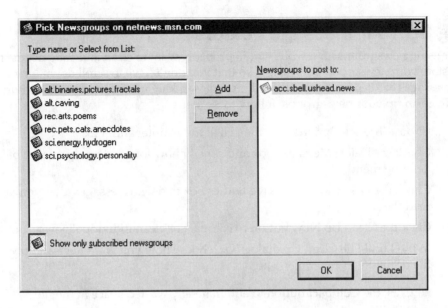

Although it may seem wise to post a message on as many newsgroups as possible so as to reach the largest audience, this technique can backfire and only offend the people you're trying to reach. Many people regularly read several newsgroups and get frustrated seeing the same message posted on many of them.

3. Type a brief subject for the post and write your message.

4. Click Post when you're finished.

*If you've got a question, try using DejaNews' search engine (**http://www.dejanews.com**) to search for a message with an answer before you post your question; chances are someone has already answered it.*

Replying to a Message

When you read a message on a newsgroup, there are two ways you can reply to the message: You can reply to the author via e-mail or you can post a reply on the newsgroup.

■ To reply to the author of the message, click the Reply button either in the main Outlook Express window or in a message window. Type your response, then click the Send button.

■ To post a reply to all newsgroups containing the message, click the Reply Group button, then compose your message and click Send.

OUTLOOK

Tidying Up Your Message Folders

After using newsgroups for a while, you'll probably want to clean and compact the files that store your newsgroup information so that you don't have to scroll down long lists of old messages or keep local copies of old messages (taking up space on your hard drive).

To clean up your newsgroups, follow these steps:

1. Choose Tools | Options, and then click the Maintenance tab.

2. Check the Delete Messages box and specify how long to keep messages before deleting them.

3. Check the Delete Read Message Bodies box to delete messages after you've read them.

4. Click the Clean Up Now button to compact or clean individual newsgroup files.

5. In the Local File Clean Up dialog box, choose how you want to clean up your file or files:

   ■ Click the Compact button to eliminate any wasted space in the file.

   ■ Click the Remove Messages button to remove the message bodies, leaving the headers.

   ■ Click the Delete button to remove all messages and headers from your file, making the newsgroup appear empty.

   ■ Click the Reset button to delete all messages and headers and read message information, making the newsgroup appear as if you've never read it before.

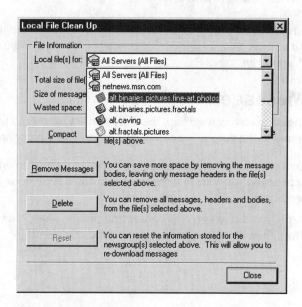

7. Click Close, then click OK when you're finished.

The Complete Reference

Office 2000

Part VI

Internet Explorer

Chapter 23

Browsing the Internet
with Internet Explorer

691

Office 2000 comes with Internet Explorer 5, Microsoft's suite of Internet software. This chapter provides an overview of what the Internet is and a fast-paced discussion of how to use the Internet Explorer 5 web browser to view and access Internet resources.

An Internet and World Wide Web Primer

In a nutshell, the Internet is a bunch of computers connected together so that people can quickly and inexpensively share information. To be extremely precise, the Internet is actually a network of networks, because the Internet is made up not only of stand-alone computers but primarily of groups of computers.

Internet Areas

The Internet allows you to share several types of information:

- You can send people electronic letters, called *e-mail* messages, that usually arrive within minutes, regardless of how far away the recipient lives. (Chapter 20 describes how to use Microsoft Outlook for e-mail. Chapter 25 briefly describes how to use Outlook Express for e-mail.)

- You can view multimedia documents, called *web pages* that companies and individuals have published. (Or you can publish your own web pages about yourself or your business.) You can also sometimes respond to the information you see using forms on web pages. For example, you can purchase products or make travel reservations over the computer from the comfort of your own home. (Later sections in this chapter describe how to use Internet Explorer to browse web pages. Chapter 25 describes how you can use FrontPage Express to create web pages of your own.)

- You can discuss issues electronically by posting messages in newsgroups. Newsgroups are a good way for subscribers to meet and send messages to people who share the same interests. (Chapter 22 describes how you do this using Outlook Express.)

- You can grab copies of files (such as tax forms, programs, hardware drivers, government and business reports, etc.) from another computer on the Internet (called an *FTP server*). You can also move files from your computer to another computer connected to the Internet (in a manner much similar to how you would move a file to another drive on your own computer).

- You can connect with other people online and type back and forth (called *chatting*), make and receive phone calls, and even send and receive live video. (Chapter 25 describes how you can do these tasks.)

Information-Sharing Methods

Because people share a variety of information over the Internet, the Internet uses a variety of methods—called *protocols*—for sharing the different types of information. Table 23-1 lists and describes some of the more common protocols that Internet programs use to move information. You don't need to remember which protocol is at work every time you move a certain type of information across the Internet. But this table may come in handy when you set up a new Internet connection or work with URLs (as described later in the chapter).

Protocol	Description
FTP	The file transfer protocol copies files to and from computers on the Internet.
HTTP	The hypertext transfer protocol allows you to view (and even upload) web pages from your computer.
HTTPS	This secure protocol allows you to send and receive sensitive information (such as credit card numbers or passwords) on the World Wide Web.
IMAP	The Internet message access protocol is one of two common protocols used to receive e-mail messages over the Internet.
IDAP	The lightweight directory access protocol allows you to search for e-mail addresses and other contact information on the Internet.
NNTP	The network news transfer protocol lets you move newsgroup messages to and from news servers.
POP3	The post office protocol is one of two common protocols used to receive e-mail messages over the Internet.
SMTP	The simple mail transfer protocol allows you to send e-mail messages over the Internet.
Telnet	The telnet protocol lets you essentially turn your computer into a dumb terminal (a monitor and a keyboard) and then log on to a server. This protocol is often used to access online library catalogs.

Table 23-1. *The Most Common Internet Protocols*

A Word About Servers and Clients

A *server* on the Internet is a computer that responds to requests for information. Servers run special software to be able to respond to requests, but any computer on the Internet can act as a server. There are several types of servers for the various types of information shared on the Internet. For example, a mail server responds to requests to send and receive e-mail messages. A news server responds to requests to view the newsgroups it stores, and a web server responds to requests to see the web pages it stores. A single computer might take several of these server roles. And it might simultaneously act as a client as well.

A *client* on the Internet is a computer that requests information from a server. Clients run client software. Office comes with a few Internet client programs—the Internet Explorer web browser is a client program. Outlook is an e-mail client, and Outlook Express is an e-mail and news client.

An Introduction to the World Wide Web

As mentioned earlier, one of the most popular uses of Internet Explorer is browsing the World Wide Web. The web, as it's often called, is popular for two basic reasons. The first, and perhaps most significant, reason is that it presents a wealth of vibrant and interesting information in an attractive way. The web contains millions of documents (web pages), many of which consist of several media. For example, a single web page may have text (one medium), pictures (another medium), sound (still another medium), and video (yet another medium). Figure 23-1 shows one example of a web page that includes several media: a United Nations page with live video footage of the General Assembly.

The other reason for the popularity of the web is that it's really easy to navigate. The web got its name because it's interconnected like a spider web so that you can move around in many directions. And programs like Internet Explorer make browsing the web a snap. The "Using Internet Explorer" section later in this chapter talks all about the ways in which you can move around the web.

Connecting to the Internet

In order to browse the Internet as described in this chapter, you need some sort of Internet connection. To connect to the Internet at work, you may likely use a permanent connection through your company's network. (For information on how to

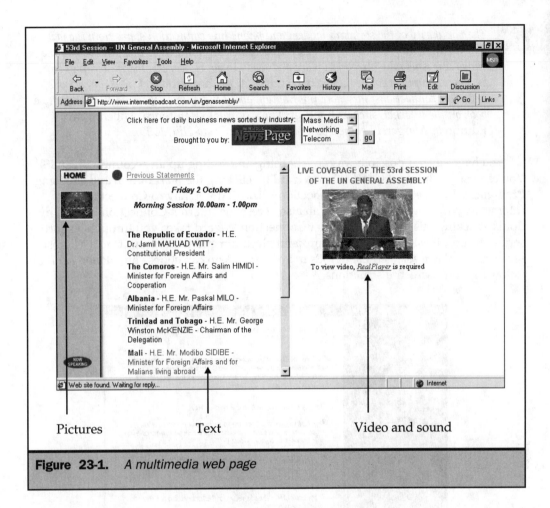

Figure 23-1. *A multimedia web page*

use this connection, contact the person in charge of your network.) To connect to the Internet from home, most people use a standard modem, your average phone line, and an account with an Internet service provider (ISP). Once you pay for an account to connect to the Internet, you can move through and visit almost all areas of the Internet for free.

Note *What's a modem? A modem is a hardware device that converts the digital language your computer speaks to an analog signal that can go across a standard (analog) phone line and vice versa.*

Note *The popularity of the standard modem and phone line connection stems from the fact that it's the cheapest and easiest to set up because the hardware is inexpensive and the phone line is usually already in place and ready to go. However, other faster (and more expensive) types of connections exist, such as ADSL connections, ISDN connections, and cable connections. For more information about these types of connections, refer to a book on the Internet, such as* Internet: The Complete Reference, Millennium Edition *by Margaret Levine Young (Osborne/McGraw-Hill, 1999).*

You have several possible ways of choosing and setting up an account with an ISP. You can use the Internet Connection Wizard by clicking the Start button and choosing Programs | Internet Explorer | Connection Wizard. If you have a Connect to the Internet icon on your desktop, you can also access the Internet Connection Wizard by double-clicking this icon. The Internet Connection Wizard takes you through a short series of steps. It asks you about your dialing location and then connects to a Microsoft server to display a selected list of ISPs in your area. You can choose an ISP and set it up following the onscreen instructions.

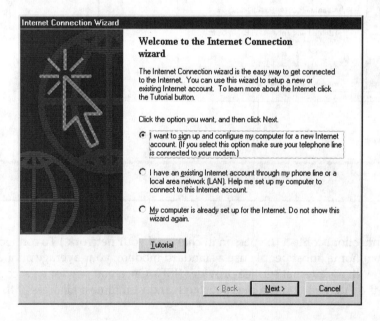

Tip *Probably the best way to choose an ISP and set up an Internet account is simply by asking around to see which ISPs the people you know use and like and which ones provide the best service in your area.*

Using Internet Explorer

This section describes how you start Internet Explorer and use its tools to browse the Internet and especially the World Wide Web.

Although Office comes with Internet Explorer, you aren't required to use it. You can install and use other Internet programs as well. For example, you may want to try out Netscape Communicator, a popular free suite of Internet programs much like Internet Explorer. This program is included on the companion CD-ROM that came with this book. Or you might want to purchase or download other programs that have additional Internet functionality not included with Office.

Starting Internet Explorer

To start Internet Explorer, double-click the Internet Explorer icon on your desktop or click the Launch Internet Explorer button on the Quick Launch toolbar. If you don't see either of these options, click the Start button and select Programs | Internet Explorer | Internet Explorer. The first time you use Internet Explorer, it may ask you for some information about your connection. If you don't know some of this information, you should be able to obtain it from your ISP or network administrator. Internet Explorer may also prompt you for sign-on information, such as your password.

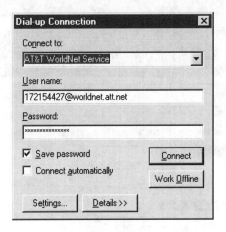

If you're connecting from home using a modem and an ISP, you need to tell Internet Explorer to prompt you to dial your ISP when you request an Internet resource. To do this, choose Tools | Internet Options and click the Connections tab. Then check the Dial The Default Connection When Needed box.

You can start Internet Explorer (or your default web browser) from Windows Explorer by requesting to open a document file (such as an HTML file) that Windows knows needs to be opened with a web browser.

After you successfully make your connection and start Internet Explorer, you see your home page. Figure 23-2 shows Internet Explorer's default home page. Note that it may take several seconds for your computer and web browser to retrieve the home page from the web server on which it resides. After Internet Explorer loads your home page, you can begin moving to other web pages in a variety of ways, as described later in the chapter.

Working with Hyperlinks and URLs

The web provides two basic ways of moving from one page to another: by clicking hyperlinks and by entering URLs. This section describes both of these methods in detail.

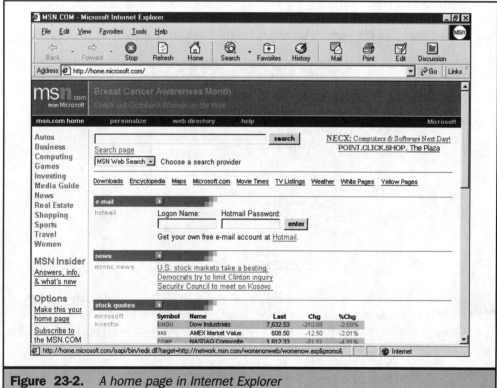

Figure 23-2.   *A home page in Internet Explorer*

Clicking Hyperlinks

A *hyperlink* is simply a bit of text or a picture that points to another web page. Hyperlinks enable you to move from web page to web page simply by clicking the mouse. You can typically identify hyperlinks in two ways:

■ The web page itself identifies the hyperlink, either by providing description text such as "click here" or by formatting the hyperlink in a certain way. Typically, for example, textual hyperlinks show in color and with underlining to stand out on the web page.

■ Internet Explorer identifies the hyperlink by changing the mouse pointer to a pointing finger. Run the mouse across your home page to give this a try. In the web page shown in Figure 23-2, if you rest the mouse pointer on top of the word Weather, the mouse arrow turns into a pointing finger. If you click this link, Internet Explorer displays the web page shown in Figure 23-3.

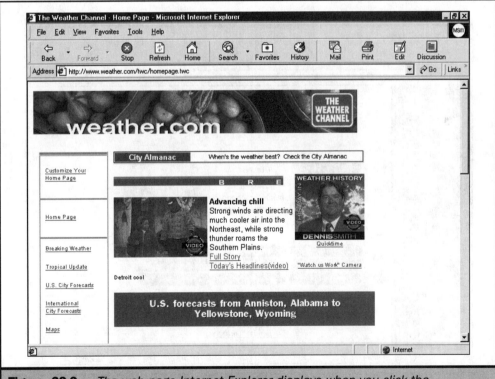

Figure 23-3.   *The web page Internet Explorer displays when you click the Weather hyperlink*

Right-click a hyperlink and choose Open In New Window from the shortcut menu to open the web page in its own window. By doing so, you can continue to view the current web page while retrieving a new one.

Using URLs

A *URL*, or uniform resource locator, identifies a specific Internet resource such as a web page or a file on an ftp server. In other words, the URL is the resource's address. This section describes what URLs are and how you use them.

UNDERSTANDING URLS   While URLs look like ciphers the first few times you see them, they're actually fairly easy to interpret and read. In general, URLs consist of three parts: the protocol, the server name, and sometimes the path and filename.

The first part of the URL is the protocol name. In Figure 23-4, for example, the protocol name is the http:// portion of the URL. The protocol specifies the

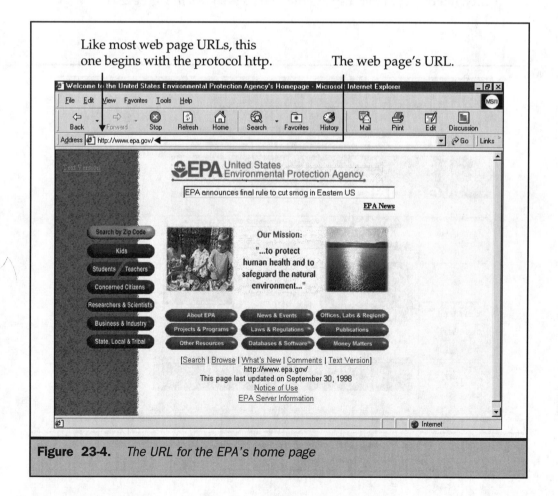

Figure 23-4.   *The URL for the EPA's home page*

information-sharing method used to move that particular Internet resource (in this case, your average web page). Table 23-1 earlier in the chapter described some of the more common protocols used on the Internet.

If an Internet resource uses another information-sharing method, the protocol or service name is different. The following illustration shows the URL for a resource that uses the ftp protocol, for example.

The URLs for ftp sites begin
with the protocol ftp.

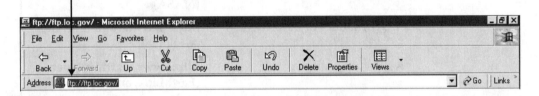

> **Note**   *You use Internet Explorer to browse FTP sites the same way you use Windows Explorer to browse folders on your hard disk. To view the files and subfolders in a folder, double-click the folder's icon. To open a file Windows recognizes (such as a text file or a .PDF file if you have Adobe Acrobat Reader), double-click the file. To download a file Windows doesn't recognize, double-click the file and click the Save This File To Disk option button. Then click OK and use the Save As dialog box to specify a storage location for the file. For more information on downloading files, see "Retrieving Files via Web Pages," later in this chapter.*

The next part of a URL is the server's domain name. This names the server on which the Internet resources you want to retrieve are stored. While it's not an ironclad convention, the first part of the domain name for web servers often uses the common abbreviation for the World Wide Web, www. The second part of the domain name identifies the company or organization. The last part of the domain name specifies the domain type. In the case of the EPA home page URL shown in Figure 23-4, for example, the server name is www.epa.gov. Similarly, in the case of the Library of Congress ftp site URL shown in the previous illustration, the server name is ftp.loc.gov.

The .gov part of the domain name specifies the type of domain. The domain type abbreviation describes what kind of publisher published the web page or web site. Table 23-2 table lists some of the most common domain types.

Other countries have their own domain type abbreviations and country abbreviations. For example:

- The United Kingdom's domain abbreviation is .uk. The British Broadcasting Corporation's home page is at **http://www.bbc.co.uk**.

- France's domain abbreviation is .fr. The Louvre museum home page is at **http://mistral.culture.fr/louvre/**.

Domain Type Abbreviation	Type of Publisher	Example
.com	A commercial organization	**http://www.henson.com/** (The Jim Henson Company)
.edu	An educational institution	**http://www.cornell.edu** (Cornell University)
.gov	A government agency	**http://www.nasa.gov** (NASA)
.mil	A U.S. military organization	**http://www.af.mil** (The U.S. Air Force)
.net	A network provider	**http://www.earthlink.net** (EarthLink, an ISP)
.org	An organization that doesn't fit any of the other standard domain types, often a non-profit organization	**http://www.now.org** (The National Organization for Women)

Table 23-2.   *Domain Types and Abbreviations*

- Japan's domain abbreviation is .jp. The Tokyo Stock Exchange's home page is at **http://www.tse.or.jp/**.
- Germany's domain abbreviation is .de. The Volkswagen home page is at **http://www.volkswagen.de**.

Note   *A web site is just a collection of web pages published by the same source and linked together. For example, a person or business might decide to categorize content and divide it among several pages instead of putting it all on one. This way, viewers do not need to wait for an enormous page to load or scroll through lots of content that doesn't interest them, but can instead click hyperlinks to individual pages containing the information they need.*

The last part of a URL supplies the path name of the Internet resource you want to retrieve. The path name starts with the / character, then names the folder (or perhaps the folder and subfolder), and then (usually) names the file.

Sometimes you can't see the path and filename of an Internet resource you're viewing. This often happens when the resource is the default resource on that server. If you visit the home page of a large corporation's web site, for example, the URL may show only the server address—that is, until you link to a folder or subfolder within the web site.

ENTERING URLS   While clicking hyperlinks and toolbar buttons is the easiest way to move from web page to web page, you (thankfully) aren't limited to following a trail of hyperlinks. You can also enter a URL directly into the Address box. To do this, click the Address box and then type the URL. For example, if you want to visit the Danish soccer association's home page at **http://www.dbu.dk**, you simply type this URL into the Address box.

You don't need to include the http:// prefix if you're visiting a web server. Internet Explorer (as well as most other web browsers) assume that the URL you've entered is for a web page if you don't specify the Internet protocol. You also typically don't need to include an actual web page document in your URL; web servers will typically supply a default home page if you don't identify some other page by name. This means that it's usually quickest to just enter the piece of the URL that falls between the http:// and the very next /. Entering this chunk of the URL takes you to the default home page, and from there you can click hyperlinks to get to the different web page documents.

Tip

As you enter URLs directly into the Address box, be sure that you enter the slashes as slashes (and not as backslashes).

Internet Explorer actually maintains a list of web pages and web sites you've visited. As you start to type a URL in the Address box, Internet Explorer displays a list of URLs you've previously visited that begin with the letters you're typing. To revisit one of these resources, select it from the list.

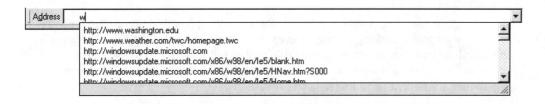

Using Telnet Sites

When you enter a URL that begins with telnet:// or click a hyperlink to a telnet site, Internet Explorer starts the telnet client that comes with Windows 95/98 and Windows NT.

Connecting to a telnet site in effect turns your computer into a dumb terminal, a monitor and keyboard connected to a telnet server. When you finish working with a telnet site, follow whatever instructions you were given for logging off of the telnet site and then choose Connect | Disconnect.

 Note *For more information about working with the Windows telnet client, refer to the Windows online help or a good book on Windows and the Internet.*

Using the Internet Explorer Toolbar

This next section describes how you use Internet Explorer's toolbar to move around in the World Wide Web and other parts of the Internet.

Using the Back and Forward Buttons

As you move from web page to web page, you may notice that Internet Explorer activates the Back and Forward buttons on the toolbar. You can click the Back button to redisplay the web page you were just viewing. If you've just clicked the Back button, you can click the Forward button to go back to the web page you were viewing before you clicked the Back button.

Because Internet Explorer caches, or stores, copies of web pages you've recently viewed on your computer, you'll find that it redisplays web pages very quickly when you click the Back or Forward button.

Stop and Refresh

The Stop button tells your web browser to stop retrieving a web page from a web server. If a web page is taking a long time to grab (more than about a minute if you're using a dial-up connection), you can use this tool to tell Internet Explorer that it should give up on the retrieval operation. You can then tell it to retry retrieving the page, or you can visit a different page instead.

The Refresh button tells your web browser to grab a new copy of a web page from the web server. You use this tool when the web page didn't load correctly or completely. You also use it if a web page changes frequently and you want the most recent version.

If you've used Netscape Navigator before, you'll recognize the Refresh button as Internet Explorer's equivalent of the Reload button. Both buttons do exactly the same thing.

Home

The home button moves you to your default starting, or home, page. Internet Explorer links to a Microsoft home page that you can customize if you like it. However, you can and should consider changing your home page to another web page, if you find yourself frequently using a different page's information as a springboard in your web browsing.

To designate a new home page, choose Tools | Internet Options, click the General tab, and then enter the URL of the home page you want Internet Explorer to display in the Address box, as shown in Figure 23-5.

Search

One of the biggest challenges in using the World Wide Web as a tool is that it's often very difficult to find information. This isn't surprising, really. Two problems confront

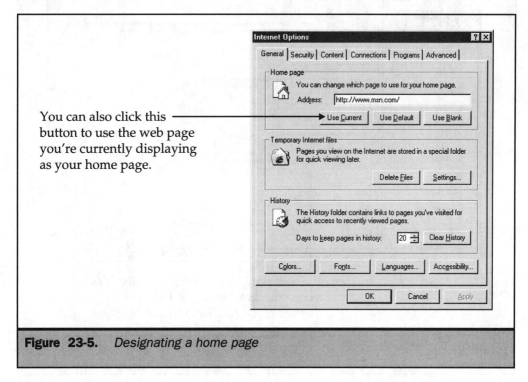

You can also click this button to use the web page you're currently displaying as your home page.

Figure 23-5. *Designating a home page*

web site visitors: the staggering volume of the information available and the varying quality and reliability of the information. Tens of thousands of web sites exist, supplying millions of pages of information. And if you sift through even a few dozen pages, you'll encounter voluminous quantities of advertising, sloppily prepared and hastily presented information, and much suspect data.

You can use search engines to deal with the quantity of information problem and you can sometimes even use them to help filter out some of the poor quality web pages. Search engines attempt to organize and bring structures to the Internet's—and in particular to the web's—vast resources.

Click the Search button in Internet Explorer to display the Search bar, as shown in Figure 23-6. You can use the Search bar's default search engine by entering a search

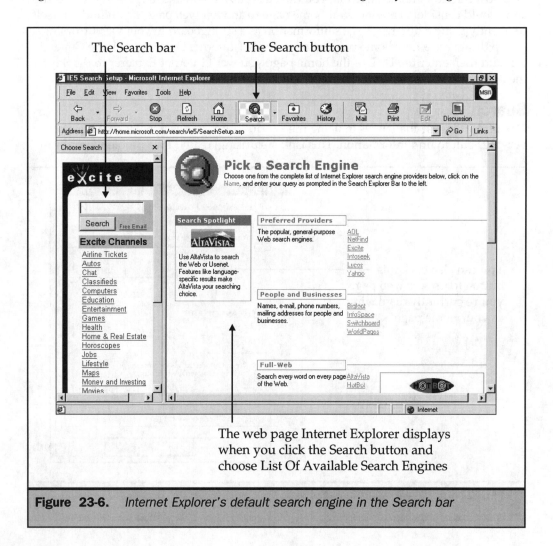

Figure 23-6. Internet Explorer's default search engine in the Search bar

phrase or browsing through the search engine's categories. If you click the down arrow on the right side of the Search button and choose the On The Internet command, Internet Explorer displays a different search engine page in the Search bar. If you click the down arrow on the right side of the Search button and choose the List Of All Search Engines command, Internet Explorer displays a list of search engines in the main pane to the right of the Search bar. To remove the Search bar, click the Search button again.

You shouldn't feel obligated to use the default search engine that Internet Explorer displays first in the Search bar. Once you find a search engine that suits your needs, you can go immediately to that engine's web page by entering its URL in the Address box or by adding the search engine's home page to your list of favorites.

WAYS TO USE A SEARCH ENGINE   Search engines work in different ways. Some use computers to index millions of web pages based on hyperlinks. Others use human resources to sort through and categorize web pages. You usually have two ways of searching the Internet:

■ If you're looking for something specific, it usually works best to supply a term or phrase to the search engine, as shown in Figure 23-7. For example, let's say you are interested in taking a train to the Indian mountain town of Darjeeling. You might enter the words **Darjeeling** and **train** in the search engine's text box as shown in Figure 23-7. When you press ENTER, the search engine then looks up the term or phrase in its index and supplies the first portion of a list (usually a lengthy list) of web pages that contain that term. You can go to a web page by clicking its hyperlink from the list.

Note   *Different search engines work differently, but, in general, if you enter more than one word, enclose the words in quotations if you want the search engine to treat the words as a phrase. For example, if you wanted to search for web pages that used the phrase "St. Augustine," you would enclose this entry in quotation marks.*

■ If you're looking for general information on a topic, you can browse through the search engine's categories and subcategories, as shown in Figure 23-8. For example, if you want to learn more about the province of Alberta in Canada, you could click the Countries subcategory under the Regional category. Then you could go through the categories clicking Canada, Provinces and Territories, and Alberta. Each time you click a subcategory, the search engine displays a new page listing the information subcategories within the selected category.

WHAT TO DO WHEN A SEARCH ENGINE DOESN'T WORK   Search engines, as you'll find as soon as you begin using them, aren't perfect. Certainly, they make it much easier to find information on the Internet, but they won't always help you find the information you need or want. For this reason, don't rely solely on search engines. If you stumble upon some interesting web site while browsing, for example, add it to your Favorites folder, which is discussed in the following section. If you hear about or see the

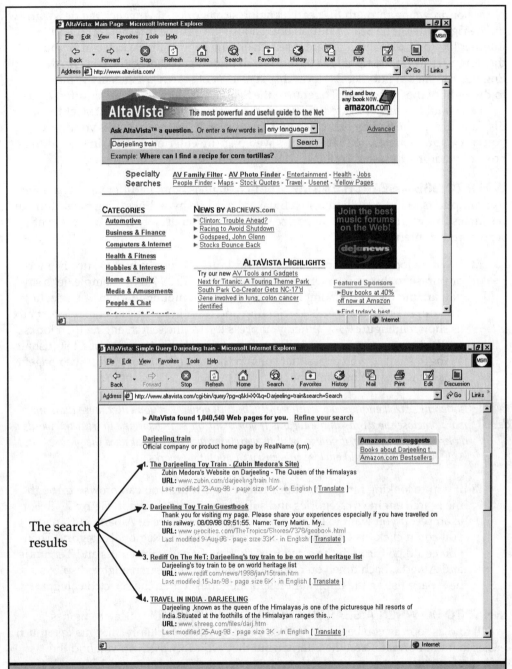

The search
results

Figure 23-7. *Entering a search phrase using the search engine AltaVista*

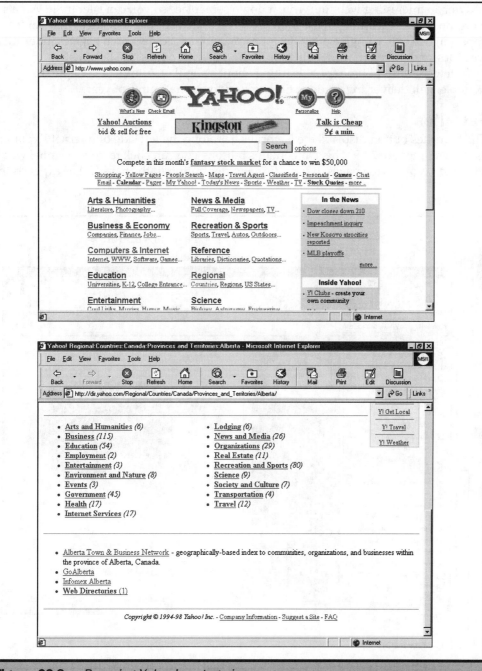

Figure 23-8. *Browsing Yahoo's categories*

URL for an interesting web site, write it down someplace so you can later try it. What's more, do consider learning to use more than one search engine. Resources that don't appear in one search engine often do appear in another. Some search engines index more web sites, and therefore work better for finding specific or obscure information.

A few minutes of time spent learning about Yahoo! or AltaVista in depth, for example, will deliver tremendous time savings over the course of year.

Favorites

The Favorites button displays the Favorites bar along the left side of Internet Explorer, as shown in Figure 23-9. This bar contains buttons you can click to go to channel web sites and favorite web pages. If you click a folder button in the bar, the bar expands to

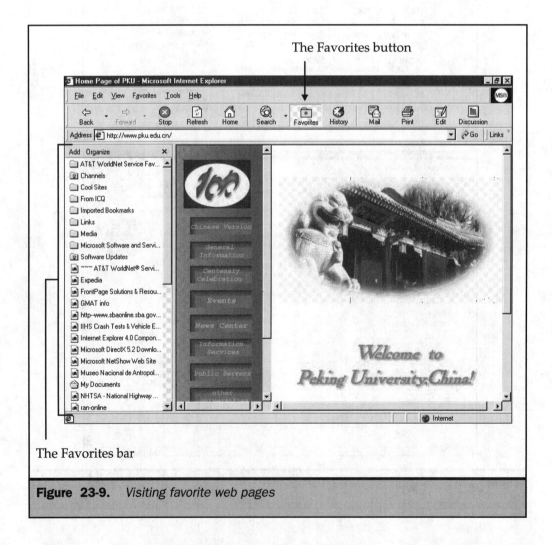

Figure 23-9. *Visiting favorite web pages*

show the web pages included in that folder. Microsoft and your ISP add some web pages to your Favorites folder for you to begin with, but you'll probably want to add your own favorite web pages to your Favorites folder so that they appear on this bar. The next sections describe how to add and work with your favorites.

ADDING A FAVORITE TO YOUR FAVORITES FOLDER   If you find or discover a web page that you want to revisit, you can tell Internet Explorer to record the web site's URL in your Favorites folder. To add the web page you're currently viewing to the Favorites folder, choose Favorites | Add To Favorites. Then, when Internet Explorer displays the Add Favorite dialog box, click the Create In button so that Internet Explorer expands the dialog box to show the Favorites folder's subfolders. Select the folder you want to store the web page's URL in, and then click OK.

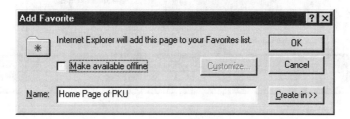

    If you want to create a new subfolder, select the folder into which you want to place the subfolder, click the New Folder button, and then enter a name for the new folder using the dialog box that Internet Explorer provides.

WORKING WITH FAVORITES   To organize your favorites, choose Favorites | Organize Favorites. Then use the Organize Favorites dialog box shown in Figure 23-10 to move, rename, delete, and edit the properties of your favorites.

- **Create a New Folder for Storing Favorites**   Click the Create Folder button. This adds a new folder to the list. To name the folder, type a name and press ENTER.

- **Add a Favorite to a Folder**   Select the favorite, drag it up or down the list, and drop it in the folder.

- **Move a Favorite Up or Down the List**   Select a favorite and drag it up or down the list. Drop it where you want the favorite to fall.

- **Subscribe to a Favorite for Offline Viewing**   Select the favorite and check the Make Available Offline box. Subscribing to web pages and channels is described later in this chapter.

- **Rename a Favorite**   Select the favorite and click the Rename button. Type a new name and press ENTER.

- **Delete a Favorite**   Select the favorite and click the Delete button.

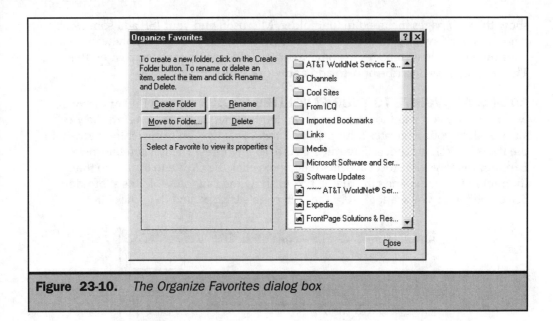

Figure 23-10. *The Organize Favorites dialog box*

History

Click the History button to display the History bar along the left side of the Internet Explorer window, as shown in Figure 23-11. To view a list of the web sites you visited within a listed range of time, click that time range's hyperlink. To view a list of the web pages you viewed within the web site, click the web site's hyperlink. To revisit a web page listed in the History bar, click the web page's hyperlink.

To delete your history list, choose Tools | Internet Options and click the Clear History button.

Mail

Click the Mail toolbar button to launch your default e-mail client. Chapter 25 discusses using Outlook Express to create and send e-mail messages. Chapter 20 discusses using Outlook for e-mail.

If you find a web page you want to share with others, you can send the web page or a hyperlink to the web page in an e-mail message. To do so, display the web page and choose File | Send. Then choose Page by Email or Link by Email.

You can change which programs you use as your default Internet programs by choosing Tools | Internet Options and clicking the Programs tab. Then select the program you use most in each category using the drop-down list boxes.

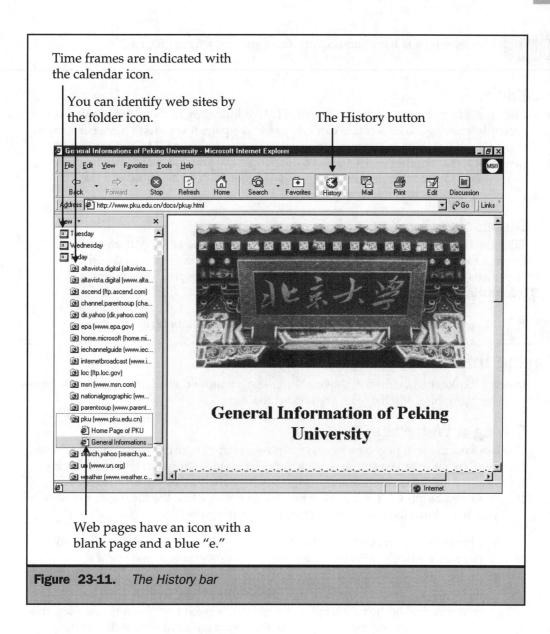

Time frames are indicated with the calendar icon.

You can identify web sites by the folder icon.

The History button

Web pages have an icon with a blank page and a blue "e."

Figure 23-11. *The History bar*

Print

You can print the web page you're viewing by clicking the Print button. When you do so, Internet Explorer prints the page using the default settings. This option works well for pages without frames. If you want to specify print settings (for example, to print only some elements of a page), choose File | Print.

For more information about printing document files, refer to Chapter 2.

Edit

Click the Edit button to use your default HTML editor copy of the web page you're currently viewing. Note that you can't repost a web page if you don't have permission to post on that web page's server. However, you can use your HTML editor to edit and save a local copy of the page. Chapter 6 describes how you use Word and the other programs in Office for web publishing, and Chapter 25 describes how you use FrontPage Express to create web pages.

Discussion

Click the Discussions button to display the Discussion pane at the bottom of the Internet Explorer window. You can use the Discussion pane to view and add comments to discussions about Office documents or web pages. See Appendix C for information on using this feature.

 You need to first set up the Discussion feature before you can begin using it.

Saving Information from the Internet

Internet Explorer lets you easily save a web page, an individual element on a web page (such as a graphic), or a file from an Internet location.

Saving a Web Page

You can save the web page you're currently viewing by choosing File | Save As. When Internet Explorer displays the Save Web Page dialog box, shown in Figure 23-12, use the Save In drop-down list box and the list box beneath it to indicate the folder where the file should be stored. Then use the File Name box to name the file. From the Save As Type drop-down list box, choose a format for saving the file:

- Choose Web Page, Complete to save each of the files that make up the web page individually in its native format, including graphics and frames.

- Choose Web Archive to save all of the web page's files in a single archive. If the web page is not very complex, this option allows you to easily save one file containing all of the web page's elements. If the web page is more complex, this option creates a self-extracting file of the web page's individual files and requires a lot of memory to extract.

- Choose Web Page, HTML Only to save only the HTML on the web page. This preserves the text formatting but does not include graphic images.

- Choose Text Only to save only the text on the web page as an unformatted text document.

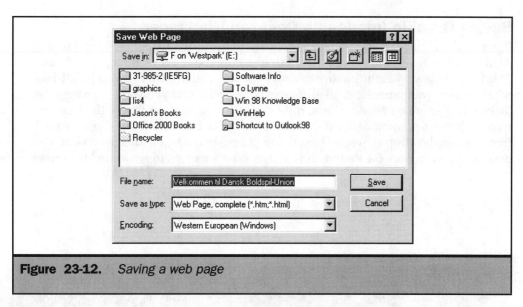

Figure 23-12. *Saving a web page*

Tip   *You can save the web page or graphic that's the target of a hyperlink by right-clicking the link and choosing the shortcut menu's Save Target As command. Use the Save As dialog box Internet Explorer displays to specify the storage location.*

Saving Graphic Images

You can save a graphic image individually by right-clicking the image and then choosing the shortcut menu's Save Picture As command. When you do this, Internet Explorer displays the Save Picture dialog box. Use the Save In drop-down list box and the list box beneath it to indicate the folder where you want to store the graphic image. Optionally, use the File Name box to provide a new name for the graphic image and the Save As Type drop-down list box to save the image as a .BMP file instead of a .GIF or .JPG file.

Saving Graphic Images as Desktop Wallpaper

If you find an image on the web that you want to use as wallpaper on your desktop, right-click the image and choose the shortcut menu's Save As Wallpaper command. This immediately adds the picture to your desktop, as shown in Figure 23-13. To see what the new wallpaper looks like, display your desktop. If you want to change the look of the picture on your desktop, right-click the desktop and choose the shortcut menu's Properties command. On the Background tab, choose Center, Tile, or Stretch from the Display drop-down list box. If you choose to center the image on your desktop, you can click the Pattern button to choose a pattern to go around the image.

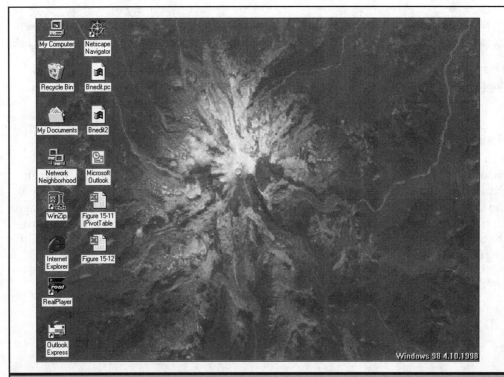

Figure 23-13. *This desktop uses a graphic image from the Internet*

Retrieving Files via Web Pages

Many web pages include hyperlinks that point not to other web pages, but instead point to files that Internet Explorer thinks you may want to save and not just view (such as hardware drivers, shareware and freeware programs, and almost anything else besides web pages). If you do click a hyperlink that points to such a file, Internet Explorer displays the dialog box that follows:

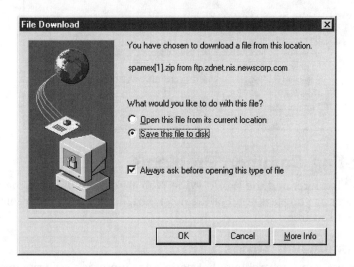

To confirm that you do indeed want to save the file, click the appropriate option button and then OK.

 *You probably want to think twice about downloading files unless you are fairly certain the source is reputable because it is very easy to get viruses from the Internet, and even if you are running an antivirus program, you aren't protected from each and every virus. A good source for general information about viruses is the comp.virus newsgroup's FAQ list. You can access the complete FAQ list or a condensed version of it from the web page at **http://www.cis.ohio-state.edu/hypertext/faq/usenet/computer-virus/top.html**. If you're indiscriminate about the files you download, you should probably acquire and regularly use virus protection software. You can't catch a virus simply by opening web pages. You can, however, catch a virus by running or opening a file you've saved on your computer.*

After you click OK, Internet Explorer next displays the Save Web Page dialog box (as shown in Figure 23-12), which you can use to specify where the file should be saved and what it should be named. When you provide this information and click OK, Internet Explorer begins downloading the file, displaying the dialog box that follows to apprise you of its progress. To stop downloading a file, of course, you just click Cancel.

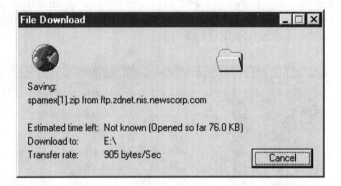

Troubleshooting Common Problems

While Internet Explorer and the World Wide Web are easy to use, you may encounter several problems as you start out. For the most part, however, these problems are relatively easy to address.

Slow Transmission Times

Perhaps the most common problem that people encounter is slow transmission. Richly illustrated HTML documents—the kind that are most fun to view—take time to retrieve. And this is especially true when you're connecting to the web site over a slow, 28.8Kbps dial-up networking connection. HTML documents that include sound, video, and other exotic objects take even longer. Fortunately, there are a couple things you can do to at least mitigate the problem of slow transmission times.

CHOOSE A SMART HOME PAGE   As mentioned earlier, Internet Explorer loads a home page every time it starts. While that's usually fine, it doesn't make sense to spend any time waiting for Internet Explorer to load a fancy home page you don't read. You can change the home page that Internet Explorer loads as described in the "Home" section earlier in the chapter.

SKIP THE SOUNDS AND VIDEOS   One other technique you can easily use to speed up transmission time is to not load the sounds and video for each web page you open. To make this adjustment, choose Tools | Internet Options and click the Advanced tab. Then you uncheck the Play Sounds and Play Videos boxes and click OK.

Web Site Connection Problems

If you can't connect to a web site, your problem typically falls into one of three categories: a problem with the connection itself, a problem with the remote web server, or a bad URL. Typically, you can easily identify all problems. And once you identify the problem, you can begin working on a solution.

BAD CONNECTIONS   The first thing you should check when you can't connect to a particular web site is the connection itself. See if you can display a new web page that you haven't just viewed. If you can, you can be sure that your connection is working.

If you've connected to the Internet using a dial-up connection, you can display a status dialog box to check on your connection. To do so, click the icon that looks like two computers with green monitors on the right end of the Windows taskbar. The middle button says Disconnect if you are currently connected. If you see the Connect button instead, it means you lost your connection. Click this button to reconnect.

BAD URLS   If you can't connect to a web site and you're sure your connection is working, you may have entered the URL incorrectly. When you enter an incorrect URL, Internet Explorer usually returns with a "This page cannot be found" message. URLs aren't exactly easy to enter. You need to make sure that you type everything just right and that you punctuate the URL correctly. You need to be careful, for example, that you use periods and not commas and slashes rather than backslashes. Once you've checked for these sorts of obvious errors, you have two other tacks you can attempt:

- You can simplify the URL so that you land at the web site's root directory. Then, once there, you can (hopefully) use hyperlinks to move to the web page you want to view. For example, if you can't open the web page at **http:// www.company.com/folder/subfolder/page1.htm**, you can enter the URL as **http://www.company.com** and then hope that the web server's default home page contains hyperlinks that point to the HTML document named page1.htm.

- You can find another web page that shows a hyperlink to the page you want and then use this hyperlink to move to the page. For example, you may be able to use a search engine to find the URL. (The "Search" section of this chapter explains how to use a search engine.)

BAD WEB SERVERS   If you know a connection is working and you know the URL is correct, the remote web server just may not be working. When this is the case, Internet Explorer usually returns with the "Navigation cancelled" or "The page cannot be displayed" message. The web server to which you're trying to connect may be too busy to respond to your request, for example. (This often happens with very popular web servers.) The web server may be temporarily shut down for regular maintenance. Or, the web server may simply have permanently disappeared. In any of these cases, your only real recourse is to just attempt a connection later.

MESSED UP CONNECTION PROPERTIES   If you or someone else may have edited your connection properties, make sure Internet Explorer knows what connection you're using, and that the connection is set up correctly. To do this, choose Tools | Internet Options and click the Connections tab. To verify a connection's settings, select the connection and click the Settings or LAN Settings button (depending on the type of connection.) Then click the tabs of this dialog box and verify that everything is entered correctly. If you need help, contact your ISP or network administrator.

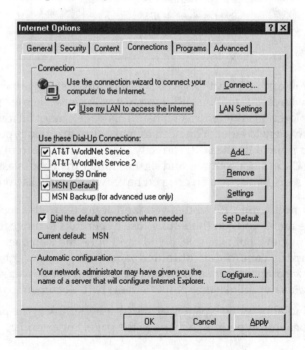

Refining Your Browsing

Internet Explorer offers several ways that you can refine your browsing to meet your preferences. For example, you can set security options to help protect yourself from downloading viruses. You can restrict web pages that contain content you don't want to view (or you don't want your children to view), and you can subscribe to web pages and special channel web sites so that you can browse Internet content at your leisure without being connected to the Internet.

Setting Security Options

To set security options in Internet Explorer, choose Tools | Internet Options and click the Security tab shown in Figure 23-14.

To set a security level for a zone, click the zone's icon in the box at the top. Then drag the slider to change the security level for that zone. Click OK when you're finished.

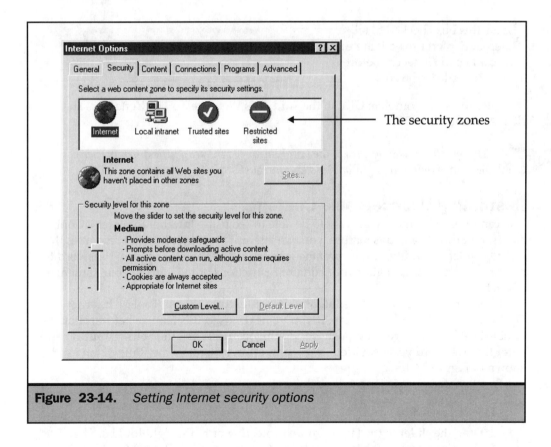

Figure 23-14. *Setting Internet security options*

To add sites that you want included in the Trusted Sites or Restricted Sites zone, select the zone's icon from the box at the top. Then click Sites to display the dialog box shown as follows:

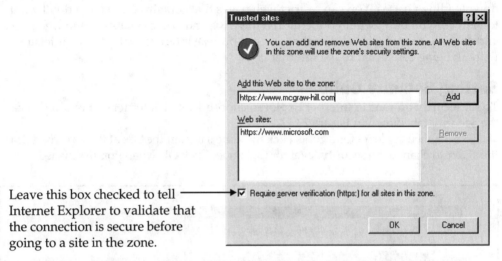

Leave this box checked to tell Internet Explorer to validate that the connection is secure before going to a site in the zone.

Enter the site's complete URL in the Add This Web Site To The Zone box. Then click Add and click OK.

   The options for adding sites to the Local Intranet zone are a little different. See your network administrator for advice about intranet security options.

Restricting Unacceptable Content

You can filter the content you want to be able to see using Internet Explorer's Content Advisor feature. Using this feature, you can attempt to restrict Internet resources that include violence, nudity, sex, or profane language. You can also create a password to prevent others from changing your content restrictions or to override your content restrictions.

To use Internet Explorer's Content Advisor feature, choose Tools | Internet Options and click the Content tab. If you've never used this feature before, click the Enable button. If you've previously set up this feature, click the Settings button and enter the password you provided. Internet Explorer displays the Ratings tab as shown in Figure 23-15.

To set content restrictions, follow these steps:

1. Select a category from the list.

2. Drag the slider to the left for more protection or to the right for less. The Description box explains what type of content you're allowed to see on the level selected.

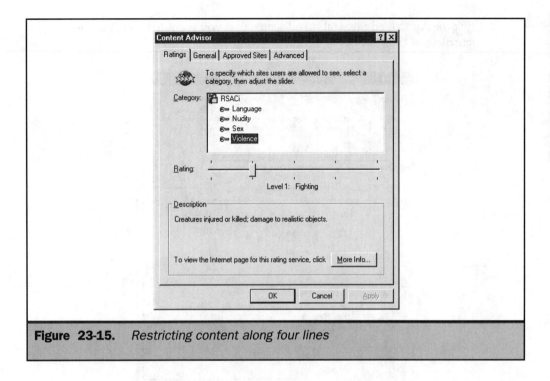

Figure 23-15. *Restricting content along four lines*

3. Click the General tab and specify whether you want to be able to view unrated sites or to enter a password to override the restriction of a web page.

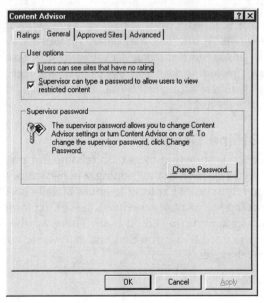

4. Click the Approved Sites tab to add sites that you want to be able to view regardless of their rating.

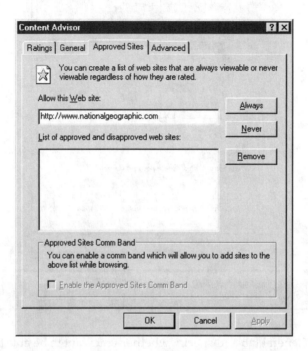

5. Click OK.

There are many shortcomings of Internet Explorer's Content Advisor, so don't count on it as the fix-all solution. At this time, the Content Advisor's main problem is that most sites aren't rated. This means that if you block unrated sites, you block access to the vast majority of the web (including the majority of valuable and reputable sites). Likewise, if you allow access to unrated sites, you allow access to almost all of the objectionable and offensive material on the web.

Subscribing to Offline Content

If your Internet connection is something less than reliable (for instance because you frequently use a dial-up connection in the evening when everyone else goes online as well), you may want to tell Internet Explorer to automatically check for and download new web content. By doing so, you can schedule Internet Explorer to connect to the Internet and download content during an off-hour. This way, the content is there and waiting for you when you need it and you don't have to waste your time trying to connect or to retrieve web pages.

You have two options when it comes to subscribing to Internet content. You can subscribe to any old web page or web site or you can subscribe to a special web site called a *channel*. The following paragraphs describe both types of subscriptions.

Subscribing to a web site or channel usually doesn't cost anything. However, some web site providers require a paid subscription in order to view all of the site's content

SUBSCRIBING TO A REGULAR WEB PAGE OR WEB SITE   To subscribe to a web page, display the web page and choose Favorites | Add to Favorites. In the Add Favorite dialog box (shown next), check the Make Available Offline box and click Customize:

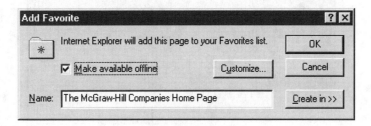

This starts the Offline Synchronization Wizard. Click Next to begin and then follow these steps:

1. Click the Yes option button to subscribe to all of the web pages directly linked to the web page you're viewing or click the No option button to subscribe to only the single web page you're viewing. Click Next.

If a web page has hyperlinks to several other pages (as many web pages do), downloading copies of all of these pages requires a long connection time. And keeping copies of all of these pages on your computer takes up a lot of hard disk space as well. So only subscribe to the web pages you intend to read offline.

2. In the wizard's next dialog box, indicate how you want to update the local copy of the web page with the current online copy. (Internet Explorer calls this updating process *synchronizing*.)

   ■ Click the first option button if you want to synchronize the web page manually. To update your subscriptions, click the Start button and choose Programs | Accessories | Synchronize.

   ■ Click the second option button if you want to create your own schedule for automatic synchronization. If you choose this option and click Next, Internet Explorer asks you how often and at what time of the day you want to automatically synchronize the web page.

■ Click the third option button if you want to automatically synchronize the web page using one of Internet Explorer's predefined schedules. Then choose Daily, Weekly, or Monthly from the drop-down list box.

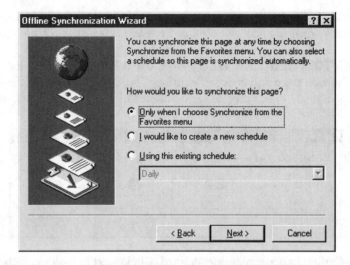

3. Click Next and tell Internet Explorer whether the web page to which you're subscribing requires you to enter a password. If the site requires a password, enter your user name and password in the boxes provided.

4. Click Finish.

SUBSCRIBING TO A CHANNEL   Channels are special web sites that include built-in synchronization schedules. To subscribe to a channel, follow these steps:

1. Click the Favorites toolbar button.

2. Click the Channels folder on the Favorites bar.

3. Click a channel or select a channel category from the list and then click a channel within that category, as shown in Figure 23-16.

To find more channels, click Microsoft Channel Guide under the list of channels. On the web page Internet Explorer displays, click the Search button to search for a specific channel or click a category to browse through the channels in that category.

4. Once you find a channel you like, click the Add Active Channel button. If you can't find the Add Active Channel button on the channel, choose Favorites | Add to Favorites. Internet Explorer displays the Add Favorite dialog box.

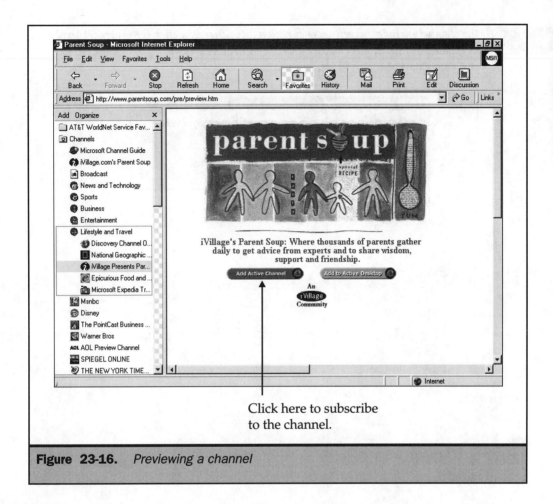

Click here to subscribe
to the channel.

Figure 23-16. *Previewing a channel*

Note   *If a channel has an Add to Active Desktop button, you can click this button to add an item (such as a stock ticker) designed by the channel's creator to your desktop. Note that to display Active Desktop items, you need to specify in Windows that you want to use the Active Desktop.*

5. Specify a location for the channel using the Create In list box. If you can't find the location you want, click Browse.

6. Make sure the Make Available Offline box is checked.

7. Click OK. Internet Explorer subscribes you to the channel and will synchronize the channel based on the channel creator's schedule.

If the channel includes screen saver functionality, after you click OK, Internet Explorer asks if you want to use the channel's screen saver. Click Yes to do so or click No to keep using your existing screen saver.

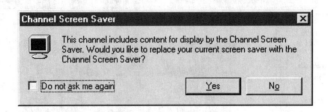

Chapter 24

Using Web Components

Microsoft developed Web Components, an amazing new collection of features of Microsoft Office, to allow unparalleled interaction with database and spreadsheet data while using your web browser. Designed mainly for large corporations and businesses, you use Web Components inside of Internet Explorer to view and manipulate data that was created in Excel or Access and published to the web. Web Components are powerful enough to let you perform the same kinds of operations on data you would perform using Excel (the main Office program that Web Components are meant to augment).

About Web Components

Web Components are small ActiveX programs that run inside of a compatible web browser (Internet Explorer 4.01 or higher) and provide a subset of the tools available in Excel and Access to view and manipulate data. Even though the components are completely new programs, they look and work very much like a miniature version of Excel or, in the case of Data Access Pages, like a subset of Access.

Web Components display information either from an HTML file with embedded XML tags to facilitate the storage of Excel data, or by accessing data directly from a database located on the server. While you can use a Web Component to manipulate and modify data, you cannot actually change the underlying data file or database unless you are explicitly given write privileges.

If you are using a computer without Office 2000 to view a web page with data intended for an Office Web Component, you can often still view the data; you just won't be able to use the intended Office Web Component to manipulate and interact with the data.

There are three main Web Components: the Spreadsheet component, the PivotTable™ component, and the Chart component, as shown in the following table:

Component	Function
Spreadsheet	Allows users to modify and recalculate data in their browser.
PivotTable	Allows users to sort, filter, outline, and pivot data in their browser.
Chart	Allows users to chart data in their browser from a published spreadsheet or linked database.

There are several additional Web Components that are of only peripheral interest. These components include the Field List component, which you use to add fields while using Excel Web Components; the Microsoft Access data access component, which you use to navigate through data from a database; and the Microsoft PowerPoint presentation control, which you use to view presentations on the web.

Creating Web Pages That Use Web Components

You create web pages that use Web Components the same way you create a normal document; the only difference is how you save it. You can specify that you wish to make the data interactive using the Microsoft Office Web Components by choosing Web Page as the file type in Excel's Save As or Save As Web Page dialog box, clicking the Selection:Worksheet option button and then checking the Add Interactivity check box. See Chapter 6 for more information on publishing web pages using Office.

Working with Web Components

You use Microsoft Office Web Components in your web browser to view and manipulate data basically the same as you would use the parts of the Office program they are designed to replicate. Use the Spreadsheet component the same way you would work with a worksheet in Excel, and use the Chart and PivotTable components just like you would use Excel's Chart and PivotTable features.

See Chapter 12 for more information on using spreadsheets, Chapter 14 on using charts, and Chapter 15 on how to create and use PivotTables.

LEARN BY EXAMPLE
To get a chance to play with some Microsoft Office Web Components, open the web pages in the Web Components directory on the companion CD. Notice how when you change a number in the Spreadsheet component, the total automatically recalculates.

Just to get you started, Figure 24-1 shows a sample web page created with Microsoft Excel and designed to be viewed in the Spreadsheet component. Just like Excel, you can change the numbers, alter underlying formulas, add columns and sort your data.

Figure 24-2 shows a simple Sales Revenues vs. Expenses chart and its associated spreadsheet. Select the chart, then click the Properties toolbox button in the Spreadsheet component, then click the Chart Type button to change the type of chart displayed.

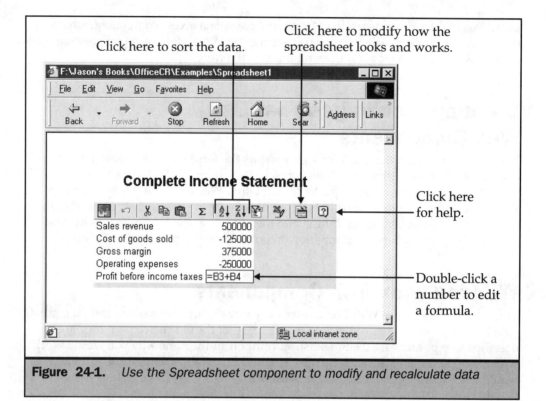

Figure 24-1.   Use the Spreadsheet component to modify and recalculate data

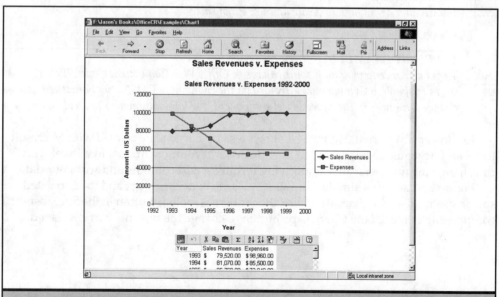

Figure 24-2.   Use the Chart component along with the Spreadsheet component to graphically view and manipulate data

Figure 24-3 shows the simple PivotTable from Chapter 15, with sales figures for different ice cream flavors. Notice how you can use the PivotTable component almost the same as you would use the PivotTable feature in Excel.

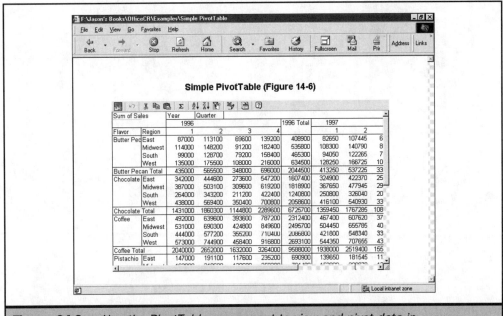

Figure 24-3.   *Use the PivotTable component to view and pivot data in Internet Explorer*

The Complete Reference

Office 2000

Chapter 25

Internet Explorer
Component Programs

I nternet Explorer comes with several add-on features and component programs you can use to enhance your web browsing and accomplish a wide variety of tasks on the Internet. This chapter explains how to use the four largest of these programs: Outlook Express, Microsoft NetMeeting, FrontPage Express, and Microsoft Chat.

Installing Internet Explorer Component Programs

You install all Internet Explorer components in the same way. To do so, follow these steps:

1. Click the Start button and choose Settings | Control Panel to display the Control Panel window.

2. Double-click the Add/Remove Programs icon to display the Add/Remove Programs Properties dialog box.

3. Select Microsoft Internet Explorer 5 from the list box and click Add/Remove.

4. Click the Add A Component To Internet Explorer option button and click OK.

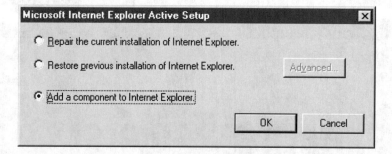

5. Click the I Accept The Agreement option button and click Next.

6. Click the Customize Your Installation option button and click Next to display the Internet Explorer 5 Setup dialog box shown in Figure 25-1.

7. Check the name of the component or components you want to add and click Next. The Internet Explorer setup program installs the components you selected. As it installs, it displays a dialog box containing a progress bar so that you can monitor the progress of the installation.

Note   *At the bottom of the list of components are the language components. Click a Language Support Pack to be able to display text in that language's alphabet. Click a language IME, or Input Method Editor, to be able to enter text in that language while using Windows in a different language.*

8. Click Finish in the dialog box the setup program displays when it finishes installing the components.

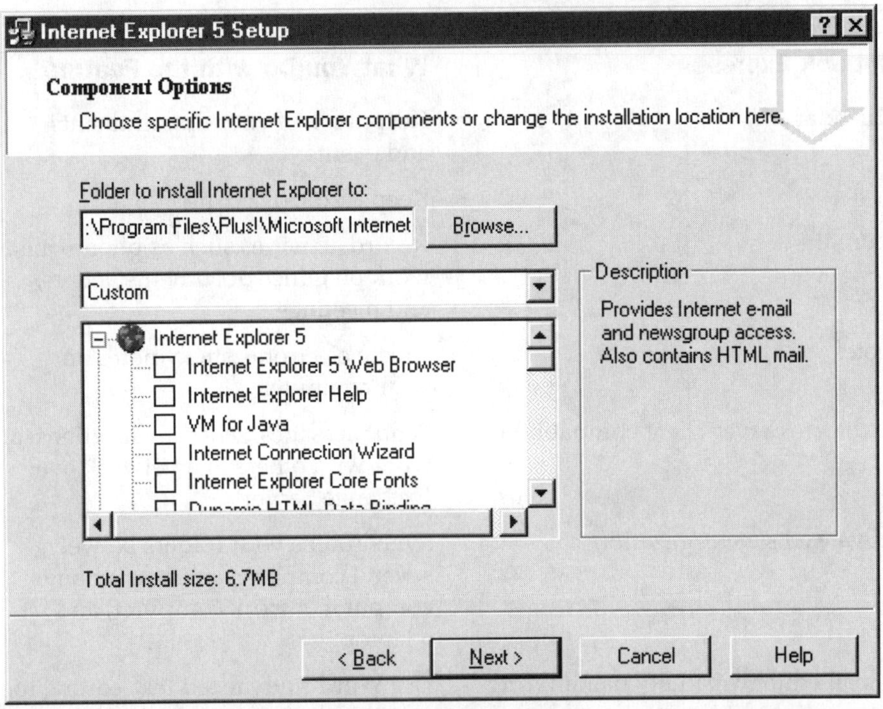

INTERNET EXPLORER

Figure 25-1.   *Adding a component to Internet Explorer*

Using Outlook Express

Outlook Express is a slick little e-mail client that comes with Internet Explorer. But because Office comes with Outlook 2000, a more robust e-mail program than Outlook Express, you may choose to use Outlook instead of Outlook Express. This section talks about Outlook Express and how it differs from Outlook, so that you can make an informed decision about which program you use for e-mailing. It then describes how you accomplish e-mailing tasks using Outlook Express.

Note   *For information about using Outlook for e-mail, see Chapter 20.*

How Outlook Express Differs from Outlook

Outlook contains many more features than Outlook Express. Table 25-1 lists the primary advantages of using Outlook as opposed to Outlook Express. If you never or

Feature in Outlook but Not Outlook Express	What You Do with the Feature
Calendar	Keep track of your appointments and events
Tasks	Keep a To Do task list
Journal	Record activities such as phone calls, work on Office documents, letters, and meetings
Notes	Create electronic sticky notes on your computer
Exchange Server client compatibility	Send messages, schedule meetings, and work with others in a network over Exchange Server
Advanced synchronization	Synchronize your folders between several computers, such as a home computer, a work computer, and a laptop
E-mail editor capability using Word	Use Word's advanced text-editing tools to create e-mail messages
Fax	Send messages as faxes
Views	Customize folder views

Table 25-1.   *Outlook's Extra Features*

rarely make use of these features, you might want to consider using Outlook Express as your e-mail client instead. Because Outlook Express is a leaner program, using it makes fewer demands on your system and speeds up your e-mailing tasks.

Note   *Outlook Express let's you work with newsgroups, while Outlook doesn't have this feature.*

Working in the Outlook Express Program Window

Not only does Outlook Express have a different set of features from Outlook, it also looks much different on screen (see Figure 25-2). If you've used Outlook Express for working with newsgroups, as described in Chapter 22, you're already familiar with the layout of Outlook Express. If you've never used Outlook Express before, this section familiarizes you with its basic layout and operation.

Outlook Express doesn't contain the Outlook bar. Instead, it contains the Folder List, which you use to make your way around the program and display your various folders. Included in the Folder List are many of the same folders you see in Outlook: Inbox, Outbox, Sent Items, Deleted Items, Drafts, Offline Errors, and Junk Mail. Also included in the Folder List are the names of the news servers you've set up and the newsgroups to which you've subscribed on those servers.

Click this button to check for new mail and send messages waiting in the Outbox.

Bold-faced messages haven't been read.

The Folder List

The Message List

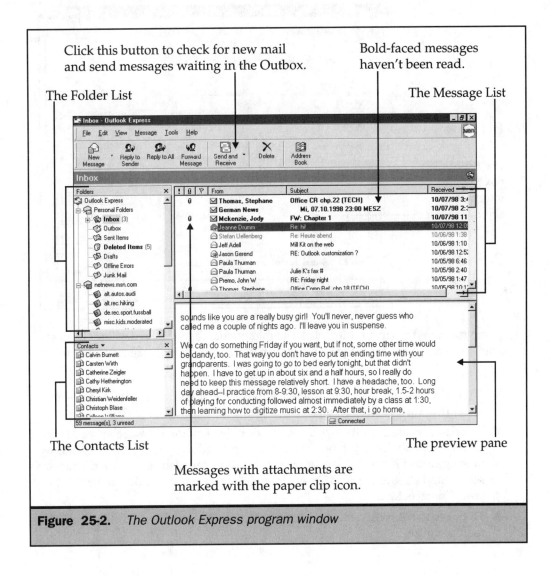

The Contacts List

The preview pane

Messages with attachments are marked with the paper clip icon.

Figure 25-2. *The Outlook Express program window*

If you choose to filter out junk mail messages (spam) in Outlook Express, you can use the Junk Mail folder to store junk mail messages separately from your Inbox. Select Tools | Message Rules | Junk Mail to tell Outlook Express how to filter your junk mail.

Below the Folder List, you find the Contacts List. You can double-click a contact's name to send a message to that contact. Or you can click the word Contacts on the bar at the top of the list and choose New Contact from the pop-up menu to add a contact to your Contacts List.

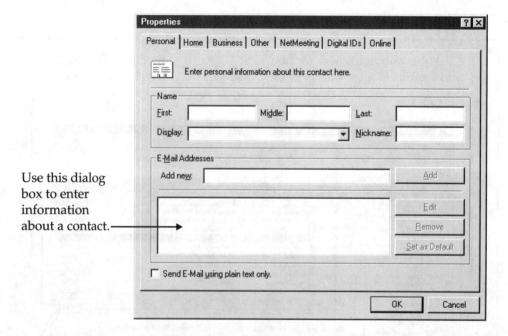

Use this dialog box to enter information about a contact.

To see the messages in a folder, click the folder's name in the Folder List. The list of messages appears in the Message List. You can work with the messages in your folders in several ways:

- To read a message, select the message in the Message List. The message's text appears in the preview pane.

- To open a message in its own window, double-click the message in the Message List. When you display a message in its own window, you can right-click any message attachments to save or open them. You can also right-click the message sender and choose the Add To Address Book command to add the sender to your Contacts List.

- To delete a message, select the message in the Message List and click the Delete toolbar button.

■ To reply to a message, select the message in the Message List and click Reply To Sender to reply only to the person who sent the message or Reply To All to reply to the message sender as well as the other message recipients. When you click one of these buttons, Outlook Express displays a message window you can use to write your reply. For more information working with this window, refer to the next section.

■ To forward a message to someone else, select the message in the Message List and click the Forward toolbar button. Use the message window that Outlook Express displays to address and add comments to the message.

Composing Messages

This section gives bare-bones instructions for composing and sending an e-mail message with Outlook Express.

Follow these steps to send an e-mail message with Outlook Express:

1. Click the New Message button. You see a New Message window like the one in Figure 25-3.

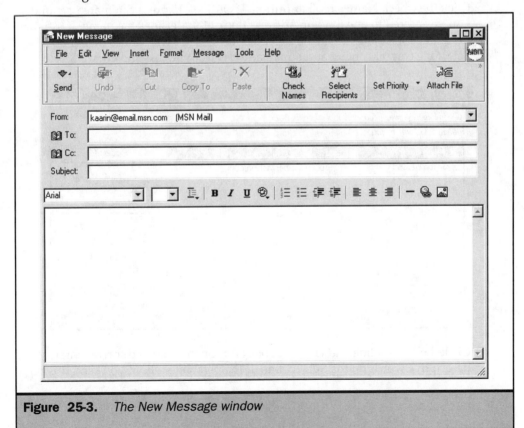

Figure 25-3.   *The New Message window*

To create a new message using an HTML stationery, click the down arrow beside the New Message button and select a stationery from the pop-up list. Be aware, however, that some mail recipients may be using a mail program which distorts these types of stationary when it receives them.

2. If you have multiple e-mail accounts, use the From drop-down list box to select the account from which you want to send the message.

3. Enter the message recipient's name on the To line. As you type the first few letters, Outlook Express tries to guess what you're typing and offers suggestions. If it guesses correctly, press TAB to accept the suggestion and move on or press ENTER to accept the suggestion and add more names to the To line.

If the person you're e-mailing isn't in your Contacts List, just type his or her e-mail address in the To box.

4. Click the Cc line and enter the names of any people you want to receive copies of the message.

5. Click the Check Names toolbar button. If Outlook Express can match a name you've entered to one in your Address Book, it underlines the name. If it finds more than one match to the name, it displays the Check Names dialog box. Select the correct contact and e-mail address from the list and click OK.

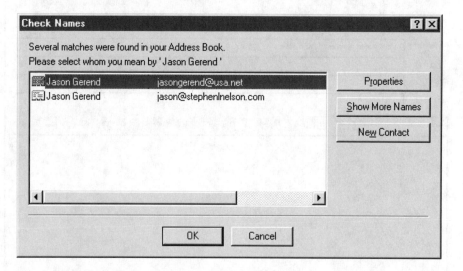

6. Click the Subject line and enter a subject for the message. Be sure to enter descriptive words on the Subject line. If the person to whom you send this

message receives lots of e-mail, he or she needs to know how important this message is and whether to answer it today or a week from now. By entering a descriptive subject, you help the recipient prioritize your message.

7. In the large box at the bottom of the window, type your message.

8. If you want to send a file with the message, click the Attach File toolbar button and use the Insert Attachment dialog box to locate and select the file you want to attach.

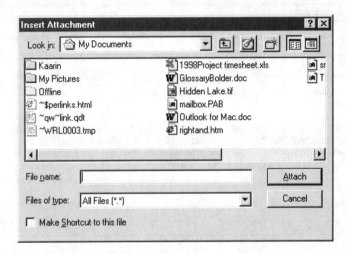

9. By default, the messages you create are categorized as Normal priority. If you want to set the message priority to High, click the Set Priority toolbar button once. If you want to set the message priority to Low, click the Set Priority toolbar button twice. When you set the priority of the message to High or Low, Outlook Express adds a banner to the top of the message window alerting you to this fact.

> **❶ This message is High Priority.**

10. Click the Send button, shown in Figure 25-4. Outlook closes the Message window and you see the Inbox screen again.

Tip *If you are in the middle of composing a message and decide you want to continue working on it later, choose File | Save to save the message to the Drafts folder. You can then close the message and retrieve it later from the Drafts folder.*

11. Depending on how you've set up some of Outlook Express' options, the program may send the message immediately or prompt you to log on to send

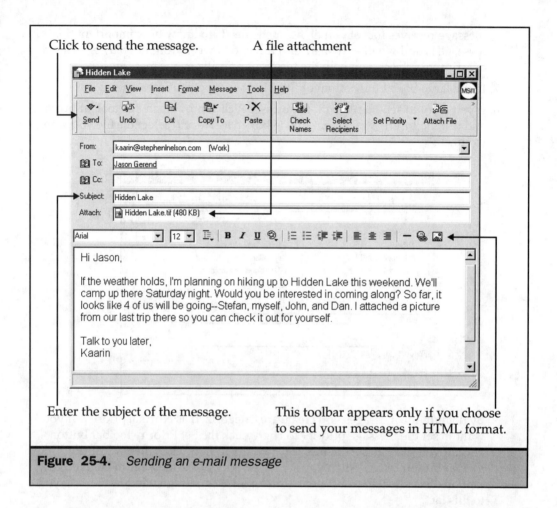

Click to send the message.   A file attachment

Enter the subject of the message.   This toolbar appears only if you choose to send your messages in HTML format.

Figure 25-4. *Sending an e-mail message*

the message. Until the message is delivered to your mail server, it stays in the Outbox. To send messages in the Outbox on their way, click the Send and Receive toolbar button.

Tip   *Clicking the Send and Receive toolbar button collects messages and sends messages using all of your e-mail accounts. If you have more than one e-mail account, you can choose to send and receive on a single account by clicking the down arrow beside the Send and Receive toolbar button and selecting the account you want to use from the pop-up menu.*

Note   *For information about using Outlook Express for newsgroups, see Chapter 22.*

Using Microsoft NetMeeting

You use Microsoft NetMeeting to hold online meetings. To receive audio, your computer needs to have speakers and a sound card. To send audio, you also need a microphone. And to send video, your computer needs a video camera.

Setting Up NetMeeting

To start Microsoft NetMeeting, click the Start button and choose Programs | Internet Explorer | Microsoft NetMeeting. The first time you use NetMeeting, it takes you through a wizard that sets up the program. Follow these steps to proceed through the wizard.

1. Click Next to begin.

2. If you plan on primarily logging on to a single server, check the Log On To A Directory Server When NetMeeting Starts box and select the server from the drop-down list box. If you think you'll frequently use different servers, leave the box unchecked. Click Next.

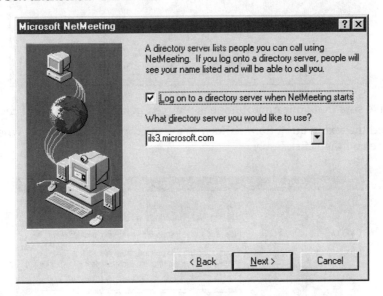

3. Enter the personal information NetMeeting requests using the boxes provided and click Next.

4. Categorize the information you'll be sharing using NetMeeting as personal, business, or adult-only and click Next.

5. Specify your connection speed and click Next.

6. If NetMeeting detects that you have a video camera installed, it asks you to verify the video device you'll use for your meetings. Click Next to accept the device NetMeeting detects or use the drop-down list box to select a different device if you have more than one.

7. Click Next to begin testing your audio.

8. Make sure your speakers are turned on and click Test to test the volume. Adjust the volume slider if necessary and click Stop to stop testing.

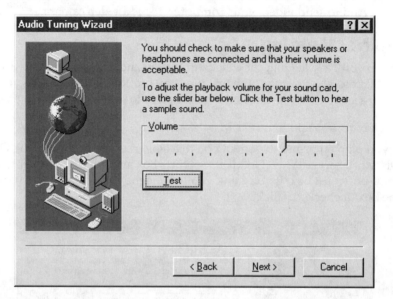

9. Make sure that your microphone is plugged in and turned on and click Next.

10. Read the text in quotation marks into the microphone. Click Next when you're done and then click Finish.

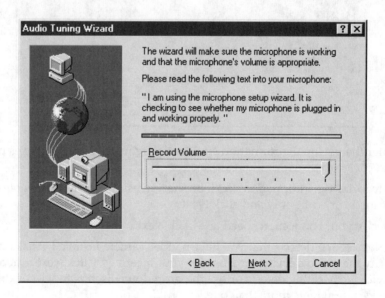

Working with Directories

NetMeeting's directories provide an easy way for you to see who's logged on to a server and to call people logged on to that server. Like a telephone book, a directory lists the names of only those people who choose to be listed. It also lists the personal information they specified.

To display a NetMeeting server's directory, click Directories in the Places bar. By default, NetMeeting displays the directory of the server you specified as you set up the program. To display the directory of a different server, select the server in the Server drop-down list box. To display a different category of content, select an entry from the Category drop-down list box. Figure 25-5 shows what a directory looks like and the symbols used to describe the people listed in the directory.

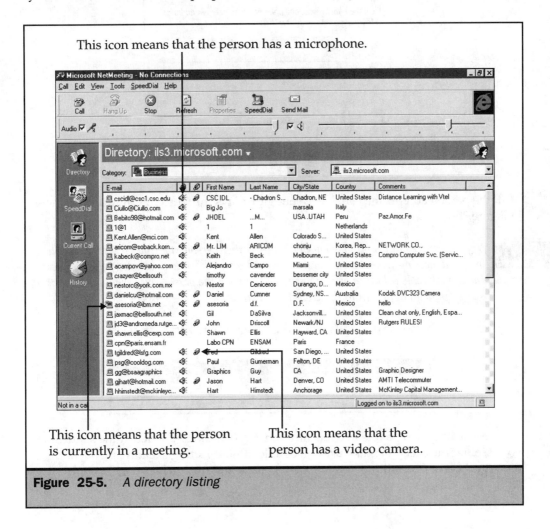

This icon means that the person has a microphone.

This icon means that the person is currently in a meeting.

This icon means that the person has a video camera.

Figure 25-5.   *A directory listing*

Conducting a Meeting

To conduct a meeting, you first need to log on to the same server as the other participants. To log on to your default server, choose Call | Log On To *Name Of Server*, where *Name Of Server* is the name of your default server. To log on to a different server, you need to first choose Tools | Options and click the Calling tab. Then choose a different server from the Server Name drop-down list box and click OK.

To call someone listed in the directory, select the person from the list and click the Call toolbar button. When NetMeeting displays the New Call dialog box, click Call.

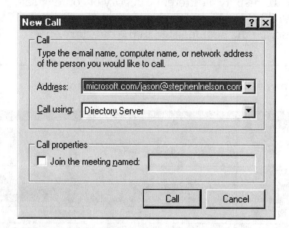

If the person accepts the call, NetMeeting displays the Current Call window shown in Figure 25-6.

 You can share audio and video with only one other person at a time. If several people attend a meeting, you can switch to share audio and video with someone else by clicking the Switch toolbar button and choosing the name of the person with whom you want to share audio and video from the drop-down menu.

Likewise, if someone else calls you, you can choose to accept or reject the call.

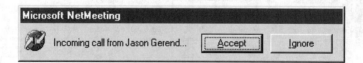

Because only two people in a meeting can share audio and video at the same time, you'll sometimes need to make use of a couple of NetMeeting's features: Chat and the Whiteboard. Chat allows you to type text back and forth with several people.

Whiteboard allows you to draw sketches for the other meeting participants to see. To begin chatting, click the Chat toolbar button. This displays the Untitled Chat window.

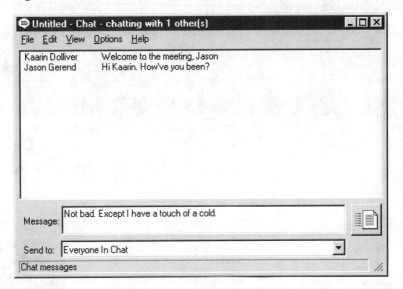

To illustrate your text with sketches, click the Whiteboard toolbar button. This displays the Untitled Whiteboard window. Use the window's tools to paint and page through paintings as your would flip through pages on an easel.

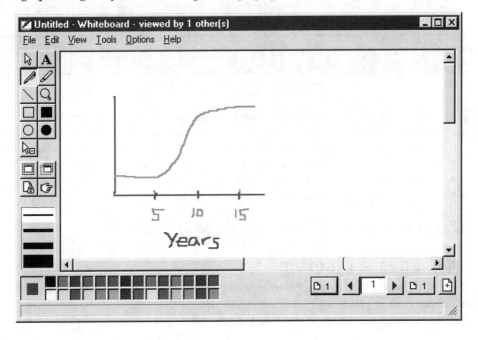

Use this slider to adjust your microphone volume if the other person can't hear you.

Use this slider to adjust your speaker volume.

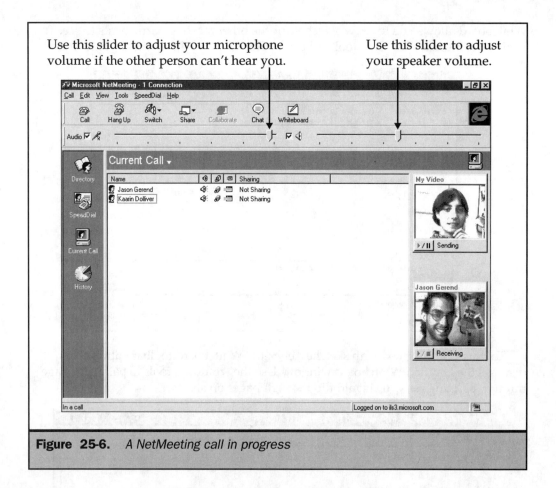

Figure 25-6.   *A NetMeeting call in progress*

| Tip | It's very common to have slow transmission times when using NetMeeting. This is because audio and video files are large and take a long time to transfer. If you find that your connection is very slow, your best remedy is usually to choose to stop sending video (by clicking the Stop button underneath your video). If this doesn't help much, you can also stop sending audio by unchecking the box beside the microphone volume slider. You can then resort to using Chat and the Whiteboard for a while. |

To end a meeting, click the Hang Up toolbar button.

Sharing Files in a Meeting

To share a file with other meeting participants, open the file and click the Share button. Then choose the file you want to share from the drop-down menu. If NetMeeting displays a message box alerting you that you're about to share a file, click OK.

You can begin working in the other application as you normally would. The other meeting participants can see your mouse and the changes you make, but at this stage, they cannot make changes of their own. To allow others to make changes, click the Collaborate toolbar button in NetMeeting. If NetMeeting displays a warning message box, click OK. The other meeting participants can now double-click somewhere in the file to begin making changes. To take control again yourself, just click somewhere in the file. To stop collaborating, click the Collaborate toolbar button in NetMeeting.

Using FrontPage Express

The Office 2000 programs come with several tools for designing and publishing a web page, but you can also use FrontPage Express to create and publish a simple web page. To start FrontPage Express, click the Start button and choose Programs | Internet Explorer | FrontPage Express. FrontPage Express displays a blank canvas for you to design your web page, as shown in Figure 25-7.

Web Page Creation Basics

You create web pages in FrontPage Express in much the same way you create web pages in Word. You add text to a FrontPage Express web page the same way you add text to Office documents. To add hyperlinks, you can simply enter the Internet resource's URL. When you finish, FrontPage Express recognizes the text as a hyperlink and formats it as such (by default, it underlines it and changes the text color to blue). You can also create new hyperlinks or edit existing hyperlinks by clicking the Create or Edit Hyperlink toolbar button. The Create Hyperlink and Edit Hyperlink dialog boxes allow you to link to one of three resources: a web page currently open in FrontPage Express, a World Wide Web resource, or a new page you want to create.

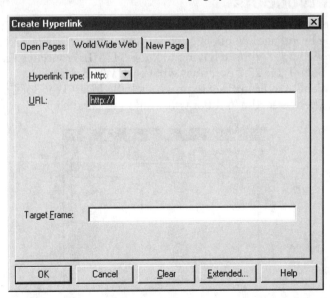

To add images to a FrontPage Express web page, click the Insert Image toolbar button. This displays the Image dialog box:

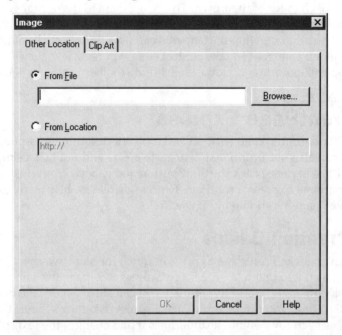

Use the Other Location tab to insert an image file from your computer or an image from the Internet. Use the Clip Art tab to insert a clip art image.

Working with WebBots

FrontPage Express provides one primary feature not included in any of the Office programs beside FrontPage: WebBots. WebBots allow you to easily add dynamic content to your web page without having to know HTML. FrontPage Express comes with three WebBots. Table 25-2 describes what each WebBot does.

To insert a WebBot in FrontPage Express, click the Insert WebBot Component toolbar button. Then select the WebBot you want to use and click OK.

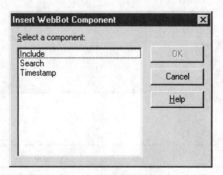

The Forms toolbar

You can recognize most of FrontPage Express'
toolbar buttons from the Office programs.

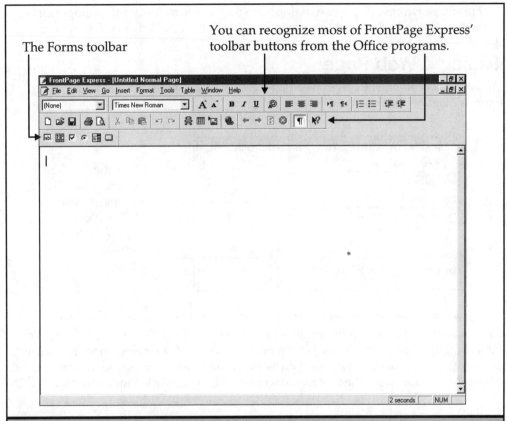

Figure 25-7.   *A new web page in FrontPage Express*

WebBot	Description
Include	Automatically updates content between web pages. With the Include WebBot, you can tell FrontPage Express that you want to insert another web page in the web page you're creating. Then, when you make changes to the inserted web page, the changes are reflected in the web page containing the Include WebBot.
Search	Creates a form that web page visitors can use to search the web page for a word or phrase.
Timestamp	Stamps your web page with the date you last saved it or the date it was last automatically updated.

Table 25-2.   *FrontPage Express' WebBots*

FrontPage Express displays a dialog box you can use to specify the component's properties. Enter the required information in the dialog box and click OK.

Publishing a Web Page

To publish a FrontPage Express web page, click the Save toolbar button. FrontPage Express displays the Save As dialog box.

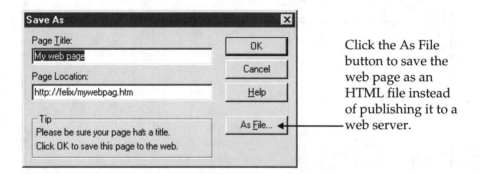

Click the As File button to save the web page as an HTML file instead of publishing it to a web server.

Enter a title for the web page in the Page Title box. Enter the location to which you want to publish the page in the Page Location text box. Click OK. This starts the Web Publishing Wizard. Follow the wizard's steps to complete your web page. The wizard will ask you a few basic questions such as the name of your server and your password. (If you don't know what these are, contact your ISP or network administrator.)

Using Microsoft Chat

Microsoft Chat is a fun and easy little program you can use to type text back and forth with groups of people in real time. To use Microsoft Chat, click the Start button and choose Programs | Internet Explorer | Microsoft Chat.

Setting Up Chat

When you start Chat, it displays the Chat Connection dialog box, shown in Figure 25-8. Use the Connect tab to select a server and tell Chat whether you want to go directly to a chat room, connect to a chat server, or see a list of chat rooms. Unless you have already planned to meet someone in a certain chat room on a certain server, or you already know in which room you'll spend the majority of your time, you probably want to accept the default server and click the Show All Available Chat Rooms option button.

Click the Personal Information tab to enter personal information about yourself that you want others to see.

Joining a Chat

To select a chat to join, display the chat room list. If you aren't currently displaying the chat room list, you can do so by clicking the Chat Room List toolbar button:

Check this box to avoid the unofficial (and sometimes objectionable or offensive) chat rooms.

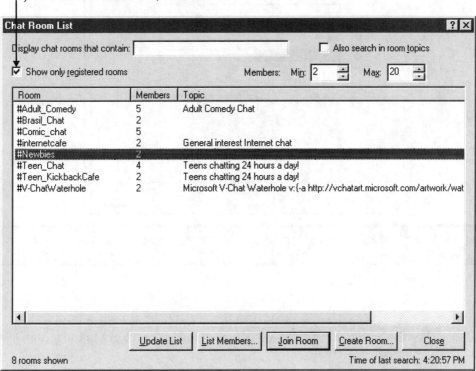

To filter the list of chat rooms, enter a keyword in the Display Chat Rooms That Contain text box or adjust a range of current participants with the Min and Max buttons. To enter a listed chat, select the chat and click Join Room. This displays the Chat window shown in Figure 25-9.

Tip   *To create your own chat room for others to join, click the Create Room button and use the Create Chat Room dialog box to describe the room.*

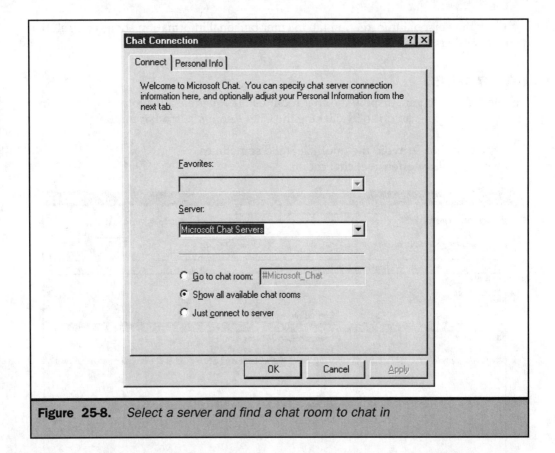

Figure 25-8. *Select a server and find a chat room to chat in*

To talk to a specific person, enter the text in the text box, click the person's head, and then click the button that describes the type of bubble you want to use for the text: Say, Think, Whisper, or Action.

You can also choose to chat using only text instead of cartoons. To do this, click the Text View toolbar button.

If you need to step away from the chat for a moment, click the Away From Keyboard toolbar button.

To see someone's identity, click the person's cartoon head and click the Get Identity toolbar button.

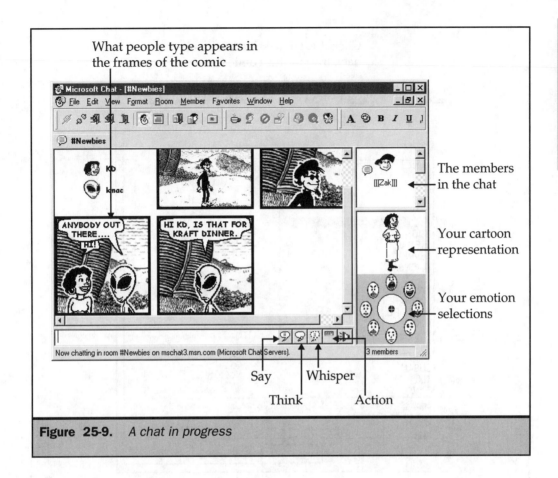

Figure 25-9. *A chat in progress*

To select a different cartoon character for yourself, double-click your cartoon character in the chat window to display the Microsoft Chat Options dialog box, shown in Figure 25-10. Select a new character from the Character list. You can change your emotion in this dialog box and in the Chat window as well by clicking a different face on the circle of emotions. If you don't know which emotion a face represents, rest the mouse over the face until a tool tip appears, naming the emotion.

To leave a chat, click the Leave Room toolbar button.

Note *Microsoft Chat is a new and fun interface, but chat rooms have been around for a while. IRC (Internet Relay Chat) continues to have many users, many of whom have been chatting over the Internet for years.*

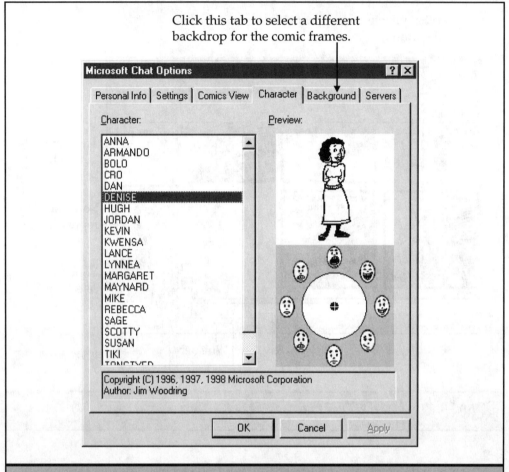

Click this tab to select a different backdrop for the comic frames.

Figure 25-10. *You can change your character and select an emotion for your character*

The Complete Reference

Office 2000

Part VII

Microsoft Access

Chapter 26

Creating a Database

This chapter explains how to create a database with Microsoft Access. Before you can create a database that will serve you well, however, you need to know a little database theory. I'll explain how the different tables in a database fit together and what a relational database is. This chapter will also define strange database terms such as records, fields, forms, and queries.

In this chapter you will find advice for structuring a database. You'll learn how to get around on the Access screen and how to create a database table as well. Because creating databases can be an onerous task and requires more know-how than the other Office 2000 programs, you can call on the wizards to do much of your database work. This chapter explains how to use the Database Wizard and the Table Wizard to create databases and database tables.

How a Database Works

Unfortunately, it is impossible to jump in and get to work in a database program like Access without knowing a bit about database theory. In a database, information is stored in very specific ways. What's more, the data in a database can be stored in more than one database table. In fact, as this chapter explains, it is to your advantage to store data in more than one table if you intend to track large numbers of people, sales items, inventory items, or whatever it is you want to track with your database. And, apart from putting data in database tables, there is more than one way to get data out of a database, too. You can query the database, filter it, or create a report, for example.

The following pages explain what you need to know about databases before you create a database of your own. They also explain what extremely dreary database terms like "filter," "relational database," and "form" mean. Of all the computer terminology, database terminology is the most dreary—and that's saying a lot, because computer terminology as a rule is the dreariest jargon on the planet. I wish one or two literate people had been in the room to object when the propeller-heads invented database terms like "relational query," "dynaset," and "primary key."

Storing the Data in Tables, Records, and Fields

The data in a database is stored in different tables. Like the tables you create in Excel or Word, database tables are divided into columns and rows. In a database table, however, rows are called *records* and columns are called *fields*. Actually, to be precise, each row in a database table is a record, and each record is divided into several fields. For example, five records have been entered in the Customers database table shown in Figure 26-1. Each record is divided into five fields—Company Name, Billing Address, City, State/Province, Postal Code, and Country.

A record comprises all the data about one person or thing. A field is one category of information. As the section "Designing Your Database," a little later in this chapter, explains, one of the most important choices you make when you design a database is

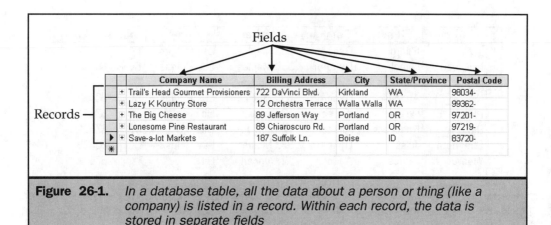

Figure 26-1.   *In a database table, all the data about a person or thing (like a company) is listed in a record. Within each record, the data is stored in separate fields*

which fields to include. Include one field for each category of information you care to know about a person or thing.

A Relational Database

Access 2000 is a *relational database*, which means that data is not stored in a single, very large table. Instead, data is stored in several different tables, all of which are related to one another in such a way that you can join the data from different tables if need be, or retrieve information from several tables at once.

To understand how a relational database works, consider Figure 26-2, which shows what is called a "flat-file database." A *flat-file database*, as opposed to a relational database, consists of a single large table, not several different tables. The flat-file database in Figure 26-2 lists the names of contacts. Notice that much of the data stored in the database table is repetitive: The contacts in the database table work for either of two companies, AirTech or DynoAir. Each time you enter information about a person or thing—that is, each time you enter a record—in a flat-file database, you have to enter all the data. In the case of the table in Figure 26-2, you have to enter the name, address, city, state, and ZIP code of either the AirTech company or the DynoAir company.

With a relational database, on the other hand, you wouldn't have to enter the name, address, city, state, and ZIP code of AirTech or DynoAir each time you entered a new contact name in the database table. All you would enter is the contact's last name, first name, and the name of the company that he or she works for. A separate table, also part of the database, would list the addresses of AirTech, DynoAir, and other companies you do business with. If you wanted a complete list like the one in Figure 26-2, you would ask the database for a report that lists contacts, the companies they work for, and the address and phone numbers of those companies.

	Last	First	Company	Address	City	State	Zip
▶	Dyer	George	DynoAir	333 Maples	Las Pulgas	TX	60432
	McCreedy	Lionel	DynoAir	333 Maples	Las Pulgas	TX	60432
	Munoz	Rebecca	AirTech	12 Duncan	Bitz	TX	67521
	Ng	Andrew	DynoAir	333 Maples	Las Pulgas	TX	60432
	Plesco	Wilma	AirTech	12 Duncan	Bitz	TX	67521
	Ritz	Roscoe	AirTech	12 Duncan	Bitz	TX	67521
	Strayhorn	Jules	DynoAir	333 Maples	Las Pulgas	TX	60432
	Weaver	James	AirTech	12 Duncan	Bitz	TX	67521
✳							

Figure 26-2.   *An old-fashioned, flat-file database. In a relational database like Access, repetitive information like this is eliminated*

In a relational database, it is possible to gather information from different tables and assemble that information in one place. In fact, you are encouraged to divide your database into tables. You save time that way, because you don't have to enter repetitive information in many different fields. Instead of entering the same address over and over again, you would enter it only once, in an Addresses table. You also cut down on data-entry errors by saving data in different tables because you don't have to enter the same data over and over.

Getting Information from Forms, Queries, and Reports

Tables are the means of storing information in a database, but storing information is only half the story. A database is also a means of getting information. Basically, the three ways to get information from a database are by means of a form, a query, or a report.

Note   *The tables, forms, queries, reports, macros, and so on. that make up a database are known collectively as database objects.*

Forms

Figure 26-3 shows a form. Most forms display one record—and they display that record very succinctly. Forms are one of the best ways to view data in a database, although you can also enter data on a form. In the form in Figure 26-3, for example, the field names are clearly labeled. You can tell precisely what each piece of information—what each field—is.

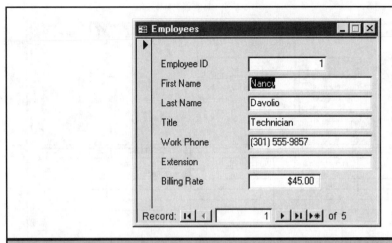

Figure 26-3. *On a form, you can see data more clearly. You can also enter or edit data on forms*

Queries

Queries are the means of gathering information from a database and organizing it in a different way. In effect, a query is a question. For example, you could query a database to gather the names of people who live in Connecticut and whose incomes are between $30,000 and $40,000 a year. Or, if your database is an inventory of the items in a store, you could query to find out how many light bulbs in the $1 to $3 price range are in stock. The simple query shown in Figure 26-4 asks a business' database for the total of each paid workorder. The results of the query produced nine customers, as shown in the figure.

Reports

Reports like the one shown in Figure 26-5 neatly organize and summarize information in a database. Reports are meant to be printed. Data from a report can come from a database table or a query. Access offers many preformatted layouts, so you don't have to be a layout artist to create a fancy report.

Designing Your Database

Before you touch the keys of the computer, you need to sit down with a scratch pad and pencil and choose a design and structure for your database. In the first place, you need to decide which fields to include in the database. How many distinct pieces of information does your database require? If you operate a video rental shop and you are putting together a database of all the videos in stock, your database obviously needs a

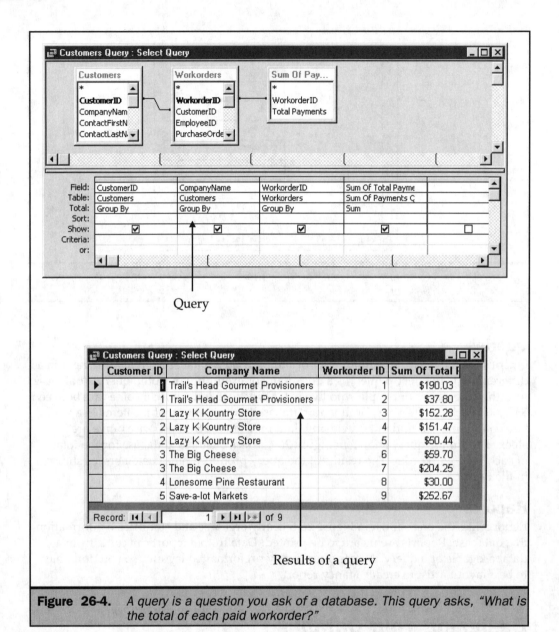

Query

Results of a query

Figure 26-4.   *A query is a question you ask of a database. This query asks, "What is the total of each paid workorder?"*

title field. How about a director field, a lead actor field, and lead actress field? What if someone asks if the shop carries biker flicks? Perhaps you should have a genre field as well. Having a Yes/No field that indicates whether each video has been checked out would be an excellent idea. In the database, include fields for each type of information you conceivably might need some day.

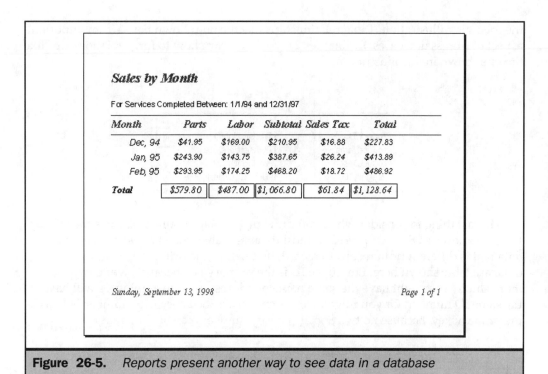

Sales by Month

For Services Completed Between: 1/1/94 and 12/31/97

Month	Parts	Labor	Subtotal	Sales Tax	Total
Dec, 94	$41.95	$169.00	$210.95	$16.88	$227.83
Jan, 95	$243.90	$143.75	$387.65	$26.24	$413.89
Feb, 95	$293.95	$174.25	$468.20	$18.72	$486.92
Total	$579.80	$487.00	$1,066.80	$61.84	$1,128.64

Sunday, September 13, 1998   Page 1 of 1

Figure 26-5. *Reports present another way to see data in a database*

When it comes to choosing which fields to include in the database, it is better to err on the side of too much than too little. In particular, you don't want to group different types of data into a single field. For example, in a database with addresses, you'll want separate fields for city, state, and ZIP code so that you can sort by any of these. You'll probably even want separate fields for first and last name for the same reason. On the other hand, don't include frivolous information or information that can be derived through a calculation. Entering data in a database is tedious work to begin with, and if you have to enter data in more fields than are really necessary, the work becomes all the more tedious.

After you have decided which fields to include, it is time to divide the fields into database tables. As I explained in the section "A Relational Database," earlier in this chapter, creating more than one table for different types of information makes it easier to enter data, because you don't have to enter repetitive information time and time again. Put repetitive information in its own table. For example, if you were creating a database of inventory transactions, you could create a Products table with the product description, unit price, and so on. Meanwhile, in the Inventory Transaction table that lists each individual transaction (withdrawing from and replenishing inventory), you could include a Product ID field. The relationship between two such tables is shown in the following illustration. Table relationships like the one shown here are an important aspect of Access databases. In Chapter 27, you will learn how to forge relationships like the one shown in this illustration:

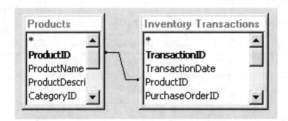

The last thing to consider when you draw up plans for your database is the *primary key*, also known as the *unique field*. In most database tables, one field should contain data that is different from record to record; that field is the primary key. In the database table shown here, Employee ID is the primary key because, while two or more employees might have the same name or address, no two employees will have the same ID number. Or you might use the employee Social Security number field as the primary key, because no two Social Security numbers can be the same.

	Employee ID	First Name	Last Name	Title	Email Name	Work Phone
▶ +	1	Nancy	Davolio	President	ndavo	(212) 555-9857
+	2	Andrew	Fuller	Treasurer	afull	(212) 555-9482
+	3	Janet	Leverling	Executive Secretary	jleve	(212) 555-3412
+	4	Margaret	Peacock	Accounting Manager	mpeac	(212) 555-8122
+	5	Steven	Buchanan	Vice President	sbuch	(212) 555-1189
*	(AutoNumber)					

Primary key fields make it easier for Access to organize and identify records in databases. When you create a database table, Access asks you to specify the primary key.

A Quick Geography Lesson

In Access, you create, open, and design tables, queries, forms, reports, macros, and modules starting from the *Database window*. The Database window, shown in Figure 26-6, is Access' Grand Central Station. Although tables, queries, reports, and all the other parts of the database are stored in one file, you open them by way of the Database window.

To create a table, query, form, or whatnot, you click a button in the Database window and then click the New button. Click the Open button to open a database object—table, query, form, or whatnot—that you have already created. The Design button is for switching to Design view so you can modify the layout and contents of a table, form, report, or whatnot. Moreover, by right-clicking on an item in the Database window, you can open it, print it, rename it, or delete it, among other things, as Figure 26-6 shows.

 Press F11 or click the Database Window button to open the Database window or get back to it when you are working in a table, query, form, or report.

Access treats the different parts of a database like files. If you open a database table, for example, and decide to work on a query, you have to save the table before you can close it. In fact, if you try to close a table or any other part of a database without saving

Figure 26-6. *In Access, the Database window works like a file manager. Use it to open, create, and redesign different parts of a database*

ACCESS

the changes you made to it, a message box appears and asks if you want to save the changes you made. Instead of closing a part of a database when you want to work on another part, you can click the Minimize button. For this illustration, I opened three of the tables shown in Figure 26-6 and then minimized them:

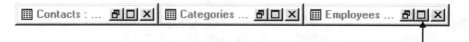

Click this button to enlarge to full-screen size.

Two Ways to Create a Database

Access offers two ways to create a database—with the Database Wizard or from scratch. Both techniques are described in the pages that follow.

 Access is different from the other Office programs in that you have to save and name the database file you create from the moment you create it. Before you create your new database, prepare a folder for storing it and be prepared to enter a meaningful name for the database file.

Creating a Database with the Database Wizard

Access offers many databases that you can create either from templates or by means of the Database Wizard. The preformatted, ready-made databases are fine for doing common database tasks such as tracking expenses or keeping tabs on the members of an organization. After you create a database with the wizard or a template, you get a handful of queries, forms, and reports, all ready to go. And if the queries, forms, and reports aren't quite right, you can always refine them.

Note *When you create a database with the wizard, Access creates what it calls the "Switchboard," another way (in addition to the Database window) to open database tables, forms, queries, and whatall. The Switchboard is a menu system that allows you to quickly perform common tasks, like entering data. It's particularly handy if you have people with little database experience accessing your database. See "Using the Switchboard to Work with a Database," later in this chapter, for more information.*

Access offers the following ready-made databases:

Asset Tracking
Contract Management
Event Management
Expenses
Inventory Control
Ledger
Order Entry
Resource Scheduling
Service Call Management
Time and Billing

Follow these steps to create a ready-made database with the help of the Database Wizard:

1. If you just started Access, click the Access Database Wizards, Pages, And Projects option button in the Microsoft Access dialog box and then click OK. If the program is running already, choose File | New and click the Databases tab in the New dialog box.

2. In the New dialog box, click the type of database you want to create and then click OK. You see the File New Database dialog box.

3. Find and double-click on the folder that the database file is to be stored in, enter a name for the file in the File Name box, and click the Create button.

4. A dialog box tells you what kind of information that database is designed to store. Click the Next button.

5. As shown in Figure 26-7, the next dialog box allows you to control which fields to include in the database table or tables. Fields you may or may not want are shown in italics in the right side of the dialog box. Click a table name in the left side of the dialog box and then click the check box next to any optional fields you want in your database.

6. Click the Next button after you have told Access which fields to include in the database table or tables. The next screen asks what screen displays should look like in your database.

7. Try clicking on a few display names. When you do so, the sample display changes. When you have found a display that suits you, click the Next button.

8. Choose a style for the reports you will generate and print from your new database. Click a few style names until you find the one you want, and then click the Next button.

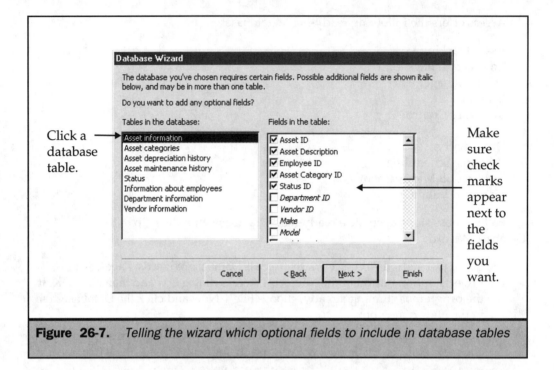

Figure 26-7. *Telling the wizard which optional fields to include in database tables*

9. In the next dialog box, enter a title for your database in the text box if you don't like the title that Access suggests. Titles appear on reports. Click Next when you have finished.

Note *To include a picture, perhaps a corporate logo, on reports, click the Yes, I'd Like To Include A Picture check box and then click the Picture button. In the Insert Picture dialog box, find and click on the clip art file whose picture you want to appear on reports, and then click OK. The picture appears in the upper-left corner of reports.*

10. The last dialog box simply asks if you want to start working with the database immediately. Click Finish in this dialog box.

Depending on how large a database you created, it can take a while for Access to create the sundry parts of your database. Twiddle your thumbs awhile. When the database has been constructed, you see a Switchboard like the one shown in Figure 26-8. A Switchboard is an alternative means of working with a database.

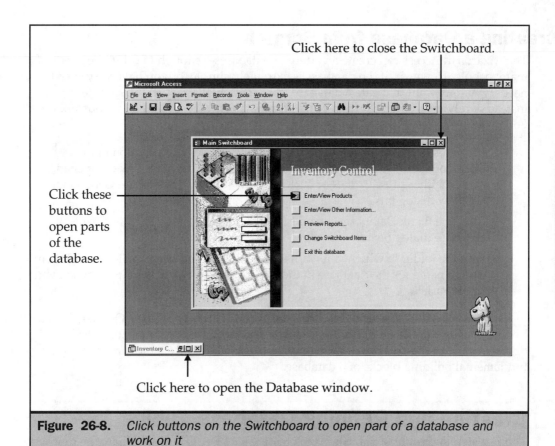

Click here to close the Switchboard.

Click these buttons to open parts of the database.

Click here to open the Database window.

Figure 26-8.   *Click buttons on the Switchboard to open part of a database and work on it*

Using the Switchboard to Work with a Database

If you created your database file with the Database Wizard, you have an alternative means for working with your database—the Switchboard, shown in Figure 26-8. It's simply a menu system that's convenient for performing common tasks, such as entering or editing data. Just click the appropriate buttons.

When you open the database, you see the Switchboard. To close the Switchboard, click the Exit button (usually the button in the upper-right corner). To open the Database window, click its Restore or Maximize button. You will find the Database window along the bottom of the screen, as shown in Figure 26-8.

Creating a Database from Scratch

The wizards in Access can create a variety of databases—enough to fulfill the needs of many people. However, if the database is extremely simple, or you have very specific needs, you may want to create a database from scratch. It's easy in the short term; instead of relying on the wizard to build your database objects, you do it yourself. Follow these steps to create a database from scratch:

1. If you just opened Access, click the Blank Database option button in the Microsoft Access dialog box and then click OK. If you have already opened Access, either press CTRL-N or click the New button. Click on the General tab of the New dialog box.

2. Click the Blank Database icon and then click OK. You see the File New Database dialog box.

3. Find the folder in which you want to save the file and double-click it, and then enter a name for the database in the File Name text box. Click Create when you have finished.

Access opens the Database window with its seven buttons: Tables, Queries, Forms, Reports, Pages, Macros, and Modules. This is the starting point for creating the different parts of the database. It also opens a blank table, since tables are the fundamental building blocks of a database.

Creating and Refining Database Tables

The first step in creating a database is to create the tables. Tables are where the raw data is stored. After you have entered data in the database tables, you can start consulting the database for information about the people or things that your database is supposed to keep track of.

The following pages explain how to design a table by adding the fields. You also learn how to select data types for the fields and establish field properties to make entering the data easier. These pages also explain how to choose a primary key for a table and how to index a table. Finally, because appearances count, you also learn how to change a table's appearance.

Creating a Database Table

Access offers three ways to create a database table. You can start in Design view and enter the field names yourself, create a table with Access' Table Wizard, or import the data from a table you already created. The Table Wizard can be very helpful when it comes to creating a table, but even if you create a table with the wizard you have to refine it to make it work for your data.

No matter which method you choose for designing a table, you start from the Database window (click the Database Window button or press F11 if you don't see it). Click the Tables button and then the New button. You see the New Table dialog box:

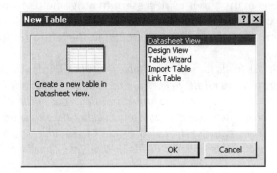

This dialog box is where you decide how to create your table:

- **Datasheet View**   Choose Datasheet View and click OK to view a blank datasheet in which you can begin entering data fields and table data.

- **Design View**   Choose Design View and click OK to design the table yourself. "Designing and Refining a Database Table" in Chapter 27 tells what to do next if you go this route.

- **Table Wizard**   Choose Table Wizard and click OK to get Access' help in designing and creating the table. The following section explains what to do next.

- **Import Table**   Choose Import Table and click OK to import a table from another Access database; an Excel spreadsheet; a dBASE, FoxPro, or other database; or from a text file. See "Importing Data from Another Table or Program," later in this chapter, to find out what to do next.

- **Link Table**   You can also choose Link Table, which is a variation of Import Table. You don't bring the data into the database; you create a link, which allows the data to continue to be worked with and updated in the other application.

Creating a Table with the Table Wizard

Choose Table Wizard, and then click OK in the New Table dialog box. In order to create a table with the Table Wizard, follow these steps:

1. In the first Table Wizard dialog box, which is shown in Figure 26-9, choose the table in the Sample Tables box that best describes the database table that you want to create.

2. In the Sample Fields box, click on a field that you want for your table and then click the topmost button, the one that points to the right. When you do so, the field name is moved into the Fields In My New Table box.

3. Repeat step 2 as many times as necessary to move fields from the Sample Fields box to the box on the right. If you make a mistake and accidentally move a field you don't want, click the arrow that points to the left to remove it.

Tip   *A fast way to choose fields for your new table is to click the double arrows that point to the right. Doing so places all the fields from the Sample Fields box into the Fields In My New Table box. With that done, move unwanted fields out of the Fields In My New Table box by selecting them one at a time and clicking the single arrow that points to the left. Conversely, if you want to start all over, click the double arrow that points to the left. It will remove all fields from the Fields In My New Table box.*

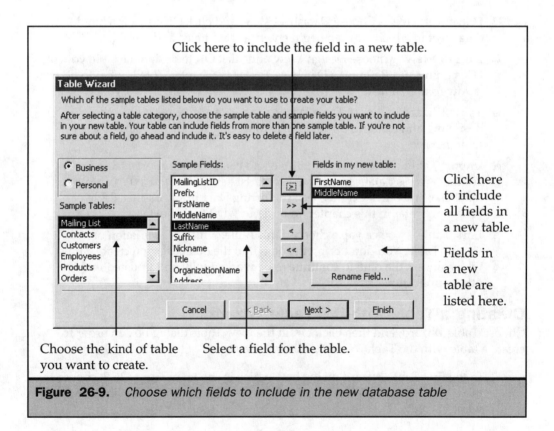

Figure 26-9.   *Choose which fields to include in the new database table*

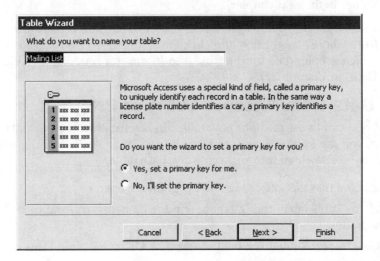

| Tip |

To rename a field, select it in the Fields In My New Table box and then click the Rename Field button. You see the Rename Field dialog box. Enter a new name and click OK. By the way, field names can include blank spaces and be more than one word long. If you plan to export information to another database system, however, it's best to omit blank spaces in field names.

4. Click the Next button. The next dialog box asks for a table name and whether you want the wizard to choose a primary key for you:

5. Enter a name for your table if Access' name doesn't suit you.

6. Click the Yes or No option button concerning whether you want to choose a primary key yourself or let Access choose one ("Designing Your Database," earlier in this chapter, explains what a primary key is). If you click No, a dialog box appears and asks which field is the primary key and what kind of data is stored in that field. It isn't really necessary to choose a primary key now, so you can bypass the question and choose one later if you want. See "Choosing the Primary Key" in Chapter 27 for more information.

7. Click the Next button.

8. If your database already includes a table, the next dialog box asks how the table you are creating relates to the table or tables already in the database. If you are lucky, the Table Wizard may be able to create a relationship for you. Whether or not the wizard can do that, however, I recommend bypassing this dialog box. In the next chapter, "Forging the Relationships Between Tables" explains how to chart the relationships between tables in a database. It isn't really necessary to do it from this unwieldy dialog box.

9. Click the Next button. You see the last Table Wizard dialog box, which simply asks what you want to do now that you have created a database table:

- ■ **Modify The Table Design** Choose this option and click Finish to go to Design view, where you can refine the design of the table (see "Designing and Refining a Database Table" in Chapter 27).

- ■ **Enter Data Directly Into The Table** Choose this option and click Finish to switch to Datasheet view and begin entering data (see "Entering Data in a Table" in the next chapter).

- ■ **Enter Data Into The Table Using A Form That The Wizard Creates For Me** Choose this option and click Finish to tell Access to create a form in which to enter data for the table (see "Forms for Entering and Viewing Data" in Chapter 27).

Importing Data from Another Table or Program

If the data you want to use for your new table already exists in another database or spreadsheet, you can import the information into a new table. Follow these steps to import data from elsewhere into an Access database table:

1. Make sure that the source file and program are open.

2. Click the Table tab in the Database window, if necessary, and then click the New button.

3. Choose Import Table from the list and click OK in the New Table dialog box. You see the Import dialog box.

4. Find and click on the database file with the data you want to import. If you are importing data from an Excel file or other database program besides Access, open the Files Of Type drop-down list and choose the type of file whose data you need. Click the Import button when you have finished.

What happens next depends on where the data comes from. If you are importing data from another Access file, you see a dialog box similar to the following. It wants to know which table to get the data from. You can click the Options button to tell Access precisely how to import the data. You can, for example, import only the structure of a table, not the data itself.

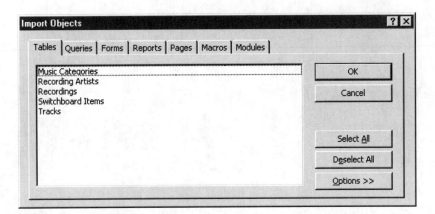

If you import data from an Excel file, Access asks which worksheet to get it from and helps you pinpoint which parts of the worksheet to import. Keep answering the questions and clicking Next in the wizard dialog boxes until the data is imported.

ACCESS

Chapter 27

Building Your
Database Tables

This chapter explains how to design a database table, establish relationships between tables so you can work with more than one at a time, change the appearance of a table, and enter the data itself. It also explains how to create and design forms for entering and viewing data.

In the course of this chapter, you will learn ways to make sure that data is entered accurately. You can do that by making rules—Access calls them "properties"—for each field in a table. For example, you can tell Access to allow only two letters to be entered in a State field (for standard state abbreviations such as CT, RI, NY, and so on). Or you can tell Access only to permit numbers, not letters, to be entered in a ZIP code field, for example.

This chapter also offers techniques for viewing tables. Eventually, you will be the judge of which view is best for displaying and entering the data in tables; this chapter explains how to change views and makes suggestions about which view is best in different situations. At the end of this chapter, you learn how to print a database table and export data to other Access files and database programs.

Opening a Database Table

To open a database table, start at the Database window. This window appears automatically if you created your database without the help of the Database Wizard. If you used the wizard to create your database, you see the Switchboard instead of the Database window when you open a new database file. To see the Database window, which is shown in the following illustration, press F11 or click the Database window button.

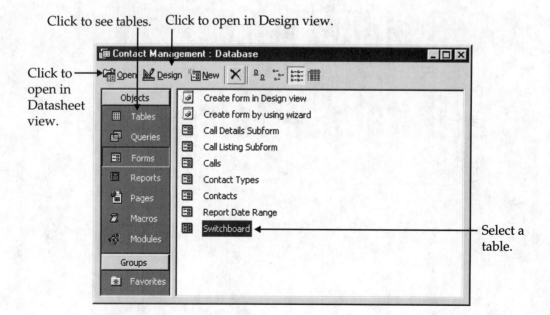

After the Database window is onscreen, click the Tables button, if necessary, to see the tables in the database, click the table you want to open, and then click either the Open or the Design button:

- **Open**   Opens the table in Datasheet view so you can view records, enter new records, or delete records.
- **Design**   Opens the table in Design view so you can change the structure of a table, add new fields, delete fields, or change field settings.

You can also open a database table by right-clicking on its name on the Tables tab. From the shortcut menu, choose Open to open the table in Datasheet view; choose Design to open the table in Design view.

Read on to find out more about the two views and why you would choose one or the other.

Ways of Viewing Tables

Access offers two ways to view database tables—in Datasheet view or Design view. Figure 27-1 shows a table in Datasheet view, and Figure 27-2 shows the same table in Design view. Use Datasheet view to enter data in a table. Design view is for designing the database table—that is, for telling Access which fields go in the table, what kind of data is allowed in each field, and how the data is formatted.

To change views of a table, choose either View | Datasheet or View | Design. The next section, "Designing and Refining a Database Table," explains how to add fields to a table and set properties for the fields. "Entering Data in a Table," later in this chapter, explains how to enter data in Datasheet view.

LEARN BY EXAMPLE
To experiment with views, open the Figure 27-1 (views) file on the companion CD.

Designing and Refining a Database Table

Designing a table is a big job, especially when it comes to choosing what kind of data goes in each field. The following pages explain how to create a new field, choose a data type for the field, and establish a field's properties (the settings that determine how data is displayed and stored). These pages also explain how to edit fields, move and copy them, and establish the primary key for a table.

Change views.

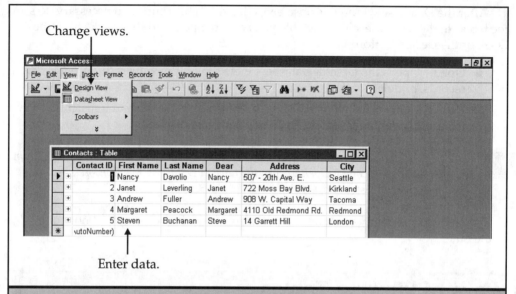

Enter data.

Figure 27-1. Datasheet view is for entering and viewing data

Enter field names.

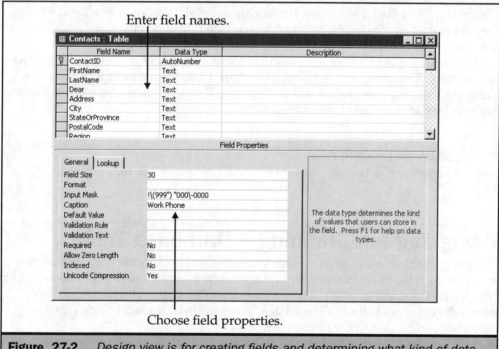

Choose field properties.

Figure 27-2. Design view is for creating fields and determining what kind of data goes in them

Tip

Access offers a thing called the Table Analyzer Wizard that looks at tables and tells you whether they should be broken into two or more tables. If you find yourself entering the same data time and time again in a table, your table might need breaking up. To use the Table Analyzer Wizard, choose Tool | Analyze, and then click Table.

Creating a Field

To create a field in a database table, follow these steps:

1. Switch to Design view, if you are not already there, by choosing View | Design, or clicking on the Design View button.

2. Tell Access where the new field is to go:

   ■ If you are creating the first field in the table, the cursor is in the first row and you are ready to go.

   ■ To insert a field between fields that are already there, select the field below where you want the new field to be and either click the Insert Rows toolbar button or right-click and choose Insert Rows from the shortcut menu. To select a field, click the small square to its left. In this database table, I want to insert a field between LastName and Dear, so I have selected the Dear field:

Click to select fields.

Field Name	Data Type	Description
FirstName	Text	
LastName	Text	
Dear	Text	
Address	Text	

Note

The order in which fields are entered in Design view determines where the fields appear in Datasheet view. The topmost field in the Design view window is the leftmost field in the Datasheet view window; the last field in the Design view window is the rightmost field in the Datasheet view window.

3. Enter a name for the field in the Field Name box. Names can be 64 characters long, but they ought to be considerably shorter so they fit onscreen in Datasheet view and don't take up too much space on forms.

Caution

Including spaces in field names in Access database tables is perfectly okay, but some database programs do not permit spaces in field names, which could trip you up if you ever export databases from Access to other database programs. In general, you're better off not including blank spaces in field names. Instead of "Last Name" as a field name, you can call it LastName or Last_Name. Click in the Data Type box to the right of the field name. The word "Text" appears in the Data Type box. However, if numbers, currency amounts, or other types of data besides text are to be stored in the field, click the down arrow in the Data Type box and choose a different data type, as shown in the next illustration (the next sidebar explains what the data types are):

ACCESS

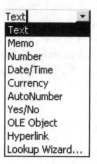

4. Enter a few words in the Description box to describe the data that is to be stored in the field. Taking a moment to do this now may help you later, since this description will appear on the status bar when you're working with a field in Datasheet view.

5. If you want, choose field properties from the bottom half of the dialog box to tell Access how to handle the data you will enter in the field. (See "Establishing Field Properties for Easier Data Entry," later in this chapter.)

You can also get Access' help to create a new field. Right-click the Field Name box below where you want the new field to be located, and then click Build on the shortcut menu. You see the Field Builder dialog box shown in Figure 27-3. Click the Business or Personal option button to tell Access what type of fields you need, and then, in the Sample Tables box, click the table that most resembles the one you are working on. New field names appear in the Sample Fields box. Click a field name and then click OK.

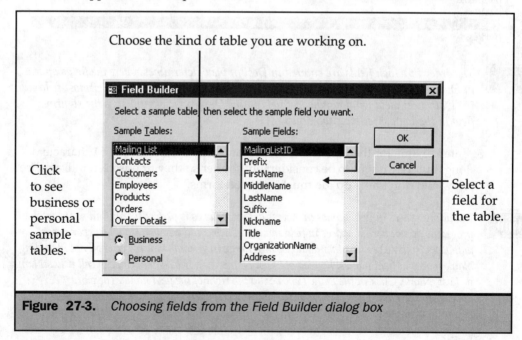

Figure 27-3. *Choosing fields from the Field Builder dialog box*

The Data Types

When you create a field, Access asks you to choose a data type. Following are explanations of the ten data types:

Data Type	Description
Text	For storing text (names, for example), combinations of text and numbers (street addresses), and numbers that aren't meant to be calculated (Social Security numbers and telephone numbers). A text field cannot be longer than 255 characters.
Memo	For storing long notes. Choose this data type when you want to include long descriptions in a database table. For really long chunks of text (say, a page or more) use the OLE Object data type instead.
Number	For storing numbers that are to be used in calculations.
Date/Time	For storing dates and times. (To choose how the date or time is formatted, click the Format box in the lower half of the Design View dialog box and choose a format from the drop-down menu.)
Currency	For storing monetary figures that are to be used in calculations.
AutoNumber	For entering numbers in sequence each time you add a new record to the table. For example, the first record is 1; the second, 2; and so on. Each number can only be used once in the field. By choosing the AutoNumber data type, you make sure that the data in the field is unique and is not repeated. Use the AutoNumber data type for the primary key field if no other field in the table stores unique, one-of-a-kind numbers such as Social Security numbers or item numbers. To make the AutoNumber field assign random numbers instead of sequential numbers, click in the New Values box on the lower half of the Design View dialog box and choose Random from the drop-down menu instead of Increment.
Yes/No	For storing either/or data, such as Yes/No, True/False, Checked Out?, Beautiful/Ugly. When you choose this data type, a box appears in the field. Checking the box means Yes, True, Checked Out, Beautiful, and so on; an empty check box means No, False, Not Checked Out, Ugly; and so on.
OLE Object	For storing text, spreadsheets, pictures, sounds, and other data created in Word, Excel, or other programs. The Memo data entry type is fine for entering a paragraph or two; but if you want a page or more to appear in a database table, you are better off choosing the OLE Object data type.

Data Type	Description
Hyperlink	For storing hyperlinks, which are described in Chapter 6 of this book.
Lookup Wizard	For retrieving values either from another database table or from a list of values in a combo box. When you choose this data type, the Lookup Wizard comes onscreen so you can designate which table to get the data from or enter the values that will appear in the combo box. See "Creating a Data-Entry Drop-Down List," later in this chapter, for more information.

Moving, Copying, Deleting, and Renaming Fields

After you have gone to the trouble of creating all the fields for the database table, you might discover to your dismay that fields are in the wrong order, that some fields don't belong in the table, or that some fields need new names. The following pages explain how to move, delete, and rename fields. You will also find instructions for copying fields.

Moving and Copying Fields

Move a field when you want it to appear in a different place in the table. To move a field, follow these steps:

1. Select the field by clicking on the box to its left. The field is highlighted.

2. Drag the field up or down across the small squares to the left of the fields. As you drag, a gray line appears between fields to show where the field will land when you release the mouse button.

3. Release the mouse button.

 You can also move fields in Datasheet view. To do so, click the field name at the top of the database table. Click again and drag it to the left or right. A black line appears between columns to show where the field will go. When the black line is in the right place, release the mouse button. However, moving fields in Datasheet view only changes the table's layout; it doesn't change its underlying structure. When you export the table, for example, its fields will be in their Design view order.

Copy a field when all its settings—its data type and field properties—can be used over again in another field. After you have copied the field, be sure to rename it. Identical fields cannot appear in the same table. To copy a field, follow these steps:

1. Select the field to be copied by clicking the box to its left in Design view.

2. Press CTRL-C or right-click and choose Copy from the shortcut menu.

3. Click on the field that you want the copy to appear above. In this illustration, for example, the copy will appear between the account numbers 610 and 620:

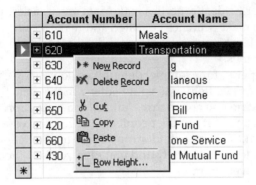

4. Either press CTRL-V or right-click and choose Paste on the shortcut menu.

5. Change the field name for the field you copied.

Renaming a Field

To rename a field, all you have to do is start in Design view, click in the box where the field's name is, delete the name that is there, and enter a new name. It doesn't matter if the field whose name you change is linked to a field in another table, because changing the name of a field doesn't affect the relationships between tables.

Caution *If you change the name of the field that you created with the Table Wizard or the Field Builder, the name change won't appear when you switch to Datasheet view. To make the name change appear in Datasheet view, either make the name change in Datasheet view by right-clicking on the column name, choosing Rename Column, and entering a new name, or else change the field's Caption property in Design view. See "Establishing Field Properties for Easier Data Entry," later in this chapter.*

Deleting a Field

Think twice before you delete a field. After you delete it, all the data contained in that field is lost from every record in the database table. You can't recover it. Follow these steps to delete a field:

1. In Design view, select the field you want to delete by clicking the little box to its left. The field is highlighted.

2. Either click the Delete Rows button or right-click and choose Delete Rows.

3. When Access asks if you really want to go through with it, click Yes.

Caution *Before you can delete a field that is related to a field in another table, you have to end the relationship. See "Forging the Relationships Between Tables" later in this chapter.*

Establishing Field Properties for Easier Data Entry

As shown in Figure 27-4, the lower half of the Design view window offers boxes for choosing properties for fields. Properties make data entry easier. They also help make entries more accurate, make searches go faster, and make sorting faster. You can do yourself and the people who enter data in your database tables a big favor by carefully choosing property settings.

The Field Size property, for example, determines how many characters can be entered in a field. For a State field, you could enter **2** in the Field Size property box and thereby make sure that no one enters three letters for a state abbreviation instead of the requisite two. Or, if the majority of the people whose records you want to enter live in California, you can make CA the default property for the State field. That way, CA appears in the State field automatically and you save yourself the trouble of entering those letters over and over again.

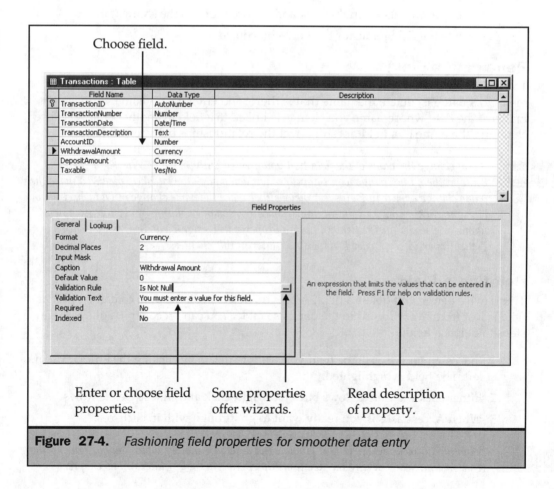

Figure 27-4. *Fashioning field properties for smoother data entry*

LEARN BY EXAMPLE
To try your hand with field properties, open the Figure 27-4 (Properties) file on the
companion CD.

Which field properties appear in Design view depends on which data type you
chose for the field you created. The following pages explain all the different field
properties, when to use them, and how to use them.

Before you choose properties for a field, make sure that the cursor is in the correct field in
the top half of the window in Design view. Property settings apply to whatever field the
cursor is in.

For detailed information about a property, click in its property box and then press F1.

Allow Zero Length

The Allow Zero Length property allows zero-length strings to appear in the field. A
zero-length string is an empty string (two quotation marks with no text between them).
It indicates that there is no value for a field. The default setting is No.

Enter a zero-length string to indicate that the field is not applicable. For example, if
you did not know a person's e-mail address, you could leave the field blank; but if you
knew that the person did not have an e-mail address, you could enter a zero-length
string to record that information in the database table.

Caption

Enter a word or two to describe the field in the Caption box if you don't care for the
field name. The word or words you enter will appear in Datasheet view, on reports,
and on forms in place of the field name. In Figure 27-4, for example, "Withdrawal
Amount" has been entered in the Caption box, so "Withdrawal Amount" and not
"WithdrawalAmount" (no space between words) will appear on reports, on forms, and
in Datasheet view.

Decimal Places

The Decimal Places property determines how many spaces can appear to the right of
the decimal point. This property only affects how numbers and currency figures are
displayed, not their real value. Choose a number from the drop-down list or choose
Auto. The Auto option displays the number of decimal places that the Format property
allows (see "Format," below).

Default Value

The Default Value property enters a value in each new record so you don't have to
enter it yourself. Enter a default value—it can be a word, abbreviation, or
number—when you know that the majority of the records you will enter require a

certain value. You can always delete the default value and enter a different value. If the majority of the people whose records you enter live in Daly City, you can make Daly City the default value; and if a person lives in Colma instead of Daly City, all you have to do is delete Daly City and enter **Colma** in its place.

When you select a field property text box and see an ellipses (three dots) next to it, it means that a wizard is available to help you set the field property value. Figure 27-4 shows the three dots next to the Validation Rule text box. Wizards are also available for the Input Mask and Default Value boxes.

Field Size

The Field Size property determines how many numbers or characters at maximum can be entered in the field. Use the Field Size property to make data entry more accurate. If the field stores phone numbers, for example, and you know that no phone number can be longer than 14 characters, enter **14** in the Field Size box.

Format

The Format property is for determining the format in which dates, times, numbers, currency figures, and Yes/No data types are displayed. Table 27-1 illustrates the different formats.

You can also format text or tell Access what should be entered in Memo and Text fields. To do so, enter one of the following four characters in the Format box:

Character	Description
@	Tells Access that a text character or a blank space is required in the field
&	Tells Access that a text character is not required in the field
<	Requires all characters in the field to be lowercase
>	Requires all characters in the field to be uppercase

Indexed

Indexes make searching and sorting operations go faster. In large databases, however, they also make table updates take longer and require more disk space for storing the data. With the Indexed property, you can tell Access that you want to index a field in a table. No is the default choice. The indexing choices are

- **No**   No indexing.
- **Yes (Duplicates OK)**   Indexes the field and allows duplicate values to appear in the field.

Format	Example
Date/Time	
General Date	7/31/98 5:29.24 PM
Long Date	Monday, July 31, 1998
Medium Date	31-Jul-98
Short Date	7/31/98
Long Time	5:29:24 PM
Medium Time	5:29 PM
Short Time	17:29
Number and Currency	
General Number	4455.78
Currency	$4,455.78
Fixed	4455.78
Standard	4,455.778
Percent	78.00%
Scientific	46E+03
Yes/No	
True/False	True
Yes/No	Yes
On/Off	On

Table 27-1. *Formats for Dates, Numbers, Currency Figures, and Yes/No Field Types*

■ **Yes (No Duplicates)**   Indexes the field and prevents duplicate values from appearing in the field.

Note   *Later in this chapter, "Indexing a Table Field" explains indexing in detail.*

Input Mask

The Input Mask property lays down blank spaces and punctuation in the field so that numbers and letters can be entered accurately. The following illustration shows an input mask for entering a telephone number. As soon as you move the cursor into a field that has a data input mask, punctuation marks and blank spaces appear so you know how many numbers or letters to type.

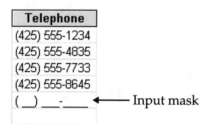

Input masks can be very sophisticated. You can create an input mask by entering the punctuation marks, a 9 where optional numbers appear, and a 0 where numbers are required. For example, to create the input mask shown in the previous illustration, enter the following in the Input Mask text box: **(999) 000-0000**. The punctuation marks—the parentheses and hyphen—will always appear in the field. The three-digit area code is optional, so 9s are used for its placeholders. The seven-digit telephone number is required, so 0s are used for its placeholders.

To create sophisticated input masks, click the three dots beside the Input Mask text box to open the Input Mask Wizard and get help there. The Input Mask Wizard may not have loaded when you installed Office. If it was set for install on first use, Access will prompt you for the Office 2000 CD.

New Values

For use with the AutoNumber data type, the New Values property determines whether the numbers are generated sequentially or at random. To make the AutoNumber field assign random numbers instead of sequential numbers, choose Random; otherwise, keep the default Increment setting.

Required

The Required property tells Access whether an entry has to be made in the field. The default value is No; but if you choose Yes for this property and then fail to enter a value in the field in question, you see the message in the following illustration.

Validation Rule

The Validation Rule lets you set down rules that have to be followed in order for data to be entered in the field. For example, you could require date entries to fall within a certain time period. Or you could require numbers or currency figures to be above or below a certain number. To create a validation rule, you enter an expression in the Validation Rule text box. In Figure 27-4, for example, the expression Is Not Null tells Access not to allow an empty or null entry in the WithdrawalAmount field. Or, if you wanted to exclude negative amounts in the same field, you might use the expression >0.

 To use dates in an expression, the dates must be enclosed by pound signs (#).

The best way to create an expression, especially if you are not up on your math, is to click the three dots beside the Validation Rule text box. You see the Expression Builder shown in Figure 27-5. By clicking buttons; choosing functions, constants, or operators; and by entering text in the text box, you can construct expressions. Click OK when you have finished constructing your expression.

Note *By choosing a data type, you are already establishing a validation rule. Letters, for example, cannot be entered in fields to which the Number or Currency data types have been assigned.*

Validation Text

If you established a validation rule for a field and someone enters data that breaks the rule, Access displays a standard error message. You can, however, write an error message of your own by entering it in the Validation Text text box. This error message, for example, warns a data-entry employee that they have to enter a value for the field:

Click a button to enter an operator.

Type
numbers
and letters
in the text
box.

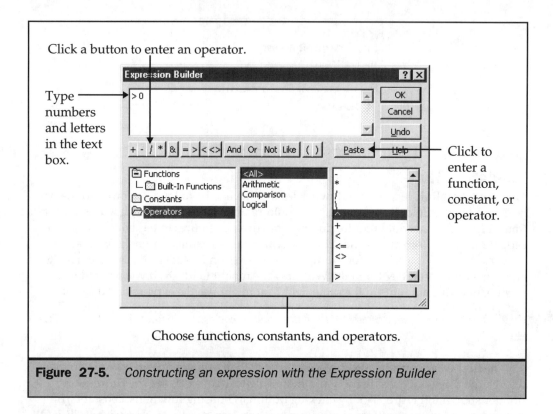

Click to
enter a
function,
constant, or
operator.

Choose functions, constants, and operators.

Figure 27-5. *Constructing an expression with the Expression Builder*

Following are some sample validation rules and their corresponding text:

Validation Rule Setting	Validation Text Setting
<>0	Please enter a nonzero value.
0 or >100	Value must be either 0 or greater than 100.
Like "K???	Value must be four characters long and start with the letter K.
<#1/1/96#	Enter a date before 1996.
>=#1/1/97# And <#1/1/98#	Date must be in 1997.

Creating a Data-Entry Drop-Down List

Instead of entering data in a field, you can choose data from a drop-down list.
Choosing data from a list not only makes entering data go faster, it makes entries more
accurate. With a list, you can be sure that you or others are entering data

correctly—and consistently—in the database table. Access offers two ways to create a drop-down list for entering data. You can type the items that appear on the list yourself, or you can get the items for the list from a column in a database table.

Both techniques are described in the following pages. Type the list yourself if the items on the list are not likely to change. By getting the items from a database table, you can access a completely up-to-date list of items. As the number and variety of items in the database table changes, so will the number and variety of items on your drop-down list, because items on the list will come from a database table.

LEARN BY EXAMPLE
Open the Figure 27-7 (Lookup) file to see examples of drop-down lists in database tables.

Creating the List Yourself

The following illustration shows a drop-down list with budgeting account names and numbers. Instead of entering this information, users can simply choose it from the list. That saves time and ensures that the account is entered correctly.

Meals	610
Miscellaneous	640
Mutual Fund	420
Power Bill	650
Rental Income	410
Second Mutual Fund	430
Telephone Service	660
Transportation	620

Follow these steps to create a drop-down list of your own:

1. In Design view, click in the field in which you want to create a drop-down list.

2. In the Data Type column, click to open the drop-down list and choose Lookup Wizard. You see the first Lookup Wizard dialog box.

3. Click the I Will Type The Values That I Want option button and then click Next. As shown in Figure 27-6, the second Lookup Wizard dialog box appears. This is where you type the values that will appear on the list.

4. Under Col1, type each item that is to appear on the drop-down list. When you have finished, click Next.

Note   *You can create a multicolumn drop-down list by entering the number of columns you want in the Number Of Columns box and entering choices under each column.*

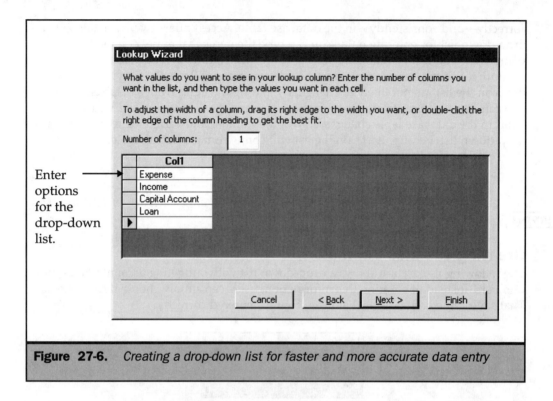

Enter options for the drop-down list.

Figure 27-6. *Creating a drop-down list for faster and more accurate data entry*

5. In the next Lookup Wizard dialog box, enter a name for the field in your database table, if necessary. Then click the Finish button.

If you click the Lookup tab on the bottom of the Design view window, you will see everything you care to know about the drop-down list:

General	Lookup	
Display Control	Combo Box	
Row Source Type	Value List	
Row Source	"Expense";"Income";"Capital Account";"Lc	
Bound Column	1	
Column Count	1	
Column Heads	No	
Column Widths	1"	
List Rows	8	
List Width	1"	
Limit To List	No	

Getting Items on the List from a Database Table

Follow these steps to get items on your drop-down list from another table or from a query in the database:

1. In Design view, click in the field in which you want to create a drop-down list.

2. In the Data Type column, click to open the drop-down list and choose Lookup Wizard. The first Lookup Wizard dialog box appears.

3. The I Want The Lookup Column To Look Up The Values In A Table Or Query option button is already selected, so click the Next button. The next Lookup Wizard dialog box asks for the name of the table or query where the column whose values you want for your list are located.

4. Click the Tables, Queries, or Both option button; if necessary, click a table; then click the Next button. As shown in Figure 27-7, the next dialog box asks for the name of the column whose values you want for the list.

5. Click a column name on the left side of the dialog box, and then click the arrow that points to the right. The column name moves to the right side of the dialog box. Repeat this step if you want to add more than one column to the combo box; otherwise, click the Next button.

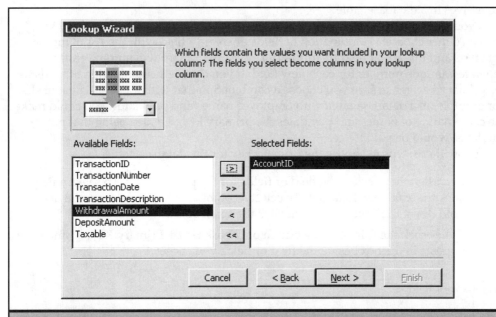

Figure 27-7. *Click the field whose values you want for the drop-down list and then click the arrow that points to the right*

6. If necessary, adjust the width of the column or columns in the next dialog box either by dragging the right side of the column heading or by double-clicking on the right side of the column heading. Then click Next.

7. In the next Lookup Wizard dialog box, enter a name for the field in your database table, if necessary. Then click the Finish button.

8. In the message box that appears, click Yes. Access has to create a relationship between your table and the other table or query so that you can draw upon values in the other table or query.

9. Switch to Datasheet view, click in the new field you created, and see if the drop-down list appears.

Choosing the Primary Key

It's so important to choose a primary key that Access reminds you if you try to leave Design view without having chosen one.

A primary key is the means by which Access identifies each record in the table. Therefore, the primary key field must be one whose entries are unique—different in every single record. Invoice numbers, social security numbers, account numbers, and check numbers are often chosen for the primary key, because these numbers always differ from record to record. A last name field, however, would be a poor choice for the primary key, because common names like Martinez and Smith are likely to repeat themselves in a database table.

If you can't find a field in your database table that can serve as the primary key, you can either choose a combination of fields or create a field with the AutoNumber data type and make that field the primary key. AutoNumber will automatically generate a unique number for each new field. If you choose a combination of fields for the primary key, make sure you choose a combination that will not ever repeat itself. For example, in a database table with employee names and pay dates, you could make the combination of names and pay dates the primary key, the idea being that no employee would be paid twice.

Follow these steps to choose the primary key for the database table:

1. In Design view, select the field or fields for the primary key. To select a field, click the small box to its left. To select a combination of more than one field, hold down the CTRL key as you click the small boxes.

2. Either click the Primary Key button or choose Edit | Primary Key. A small key appears in the box beside the field or fields you chose:

Primary key field

	Field Name	Data Type	Description
💡	Social Security Number	Text	
	Last Name	Text	
	First Name	Text	

Indexing a Table Field

By indexing a field in a table, you can make data searches go faster. You can also sort table records faster and generate reports faster. Indexing a field tells Access that the field is an important one and that you intend to use it for sorting, searching, and generating reports.

When you choose which fields to index, choose the pivotal fields in the table from which you expect to gather data. For example, in a table of products, the Product Number field would be the primary key field because product numbers are unique and can't be repeated. But you would likely generate reports based on product names, in which case you would index the Product Name field.

 It takes Access longer to update tables, especially large ones, in which fields have been indexed.

Choose View | Indexes, or click the Indexes button. This opens the Indexes dialog box, which shows which fields in a table have been indexed, as well as which field is the primary key field. Figure 27-8 shows the Indexes dialog box.

 LEARN BY EXAMPLE
To experiment with indexes, open the Figure 27-7 (Indexes) file on the companion CD.

Indexing One Field

Follow these steps to index a table field:

1. In Design view, click the field that you want to index.

2. Click the General tab, if necessary, at the bottom of the Design view window.

3. Click the down arrow in the Indexed box at the bottom of the General tab and choose an indexing option:

   ■ **No** No indexing (the default setting).

   ■ **Yes (Duplicates OK)** Indexes the field and allows duplicate values to appear in the field.

   ■ **Yes (No Duplicates)** Indexes the field and prevents duplicate values from appearing in the field.

Tip *By default, indexed fields are sorted in ascending order. To index a field in descending order, choose View | Indexes to open the Indexes dialog box (see Figure 27-8), click in the Sort Order column beside the field whose index order you want to change, and choose Descending from the drop-down list.*

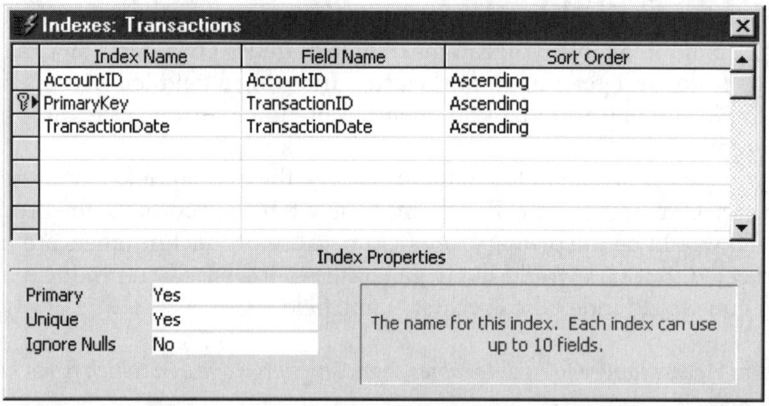

Figure 27-8. The Indexes dialog box shows which fields in the table have been indexed. Use this dialog box as well to create an index based on two or more fields

Indexes Based on More Than One Field

Sometimes it is necessary to index two or even three fields at the same time. For example, if you index the Last Name field and two or more people in the database table have the same last name, you might want to index the First Name field. That way, if there are two Johnsons, two Martinezes, two Wongs, Access can more easily look to the First Name field to "break the tie" and sort Billy Bob Johnson before Laree Johnson, for example.

Follow these steps to create an index based on two fields instead of one:

1. In Design view, click anywhere in the database table.

2. Choose View | Indexes or click the Indexes button on the Standard toolbar. You see the Indexes dialog box (see Figure 27-8).

3. On a blank line in the Index Name column, enter a name for the new index you want create.

4. Click in the Field Name column beside the name you just entered. An arrow appears in the column.

5. Click the arrow to open a drop-down list of all the fields in the database table.

6. From the list, choose the first field for the index. For a Withdrawals index, for example, choose TransactionDate.

7. Click the Field Name box immediately below the one from step 6. Open the drop-down list, and choose the second field for the index. When you have finished, the Indexes dialog box looks something like the one shown in this illustration:

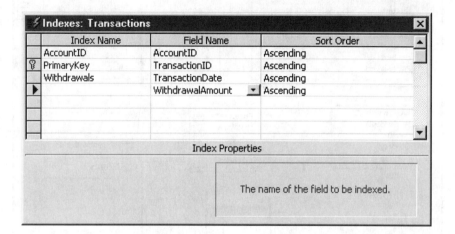

Forging the Relationships Between Tables

As the section "A Relational Database" in Chapter 26 explained, you don't have to store all the data in a single table. In fact, you shouldn't, because that makes entering the data harder and it uses up valuable disk space. Instead, you can store the data in several tables, pass information back and forth between tables, query several tables at the same time, create forms that draw data from different tables, and generate reports from different tables. The hitch is this: Access cannot work with several tables or create queries, forms, or reports from several different tables until you have established relationships between the tables.

A relationship matches data from fields in different tables, usually from fields that have the same name. Figure 27-9 shows the relationships among eight tables in a database. In the figure, a line has been drawn from table to table when two tables have a relationship. Notice that relationships are forged so that data from one table can be used in another table. Moreover, relationships are usually forged by using the primary key fields from tables. In Figure 27-9, for example, the Workorders table (top row, second from the left) gets employee ID numbers from the EmployeeID field—a primary key—in the Employees table beneath it. In turn, the Workorders table "lends" its primary key, the WorkorderID field, to three other tables: Payments, Workorder Parts, and Workorder Labor.

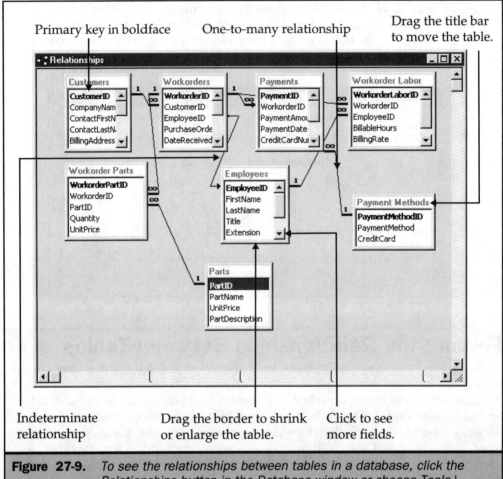

Primary key in boldface   One-to-many relationship   Drag the title bar to move the table.

Indeterminate relationship   Drag the border to shrink or enlarge the table.   Click to see more fields.

Figure 27-9. *To see the relationships between tables in a database, click the Relationships button in the Database window or choose Tools | Relationships*

This section explains how to view relationships between tables like the ones shown in Figure 27-9, forge new relationships, and change or sever relationships. You'll also learn about the different relationships that can be forged and what referential integrity is.

LEARN BY EXAMPLE

To experiment with forging relationships between tables, open the sample database file called Figure 27-9 (Relationships) on the companion CD.

Seeing the Relationships Between Tables

When you create a database with the Database Wizard, Access forges relationships between the tables in the database automatically. And when you create a database table with the Table Wizard, Access asks if you want to forge a relationship with the table or tables that you already created. Therefore, relationships may already exist between the tables in your database.

Viewing Tables in the Relationships Window

It is easy to find out where relationships have been forged between tables. Choose Tools | Relationships or click the Relationships button. You see the Relationships window (see Figure 27-9) if relationships have already been forged. If they haven't been forged, you see the Show Table dialog box (see Figure 27-10).

 To see only the relationships between one table and the tables to which it is related, click the table and then click the Show Direct Relationships button on the Relationship toolbar. Click the Show All Relationships button when you want to see the relationships among all the tables in the database.

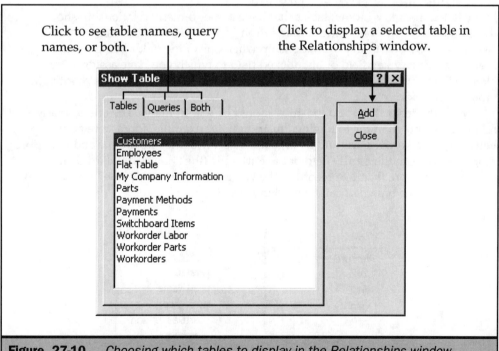

Figure 27-10.   *Choosing which tables to display in the Relationships window*

In the Relationships window, each table is represented by a box and lines are drawn to show the relationships between tables. Field names in boldface are primary key fields. If yours is a database with a lot of tables, you might have to do some dragging and clicking in the Relationship window to untangle the tables and see precisely where the relationships are.

- ■ **Moving Tables**   To move a table box in the window, drag its title bar to a new place.

- ■ **Changing Table Size**   To make a table box larger or smaller, move the pointer over its border, and when you see a two-headed arrow, click and drag the border.

- ■ **Seeing the Field Names**   A scroll bar appears in the table box if all the fields can't be displayed at once. Click the arrows in the scroll bar (or enlarge the table box) to read the field names.

   To remove a single table from the Relationships window, right-click it and choose Hide Table from the shortcut menu. Click the Show All Relationships button to get it back again.

Relationships Between Tables

In the Relationships window, tables that have a one-to-many relationship show the number 1 on the "one" side and an infinity symbol (∞) on the "many" side. Access creates a one-to-many relationship when one of the fields being related is either a primary key field or an indexed field to which you have assigned the No (No Duplicates) setting (see "Indexing a Table Field," earlier in this chapter, for more information).

By far, the majority of relationships should be one-to-many. The one-to-many relationship shown in the following illustration, for example, forges a relationship between a Workorder Parts and a Parts table. Part IDs must be unique and not appear more than once in the PartID field of the Part table (the "one" side). Part ID numbers can appear in more than one record in the Workorder Parts table (the "many" side), because the same type part can be used in many repair jobs.

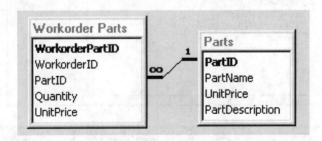

Besides one-to-many relationships, you can forge one-to-one, indeterminate, and many-to-many relationships. One-to-one relationships show a 1 on each side of the relationship line. A simple line is drawn between tables whose relationship is indeterminate. Many-to-many relationships are rare. They require a third, intermediary table. Look up "Relationship" in the Access Help program for more information.

Mapping Relationships Between Tables

To forge relationships between tables, you start by displaying the tables in the Relationships window. Then you draw lines between fields on the tables.

Displaying Tables in the Relationships Window

Follow these steps to display the tables that you want to form relationships between in the Relationships window:

1. If necessary, close all the tables in the database.

2. Click the Relationships button or choose Tools | Relationships. The Relationships window appears. The Show Table dialog box shown in Figure 27-10 will also appear if you have no relationships established yet. If the Show Table dialog box does not appear automatically, click the Show Table button.

3. Click the Queries tab or Both tab, if necessary, to see the names of queries or of both tables and queries.

4. Click the table or query you want to place in the Relationships window.

5. Click the Add button.

6. Repeat steps 3 through 5 until all the tables or queries which you want to relate are in the Relationships window.

7. Click the Close button.

 Right-click a table and choose Hide Table from the shortcut menu to remove a table from the Relationships window. Click the Show All Relationships button to get the table back again.

Drawing the Lines Between Tables

After the tables (and/or queries) you want are in the Relationships window, you can forge relationships between them. Follow these steps:

1. Drag a field from one table box and drop it in the field in another table box. When you drag the field into the second table box, the pointer changes into a rectangle. By the way, it doesn't matter which table box you start from. In other words, you can drag the field from table to table in either direction.

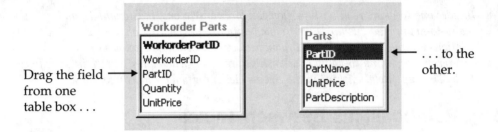

Drag the field from one table box . . .

. . . to the other.

Caution *You can't create a relationship using fields that aren't of the same data type. For example, you can't create a relationship between a number field and a text field.*

2. Release the mouse button. The Edit Relationships dialog box appears, as shown in Figure 27-11. The name of the field you dragged and the field you dropped it on appear in the dialog box. At the bottom of the dialog box, you can see what kind of relationship you are creating.

3. Click the Enforce Referential Integrity check box if you want the rules of referential integrity to apply to the relationship. See the sidebar "What Is Referential Integrity?" to find out what those rules are. The sidebar also

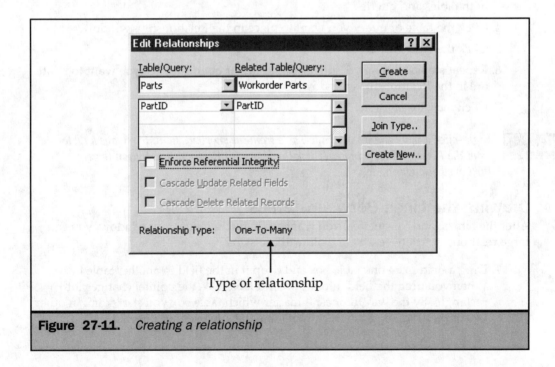

Type of relationship

Figure 27-11. *Creating a relationship*

explains what the Cascade Update Related Fields and Cascade Delete Related Records check boxes are for.

Note *If you opt against applying the rules of referential integrity, the line that is drawn between the tables will show an indeterminate relationship without 1s or the infinity symbol.*

4. Click the Create button. You go straight to the Relationships window, where a line has been drawn to mark the relationship.

Tip *Click the Join Type button to open the Join Properties dialog box and tell Access how to display records by default when you create a query with the two tables in the relationship. Queries are discussed in the next chapter.*

When you have finished forging relationships between tables and close the Relationships window, Access asks if you want to save your changes to the layout in the window. The relationships themselves have already been saved—you saved them when you clicked the Create button in the Relationships dialog box. Access only wants to know whether to save the positions of the table boxes onscreen so that the table boxes appear in the same places next time you open the Relationships window. Click Yes or No.

ACCESS

What Is Referential Integrity?

Referential integrity, a particularly hideous database term, refers to the rules by which Access makes sure that relationships between tables are valid and that you don't delete or change field values in one table that are necessary for another table. By clicking the Enforce Referential Integrity check box in the Edit Relationships dialog box, you make sure that one side of the relationship works in tandem with the other side in the following ways:

■ A value in a field on the "many" side of the relationship is valid only if it matches a value on the "one" side. For example, suppose there is a relationship between two tables, one called Health Plans and one called Employees, and the relationship is forged on a field in each table called Plan Number. In this case, you couldn't enter a health plan number in the Employees table (the "many" side) unless it was listed already in the Plan Number field of the Health Plans table (the "one" side). You could, however, leave the Plan Number field blank in the Employees table under the rules of referential integrity. If you tried to enter a health plan number in the Employees table that didn't match any values in the Health Plans table, you would see the dialog box shown next.

■ A value on the "one" side of the relationship cannot be deleted or changed if it is matched by a value that has been entered on the "many" side. To use the example of the Health Plans and Employees table again, the Health Plans table holds the master list of plan numbers, all or some of which have already been entered in the Employees table. If you try to change or delete a plan number in the Health Plans table, Access will not permit it under the rules of referential integrity—it would leave employees assigned to a non-existent health plan. If you try to delete or change a value on the "one" side that has been entered on the "many" side, you see this dialog box:

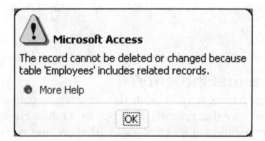

The Edit Relationships dialog box offers two check boxes for keeping referential integrity but also allowing records on the "one" side to be deleted or changed:

■ **Cascade Update Related Fields**   Click this check box and Access allows you to change values on the "one" side of the relationship even if the values have already been entered on the "many" side. When you change a value on the "one" side, matching values in related records on the "many" side are likewise changed.

■ **Cascade Delete Related Records**   Click this check box and Access lets you delete values on the "one" side of the relationship. When a value is deleted on the "one" side, matching values in related records on the "many" side are also deleted.

The term "cascade" in this case refers to the way Access will change the affected records, moving sequentially from table to table, making changes in the next table based on changes in the previous one.

Changing and Severing Table Relationships

Follow these steps to change a relationship between two tables or end the relationship altogether:

1. In the Relationships window (click the Relationships button or choose Tools | Relationships), right-click on the line that marks the relationship between two tables. You see the following shortcut menu:

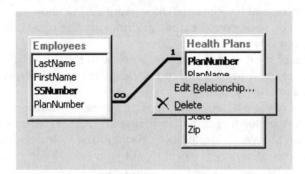

Note   *Sometimes when you click the line between tables, you see a shortcut menu with options for displaying tables in the Relationships window. Keep right-clicking. Eventually, you see the shortcut menu for editing and deleting relationships.*

2. Either edit the relationship or delete it:

   ■ **Edit the Relationship**   Click the Edit Relationship option to open the Edit Relationships dialog box (see Figure 27-11). From there, you can choose options to change the relationship.

   ■ **Delete the Relationship**   Click the Delete option to sever the relationship between the two tables.

Changing a Table's Appearance

Thus far in this chapter, you have learned how to design database tables and forge relationships between them. To actually see the data in a table, however, you must switch to Datasheet view. To do so, either choose View | Datasheet or, if you are starting from the Database window, click the Tables button, then double-click a table name or click it and then click the Open button.

One way to enter data is to do it in Datasheet view, so taking the time to make the table more legible is definitely worthwhile if you have a lot of data to enter. The following pages explain how to make columns wider and rows taller, change the arrangement of columns, and change the look of a datasheet.

ACCESS

LEARN BY EXAMPLE
To experiment with the commands for changing a datasheet's appearance, open the Figure 27-12 (Datasheet) file on the companion CD.

Changing the Look of a Datasheet

To change the way that a datasheet looks onscreen, you can do any number of things. You can change the font of the text or change what Access calls the "cell effects"—the gridline, gridline color, and background color. Figure 27-12 shows four data sheets whose fonts, font sizes, background colors, gridlines, and gridline colors have been formatted in different ways.

Change the font of the text in a datasheet by choosing Format | Font. In the Font dialog box, choose a font, font size, and font style for the text. You can also change the color of text in the Font dialog box.

Change the look of the datasheet by choosing Format | Datasheet. You see the Datasheet Formatting dialog box shown in Figure 27-13. By experimenting with the Cell Effect, Gridlines Shown, Gridline Color, Background Color, and Border and Line Styles options, you can design a datasheet to suit your taste. Keep your eye on the Sample box as you experiment to see what your design looks like. Click OK when you have put together the perfect datasheet design.

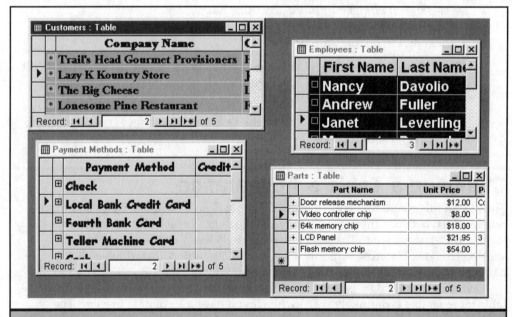

Figure 27-12.   *By changing fonts and experimenting with "cell effects," you can radically change the way a datasheet looks*

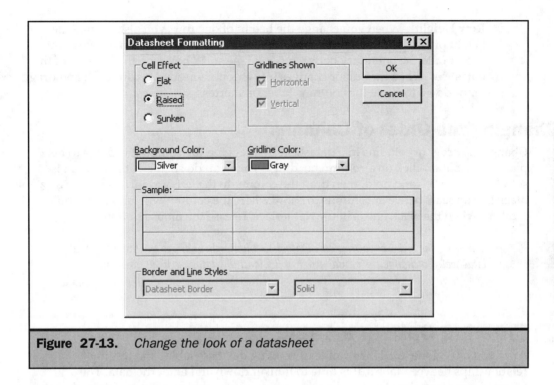

Figure 27-13.   *Change the look of a datasheet*

    Another way to change the appearance of a datasheet is to click the Fill/Back Color, Font/Fore Color, Gridlines, and Special Effects buttons on the Formatting toolbar. Clicking these buttons and choosing options from the drop-down menus is a quick way to experiment with a datasheet's appearance.

Changing the Width of Columns and the Height of Rows

The techniques for changing the width of columns and the height of rows are the same in Access as they are in Excel:

■ **Column Width**   To change the width of a column, move the pointer into the right side of the heading of the column. The column heading is the gray field name at the top of the column. When the pointer changes into a double-headed arrow, click and drag the boundary between column headings to make the column wider or narrower.

    The fastest way to adjust the width of a column is to double-click on the right side of its column heading (the field name at the top of the column). Double-clicking there tells Access to make the column wide enough for its widest entry.

■ **Row Height** When you change the height of one row, you also change the height of all the rows in the table. To change the height of the rows, move the cursor onto the boundary between two of the small boxes on the left side of the datasheet. When the cursor changes into a double-headed arrow, click and drag up or down to make the columns taller or shorter.

Changing the Order of Columns

Change the order of columns in a datasheet by dragging the column headings to new places. To do that, click on a column heading. When you do so, the entire column is selected. Now click and hold, then drag the column to the left or right. As you drag, a black line appears between columns to show where the column will land after you move it. When the black line is in the right place, release the mouse button.

Changing the order of columns in Datasheet view only changes the layout of the datasheet. To change the actual order of fields in the database itself, do so in Design view.

Entering Data in a Table

After you have gone to all the trouble of creating database tables and forging relationships between tables, it is time to hunker down and enter the data. The following pages explain tried-and-true techniques for entering data quickly and accurately. They also explain how to edit the data in a database table, in case you don't enter it correctly the first time.

Access offers two ways to enter data in a table: on the datasheet and on a form. Creating a form for entering data in a database table is explained in "Forms for Entering and Viewing Data," later in this chapter. To open the datasheet and start entering data in a table, choose View | Datasheet. Or, if you are starting from the Database window, click the Tables button and double-click a table name, or click it and click the Open button.

LEARN BY EXAMPLE
To test drive the techniques described in the following pages for entering data in a datasheet, open the Figure 27-14 (Enter Data) file on the companion CD.

Entering Data in a Datasheet

The pages that follow explain how to enter data in a datasheet, as well as how to enter data in Memo fields, and how to hide and freeze columns so you never lose sight of where you are entering data in a datasheet.

Don't worry about whether you are entering data in the first record or last record in a datasheet. It doesn't matter where you enter the data. Access gives you lots of opportunities to sort or rearrange records on the datasheet, as the next chapter explains.

To enter data in a datasheet, go to the last record. To get there, either click the New Record button or scroll to the bottom of the datasheet and click in the first field of the last empty record. After you type the first character in the new record, a picture of a pencil appears to the left of the record so you know where you are entering data. Meanwhile, Access inserts a new blank row at the bottom of the table and marks the new row with an asterisk (*):

	$30.00	2/2/95
	$252.67	2/9/95
🖉	236.	
*		

Enter data in the first field and press the TAB or ENTER key when you have finished. The cursor moves to the next field so you can enter data there. When you have entered data in all the fields in the record, press ENTER or TAB again. The cursor moves to the next row so you can enter another record.

Note *At the bottom of the datasheet, Access tells you how many records are in the database table and which record the cursor is in.*

Formatted Fields, Input Masks, and Drop-Down Lists

The only unusual things to notice about entering data on a datasheet is that you don't have to worry about formatting when you enter data in a field that has been formatted in a certain way. You encounter punctuation marks when the cursor is in a field with an input mask, and you see an arrow when the cursor is in a field to which you have attached a drop-down list, also known as a *lookup table*. The following illustrations show a field that has been formatted for entering currency figures, a field with an input mask, and a field with a drop-down list (from left to right):

	Payment Amo
	$190.03
	$37.80
	$152.28
	$151.47
	$50.44
	$59.70
	$204.25
	$30.00
	$252.67
🖉	$0.00
*	

Phone Number
(301) 555-8257
(301) 555-7969
(403) 555-3612
(403) 555-9573
(360) 555-8097
(4 █) __-____

Music Category ID
Rock
Rock
Rock
Jazz
New Age
Classical
Rock
▼
Classical
Country
Jazz
New Age
Rock

Do the following when you encounter formatted fields, input masks, and drop-down lists:

- **Formatted Fields**   Enter the value and let Access format the field for you. For example, if you type **4321.1** in the Payment Amount field shown in the previous illustration and press TAB or ENTER, Access formats the entry as follows: $4,321.10. You don't have to worry about entering the dollar sign, comma, or trailing zero because the field has been formatted with the Currency data type.

- **Input Masks**   Enter the numbers or letters without any concern for punctuation marks. Access bypasses punctuation marks and moves the cursor directly to the next place where a number or letter needs to be entered.

- **Drop-Down Lists**   Click the down arrow and choose an item from the list.

Entering Data in Memo Fields

As you know if you read "Creating a Field" earlier in this chapter, Access gives you the opportunity to create Memo fields for storing long notes in a database table. However, entering a long note on the datasheet is well-nigh impossible. To enter a note in a Memo field, move the cursor into the field and press SHIFT-F2. You see the Zoom dialog box shown in Figure 27-14. Enter your note and click OK or press ENTER. Only the first few words of a note appear on the datasheet, but you can read a note on a datasheet by moving the cursor into the Memo field and pressing SHIFT-F2.

Freezing and Hiding Columns So You Can See What You Are Doing

As you enter data on the outskirts of a datasheet, it is sometimes hard to tell what data to enter. When the cursor is in the eighth or ninth column, for example, you lose sight of the fields in the first and second column that usually identify the name of the person or thing whose data you are entering. You can, however, "freeze" the first and second column—or any column for that matter—so that columns stay onscreen no matter how far you stray to the outskirts of the datasheet. And you can also hide columns so that fewer appear on the datasheet.

FREEZING COLUMNS IN ONE PLACE   Follow these steps to "freeze" a column or columns so that they can always be seen:

1. Select the column or columns that are to stay onscreen. To select a single column, click its column heading. To select several columns, click the first column heading, then hold down the SHIFT key as you click the last one. Columns are highlighted onscreen after they have been selected.

2. Choose Format | Freeze Columns.

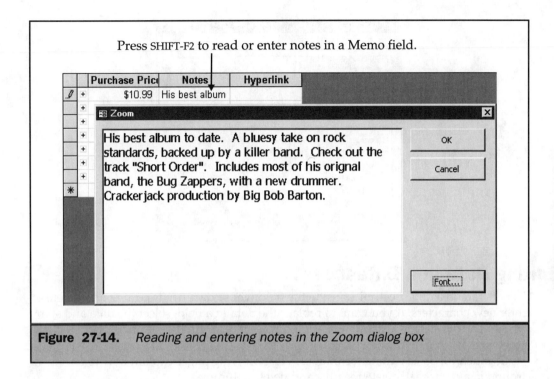

Figure 27-14.   *Reading and entering notes in the Zoom dialog box*

Now when you move around in the datasheet, the columns you "froze" stay onscreen. To "unfreeze" a column or columns, choose Format | Unfreeze All Columns.

HIDING COLUMNS ON THE DATASHEET   Follow these steps to hide a column or columns:

1. Select the column or columns that you want to hide. To select a column, click its column heading. Select several columns by clicking the first column heading, then holding down the SHIFT key as you click the last one.

2. Choose Format | Hide Columns.

The columns disappear. You can hide as many different columns as you want. When you need to see the columns again, choose Format | Unhide Columns, click beside the names of the columns you want to unhide in the Unhide Columns dialog box, shown next, and click the Close button.

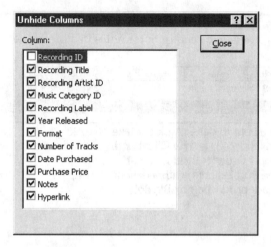

Editing Data in a Datasheet

To edit data in a datasheet, click inside the field whose data needs editing and delete or enter new characters. If you want to replace the data in a field, select the data and start typing. The old data is instantly erased and is replaced with the numbers or characters you type.

So much for basic editing techniques. The following pages explain how to move around in a datasheet, delete records, and delete columns.

 You can't edit data in the following kinds of fields: AutoNumber fields, locked fields, fields in queries that establish relationships between fields, and calculated fields.

Moving Around a Datasheet

Table 27-2 explains keyboard techniques for getting around in a datasheet. Besides pressing keys, you can click the buttons or work the scrollbar on the bottom of the datasheet to move the cursor. Figure 27-15 explains what the buttons on the bottom of the datasheet do.

Deleting Records and Columns

Deleting a record on a datasheet isn't a big deal, but deleting a column is.

 When you delete a column or record, you can't get the data back. It is gone forever. Access doesn't let you click the Undo button, for example, to get it back.

DELETING A RECORD   To delete a record, follow these steps:

1. Select the record you want to delete by clicking the small box to its left. To select several records, click the box to the left of the first one, and then SHIFT-click the box to the left of the last one.

Press	To Move
↑	To the previous record
↓	To the following record
TAB or ENTER	To the next field in the record
SHIFT-TAB	To the previous field in the record
CTRL-HOME	To the first field in the record
CTRL-END	To the last field in the record
PAGE UP	Up one screen
PAGE DOWN	Down one screen

Table 27-2.   *Moving Around in a Datasheet*

2. Click the Delete Record button or press the DELETE key.

3. Click Yes when Access asks if you really want to delete the record.

Caution   *If the record you want to delete is related to records in another table, deleting the record deletes the records in the other table as well. Access displays a dialog box to warn you about it. Click No in the dialog box to keep from deleting the records, then choose Tools | Relationships to open the Relationships window and investigate the relationship. Refer to "Seeing the Relationships Between Tables," earlier in this chapter, for more information.*

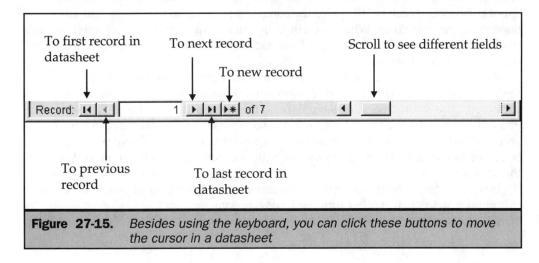

Figure 27-15.   *Besides using the keyboard, you can click these buttons to move the cursor in a datasheet*

DELETING A COLUMN   When you delete a column, you delete an entire field in the database. In other words, you delete part of each record you have entered so far. Think twice before doing that. In fact, I recommend switching to Design view to delete a field because Design view offers a better look at the structure of the table and how the fields fit together. (See "Moving, Copying, Deleting, and Renaming Fields," earlier in this chapter, to learn how to delete a field in Design view.)

| Caution | *Deleting a field may adversely affect the forms and reports that get their data from the table.* |

If you disregarded my advice about deleting columns and want to delete columns in Datasheet view anyway, follow these steps:

1. Select the column or columns you want to delete. To do so, either click the column heading or SHIFT-click column headings to select more than one.
2. Choose Edit | Delete Column.
3. Click Yes in the dialog box that asks if you really want to go through with it.

| Caution | *Before you can delete a field that is related to a field in another table, you have to end the relationship. See "Forging the Relationships Between Tables," earlier in this chapter.* |

Forms for Entering and Viewing Data

Forms are the chief means of viewing and entering data in a database table, aside from Datasheet view. Access forms are very much like the forms you fill out to apply for a job or a driver's license. Each field is labeled and asks for or offers information of some kind. The form shown in Figure 27-16, for example, solicits and displays information about customers. There are fields for the company name, who to contact, address, phone number, and so on. When you enter data in a form like this, it is entered into the underlying database table. When you view data or query data by means of a form, the data comes from a database table.

Forms can be far more sophisticated than datasheets. For one thing, you can usually see all the fields in a record on a form. And you can also clearly see where data is supposed to be entered because each place on the form is clearly labeled. Moreover, you can create more than one form for a database table—or you can link a form to several database tables and assemble information from several different places at once. For example, this particular form includes a datasheet showing work orders for that customer.

Items on a form are called *controls*. You can include other controls, such as buttons that allow you to open another form and view its data.

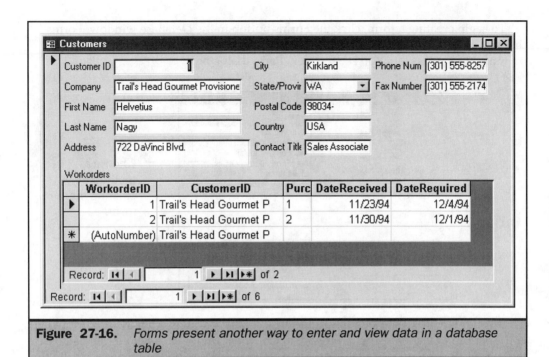

Figure 27-16.   *Forms present another way to enter and view data in a database table*

The following pages explain how to create a form, print a form, enter data in a form, copy data from one form to another, and delete a record from a form.

LEARN BY EXAMPLE
To experiment with the techniques in this chapter for creating forms, open the Figure 27-16 (Forms) file on the companion CD.

Creating a Form

Access offers no less than three ways to create a form: in Design view, with an AutoForm option, and with the Form Wizard. The least sophisticated but simplest method of creating a form is to use an AutoForm option. With an autoform, you get one text box, check box, or drop-down menu for each field in your database table. To create forms that draw upon data from more than one table or query, create your form with the Form Wizard or in Design view. By the way, if you used the Database Wizard to create your database, chances are that Access already created a form or two for your database.

To begin creating a form, click the Forms button in the Database window. Forms that you or Access already created will appear. To create a new form, click the New button on the Forms tab. You see the New Form dialog box:

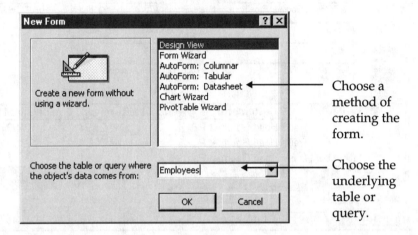

If you intend to create an autoform, choose a table or query from the drop-down list at the bottom of the dialog box. Access will create a form for each field in the database table. You need not choose a table or query to create a form in Design view, or with the Form Wizard, Chart Wizard, or PivotTable Wizard options in the dialog box.

Choose one of the following means of creating a new form:

- **Design View**   Create the form yourself, one control—that is, one text box, check box, or command button—at a time. For more information, look up "Design view, forms" in the Index tab of the Help dialog box.

- **Form Wizard**   Let the Form Wizard do the work. The Form Wizard asks questions about which fields to include in the form and creates the form when you are finished answering questions. See "Creating a Form with the Form Wizard," later in this chapter.

- **AutoForm: Columnar**   Create a two-column form in which the text boxes and other controls are left-aligned, one below the other. The form in Figure 27-16 is a columnar form, as is the topmost form in Figure 27-17. To learn about this and the other AutoForm options, see "Creating a Form with Access' AutoForms," later in this chapter.

- **AutoForm: Tabular**   Create a form in which the text boxes and other controls appear in a table format, as shown in Figure 27-17.

- **AutoForm: Datasheet**   Create a form that looks exactly like a datasheet, as shown in Figure 27-17.

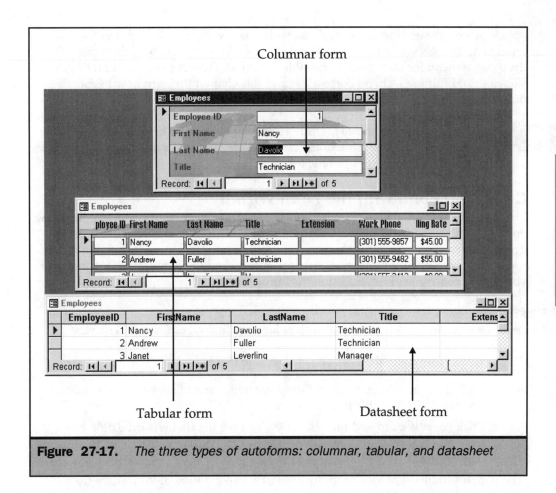

Figure 27-17. *The three types of autoforms: columnar, tabular, and datasheet*

- **Chart Wizard** Create a form with the Chart Wizard that shows data from a chart.
- **PivotTable Wizard** Create a form that gathers information from an Excel pivot table.

> **Tip** *Data input masks, formats, drop-down lists, and data type settings made to a table in Design view appear on the form you create as well. You can create special formats for entering data in a form, but it is far easier to do that in Design View.*

Creating a Form with Access' AutoForms

After you have clicked the New button in the Database window, chosen which table or query to be the basis of the form in the New Form dialog box, and chosen an AutoForm option, Access creates the form nearly instantaneously. Figure 27-17 shows the three types of autoforms you can create. On your new form is one text box, check box, or drop-down menu for each field in the table. That's all there is to it. See "Entering, Viewing, and Editing Data on Forms," later in this chapter, to learn how to enter data in forms.

Access offers a very fast way to create a columnar autoform. Click the Tables or Queries button on the Database window and click the table or query for which you want to create a form. Then choose Insert | AutoForm.

Creating a Form with the Form Wizard

The Form Wizard is the way to go if you want to create a sophisticated form that draws on data from more than one table without the complexities of Design view. Besides drawing upon data from more than one table or query, forms created with the wizard can include command buttons and other amenities. And they look good, too, because you get to choose one of Access's designs for your form.

To create a form with fields from more than one table, the tables must be related to one another. See "Forging the Relationships Between Tables," earlier in this chapter.

To create a form with the Form Wizard, follow these steps:

1. Click the Forms button on the Datasheet window and click the New button. You see the New Table dialog box.

2. Click Form Wizard and then click OK. You see the first wizard dialog box shown in Figure 27-18. This dialog box wants to know which fields to include on the form.

3. In the Tables/Queries drop-down list, choose the first table or query from which to get fields for the form.

4. Click a field in the Available Fields box, and then click the right-pointing arrow to the right to enter the field in the Selected Fields box. You can click the double-arrow to enter all the fields in the Available Fields box into the Selected Fields box.

5. Repeat steps 3 and 4 until all the fields you want for the form are assembled in the Selected Fields box.

6. Click the Next button. As shown in Figure 27-19, you see a dialog box that asks how you want to view your data. What this dialog box really wants to know is which of the tables or queries whose fields you chose for the form should take precedence over the others. Fields from the table or query you click in the box on the left side of the dialog box appear in the top half of the form.

Choose the table or query for fields in the form.

Adds fields to the form

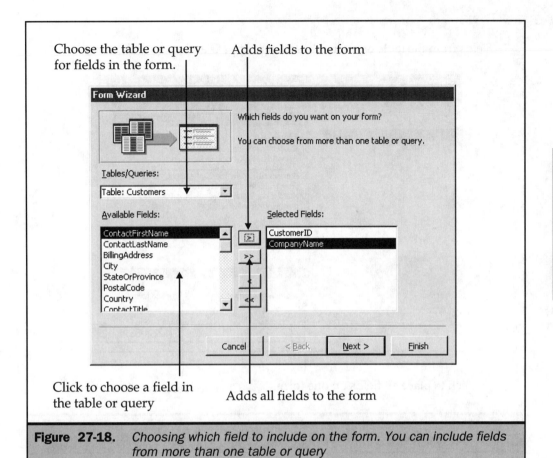

Click to choose a field in the table or query

Adds all fields to the form

Figure 27-18. *Choosing which field to include on the form. You can include fields from more than one table or query*

Note *If you are including fields from only one table or query on the form, the wizard bypasses the dialog box shown in Figure 27-19. Instead, you see a dialog box for choosing a columnar, tabular, datasheet, or justified form. Figure 27-17 demonstrates what three of the forms are. The Justified option creates columnar, right-aligned fields on the form.*

7. In the box in the upper-left corner of the dialog box, click on the name of the table or query whose fields are to appear on the top of the form.

8. Choose the Form With Subform(s) or Linked Forms option button:

■ **Form With Subform(s)** Places fields from secondary tables or queries at the bottom of the form.

■ **Linked Forms** Creates a button on the form that you can click to access fields from the secondary tables or queries.

Fields from the table or query chosen here appear at the top of the form.

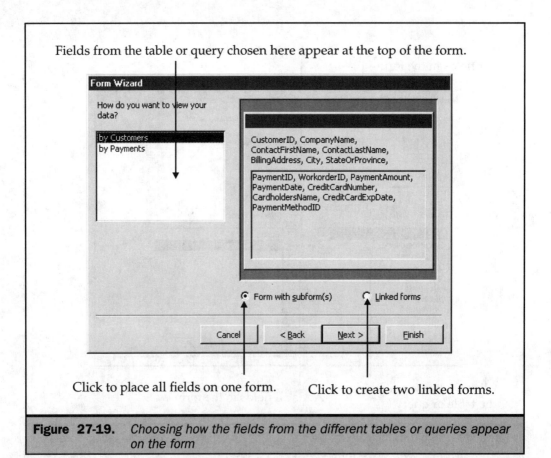

Click to place all fields on one form.   Click to create two linked forms.

Figure 27-19.   *Choosing how the fields from the different tables or queries appear on the form*

9. Click the Next button. The next dialog box asks you to choose a layout for the form.

10. Click option buttons until you see a preview form in the dialog box that suits you, and then click the Next button. The next dialog box asks you to name forms and subforms that comprise your new form.

11. Enter form and subform names and click the Finish button. Your new form appears onscreen.

Entering, Viewing, and Editing Data on Forms

After you have created a form, you can start entering data in it. The following pages explain how to enter data, move from record to record in a database table while forms are onscreen, delete a record, copy data from one record to another record, and print a form.

To open a form, click on the Forms button on the Database window and either double-click the form you want to open or click the form and then click the Open button.

"Finding Data in a Database Table" at the start of the next chapter explains how to find a record in a table.

LEARN BY EXAMPLE
To practice entering data on forms, open the Figure 27-A (Forms) file on the companion CD.

Entering Data in Forms

To enter data in a form, click the New Record button in one of two places—on the toolbar or among the record navigation buttons at the bottom of the form. When you do so, an empty form appears onscreen. Enter data in the fields. To move to the next field, press the TAB or ENTER key. You can also move to a field by clicking on it or by pressing the UP ARROW or DOWN ARROW key.

When you press the TAB or ENTER key after you have entered data in the last field, the data on the form is saved on disk and you see a new, empty form onscreen. (If you are working on a form/subform, pressing TAB or ENTER either moves the cursor to the subform or to a new record on the subform.)

Viewing Records on Forms

Use the toolbar along the bottom of the Form window to move from record to record and view the data in forms:

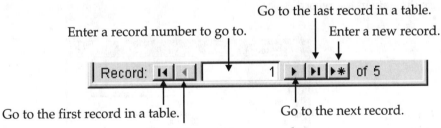

You can also use the following keyboard techniques to move from record to record:

Press	To Move
HOME	To the first field in a record
END	To the last field in a record
PAGE UP	To the previous record
PAGE DOWN	To the next record

And these keyboard techniques can come in handy when you are entering data in a multitable form with subforms:

Press	To Do This
CTRL-TAB	Leave a subform and move to the next field in the main form.
CTRL-SHIFT-HOME	Move to the first field in the main form.
CTRL-SHIFT-TAB	Leave a subform and move to the previous field in the main form.

Deleting Records

To delete a record on a form, display it onscreen and click the Delete Record button on the Form View toolbar. Click Yes when Access asks if you really and truly want to delete the record. But remember, you can't get the data back after you delete a record. Deleted records are gone for good.

Copying Data from One Record to Another

Oftentimes the data in one record is similar to the data in another. To save a little time, you can copy a record and then change whatever needs changing in the new record. Follow these steps to copy data from one record to another:

1. Display the record that you want to copy.

2. Click in the vertical bar on the left side of the form. Clicking the vertical bar selects the data in the record.

Click here to select a record's complete data.

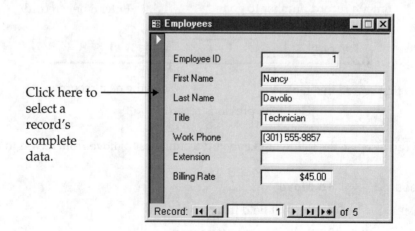

3. Copy the data one of three ways: Choose Edit | Copy, click the Copy button, or press CTRL-C.

4. Click the New Record button.

5. Click the vertical bar on the left side of the blank form.

6. Paste the data one of three ways: Choose Edit | Paste, click the Paste button, or press CTRL-V. Except for primary key data and/or data in an indexed field that is supposed to be unique, the data is copied to the new record.

7. Edit the data in the form as necessary.

Printing a Form

Follow these steps to print one or more records in Form view:

1. To print a single record, display it onscreen. To print several records or all of the records on the forms, it doesn't matter where you start.

2. Press CTRL-P or choose File | Print. You see the Print dialog box.

3. Tell Access what you want to print:

   ■ Click the Selected Record(s) option button to print the form that is displayed onscreen.

   ■ Click the All button to print forms for all the records in the table.

   ■ To print a range of records, click the Pages button. Enter record numbers in the From and To boxes.

4. Click the OK button.

Printing a Database Table

Follow these steps to print all or some of the records in a database table:

1. Click the Tables tab on the database table and open the table by double-clicking on it.

2. If you want to print a single record, select it. Otherwise go straight to step 3.

3. Choose File | Print or press CTRL-P.

4. Tell Access what you want to print:

   ■ To print one or more selected records, click the Selected Record(s) option button.

   ■ Click the All button to print all the records in the table.

■ To print a range of records, click the Pages button. Enter record numbers in the From and To boxes.

5. Click the OK button.

 Click the Print Preview button to see beforehand what the records will look like after they are printed.

Exporting Data to Other Programs and Databases

After you have carefully and thoughtfully entered data in an Access database table, you might decide that your data is needed elsewhere. The following pages explain how to copy data to another database program and how to copy data from one Access database to another Access database. You will also find instructions for copying a table's design but not its data from one Access database to another.

Copying Data to Another Program

Use the File menu's Export command for copying a database table to a new file so that other database programs, as well as programs like Excel and Word can make use of the data. Follow these steps to make a copy of an Access database table to use in other programs:

1. Click the Table button of the Database window, then click on the table whose data you want to copy. It's not necessary to actually open the table.

2. Choose File | Export. You see the Export Table As dialog box:

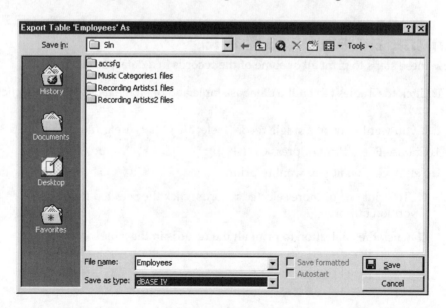

3. In the Save As drop-down list, choose the appropriate file format.

If the program you want to use isn't listed, there are two ways around this. You could choose the Rich Text Format option. It's the lingua franca of the computer world and allows programs to pass data back and forth without losing sophisticated data formats. Or you could choose an intermediate program format. For example, if the other program imports from dBase IV, export the Access file in the dBase IV format. Enter a name for the copy in the File Name box.

4. Choose a folder to store the file in.

5. Click the Save button.

Depending on the type of export you are performing, Access may start a wizard to help you copy the data. Follow the instructions in the wizard dialog boxes until the copy procedure is completed.

Copying Data to Another Access Database

Follow these steps to copy the data in a database table from one Access database to another Access database:

1. Click on the table button in the Database window.

2. Click on the table you want to copy. It's not necessary to open the table.

3. Choose Edit | Copy. The entire database table is copied to the Clipboard.

4. Close the Access database.

5. Open the Access database into which you want to copy the table.

6. Choose Edit | Paste. You see the Paste Table As dialog box:

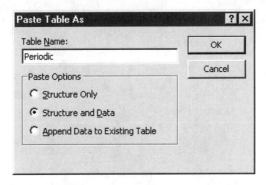

7. Make sure that the Structure And Data option button is selected. With this option, you copy the design of the database table and the data as well.

To copy the design of a table, but not its data, from one Access database to another, choose the Structure Only option. To merge the copied data with data in an existing table, choose the Append Data To Existing Table option.

8. Enter a name for the table in the Table Name box.

9. Click OK.

Copying a Table Within a Database

You can copy an *object*—a table, form, query, report, or data access page—and place the copy within the same database. You can also save the copy as a different object—save a table as a form, for example. Follow these steps:

1. Select the object. It's not necessary to open the object.

2. Choose File | Save As. Access displays the Save As dialog box:

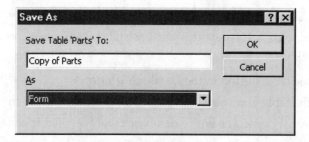

3. Rename the new object you're creating, if desired.

4. In the As drop-down box, select the type of object you want the copy to be.

5. Click OK.

The Complete Reference

Office 2000

Chapter 28

Sorting, Filtering, and Querying a Database

The last two chapters explained how to enter and view data in a database. In this chapter, you learn how to ask a database for the information you have so carefully and thoughtfully stored there. You will also learn how to find specific records in a database, filter data to derive information of a certain kind, and sort data to arrange it in a new way.

No doubt you have received lots of junk mail in your life. You might be interested to know that your name was chosen as the result of a query. That's right—you lived in a certain postal code, purchased products from certain mail order or retail operations, or met some other condition that deemed you worthy of being sent a solicitation of some kind. In this chapter, you learn the same techniques the big companies use to cull information from a database.

In general terms, there are four ways to draw data out of a database:

- **Find It**   Find specific records; the simplest form of data manipulation.

- **Filter It**   Find all the records that share a field value in a database table. For example, you can find the records of all the people who live in Florida. Or you can find the records of all the inventory items that cost more than $400.

- **Sort It**   Rearrange the records in a database table in a new way to make records easier to find.

- **Query It**   Find records throughout an entire database that meet certain criteria. If you set up and enter data correctly in a database, for example, you can find all the people in three Los Angeles ZIP codes who own sports utility vehicles and have incomes over $50,000 a year.

Each method of getting data out of a database is described in the following pages.

Finding Data in a Database Table

To find a single record in a table, use the Edit menu's Find command. You might use this command to find records that need changing or deleting. The following pages explain how to find data in a database table and how to replace the data if it needs replacing.

Finding Specific Records

Follow these steps to find data in a database table:

1. Open the table containing the data you want to find.

2. Click in the field you want to search if you happen to know in which field the data you are looking for is located. If the data might be found in more than one field, it doesn't matter which field the cursor is in when you start the search.

Be sure to complete step 5 in this list of instructions if you want to search in more than one field.

3. Press CTRL-F, click the Find button, or choose Edit | Find. You see the Find and Replace dialog box shown in Figure 28-1.

4. Enter the text or numbers you are looking for in the Find What box.

5. In the Look In box specify the specific field or the entire database to be searched.

6. To speed up the search, choose an option from the Match drop-down list:

- **Any Part Of Field**   The search stops on the letters or numbers you entered in the Find What box no matter where it encounters them in fields. This is the broadest way to search. For example, a search for the letters "con" finds "Conner," "Deacon," "con," "113 Condor Dr.," and "University of Connecticut."

- **Whole Field**   The search stops on the letters or numbers you entered only if the letters or numbers stand by themselves in a field. This is the narrowest way to search. A search for "con" finds "con" and "Con," but not "Conner," "Deacon," "113 Condor Dr.," or "University of Connecticut" because in those records "con" is part of the field, not the whole field.

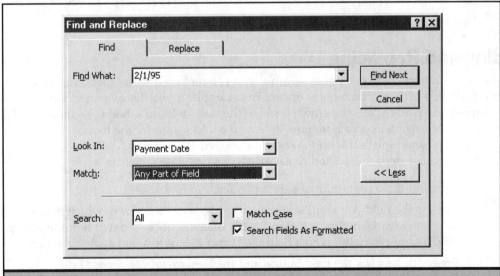

Figure 28-1.   *Telling Access how to search the database table*

■ **Start Of Field** The search stops on the letters or numbers you entered if they appear at the start of a field. A search for "con" finds "Con" and "Conner," but not "Deacon," "113 Condor Dr.," or "University of Connecticut."

7. To access further options, click the More button.

8. In the Search drop-down list, choose Up or Down instead of All if you know where the record is and you want to search in one direction.

9. Click the Match Case check box if you know the correct combination of upper- and lowercase letters you are looking for and you entered the right combination of letters in the Find What box.

10. Click the Search Fields As Formatted check box if you are searching in a field that has been formatted a specific way. Dates, times, numbers, currency figures, and Yes/No data types are formatted in specific ways (see "Establishing Field Properties for Easier Data Entry" in Chapter 27). To find data in a field that has been formatted, the Search Fields As Formatted check box must be checked and the text or numbers in the Find What box must be formatted correctly as well. For example, the search in Figure 28-1 will find 2/1/95 but will bypass February 1, 1995 in the Payment Date field.

11. Click the Find Next button. If the letters or numbers can be found, Access highlights the first place where they appear in the database table.

12. You can click Find Next as many times as it takes to find the record you're seeking.

13. Click the Close button when your search is over.

Finding and Replacing Data

As well as finding data in a database table, you can replace it with other data. You might do this to correct data-entry errors. For example, if you discovered to your dismay that "Waukegan," the crown jewel of the state of Illinois, had been misspelled time and time again in your database table, you could search for the incorrect "Woukigan" and replace it with the correctly spelled "Waukegan."

Follow these steps to find and replace data in a database table:

1. Open the table containing the data you want to find.

2. Click in the field you want to search if you happen to know in which field the data you are looking for is located. If the data might be found in more than one field, it doesn't matter which field the cursor is in when you start the search.

3. Press CTRL-H, click the Find button and the Replace tab, or choose Edit | Replace. You see the Find and Replace dialog box shown in Figure 28-2.

4. Enter the text or numbers you are looking for in the Find What box.

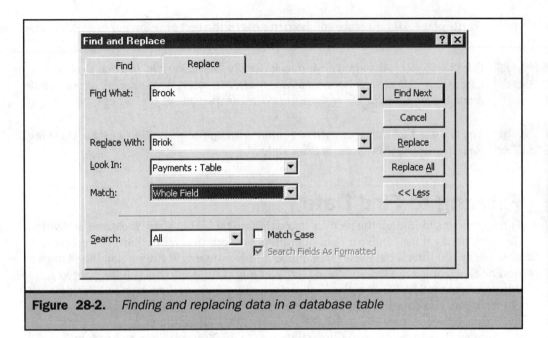

Figure 28-2.   *Finding and replacing data in a database table*

5. Enter the replacement text or numbers in the Replace With box. Be sure to enter the correct combination of upper- and lowercase letters.

6. If you want to search and replace in a certain direction, open the Search drop-down menu and choose Up or Down.

7. Click the Match Case check box if you know the correct combination of upper- and lowercase letters you are looking for.

Caution   *You should always select Match Whole Field from the Match drop-down list. If you do not select Match Whole Field, Access replaces parts of field entries, which can have unwanted consequences. For example, a search for "Brook" would also find "Brooklyn," and if the replacement text were "Briock," the result would be a new entry, "Briocklyn."*

8. Click the Find Next button. Access finds the text or numbers you are looking for if they are in the database table.

9. Either click the Replace or Replace All button:

   ■ **Replace**   Replaces the text or numbers that Access found with the replacement text. Click Find Next again to find the next instance of the text or numbers.

ACCESS

- **Replace All**   Replaces all occurrences of the text or numbers in the database with the replacement text.

Click the Replace All button at your own risk. By "replacing all," you don't get the chance to review each replacement as it is made. Moreover, Access doesn't offer an Undo command for reversing the replacements. They are permanent.

You can also find and replace data by running an update query. See "Update: Updating Records in a Database" later in this chapter.

Filtering to Find Data

Filtering means to find all the records in a database table that share the same or nearly the same field values. Unlike a Find operation, you can find more than one record at a time when you filter a database table. For example, you might filter a database table to find all the people who live in Florida. Or you might filter it to find all the people whose income is $40,000 or more. You can use more than one criterion to filter data. For example, you could filter a database to find the records of all the people who live in Florida, have incomes above $40,000, and own their own homes.

Access offers three ways to filter a database table. You can filter by form, by selection, or by exclusion. Either way, the general idea is to choose a field value from the database table and then filter the table to find or exclude all records that have the same value.

- **By Form**   Choose values from drop-down lists to tell Access which records you want to get, and then give the filtering command. Filter by form when you want to filter a database table using several different criteria. For example, you could search in a Videos database table for all movies that star either Humphrey Bogart or George Raft. What's more, you can use comparison operators in a filter by form. For example, you can search for videos that cost less than $35.

- **By Selection**   Starting in Datasheet view, select a value or values in a single record that you want to find throughout the database table, and then give the filtering command. For example, to find all movies with Humphrey Bogart in them in a Videos database table, select Bogart's name. The filtering operation will throw up the names of all movies in which Humphrey Bogart played. Combining two or more filtering criteria with the "by selection" method is extremely limited. You could, for example, find all the movies starring Humphrey Bogart that were directed by John Huston. You would filter the star field for Humphrey Bogart, then filter the director field for John Huston. But you couldn't, for example, filter the star field for Humphrey Bogart and George Raft at the same time. And you can't use comparison operators with this method, either.

■ **By Exclusion**   Starting in Datasheet view, select a value or values and then filter the database. You see all the records in the database except those in which the value or values you selected are found. For example, by selecting Humphrey Bogart's name and then filtering by exclusion in a Videos database table, you could find all the movies in the table except those in which Humphrey Bogart starred.

Filtering by form, by selection, and by exclusion are discussed on the following pages. You'll also learn how to save the results of a filtering operation on a form or in a report. There is another method of filtering called Advanced Filter/Sort. However, it has more in common with query operations and is discussed later in this chapter under "Advanced Filter/Sort: Sorting on Two Fields."

EXAMPLES

LEARN BY EXAMPLE
To try your hand at filtering a database table, open the Figure 28-3 (Filter) file on the companion CD and filter away.

Filters vs. Queries

Filtering is a sophisticated means of finding more than one record in a database table. Query a database table if you frequently use the same criteria to gather information or you want to include information from more than one database table.

When you filter a database table, you can use standard comparison operators to find records whose values are greater than, less than, equal to, less than or equal to, greater than or equal to, or not equal to a value that you enter. For example, you could find items of a certain kind that cost $20 or more. However, you can't use expressions to find records whose values fall within a certain range. In other words, to find items that cost between $20 and $22, you can't filter a database table. To do that, you have to construct a query.

Access remembers the last filtering operation you did so you can filter in the same way a second time, but you can't store several different filtering criteria and call on each one whenever you need it. You can, however, save the results of a filtering operation in a form or report.

By the way, it is possible to filter the results of a query. To do so, open the query on the Queries tab of the Datasheet window and then give a filtering command.

Filtering by Form

Follow these steps to filter a database by form:

1. Open the database table you want to filter by and click the Tables button on the Database window, then double-click the table's name.

2. Click the Filter by Form button on the Table Datasheet toolbar or choose Records | Filer | Filter by Form. The datasheet changes into a tabular form, as shown in Figure 28-3.

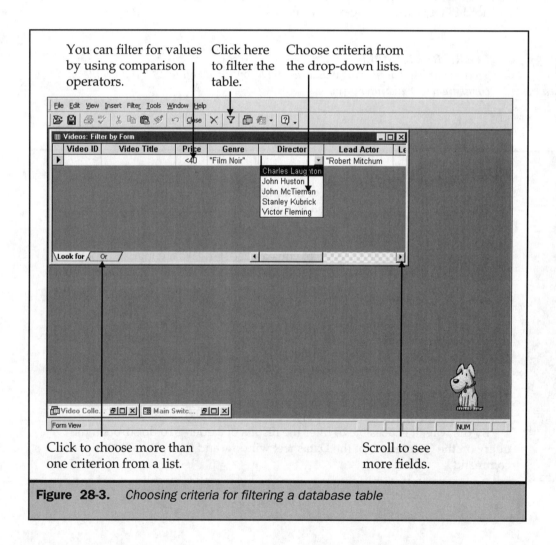

Figure 28-3.   *Choosing criteria for filtering a database table*

Tip *If you or someone else filtered the database already, criteria from the last filtering operation appear in the first row of the form. Click the Clear Grid button on the Filter/Sort toolbar to remove the criteria and start anew.*

Field names appear across the top of the form. Notice the down arrow in the first field. By clicking that down arrow, or by moving to another field and clicking the down arrow there, you can open a drop-down list with all the values that were entered in each record of the database. In Figure 28-3, an inventory database table called Videos is being filtered to locate *film noirs* that cost less than $40, were directed by Charles Laughton, and star the great Robert Mitchum. On the Director drop-down list are the names of all the directors that were entered in the database table.

3. Enter the criteria for the filtering operation:

   ■ **Choosing Criteria from Lists**   To search for values in the table, open as many drop-down lists as necessary and choose values. Values are listed in alphabetical order. You might have to scroll to get to the bottom of the list and find the value you are looking for.

   ■ **Using the Or Operator for Making More Than One Selection from the Same List**   To choose more than one value from the same drop-down list, click the Or tab along the bottom of the window and then make another selection from the list. A new Or tab appears each time you make another selection from the same list.

   ■ **Using Comparison Operators to Choose Relative Values**   Enter a number and a comparison operator in a numeric field to look for monetary and numerical values in the database table. In Figure 28-3, the <40 tells Access to look for videos that cost less than $40. Table 28-1 describes the comparison operators you can use.

Tip *To remove a criterion from the form, select it and press the DELETE key. To remove a criterion you entered by means of an Or operator, click the Or tab for the criterion you entered and then choose Edit | Delete.*

4. Click the Apply Filter button when you are done entering the filtering criteria. The results of the filter appear in the Form window. My search for a film noir directed by Charles Laughton and starring the great Robert Mitchum turned up—what else?—*Night of the Hunter,* as the following illustration shows. If I was a clerk at a video store and someone called to ask if the store carried that movie with Robert Mitchum directed by that fat English guy, Charles Laughton,

Operator	Name	Example (27..23)
<	Less than	<25 finds 24, 23
<=	Less than or equal to	<=25 finds 25, 24, 23
>	Greater than	>25 finds 27, 26
>=	Greater than or equal to	>=25 finds 27, 26, 25
=	Equal to	=25 finds 25
<>	Not equal to	<>25 finds 27, 26, 24, 23

Table 28-1. *Comparison Operators for Filtering Operations*

I could find out very quickly if the store carried that video and what its title is by filtering the Videos database table:

Video ID	Video Title	Price	Genre	Director	Lead Actor	Le
▶	Night of the Hunter	$19.99	Film Noir	Charles Laughton	Robert Mitchum	

5. Click the Remove Filter button to return to the database table.

Next time you click the Filter by Form button and see the form onscreen, the filtering criteria you so laboriously constructed appears on the form in case you want to filter the database table all over again. Click the Clear Grid button on the Filter/Sort toolbar if you want to start all over and enter new criteria. To conduct the same filtering operation, simply click the Apply Filter button.

After you have filtered records from a database table, you can filter the records that are left. In this way, by filtering and filtering, you can trim the database table down to size and find the records you are looking for.

Filtering by Selection

Filtering by selection is a primitive version of filtering by form. It is harder to do, makes it hard to enter more than one search criterion, and doesn't permit the use of comparison operators. As far as I know, the only advantage of filtering by selection is that you can do it in a hurry.

Follow these steps to filter by selection:

1. Open the database table you want to filter by clicking the Tables button on the Database window, then double-clicking the table's name.

Creating a Form or Report with the Results of a Filtering Operation

After you have finished a filtering operation, you can save the results in a form or report (Chapter 29 explains reports). To save filtering results in a form or report, follow these steps:

1. With the results of the filtering operation onscreen, click the down arrow beside the New Object button and choose either AutoForm or AutoReport.

2. Click Yes in the message box that appears and advises you to save the database table from which you filtered data.

3. If you created a form, it appears onscreen; if you created a report, you see your report in the Print Preview screen.

4. Click the Save button if you created a form: Press CTRL-S or choose File | Save to save a report.

5. In the Save As dialog box, enter a name for your form or report and click OK:

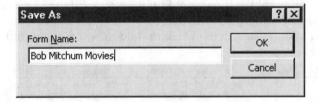

6. Close the form or report to see the filtering results again.

7. Click the Remove Filter button to get back to the database table.

Forms are kept on the Forms tab of the Database window; reports are kept on the Reports tab. Go to the Forms or Reports tab and double-click a form or report to open it.

2. Choose criteria for the filtering operation:

- **Search for One Field Value**   Click in a field whose data value you want to search for. In the following illustration, I clicked on McTiernan, John in the

Director field. This filtering operation will turn up all movies in the Videos database table that were directed by John McTiernan:

Video ID	Video Title	Price	Genre	Director	Lead Actor
1	Gone with the Wind	$49.99	Drama	Victor Fleming	Clark Gable
▶ 2	Die Hard	$29.99	Action	John McTiernan	Bruce Willis
3	A Clockwork Orange	$34.99	Sci-Fi	Stanley Kubrick	Malcolm McDowell
4	Maltese Falcon, The	$29.99	Film Noir	John Huston	Humphrey Bogart
5	Night of the Hunter	$19.99	Film Noir	Charles Laughton	Robert Mitchum
* (toNumber)		$0.00			

- **Search for Two or More Values in the Same Field**   Select two or more values in the same field to search for values in the same field. In the following illustration, for example, I have selected Victor Fleming, John McTiernan, and Stanley Kubrick to find all movies in the database table that were directed by those three directors:

Video ID	Video Title	Price	Genre	Director	Lead Actor
▶ 1	Gone with the Wind	$49.99	Drama	Victor Fleming	Clark Gable
2	Die Hard	$29.99	Action	John McTiernan	Bruce Willis
3	A Clockwork Orange	$34.99	Sci-Fi	Stanley Kubrick	Malcolm McDowell
4	Maltese Falcon, The	$29.99	Film Noir	John Huston	Humphrey Bogart
5	Night of the Hunter	$19.99	Film Noir	Charles Laughton	Robert Mitchum

- **Search for Values in Two or More Different Fields**   Select two or more values in different fields to search for values in different fields. In the following illustration, for example, I have selected Film Noir in the Genre field and John Huston in the Director field to search for all film noir directed by John Huston:

Video ID	Video Title	Price	Genre	Director	Lead Actor
1	Gone with the Wind	$49.99	Drama	Victor Fleming	Clark Gable
2	Die Hard	$29.99	Action	John McTiernan	Bruce Willis
3	A Clockwork Orange	$34.99	Sci-Fi	Stanley Kubrick	Malcolm McDowell
▶ 4	Maltese Falcon, The	$29.99	Film Noir	John Huston	Humphrey Bogart
5	Night of the Hunter	$19.99	Film Noir	Charles Laughton	Robert Mitchum

Selecting field values this way is kind of tricky. To do it, move the pointer to the left side of the first field value you want to select, and when the pointer changes into a cross, drag downward or across to select the other values.

Tip *Unfortunately, you can only select more than one value in the same field or more than one value in two different fields if the values are next to each other in the database table. You can, however, move records (rows) or move fields (columns) in the database table so that they are next to each other, and then select them. But why bother? Filter by form, not by selection, when you want to select criteria from more than one field or in more than one field.*

3. Click the Filter by Selection button on the Table Datasheet toolbar. The table shrinks considerably and you see the results of the search in the Table window.

4. Click the Remove Filter button or choose Records | Remove Filter/Sort to see all the records in the database table again.

Filtering by Exclusion

Filtering by exclusion is done very much like a filter by selection. Open the database table, click a field whose value you want to exclude from the database table, choose Records | Filter, and click Filter by Excluding Selection. In spite of its name, you can't select more than one value to exclude with the Filter by Excluding Selection command.

In the following illustration, for example, I clicked Film Noir in the Genre field. When I choose the Filter by Excluding Selection command, Access will show me all the movies in the database table except records containing the genre of film noir.

	Video ID	Video Title	Price	Genre	Director	Lead Actor
	1	Gone with the Wind	$49.99	Drama	Victor Fleming	Clark Gable
	2	Die Hard	$29.99	Action	John McTiernan	Bruce Willis
	3	A Clockwork Orange	$34.99	Sci-Fi	Stanley Kubrick	Malcolm McDowell
▶	4	Maltese Falcon, The	$29.99	Film Noir	John Huston	Humphrey Bogart
	5	Night of the Hunter	$19.99	Film Noir	Charles Laughton	Robert Mitchum

Click the Remove Filter button to see all the records again, including the ones you excluded.

Sorting, or Arranging, Records in a Database Table

Sorting means to arrange the records in a database table in an entirely new way. By sorting a database table, you can locate information faster. And before you print a database table, you should sort it so that the records appear in the order you want them to appear. To sort a table, you start by selecting the field, or column, on which the table is to be sorted, and then you click either the Sort Ascending or Sort Descending button to sort the records in the column in ascending or descending order:

■ **Ascending Order**   Arranges text entries in alphabetical order from A to Z (California, Nebraska, Wisconsin); numbers from smallest to largest (4, 27, 146); and dates from earliest in time to latest in time (31-Jul-58, 4-Mar-97, 16-Oct-06). In case you are wondering, yes, Access is year 2000 compliant.

■ **Descending Order**   Arranges text entries from Z to A (Wisconsin, Nebraska, California); numbers from largest to smallest (146, 27, 4); and dates from latest in time to earliest in time (16-Oct-06, 4-Mar-97, 31-Jul-58).

ACCESS

Sorting a table only changes its appearance onscreen. The records revert to their primary key order when the table is closed. If you find yourself sorting records often, create a query that permanently sorts the records in the way you want them to appear onscreen.

The following two illustrations show the same information in the same database table. However, in the illustration on the left, the records have been sorted in ascending order in the Video Title field; in the illustration on the right, the records have been sorted in descending order on the Price field:

Video Title	Price
Clockwork Orange, A	$34.99
Die Hard	$29.99
▶ Gone with the Wind	$49.99
Maltese Falcon, The	$29.99
Night of the Hunter	$19.99

Video Title	Price
▶ Gone with the Wind	$49.99
Clockwork Orange, A	$34.99
Maltese Falcon, The	$29.99
Die Hard	$29.99
Night of the Hunter	$19.99

Follow these steps to sort a database table:

1. In Datasheet view, click anywhere in the field, or column, that the table is to be sorted on.

2. Click the Sort Ascending or the Sort Descending button on the Table Datasheet toolbar.

 To sort a table on two or three fields instead of one, you have to query it. For example, to sort by last name, then by first name so that Smith, Michael comes before Smith, Steven, you have to query the table. See "Advanced Filter/Sort: Sorting on Two Fields," later in this chapter.

Querying a Database for Information

The term *query* means simply to ask. When you query a database, you ask it for information of some kind.

The rest of this chapter concerns queries. It explains how queries work and what the different kinds of queries are. It describes how to construct a query using expressions and numeric-, date-, and time-based criteria. You also learn how to save a query and run it again, as well as modify a query so it digs up the information you are looking for. Finally, this chapter explains the details of constructing and running queries with Access.

LEARN BY EXAMPLE
To try your hand at querying a database, open the Figure 28-4 (Query) file on the companion CD.

An Introduction to Querying

Queries run the gamut from the very simple to the very complex. For example, you could construct a query that finds purchase orders submitted on a particular date for a particular item. Or you could construct a query that finds purchase orders for the same item made during a three-month period in states where sales tax is charged, and obtain the total amount of sales tax that was charged for the item during the three months.

> **Note**   *These pages outline the procedures for creating a query from scratch. However, you can also create a query with the Query Wizard. How to use the Query Wizard to create different kinds of queries is discussed throughout this chapter.*

Unlike a filtering operation, which can look in one table only, a query can gather information from all the tables in a database. Figure 28-4 shows two tables being queried—Products and Inventory Transactions. When you construct a query, the first thing you do is tell Access which tables to look in.

After you have told Access which tables to query, the next step is to tell the program which fields to look in. In Figure 28-4, the first row of the query grid shows that five fields will be queried, two from the Products table (Product ID and

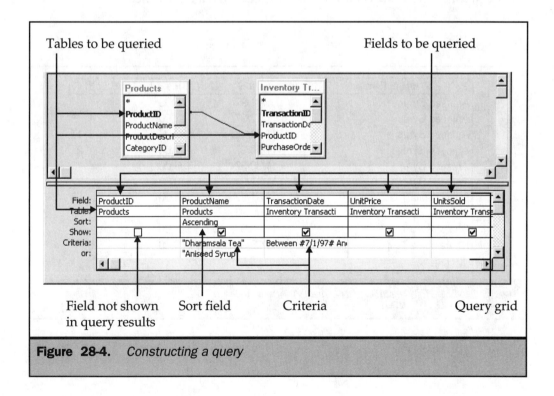

Figure 28-4.   *Constructing a query*

ACCESS

ProductName) and three from the Inventory Transactions table (TransactionDate, UnitPrice, and UnitsSold).

As you construct a query, you can ask Access to sort the results. To do so, make a choice on the Sort row of the query grid. In Figure 28-4, the results of the query will be sorted in ascending order—that is, alphabetical order—by product name.

A query tells Access which fields to look in to gather information, but that doesn't mean that each field in which Access looks has to be on the results table. By removing the check mark from the box in the Show row, you tell Access not to include a field in the query results. In Figure 28-4, no check mark appears in the ProductID check box, so this field will not appear in the query results.

The bottom of the query grid is where you establish the criteria, also known as the *conditions*, for the query. This query asks for information about two products— Dharamsala Tea or Aniseed Syrup. For the period between 7/1/97 and today's date, this query wants to know when units of these products were sold, what the unit price of each transaction was, and how many units were sold as part of each transaction.

To run a query after you have finished constructing it, click the Run button or choose Query | Run. When I clicked the Run button, I got the results shown in Figure 28-5. Now I can see price fluctuations and judge which of my two exotic products is most popular with the health food set. Query results appear on a datasheet like the one you see in Datasheet view when you are working on a database table.

Product Name	Transaction Da	Unit Price	UnitsSold
Aniseed Syrup	11/1/97	$6.00	4
Aniseed Syrup	11/2/97	$3.00	3
Aniseed Syrup	11/27/97	$43.00	17
Aniseed Syrup	11/30/97	$22.00	22
Aniseed Syrup	11/30/97	$33.00	3
Aniseed Syrup	11/12/94	$10.00	
Dharamsala Tea	11/1/97	$4.00	3
Dharamsala Tea	11/5/97	$11.00	5
Dharamsala Tea	11/26/97	$33.00	4
Dharamsala Tea	11/30/97	$43.00	5

Figure 28-5.   *The results of the query shown in Figure 28-4*

After you finish constructing a query, the next step is to save it and give it a name. The names of queries that have been saved and named appear on the Queries tab of the Database window so you can run them over and over again.

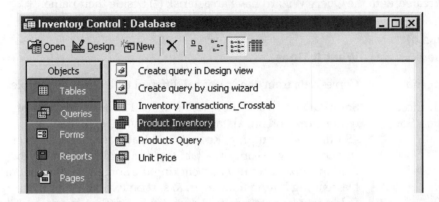

A query doesn't actually store any data. It stores criteria, table names, field names, and other information for searching in database tables. However, you can enter data in a query datasheet. The data you enter is stored in the tables that were accessed when the query was created. For example, if I enter a record or change a value in the query datasheet shown in Figure 28-5, the new data is stored in the Products and Inventory Transactions tables, the two tables from which I constructed the query.

By keeping a query on hand on the Queries tab of the Database window, you can run the query time and time again. Each time you run it, you get an up-to-date picture of the records in the database tables that the query was designed to access.

You can create forms and reports from queries. To do so, click the arrow beside the New Object button when the query results are onscreen and choose either AutoForm or AutoReport on the drop-down menu.

Constructing a Select Query

No matter which way you query a database, the techniques for creating the query, choosing which tables to query, choosing which fields to query, entering the criteria, and running the query are the same. The following pages explain how to create and generate a select query, the standard type of query on which all the others are built.

The following pages describe how to construct a select query yourself, but you can also construct one with the Query Wizard. See "Constructing a Select Query with the Query Wizard," later in this chapter.

The Fifteen Types of Queries

Access offers no less than 15 kinds of queries. Queries in the following list that can be created with the Query Wizard have an asterisk (*) beside their name.

Type of Query	What It Does
Append	Copies data from one or several different tables to a single table.
Advanced Filter/Sort	Sorts data on two or more fields instead of one. This type of query works on one database table only. As explained in "Sorting, or Arranging, Records in a Database Table," earlier in this chapter, you can sort a table on one field by selecting the field in Datasheet view and clicking the Sort Ascending or Sort Descending button. However, to sort on two, three, or more fields, you have to run an Advanced Filter/Sort query.
AutoLookup	Automatically enters certain field values in new records.
Calculation	Lets you add a field in the query results table for making calculations with data that the query returns. In a database that tracked rental properties, for example, you could query to find out how much rental income each property generates, and then see how much income each property would generate if rents were increased across the board by 7 percent.
Crosstab*	Displays information in a matrix instead of a standard table. Crosstab queries make it easier to compare the information in a database.
Delete	Permanently deletes records that meet certain criteria from the database. Use this type of query, for example, to remove outdated records that were entered before a certain date.
Find Duplicates*	Finds all records with field values that are also found in other records. This query is useful for finding all the people in a database who live in the same ZIP code or have the same blood type, for example.
Find Unmatched*	Compares database tables to find records in the first table for which a match cannot be found in the second table. This query is useful for maintaining referential integrity in a database.

Type of Query	What It Does
Make-Table	Creates a table from the results of a query. This type of query is useful for backing up records.
Parameter	Displays a dialog box that tells the data-entry person what type of information to enter.
Select*	Gathers information from one, two, or more database tables. The select query is the standard query on which all others are built. Also known as a *simple query*.
SQL	Uses a SQL (structured query language) statement to combine data from different database tables. There are four kinds of SQL queries: a Data Definition query creates or alters objects in a database; a Pass Through query sends commands for retrieving data or changing records; a Subquery queries another query for certain results; and a Union query combines fields from different queries.
Summary	Finds the sum, average, lowest or highest value, number of, standard deviation, variance, or first or last value in the field in a query results table.
Top-Value	Finds the highest or lowest values in a field. You can find, for example, the five highest or lowest values. Or you could find the highest or lowest 5 percent of the values.
Update	Finds records that meet certain criteria and updates those records en masse. This query is useful for updating records. For example, to increase the price of all items in a database by a certain percentage, use an update query.

ACCESS

Creating the Query

To tell Access that you want to create a query, click the Query button on the Database window and either click the New button or choose Insert | Query. You see the New Query dialog box shown in the following illustration. Query Wizards are available for creating simple (select) queries, crosstab queries, and queries for finding duplicate records and unmatched records. Choose a Wizard option to create one of those queries. To design your own query, make sure Design View is selected in the New Query dialog box, and then click OK.

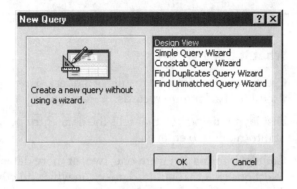

The Query Design window and Show Table dialog box appear so you can tell Access which tables to query. Read on.

Choosing Which Tables to Query

Choose which table or tables to query from the Tables tab of the Show Table dialog box shown in the following illustration. And yes, you can construct queries from queries you have already constructed by choosing them on the Queries tab. The Both tab lists both tables and queries in case you want to start from there.

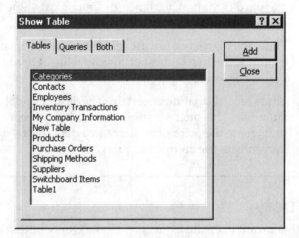

To choose each table or query that your new query will gather data from, click it in the Show Table dialog box and then click the Add button. Keep clicking tables or queries and clicking the Add button until you have "loaded" all the tables or queries you need for the new query. Click the Close button when you are done. The tables and queries you chose appear on the top of the Query Design window, as shown in Figure 28-6.

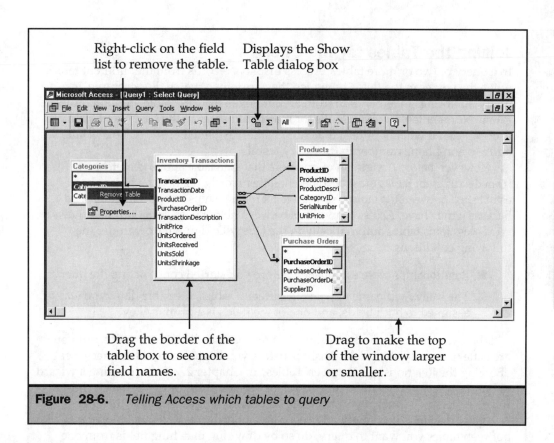

Right-click on the field list to remove the table.

Displays the Show Table dialog box

Drag the border of the table box to see more field names.

Drag to make the top of the window larger or smaller.

Figure 28-6. *Telling Access which tables to query*

Tip *If you loaded a table in the Query Design window but regret having done so, right-click on its field list box and choose Remove Table from the shortcut menu. To add a table you forgot to add, click the Show Table button on the Query Design toolbar to bring back the Show Table dialog box.*

The next step in constructing the query is to tell Access which fields to include. To get a fix on which fields are in each table, and to make it easier to work with the fields, drag the border that divides the top half of the Query Design window from the query grid downward. That gives you more room to work. Drag the bottom border of the table boxes downward as well so you can see all the field names. Later, when it is time to focus on the query grid, you can drag the upper border of the grid upward.

Choosing Which Fields to Query

The next step is to tell Access which fields from the tables to include in the query. Drag and drop field names from the table box or boxes to the Field row in the query grid (the

Joining the Tables for the Query

In a query of two or more tables, Access displays records from the different tables when the values in the fields by which they are joined match. For example, in a query that brings together data from an Employee Address table and an Employee Phone Number table, Access looks for matching names in the Last Name field of each table, and when it finds a matching name, say, Jane Perez, it displays Jane's address and phone number in the query results.

However, before Access can query more than one table and find matches, fields from the different tables must be joined. In other words, relationships must be established between the tables. You can tell if relationships have been established because if they have, Access draws lines between field names, as Figure 28-6 shows.

Access joins tables automatically in the Query Design window under the following conditions:

- Relationships were established before you started constructing the query.

- The same field name appears in different tables, the same data type was assigned to both fields, and one of the fields is a primary key.

The Query Design window provides a mechanism for joining tables, but you are better off establishing relationships before you begin to build the query. See "Forging the Relationships Between Tables" in Chapter 27. If you're using a wizard to build a query and relationships have not been established yet between chosen fields, Access will prompt you to create them. You'll have to restart the query.

If you decide to ignore my advice, or if you need to establish relationships between tables you want to query, do so by dragging matching fields from one table or query to another. For example, click, drag, and drop the ProductID field from one table to another. Access draws a line between the two tables to show the relationship.

Whatever you do, don't run a query on tables that haven't been joined. The query will be useless, because Access will join every record in one table with every record in the other and you could end up with thousands of records in the query results.

lower half of the Query window). Each field you add will appear on the query results table (unless you clear the Show button; that subject is covered a little later in this chapter).

Following are instructions for choosing which fields to query and rearranging the field names—that is, the columns—on the query grid.

Use the techniques outlined in Figure 28-7 and described here to copy field names onto the Field row in the query grid:

- **Choose Tables and Fields from Menus**   Click on the Table row, open the drop-down list and choose a table name. Then click directly above in the Field

Rearranging Columns on the Query Grid

The order in which field names appear in the columns on the query grid is the order in which they will appear in the query results. In Figure 28-7, for example, the PurchaseOrderID field comes first, then the PurchaseOrderNumber field, then the OrderDate field. Follow these steps to change the order of columns on the query grid:

1. Move the pointer to the small rectangle at the top of the column you want to move.

2. When you see an arrow that points downward, click to select the column. The column is highlighted, as shown in this illustration:

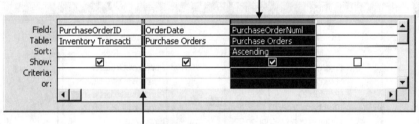

Click here to select and move the column.

The black line shows where the column will move.

3. Click again on the small rectangle at the top of the column and drag toward the left or right. As you drag, a black line appears between columns to show where the column will land when you release the mouse button.

4. When the black line is in the right place, release the mouse button.

row, open the drop-down menu, and choose a field name. In Figure 28-7, the OrderDate field is being chosen this way.

- **Drag a Field** Drag a field name from the table box to the Field row.

- **Double-Click a Field Name** Double-clicking a field name copies the field name to the Field row in the next available column.

- **CTRL-Click Field Names** By CTRL-clicking the field names in a table box, you can select several field names at once and copy them onto the Field row. Hold down the CTRL key and click each field name you want to copy. Then point to one of the selected fields and drag the field names en masse onto the query grid. The first field name in the block lands in the first empty Field column, and the others land to its right.

You may use the scroll bars below the Design window and query grid to scroll side to side and see the tables and different field columns. Try dragging the boundary lines between columns in the query grid if you are having trouble reading field names.

Tip   *If you mistakenly copy the wrong field name to the Field row, either delete it and substitute the right name or open the drop-down list on the Field row and choose the correct field name.*

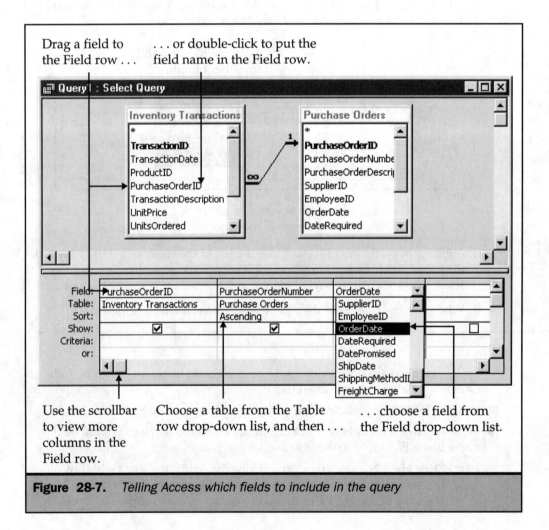

Drag a field to the Field row . . .   . . . or double-click to put the field name in the Field row.

Use the scrollbar to view more columns in the Field row.   Choose a table from the Table row drop-down list, and then . . .   . . . choose a field from the Field drop-down list.

Figure 28-7.   *Telling Access which fields to include in the query*

By double-clicking the asterisk at the top of a table box or dragging it onto the Field row, you can copy all the fields in a table to the Field row at once. Use the asterisk method only to tell Access to include all the fields in a table in a query. When you copy fields with the asterisk method, only the table name and an asterisk appear on the Field row. Field names do not appear across the columns of the query grid.

Deciding How to Sort the Query Results

Unless you tell it otherwise, Access sorts query results on the primary key field or, if there isn't a primary key field, on the leftmost field in the query grid. You can, however, decide for yourself which field is the one on which the query results are sorted, and if you want to sort on more than one field, you can do that as well by following these steps:

- **Sorting on One Field**   To choose a single field on which to sort the results, click on the Sort row in the field, open the drop-down menu, and choose Ascending or Descending, as shown in the following illustration:

Field:	ProductName	TransactionDate	UnitPrice	UnitsSold	
Table:	Products	Inventory Transacti	Inventory Transacti	Inventory Transacti	
Sort:	Ascending	Ascending			
Show:	☑	☑	Ascending	☑	☐
Criteria:	"Dharamsala Tea"	Between #7/1/97# An	Descending		
or:	"Aniseed Syrup"		(not sorted)		

The leftmost field is sorted first, then the next field, and then the next.   Choose the type of sort from the drop-down menu.

- **Sorting on More Than One Field**   To sort the results on more than one field, click on the Sort row in each field and choose Ascending or Descending from the drop-down list. Then, make sure that the first field to be sorted appears to the left of the other fields to be sorted on the query grid, that the second field to be sorted appears directly to the right of the first field to be sorted, and so on. In the illustration, for example, the query results will be sorted in ascending order by product name, transaction date, then unit price.

 "Sorting, or Arranging, Records in a Database Table," earlier in this chapter, explains the difference between ascending and descending sorts.

Deciding Which Fields Appear in the Query Results

It isn't necessary to include all the fields that you query in the query results. In fact, sometimes including all the fields is pointless. For example, if you design a query to find people who live in a single county or ZIP code, you need not include the County or ZIP Code field in the query results, because that would be redundant. Every record the query turns up would list the same county or ZIP code.

To keep a field from appearing in query results, click to remove the check mark from the Show box. In this illustration, the Birthdate, Squires, Province, and Castle fields will be queried; and the query will list, from oldest to youngest, each squire, the province where he lives, and the castle he inhabits. However, the squires are getting quite old, and to spare them any embarrassment concerning their ages, the Birthdate field will not appear in query results, because no check mark appears in its Show box:

Field:	Birthdate	Squires	Province	Castle
Table:	Vitals	Castles	Castles	Castles
Sort:	Descending			
Show:	☐	☑	☑	☑
Criteria:				
or:				

Entering the Query Criteria

Include criteria on the Criteria line of the query grid when you want to query for certain kinds of records. For example, to query for the records of people who live in San Francisco, the query grid looks like this:

Field:	Last Name	City	Annual Income	Birthdate
Table:	CityAddress	CityAddress	Vitals	Vitals
Sort:				
Show:	☑	☑	☑	☑
Criteria:		"San Francisco"		
or:				

In a similar way, by making an entry in the Criteria line of the Annual Income field, you could query for people who earn between $45,000 and $65,000 a year. By making an entry in the Criteria line of the Birthdate field, you could query for people born after 1 January 1958. Or, you might query for the records of people who meet all three of those criteria, in which case the query grid looks like this:

Field:	Last Name	City	Annual Income	Birthdate
Table:	CityAddress	CityAddress	Vitals	Vitals
Sort:				
Show:	☑	☑	☑	☑
Criteria:		"San Francisco"	Between 45000 And 65000	>=#1/1/58#
or:				

Besides querying for records that meet criteria in different fields, you can require records to meet more than one criterion in the same field. Consider the criteria in the following illustration. This query not only seeks the records of people who earn between $45,000 and $65,000 annually, were born after 1 January 1958, and live in San Francisco, but it seeks people in Los Angeles, San Diego, and San Jose. So this query asks the database for the records of people living in San Francisco, Los Angeles, San Diego, and San Jose who earn between $45,000 and $65,000 annually and were born after 1 January 1958:

Field:	Last Name	City	Annual Income	Birthdate
Table:	CityAddress	CityAddress	Vitals	Vitals
Sort:				
Show:	☑	☑	☑	☑
Criteria:		"San Francisco"	Between 45000 And 65000	>=#1/1/58#
or:		"Los Angeles"		
		"San Diego"		
		"San Jose"		

Notice that the Criteria line on the query grid in the previous two illustrations includes two *expressions*: Between 45000 And 65000, and >=#1/1/58#. By building expressions like these, and by entering criteria in different fields and in the same field, you can construct very sophisticated queries and get very specific kinds of information from a database.

The following pages explain how to query a database by using text, numeric, and date expressions, as well as wildcards. You also learn how to enter criteria on the Criteria lines of the query grid.

Guidelines for Entering Criteria on the Query Grid

Unless you enter the criteria correctly, Access can't query a database. In fact, if you enter criteria incorrectly, the program shows you a message window with a cryptic explanation of why your criteria are wrong. Following are guidelines for entering criteria on the query grid:

- **Quote Marks (") and Pound Signs (#)**   As the previous two illustrations show, Access puts quotation marks around text criteria and pound signs around date criteria. However, you do not need to enter those symbols yourself. The program enters them for you after you move the cursor out of the criteria box.

- **Number Formats**   Do not enter commas when you enter numbers on the query grid. For example, to enter the number 45,000, you need only enter 45000. If you include a comma in numbers or currency figures, Access flashes a message that says you created the expression incorrectly.

- **Date Formats**   You can enter dates in all three of Access' date formats. For example, to find records dated December 31, 1978, you can enter the date in the query grid in any of the following ways: 12/31/78, 31-Dec-78, or December 31, 1978. Whichever way you type the date, Access puts pound signs around it and changes it to this format on the query grid: #12/31/78#.

■ **Operator Names**   It doesn't matter whether you enter operator names such as Not and Between in all uppercase or all lowercase letters. Access capitalizes the first letter and lowercases the other letters for you.

Text Criteria

Text criteria are the simplest and easiest types of criteria, not to mention the most common type of criteria you can use in queries. To enter text criteria, all you do is enter letters on the query grid. For example, to query a database for people who live in Rome, you include the City field in the query and the name "Rome" on the Criteria line in the City field:

Field:	Last Name	City	Annual Income	Birthdate	
Table:	CityAddress	CityAddress	Vitals	Vitals	
Sort:					
Show:	☑	☑	☑	☑	
Criteria:		"Rome"			
or:					

Two operators, Not and Like, can come in handy when you are working with text criteria. The Not operator tells Access to exclude a criterion from the search. By using the Like operator along with the asterisk wildcard, you can search for groups of records. For example, entering **Like F*** in the Shipped To field of a query grid finds the records of companies whose names begin with the letter "F." Entering **Like [A-E]*** finds the records of companies whose names begin with the letters "A," "B," "C," "D," and "E." Entering **Like *Ltd.** finds the records of companies whose names end with the "Ltd." suffix.

In the following illustration, the query finds people whose last name starts with "T" who live in Rome, but not in Rome, Italy. A query like this one would turn up Lucas Tarantino in Rome, New York, USA; but not Luciano Tarantino in Rome, Italy:

Field:	Last Name	City	Country		
Table:	CityAddress	CityAddress	CityAddress		
Sort:					
Show:	☑	☑	☑	☐	
Criteria:	Like "T*"	"Rome"	<>"Italy"		
or:					

Numeric Criteria

Use numeric criteria in Number and Currency fields to find specific kinds of records. Table 28-2 lists the operators you can use in Numeric and Currency fields. Use these operators liberally and often to query databases and get detailed information about the people or things that your database is meant to track.

Operator	Name	Example (in Cost Field)	Query Results
=	Equal to	=49.95	Items that cost exactly $49.95
<>	Not equal to	<>49.95[49.95]	Items that do not cost $49.95
<	Less than	<49.95	Items that cost less than $49.95
<=	Less than or equal to	<=49.95	Items that cost $49.95 or less
>	Greater than	>49.95	Items that cost more than $49.95
>=	Greater than or equal to	>=49.95	Items that cost $49.95 or more
Between... And...	Between	Between 49.95 And 59.95	Items that cost between $49.95 and $59.95

Table 28-2.   *Operators for Use in Numeric Fields in Queries*

As an example of how to use numeric operators to pinpoint specific records in a database, the following query finds donors whose annual income is between $150,000 and $200,000 and who donated $15,000 or more to charities:

Field:	Last Name	First Name	Total Charity Contribution	Income
Table:	Generous People	Generous People	Generous People	Generous People
Sort:	Ascending			
Show:	☑	☑	☑	☑
Criteria:			>=15000	Between 150000 And 200000
or:				

Date Criteria

All the numeric operators that can be used in numeric fields on a query grid can also be used in date fields (see Table 28-2). For example, entering **<3/8/97** in a field called Ship Date finds all shipments that were made before (are less than) 8 March 1997. Entering **Between 3/8/97 And 3/15/97** finds shipments that were made between 8 March and 15 March 1997.

The Expression Builder for Creating Expressions

Besides creating expressions yourself, you can do it by getting the Expression Builder's help. The Expression Builder offers buttons and tools for creating expressions. To use it, right-click on the query grid where the expression will go and choose Build from the shortcut menu. You see the Expression Builder dialog box shown in Figure 28-8.

By clicking buttons; by choosing functions, constants, or operators; and by entering text in the text box, you can construct expressions. Click OK when you are done constructing your expression.

Tip   *Access offers a function called Date() that represents today's date and can be useful in date expressions. For example, to find shipments made between today's date, whatever it happens to be, and 1 April 1997, you can enter the following expression:* **Between 4/1/97 And Date().**

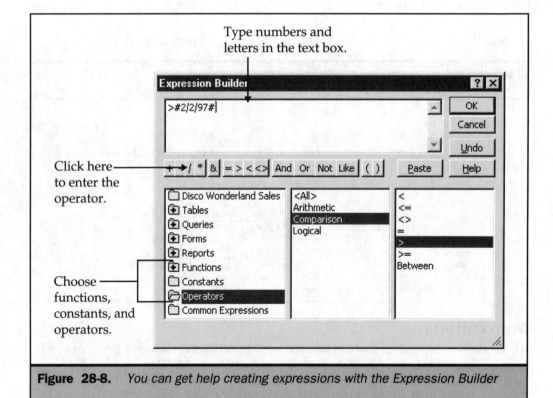

Figure 28-8.   *You can get help creating expressions with the Expression Builder*

As an example of using date criteria in a query, the following query finds the records of people born in the years 1946 to 1958 to whom a CD called "Disco Wonderland Retrospective" was shipped after 2 February 1997:

Field:	Name	Birthdate		Date Shipped	[CD: Disco Wonderland]	
Table:	Baby Boomers	Baby Boomers		Baby Boomers	Baby Boomers	
Sort:	Ascending					
Show:	☑		☑	☑	☑	
Criteria:		Between #1/1/46# And #12/31/58#		>#2/2/97#		
or:						

Seeing and Saving the Results of a Query

After you have constructed your query, it is time to run it. Either click the Run button or choose Query | Run. The results of the query appear on a datasheet that looks like a table in Datasheet view.

In database parlance, the datasheet is called a *dynaset*. It's called that because the results of a query represent a set of data that is "dynamic"—you can alter the date in the dynaset and the underlying tables are altered as well.

Many Access users find entering data on a query datasheet, or dynaset, easier, because they can work with a subset of the fields in a table. However, unless all the fields in a database table also appear on the query results table, records that are entered in the query results table are incomplete. For example, if you queried a table for six of its eight fields, six fields appear on the query. If you then enter a record on the query, it is recorded on the table, but the data is recorded in only six of the eight fields.

What's more, all the formats that apply to fields in the database table also apply on the results table. For example, if the database table stipulates that a field name be no longer than 20 characters, the same is true on the query results table.

You can remove fields, insert fields, or change the order of fields on the dynaset. To do so, see "Moving, Copying, Deleting, and Renaming Fields" in Chapter 27. The same techniques for working on a table in Datasheet view also apply to working on the table that shows the results of a query.

After you have finished examining the results of a query, save it by clicking the Save button. A box appears so you can give the query a name. Enter a name and click the OK button.

Viewing, Running, and Modifying Queries You Already Created

Queries that have been constructed and saved appear under Queries on the Database window. To open a query so you can view its results, run it again, or perhaps modify it, click the Queries button, click the query you want to use again, and then click either the Design or the Open button:

- **Design Button** Opens the query in Design view so you can modify it or run it. To modify it, click the Show Table button to add new tables to the query if that's what you want to do, or else change the field names and criteria on the query grid. When you are ready to run it again, click the Run button or choose Query | Run.

- **Open Button** Runs the query and displays the results.

The Different Kinds of Queries

Thus far, you have learned how to construct a select or standard query, the foundation on which all the other queries are built. The remainder of this chapter describes how to create the other kinds of queries, as well as the select query, with the Query Wizard. If you need instructions for selecting tables for a query, or selecting fields for a query, or doing all the other standard things that have to be done to construct a query, refer to the preceding pages in this book. Meanwhile, read on to learn about the different kinds of queries you can create with Access.

Constructing a Select Query with the Query Wizard

You can create a select query with the Query Wizard by following these steps:

1. In the Database window, click the Queries button, then the New button. You see the New Query dialog box.

2. Click the Simple Query Wizard option and then click OK. You see the first wizard dialog box, shown in Figure 28-9, which asks which tables to query and which fields in those tables to query.

3. Open the Tables/Queries drop-down list and choose the first table or query that you intend to query. Its fields appear in the Available Fields box.

4. To move all the fields from the Available Fields box to the Selected Fields box, click the double arrows that point to the right. To move fields one by one, click on fields one at a time and then click the single right-pointing arrow. If you make a mistake you can remove fields with the left-pointing arrow.

5. Repeat steps 3 and 4 until you have selected all the tables and all the fields you want to query.

6. Click the Next button to open the next wizard dialog box. It asks if you want a detailed or summary query.

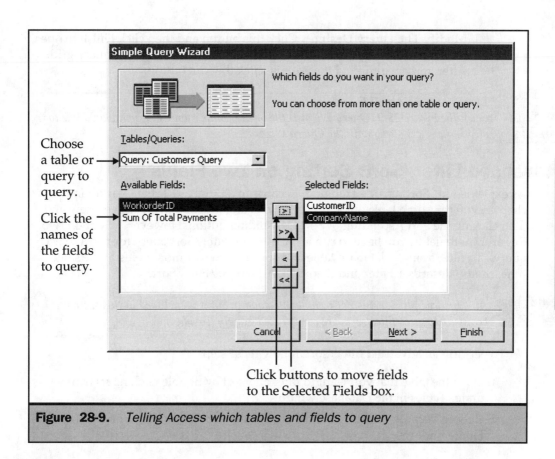

Choose a table or query to query. →

Click the → names of the fields to query.

Click buttons to move fields
to the Selected Fields box.

Figure 28-9. *Telling Access which tables and fields to query*

ACCESS

Note   *Later in this chapter, "Summary: Getting Comprehensive Information About Data in a Field" explains how to run a summary query.*

7. Click Next to create a detailed query. The next dialog box asks for a query name. The name you enter will appear under Queries in the Database window.

8. Enter a name for your query.

9. Click one of the option buttons on the dialog box:

■ **Open The Query To View Information**   Click this button and then click Finish to run the query. You see the query results on a datasheet.

■ **Modify The Query Design**   Click this button and then click Finish to open the Query in Design view, where you can enter criteria on the query grid. After you have entered the criteria, click the Run button.

LEARN BY EXAMPLE
Open the Figure 28-9 (Query Wizard) file on the companion CD if you would like to try creating a select query with the Query Wizard.

Advanced Filter/Sort: Sorting on Two Fields

As explained in "Sorting, or Arranging, Records in a Database Table," earlier in this chapter, you can sort a table on one field by selecting the field in Datasheet view and then clicking the Sort Ascending or Sort Descending button. However, to sort on two, three, or more fields, you have to run an Advanced Filter/Sort query (or run a select query). To filter a single database table and sort it on two or more fields at the same time, choose Records | Filter and then click Advanced/Filter Sort.

An advanced filter/sort is not technically a query, but it is included in this section because advanced filter/sorts are constructed exactly like queries.

To perform an advanced filter/sort, follow these steps:

1. Open the table that you want to filter and sort by double-clicking its name under Tables in the Database window.

2. Choose Records | Filter and then click Advanced/Filter Sort. You see the Filter window:

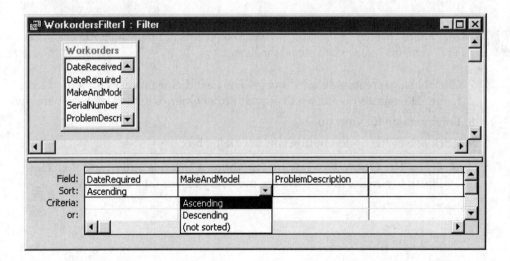

Note   *If instructions from a previous filter appear on the filter grid, click the Clear Grid button.*

3. Tell Access which fields to include in the filter operation by displaying them on the Field row (see "Choosing Which Fields to Query," earlier in this chapter, if you need help).

4. On the Sort box of each field you want to sort by, open the drop-down menu and choose Ascending or Descending:

   ■ **Ascending Order**   Arranges text entries in alphabetical order from A to Z (Cleveland, New York, West Hollywood); numbers from smallest to largest (5, 26, 144); and dates from earliest in time to latest in time (31-Jul-57, 4-Mar-96, 16-Oct-05).

   ■ **Descending Order**   Arranges text entries from Z to A (West Hollywood, New York, Cleveland); numbers from largest to smallest (144, 26, 5); and dates from latest in time to earliest in time (16-Oct-05, 4-Mar-96, 31-Jul-57).

5. When Access sees that more than one field needs to be sorted, it sorts the leftmost field first. If necessary, move the field you want to sort by first to the left of the other fields to be sorted. To learn how to move a field in the query grid, see "Rearranging Columns on the Query Grid," earlier in this chapter.

6. Click the Apply Filter button.

Tip   *You can enter criteria on the query grid as part of an advanced filter/sort operation. See "Entering the Query Criteria," earlier in this chapter.*

Calculation: Performing Calculations on Query Returns

By performing a calculation query, you can make a query results table work like a spreadsheet and have it perform calculations on the data that the query returns. In a database that tracks sales prices, for example, you can query to find many different items and have the query results show how much each item would cost if prices were increased by 3 percent.

LEARN BY EXAMPLE
To try your hand at calculating the results of a query, open the Figure 28-10 (Calculation Query) file on the companion CD.

EXAMPLES

Follow these steps to create a calculation query:

1. Create a new query, choose which tables to query, and choose which fields to query.

2. Click the Table row of a blank column.

3. From the drop-down list, choose the table with the field that you want to use in the calculation. For example, if the field you want to use is called Price and it is in the Items table, choose the Items table from the drop-down list.

4. Click directly above the Table row, in the Field row.

5. Click to open the drop-down list and choose the name of the field you want to use in the calculation. Figure 28-10 shows the UnitPrice field being chosen.

6. Click directly to the right of the field name you just entered and type an operand and number. In Figure 28-10, I entered ***1.03** to calculate a 3 percent rise in prices.

7. Press the ENTER key. When you do so, Access inserts the letters Expr1 (for Expression 1) and encloses the field name in brackets, as shown in Figure 28-10.

8. Run the query by clicking the Run button.

The following illustration shows the results of the query shown in Figure 28-10. For this query, I did two calculations on the items in the Price field, one to see how much prices would rise if I increased them by 3 percent, or 1.03 (Expr1); and one to see how much prices would rise if I increased them by 7 percent, or 1.07 (Expr2):

Product Name	Unit Price	Expr1	Expr2
Dharamsala Tea	$18.00	18.54	19.26
Tibetan Barley Beer	$19.00	19.57	20.33
Aniseed Syrup	$10.00	10.3	10.7
Chef Anton's Cajun Seasoning	$22.00	22.66	23.54
Chef Anton's Gumbo Mix	$21.35	21.9905	22.8445

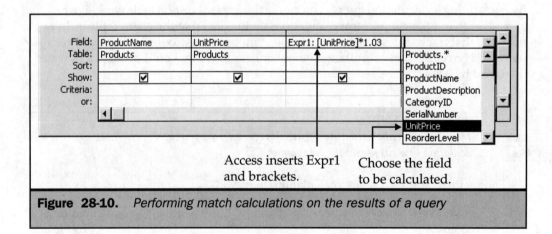

Figure 28-10.   *Performing match calculations on the results of a query*

Crosstab: Displaying Query Results in a Matrix

A crosstab query makes it easier to compare, or cross-tabulate, information. To see the advantages of a crosstab query, study the following two illustrations. The first shows a table with horses' names, races in which the horses ran, and the prize money they won. However, horses' names and sweepstakes' names repeat themselves in the first two columns, so it is hard to make a realistic comparison of the horses to see which won more money.

Race ID	Horse	Sweepstakes	Prize Money
1	LaSerella	The Brown Derby	$4,400.00
2	Lady Fair	Kentucky Home	$65,000.00
3	Swan's Delay	The Freakness	$115,000.00
4	Lady Fair	The Brown Derby	$23,000.00
5	Swan's Delay	Kentuck Home	$32,000.00
6	Sky's Limit	The Brown Derby	$13,000.00
7	LaSerella	Kentucky Home	$23,000.00
8	Lady Fair	The Freakness	$78,000.00

The following illustration shows the results of a crosstab query on the table. Horses' names have been grouped in the left-hand column and you can clearly see how much money each horse won, if any, in each sweepstakes race. Moreover, the crosstab query has added a "total of" column so you can see each horse's total winnings:

Horse	Total Of Prize Money	Kentucky Home	The Brown Derby	The Freakness
Lady Fair	$166,000.00	$65,000.00	$23,000.00	$78,000.00
LaSerella	$27,400.00	$23,000.00	$4,400.00	
Sky's Limit	$13,000.00		$13,000.00	
Swan's Delay	$147,000.00	$32,000.00		$115,000.00

EXAMPLES

LEARN BY EXAMPLE

Open the Figure 28-11 (Crosstab Query) file on the companion CD to try your hand at creating a crosstab query.

When you construct a crosstab query with the Query Wizard, the wizard asks three questions about how to translate the data on the table into the data on the query results:

- **For Row Labels in the Left-Hand Column of the Query Results**   From which column in the database table should the query get row labels? In the query results shown in the preceding illustration, row labels came from the Horse column of the database table. For each name in the Horse column of the table, Access created a row on the query results.

- **For Column Headings in the Query Results**   From which column in the database table should the query get column headings? In the previous illustration, column headings came from the Sweepstakes column. For each sweepstakes name in the Sweepstakes column, Access created a column in the query results.

- **For the Numeric Data in the Query Results**   From which column heading in the table should the query get the numeric data that fills most of the table? In the illustration, numeric data came from the Prize Money column.

The Query Wizard asks a fourth question, too. It asks if you want to total, average, count the number of, or do a number of other mathematical things to the data in the table. For the sample illustration, I had the Query Wizard total the prize money won by each horse.

To run a crosstab query, the table you are querying must include at least one field that stores numbers—that is, one numeric, date, or currency field. Moreover, if the data is to come from two or more tables, query the tables with a simple, select query. After you have assembled the data from the different tables in a select query, run a crosstab query on the select query.

By far the easiest way to create a crosstab query is to do so with the Query Wizard. Follow these steps to create a crosstab query:

1. Click the Queries button on the Database window. Click the New button.

2. In the New Query dialog box, choose Crosstab Query Wizard and click OK. You see the first wizard dialog box, which asks which table or query you want to query.

3. Choose a table or query. If necessary, click the Queries or Both option button to see the query that you want to query.

4. Click the Next button. The next dialog box asks, "Which Field's Values Do You Want As Row Headings?" The wizard is asking you question number 1 in the list of questions above. The wizard wants to know where to get the names or numbers that will go in the left-hand column of the query results and identify each row of data.

5. Click one field name in the Available Fields box and then click the arrow that points to the right to move that field into the Selected Fields box.

Watch the Sample box in the Query Wizard dialog box. It gives a fair idea of what the query results table will look like when you are done creating it.

6. Click the Next button. The next dialog box asks, "Which Field's Values Do You Want As Column Headings?" This is question 2 in the list above. The wizard is

asking where in the table or query being queried to get the column names for the query results table.

7. Click the field whose values you want to appear in the column headings across the top of the query results table you are about to create.

8. Click the Next button. As shown in Figure 28-11, the next dialog box wants to know which numeric value to place in the query results table and whether or not to summarize the data in each row.

9. Click the name of the numeric field in the table you are querying that holds the values you want to compare in your crosstab query.

10. If you want to add a column to the query results table that summarizes each row, make sure a check mark appears in the Yes, Include Row Sums check box, and then choose the means by which the data will be summarized by clicking

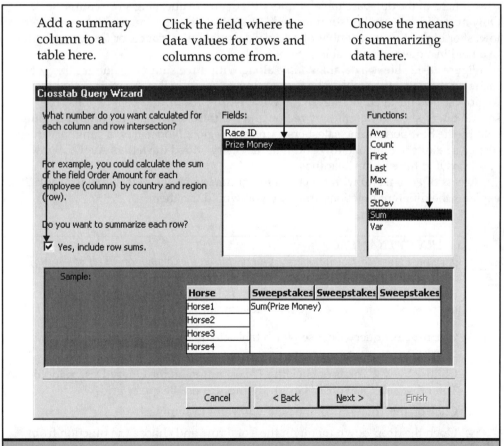

Figure 28-11.   *From which field in the table being queried do you want to get the numbers that fill your query results?*

an option in the Functions box. For example, SUM totals the rows and adds a "total of" column. AVG averages the numbers in the rows. Count counts how many entries are in each row.

11. Click the Next button.

12. Enter a name for the crosstab query. The name you enter will appear on the Queries tab in the Database window.

13. Click the Finish button. The results of the query appear onscreen.

Summary: Getting Comprehensive Information About Data in a Field

The previous section explained how to summarize a row of data in a crosstab query. You can create a query that summarizes all the data in a field as well, as long as the row or field in the database table or query that you are querying stores numeric data. Only numeric data can be "summarized." A summary query can find the sum, average, lowest or highest value, number of, standard deviation, variance, or first or last value in a field in a query results table.

Figure 28-12 shows a database table along with three summary queries that were made on the data in the table. The first summary query, called Average Sales by Region, shows the average sales in the West, North, South, and East regions. The second query shows total sales by region and the third shows the maximum amount sold by the best-performing salesperson in each region. Notice how a summary query displays results in only one row and that the query added the letters AvgOf, SumOf, and MaxOf to the column headings.

Access offers a menu with functions for summarizing the data in a field. Table 28-3 explains the different functions and why you would use them.

EXAMPLES

LEARN BY EXAMPLE
Open the Figure 28-12 (Summarize Query) file on the companion CD if you want to experiment with summary queries.

Follow these steps to create a query that summarizes data in a query results table:

1. Create a new query, choose which tables to query, and choose which fields to query.

2. Choose View | Totals or click the Totals button on the Query Design toolbar. A Total row and the words "Group By" appear on the query grid.

3. Click on the Total row of the field you want to summarize.

4. Open the drop-down menu on the Total row and choose the function from

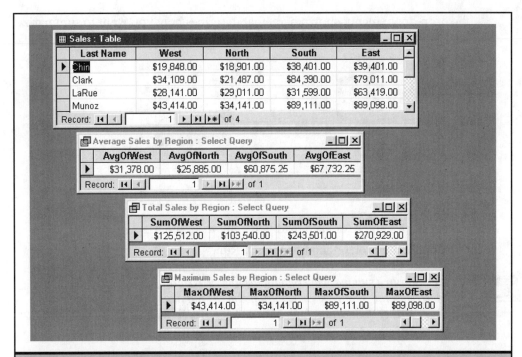

Figure 28-12.   *A database table (top) and three summary queries made from it: Average Sales, Total Sales, and Maximum Sales, all by region*

Function	What It Does
Sum	Totals the values in the field
Avg	Finds the average value in the field
Min	Finds the lowest value in the field
Max	Finds the highest value in the field
Count	Counts the number of values in the field
StDev	Finds the standard deviation of the values in the field
Var	Finds the variance of the values in the field
First	Finds the first value in the field
Last	Finds the last value in the field

Table 28-3.   *Functions for Use with Summary Queries*

the drop-down menu, shown here, that describes how you want to summarize the row (see Table 28-3):

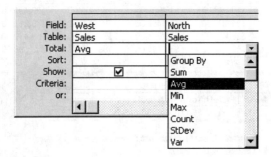

5. Repeat steps 3 and 4 for each field you want to summarize.

6. Click the Run button or choose Query | Run.

You can also run a summary query with the Query Wizard. In the wizard's second dialog box, click the Summary radio button and the Summary Options button. In the next dialog box, click the Sum, Avg, Min, or Max check box for each field you want to summarize.

Top Value: Finding High and Low Values in Fields

We've seen how to find the highest and lowest value in a field by performing a summary query. However, if you want to find high and low values, there is a quicker way. You can find the highest or lowest 5, 25, 100, or whatever values, or find the values in the highest or lowest percentile of a database table, by following these steps:

1. Create a new query, choose which tables to query, and choose which fields to query.

2. On the query grid in the field in which you want to find the highest or lowest values, click the Sort row.

3. Click Ascending or Descending on the drop-down menu.

   - **Ascending** Click to find low values in the field.
   - **Descending** Click to find high values in the field.

4. Click to open the Top Values menu on the Query Design toolbar:

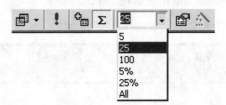

5. Enter or choose a number or percentage to find the low or high value. To enter a number, click in the Top Values box, type the number, and press the ENTER key. To enter a percentage, enter a number followed by the percent sign, and then press the ENTER key.

6. Click the Run button to run the query.

Update: Updating Records in a Database

An update query finds records that meet certain criteria and updates those records en masse. Update queries are especially useful for updating telephone numbers, addresses, and other types of information that typically are stored in several different database tables.

EXAMPLES

LEARN BY EXAMPLE
To practice working with update queries, open the file Figure 28-13 (Update Query) on the companion CD.

Finding Duplicate Fields and Unmatched Records

The New Query dialog box—the one you see when you click the New button—offers Query Wizards for finding duplicate fields in a table and records in one table for which matches can't be found in another:

- **Find Duplicates**   The Find Duplicates Query Wizard lists all the records in a table that share field values with other records. For example, the records of people who live in the same ZIP code are listed, as are the records of people who live in the same city or have the same blood type. Besides running the Find Duplicates Query Wizard to locate like-minded records, you can also use it before you choose the primary key field or index a field to find out whether duplicate values exist in a field. As you surely must know, duplicate values cannot appear in a primary key field.

- **Find Unmatched Records**   The Find Unmatched Query Wizard compares two tables to find out whether matches exist between the records in one table and the records in another. Records for which matches can't be found are listed. For example, in a comparison of an Inventory table and a Product Description table, the Find Unmatched Query Wizard could find items in the Inventory table that haven't been assigned a product number that is listed in the Product Description table. Finding records for which matches don't exist is useful for maintaining referential integrity in a database (see the box "What Is Referential Integrity?" in Chapter 27 if the concept is foreign to you).

To see how an update query works, suppose you keep a database in which one table lists college courses and the other lists information about professors. Each course is assigned one professor, but Professor Jacobson leaves and is replaced by Professor Hernandez. Rather than go into the college courses table, find courses taught by Jacobson, and change Jacobson to Hernandez in the Professor field, you could run an update query that finds Jacobson and changes her name to Hernandez. In a very large database, being able to make updates automatically is invaluable.

Caution   *Update queries can have unforeseen consequences. Moreover, the changes they make are permanent and can't be reversed. Before you run an update query, create and run a select query to see which records will be affected by the update query. If the results are satisfactory, then change the query type to an update query. The instructions here explain how.*

Follow these steps to run an update query:

1. Create a new query and make sure to add the table with the data you want to change and the table from which the new data will come.

2. Choose the fields that you want to appear in the query results table.

3. Click on the Criteria row of the field that you want to update and enter the value that is to be updated. In Figure 28-13, Professor Jacobson is going to be "updated" and replaced by Professor Hernandez.

4. Click the View button to switch to Datasheet view. Access shows you the table that will be updated when you finish the update query.

Caution   *Make absolutely certain that the table you see after you switch to Datasheet view is indeed the one that you want to update and that the selection criteria was entered correctly.*

5. Click the View button again to return to Design view.

6. Click the down arrow beside the Query Type button and choose Update Query from the drop-down menu. A new row called Update To appears on the query grid.

7. On the Update To row, enter the new, updated value. In Figure 28-13, the value is a name, Hernandez.

8. Click the Run button or choose Query | Run. A dialog box asks if you want to go through with it. Changes made by an update query are permanent and can't be reversed.

9. Click the Yes button.

Note   *An update query does not produce a dynaset. To see the result of an update query, close the query without saving it, and then open the source table to see the result of the update.*

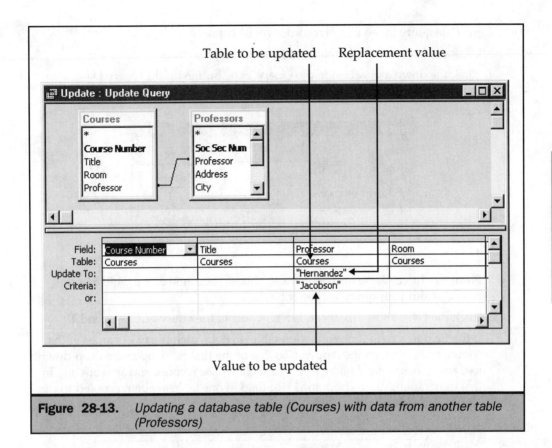

Table to be updated   Replacement value

Value to be updated

Figure 28-13.   *Updating a database table (Courses) with data from another table (Professors)*

Append: Copying Data to a New Table

An append query copies records from one table and pastes them into another table. When you create an append query, you formulate the query that will retrieve the records you want to copy to a table. Then you tell Access which table to copy the records to. For an append query to work, field types in both tables must be the same.

LEARN BY EXAMPLE
To try your hand at running an append query, open the Figure 28-B (Append Query) file on the companion CD.

EXAMPLES

Follow these steps to create and run an append query:

1. Create a query that retrieves the records you want to copy into a table. Choose which tables to query and choose which fields to query.

2. Run the query to see which records will be copied.

3. Click the View button to return to Design view.

4. Click the down arrow beside the Query Type button on the Query Design toolbar and choose Append Query. You see the Append dialog box:

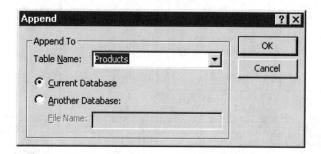

5. From the Table Name drop-down list, choose the name of the table that the records from your query will be copied to.

6. Click the OK button. Access adds a new line to the query grid: Append To.

7. If the field names in the destination table do not match the field names in the source table, click on the Append To line of the first field, open the drop-down list, and choose a field name from the table whose records you are copying. In this illustration, values from the Price field in one table are being copied to the UnitPrice field in another table:

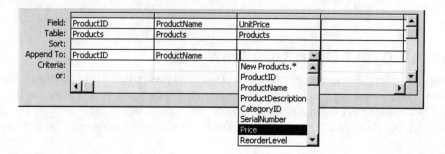

Caution *In order to copy values from a field in one table to another, the fields must have been assigned the same data type. For example, only data in currency fields can be copied to a currency field in another table. In the illustration shown here, you couldn't copy values from the SerialNumber field into the Cost field, because SerialNumber has been assigned the Text data type and Cost has been assigned the Currency data type.*

8. Repeat step 7 for each field whose name does not have a matching field name in the destination table.

You cannot copy records with fields to which the AutoNumber data type has been assigned from one table to another. When you copy records to a table that includes a field with autonumbers, the copied records are assigned new autonumbers.

9. Choose Query | Run or click the Run button.

10. Click Yes in the dialog box that asks if you really want to go through with it.

Make-Table: Creating a Table from Query Results

Use a make-table query when you want to back up or archive records. A make-table query copies records from database tables and stores the records in a new table. Follow these steps to create and run a make-table query:

1. Create a new query, choose which tables to query, and choose which fields to query.

2. On the query grid, carefully enter criteria for choosing the records for the new table. For example, to create a backup table of sales transactions made in 1995, you might enter **Between 1/1/95 And 12/31/95** in the Transaction Date field of your query. See "Entering the Query Criteria," earlier in this chapter.

3. Run the query to see which records will be included in the new query.

4. Click the View button to return to Design view.

5. Click the down arrow beside the Query Type button on the Query Design toolbar and choose Make-Table Query. You see the Make Table dialog box:

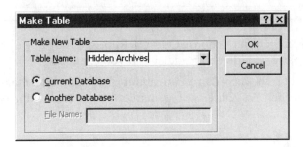

6. Enter a name for your new table in the Table Name box and click OK.

7. Click the Run button or choose Query | Run. A dialog box appears and tells you how many records (rows) are in your new table.

8. Click the Yes button.

You can find your new table under Tables in the Database window. Take note, however, that the new table does not have a primary key field. If you intend to create a relationship between the new table and other tables in the database, open the new table in Design view and designate a primary key.

Delete: Querying to Delete Records from Tables

Before you read about delete queries, take heed: Delete queries permanently delete records from a database. Before you run a delete query, run a make-table query that assembles all the records you intend to delete. That way, if you regret deleting the records, you can get them from the table you made.

That said, delete queries are excellent for removing the dead wood from a database. Use this type of query to remove outdated records that were entered before a certain date or are otherwise obsolete.

Follow these steps to create and run a delete query:

1. Create a new query, and, on the query grid, carefully enter criteria for choosing which records to delete. To delete records that were entered before a certain date, for example, you could enter an expression in the Date of Sale field. See "Entering the Query Criteria," earlier in this chapter.

2. Click the down arrow beside the Query Type button on the Query Design toolbar and choose Delete Query. As shown in this illustration, a new row called Delete appears in the query grid and the word "Where" appears on each line in the Delete row:

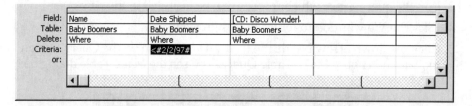

3. Click the Run button or choose Query | Run. A dialog box appears and tells you how many records will be deleted if you click Yes.

4. You backed up the records you are about to delete with a make-table query, right? If so, click Yes. Otherwise, you might want to click the No button.

Chapter 29

Generating Reports and Mailing Labels

N o doubt, one of the reasons people go to such lengths to create databases is so they can present the data in printed form for others to admire. This chapter explains how to create and print reports. Of course, you can also view data on the computer screen, but reports are especially designed to be printed. As the following pages explain, Access offers several different kinds of reports, and you can get quite fancy if you want to.

One special—and handy—type of Access report is mailing labels. This chapter explains how to print mailing labels suitable for use in mass mailings and bulk mailings from the names and addresses in a database table or query. Since the post office requires bulk mailings to be sorted by ZIP code, you can sort the addresses before you print them and save yourself the trouble of sorting envelopes later.

Generating Reports

Access offers three ways to generate a report: with an AutoReport, with the Report Wizard, or from scratch. AutoReports and the Report Wizard are covered in the following pages. Creating a report from scratch is a bit beyond the scope of this book, but we will discuss how to modify the design of reports created in AutoReport or with the Report Wizard.

Choosing How to Create Your Report

No matter which method you choose to create a report, you start the same way:

1. From the Database window, click the Reports button.

2. Click the New button in the Reports window. You see the New Report dialog box shown in Figure 29-1.

Time-Saving Tips for Creating Reports

Like a query, reports can pull data off more than one table or query—the process is similar. You can create a query to gather all the data into place, then simply generate a report off the query (and if you're using AutoReport, which only takes data from one table or query, this is the way you'll have to go). But if you're not going to use the intermediate query for other purposes (such as building a crosstab query) and you're using the Report Wizard, then you can save yourself a step and collect the data directly into the report.

Another shortcut for creating reports is to give the query the name that you want the report to have. In the case of AutoReports, Access simply names the report after the table or query from which the data came. By carefully naming the query, you make sure that the AutoReport has a descriptive name.

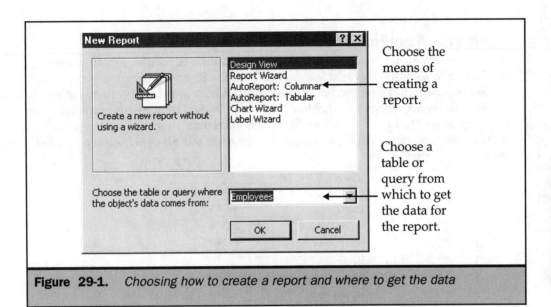

Figure 29-1.   *Choosing how to create a report and where to get the data*

1. Choose the table or query from which to get the data for the report from the drop-down list at the bottom of the dialog box.

2. Choose a means of creating a report:

   ■ **Report Wizard**   Opens the wizard, after which you are asked a bunch of questions about what the report should look like. See "Creating a Report with the Report Wizard," later in this chapter.

   ■ **AutoReport: Columnar**   Creates a report in which the data is displayed in a single column. See the following section.

   ■ **AutoReport: Tabular**   Creates a report in which data is shown in a table. See "Creating an AutoReport" next.

3. Click OK.

Creating an AutoReport

To create an AutoReport, click the Reports button on the Database window, click the New button, choose a Table or Query from the drop-down list box, and then choose AutoReport: Columnar or AutoReport: Tabular in the New Report dialog box. That's it; AutoReport does everything else.

When you first see it, an AutoReport appears on the Print Preview screen, as shown in Figure 29-2. (See "Using Print Preview" in Chapter 2 if you don't know your way around the Print Preview screen.) If you like the looks of your AutoReport and want to

Columnar, Tabular, or Justified Reports?

AutoReport gives you the choice of creating a columnar or tabular report (there's another option, justified, available when you use the Report Wizard).

Below is a columnar report, which presents data with each field below the other. A columnar report looks somewhat like a form and is good for listing information, such as pertinent facts on a customer. These reports typically take more page space to show a given amount of data. Labels appear on the left and the data itself is presented in a single column:

Horse	Lady Fair
Total Of Prize Mon	$166,000.00
Kentucky Home	$65,000.00
The Brown Derby	$23,000.00
The Freakness	$78,000.00
Horse	LaSerella
Total Of Prize Mon	$27,400.00
Kentucky Home	$23,000.00
The Brown Derby	$4,400.00
The Freakness	

Tabular reports present data in a table format. These reports typically allow you to get more records on a page and are good for comparing data, as the following illustration demonstrates. Create a tabular report when you want to show a list of the data in the database table or query. A tabular report might resemble an Excel spreadsheet and will typically get more data onto a page.

Horse	*Total Of Prize Money*	*Kentucky Home*	*The Brown Derby*	*The Freakness*
Lady Fair	$166,000.00	$65,000.00	$23,000.00	$78,000.00
LaSerella	$27,400.00	$23,000.00	$4,400.00	
Sky's Limit	$13,000.00		$13,000.00	
Swan's Delay	$147,000.00	$32,000.00		$115,000.00

A justified report is a hybrid between a columnar and a tabular report, and can only be created if you don't choose any grouping levels. In a justified report, fields and values appear in rows, and values appear directly below field names:

Horse	*Total Of Prize Money*	*Kentucky Home*	*The Brown Derby*	*The Freakness*
Lady Fair	$166,000.00	$65,000.00	$23,000.00	$78,000.00

Horse	*Total Of Prize Money*	*Kentucky Home*	*The Brown Derby*	*The Freakness*
LaSerella	$27,400.00	$23,000.00	$4,400.00	

Horse	*Total Of Prize Money*	*Kentucky Home*	*The Brown Derby*	*The Freakness*
Sky's Limit	$13,000.00		$13,000.00	

Horse	*Total Of Prize Money*	*Kentucky Home*	*The Brown Derby*	*The Freakness*
Swan's Delay	$147,000.00	$32,000.00		$115,000.00

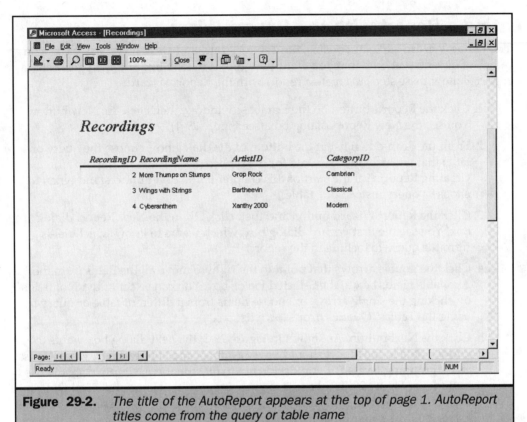

Figure 29-2. *The title of the AutoReport appears at the top of page 1. AutoReport titles come from the query or table name*

keep it, choose File | Save, enter a name for your report in the Save As dialog box, and click OK. The names of reports that have been saved appear on the Reports tab of the Database window.

An AutoReport gets its title from the query or table from where it came. For example, the AutoReport shown in Figure 29-2 came from a table called "Recordings," so the word "Recordings" appears at the start of the report. Along the bottom of each page of an AutoReport is a footer with the day of the week, date, page number, and total number of pages in the report, as shown here:

Sunday, September 20, 1998   *Page 1 of 1*

You can create a columnar AutoReport from a database table or the results of a query by clicking the arrow that points down beside the New Object button and choosing AutoReport while the table or query results are onscreen.

Creating a Report with the Report Wizard

The Report Wizard—like its cousins, the Table Wizard and Design Wizard—asks you a bunch of questions about what you want your report to look like and then generates a report. Follow these steps to create a report with the Report Wizard:

1. Click the Reports button on the Database window, then click the New button. You see the New Report dialog box (see Figure 29-1).

2. From the drop-down list at the bottom of the dialog box, choose the query or table that will provide raw data for the report. (See "Time-Saving Tips for Creating Reports" at the start of this chapter if you don't understand when to choose a query instead of a table.)

3. Click the Report Wizard option and then click OK in the New Report dialog box. You see the first wizard dialog box, which wants to know which fields from the query to include in the report.

4. Click the double arrows that point to the right to move all the fields from the Available Fields box to the Selected Fields box. You can select individual fields by clicking the single arrow, or choose fields from a different table or query by using the Tables/Queries drop-down list box.

5. Click the Next button. As shown in Figure 29-3, the next dialog box wants to know if data in the report should have headings and subheadings, what Access calls "grouping levels." If you decide not to include them, simply click the Next button. For Figure 29-3, I chose two grouping levels—Horse and Total Of Prize Money. The following illustration shows what a report with these two grouping levels looks like after it has been printed:

Lady Fair

Total Of Prize Money		$166,000	
	Kentucky Home	The Brown Derby	The Freakness
	$65,000.00	$23,000.00	$78,000.00

LaSerella

Total Of Prize Money		$27,400	
	Kentucky Home	The Brown Derby	The Freakness
	$23,000.00	$4,400.00	

Sky's Limit

Total Of Prize Money		$13,000	
	Kentucky Home	The Brown Derby	The Freakness
		$13,000.00	

6. For each field you want as a "grouping level," if you indeed want grouping levels, click its name in the box on the right and then click the button with the arrow that points to the right. The field name moves into the box on the right. You can include as many grouping levels as you wish. Click the Priority button to change the hierarchy of grouping levels.

7. Click the Next button. The next dialog box wants to know how to sort the records in the report. Choose the first field you want to sort by from the first drop-down list box, then choose the next fields from the other drop-down list boxes.

8. Click the Next button. The next dialog box asks if you want a columnar, tabular, or justified report, and whether to print the report in landscape mode. If you opted for grouping levels, you must also choose between stepped, block, two types of outlines, and two types of left alignment choices.

Tip *Click the Landscape option button if the query on which you base your report includes a lot of fields and you are creating a tabular or justified report. With a landscape report, you can fit more fields across the page.*

9. Click a button to tell Access what kind of report you want. "Columnar, Tabular, or Justified Reports?" earlier in this chapter explains the three main kinds of reports.

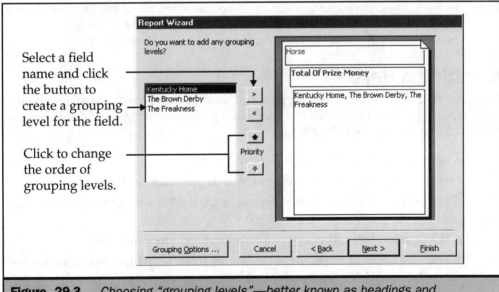

Figure 29-3. *Choosing "grouping levels"—better known as headings and subheadings for the report*

10. Click the Next button. The next dialog box asks what you want the report to look like:

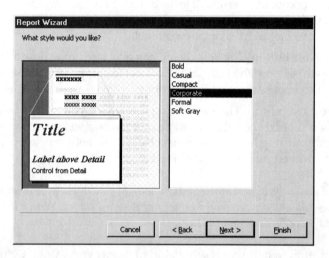

11. Click style options until you've found the one that looks good, and then click the Next button.

12. In the last wizard dialog box, enter a name for your report and then click the Finish button. The name you enter will appear at the top of the first page in the report and appear as well on the Reports tab of the Database window. Your new report appears on the Print Preview screen (see Figure 29-2).

Customizing a Report

Once you've created a report using the Report Wizard or AutoReport, you may want to add text, change labels, or add fields to your existing reports using Access' design tools.
   To customize a report, follow these steps:

1. Click the Reports button in the Database window.

2. Select the report you want to customize and then click the Design button.

3. Click on a text box and modify the text or use the Formatting toolbar to change the text's formatting (see Figure 29-4).

4. Click on a text box and drag it to a new location to move the text.

5. Click the Text Box button on the toolbox, to create a new text box. If the toolbox isn't visible, click the Toolbox toolbar button.

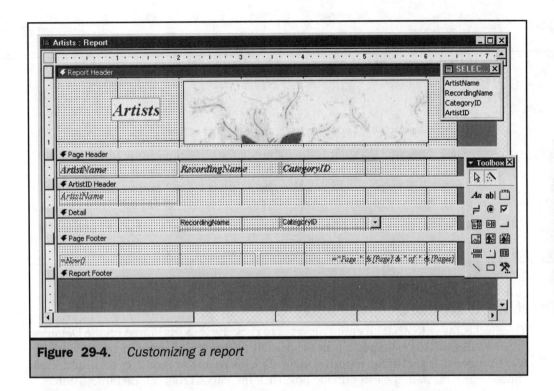

Figure 29-4.   *Customizing a report*

6. Click the Field List toolbar button and drag a field name into your report to add a new field.

7. Click the Image button on the toolbox, to insert a picture in your report.

8. Click the Sorting and Grouping toolbar button to change how you group and sort your fields, and then choose your fields from the Field/Expression box and the sort order from the Sort Order box.

9. Click the Close button and click Yes to save your changes.

Opening a Report You Already Created

To open a report, click the Reports button on the Database window and double-click the report's name. Reports remain up to date as the data in the database changes. For example, if you enter a new record or change part of an existing one and then open a report that "reports on" the data you entered or altered, the report shows the changes you made.

Saving a Report As a Word Document

You can save a report as a Word document. Once the database is in Word, you can change the fonts, headers and footers, and other formats. Follow these steps to save a report in Word:

1. In Access, open the report in the Print Preview screen.

2. Click the arrow that points down beside the OfficeLinks button on the Print Preview toolbar and choose Publish It With MS Word from the drop-down menu. A dialog box tells you that the report is being "output" to MS Word. Soon the report opens in Word as a rich text format (RTF) file.

3. In Word, choose File | Save As to save the file under a name and in a folder of your choice.

Printing a Report

The quickest way to print an entire report is to click the Reports button on the Database window, right-click on the report, and choose Print from the shortcut menu. If you want to print just part of the report, double-click the report's name to open it, and then choose File | Print. In the Print dialog box, click the Pages From option button, enter the number of the first page to print in the From box and the last page to print in the To box, and then click OK.

Generating Mailing Labels

One of the nicest features of Access is being able to produce mailing labels quickly. All you have to do is query the database to produce the names and addresses for which you want to make labels. With that done, you take a very serious look at the labels on which you want to print the addresses. Make sure you know the manufacturer and product number or the dimensions of the labels you intend to print on, because Access needs to know that in order to print labels. Once you have assembled the names and addresses and examined the labels, you can let the Label Wizard do the rest of the work.

 If you are printing the labels for a bulk mailing, sort the query results on the Zip Code field before you create the labels. That way, you can save a lot of time sorting the mail.

Follow these steps to generate mailing labels with Access:

1. Click the Reports button on the Database window. Click the New button. You
   see the New Report dialog box:

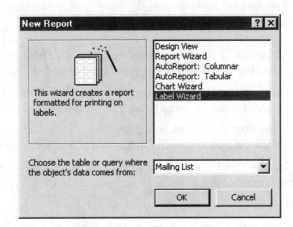

2. Choose the query from which the names and addresses will come from the
   drop-down list at the bottom of the dialog box.

3. Click the Label Wizard option and then click OK. You see the first wizard
   dialog box. It wants to know what size labels you will print on, as well as other
   information:

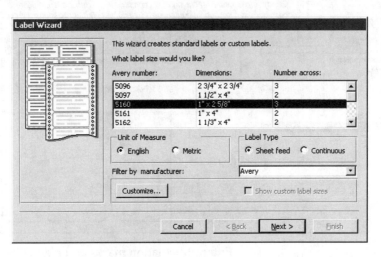

4. In the scroll list, find and click on the kind of labels you will print on. The
   Dimensions column shows label sizes (click the Metric option button if
   appropriate) and the Number Across column shows how many labels appear

across the page. If you are using Avery brand labels, all you have to do is look at the number on the package the labels came from and click that number in the dialog box.

> **Note**   *If labels are fed to your printer continuously, not one sheet at a time, click the Continuous option button.*

5. Click the Next button. The next dialog box asks about font name, font size, and other settings having to do with the appearance of text on the labels.

6. Choose new font and text color settings to your heart's desire, but make sure that the text doesn't grow so large it can't fit on the labels.

7. Click the Next button. As shown in Figure 29-5, the next dialog box asks you to construct a prototype label from the fields in the Available Fields box.

8. Click the field name that is to appear first in the label, and then click the button with the arrow on it to move the field name into the Prototype Label box.

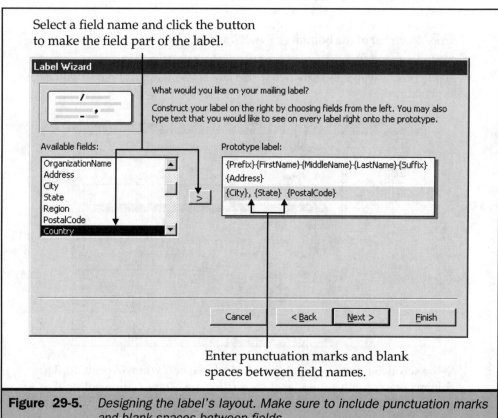

Figure 29-5.   *Designing the label's layout. Make sure to include punctuation marks and blank spaces between fields*

9. Enter a space, line breaks, or a punctuation mark, or other text as shown in Figure 29-5. To go from line to line, press ENTER or use your arrow keys.

10. Repeat steps 8 and 9 for each field that is to appear on the label. Be sure to enter blank spaces, line returns, and perhaps punctuation marks between fields.

11. Click the Next button. The next dialog box wants to know how to sort the fields, but if you sorted them before you started the Label Wizard, you can skip this step.

12. Click the Next button.

13. Enter a name for the labels. The name you enter will appear on the Reports tab of the Database window.

14. Click the Finish button. The labels appear on the Print Preview screen.

15. To print the labels now, insert the labels in your printer, choose File | Print, and click OK in the Print dialog box.

To print the labels in the future, all you have to do is put labels in your printer, open the Reports tab of the Database window, right-click on the labels report, and choose Print from the shortcut menu.

The Complete Reference

Office 2000

Part VIII

Microsoft Publisher

The Complete Reference

Office 2000

Chapter 30

Laying Out a Publication

This chapter explains how to create and set up a Publisher document, called a *publication*, both using a wizard and from scratch.

Creating a Publication Using a Wizard

You can use Publisher's wizards to quickly create professionally designed publications. With Publisher's wizards, you need to only answer a series of questions and then fill in the content blanks that the wizard creates for you. To create a publication using a wizard, follow these steps:

1. When you start Publisher or choose File | New, click the Publications By Wizard tab, and then select a wizard from the list of wizards, as shown in Figure 30-1. Then select a design for the publication by clicking an example design from the list box on the right. This section describes the steps of the Newsletter Wizard. The steps of the other wizards are quite similar.

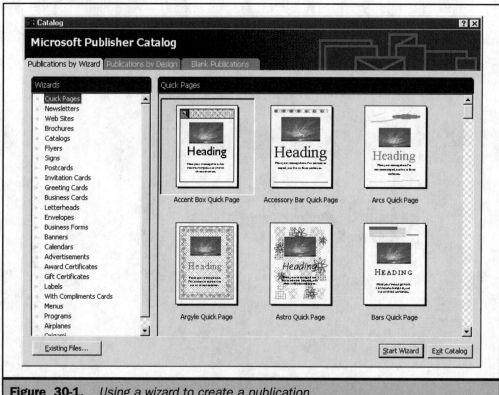

Figure 30-1. *Using a wizard to create a publication*

Note *Click the Publications By Design tab to browse the publication wizards by design as opposed to browsing them by publication type. The majority of the publications—all that use a standard design—are available on this tab. Using the Publications By Design tab is an easy way to take on a uniform design presence for all of the publications you create.*

2. Click Start Wizard. The first time you go through a wizard, Publisher prompts you to fill out a personal information set. You only have to fill this out once. Publisher uses your personal information sets in future publications.

3. Click Next to begin the wizard. The steps of each wizard vary; these are the steps you take for the Newsletter Wizard.

4. Select a color scheme. This is the first step in most wizards. Select a group of colors from the list and observe the color changes in the publication on the right, as shown in Figure 30-2.

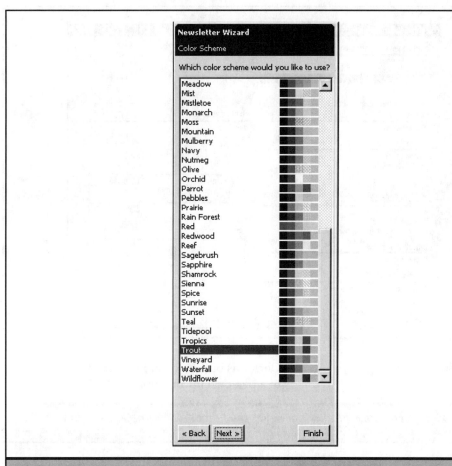

Figure 30-2. *The wizard allows you to choose a color scheme*

Note *If you're using a black-and-white printer to print your publication, it probably makes sense to choose the Black & Gray scheme so that the shades of gray print as you see them on screen.*

5. Specify how many columns you want and click Next.

6. The Newsletter Wizard, like the other wizards for publications that are commonly mailed out, asks if you want a placeholder for a mailing address. Click Yes or No and click Next.

7. Use the print options to specify single or double-sided printing and click Next.

8. Select the personal information set you want to use in the publication, as shown in Figure 30-3. Click Update to add an information set or review or edit an existing set.

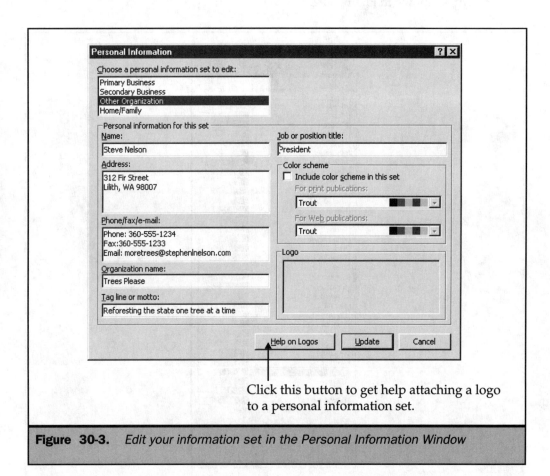

Click this button to get help attaching a logo to a personal information set.

Figure 30-3. *Edit your information set in the Personal Information Window*

9. Click Finish to begin working with the pages of the publication.

Note   *Chapter 6 describes how to use the Web Sites Wizard.*

When you create a publication using a wizard, the wizard sticks around as you work on the publication. If you want to edit a choice you made while using the wizard to create the publication, you can do so at any time by selecting new options in the wizard.

Creating a Standard Publication from Scratch

If you don't want to create a publication using one of Publisher's design templates, but instead want to start with a blank sheet of paper and add elements individually, you can use the Blank Publications tab of the Microsoft Publisher Catalog to create a publication from scratch. To create a publication from scratch, follow these steps:

1. Click the Blank Publications tab of the Microsoft Publisher Catalog, shown in Figure 30-4.

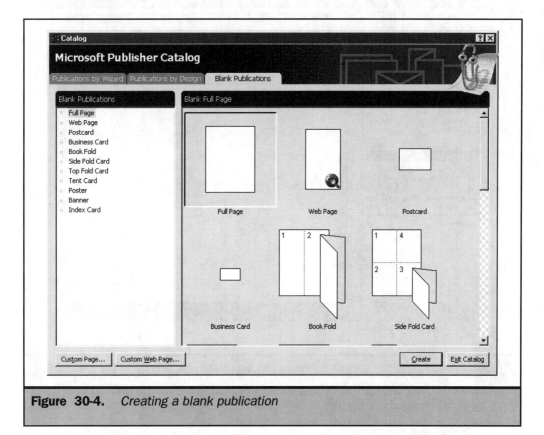

Figure 30-4.   *Creating a blank publication*

PUBLISHER

2. Select the type of publication you want to create by clicking a picture in the list on the right.

3. Click Create. Publisher creates the publication and displays the Quick Page Wizard (shown in Figure 30-5), which you can use to easily add elements to your publication.

Creating a Custom Publication

To create a custom publication on a special size of paper or envelope, or to specify a special fold, you can create a custom publication. To create a custom publication, follow these steps:

1. Click the Blank Publications tab of the Microsoft Publisher Catalog.

2. Click the Custom Page button. Publisher displays the Page Setup dialog box shown in Figure 30-6.

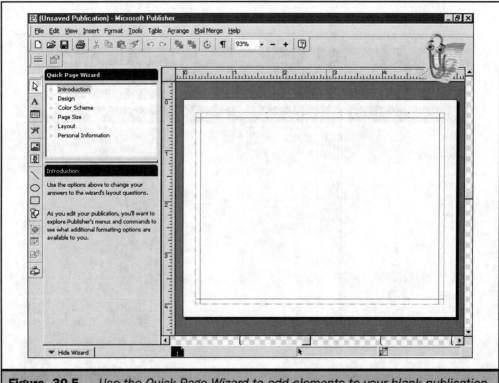

Figure 30-5. *Use the Quick Page Wizard to add elements to your blank publication*

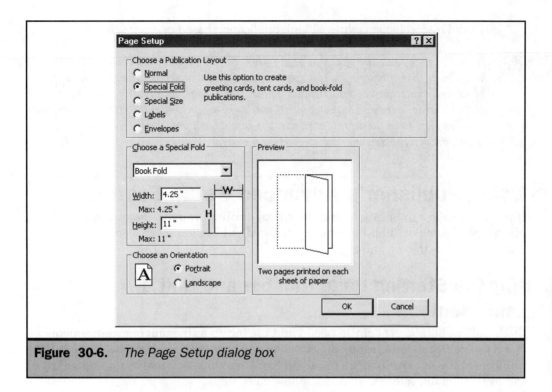

Figure 30-6.   *The Page Setup dialog box*

3. In the Choose A Publication Layout section, click a button to tell Publisher what you want to customize.

4. Use the boxes and buttons for the layout option you chose to specify the custom settings:

   ■ For Normal layout, select the page orientation.

   ■ For Special Fold, select how the publication should fold, the dimensions of the paper, and the orientation of the page.

   ■ For Special Size, enter the dimensions of the paper and select the page orientation.

   ■ For Labels, select the label style number.

   ■ For Envelopes, select a standard envelope size or enter custom envelope dimensions.

5. Click OK. Publisher creates a blank publication based on your settings.

To change the page setup after you've already created a publication, choose File | Page Setup. Note that although you can use the Page Setup dialog box to change the page layout and dimensions of a publication you created using a wizard, it's usually not advisable to do so unless the adjustments you make are only slight. Publisher's templates were designed to fit the default page size and layout, so if you change the page size or layout, the designs may not look as good on the page.

Using Publisher's Advanced Setup Features

If you're creating a publication for professional printing, you may want to take advantage of some of Publisher's more advanced publication setup features. This section describes these features.

Setting the Starting Page Number and Unit of Measurement

By default, publications begin on page 1 and use inches as the unit of measurement. But if you're creating, for instance, an issue of a journal that uses consecutive page numbers or if you're printing on paper cut to metric units, you may want to change Publisher's default settings. To do so, follow these steps:

1. Choose Tools | Options to display the General tab of the Options dialog box, as shown in Figure 30-7.

2. Enter a starting page number in the Start Publication With Page text box.

3. Use the Measurement Units drop-down list box to change the unit of measurement.

A pica is a common unit of measurement in publishing. A pica equals 12 points, or approximately 1/6 inch. A point is another common unit of measurement in publishing. A point equals about 1/72 of an inch. Typographers often specify leading (the space between lines of text) in points.

Setting the Hyphenation Zone

Publisher offers two ways to hyphenate text in text frames: manually and automatically. Usually, you want to use Publisher's automatic hyphenation because it means less work for you. To set the hyphenation zone, which tells Publisher how often it can hyphenate, follow these steps:

1. Choose Tools | Options.

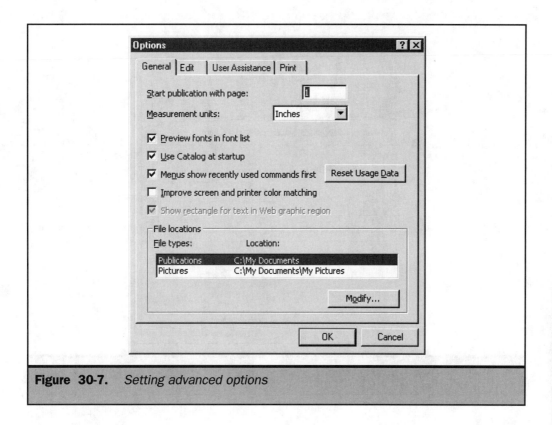

Figure 30-7.   *Setting advanced options*

2. Click the Edit tab, shown in Figure 30-8.

3. Enter a value in the Hyphenation Zone box. If you increase the value, Publisher hyphenates fewer words, but you have more white space between words. If you decrease the value, Publisher hyphenates more words and you have less white space between the words.

Creating Layout Guides

You use Publisher's Layout Guides to help position objects on the page. You can tell Publisher that you want objects to snap to the guides so that you can be sure they are in

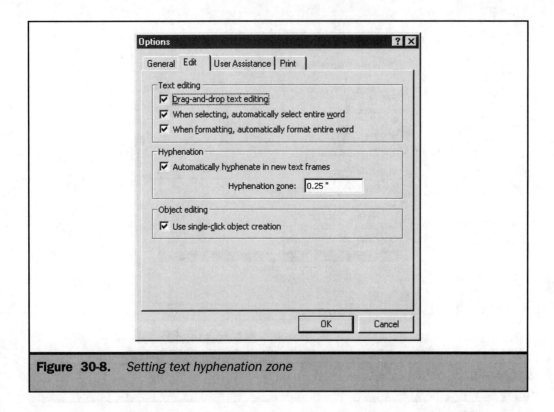

Figure 30-8. *Setting text hyphenation zone*

line. You also use Publisher's layout guides to specify margins. To set layout guides for a publication, follow these steps:

1. Choose Arrange | Layout Guides to display the Layout Guides dialog box shown in Figure 30-9.

2. Use the Margin Guides options to set the left, right, top, and bottom margins.

3. Use the Grid Guides options to specify the number of column and row guides.

Note   *Publisher unfortunately only allows equally spaced grid guides. So if you want a vertical guide, say, 1/6 of the way across the page, you need to create six columns, even though you won't use the other column guides.*

4. Click OK.

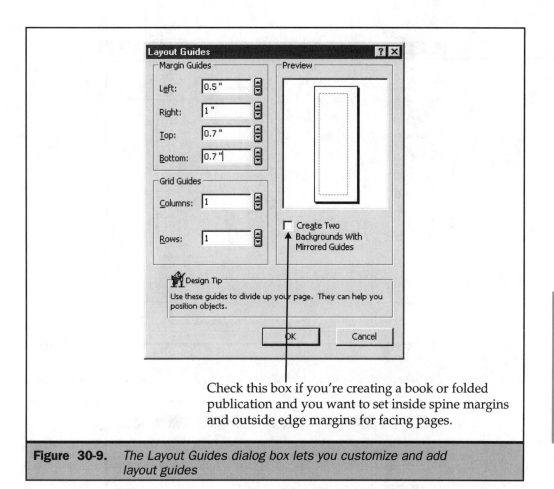

Check this box if you're creating a book or folded publication and you want to set inside spine margins and outside edge margins for facing pages.

Figure 30-9.   *The Layout Guides dialog box lets you customize and add layout guides*

Creating a Custom Color Scheme

Publisher's wizards allow you to select a color scheme for your publication. But if your company or organization has its own colors, you can also create a custom color scheme and save it for use in all of your publications. To create a custom color scheme, follow these steps:

1. Choose Format | Color Scheme and click the Custom tab, shown in Figure 30-10.

2. Use the New drop-down list boxes to select the colors of the color scheme. You can select a different basic color by clicking it or you can click the More Colors button to specify a custom color. If you click More Colors, Publisher displays the Colors dialog box shown in Figure 30-11.

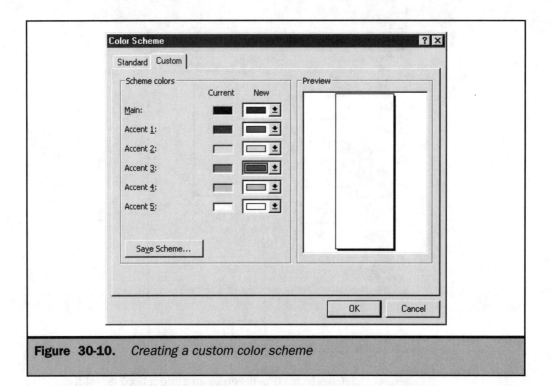

Figure 30-10. *Creating a custom color scheme*

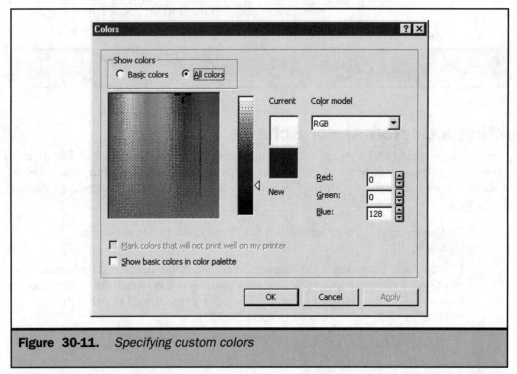

Figure 30-11. *Specifying custom colors*

You probably want to select the darkest color in your scheme in the first drop-down list box and then go down the colors in the scheme to the lightest color, as shown in Figure 30-11.

3. Click the All Colors option button.

4. Select a color system from the Color Model drop-down list box.

5. Use the options Publisher provides to specify your color in that system:

   ■ For RGB colors, enter red, green, and blue values.

   ■ For CMYK colors, enter cyan, magenta, yellow, and black values.

   ■ For Pantone colors, Publisher displays the Pantone dialog box, which you can use to select a solid or process Pantone spot color.

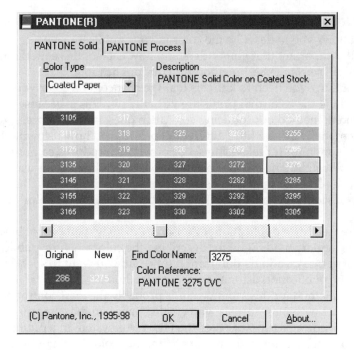

   ■ For HSL colors, enter hue, saturation, and luminance values.

6. Repeat the steps for each color in your color scheme.

7. When you're finished selecting the colors in your scheme, click OK to return to the Color Scheme dialog box.

8. Click Save Scheme to save your custom scheme.

9. Enter a name for the new scheme in the Save Scheme dialog box and click OK. This includes your custom scheme on the color scheme list so that you can select it in future publications.

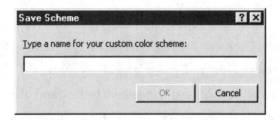

About Color Systems

Publisher allows you to describe the color in your publications using a variety of methods. It's important that you understand how each of these methods works to so that you can select the best method for your publication.

The first thing you need to know is that the chances of a color you see on your screen matching the color that prints are virtually nil. This is because your monitor uses a different method of producing color than does a printing press. Along with that, every monitor looks a little different depending on how its owner has adjusted it. A monitor (or television set or projector) produces color by adding red, green, and blue light. The ink that prints on paper produces color using a completely different method: by absorbing (or subtracting) light. This means that the color you see when you look at ink on paper is the leftover color that the ink reflects.

If you're creating a publication for onscreen display, you probably want to use the additive light method, RGB, for describing the colors in your publication. However, if you're creating a publication for print, you want to specify the colors you use in the publication using the printer's method.

The HLS method for describing color is probably the least common method. But it's popular with many artists who create images on the computer. This means that if you include a picture that uses the HLS color system in a publication and you want to match a color in the picture to another color in the publication, you probably want to use the HLS color system for the publication to make sure that the colors match.

You have two options when it comes to describing the ink used in printing a publication: You can use spot colors or you can use process colors. A spot color is a solid swatch of premixed ink. If your publication only includes a couple of colors, you probably want to use a spot color because it's cheaper. This means that you use the Pantone color system. Selecting a spot color is like buying paint based on a swatch at the paint store. The paint store employee mixes the colors of paint according to the formula, and you can be almost sure to get the same color if you go back for more paint of the same swatch number (although some inconsistencies between batches of paint can't be completely avoided). If your publication includes several colors (as would be the case for color photographs), you probably want to use process colors because it will be cheaper. Using process colors is sort of like going to the paint store and buying a box of the primary colors and mixing them to paint a picture with hundreds of different colors and shades of color. When professional printers use process colors, they add four colors to the paper individually: cyan (a blue-green color) magenta (a red-pink color), yellow, and black. The ink isn't actually mixed: The different colored dots on the page are combined by your eye to look like a solid color.

Chapter 31

Adding Content to a Publication

The previous chapter described how to create and set up a publication. This chapter first familiarizes you with the look and features of Publisher, and then describes how to add and work with the substance of a publication: text, pictures, and so on. Lastly, this chapter describes how to add and delete pages in a publication and how to check your publication for possible errors.

An Introduction to the Publisher Working Environment

Publisher looks and feels different from the other Office programs, so it takes a little getting used to before you can become efficient in Publisher and exploit its tools. This section describes the basics of how Publisher works and how to move around a publication. Figure 31-1 shows details the parts of the Publisher program window.

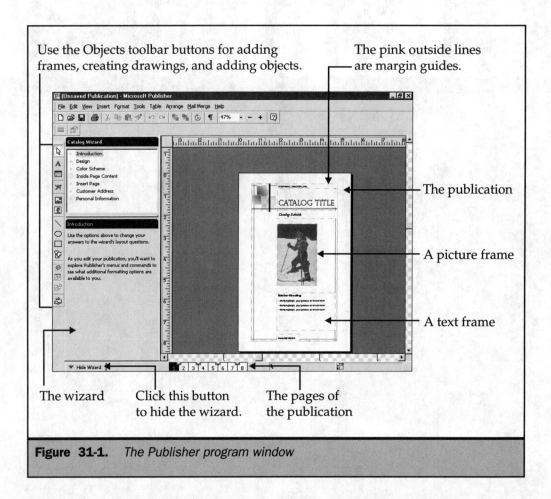

Figure 31-1.   *The Publisher program window*

Zooming

As you're ready to begin adding content to a publication, you'll probably notice right off the bat that it's hard to see what you're doing at the publication's default magnification level. Figure 31-2a shows a publication in Whole Page view. This page is sized at 75%. Here are some tips for zooming in and out on a publication:

■ Use the Zoom toolbar button to select a magnification percentage or use the Zoom In and Zoom Out toolbar buttons to zoom in or out incrementally.

■ Press the F9 key to view the publication at its actual size (100%), as shown in Figure 31-2b. Press F9 again to go back to the previous magnification level.

■ To zoom in on an object in a page, right-click the object and choose the shortcut menu's Selected Object command.

Using Frames

You work with all of the various types of content in Publisher using frames. Frames are like little boxes that, as their name implies, frame the content. If you used a wizard to create your publication, Publisher provides you with several frames to start from. You can replace the content in these frames with your own content. You can also add your own frames. Later chapter sections talk about adding framings, adding content to frames, and customizing frame settings. This section describes some basic frame tasks common among all types of frames.

Moving Frames

To move a frame, select the frame by clicking it. Then rest the mouse pointer over an edge of the frame until it becomes the Move pointer with a little moving truck icon. Then drag the frame to a new location.

Resizing Frames

To resize a frame, select the frame by clicking it. Then rest the mouse pointer over one of the frame's corner or side handles until the mouse pointer becomes the Resize pointer with the double arrows. Drag the side or corner of the frame inward or outward to make the frame larger or smaller.

Deleting Frames

To delete a frame and all of its contents, right-click the frame and choose the shortcut menu's Delete Object command.

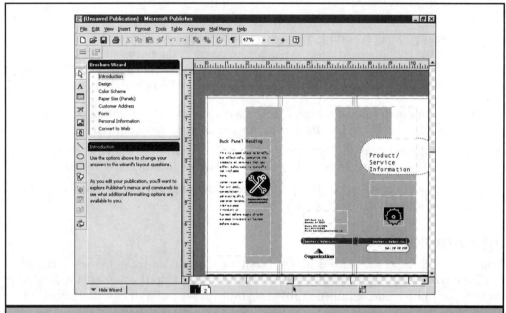

Figure 31-2a. *A publication at Whole Page view*

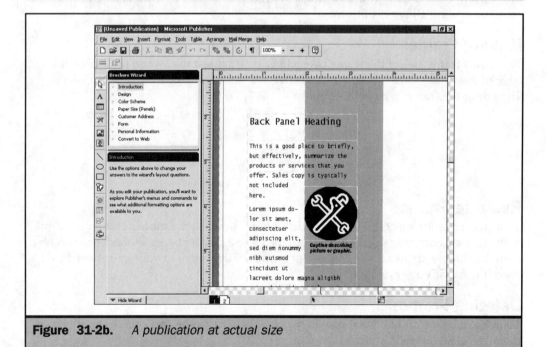

Figure 31-2b. *A publication at actual size*

Adding Background Color and Borders to Frames

To add a background color to a frame, select the frame by clicking it and click the Fill Color toolbar button. Use the color options from the pop-up menu to select a fill color. To add a border to a frame, select the frame and click the Border Style toolbar button. Use the border options from the pop-up menu to select a border for the frame.

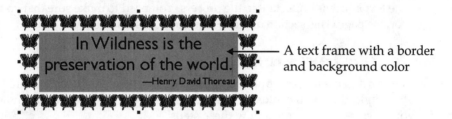

A text frame with a border and background color

Grouping and Ungrouping Frames

Some of the placeholder frames that Publisher adds to the publication are actually multiple frames grouped together. For example, what looks like a single picture frame might actually include a picture frame and a text frame for the picture's caption. To work with the picture and text components individually (for example, if you want to rotate or resize the picture but not the text), you need to first ungroup the frame elements. You can tell when multiple elements are grouped because when you select the frame, Publisher displays colored boxes around the individual elements in the group and the Ungroup Objects button at the bottom of the frame. (This button looks like two interlocked puzzle pieces.) To ungroup the frame components, select the frame and click the Ungroup Objects button.

 To group frames that you want to move or work with together, select the first frame, hold down the CTRL key and select the other frame(s), and then click the Group Objects button.

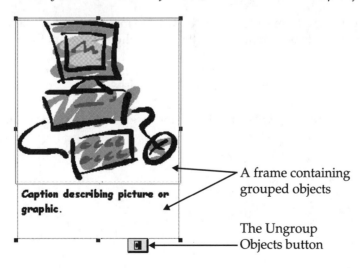

A frame containing grouped objects

The Ungroup Objects button

Adding Textual Content

While a good design can make or break the success of a publication, it's the text that carries the message, so it's the text that's the most important piece in any publication. Therefore, when creating a publication, you'll probably want to spend a sufficient amount of time composing and polishing your text. But your work with the text shouldn't end there. Laying out the text is just as important in the process. You need to make sure that your text reads easily on the page. This section describes how to do just that.

Inserting Text in Text Frames

If you use a wizard to create your publication, Publisher adds a handful or more text frames in the publication. You can use these text frames by replacing the placeholder text with your own text. To do so, follow these steps:

1. Select a text frame by clicking it. This selects the text frame's text if it's a placeholder text frame.

2. Type your own text. If the text runs too long, Publisher adjusts the font size and sometimes also the leading so that the entire text fits in one frame. You can tell Publisher to stop doing this (for example if you want the text to continue into another frame) by choosing Format | AutoFit and then choosing None.

Inserting Text Files in Text Frames

If you've already composed the text you want to include in a publication using another program (such as Word), you can insert this text into Publisher's text frames as well. As a matter of fact, Publisher has a pretty slick way of flowing text into multiple text frames and even creating frames for text that doesn't fit. To insert a text file into a publication, follow these steps:

1. Select the text frame into which you want to insert the text. If you want the text to go in multiple text frames, select the frame where you want the text file to begin.

Note *If you don't want Publisher to try to fit all of the text in one frame, you need to make sure you turn off the AutoFit options for the frame first.*

2. Choose Insert | Text File to display the Insert Text dialog box, shown next.

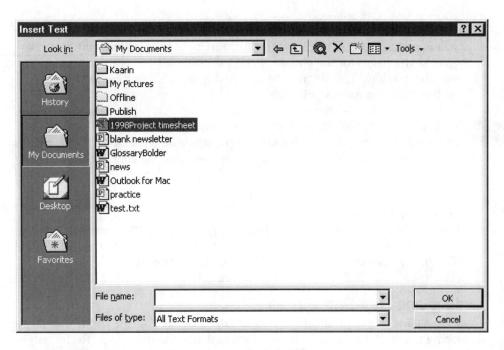

3. Select the file you want to insert and click OK.

Publisher can insert a wide range of files, including files created in various versions of Word, Works, and WordPerfect, as well as formatted and plain text files, and even Excel and Lotus 1-2-3 spreadsheets.

4. If the file contains more text than can fit in one frame, the Office Assistant asks you if you want to AutoFlow the text into other frames. If you've already created the other frames for the text, or if you want Publisher to create them on separate pages of the publication, go ahead and use AutoFlow. If you want to create custom-size text frames and connect the frames manually yourself (as described later in the chapter), don't use AutoFlow.

5. If you choose to use AutoFlow and have empty frames, the Office Assistant selects an empty frame and asks if you want to continue text into that frame. Click Yes to flow the text into that frame or click No to have Publisher select a different frame.

6. If Publisher runs out of empty frames for your text, the Office Assistant asks if you want to AutoCreate frames for the remaining text. If you want Publisher to create extra pages for the remaining text, click Yes. If you want to work the text into the existing pages (by resizing the text frames, formatting the text, or adding new text frames), click No.

If you decide not to flow the overflow text into existing or new frames, Publisher does not get rid of the overflow text. Instead, it alerts you to the fact that the frame contains more text than it can show by displaying a small box with the letter A and an ellipses (…) at the bottom of the frame.

LEARN BY EXAMPLE
To see how AutoFlow and AutoCreate work, open the Figure 30-A (inserting text files) publication file on the companion CD and flow the Word document in the Figure 30-A (Text file for insertion) file into the publication's first text frame.

Adding and Deleting Pages

To delete a page from a publication, choose Edit | Delete Page. If you're displaying two facing pages, Publisher asks if you want to delete the right page, the left page, or both.

To add pages to a publication, display the page after which you want to insert a new page. Then choose Insert | Page to display the Insert Pages dialog box. Use this dialog box to specify the style of the page or pages you want to add.

Click this button to specify how many pages you want to insert and whether you want them to come before or after the page you're currently displaying. ──▶

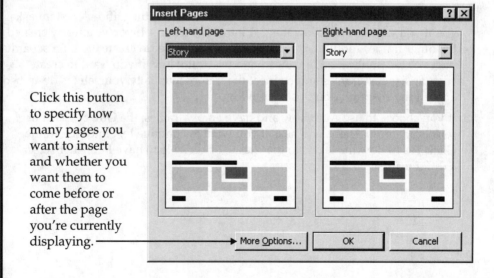

Creating New Text Frames

If you want to add text where there is no text frame in the template, or if you created a blank publication, you need to create a text frame before you can insert text. To create a text frame, follow these steps:

1. Click the Text Frame Tool button on the Objects toolbar.

2. Drag diagonally from where you want one corner of the frame to go to where you want the other corner of the frame. Figure 31-3 shows what a new empty text frame looks like.

3. Begin typing to add text to the frame.

Tip   *You can create individual text frames for personal information items by choosing Insert | Personal Information and then choosing the item you want to insert from the submenu.*

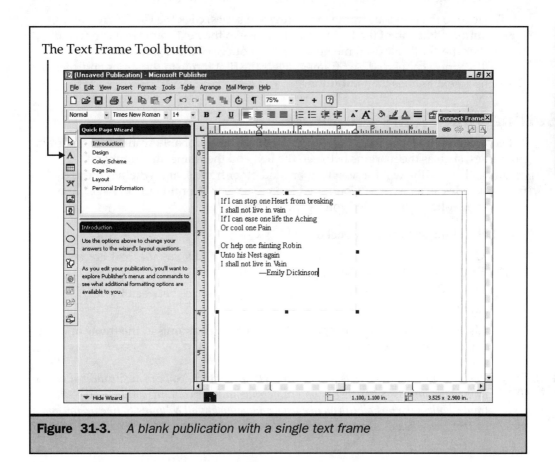

Figure 31-3.   *A blank publication with a single text frame*

Working with Connected Frames

In publications such as newsletters, it's common to have text begin on one page or column and continue on another page or column. Publisher makes this process of connecting pieces of a story together easy. This section describes how to connect and disconnect text frames and how to move between connected frames as you edit a story.

To connect text frames, follow these steps:

1. If necessary, create a new frame into which you want the text to continue.

2. Select the frame containing the text you want to flow into a second frame.

3. Click the Connect Text Frames button on the Connect Frames toolbar. (If you can't see this toolbar, choose View | Toolbars | Text Frame Connecting.) The mouse pointer turns into an icon of a little pitcher.

4. Click the empty text frame into which you want to flow the extra text. Publisher flows the remaining text into this frame, as shown in Figure 31-4.

To move to the previous frame in a connected series, click the Go To Previous Frame button at the top of the text frame. To move to the next frame in a connected series, click the Go To Next Frame button at the bottom of the text frame.

To disconnect connected text frames, select the first frame in the series and click the Disconnect Text Frames toolbar button.

Setting Text Frame Properties

After you create and insert text in your text frames, you probably want to set text frame properties, such as the margins between the text and the frame, the number of columns, the way the text frame wraps around other frames, and whether the text frame includes an area for a "Continued From Page" or "Continued On Page" line.

To set text frame properties, follow these steps:

1. Select the text frame by clicking it.

2. Click the Text Frame Properties toolbar button to display the Text Frame Properties dialog box shown in Figure 31-5.

3. Use the Margins boxes to specify the amount of space between the text and the frame.

4. Use the Columns boxes to specify the number of columns in the frame and the space between the columns.

Note *Publisher provides two ways for creating columns of text: You can create individual text frames and link them together or you can create multiple columns within a single text frame. Unless the text all fits on one page and you want all columns to line up top and bottom, you'll want to use the former option.*

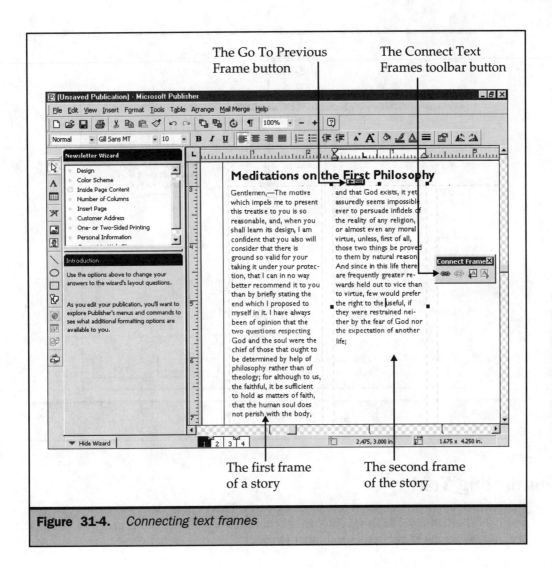

Figure 31-4. *Connecting text frames*

5. Use the Options check boxes to specify whether you want the text in the frame to go around any overlapping objects (such as picture frames) and whether you want the frame to include a line alerting readers that the frame is connected to another frame on a different page.

6. Click OK.

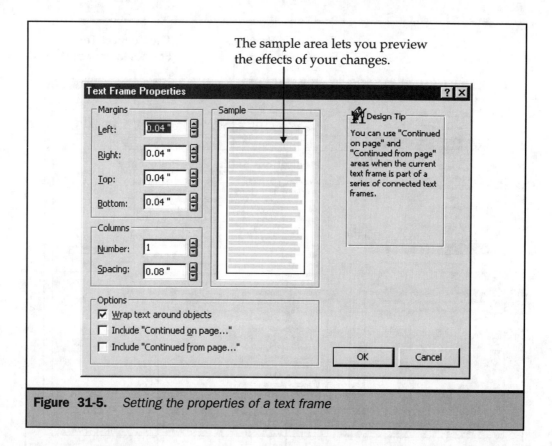

Figure 31-5.   *Setting the properties of a text frame*

Formatting Text

Publisher allows you to format text in many ways. This section describes how you can use Publisher's text styles, how you can set character and line spacing, and how each of the buttons on the Measurements toolbar works.

Formatting fonts, creating lists, and specifying indentation works in much the same way as it does in Word. The dialog boxes you use to specify these features look a little different from those in Word, but the options are almost the same.

Using Styles

As with the other Office programs, you can use the Style button on the toolbar to apply styles. This section describes how you create, change, rename, delete, and import styles.

To work with text styles, choose Format | Text Style. This displays the Text Style dialog box shown in Figure 31-6.

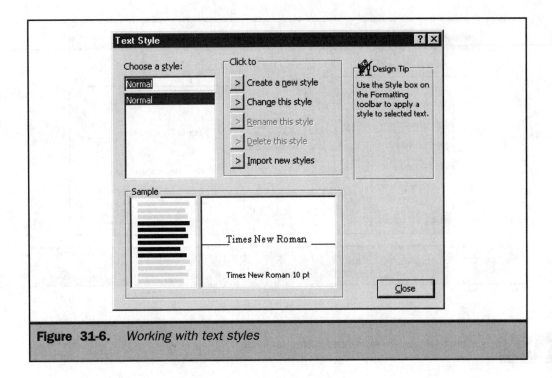

Figure 31-6. *Working with text styles*

To create a new style, follow these steps:

1. Click the Create A New Style button. This displays the Create New Style dialog box shown in Figure 31-7.

2. Enter a name for the style in the Enter New Style Name text box.

3. Click the Character Type And Size button to display the Font dialog box, which you can use to select the font, font size, text color, and such formatting options as bold, italic, and underline.

4. Click the Indents And Lists button to display the Indents And Lists dialog box, which you can use to select bulleted and numbered list options, as well as indentation and alignment options.

5. Click the Line Spacing button to display the Line Spacing dialog box, which you can use to specify the spacing between lines in a paragraph and before and after paragraphs.

Tip *Click the Show Toolbar button in the Line Spacing dialog box to display the Measurements toolbar in Publisher. Later in this chapter, "Using the Measurements Toolbar" describes the toolbar's tools and how they work.*

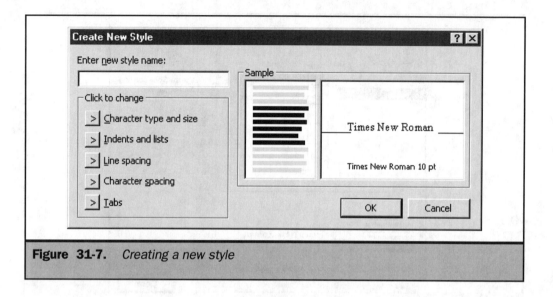

Figure 31-7. *Creating a new style*

Note   *The next section describes line spacing in detail.*

6. Click the Character Spacing button to display the Character Spacing dialog box, which you can use to shrink or stretch the font and to specify tracking (the space between letters in a block of text) and kerning (the space between a pair of letters).

Note   *The next section describes character spacing in detail.*

7. Click the Tabs button to display the Tabs dialog box, which you can use to set tab stops and the alignment and leader of each stop.

To change an existing style, select the style you want to change from the list and click the Change This Style button. Publisher displays the Change Style dialog box, which works just like the Create New Style dialog box.

To delete a style, select the style and click Delete this Style. When the Office Assistant asks you to confirm the deletion, click Yes.

To import styles from an existing document or publication, click the Import New Styles button. Publisher displays the Import Styles dialog box. Use the dialog box to select the file containing the styles you want to import and click OK.

If a style you import contains a font that you don't have on your computer, Publisher replaces the style's font with a font it does have. To avoid the extra work of replacing fonts in all of the imported text, make sure you first install the fonts you need before importing styles.

Setting Character and Line Spacing

To specify the character spacing in a block of text, follow these steps:

1. Select the text you want to adjust. To adjust scaling or tracking, select a block of text. To adjust kerning, select the pair of adjoining characters.

2. Choose Format | Character Spacing. This displays the Character Spacing dialog box shown in Figure 31-8.

3. Use the Scaling options to shrink or stretch the font. Note that this stretches the letters themselves but has no effect on the spacing between the letters.

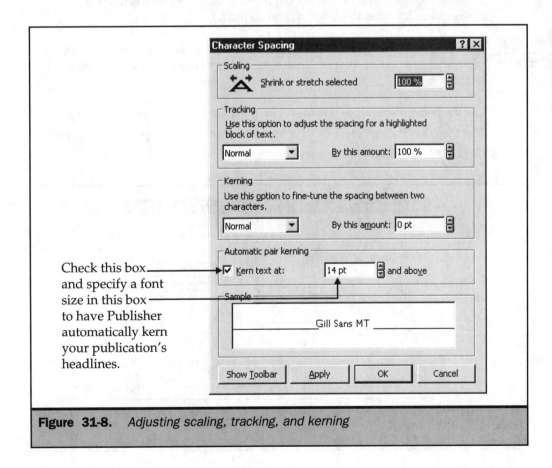

Figure 31-8.   *Adjusting scaling, tracking, and kerning*

4. Use the Tracking options to set spacing between characters in a block of text.

5. Use the Kerning options to set spacing between two letters. You use kerning because different letters have different shapes and therefore some combinations of letters appear closer together than other pairs of letters in the surrounding text.

6. Click OK.

Because you typically use kerning on a letter-pair basis, kerning is most often used only for highly visible text such as headlines.

To specify line spacing (also referred to as *leading*), follow these steps:

1. Select the text you want to format and choose Format | Line Spacing. This displays the Line Spacing dialog box shown in Figure 31-9.

2. Use the Between Lines box to specify spacing between lines in a paragraph. (The "sp" spacing unit stands for the number of spaces between the line: 1 is single-spaced, 2 is double-spaced, and so forth.)

Note

When you increase leading to 1.25 spaces, Publisher adds the extra space to the top and bottom of the line of text. Beyond 1.25 spaces, Publisher adds the additional space below the text.

3. Use the Before Paragraphs box to specify the space before the paragraph in points.

4. Use the After Paragraphs box to specify the space after the paragraph in points.

5. Click OK.

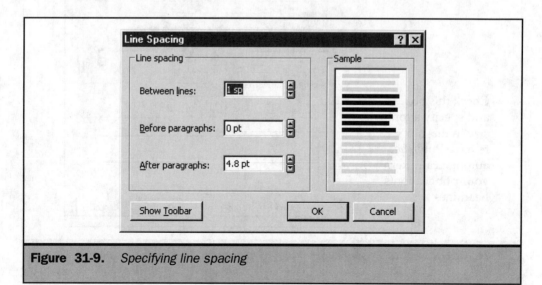

Figure 31-9. *Specifying line spacing*

Using Drop Caps

Like Word, Publisher has a Drop Cap feature you can use to emphasize the first letter in a story. A drop cap increases the size of the first letter of text and often changes the font or allows the letter to hang down into the next lines of the story. To use Publisher's Drop Cap feature, follow these steps:

1. Select the letter you want to turn into a drop cap.

2. Choose Format | Drop Cap. This displays the Drop Cap dialog box shown in Figure 31-10.

3. Select a drop cap style from the list box.

4. Click OK to convert the letter to a drop cap or click the Custom Drop Cap tab to customize the drop cap style you chose.

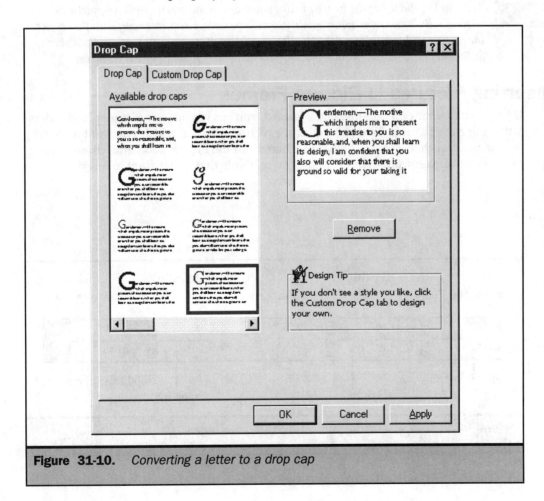

Figure 31-10.   *Converting a letter to a drop cap*

PUBLISHER

Using the Measurements Toolbar

Publisher comes with a handy toolbar that you can display as you work with text formatting. To display the Measurements toolbar, choose View | Toolbars | Measurements. Figure 31-11 shows the Measurements toolbar, and Table 31-1 describes what each Measurements toolbar button does.

Adding Pictures

The first section of this chapter described the ways you can work with text and text frames. This section describes how to work with pictures and the various types of picture frames.

You can tell Publisher the image quality you want to use when displaying pictures onscreen. By choosing a higher quality, you have a more accurate representation of how the picture will print. If you choose a lower quality, it makes your work in Publisher faster because your publication places fewer demands on your system resources.

Inserting Pictures in Picture Frames

If you created your publication using a wizard, you can replace any picture placeholders with your own pictures. To do so, select the picture frame in which you want to insert the picture and choose Insert | Picture. Then, from the Picture submenu, choose the type of picture you want to insert in the frame. (Note that if you want to insert a

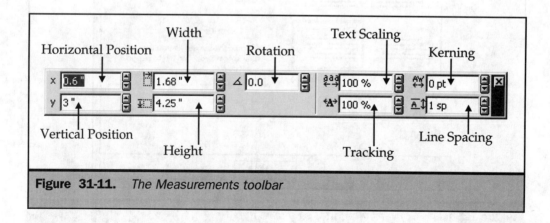

Figure 31-11. *The Measurements toolbar*

Button	Description
Horizontal Position	Describes the distance from the left edge of the publication to the left side of the text frame. Enter a different value to position the text frame horizontally.
Vertical Position	Describes the distance from the top edge of the publication to the top side of the text frame. Enter a different value to position the text frame vertically.
Width	Describes the width of the text frame. Enter a different value to resize the text frame width.
Height	Describes the height of the text frame. Enter a different value to resize the text frame height.
Rotation	Describes the text frame's angle of rotation. Enter a different value to rotate the text frame counterclockwise that number of degrees.
Text Scaling	Describes the text stretch percentage. Select a block of text and enter a value larger than 100 to stretch the text or smaller than 100 to shrink the text.
Tracking	Describes the spacing between text. Select a block of text and enter a value larger than 100 to make the text looser or smaller than 100 to make the text tighter.
Kerning	Describes the spacing between two characters. Enter a value larger than 0 to spread the characters apart.
Line Spacing	Describes the spacing (leading) between two lines of text. Enter a value larger than 1 to increase the line spacing.

Table 31-1.   *The Measurements Toolbar Buttons*

PUBLISHER

picture in an area of the publication that has no picture frame, you first need to create a picture frame, as described in the next section.)

- Choose Clip Art to display the Insert Clip Art window and select a clip art image to insert.

- Choose From File to display the Insert Picture dialog box and select an existing image file you have.

- Choose From Scanner or Camera and then choose Select Device to display the Select Source dialog box. Use this dialog box to select the hardware device on your computer that you want to use for acquiring the image. Choose the Acquire Image command to display a window for capturing or scanning an image.

- Choose New Drawing to display the AutoShapes and Drawing toolbars, which you can use to draw your image.

Creating New Picture Frames

To create a new picture frame in a publication, click the Picture Frame Tool button on the Objects toolbar. Then drag in the publication to create a rectangle where you want the picture frame to go, as shown in Figure 31-12.

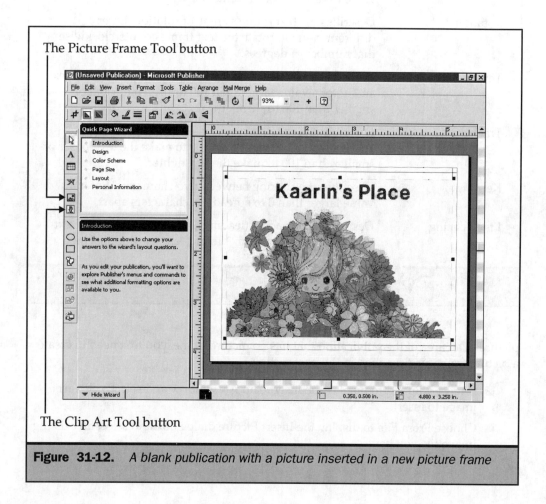

Figure 31-12.   *A blank publication with a picture inserted in a new picture frame*

Tip   *To create a picture frame in which you want to insert clip art, click the Clip Art Tool button on the Objects toolbar. After you drag to create the picture frame, Publisher automatically displays the Insert Clip Art window, so you can select the clip art image you want to insert. If you later decide to insert a different kind of image, you can select the frame and insert a different kind of image following the steps described in the previous section.*

Note   *For more information about working with clip art, see Chapter 3.*

Setting Picture Frame Properties

To set picture frame properties, follow these steps:

1. Click the picture frame to select it.

2. Click the Picture Frame Properties toolbar button. This displays the Picture Frame Properties dialog box shown in Figure 31-13.

3. Choose a Wrap Text Around option to specify how close you want text to run against a non-rectangular picture. Which option you choose only makes a difference if the picture is an odd shape and doesn't take up all corners of the frame. This is often the case with clip art, for example, but it's not as common with photographs, scanned images, and many image file types.

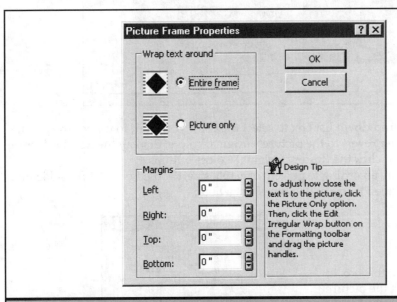

Figure 31-13.   *Setting properties of a picture frame*

4. If you chose to wrap the text around the entire frame, use the Left, Right, Top, and Bottom Margins options to specify the distance between the sides of the picture and the picture frame. If you chose to wrap the text around the picture, use the Outside Margin option to specify the distance between the picture and the text.

Note   *If you increase the margins, the frame stays the same size and the picture decreases in size.*

5. Click OK.

Recoloring and Scaling Pictures

If you want to use a color picture in a black and white publication, it makes sense to transform the picture to grayscale so that you can better see how it will look when printed. Or if you want to print a picture using percentages of a spot color, it also makes sense to recolor the picture. To recolor a picture, select the picture and choose Format | Recolor Picture. This displays the Recolor Picture dialog box shown here:

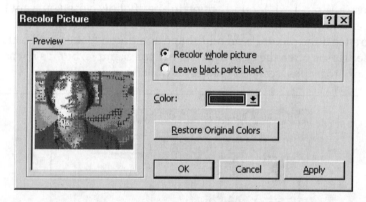

Use the Color drop-down list box to select the color you want to use for the picture and click OK. To later revert to the picture's original colors, display the Recolor Picture dialog box again and click the Restore Original Colors button.

To resize a picture according to percent of actual size, choose Format | Scale Picture. This displays the Scale Picture dialog box shown here:

Check this box to revert the picture to actual size.————

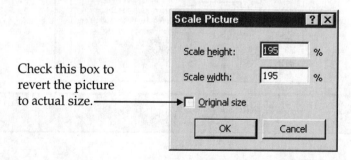

Enter values in the Scale Height and Scale Width boxes for the percent of actual size. To scale the picture proportionally, enter the same value in both boxes.

Adding Other Objects

In addition to letting you add and work with regular text and picture frames, Publisher lets you add a variety of special text and graphic objects to your publications. This section describes how to add and work with Publisher's predesigned elements, WordArt, and tables.

Working with the Design Gallery

Publisher comes with a large collection of predesigned common publication elements. Instead of creating these elements yourself, you can simply insert them and then edit them as necessary. To work with Publisher's Design Gallery, click the Design Gallery Object button on the Objects toolbar. Publisher displays the Design Gallery dialog box shown in Figure 31-14.

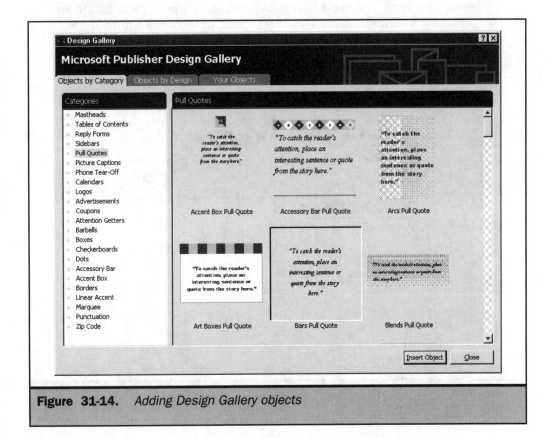

Figure 31-14.   *Adding Design Gallery objects*

Use the Objects By Category tab to select an Object category from the Categories list. Then click the picture of the design you want to use from the list on the right and click Insert Object. Alternatively, to browse objects by design, click the Objects By Design tab and select a design from the Design Sets list. Then click the picture of the object you want to insert and click Insert Object.

 If you spend a long time working on an object (such as a logo) that you want to add to the Design Gallery for future use, select the object you created and click the Your Objects tab of the Design Gallery window. Then click the Options button to display the Add Object dialog box. Enter a name for the object, choose an object category from the Category drop-down list box, and click OK to add the object.

Adding WordArt

To add a WordArt element to a publication, follow these steps:

1. Click the WordArt Frame Tool button on the Objects toolbar.
2. Drag in the publication where you want to place the WordArt frame. Publisher displays the Enter Your Text Here dialog box and replaces the Standard and Formatting toolbars with the WordArt toolbar, as shown in Figure 31-15.

Figure 31-15. *Adding WordArt*

3. Enter the WordArt text in the Enter Your Text Here dialog box and click Update Display.

Tip *You can drag the Enter Your Text Here dialog box to another location if it covers the WordArt frame. You can also close the dialog box by clicking its Close button. If you close the dialog box and later want to change the WordArt text, you can redisplay the dialog box by double-clicking the WordArt frame.*

4. Use the WordArt toolbar's buttons (described in Table 31-2) to format the text.

5. When you're finished creating the WordArt and want to return to working with the publication's other objects, click anywhere in the publication outside a WordArt frame.

Button	Description
Shape	Changes the shape of the WordArt text.
Font	Changes the font.
Font Size	Increases or decreases the font size.
Bold	Boldfaces the WordArt text.
Italic	Italicizes the WordArt text.
Even Height	Makes all letters in the WordArt text the same height, even if some are capitalized and some are not, or some have tails (descenders) hanging below the baseline while others do not.
Flip	Flips the text 90 degrees to the left (counterclockwise).
Stretch	Stretches the text to fill up the width of the WordArt frame.
Alignment	Centers, left-aligns, or right-aligns the text in the WordArt frame.
Character Spacing	Adjusts the tracking of the WordArt text.
Special Effects	Specifies the degree of rotation, and the angle of arch or the slope.
Shading	Applies a background color and a color and pattern for the WordArt text.
Shadow	Applies a shadow effect to the WordArt text.
Line Thickness	Specifies the border thickness around the WordArt text.

Table 31-2.   *WordArt Toolbar Buttons*

PUBLISHER

Inserting Tables

To create tables in Publisher, you use table frames. Table frames are especially useful for aligning objects in web page publications.

To insert a table frame, click the Table Frame Tool button on the Objects toolbar. Then drag to create a frame in the publication where you want to place the table. Publisher displays the Create Table dialog box shown in Figure 31-16.

Use the Number Of Rows and Number Of Columns boxes to specify the number of rows and columns in the table. Select a table format from the Table Format list to specify the look of the table and the type of information it will hold. Click OK when you're done.

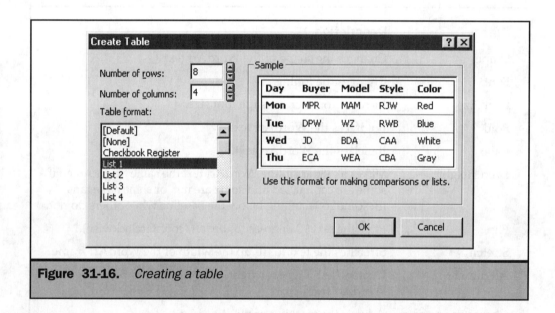

Figure 31-16. *Creating a table*

The
Complete
Reference

Chapter 32

Publishing

With Publisher, you have two options for printing your publication: You can print it yourself on your own printer, or you can take your publication files to a professional printer for printing. This chapter describes how to run a last-minute check for errors in the publication and how to prepare the publication for each printing method.

Checking Your Design

Before you print a publication, it's wise to check the publication for errors. You should make sure that you didn't accidentally create, move, or resize objects so that they overlap, spill into the margins, or otherwise just look funny. To check your publication for errors, choose Tools | Design Checker. This displays the Design Checker dialog box:

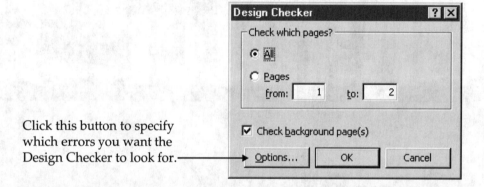

Click this button to specify which errors you want the Design Checker to look for.

Select the All option button to check all of your publication's pages and click OK.

If Publisher spots a potential problem in your publication, it alerts you to the problem and provides a suggested solution. You can choose to ignore the problem or to solve it.

Printing a Publication Yourself

It's easy to print a publication using your own printer. To do so, just choose File |
Print. This displays the Print dialog box shown in Figure 32-1. It bears a striking
resemblance to the Print dialog boxes discussed in Chapter 2.

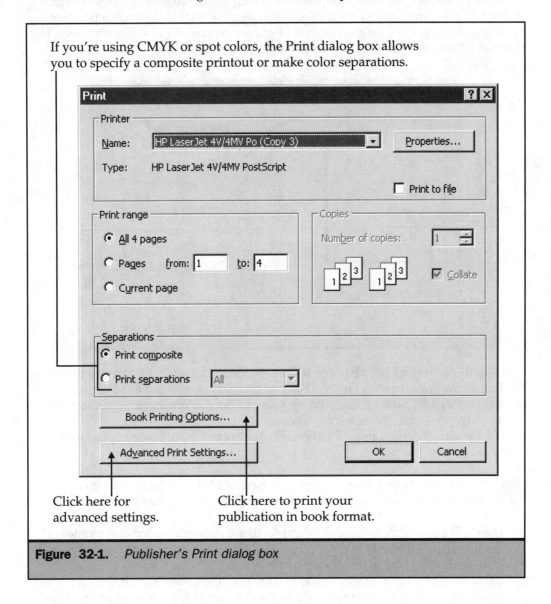

If you're using CMYK or spot colors, the Print dialog box allows
you to specify a composite printout or make color separations.

Click here for advanced settings.

Click here to print your publication in book format.

Figure 32-1. *Publisher's Print dialog box*

A composite printout is a single printout with all colors. Color separations are individual printouts for each spot color, or individual printouts of cyan, magenta, yellow, and black (CMYK) in a four-color publication.

Some publication types include a Book Printing Options button. Click this button to tell Publisher whether you want to print the pages of an 8½ × 11 book separately on 8½ × 11-inch paper or whether you want to print two pages on 11 × 17-inch paper. The following illustration shows the Book Printing Options Dialog box:

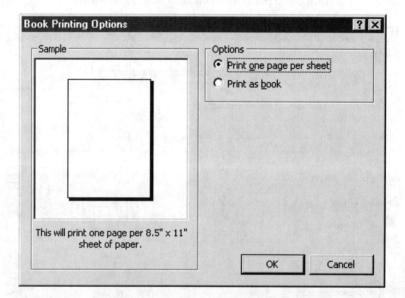

Click the Advanced Print Settings button shown in Figure 32-1 to display the Print Settings dialog box shown in Figure 32-2. You probably don't need to adjust any of the settings on this tab unless you're printing your publication on your own printer to be used as a reference for a commercial printer.

Use the Graphics options to tell Publisher not to print graphics or to print them at a lower resolution.

If you have a slower printer, and are printing only a rough draft of a publication, it usually makes sense to print low-resolution graphics to save yourself some time.

Use the Fonts options to tell Publisher whether it's acceptable for your printer to replace fonts that it doesn't have with those it does. Keep in mind that this can give you really unpredictable (and generally not good) results in the final version.

If you're using CMYK or spot colors and are printing a reference copy for a commercial printer, use the Printer's Marks check boxes to specify what you want to print. Most commercial printers like you to print all of the available printer's marks, but consult with your printer first.

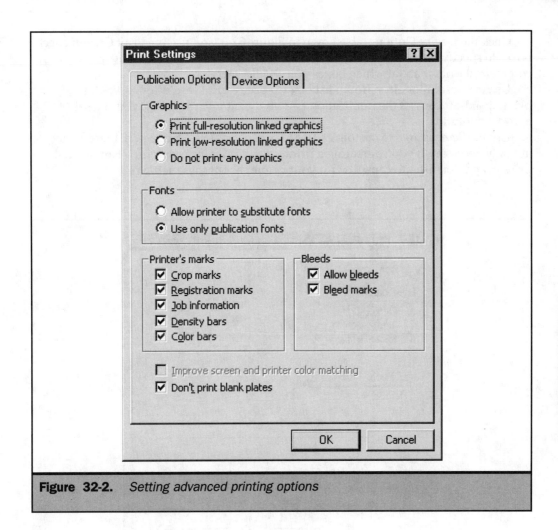

Figure 32-2. *Setting advanced printing options*

If you are not printing a reference copy for a commercial printer, you still may want to print crop marks if you plan on trimming the publication yourself.

Registration marks verify that elements align on a page, which is especially important in color separations. Density and color bars allow the printer to proof the colors and density.

Use the Bleeds options to tell Publisher whether or not ink can bleed off the edge of the pages past the crop marks. If you're printing a reference copy for a commercial printer, consult with your printer about bleeds. If you're printing a publication solely on your own printer, you can use bleeds if you plan on cropping the publication and want to make sure that you don't have any slivers of white between elements bumped up against the edge of the page.

Click the Device Options tab, shown in Figure 32-3, and use the Print Output check boxes to specify the image setter film your commercial printer uses. Consult with your commercial printer about which boxes you should check.

Use the Resolution drop-down list box to specify print resolution. If you're printing a draft copy of the publication and you want it to print fast, you can select a lower resolution.

Use the Screens area to customize CMYK or spot colors. Once again, these options are only necessary if you're creating a printout as a reference copy for a commercial printer, and you need to consult with your printer about these settings.

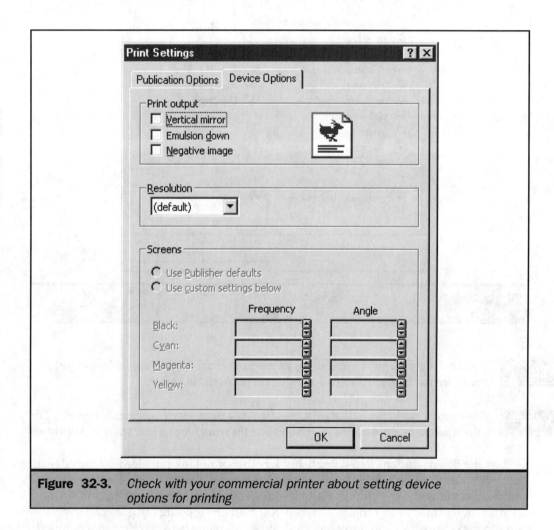

Figure 32-3. *Check with your commercial printer about setting device options for printing*

Using Publisher's Commercial Printing Tools

If you're going to take a publication to a printer for commercial printing, you need to prepare the publication according to the printer's press. Communication plays a key role in the commercial printing process. It's important to talk to your printer before you set any of these options. If your printer isn't familiar with the workings of Microsoft Publisher, you can capture the various commercial printing dialog boxes and show the printer your available options. To do so, display the dialog box and press CTRL-PRINT SCREEN. Then start a program such as Paint and press CTRL-V to paste the image of your screen. Use the program to save or print the image.

Colors

If you're printing a color publication, you need to specify the color system you're using and the colors in the publication. To do so, follow these steps:

1. Choose Tools | Commercial Printing Tools and then choose Color Printing to display the Color Printing dialog box:

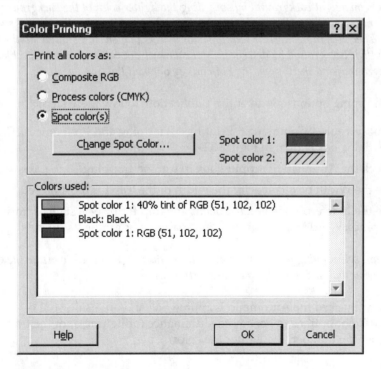

2. Select the option button that corresponds with the color system you want to use.

Note   *See the sidebar at the end of Chapter 30 for more information about color systems.*

3. If you're using spot colors, click Change Spot Color to display the Choose Spot Color dialog box, which you can use to select a different spot color.

4. Click OK.

Trapping

Trapping is specifying an intentional overlap when two colors of ink adjoin on a page. You need to trap colors when printing separations because printing presses aren't perfect, and when the paper shifts in the press, the misregistration can cause white lines between colors that don't quite meet and dark bands from colors that overlap.

Note   *Publisher uses the spread trapping technique for light objects on a dark background by spreading a band of the lighter color onto the dark background. This technique is called "spread" because it makes the object larger. Publisher uses the choke technique for dark objects on a light background by spreading the lighter color of the background onto the darker object. This technique is called "choke" because it makes the object smaller. Publisher uses the centerline technique for objects that share a similar luminance value with their background by determining the darkest ink values for both the object and the background, and then spreading both out by one-half the trap width.*

To set trapping options for an entire publication, follow these steps:

1. Choose Tools | Commercial Printing | Trapping and Preferences. This displays the dialog box shown in Figure 32-4.

2. Check the Automatic Trapping box to turn on trapping.

3. Use the Width box to specify the width of the trap for most objects.

4. Use the Indeterminate box to specify the trap for objects such as imported graphics, WordArt, and objects with patterns or gradients (blends).

Note   *Always set trapping for imported graphics in the program used to create the graphics. Publisher will maintain the trapping settings.*

5. If you checked the Automatic Trapping box and are using spot colors, use the Spot Color options to specify the luminance (or lightness) of the trap. The higher the number, the lighter the color.

Click this button to define when Publisher should trap.

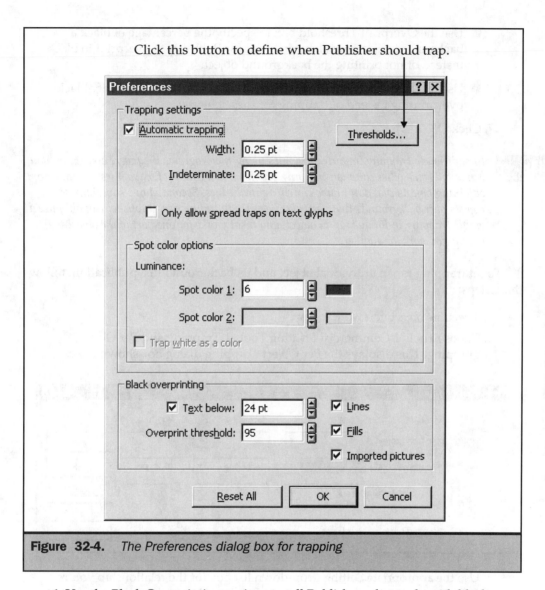

Figure 32-4.   *The Preferences dialog box for trapping*

6. Use the Black Overprinting options to tell Publisher what to do with black objects that overlap other objects.

■ Check the Text Below box to have Publisher overprint black text. Then use the text box to specify the font size at or above which Publisher does not print the background behind the text instead of overprinting the text on the background.

- Use the Overprint Threshold box to specify the percentage of black a background object must have in order for Publisher to overprint in black instead of not printing the background object.

- Use the Lines, Fills, and Imported Pictures check boxes to specify black overprinting instead of trapping for these objects.

7. Click OK.

In addition to trapping imported graphics using the programs they were created in, you can avoid some other common trapping problems in a couple of ways. First, refrain from adjoining objects that don't have clearly defined edges. Second, don't superimpose objects over backgrounds that vary significantly in luminance. Publisher can only use a single trapping technique for an object, and what works for one part of the object will surely not work for another.

To set trapping for an individual object and its background in a publication, follow these steps:

1. Select the object you want to trap.

2. Choose Tools | Commercial Printing Tools | Trapping and Per Object Trapping. This displays the Per Object Trapping dialog box shown next:

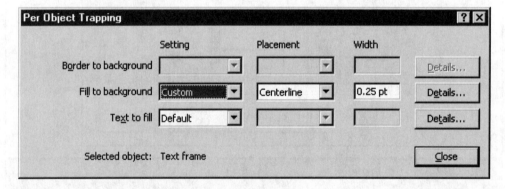

3. Use the appropriate Setting drop-down list box for the relationship you're trapping to specify whether you want Publisher to use default trapping settings, overprint the object, knockout the object (don't print it), or trap the object according to your custom settings.

4. If you choose Custom, use the Placement drop-down list box to choose centerline, choke, or spread trapping, then use the Width drop-down list box to specify the width of the trap.

5. Click Close.

Fonts

You can tell Publisher if and how to embed the fonts you use in a publication. By embedding the fonts, other people (including the printer) can open the publication on a different computer and still see the fonts correctly, even if they don't have the fonts you used installed on their computers. If you're worried about the size of your file (embedding fonts increases file size), you can embed the font information for only the characters you used in the publication. However, this could pose problems if someone needs to edit the publication and add a character you didn't use.

To set font embedding options, choose Tools | Commercial Printing Tools | Fonts. This displays the Fonts dialog box, shown in Figure 32-5.

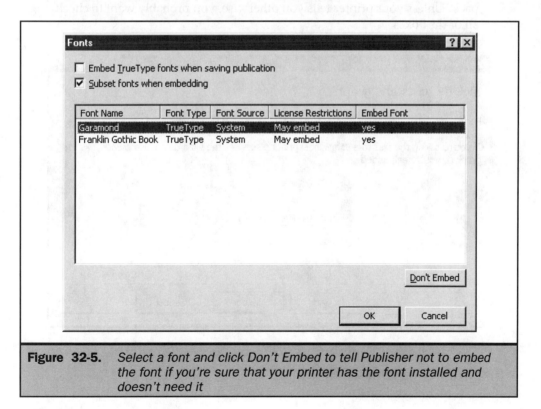

Figure 32-5.   *Select a font and click Don't Embed to tell Publisher not to embed the font if you're sure that your printer has the font installed and doesn't need it*

Using the Pack and Go Wizard

Publisher includes a Pack and Go Wizard that can pack all of the various files your publication uses into a neat little bundle, so that you can take the pack to a commercial printer or another computer. To run the Pack and Go Wizard, follow these steps:

1. Choose File | Pack and Go | Take to a Commercial Printing Service.

 The Pack and Go Wizard for taking your publication to another computer just includes a subset of the options available in the wizard for taking your publication to a commercial printing service.

2. Click Next to begin the wizard.

3. Select a location for storing the publication (probably a removable storage device) and click Next.

4. Check the boxes beside the graphics and fonts you want to include in the pack. Unless your printer tells you otherwise, you probably want to check all of the boxes.

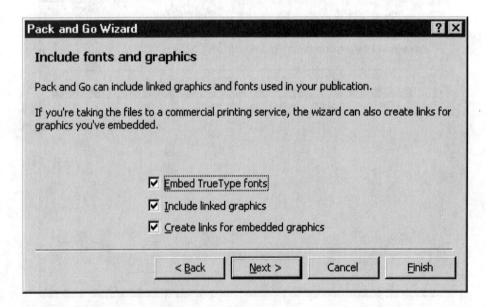

5. Click Next.

6. Click Finish to pack the files.

The Complete Reference

Office 2000

Part IX

Appendixes

Appendix A

Installing Microsoft

Office 2000

This appendix describes how to install and maintain Office 2000. It explains the questions you need to ask yourself before you install the program, what to do before you start installing it, how to install Office 2000 for the first time, and how to add or subtract features, as well as repair any broken parts of Office.

To install Office 2000, you need

- The Office 2000 CD-ROM.

- Windows 95, Windows NT 4.0, or a higher version of Windows on your computer.

- At least 16MB of memory. Actually, to run Office 2000 and not be frustrated by delays and slowdowns, you should have 32MB of memory, especially if you intend to install and run the two memory-hungry programs in the Office 2000 suite, PowerPoint and Access.

- At least 250MB of empty disk space for what Microsoft calls a "typical" installation, or about 400MB if you want to install most or all parts of Office 2000.

Tip *To find out how much empty disk space—also known as free space—is on your computer, open the My Computer utility by double-clicking it on the Windows desktop. When the My Computer window appears, right-click on the icon that represents the part of the computer on which you will load Office 2000 (most likely the C drive, Disk1_vol1 [C:]). On the shortcut menu, choose Properties. The General tab of the Properties dialog box appears and tells you how much free, or empty, space is on your computer.*

Before You Install Office 2000

Microsoft recommends closing all the programs before installing Office 2000. Microsoft also says you should back up important files—not program files, but personal files: letters to your mom, novels, legal documents, and the like. During the course of writing this book and others about the Office 2000 programs, I have installed and reinstalled the program many times and never lost a file. However, for the record, I want you to know what Microsoft recommends.

When you install Office 2000, the program asks if you want a Typical installation, a Custom installation, or a Run from CD-ROM installation:

- **Typical or Upgrade** Installs the most widely used features of all the Office programs—Word, Excel, PowerPoint, Outlook, and Access—as well as popular features that are common to all the programs, such as the spell checker and clip art utility.

- **Custom** Lets you pick and choose which programs to install, as well as which features of each program to install and which common features to install.

> **Tip**   *Microsoft says that the Custom installation is for "expert users." Not so. The Custom installation is for anyone who wants to decide for him or herself what to put on the computer. As the following pages will show, a Custom installation is not as difficult as Microsoft makes it out to be. If you're running short on disk space, or if you don't care to use one or two or three of the Office 2000 programs, by all means opt for a Custom installation.*

The important thing to remember about installing Office 2000 is that it doesn't matter if you get it right the first time. If you forgot to install a certain feature or a certain program, or if you regret installing a certain feature or a certain program, all you have to do is use Office 2000's Maintenance Mode to add, remove, or repair features.

Installing Office 2000 for the First Time

Follow these steps to install Office 2000 for the first time:

1. Close the programs that are open on your computer, if any are open.

2. Put the Office 2000 CD in the CD-ROM drive and wait for the installation program to launch.

> **Tip**   *If the installation program does not start automatically, click the Start button and choose Settings | Control Panel. Double-click the Add/Remove Programs applet, then click the Install button.*

Retaining an Old Version of an Office Program

If Office 97 or 95 is loaded on your computer and you install Office 2000, the setup program searches for old versions of the Office programs, deletes them, and replaces them with the brand-new 2000 versions. No problem there. However, what if you want to keep an old version of an Office program? For example, suppose you want to keep Word 95 and Word 2000 on your computer?

The only way to keep an old Office program on your computer and still load Office 2000 programs is to install Office 2000 into a different directory than your older version of Office. When the install program asks for the installation location, enter **C:\Program Files\Microsoft Office 2000** if you wish to keep your old Office applications. If you wish to remove one or all of your old Office programs later, use the Control Panel's Add/Remove programs applet.

APPENDIXES

3. Enter your name and, if you are so inclined, the company you work for. Then type your CD key and click OK. You can find the CD key on the back of the case that the CD was shipped in. Do not lose this number. You will be asked for it if you ever need to completely reinstall the program.

Caution *What you enter in the Name and Organization dialog box is more important than you may think. The name and company name you enter appear all over Office 2000. For example, by choosing Insert | AutoText and then clicking Signature in Microsoft Word, you can make the name you enter in the dialog box appear automatically. Make sure what you enter in the dialog box is accurate.*

4. The next dialog box lists the user information you entered, as well as a product ID number for your copy of Office 2000. Jot down the number in case you need to identify yourself to Microsoft's Customer Support staff in the event of an emergency.

5. Speed-read the copyright warning, choose the I Accept option, and click the Next button.

6. If you are upgrading from a previous version of Office and wish to use all of the default settings for Office 2000, click the Upgrade Now button. Otherwise click the Customize button (see the sidebar "Custom Installations: Choosing What Parts of Office 2000 to Install").

Note *In the next few minutes, the Office 2000 setup program examines your hard disk to see what is there and which files need to be loaded.*

7. Click OK when you see the dialog box that tells you that the setup process is complete.

Running Outlook for the First Time

The first time you run Outlook after installing Office 2000, the Outlook Startup Wizard will launch, walking you through setting up Outlook to work with your messages, contacts, and calendar, as described in the following steps:

1. After launching Outlook, click Next to begin the Startup Wizard.

2. If you have a previous version of Outlook installed on your computer, the setup program will ask you if you currently use it for your e-mail. Click Yes to keep all of the settings from your old version of Outlook, or No to specify different settings.

3. You will then see a window showing a list of installed e-mail programs that Outlook can import data and addresses from, as shown in Figure A-1. If you wish to migrate the settings from one of these programs, select it and then click Next; otherwise, select None Of The Above and click Next.

Custom Installations: Choosing What Parts of Office 2000 to Install

When you choose the Custom installation option, you get a chance to tell the installation program exactly how you want Office 2000 setup. Follow these steps to customize your installation:

1. After clicking the Customize button in step 6 in the section "Installing Office 2000 for the First Time," the setup program will recommend installing Office 2000 in the C:\Program Files\Microsoft Office folder. Click Next in this dialog box.

   Caution: If you're upgrading from an earlier version of Office, don't change the installation location unless you wish to keep your old version of Office. If older Office programs are already in the C:\Program Files\Microsoft Office folder and you want to keep an older program or two, see "Retaining an Old Version of an Office Program" earlier in this appendix. If you're not upgrading, it's okay to change the folder, but make sure you have a good reason first.

2. The next dialog box shows you any previous Office programs you have installed. Click Next.

3. Select the Internet Explorer 5 setup option you would like, either Minimum Install, Typical Install, Full Install, or Do Not Upgrade IE to keep your current version of Internet Explorer. Click Next.

4. The next dialog box is the Select Features box, as shown in Figure A-2. Click the plus sign next to the application you wish to customize to display its options. Click the triangle next to the option to choose an installation option:

   ■ **Not Available**   This option will not be available without using Office's Maintenance Mode (see "Using Office 2000's Maintenance Mode" later in this appendix). It saves hard disk space, and is good for when you don't have ready access to the installation files.

   ■ **Run From My Computer**   This option will be installed to your hard drive. It provides the fastest performance but uses more hard disk space.

   ■ **Run From CD**   This option will be loaded from the CD-ROM every time you use it. It saves hard disk space, but requires the CD-ROM and can be very slow.

   ■ **Installed On First Use**   This option will not be installed, but will appear as if it were installed inside the Office program. The first time you use the feature, Office installs it from the CD-ROM.

5. When you're finished choosing your options, click Install Now.

APPENDIXES

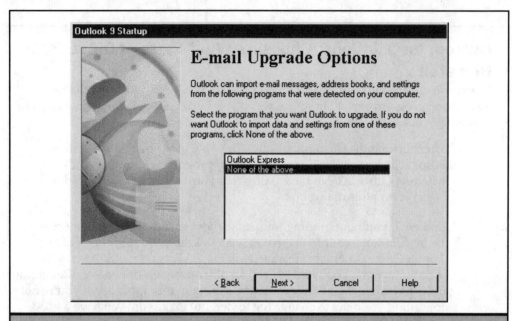

Figure A-1. Choosing an e-mail program from which to import data and settings into Outlook

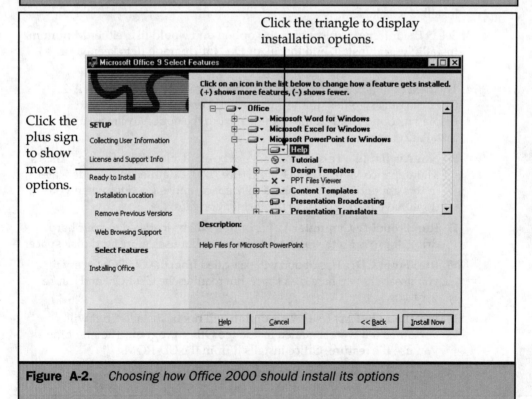

Figure A-2. Choosing how Office 2000 should install its options

4. The next window gives you three installation options for Outlook, as shown in Figure A-3:

   ■ **Internet Only**   Use this for fast Internet e-mail and faxing.

   ■ **Corporate Or Workgroup**   Use this if you need to access Microsoft Exchange servers, Microsoft Mail service, or other third party mail services in addition to or instead of Internet e-mail and fax.

   ■ **No E-mail**   Choose this if you don't wish to use e-mail or fax at all.

If you change your mind later about which Outlook installation you want, you can use the Office Maintenance Mode to change your Outlook installation.

5. Choose an option and click Next to finish the Outlook Startup Wizard. Outlook may ask additional questions if your message accounts are not currently set up. If you have any questions, contact your ISP or network administrator.

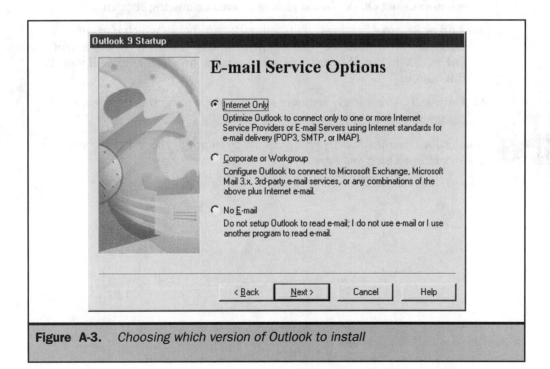

Figure A-3.   *Choosing which version of Outlook to install*

Using Office 2000's Maintenance Mode

You can use Office's Maintenance Mode to repair Office or to add and remove features. To start Office 2000's Maintenance Mode, follow these steps:

1. Insert the Office CD-ROM and wait for the Maintenance Mode program to launch.

If the Maintenance Mode program doesn't start, click Window's Start button and choose Settings | Control Panel. Double-click on the Add/Remove Programs applet, then select Microsoft Office 2000 from the list of installed programs and click the Add/Remove button.

2. Click either the Repair Office 2000 button, the Add or Remove Features button, or the Uninstall Office 2000 button:

   ■ **Repair Office 2000**   Scans all files and your registry for any changes from their original installation state and reinstalls any damaged files. Choose whether Office should reinstall itself or just repair any errors, and also whether or not Office should restore deleted or missing shortcuts.

   ■ **Add or Remove Features**   Lets you pick and choose which parts of Office 2000 to install. See "Custom Installations: Choosing What Parts of Office 2000 to Install," earlier in this appendix, to see what to do if you click this button.

   ■ **Uninstall**   Completely removes all Office 2000 programs from your computer.

You can also repair individual Office programs by launching the desired program and choosing Help | Detect and Repair.

The
Complete
Reference

Office 2000

Appendix B

Introducing the Office Small Business Programs

The Small Business, Professional, and Premium versions of Office 2000 come with a handful of useful tools for small businesses, including the Business Planner, Direct Mail Manager, Small Business Customer Manager, and the Small Business Financial Manager. This appendix briefly describes these tools.

The Business Planner, shown in Figure B-1, takes you through an interview and, based on your answers, creates wizards that help you formulate a business plan and develop a marketing campaign. The Business Planner Wizard and Marketing Campaign Wizard include articles, tips, examples, and links to Internet resources. The Business Planner also includes templates you can use to create business documents in Office.

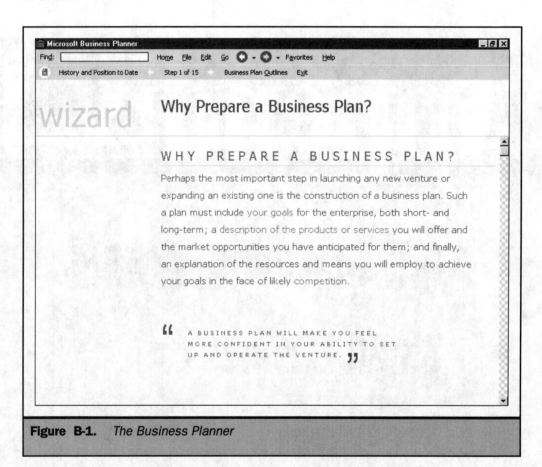

Figure B-1. *The Business Planner*

The Direct Mail Manager, shown in Figure B-2, helps automate direct mail campaigns. With the Direct Mail Manager, you can import mailing list data from an Access database, an Excel spreadsheet, or an Outlook Contacts folder. You can also choose to purchase a mailing list. Then you use the Direct Mail Manager to filter unnecessary fields, records, or duplicate entries out of the mailing data and verify mailing lists for correct addresses. The Direct Mail Manager even connects you to the U.S. Postal Service Reference Guide for correct and complete postal codes.

The Customer Manager, shown in Figure B-3, is an add-on Access tool that helps you import information from an accounting program (such as QuickBooks or Peachtree Accounting) and Outlook to monitor customer and sales information. With the Customer Manager, you can combine sales and address information and easily sort and analyze the data.

The Financial Manager, shown in Figure B-4, is an add-on Excel tool and bundle of templates that allow you to take information from an accounting program (such as QuickBooks or Peachtree Accounting) and import it into Excel to make financial forecasts and check your company's financial health. The extra wizards included in the Financial Manager allow you to set up "what-if" scenarios, for instance to find the

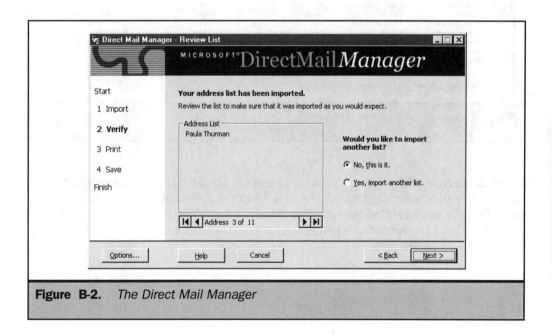

Figure B-2.   *The Direct Mail Manager*

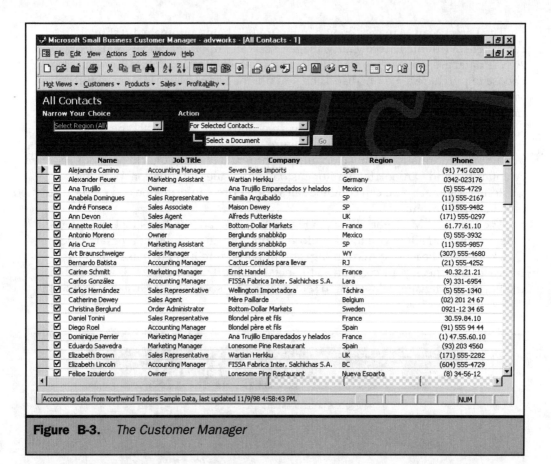

Figure B-3. *The Customer Manager*

effects of changing the price of a product or service. The wizards also allow you to easily create and customize financial reports. With the Financial Manager, you can compare your business along several lines (such as debt to equity ratio, sales to total assets ratio, and net income as a percentage of sales) against another businesses in your industry based on SIC codes.

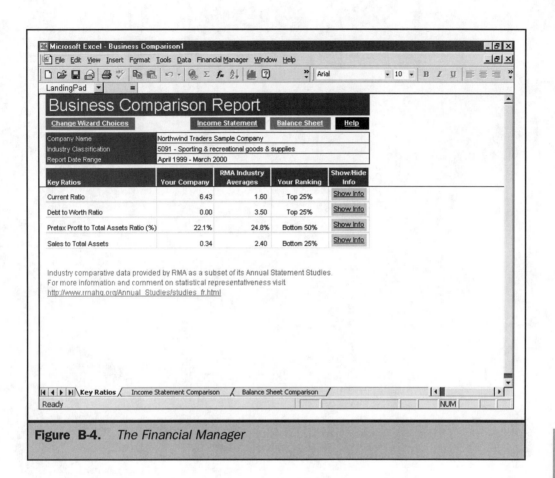

Figure B-4.   *The Financial Manager*

Office
2000

Appendix C

Using Server Extensions

Microsoft supplies all interested Internet Service Providers (ISPs) with server extensions, which are small programs that run on a web server and allow Internet users to more easily perform a variety of web-related tasks. Microsoft offers two types of server extensions: FrontPage Server Extensions and Office Server Extensions. Most Microsoft Office users find that FrontPage Server Extensions provide all of the services they need, but corporate Office users who need to collaborate with others across the Internet or an intranet may also find Office Server Extensions useful.

FrontPage vs. Office Server Extensions

FrontPage Server Extensions were designed to make common web page creation tasks easier. Office Server Extensions enlarge these capabilities to include advanced group collaboration and file management tasks. Table C-1 lists the features that FrontPage Server Extensions have in common with Office Server Extensions. Table C-2 lists the additional features specific to Office Server Extensions.

Using Office Server Extensions

Microsoft Office Server Extensions provide powerful tools for collaborating with co-workers, editing web-based documents while offline, and finding files on web servers with ease. To perform these tasks most effectively, everyone involved needs to use Internet Explorer 5 or newer. However, older versions of Internet Explorer, as well as Netscape Navigator, also work, but with only a subset of the potential functionality.

Feature	Use
Publish to the Web	Easy, one-button uploading of files to supported web servers. Previously accomplished with FTP or HTTP commands.
FrontPage Components	Small server-based applications for performing common web site tasks such as displaying a hit counter, a dynamic table of contents, or a search form. Previously performed with CGI scripts.

Table C-1. *Common Features of FrontPage and Office Server Extensions*

Feature	Use
Web Discussions	Allows users to write comments inside a web document while inside their browser.
Web Subscriptions	Allows users to sign up to be notified when any changes are made to a document.
Searching	Allows users to perform advanced searches on a web server.
AutoNavigation	Allows users to sort and filter files on a web server, allowing for easier file navigation.
Offline Editing	Allows users to edit a document that resides on a web server while offline.

Table C-2. *Features Added by Office Server Extensions*

This section covers a few of the Microsoft Office Server Extension's features; the rest, such as enhanced search pages and better file displays on web sites, are mostly transparent to you as an Office user.

Using Web Discussions

You can use Web Discussions to mark comments and carry on a dialog about a document or web page with co-workers.

Setting Up Web Discussions

To set up a server for Web Discussions, follow these steps:

1. In Internet Explorer 5 or later, choose View | Explorer Bar | Discussions.

2. If you haven't used Web Discussions before, the Add or Edit Discussion Server dialog box will ask for your discussion server. Enter the server name, give it a friendly name to refer to it by, and then click OK.

3. The Discussion Options dialog box will then appear, as shown in the following illustration. It allows you to specify what fields you want displayed in discussions. Make your selections, then click OK.

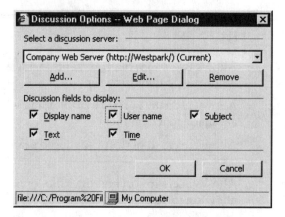

Viewing and Commenting on a Document

To view comments in and about a document and to write your own comments, follow these steps:

1. Choose View | Explorer Bar | Discussions to view the Discussions toolbar at the bottom of your browser window.

2. Browse to the document you wish to comment or view comments on.

3. Click the Insert in the Document button to comment directly inside the document, or click Insert about the Document to comment in the general discussion pane below the document (see Figure C-1).

4. Click an insert marker to open the Enter Discussion Text dialog box.

5. Enter a subject and then type your comments in the Discussion Text box as shown in the following illustration:

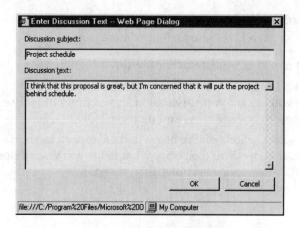

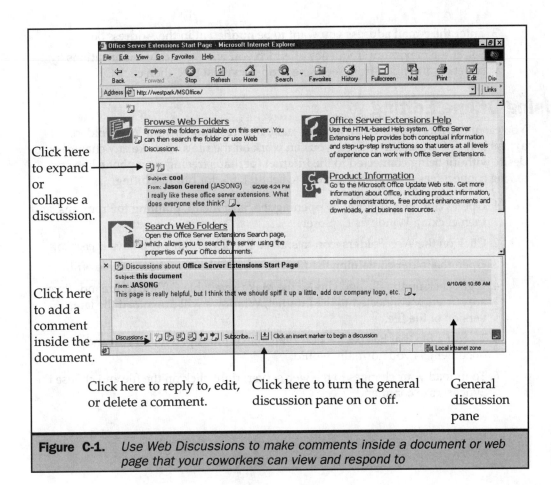

Click here to expand or collapse a discussion.

Click here to add a comment inside the document.

Click here to reply to, edit, or delete a comment.

Click here to turn the general discussion pane on or off.

General discussion pane

Figure C-1. *Use Web Discussions to make comments inside a document or web page that your coworkers can view and respond to*

6. Click OK when you're finished.

Subscribing to a Document

To subscribe to a web page or Microsoft Office Document located on a web server using Office Server Extensions, follow these steps:

1. Browse to the web page or document you wish to subscribe to and click the Subscribe button on the Discussions toolbar (see the previous section for more help on this).

2. Specify when you wish to be notified by selecting an option from the When drop-down list box.

3. Enter the e-mail address you want to be notified at in the Address box.

4. Select the maximum frequency at which you wish to receive notifications by selecting an option from the Time drop-down list box, then click OK.

Using Offline Editing

You can use Office Server Extensions to make files residing in your Web Folders available for offline editing. Then, you can work on the file and make any changes you desire without being connected to the Internet (perhaps freeing up a phone line and saving connect fees). Follow these steps to set up a file for offline editing:

1. Open Windows Explorer by opening the Start menu, pointing to Programs, and then clicking Windows Explorer.

2. Click on the Web Folders icon to show a list of web sites you have access to.

3. Open the folder containing the file you would like to make available offline.

4. Right click on the file and choose the Make Available Offline command. If you are currently connected to the Internet, Windows will download the latest version of the file.

5. To edit a file that has been made available offline, open it and edit and save the document as you normally would.

6. To upload your changes to the web server, right click on the file and choose the Synchronize command.

Appendix D

Introducing the Office Development Tools

M icrosoft Office includes two powerful tools for integrating and expanding its capabilities: the Visual Basic Editor and the Microsoft Script Editor. You can access both tools from the Tools | Macro submenu in any Office program. Both the Visual Basic Editor and the Microsoft Script Editor are complicated enough to be worthy of their own books, but you'll find an introduction to each tool below that should answer some basic questions and hopefully pique your interest.

Note *For information about programming in Visual Basic Editor or the Microsoft Script Editor, conduct an Internet search on the words VBScript or JavaScript. Or check out a book such as JavaScript Annotated Archives by Jeff Frentzen and Henry Sobotka (Osborne/McGraw-Hill, 1998) and Visual Basic 6 Programmer's Reference, 2nd edition, by Dan Rahmel (Osborne/McGraw-Hill, 1999).*

Visual Basic Editor

The Visual Basic Editor, known in technical lingo as an Integrated Development Environment (IDE), is simply a convenient and helpful place for editing and debugging the Visual Basic for Applications (VBA) programming language. It is to VBA what Word is to documents or Excel is to spreadsheets. The editor, as shown in Figure D-1, is noticeably different from Word or Excel and might appear a little strange to you if you're new to IDEs or programming. But really, it's just another set of buttons and menus waiting for your next creation. The real magic happens when you begin to code in VBA.

Visual Basic for Applications is a programming language designed specifically for the applications found in Microsoft Office. It has its roots in and inherits many characteristics from one of the most popular programming languages of our time, Visual Basic. Like all programming languages, VBA has a unique syntax and grammar that can be a little intimidating at first. But if you've learned other programming languages you might find it strangely familiar or even easier to use than other languages.

The beauty of VBA, since it is tailor-made for Office, is that its language includes familiar Office concepts such as opening a document, copying data, or calculating formulas. Experienced programmers know that by cleverly stringing together VBA commands, it is possible to greatly enhance off-the-shelf applications or automate cumbersome tasks that would normally be done by hand.

Your imagination won't need to roam too far before you begin to see powerful uses of VBA. For example, imagine that you, as an accountant in the central office of a corporation, are responsible for merging and reporting sales statistics for 100 satellite offices located throughout North America. An important first step in managing this task would be to create and distribute a standardized Excel spreadsheet that all satellite offices would use to report their individual statistics back to you. But to go through all 100 spreadsheets and extract statistics might still take several days. A crucial second step would be to create a small VBA program that opens each spreadsheet, extracts only the information you need, performs complex calculations to analyze and merge

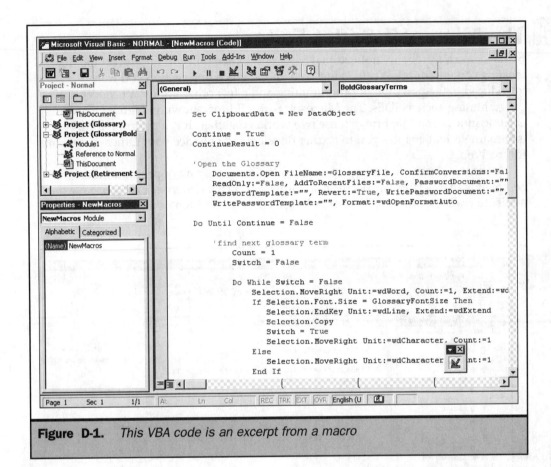

Figure D-1.   *This VBA code is an excerpt from a macro*

the data, and neatly formats the end result in another Excel spreadsheet for safe keeping and readability. A VBA program like this would complete its job in minutes and could be used over and over again, saving you time.

> **Note**
>
> *VBA is especially useful to businesses that have a desire to customize documents, drawings, or spreadsheets to meet their specific business needs. VBA has two enormously attractive qualities. First, since the language is quite similar to the ever-popular Visual Basic, businesses can more easily find programming staff from the estimated pool of over 3 million VB programmers. And second, instead of starting a project from scratch, businesses get a huge break in their project expense by incorporating all of the features and functionality of a powerful application like Word and simply building on top of it.*

The Microsoft Script Editor

By now, you've probably noticed that Microsoft Office is becoming a great tool for creating content for the World Wide Web. In the preceding section you were introduced to the potential of programming and a few other important concepts of programming such as IDEs. The Microsoft Script Editor, shown in Figure D-2, is an exciting innovation that brings these two worlds together. It is a programming environment that enables you to further develop and enhance your Office documents for the Web.

A script is similar to a program in that it's simply a string of programming commands that perform a specific task. Browsers such as Internet Explorer have the ability to read and interpret scripts as long as they are written in recognizable scripting

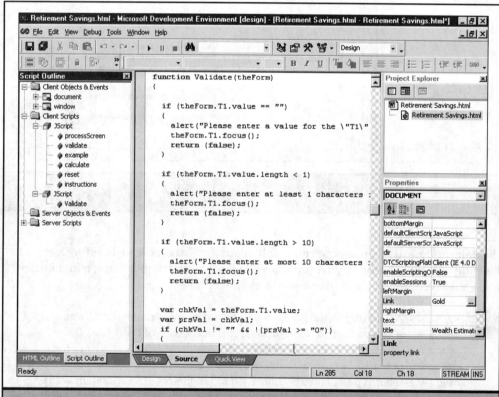

Figure D-2.   *A sample piece of JavaScript created in the Microsoft Script Editor*

languages. The Microsoft Script Editor allows you to build scripts in two languages: VBScript and JavaScript. VBScript is a descendent of Visual Basic. JavaScript is really its own language but has some vague similarities to popular programming languages like C++ and Java. Both are tailored for Internet programming and are gradually becoming more sophisticated, but are limited by the ability of the browser.

Note *If you use a web browser that is a couple years old and stumble across a web site that contains a script using a brand new scripting feature, your browser might report an error message because it's not capable of recognizing the new commands.*

Appendix E

Using the
Companion CD

O n the CD that comes with this book are more than 50 prefabricated templates that you can use to create Word files, Excel spreadsheets, and PowerPoint presentations. Also on the CD are nearly 200 sample files that you can use to experiment with the Word, Excel, PowerPoint, and Access commands described in this book. You will also find ten shareware programs.

The CD also contains a series of multiple choice tests that you can use to assess your skills with Office 2000. These Personal Testing Center TEST YOURSELF exams are especially useful if you are studying for the Microsoft Office User Specialist (MOUS) Certification tests. However, even if you're not interested in obtaining a MOUS certificate, the exams offer an excellent opportunity to test your Office 2000 skills and knowledge.

   MOUS certification includes a series of tests designed by Microsoft to assess proficiency in Office Programs.

This appendix explains how to install the CD and how to best use the templates, files, and TEST YOURSELF software. It tells you how to load templates onto your computer from the CD and explains what the different templates are. It also tells you how to make use of the sample documents and how to load the shareware on your computer.

   "Creating New Document Files" in Chapter 2 explains how to create a file with a template.

Copying Templates to Your Computer

On the CD, Word templates, Excel templates, and PowerPoint templates are each in their own folder. Follow these steps to copy the templates from the CD to your computer:

1. Place the CD in the CD drive.

2. Click the Start button on the taskbar and choose Programs | Windows Explorer to open the Windows Explorer.

3. In the left window pane in the Windows Explorer, click the plus sign next to the drive D icon (or whichever drive your CD is on). You'll see the folders on the CD.

4. In the right window pane, click the Headstart Templates folder and then double-click the folder whose templates you want to use. The templates appear in the right window pane.

5. Find the C:\Windows\Application Data\Microsoft\Templates folder in the left window pane. To get there, click the plus sign next to the Windows folder, then click the plus sign next to the Application Data folder, and then click the plus sign next to the Microsoft folder. You see the Templates folder, shown next. If you open the Templates folder you will display its contents in the right window pane.

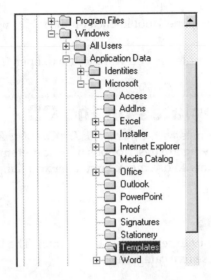

6. On the right window pane, which should still display the contents of the folder you selected in step 4, select the templates to be copied.

7. Drag the templates in the right window pane to the Template folder on the left window pane.

8. Click the Close button to close the Windows Explorer.

How to Use the Sample Documents

Throughout this book are "Learn by Example" notes that mention sample documents on the CD, which contains about 175 sample files. To try out a Word, Excel, PowerPoint, or Access sample file, you don't have to copy it to your computer. You can simply open a sample file on the CD, experiment with it, and close it. If you try to save a sample file, your computer will tell you that it is "read-only" and therefore can't be changed. You can commandeer a sample file and use it on your own, but to do so you have to copy it from the CD to your computer first. You can do whatever you please with sample files that have been copied from the CD to your computer's hard disk.

Sample files are organized into folders, with one folder for each part of the book. Follow these steps to open a sample file:

1. Make sure that the CD is in the CD drive.

2. Click the Start button on the taskbar and choose Programs | Windows Explorer to open the Windows Explorer.

3. In the Windows Explorer's left window pane, click the plus sign next to the drive D icon (or whichever drive your CD is on). You'll see the folders on the CD.

APPENDIXES

4. In the right window pane, double-click on the folder with the sample file you want.

5. Double-click the sample file you want to use to open it.

Headstart Templates on the CD

The companion CD that comes with *Office 2000: The Complete Reference* offers more than 50 Office templates. Following are descriptions of the different templates and explanations concerning how to use them. First, the Excel templates, since they are the most complicated.

The Excel Templates

On the companion CD are 19 Excel workbook templates. The Excel templates fall, roughly speaking, into these five categories:

- Business planning templates
- Capital budgeting templates
- Loan amortization templates
- Future value compounding templates
- Personal financial planning templates

Templates in each category work in a different manner, so the paragraphs that follow briefly describe what they do.

Business Planning Templates

On the companion CD are three business planning templates: 12moplan.xls, 5yrplan.xls, and Pvcanal.xls. The first two templates, 12moplan.xls and 5yrplan.xls, collect a large set of inputs and then make the calculations necessary to create a pro forma financial statement (an income statement, a balance sheet, and a cash flow statement). What's more, both templates also calculate many standard financial ratios. Figure E-1 shows the Forecasting Inputs worksheet of the Excel template that lets you build a five-year business plan.

The 12moplan.xls and the 5yrplan.xls templates work in almost the exact same way. The only difference is that the 12moplan.xls template forecasts profits, cash flows, and financial conditions on a monthly basis for a year, whereas the 5yrplan.xls template forecasts profits, cash flows, and financial conditions on an annual basis for five years. (The 12moplan.xls template does summarize its monthly amounts by also showing annual profits and cash flows, as well as the year-end financial condition.)

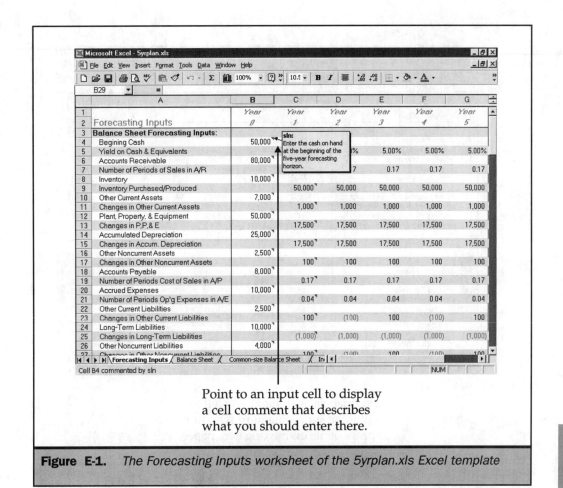

Point to an input cell to display
a cell comment that describes
what you should enter there.

Figure E-1.   *The Forecasting Inputs worksheet of the 5yrplan.xls Excel template*

Figure E-2 shows the Balance Sheet worksheet for the 5yrplan.xls template. The Balance Sheet worksheet (as well as the other worksheet pages that show calculation results) do not provide cell comments to describe their values. If you use the 5yrplan.xls or the 12moplan.xls template, I assume that you understand enough about financial and managerial accounting to work comfortably with simple financial statements.

Caution   *Both the 12moplan.xls and the 5yrplan.xls templates are very large—more than 2MB in size. Because the templates are so large, you need to use them on a computer that has plenty of memory (probably at least 16MB). Either that, or make sure that you don't open other large document files at the same time.*

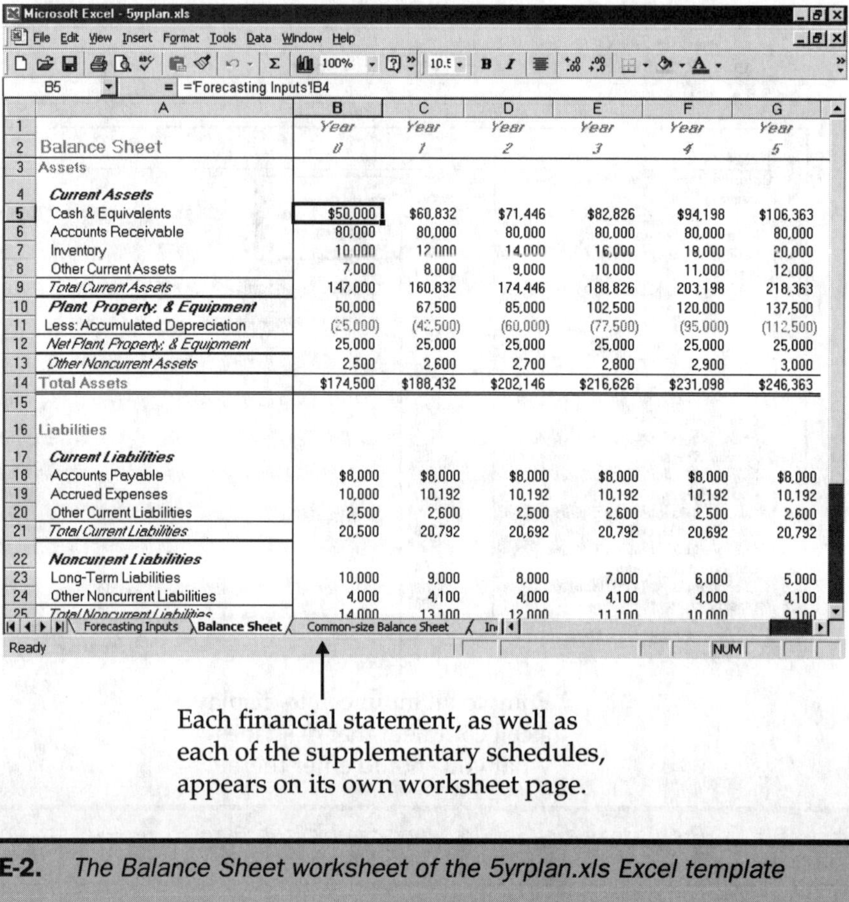

Each financial statement, as well as each of the supplementary schedules, appears on its own worksheet page.

Figure E-2. *The Balance Sheet worksheet of the 5yrplan.xls Excel template*

The third business planning template, Pvcanal.xls, makes profit-volume cost calculations, including the break-even point calculations. Like the other two business planning templates, Pvcanal.xls uses separate worksheet pages to organize information. The first worksheet page, for example, lets you collect and store the inputs for a profit-volume cost analysis, as shown in Figure E-3.

Other worksheet pages show the results of the profit-volume analysis. For example, one worksheet page describes a business' break-even point (the sales volume at which a firm makes no money but also loses no money). Another worksheet page shows how profits and costs vary as sales revenue changes. Still another page—this one a chart sheet page—plots profit-volume cost data in an area chart. Figure E-4 shows the Break-even Analysis worksheet page.

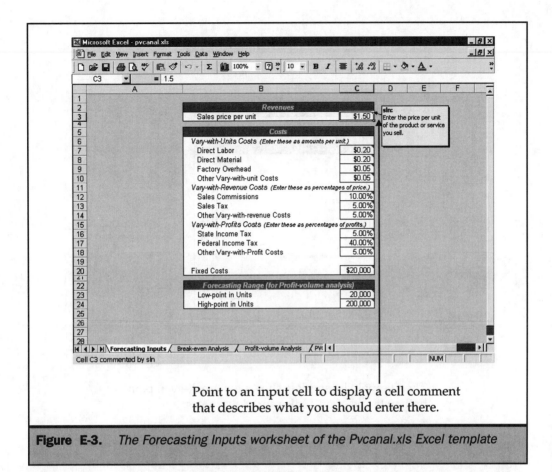

Point to an input cell to display a cell comment
that describes what you should enter there.

Figure E-3.   *The Forecasting Inputs worksheet of the Pvcanal.xls Excel template*

Note   *Compared to the 12moplan.xls and 5yrplan.xls templates, the Pvcanal.xls template is less complicated to use, primarily because it requires fewer input values and creates simpler reports. For this reason, many users who aren't financial experts can use this tool.*

Capital Budgeting Templates

The companion CD supplies two capital budgeting templates: 60mocash.xls and 10yrcash.xls. These two templates are essentially the same. Each is set up for forecasting the pre-tax and after-tax cash flows and rates of return from a capital investment (such as a new manufacturing plant or a real estate development). The difference between the two is that each uses a different forecasting horizon.

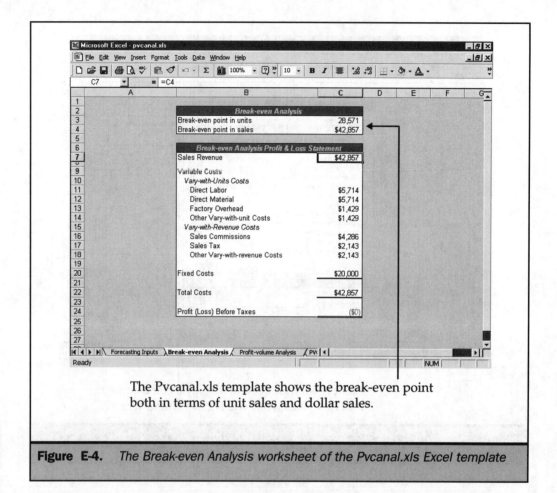

The Pvcanal.xls template shows the break-even point both in terms of unit sales and dollar sales.

Figure E-4. *The Break-even Analysis worksheet of the Pvcanal.xls Excel template*

Both capital budgeting templates collect a large set of inputs and then make the calculations necessary for creating pro forma financial statements that summarize the following:

- Operating profits (or losses)

- Capital gains (or losses) that stem from the ultimate sale or liquidation of the capital investment

- The income tax effects of the operating profits (or losses) and capital gains (or losses)

- The pre-tax and after-tax cash flows stemming from an investment

The templates then use the cash-flow information to calculate several standard, capital budgeting benchmarks, including pre-tax and after-tax net present values, pre-tax and after-tax internal rates of return, and pre-tax and after-tax payback periods. Figure E-5 shows the Forecasting Inputs worksheet of the Excel template that lets you build a 10-year capital budgeting plan.

Figure E-6 shows the operating cash flows worksheet for the 10yrcash.xls template. The operating cash flow worksheet—along with the other worksheet pages that show calculation results—do not provide cell comments to describe their values. I assume that if you're using either the 10yrcash.xls or the 60mocash.xls template, you understand enough about standard capital budgeting techniques to work comfortably with simple financial analysis tools like the templates.

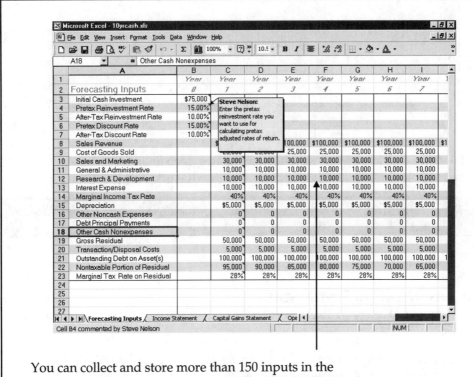

You can collect and store more than 150 inputs in the Forecasting Inputs worksheet of the 10yrcash.xls template.

Figure E-5.   *The Forecasting Inputs worksheet of the 10yrcash.xls Excel template*

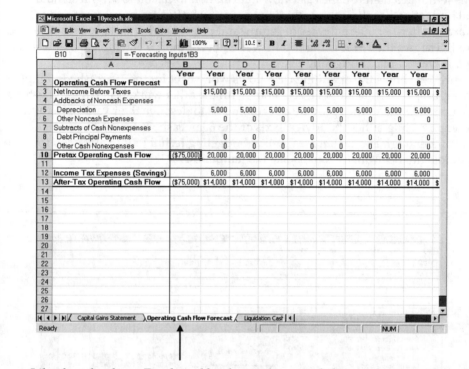

Like the other large Excel workbook templates, each financial statement and supplementary schedule appears on its own worksheet page.

Figure E-6. *The operating cash flow statement of the 10yrcash.xls Excel template*

Loan Amortization Templates

The companion CD offers six Excel workbooks that let you create loan amortization templates:

- 15yr-adj.xls lets you create a loan amortization schedule for a 15-year, adjustable interest rate mortgage or loan

- 15yrloan.xls lets you create a loan amortization schedule for a 15-year, fixed interest rate mortgage or loan

- 30yr-adj.xls lets you create a loan amortization schedule for a 30-year, adjustable interest rate mortgage or loan

- 30yrloan.xls lets you create a loan amortization schedule for a 30-year, fixed interest rate mortgage or loan

- 60moadj.xls lets you create a loan amortization schedule for a 60-month, adjustable interest rate mortgage or loan

- 60moloan.xls lets you create a loan amortization schedule for a 60-month, fixed interest rate mortgage or loan

You work with each of these templates in the same basic way. Specifically, you describe the loan's interest rate, term, and initial balance. Then you document the payment due dates. Figure E-7 shows the first portion of the 30yr-adj.xls workbook.

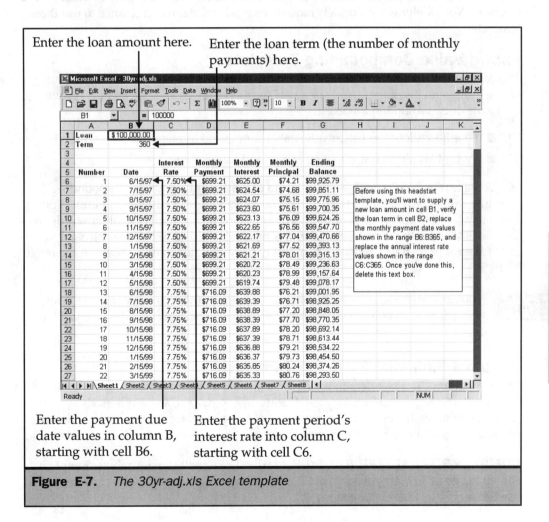

Figure E-7.   *The 30yr-adj.xls Excel template*

All of the loan amortization templates assume monthly loan payments.

The easiest way to enter the payment due values is by entering the first two payment due dates into cells B6 and B7, selecting the range B6:B7, and then dragging the AutoFill handle into the remaining rows of the loan amortization schedule.

If you understand (even roughly) how loan payments work, you should be able to use any of the loan amortization templates to estimate the breakdown of loan payments into principal and interest and the outstanding loan balance after each payment. You don't need an undergraduate or graduate degree in finance to use these templates.

Future Value Compounding Templates

The companion CD provides two future value compounding templates for estimating how a lump-sum investment and stream of payments (also called an *annuity*) grows over time due to compound interest:

- Fv-adj-i.xls lets you use an adjustable compound interest rate.
- Fv-fix-i.xls lets you use a fixed compound interest rate.

As the text box in Figure E-8 indicates, to use either future value compounding schedule, you supply an initial deposit amount and a regular payment amount. You indicate whether your payments will occur as an ordinary annuity (in other words, at the end of the month rather than at the beginning of the month) by entering **Y** for yes or **N** for no, and then you replace the monthly payment date values shown in the range B7:B186.

You can copy the last row of the compound interest schedule to extend the forecasting horizon. You can also delete rows from the compound interest schedule if you want to shorten the forecasting horizon.

Personal Financial Planning Templates

The companion CD also offers half a dozen personal financial planning templates: Cc_mgr.xls, College.xls, Homebuy.xls, Lifeinsr.xls, Retire.xls, and Savings.xls. Everyone who reads this book can make use of these Excel templates, so the following paragraphs describe each of these tools in detail.

CREDIT CARD ANALYZER (CC_MGR.XLS)   The Credit Card Analyzer template shown in Figure E-9 lets you estimate how quickly you can repay credit card debts. To use this template, follow these steps:

1. Enter your current credit card balance in cell D5.

2. Enter the annual credit card interest rate in cell D6.

3. Enter the minimum payment in cell D7.

4. Enter the largest monthly payment you can afford in cell D10.

5. Enter the number of months over which you want to completely repay the credit card debt in cell D11.

Using these inputs, the Credit Card Analyzer template calculates the number of months it will take you to repay the credit card debt if you make a minimum payment, the number of months it will take you to repay the debt if you make the largest monthly payment you can afford, and the size of the payment necessary to repay in the specified number of months shown in cell D11.

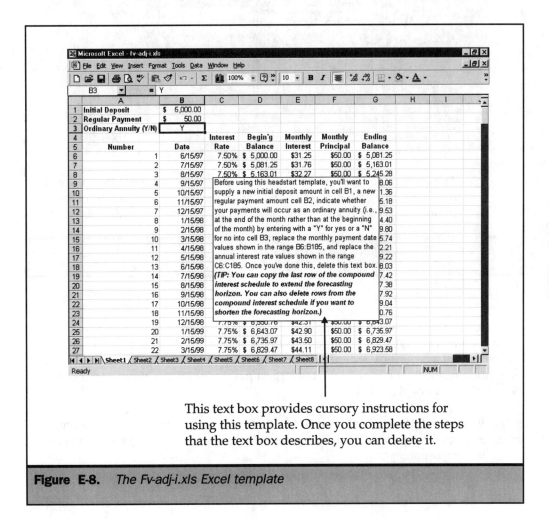

This text box provides cursory instructions for using this template. Once you complete the steps that the text box describes, you can delete it.

Figure E-8.   *The Fv-adj-i.xls Excel template*

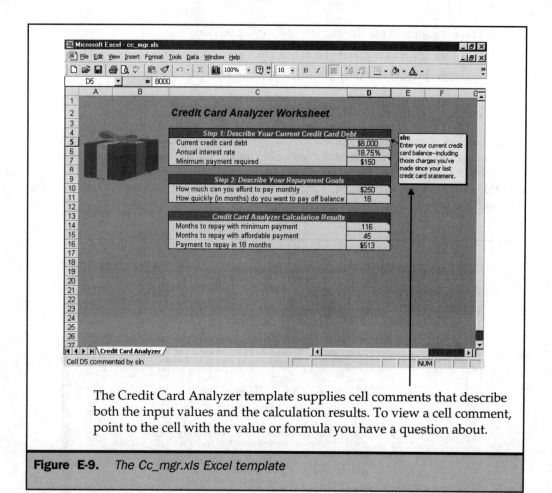

The Credit Card Analyzer template supplies cell comments that describe both the input values and the calculation results. To view a cell comment, point to the cell with the value or formula you have a question about.

Figure E-9. *The Cc_mgr.xls Excel template*

If the Credit Card Analyzer template returns an error value for the calculation result shown in cell D14, the minimum payment amount may not ever pay off the credit card balance. If the Credit Card Analyzer template returns an error value for the calculation result shown in cell D15, the largest payment you can afford may not ever pay off the credit card balance.

Caution *View the calculation results provided by the Credit Card Analyzer template as rough estimates. Your credit card company may calculate its interest charges differently than the template does.*

COLLEGE SAVINGS WORKSHEET (COLLEGE.XLS)   The College Savings
Worksheet template shown in Figure E-10 is for estimating how much money you need
to save for a child's future college expenses. To use this template, follow these steps:

1. Enter the student's current age in cell D5.

2. Enter the student's age when he or she starts college in cell D6.

3. Enter the annual estimated cost of college in current-day dollars in cell D7.

4. Enter the number of years a student will attend college in cell D8.

5. Enter the annual return on investment that you think your college savings will
   return in cell D11.

6. Enter the annual inflation rate you expect for the cost of attending college in
   cell D12.

7. Enter the amount you've already saved for the student's future college costs in
   cell D13.

8. Enter the amount you expect the student to contribute annually to his or her
   college education (these contributions can include money from scholarships,
   summer jobs, or part-time employment during the school year) in cell D14.

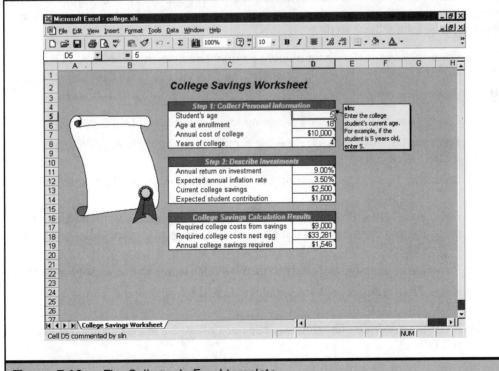

Figure E-10.   *The College.xls Excel template*

The College Savings Worksheet assumes that either your investment profits won't be subject to income taxes or that you will pay any income taxes on these profits out of your pocket and not out of the investment profits.

Using these inputs, the College Savings Worksheet template calculates the annual college costs you need to fund through savings, the amount you need to have saved by the time the student enters college to completely pay for college, and the annual college savings required between now and the time the student enters college.

By the way, the College Savings Worksheet makes one rather conservative assumption: It assumes that you will have saved the funds necessary for college by the time the student starts college. You can, however, continue to contribute to a child's college expenses out of your current income even after the student begins college.

In using the College Savings Worksheet, be sure to experiment with a variety of input values—particularly with a range of return on investment and annual inflation rate inputs. If you underestimate the inflation rate or the annual costs of attending college or you overestimate the return on investment or the student's contribution, you won't save enough to fully fund the student's college education.

HOME AFFORDABILITY ANALYZER WORKSHEET (HOMEBUY.XLS)   The Home Affordability Analyzer Worksheet template shown in Figure E-11 is for estimating how expensive a home you can purchase based on your current financial situation. To use this template, follow these steps:

1. Enter the cash available for a down payment and closing costs in cell D5.

2. Enter your gross monthly income (your income before income taxes) in cell D6.

3. Enter the total debt payments you pay monthly in cell D7.

4. Enter the annual mortgage interest rate you'll pay in cell D10.

5. Enter the term of the mortgage—the number of monthly loan payments you'll make—in cell D11.

6. Enter the closing costs you expect to pay as a percentage of the home purchase price in cell D12.

7. Enter the additional monthly housing costs you expect to pay (in addition to the mortgage payment) in cell D13. This amount, for example, includes items such as property taxes and private mortgage insurance.

8. Enter the down payment percentage the lender wants you to supply in cell D16.

9. Enter the maximum debt service percentage the lender wants you to bear in cell D17.

10. Enter the maximum housing expense percentage the lender wants you to pay in cell D18.

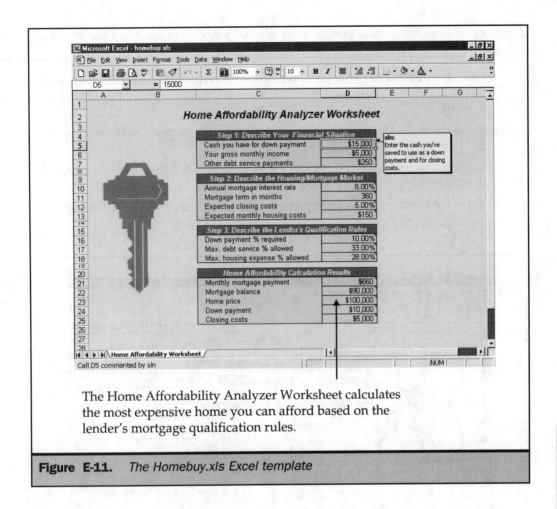

The Home Affordability Analyzer Worksheet calculates
the most expensive home you can afford based on the
lender's mortgage qualification rules.

Figure E-11.   *The Homebuy.xls Excel template*

Using these inputs, the Home Affordability Analyzer Worksheet calculates the
largest monthly mortgage payment you can afford (according to the lender's mortgage
qualification rules), the largest mortgage you can afford, the most expensive home you
can afford, the down payment you'll make, and the closing costs you'll pay.

*You should not place too much reliance on the Homebuy.xls template's results until you
enter an up-to-date mortgage interest rate and confirm the lender's mortgage
qualification rules, including the down payment percentage, the maximum debt service
percentage, and the maximum housing expenses percentage.*

LIFE INSURANCE PLANNER WORKSHEET (LIFEINSR.XLS)   The Life Insurance
Planner Worksheet template shown in Figure E-12 is for estimating how much life

insurance you need to replace your income (should you die) so that your dependents can still manage financially. To use this template, follow these steps:

1. Enter the number of earning years you want to replace in cell D5. (This might be the number of years until your youngest child graduates from college, for example.)

2. Enter the annual income you want your life insurance proceeds to replace in cell D6.

3. Enter the annual return on investment you expect your life insurance proceeds to earn in cell D10.

4. Enter the annual inflation rate you expect over the years you're replacing earnings in cell D11.

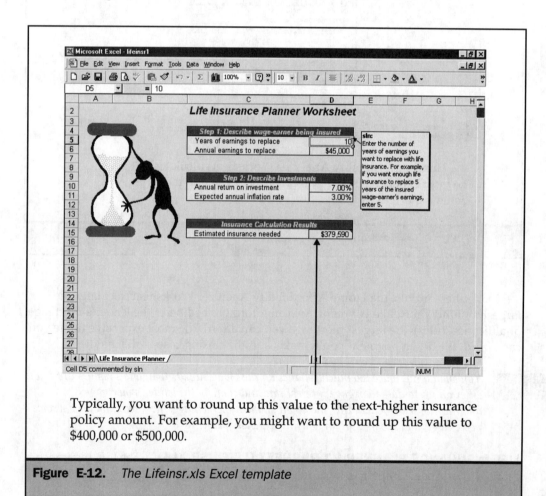

Typically, you want to round up this value to the next-higher insurance policy amount. For example, you might want to round up this value to $400,000 or $500,000.

Figure E-12.   *The Lifeinsr.xls Excel template*

Using these inputs, the Life Insurance Planner Worksheet estimates the size of the life insurance policy you should purchase to replace your income. The insurance proceeds, when invested, will produce a stream of payments that will initially equal the amount you entered into cell D6 and then over the years grow at the inflation rate.

RETIREMENT PLANNER WORKSHEET (RETIRE.XLS)   The Retirement Planner Worksheet template shown in Figure E-13 is for estimating how much money you need to save in order to retire with a specific level of retirement income. To use this template, follow these steps:

1. Enter your current age in cell D5.

2. Enter the age at which you want to retire in cell D6.

3. Enter the desired retirement income in cell D7.

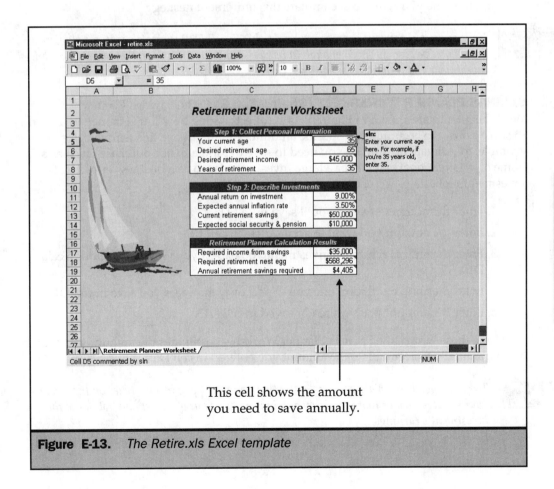

This cell shows the amount you need to save annually.

Figure E-13.   *The Retire.xls Excel template*

4. Indicate the number of years you'll be retired by entering a value in cell D8. (By adding your retirement age to the number of years you expect to enjoy retirement, you are implicitly estimating how long you expect to live.)

5. Enter the annual return on investment you expect your retirement savings to earn in cell D11.

6. Enter the annual inflation rate you expect over both the years you work and the years you will be retired in cell D12.

7. Enter the amount you've already saved for retirement in cell D13.

8. Enter the annual pension or social security benefit you expect in cell D14.

Using these inputs, the Retirement Planner Worksheet estimates the amount of income you want your retirement savings to produce, the retirement nest egg you need in order to produce this income, and the amount you need to save annually between now and the time you retire to accumulate this retirement nest egg.

If the annual retirement savings required value in cell D19 shows a negative value, it means you've already saved enough to retire—assuming, of course, that your return on investment and inflation estimates are correct.

SAVINGS PLANNER WORKSHEET (SAVINGS.XLS)   The Savings Planner Worksheet template shown in Figure E-14 is for estimating how much money you need to save in order to accumulate a specific amount. You might use this template, for example, to estimate how much you need to save to fund a major purchase (such as a home or a recreational vehicle) or a large investment (such as a business or piece of investment real estate). To use this template, follow these steps:

1. Enter the number of years you'll save in cell D5.

2. Enter the amount you want to accumulate in cell D6.

3. Enter the annual return on investment you expect your savings to earn in cell D10.

4. Enter the annual inflation rate you expect over the years you save in cell D11.

5. Enter the amount you've already saved in cell D13.

Using these inputs, the Savings Planner Worksheet estimates the amount you need to save annually to accumulate the amount you entered in cell D6.

The Savings.xls template assumes either that you won't pay income taxes on the interest your savings earn or that you'll pay any income taxes out of pocket and not out of the investment's earnings.

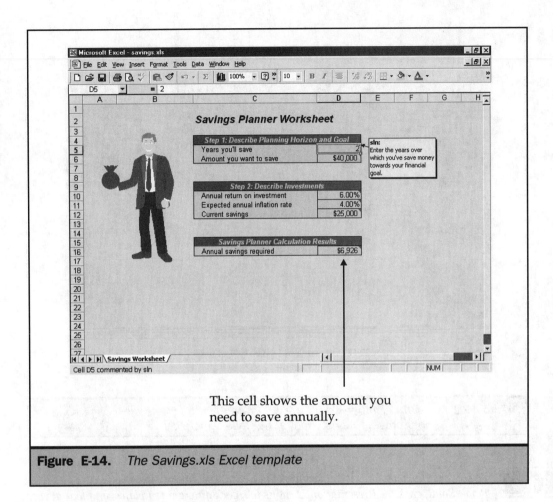

This cell shows the amount you
need to save annually.

Figure E-14. *The Savings.xls Excel template*

The PowerPoint Templates

The design templates that come with PowerPoint are superb, but they have one major drawback: Everybody who owns the software has them. In other words, because so many people have the same designs, the design templates that come with PowerPoint are downright conventional.

To remedy that, this book comes with 33 PowerPoint templates. Figure E-15 shows the Cello template. To use the 33 templates for your presentations, copy them to the C:\Microsoft Office\Templates\Presentation Designs folder.

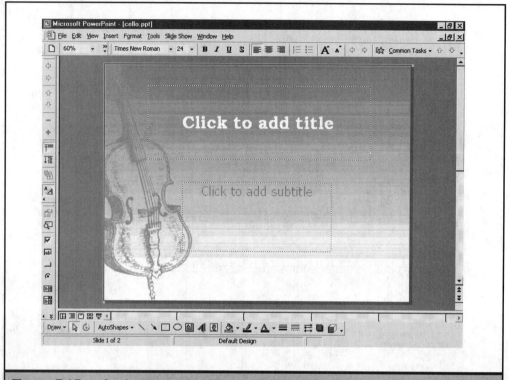

Figure E-15.   *On the companion CD are 33 PowerPoint templates you can use for your presentations. This is the Cello template*

Tip   *To see what the templates look like, open the New Presentation dialog box in PowerPoint, click the Presentation Designs tab, click different templates, and look at the Preview screen in the dialog box. To open the New Presentation dialog box, either choose File | New or, in the PowerPoint dialog box that appears when you start the program, click the Template button.*

The Word Templates

On the companion CD are also 13 Word templates. To make use of these templates in your Word documents, copy the templates to the C:\Program Files\Microsoft Office\Templates folder. Choose File | New to create a file with one of the templates. You will find the templates on the General tab of the New dialog box if you copy them to the C:\Microsoft Office\Templates folder.

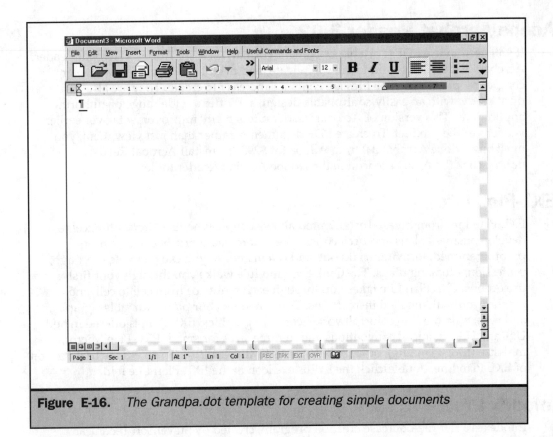

Figure E-16. *The Grandpa.dot template for creating simple documents*

All but one of the templates provide unusual backgrounds for the page. However, the Grandpa.dot template, shown in Figure E-16, offers a streamlined version of Word. Instead of the numerous commands and buttons, only essential commands and buttons are available when you create a file with this template. Use Grandpa.dot to write letters, notes, and other simple documents.

Shareware on the CD

Also on the CD are ten shareware programs. Following are descriptions of the programs and instructions for installing them on your computer.

Adobe Acrobat Reader 3.02

If you need to use PDF (Portable Document Format) files, try Adobe's Acrobat Reader. Acrobat Reader allows you to view, navigate, and print PDF files across all major computing platforms. PDF files are compact and easy to create. They are also print-ready, with an easily controllable design, and offer a wide range of authoring applications. This version of Acrobat Reader offers many improvements over earlier versions of the product. To create PDF documents, rather than just view them, you must buy Adobe Acrobat 3.0 from Adobe for $295. To install Acrobat Reader, double-click the Ar302.exe icon in the Adobe Acrobat Reader folder.

EXL-Plan Lite

EXL-Plan Lite from Invest-Tech Limited allows people who use Microsoft Excel to develop business plans and projections. The automated worksheets have been preprogrammed, formatted, laid out, and calculated, so you can generate thorough, professional-looking plans. The Quik-Start module walks you through your first projections. EXL Plan Lite takes you through each sequence from cell to cell, and coaches you with detailed instructions. You can view your plan with tables, graphs, and reports, laid out in colorful worksheets and graphics. EXL-Plan is offered in both U.S. and U.K. financial conventions and in three sizes for small (EXL-Plan Micro), mid-size (EXL-Plan Lite), or large businesses (EXL-Plan Pro). To access the trial version of EXL-Plan Lite, double-click the Exllus.exe icon in the EXL-Plan Lite folder.

Infodex Pro

Infodex is a flat-file-database creation program, created by Stevenson Technical Services, which allows you to build searchable lists for just about any type of data. You can format your data into nine field types, including text, memo, number, date/time, picture, and calculated fields. Then, place them on your form and set the font, alignment, and an entry instruction line. Infodex Pro allows you to search on any of the fields, sort them, and print tagged records or the whole list. Set up the fields and labels with tools to make professional-looking forms. With this tool, you can organize your business contacts, team rosters, charity mailing lists, or just about any type of data. To use Infodex Pro, click Ipro306.exe in the Infodex Pro folder.

iSpeed

High Mountain Software's iSpeed allows you to optimize your networking connections. To do this, it manipulates your computer's Maximum Transmission Unit (MTU), Maximum Segment Size (MSS), Receive Window (RWIN), Time To Live (TTL), MTU Auto Discover, and Black Hole detection. Fine-tuning these functions can have a dramatic effect on your throughput. (*Note:* You can click the Restore button to return all of your adjustment values to the Windows default.) iSpeed allows you to change these settings manually, one at a time, or choose from one of several buttons, which change the settings as a group. Group settings include Optimal, Default, and PPP, among others. iSpeed has comprehensive instructions and lets you adjust the settings as much as you like until you find the best settings for your application. To install iSpeed, double-click the Ispeed.exe icon in the iSpeed folder.

Microsoft Project 98

The Microsoft Project 98 Evaluation Kit provides the 60-Day Trial version of Microsoft Project 98 as well as other informational components to get you started on your evaluation process. Project 98 is a project management program, which incorporates a flexible scheduling engine which you can use to track your projects more effectively and respond to conflicts before they happen. You can schedule and track project information by hour, day, week, or month and track resource and cost information, so you can make schedule changes as they occur. You can also share information, delegate tasks, and track project status over e-mail using your company's intranet or even over the Internet. To install Microsoft Project 98 Evaluation Edition, double-click Start.exe in the Microsoft Project 98 folder.

Netscape Communicator

Netscape Communicator offers a complete set of Internet components that integrate open e-mail, editing, messaging, and browsing applications. You can browse the Internet with Netscape Navigator. You can exchange messages with Netscape AOL Instant Messenger. You can write, send, and receive encrypted e-mail on the web with Netscape Messenger. And, you can create and publish HTML documents with Netscape Composer. This installation includes import utilities for Eudora, Outlook Express, and Outlook 97/98 e-mail and address books; the Macromedia Flash Plug-in for vector graphics; and the Headspace Beatnik Shell Plug-in for audio. Other versions are available with more features at **www.netscape.com**. To install Netscape communicator, double-click the Cc32e45.exe icon in the Netscape Communicator folder.

Norton AntiVirus 5.0

Norton AntiVirus™ from Symantec protects you at home and on the Internet. New features in version 5.0 let you quarantine infected files and easily get help directly from Symantec researchers. It automatically protects you against viruses as well as malicious ActiveX and Java applets. Web browser integration ensures that all transfers are scanned on the fly, and scheduled live updates can be set up to retrieve new program enhancements automatically. It can keep your computer safe from viruses that might come in from e-mail attachments, Internet downloads, floppy disks, software CDs, or a network. And it can be scheduled to automatically retrieve new anti-virus definitions from Symantec as often as once a week. To activate the trial version of Norton AntiVirus 5.0, click the Nav95tr.exe icon in the Norton AntiVirus folder.

*This trial version only works with Windows 95/98. Other versions are available for download at **www.symantec.com**.*

Paint Shop Pro 5.01

Paint Shop Pro by Jasc Software, Inc. is a graphics program that has the tools you need to paint, edit, and retouch your images, plus a browser to help manage your graphics files. It supports over two dozen raster image formats (such as .BMP, .JPG, and .PCX) for read-write, and can read nine meta and vector image formats (such as .WPG, .CDR, and .WMF) with a broad range of editing tools. It offers image layers, which make image compositing easy and let you edit parts of an image without affecting other areas. It also includes multilevel Undo with Undo history, and a picture tube brush, among other features. To install the trial version of Paint Shop Pro Version 5.01, click the Psp501ev.exe icon in the Paint Shop Pro folder.

SmartDraw

SmartDraw Software, Inc. has created this business graphics drawing package. Even if you aren't an artist, you can create diagrams, flowcharts, and other drawing items by dragging and dropping items onto the page. It comes with hundreds of predrawn shapes and symbols. You'll be able to create perfectly formatted organization charts, fishbone diagrams, network diagrams, timelines, and other arrays of shapes automatically with intelligent connector objects. You select from a variety of predrawn shape libraries and templates to create common diagrams and flowchart designs. SmartDraw is a sophisticated and well-designed program that can go head-to-head with commercial business graphics packages. To open SmartDraw, double-click the Smartdraw_install.exe icon in the SmartDraw folder.

WinZip for Windows 95/98/NT Version 7.0

Use WinZip to view and extract zipped archives. WinZip's new toolbar is user-friendly and makes unzipping ZIP, TAR, and GZIP archives a snap. Its Wizard feature also makes installing zipped programs easier. To install WinZip, double-click Winzip95 in the WinZip folder on the companion CD. If you want to keep WinZip after the free trial period, you must register the program for $29 with Nico Mak Computing, Inc.

The Personal Testing Center TEST YOURSELF Software

As noted earlier, the CD contains exams that you can use to assess your Office 2000 skills. You can use the Personal Testing Center TEST YOURSELF exams to study for MOUS Certification tests or merely to challenge your own knowledge in an effort to improve your skills.

How to Use the Test Software to Prepare for MOUS Certification

The CD contains multiple choice questions that are drawn from the contents of this book. The actual MOUS tests are not presented in a multiple-choice format. Instead, you will be working within Office and will be asked to perform certain functions; your mouse clicks, menu selections, and actions will be recorded as the right or wrong answers. The TEST YOURSELF test component on the CD provides a drill so that you become familiar with each of the Office objectives (as determined by Microsoft). Hence, you can review the items on which you will be tested.

How to Use the Test Software If You Are Not Preparing for MOUS Certification

If you are not preparing for MOUS Certification, the TEST YOURSELF test components provide a turnkey solution for you to assess your own Office knowledge and to discover which product areas you may want to review or look at more closely.

Installing the TEST YOURSELF Software

Follow these steps to install the software:

Note   *Internet Explorer must be your default browser to run the testing software. If you don't have IE installed already, you can install it from this CD, as mentioned in step 5.*

1. Insert the CD into your CD-ROM drive.

2. Click the Start button on the taskbar and choose Programs | Windows Explorer to open the Windows Explorer.

3. In the left window pane in the Windows Explorer, click the plus sign next to the drive D icon (or whichever drive your CD is on). You'll see the folders on the CD.

4. Click the Office 2000 Complete Reference Personal Testing Center folder and double click the Setup.html icon.

5. You will now be presented with step-by-step instructions on how to run the self test software. If you do not have Internet Explorer 4.0 installed, you can install it by clicking the Click Here To Install Internet Explorer 4.0 hyperlink.

6. Click the Next button at the top of the screen to continue to the next set of instructions. Here you choose whether you want to install the software or run it from the CD. You must click on one of these options to initiate the software.

7. Now you can choose which Office programs on which to test yourself and what type of test you would like to take: Live, Practice, or Review. (See the next section for more explanation on these choices.)

8. Click Go to start the test.

About the Personal Testing Center Software

The Personal Testing Center software provides three different testing options: Practice Exams, Live Exams, and Review Exams. Each test option draws from a pool of more than 100 questions, the content of which is taken from the information contained in *Office 2000: The Complete Reference*. To decide which test option to choose, first determine your objective for taking the exam: (1) you want instant feedback on your answer choices, (2) you're looking for an exam simulation (a timed test), or (3) you want to review test concepts on questions you answered incorrectly.

Personal Testing Center Exam Choices

The Exam Choice information is included on the Quick Start Screen on the CD and is also summarized below.

Practice Exams

The Practice Exams present you with questions on a specific Office application, and actual test content is based on which objectives, or topic areas, you select. Each of the topics you choose from largely maps to MOUS Certification objectives and skill sets. However, you should review the specific MOUS requirements for the certificate you need. If you choose the Practice Exam option, you will be asked to select any number of topic areas. Once you select your topic areas of choice, you will be presented with an exam based on the areas you selected. For best use, select a few topic areas at a time on which to test yourself. However, there is no limit on how many topic areas you can select.

The Practice Exams are not timed tests. Once you have selected your answer, you can click on the Answer icon to reveal the actual answer on the spot. If you'd like more information about any answer given, click on Answers In Depth to access additional information aimed at exposing the logic behind the correct answer.

Note   *If you don't want to reveal the answer right away, you have the option of continuing through the entire exam without seeing the correct answers.*

When you are done with the Practice Exam, click the Done icon to view the Assess Yourself evaluation page, described later. After you view your score, if you'd like to take another Practice Exam (with the same or different content areas selected), click the Home icon to return to the Personal Testing Center topic selection page.

Tip   *You can end the Practice Exam at any time, but your exam score may reflect an incorrect percentage of questions wrong since questions that are skipped are counted as incorrect and will lower your overall test score.*

Live Exams

The Live Exams consist of a selection of questions drawn from the overall pool of question on the CD and offer a timed-test environment to simulate an actual exam. Take the Live Exam to assess your current product knowledge. Once you have completed the Exam, use the Assess Yourself scoring feature (described in the next section) to show what topic areas you have mastered and what areas need further study.

Note *The MOUS Exams will not contain multiple choice questions, but will be situation-based and activity-oriented instead.*

Before you take a Live Exam, you must select the topics you'd like to be tested on—select all topics for the best assessment of your skills. During the Live Exam, you'll notice an Exam Timer on the left-hand side of your screen—you are allotted 90 minutes to complete a Live Exam. Navigation icons at the bottom of the screen give you the option to skip questions and return to them later, move to the previous question, or end the exam. Once you have completed the exam, there are two scoring features available: Assess Yourself and Benchmark Yourself, both described in the next section.

Review Exams

The Review Exams are drawn from the same pool of questions as are the Practice and Live Exams. However, in the Review Exam, the Answers icon is not present. Instead, the correct answers are posted near the bottom of your screen, and you have the option of answering the question without looking at the correct answer. In the Review Exam, you can return to previous questions and skip to the next question.

We recommend you take the Review Exam once you have completed the Live Exam once or twice and would like to determine which questions you did answer correctly.

Scoring the TEST YOURSELF Personal Testing Center

Once you have completed either a Practice Exam or a Live Exam, press the Stop button to indicate you are finished with the exam. These two exam types have different evaluation features: Assess Yourself and Benchmark Yourself.

Assess Yourself

The Assess Yourself evaluation feature shows you how many questions you answered correctly out of the total pool of questions on that topic, along with the percentage of correct answers overall.

Benchmark Yourself

The Benchmark Yourself evaluation feature displays the results for each section you chose to be tested on, and includes a bar graph which displays the percentage of correct answers. You can compare your percentage to the pre-established passing percentage for each section. You'll also see the number of questions you answered correctly compared to the total number of questions on which you were tested. If you chose to skip a question it will be marked as incorrect. If you take the Live Exams over and over, and we recommend that you do, the Benchmark Yourself feature will show you your past performance so you can see where you have improved and what areas need further review.

How Your Exam Scores Are Saved

Your exam scores are saved as browser cookies. If you've configured your browser to accept cookies, your scores will be stored in a cookie named History. If your browser does not accept cookies, you cannot permanently save your scores. If you delete the History cookie, your scores will be deleted permanently.

Index

G

H

O